1995 1910   1915   1920   1925

1915
David Sarnoff writes famous memo
on the future of wireless.

Radio...

1919
Owen T. Young negotiates the
formation of RCA.

Case of *U.S. v. Zenith
Radio Corp.*

President Roosevelt uses radio for
"fireside chats" with the public.

1917
Alexanderson's alternator takes on
increased importance for
international communication.

1927
Radio Act of 1927 is passed. Forms
five-member Federal Radio
Commission (FRC).

1923
V.K. Zworykin patents the
iconoscope pickup tube for
television.

1933
Edwin Armstrong demonstrates
FM broadcasting for RCA.

1931
Zworykin and RCA officials visit
Farnsworth labs in California.
RCA later enters royalty agreement
with Farnsworth.

1914
Amateur radio operators form the
American Radio Relay League
(A.R.R.L.).

1909
Charles David Herrold's station
broadcasts from San Jose.

1932
Closed Circuit ETV begins at State
University of Iowa.

1922-1925
National Radio Conferences. (Four
held before new legislation)

1932
Shuler case is decided.

1921
Philo Farnsworth outlines to his
science teacher the concept of
electronic television.

1930
Philo Farnsworth applies for
permission to experiment with
300-line TV system.

1924
International Business Machines
Corporation (IBM) is formed.

1934
Communications Act of 1934 is
passed. Forms seven-member
Federal Communications
Commission (FCC). Independent
regulatory body.

1912
Wireless gains publicity by aiding
rescue efforts from the *Titanic.*

1926
RCA forms subsidiary NBC to
operate Red and Blue networks.

1919
9XM at the University of Wisconsin,
Madison, signs on the air. Becomes
WHA in 1922.

1934
Mutual network begins as
four-station cooperative.

1928
CBS begins when interests are
purchased by Wm. S. Paley and
Congress Cigar Company.

1930
Zworykin visits Farnsworth labs in
California to examine 300-line TV
scanning system.

1912
Radio Act of 1912.

1929
First NAB "Code of Ethics"
is passed.

1910
Wireless Ship Act of 1910.

1920
WWJ in Detroit begins intermittent
broadcasting schedules in August.

1929
First broadcast rating by Crosley
Radio Company.

1920
KDKA in Pittsburgh begins regular
programming in November.

1914-1918
Wireless used extensively in
World War I.

1922-1923
National Association of
Broadcasters (NAB) is formed.

1933
Press-Radio War ends with Biltmore
agreement.

1922
Toll broadcasting begins at WEAF.

1931
KFKB (*Brinkley*) case is decided.

1910   1915   1920   1925   1930   1935

2nd edition

BROADCASTING
and
TELECOMMUNICATION

an introduction

John R. Bittner , *1943*
The University of North Carolina at Chapel Hill

PRENTICE-HALL, INC., ENGLEWOOD CLIFFS, NEW JERSEY 07632

Library of Congress Cataloging in Publication Data

Bittner, John R., 1943–
   Broadcasting and telecommunication.

   Rev. ed. of: Broadcasting. c1980.
   Includes bibliographies and index.
   1. Broadcasting.   I. Bittner, John R., 1943–
Broadcasting.   II. Title.
PN1990.8.B5   1985   384.54   84–13344
ISBN 0–13–083551–X

Editorial/production supervision and
   interior design: Virginia McCarthy
Cover design: George Cornell
Page layout: Diane Koromhas
Manufacturing buyer: Barbara Kelly Kittle

Printed in the United States of America

10 9 8 7 6 5 4 3

ISBN 01 0-13-083551-X

Prentice-Hall International, Inc., *London*
Prentice-Hall of Australia Pty. Limited, *Sydney*
Editora Prentice-Hall do Brasil, Ltda., *Rio de Janeiro*
Prentice-Hall Canada Inc., *Toronto*
Prentice-Hall of India Private Limited, *New Delhi*
Prentice-Hall of Japan, Inc., *Tokyo*
Prentice-Hall of Southeast Asia Pte. Ltd., *Singapore*
Whitehall Books Limited, *Wellington, New Zealand*

CONTENTS

PREFACE

Today, the field of broadcasting is changing almost as fast as books and journals can record the transition. No longer can we be content to study electronic media by concentrating on radio and television stations, or, for that matter, even cable and satellites. We have arrived at the age of telecommunications. It encompasses a multitude of new media and demands the integration of these media in both theory and practice.

This new edition, also for introductory courses, incorporates this total approach to the study of electronic communication, examining everything from the history of the telegraph to the future of personal computers. In addition to the strengths of the first edition, which have been retained, this new edition includes:

* A new chapter on computers and data processing, including an examination of how personal computers are affecting the changing world of broadcasting and telecommunication.
* A new chapter on emerging telecommunication and consumer technologies, including cellular radio, digital audio and television, videodiscs, and others.
* A new chapter on the telegraph and telephone and how they evolved to complement such modern technologies as television and the computer.

* A new chapter on teletext and videotex and what the future holds for these experimental media.
* A new chapter on programming from the view of the program director, who must make the strategic decisions in a competitive marketplace.
* New material on common carrier regulations.
* New material on national and international controls over telecommunication.
* An expanded chapter on cable.
* Updating of important material on satellite communication.
* Updating of information on research into the uses and effects of broadcasting and telecommunication.

The text continues to examine traditional fields of study found in the first edition, including the historical basis of radio and television, educational and public telecommunication, corporate telecommunication, ratings, the research process, economics, and international broadcasting. It also includes a glossary and a library and database search guide for broadcasting and telecommunication.

A comprehensive Instructor's Manual also accompanies the text.

J.R.B.

ACKNOWLEDGMENTS

When the first edition of this text appeared, both the author and the publisher were unprepared for the warm and enthusiastic acceptance it received. It is not without a sincere desire to thank every colleague and friend that I must resort to a blanket "thank you." It is, instead, a desire not to miss any individual who deserves my gratitude for offering comments, suggestions, and reviews to change, expand the scope, and make improvements in this new edition.

I would be remiss not to thank Virginia McCarthy, my production editor on this text, who brought her expertise and patience to bear on the development of the book from manuscript to finished product. The production, marketing, editorial, and sales organization of Prentice-Hall, Inc. also deserve my gratitude. When this book arrives on the shelf, it will mark a ten-year anniversary with the same publisher, a time that has developed into a productive, but most importantly, a warm and supportive relationship.

As an author, I am deeply indebted to the students in my classes at The University of North Carolina at Chapel Hill, to the staff I had when serving as general manager of a broadcasting station, and also to the staff I worked with as a television journalist and radio news director. These acknowledgments are insufficient to express my deep thanks and the many contributions you have made to this book.

So many people in the broadcasting industry have contributed that it is almost impossible to keep count. The networks, professional organizations, stations, attorneys, state broadcasting organizations, including those in Indiana and North Carolina, and others have been of tremendous assistance.

This edition, like the first, has demanded the finest resource librarians to help an author negotiate the maze of new library technologies. Staff at The University of North Carolina at Chapel Hill, Duke University, DePauw University and the Durham and Chapel Hill public libraries were extremely helpful.

Living near the Research Triangle Park made the latest information on new technologies readily available. A number of firms in the Park helped, but IBM, G.E., Corning Glass Works, and Burroughs Wellcome deserve special mention.

Faculty and staff of the Department of Radio, Television and Motion Pictures, the Department of Speech Communication, and the School of Journalism at UNC helped with their supportive comments, review of new material, and assistance in locating sources and citations.

This new edition arrives a bit later than either the author or publisher planned. That it arrived at all is to the credit and faith that came from people such as Bryce and Pam Dodson. It was also helped by the friendship and warmth of my own faculty in the Department who were there when needed during a year that needed a lot.

No one deserves more credit than Denise.

for Denise
    John
    Donald
    Dorothy
    Smokey
    especially Mother
    and the memory of Dad

INTRODUCTION

The alarm clock, set earlier in winter since the ferries run only a staggered schedule, goes off at 5:00 A.M.. By the time the car's headlights slice through the fog over the Neuse River three hours later, the cup of hot chocolate on the dashboard tastes like a weak milk shake. The weather report on the car radio has changed from North Carolina inland crop reports to coastal tide levels. Now and then the waters of Pamlico Sound peek through the fog, and the lights of businesses greeting the dawn break through to join the sun's first rays.

Ahead lies Cedar Island, a corner of detached land lopped off the end of a peninsula that carries a roadway to its end at the ferry dock. There waiting for its first run of the day is the Cedar Island ferry. A crew member wearing a fluorescent orange vest asks for your ferry reservation number, motions you into line, and, if you timed your drive just right and didn't meet the drawbridge at Morehead City, directs you onto the ferry that will take you on the two-hour ride to Ocracoke Island.

If you are observant, you will find the ride to Ocracoke Island one of stark contrast. As the other passengers begin to emerge from their cars to go topside for a better view, the crew casts off the heavy lines, just as crews have been casting off heavy lines for thousands of years. The big vessel grinds and inches forward, the pilings scraping and squeaking against the steel plates welded to the port and starboard. Gradually the speed increases and the bow begins to produce the first splash, which, against the churning foam from the propellers, is almost unnoticed.

As you look beyond the marsh grass of the harbor, beyond the loons poised for their first morsel of morning seafood, you see the markers showing where crab traps, called *pots,* have been lowered to the bottom of the sound by people who make a living from commercial fishing. Their catch will grace the tables of gourmet restaurants and the stick-to-the ribs fare of all-you-can-eat diners. They will put down dozens of crab pots and dozens of markers. To the passengers on the passing ferry it will seem impossible for anyone to locate the traps, even with markers. The small white buoys, many made from discarded plastic bleach bottles, seem randomly thrown across hundreds of square miles of open water.

Soon the sights of land disappear and the passengers turn to walking around the decks, venturing inside the lounge, and leisurely breaking out a picnic brunch. If you are still observant, as you glance at the pilot house, where the crew navigates, you will see an array of sophisticated equipment that includes the green-glowing digital readouts of the depth finders, the frequency markers on the marine radio, and the readout of the radar antenna circling a few feet above. In the distance you may occasionally catch a glimpse of a marine research vessel with its dishlike antenna transmitting data 22,000 miles into space, to be relayed by the same satellite that will tell the vessel its exact location within feet, a job in years past delegated to the mariner's sextant.

On board the conversations pick up. People who have never met begin dialogues with each other. The inhibitions and barriers to talking with strangers are lessened. Everyone has something in common—they are all on the same vessel at the same time going to the same destination. Most are dressed casually. The conversations will be about where they live, where this trip is eventually taking them, where the best place to eat and stay on Ocracoke Island is. Some will be retirees enjoying the freedom to travel to places they have never been. Others are businesspeople who have people to see on Ocracoke. Others are couples looking forward to a romantic weekend on the unspoiled beaches and to the fresh seafood of the island restaurants.

About two hours from Cedar Island the outline of Ocracoke Island begins to appear on the horizon. First the water tower, then the line of trees, then the old lighthouse, then the telephone company's microwave tower. With all the sophisticated navigation equipment aboard oceangoing vessels, the lighthouse still shines as a beacon to craft of all sizes. It is perhaps Ocracoke's most famous landmark, but certainly not what the island is most famous for. That distinction is reserved for Blackbeard, the pirate who used Ocracoke's protected harbor as a refuge from the Crown governor.

As the ferry gets closer to Ocracoke the Coast Guard station begins to appear, and in a short time the ferry bears around the channel marker and heads into the harbor. Most of the cars venture toward motels or the beaches, or to the end of the island, where another ferry will take them north to Cape Hatteras. A telephone-company engineer will spend the afternoon on Ocracoke working at the telephone company's microwave relay station. The high-technology substation is critical to the island's communication links. It provides telephone service for the islanders. For some of the summer residents it links personal computer terminals with data banks thousands of miles away. For the island's only doctor it is a vital link with the mainland.

The day will go quickly for everyone who

made the trip. The day on the beach is always too short, the things to see too many. Soon evening will send shadows of twisted cedar trees across sandy sidewalks and shell-laced roadways.

The sun is beginning to set on Ocracoke. Before it rises tomorrow, the radio stations on the mainland will be echoing the tide levels, the fishermen will have found their crab-pot markers, the passengers on the early ferry will be chatting and exchanging greetings, and the substation will be receiving and transmitting data at the speed of light. It is truly an island of contrast.

An understanding of these contrasts is necessary to an understanding of this book.

Broadcasting and telecommunication are part of this contrast. In addition, broadcasting and telecommunication are part of rapid technological change—change that is just as far-reaching as the differences between the hand-held sextant of a ship and the satellite-navigation equipment of today's oceangoing vessel. To fully understand and appreciate these changes it is necessary to first understand the process of communication and then explore how broadcasting and telecommunication fit into the process. We will begin not with the radio station or the satellite-navigation system but with crab pots and people who fish the open water off Ocracoke Island.

1

THE PROCESS
OF COMMUNICATION

For the fishing boats leaving Ocracoke Island to plant crab pots, communication is an important part of their captain's day. Although they may check a local marine radio station for the weather forecast, or even use a home computer to access the prices of fish, their most important asset is their ability to communicate with themselves. That may sound somewhat strange when we consider we are studying broadcasting and telecommunication, but *intra*personal communication, *communication within ourselves,* is the foundation of all other types of communication.

The people who are scattering the crab pots across open water must go back and find those same pots without the aid of anything but their own instinct and knowledge of the water. The local radio stations do not tell them where their crab pots are located. Nor do their friends. Through years of accumulating bits of information too small to notice, they are able to navigate back to where the traps were set and harvest the crabs.

To better understand this process of communication we will begin by examining three terms: *transmit, transfer,* and *transact.*

UNDERSTANDING THE PROCESS OF COMMUNICATION

How would you describe the process of communication? If at first it seems difficult, do not be too disappointed. People who spend their lives researching the subject continue to argue about the process.

Transmit

Whenever we begin discussing communication the term *transmit* pops up. Transmit means to *send information.*[1] Yet if we transmit something, are we communicating? Consider the person who stands on a hilltop and shouts across the valley to hear the echo. Is that person communicating? Consider the football coach who comes off the sidelines to yell at a referee. Certainly the football coach is transmitting information. But is the coach communicating? Consider the student who tells her roommate to clean up their room. She has transmitted information, but two days later the room remains a mess. What if a television anchorperson asks viewers to write to the station about a community issue but only one viewer replies? Did communication take place? What about the disk jockey who finds she had the smallest number of listeners in the station's coverage area and is told by her boss to begin looking for another job? Was the disk jockey communicating with the listeners?

In all of our examples information was transmitted, but in each case we must ask if the information was *received.* If it was not, did communication take place?

Transfer

Another term that frequently pops up when we discuss communication is *transfer.* Transfer means to *send and receive information.* Stop and consider the examples we used. Is the television anchorperson who asks viewers to write the station transferring information? Is the person who stands on the hilltop shouting across the valley to hear the echo transferring information? Certainly that person is transmitting, but does transfer take place if no one hears the shouting? What occurs if someone on the other side of the hilltop shouts back? Does communication take place? Now let's consider the roommate. What if she heard the request but was too busy to clean up the room and did not respond? Was information transferred? Did communication take place? What about the football coach? What if the referee refuses to change the call after the coach yells from the sidelines? A transfer of information took place, but did communication take place? What about the disk jockey who had the smallest number of listeners? Transmission took place, but did transfer occur? Suppose the boss who tells the disk jockey to find work elsewhere leaves but the disk jockey is so shocked by the ratings that she blocks out of her mind the words from her boss. The boss has transmitted information, but did she transfer information?

Transaction

A third word that frequently crops up in discussions of communication is *transact.* What happens during transaction? Transaction means *information is sent and received and feedback occurs.* For example, if the anchorperson's request for mail results in a flood of letters, then information has been transmitted and received and more information sent back to the station through viewers' letters. We might suggest that if the person yelling across the valley hears a reply and then decides to yell back, transaction has taken place. If the roommate at least acknowledges she heard the request to clean up the room, even though she doesn't clean it, transaction has occurred. And what if the referee refuses to change the call but nevertheless has a healthy argument with the football coach? Transaction has occurred. If the disk jockey replies to her boss, "I guess you're right—I'll start looking tomorrow,'' has communication taken place?

The Dictionary Examines Communication

To go one step further in better understanding what lies behind the process of communication we can consult the dictionary. Our dictionary definition of *communicate* uses the phrase "to make known; impart; transmit." All of our examples would agree with this phrase—the television anchorperson, the person shouting from the hilltop, the roommate, the football coach, and the disk jockey and her boss. The dictionary next defines communication as follows: "to have an interchange, as of thoughts or ideas." This phrase is closest to our term *transaction,* but certainly includes *transfer* as well. If we are talking with our instructor about grades on an examination, we are having an interchange of thoughts and ideas. If we are participating in a class discussion, we are having an interchange of thoughts or ideas.

Now let's consider further the dictionary definition of communication and see how it might apply even more directly to the major emphasis of this text. According to our dictionary, communication can also be defined as "a system of sending and receiving messages, as by telephone, television, or computer." We will find later in the text that all three of these technologies play an important role in our understanding of broadcasting and telecommunication. For example, telephone cables may be used to carry television signals between cities. These same cables may provide two-way communication between points hundreds of miles away. This two-way data link is, as we will learn, more characteristic of telecommunication than broadcasting. As the operator interacts with the computer, electronic transaction is taking place. The operator sends informa-

tion and the computer responds with information that appears on the operator's display terminal. Thus, whereas the examples we first used—the television anchorperson, the football coach, the roommate, the person shouting from the hilltop, and the disk jockey and her boss—were primarily examples of human communication, broadcasting and telecommunication are forms of electronic communication.

Up to this point we have discussed three key terms in understanding communication—*transmit, transfer,* and *transact*—and we have examined the dictionary definition of communication. We now need to examine how researchers have defined communication.

Research Definitions of Communication

Some researchers have defined communication as "the process of creating meaning."[2] Others have defined it as "a dynamic process in which man consciously or unconsciously affects the cognitions of another through materials or agencies used in symbolic ways."[3] Still others stress the importance of viewing communication as "an act of sharing, rather than as something someone does to someone else."[4]

All three of these definitions are relevant to our examples. Our television anchorperson and our disk jockey and her boss are part of the communication process. The person standing on the hilltop obviously gave some meaning to the words he was shouting across the valley. Perhaps he was shouting "I love you," "Help!" or merely "Hello there." Definite meanings are expressed in all of those words. Certainly the roommate who wanted the mess cleaned up and the football coach who wanted the referee's call changed were also creating meaning, if not for the person receiving their communication, then surely in their own mind when they transmitted it. And there is little doubt that communication is a dynamic process that "consciously or unconsciously" affects others. We have all had experiences in which we both consciously made an effort to communicate to someone but unconsciously communicated something entirely different than what we had intended. On the other hand, it would be difficult to characterize the football coach's communication as "an act of sharing, rather than . . . something someone does to someone else."

We can see how difficult it is to arrive at a single definition of communication. Yet all of the definitions we have considered are correct. It's a dynamic process. It involves information that is transmitted and transferred, and information that becomes part of a communicative transaction. Keeping in

mind that there are hundreds of definitions of the term, we will settle on a specific definition for the purposes of this book: communication is the *movement of messages between senders and receivers.*

DISTINGUISHING AMONG TYPES OF COMMUNICATION

Not only are there characteristics that differentiate *types* of communication such as broadcasting and telecommunication but there are more general distinctions among intrapersonal, interpersonal, and mass communication. As we have seen, intrapersonal communication is communication within ourselves. *Inter*personal communication is *communication between two or more per-*

FIGURE 1-1 Basic model of communication. This basic model of communication differs from the model of mass communication which includes the gatekeeper organization. Central to all forms of communication is *intrapersonal* communication. *Interpersonal* communication involves communication in a face-to-face situation, whereas mass communication involves the addition of a mass medium and other distinguishing characteristics described in the chapter.

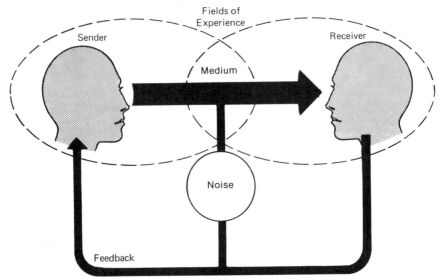

Fields of Experience

Sender

Receiver

Medium

Noise

Feedback

sons in a face-to-face situation. Mass communication usually involves a large number of people, and other factors as well. We will define it later. To learn more about the process of communication and to see how broadcasting and telecommunication fit into this process let us examine a communication model, *a stop-action picture of the communication process* (Figure 1-1).

A communication model is one of many models used by communication scholars to help clarify the process of communication.[5] Along with being a stop-action picture, it is also like a road map that tells us where messages travel and what these messages encounter along the way. For example, we can see in our basic model of communication (Figure 1-1) that it consists of a sender, a receiver, noise, a medium, and feedback.

INTRAPERSONAL COMMUNICATION

As we have learned, the people who spread traps over open water to catch crab use intrapersonal communication to process the information that tells them where the trap markers can be found. For the people who make their livelihood in this way, a degree of what they might call pure instinct comes into play. The psychologist might call such instinct intrapersonal communication.

Our senses, our nervous system, and our brain are the main physiological components of the communication process. For example, if we are watching an instructional television program about basic mathematics, our eyes and ears respond to what is on the screen. These two senses of sight and hearing send electrochemical impulses through our nervous system to our brain. After receiving the impulses, our brain feeds back other impulses to our motor nerves, the

nerves that influence movement and enable us to pick up a pencil and paper and work the math problem. Different components of the communication process have come into play: the *sender* (eyes and ears), *message* (electrochemical impulses), *medium* (nervous system), *receiver* (brain and central nervous system), and *feedback* (electrochemical impulses).[6] Another component, *noise,* can interfere with the communication process. Your head may ache to the point where you cannot think. A sickness or injury may damage your nervous system, either interrupting the passage of electrochemical impulses or interfering with your ability to respond to commands given your motor nerves by your brain. All of these are examples of one type of noise, physical noise.

To understand the process better, let's return to Figure 1-1. Note where each of the components of intrapersonal communication fits into our communication model: sender, message, medium (sometimes called *channel*), receiver, feedback, and noise.

Remember, for human communication of any kind to occur, intrapersonal communication must be present. In examining our dictionary definition of *communicate,* we see that someone must first *think* about information before it can be made known or imparted. Before an interchange of thoughts or ideas can take place between two persons, each must first employ the process of intrapersonal communication in order to react to the other's message.

We use intrapersonal communication in a number of ways every day. Consider how we adapt to stress. Stress is a stimulus, and any stimulus causes one or more reactions. We may have a headache under stress. We may sweat under stress. Each of these is a biological reaction—our body is signaling us that we are overloading our sensory system.

How do we adapt to stress? We may decide to overeat. Yet overeating may produce just the opposite effect we desire, especially if a stress-prone digestive system can't handle that much food. We may decide to overdrink, but find the consequences of visiting the local pub worse than the cure. Or we may lie awake at night trying to solve a stressful problem and pay for that wakefulness the next day. As we can see, these negative biological adaptations can cause more stress, not less.[7]

One of the most recently acclaimed methods of handling stress through intrapersonal communication is biofeedback. You've probably heard about it or read about it in popular magazines or scholarly journals. Among other things, biofeedback uses a machine to help people monitor their own body stresses. Then, through a system of trained relaxation incorporating everything from relaxing muscles to imagining relaxing scenes, people are able to minimize their reactions to stress.

Memory is another form of intrapersonal communication. It involves retrieving and encoding information stored in our brain. A person I know likes to visualize an image in order to remember a name. She easily remembers everyone she meets named Sarah, because she always thinks of a Sarah as sitting on the seat of a covered wagon. Although these associations may seem humorous and have no relation to the people we meet, they are simply ways to aid memory and stimulate the process of intrapersonal communication.

Intrapersonal communication is the foundation for adapting interpersonally to others. We process all kinds of stimuli when we communicate with other people. Using that intrapersonal processing to communicate interpersonally is one of the most important functions of our internal processing

systems. For example, many psychologists feel that to successfully manage worry, stress, and anxiety, we must communicate with others about our problems. Other research suggests that the least damage from stressful situations is done to people who discharge their fears through interpersonal relations.

INTERPERSONAL COMMUNICATION

On the Ocracoke ferry, despite the whir of the radar and the flashing digital navigation devices, interpersonal communication dominates. People talk with other people more freely than they would elsewhere. As we have mentioned, they all have something in common—they are on the same vessel going to the same destination.

As we have learned, *interpersonal communication* is communication in a face-to-face situation between at least two persons, and often many more, such as a group discussion or a speech to a crowd. In interpersonal communication the names of the components of communication are the same as in intrapersonal communication, but the components themselves are different. To continue with our previous example, imagine that instead of watching an instructional television program about mathematics you are attending the instructor's class in person. Now the instructor becomes the sender of communication; the messages become the words spoken by the instructor; the medium is the human voice; and you are the receiver of communication. If you do not understand something the instructor is saying, you can immediately raise your hand to ask a question. Your hand being raised is a form of feedback to the instructor.

Noise

Noise can also be present in interpersonal communication. Physical noise may occur if the lights go out and you cannot see the instructor. Or a student next to you may drop a pile of books, distracting you. A second type of noise can be present—semantic noise. Semantic noise can occur when the instructor uses a word or phrase having many different meanings but does not specify which meaning she wants to convey.

Sharing and Homophily

Using our example of the lecture, we can begin to see the reason communication can be referred to as a *sharing* process.[8] If constructive communication is to take place, we must share certain things with the instructor. One way of examining the process of sharing is to understand that each individual has a *field of experience*—the accumulation of knowledge, experiences, values, beliefs, and other qualities that constitutes one's self. For effective communication to take place, these fields of experience must overlap, also as seen in Figure 1–1. We must share certain things with another individual. In our example, we must first understand the language being used, both written and oral. Second, we must know something about the subject of mathematics; otherwise, the lecture would have little value for us and we could not begin to work the problems. We may also respect the instructor's ability to teach, perceiving her as having a genuine interest in mathematics whether or not we are able to comprehend the subject. If we have proved ourselves good students, the instructor will probably consider us as being interested in the subject, respect our ability to learn, and perceive us as having a genuine interest in learning. We can also stress this concept of sharing as an *identification,* not only be-

tween people's experiences but between language symbols as well.[9]

Communication researchers have used behavioral-research methods to examine the concept of sharing in more detail. Sharing has also been examined by such well-known social scientists as Paul Lazarsfeld and Robert Merton. The technical term for sharing is *homophily.* Homophily can best be understood as overlap. As McCroskey and Wheeless state, "To the extent that the attitudes, beliefs, experiences, education, background, culture, and so forth, of the source [sender] and the receiver overlap, they are more likely to attempt communication with each other, and equally as important, they are more likely to be effective in their communication attempts."[10] This concept—whether we call it *sharing interaction* or *homophily*—is important to remember, because it focuses on how we react to all communication.

MASS COMMUNICATION

Now that we have a basic understanding of the processes of intrapersonal and interpersonal communication, we need to understand the process of mass communication and, specifically, where broadcasting and telecommunication fit into the process (Figure 1–2). Mass communication is different from intrapersonal and interpersonal communication, but all three types play an important part in our lives. For the people fishing off Ocracoke Island, the weather report from the radio stations on the mainland is just as important as their instinctive ability to find their crab-pot markers. And when they bring their catch in, their ability to use interpersonal communication to bargain with the wholesalers directly affects their livelihood.

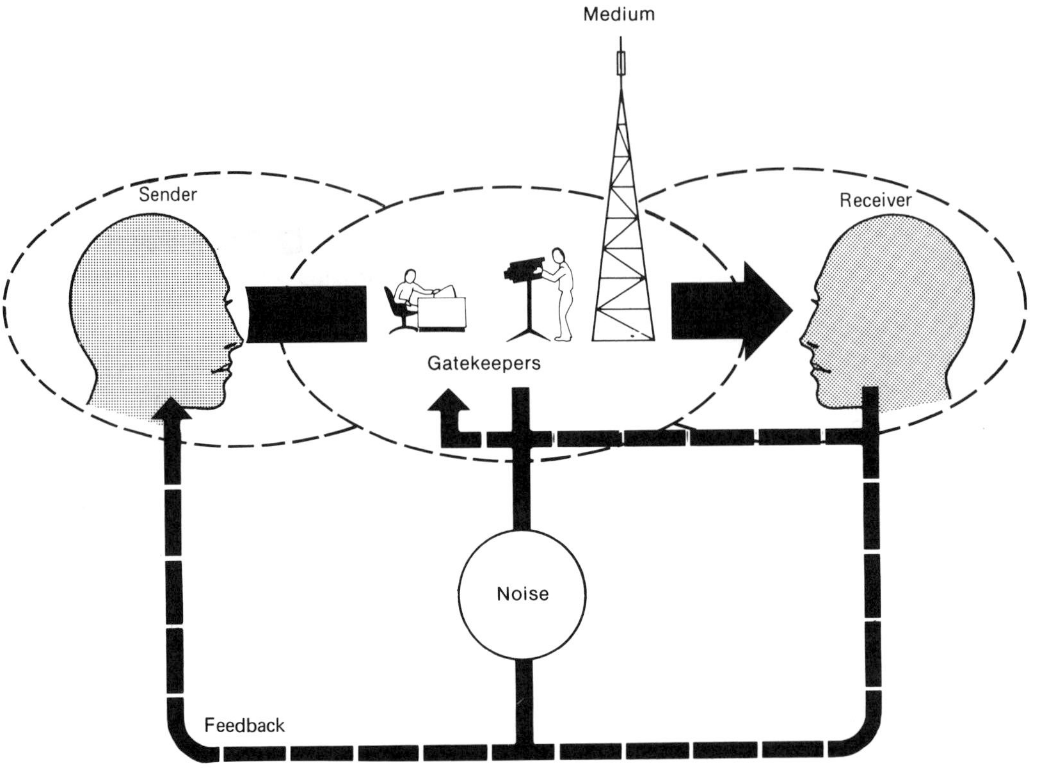

FIGURE 1–2 Model of mass communication. Gatekeepers can be one individual or an entire organization. The presence of a mass medium, limited sensory channels, a gatekeeper, and delayed feedback are characteristics which distinguish mass communication from intrapersonal and interpersonal communication.

Defining Mass

First, as the word *mass* suggests, mass communication can reach a large number of people through a mass medium. The number of people who could attend the lecture on mathematics was determined by the size of the classroom. However, if the lecture were televised, it could be made available to many thousands, perhaps millions, of people.

The Medium

To make the lecture available to all those people, it is necessary for us to alter our concept of medium. No longer is the medium just the human voice or the nervous system; we add a mass medium such as television, the radio, books, or newspapers, depending upon the applicability of the medium to our task. It may be somewhat difficult, although certainly not impossible, to teach our mathematics section by radio. We may even produce a series of articles for the newspaper. If we want to teach music appreciation, radio might be just as effective as television and considerably cheaper. On the other hand, if we want to teach surgical techniques, television would be far superior (Figure 1–3). In every case, in order to transcend the limitations of interpersonal communication, we

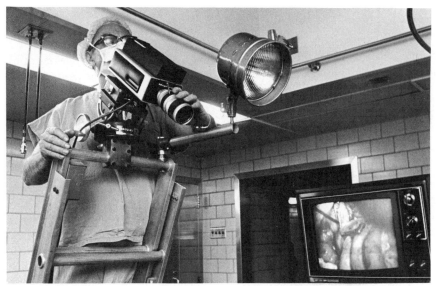

FIGURE 1-3 In many situations, television is an effective teaching tool, sometimes superior to other methods of instruction. The ability of the television camera to look directly at the surgical techniques employed in this operation makes it possible for medical students to view the procedure much more closely than would be possible if they were in an observation area. (Division of Audio/Visual Services, Johns Hopkins Medical Institutions)

would need a mass medium to reach our audience. For our purposes, therefore, we will define mass communication as *messages directed toward a group of people through a mass medium*.

Limited Sensory Channels

A mass medium also limits the number of sensory channels operating between the sender and receiver of communication. In interpersonal communication, all of our senses participate in the process of communication—our sight, hearing, smell, even touch. In mass communication these senses are limited. With radio, for example, we may be able only to hear someone deliver a speech. With television we could hear and see the person but not shake hands.

The Gatekeeper

Besides the presence of a mass medium, another factor traditionally differentiating mass communication from intrapersonal and interpersonal communication is the presence of a gatekeeper. With the addition of these two concepts, our basic model of communication now represents the process of mass communication.

The term *gatekeeper* was first applied to the study of communication by Austrian psychologist Kurt Lewin, who defined it as "a person or groups of persons governing the travels of news items in the communication channel."[11] Today, the term applies not only to groups of persons but to entire institutions. Within these institutions are both people and technology, all interacting to "govern the travels" of information between senders and receivers. That information is much more than news, as Lewin suggested. It may be strictly informative, such as an evening television news program compiled and produced by hundreds of reporters (Figure 1-4), camera-operators, editors, engineers, specialists in audio and video recording, researchers, writers, and many others. Or the message may be entertaining and involve producers, directors, costumers, scene designers, musicians, and countless more. The gatekeeper now becomes not only a person or group of persons but people and technology through which the message must pass and be acted upon, and sometimes altered, before it reaches the consuming public.

FIGURE 1-4 Gatekeeper institutions consist of all of those individuals who "govern the travels" of information between senders and receivers of communication. Reporters as well as camera persons are gatekeepers in television news departments and aid in bringing information to the public. That same news department could include such people as researchers, writers, directors, producers, and engineers. (Reprinted by permission of the Magnetic Audio/Video Products Division, 3M Company, St. Paul, Minnesota)

Functions of the Gatekeeper

The function of the gatekeeper is to alter, limit, and expand what we receive from the mass media. Assume one morning that a television assignment editor dispatches a news crew to cover a music festival. When they arrive, the crew finds the festival spread out over a city block. In addition to violinists, pianists, and guitar players, there are groups of musicians playing everything from bagpipes to kazoos.

Upon seeing the television crew arrive, all of the musicians begin to play, each trying to gain attention. The reporter in charge of the story decides to focus on the bagpipe players. She bases this decision on a number of things. For one, the colorful costumes of the musicians will look good on color television. The bagpipes are also something the average viewer does not have the opportunity to see very often. In addition, the leader of the group is from Scotland and has a distinct Scottish accent. His voice alone will help hold the viewers' attention. That night our bagpipe players appear on the evening news.

Now let's examine how gatekeepers—in this case, the news crew—affected the information we received. First, they *expanded* our informational environment by offering us information we otherwise would not have received. The music festival may have been in an outlying community, and we either may not have had the time or may not have wanted to go to the trouble of driving all that way to attend it in person. On the other hand, the crew also *limited* the information we received. For instance, many more performers were at the music festival than just those who played bagpipes. However, because the news crew chose to focus upon that one group, we were not exposed to any of the other performers. Had we been present at the music festival, we probably would have seen everyone perform. But because we watched a report of it on the evening news, we were greatly restricted in the amount of information we received.

In summary, gatekeepers serve three functions: (1) they can alter the information to which we are exposed; (2) they can expand our information by making us privy to facts of which we would not normally have been aware; and (3) they can limit the information we receive by making us aware of only a small amount of information compared with the total amount we would have been exposed to if we had been present at an event.

Delayed Feedback

Another distinction between mass communication and other types of communication is delayed feedback. Remember when you were sitting in the classroom listening to the mathematics lecture? There, as we noted, you could give instant feedback to the instructor. You could raise your hand, ask a question, and probably have your question immediately answered. However, when you were watching the mathematics lecture on television this immediacy vanished. If you did not understand something and wanted to ask a question, you could only telephone the station, if the program were live, or write a letter to the professor. Either of these alternatives is feedback, but this time it is *delayed* feedback.

New Technology: Altering Delayed Feedback

New developments in broadcast technology have in some cases altered the delayed feedback of mass communication. New two-way media do permit instant feedback under some circumstances. For instance, the instructor teaching the mathematics course via television may have two different television monitors in front of the lectern, which permit her to view students in two different classrooms hundreds of miles away. In turn, all of the students can see and hear the instructor on the television monitors located in each classroom. A two-way voice connection permits the instructor to hear any questions the students may ask and to answer them immediately. Although messages are being directed toward a large number of people through a mass medium, instant feedback is possible.

Altering the Definition of Mass

At first glance, it may seem as if the appropriate wording of our definition should be messages directed toward a *mass audience,* or large number of people, through a mass medium. Although this traditional definition has merit and in some ways is correct, it has been altered by new applications of mass media, such as the use of radio and television for internal corporate communication. We now find television connecting the boards of directors of two corporations located on different sides of the continent, or even oceans away, for executive conferences. Meetings whose participants are scattered hundreds of miles apart take place regularly in this way. Television is also used to disseminate messages to rather small audiences that cannot communicate face to face. A state-police commander may give a training lecture in front of a television camera. The videotape of the lecture is then played back at regional command centers throughout the state at which groups of ten or twelve troopers view the lecture. In each case the audience is relatively small, far from what we would normally consider a mass audience.

If we consider computers in our definition of mass, we must again alter the way we traditionally perceive the mass audience. For example, we might publish a magazine electronically by placing its contents in a data bank accessed via computer (Figure 1–5). Let us assume that our magazine is a highly specialized mass medium that reaches a small audience, such as ranchers living in Montana. In addition to obtaining this visual display, our audience has access to an index listing each article in the magazine. A rancher may need only to read an article dealing with beef pricing and disregard the other information contained in the publication. Thus, although the magazine is a mass medium, it is published only in an electronic edition and reaches only a highly specialized audience. Compared with a national television audience the readership of the electronic edition of our magazine is very small—so small we might fail to recognize that it, too, is a mass audience, though not a large one.

The use of new technology such as interactive media is continuing to alter the traditional definition of mass communication. The important thing to remember is that it is not necessarily how many people are exposed to a message, but how many people have access to the message and how it is delivered, that helps distinguish mass communication from intrapersonal and interpersonal communication.

Communicative Noise

Noise can exist in mass communication just as it can in intrapersonal and interpersonal communication. Noise can appear in the processing of information through the gatekeeper. Keep in mind that the network of gatekeepers can consist of many different persons or groups of people, all of whom are part of the processing of information. When information is passed from one gatekeeper to another it can become distorted.

One example of noise in the communicative process occurred when a group of reporters covered an incident along an interstate highway in the Midwest. A truck carrying two canisters of phosgene gas stopped at a truck stop. The driver of the truck smelled a peculiar odor and decided that one of the canisters was leaking. He became sick and was taken to a local hospital. When state

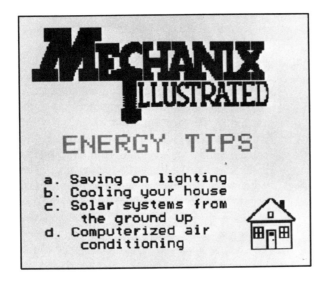

FIGURE 1-5 The traditional definition of mass communication is being altered by such interactive video systems as two-way cable and videotex, both discussed in Chapters 8 and 9, respectively. Using videotex to access an electronic data bank, the subscriber can obtain electronic editions of magazines, newspapers, and other information materials once restricted to the print media. These new media, because of the active participation of the individual, are considered more personalized than traditional mass media.

police learned from the invoice what the truck was carrying, they notified authorities at a local army depot. The state police then blocked off an exit on the interstate highway almost twenty miles away. It was the logical place to divert traffic since it was next to a main feeder highway, which made an excellent detour in case the highway immediately adjacent to the truck stop had to be blocked off.

When all of this information was processed into the news media, all under the pressure of deadlines and semicrisis conditions, it was distorted considerably. First, news reports left the impression that the truck was loaded with phosgene gas, and not merely two canisters of it. Obviously, a leak in a tank of gas the size of a gasoline tanker would be much more serious than a leak in a single canister about five feet high and less than two feet in diameter, strapped to the back of a flatbed truck. Second, because phosgene gas had been used in World War I, the wire services began to refer to the canisters as containing "war gas." Added to this was the news of the roadblock twenty miles away, which left the impression that everyone in a twenty-mile radius of the truck stop was in danger of inhaling war gas.

The network of gatekeepers that covered the story included a group of reporters from three radio stations, at least two newspapers, two wire services, and two television stations, and the local and military authorities, who also were dispensing information. The "institution" of gatekeepers was substantial, and much information was processed and eventually distorted.

Reducing Communicative Noise

Just as new technology has altered the concept of delayed feedback, it has altered noise, primarily by reducing it. In 1950 it would have been almost impossible to carry live pictures and sound from one continent to another. Back then, the speech of a European leader would have been reported first by a correspondent and then fed to a wire-service editor in the United States. The wire-service editor would have then rewritten the correspondent's report before sending it over the teletype to subscribers. This entire process was subject to much distortion and noise, because of the number of gatekeepers involved.

Today, although that process still takes place, it is now possible for a videotape of a speech to be sent by satellite into the homes of viewers thousands of miles away. On the evening news the viewer watches the picture and listens to the voice of the political leader in place of the correspondent's interpretations; this reduces the possibility of noise. Even the newspaper reporter can carry a small recorder, almost as inconspicuous as a note pad, and reduce the chance of misquoting a source. Still, few systems of processing information are perfect. Remember that although broadcast technology can reduce noise, the human factor is always present to return some noise to the system.

THE SOCIAL CONTEXT OF MASS COMMUNICATION

Our discussion thus far has concerned messages being sent, processed, and received. Although we have seen how gatekeepers act upon those messages, we should also realize that social forces act upon senders, gatekeepers, and receivers, influencing how they react to and process messages.

Consider the analogy of the computer. Data is fed (sent) into the computer, where it is processed and then presented, usually in the form of a printout. You might feed the computer a series of numbers, of which the computer will add and print out the answer. If you fed the same set of numbers into the computer each time, the computer's answer would be the same each time. Such is not the case with messages sent, processed, and received by means of mass communication. People are not computers, and we do not live in a vacuum. Messages causing one reaction at one time may cause an entirely different reaction another time. A politician's speech that attracted one gatekeeper's attention might not attract another's. Let's examine this in more detail.

Social Context of Senders

Assume that you have decided to run for a political office and it is time to begin the long, arduous trail to election day. In writing the speech that will kick off your campaign, you want to convey to the crowd those qualities you feel will truthfully express your character, your position on the issues, your background, and your intentions. As you approach the podium in a small rural community you think about the times you have seen scenes like this before. The serenity of your childhood, the familiar faces of people you do not know but really do know, the soft, mellow breeze—everything is there, including two gatekeepers, a reporter from each of the two local radio stations.

You begin your speech. You talk about things and individuals that have influenced your life. You talk about farm prices, having grown up on a farm, and you know what you are talking about. You relate your experiences of meeting expenses during the harvest season and borrowing money to buy tractors. You also talk about the plight of those in small business, for after the farm failed your family opened a clothing store. All of these social forces had a direct effect

on your campaign speech. Now how did your speech affect the two gatekeepers?

Social Context of the Gatekeeper

When you listen to the newscasts of the two radio stations later that afternoon, you are surprised to find that each reporter covered a different part of your speech. One reported your comments on farm prices and only briefly mentioned statements about small businesses. The other station detailed your statements about small businesses but skimmed your comments about farm prices. Although you considered both reports objective, you wondered why they focused upon different subjects. You discover later that the reporter who reported your comments on farm prices not only grew up on a farm but also owned one. The other reporter grew up in the suburbs, his father had a small business, and he had no love whatsoever for farming. Each reporter had interpreted your speech in accordance with his own background. Unlike a computer programmed to select and process certain information, the two reporters were as different as the forces influencing them.

In research these phenomena have been called *selective perception* and *selective retention*. Selective perception means we perceive only certain things, such as those that are most familiar to us or that agree with our preconceived ideas. The reporters' backgrounds and resulting selective perception created two different interpretations of the speech. Selective retention means we tend to remember things that are familiar to us or that we perceive as corresponding to our preconceived ideas. Research implies that what reporters selectively perceive and retain can become even more prominent when they cover controversial issues.[12]

Another influence on the story might be

the reporters' peers. The reporters may belong to a professional association and adhere to a code of ethics. This code could in turn directly affect the stories processed by these gatekeepers and consequently received by the public. What if the music festival we discussed earlier had charged a ten-dollar admission fee? And what if the assignment editor, as part of his professional ethics, had prohibited any of the staff from accepting free tickets to any event while assigned to cover that event? Admission to the festival for the news crew would have come to thirty dollars. But what if the manager of the station had refused to pay the thirty-dollar admission fee for "something as unimportant as a music festival." The editor might have decided finally not to assign a news crew to the festival. Do you agree with that decision?

Social Context of Receivers: Opinion Leaders

Just as gatekeepers do not operate in a vacuum, neither do receivers of mass communication. Our family, co-workers, peer groups, and organizations all affect how we receive and how we react to messages from the mass media. In this social realm, interpersonal communication is also very important. For instance, upon hearing the report of your campaign speech over one of the radio stations, one local listener thinks your speech has some strong merits. Yet her friend has an entirely different opinion. Since the listener respects her friend's opinion, she in turn changes her opinion of your speech. In this case, the friend acted as an *opinion leader, a person upon whom we rely to interpret messages originally disseminated through the mass media.*[13]

Consider another example. Suppose you are watching television and see a commercial about a new headache remedy. The remedy claims to be better than aspirin, to cause fewer side effects, and to work much faster. You have been having trouble with headaches, but instead of running out to buy the new remedy you call your friend, a nurse whose opinion you respect. The nurse recommends the new remedy, and the following day you purchase it and take two pills. It works. Notice, however, that it was not the commercial that convinced you to purchase the medicine. Although the commercial helped, your friend ultimately convinced you. She served as an opinion leader. Had she not recommended the remedy, chances are you might not have bought it then.

Interrelationships of Senders, Gatekeepers, and Receivers

In reviewing our examples of what occurs when information is processed through the mass media, you should begin to see many relationships among senders, gatekeepers, and receivers. For example, it was homophily—the perceived sharing or overlap of experiences between you and the two radio reporters—that caused each reporter to report a different part of your campaign speech to listeners. Similarly, the radio listeners interpreted your speech in certain ways, also because of this sharing or perceived sharing of experiences, attitudes, and other things. In fact, listeners may even have selected one radio station over the other because of similarities they perceived between themselves and the reporter.

Selecting one radio station over another is an example of *selective exposure,* whereby we expose ourselves to information that we perceive to support our beliefs or ideas. By studying the functional uses of mass media we can examine how we selectively expose ourselves to certain media because those media fulfill a particular need. For example, people waiting out a storm to fish near Ocracoke Island will exhibit selective exposure. They will turn to the radio stations that provide the most accurate weather information, selectively exposing themselves to that station over others. Or they may own a special weather radio locked on a frequency that broadcasts weather reports twenty-four hours a day.

BROADCASTING AS MASS COMMUNICATION

In its most basic sense, *broadcast* can mean "scattered over a wide area" or "in a scattered manner; far and wide." The dictionary also includes such definitions as "to make known over a wide area: broadcast rumors." Certainly a disgruntled loser of an election would agree with that definition. Or consider the definition "to participate in a radio or television program." The guest home economist on an afternoon radio program for consumers would agree with that definition. The farmer in the 1800s, who had never heard of radio or television, would have agreed with the dictionary's definition that broadcast means "to sow (seed) over a wide area, especially by hand." So would the people scattering crab pots in the open water off Ocracoke Island.

FIGURE 1-6 Television has the ability to reach mass audiences with high-quality programming. For example, public broadcasting has achieved recognition for cultivating an interest in the arts and making it available to the public through programs such as the "Dance in America" series produced by WNET/13 in New York. The dancers are from a scene in "Adorations." (WNET/13)

Consulting a thesaurus, we find that words similar in meaning to *broadcast* include *disperse, generalize, let fall, cultivate, communicate, publish, telecommunication, oration,* and *waste.*[14] We would not have to travel far to encounter people who would agree with all of those meanings. The advertising executive would *disperse* knowledge about a client's product through broadcasting commercials. The supporter of noncommercial public broadcasting would argue that quality programming *cultivates* an interest in culture and the arts (Figure 1–6). The broadcast journalist subpoenaed before a grand jury and asked to divulge the source of her latest investigative report would argue that under the First Amendment to the U.S. Constitution *broadcast* means the same as *publish,* and that her rights to protect the confidentiality of her news sources are the same as those of newspaper reporters. To the corporate executive, *broadcast* might be associated more closely with *telecommunication.* For example, the image of two executives sitting in a corporate boardroom can be reproduced on television monitors one continent away. There, other corporate executives talk back to the boardroom executives via a two-way television system. For the person highly critical of television programming the term *waste* might be more appropriate. The term *vast wasteland,* coined by former chairman of the Federal Communications Commission Newton Minow, has become a favorite of critics of commercial television.[15] For our part, we will define *broadcast* as *signals sent via radio or television.*

By now you should have begun to see how broadcasting enters into the process of mass communication. Notice that between the senders and receivers of broadcast communication are the broadcasting stations. These, along with supporting and allied organizations, directly affect the messages sent through this medium of mass communication. Broadcasting stations consist of standard-broadcast radio and television stations as well as cable television—commonly called community antenna television (CATV)—and closed-circuit television (CCTV).

SUPPORT STRUCTURES OF ELECTRONIC MEDIA

The role of broadcasting and other electronic media as forms of mass communication are affected by numerous support structures (Figure 1–7). These range from the committees of Congress who hammer out legislation affecting the industry to small-town municipalities debating a cable-television ordinance, from creative minds at a metropolitan production center to the local merchant preparing a drugstore commercial. We will divide these support structures into program suppliers, supporting industries, professional organizations, control mechanisms, technical services, audience-measurement services, and management services.[16]

Program Suppliers

Program suppliers provide stations, cable operators and others with programming ranging from Hollywood game shows to spectaculars. Many of these suppliers are already familiar to us. They include such major television networks as CBC in Canada; BBC in Great Britain; NHK in Japan; and ABC, CBS, NBC, and PBS in the United States. Television production houses, such as MTM Enterprises, are other program sources. Their programs are either sold directly to the networks or distributed through major distribution companies, such as Viacom. Not all program sources deal

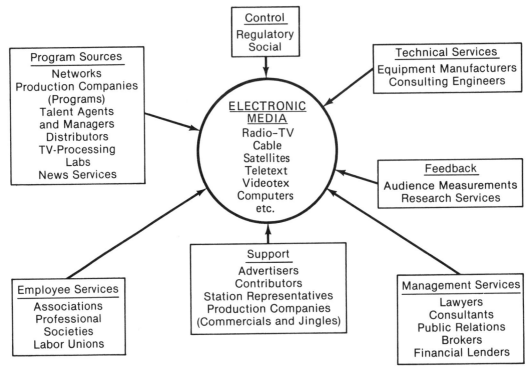

FIGURE 1-7 The institutions of electronic media include many support systems. The program we view on television can be affected by the program source, regulatory and social controls, technical services, feedback from the audience, management, advertising, and employee services such as professional societies and labor unions. (Adapted from Wilbur Schramm and Janet Alexander, "Broadcasting," in *Handbook of Communication*, ed. Ithiel de Sola Pool and others, p. 586, © 1973 Rand McNally College Publishing Company, reprinted with permission)

with entertainment. News program sources have become increasingly important as communication links with satellites continue to shrink the world and whet our interest in international events. Two widely used radio news program sources are United Press International Audio and Associated Press Radio.

Supporting Industries

These consist of advertising agencies, which place commercials on stations, and station representatives, who act as national sales-

persons for a station, group of stations, or cable systems and other forms of electronic media.

Professional Organizations

Within any industry or profession are services that link employees together for a variety of reasons, from professional to purely social. For example, broadcasting's version of such a service is the National Association of Broadcasters (NAB). More narrowly defined professional organizations include the Radio Television News Directors Association (RTNDA) and American Women in Radio and Television (AWRT). There are over one hundred other broadcast-employee services in the United States alone. Labor unions constitute a large share of the broadcast-employee membership, especially in metropolitan stations and the networks. Major unions having a foothold in broadcasting include the International Brotherhood of Electrical Workers (IBEW) and the Communication Workers of America (CWA).

Control Mechanisms

Control of electronic media ranges from governmental to social. At the national level, governmental control is represented by the Federal Communications Commission (FCC) and the National Telecommunications and Information Administration (NTIA). In the former, control takes the form of specific laws and regulations. In the latter, it is oriented more toward policy issues. State and local governments may also control broadcasting, cable in particular.

In the social-control arena public-interest groups, such as Action for Children's Television (ACT), lobby both legislators and the stations themselves. Hearings on television violence held by another group, the National Congress of Parents and Teachers (PTA), culminated in a report to the industry and pressure to reduce violence on television.

Advertisers and stockholders also exercise control over broadcasting. In fact, a small-market radio station may fear the loss of its biggest advertiser just as much as a visit from an FCC inspector. Why? Because advertisers, especially in smaller communities, can often "influence" the content of broadcast programming. If the local car dealer spends a huge sum of advertising money on a station, his drunk-driving charge may conveniently be absent from the morning news, all on the strong suggestion of the station manager. Or sponsors may refuse to air their ads during violence-filled programs.

Technical Services

The hardware components of electronic media have spawned a giant industry consisting of everything from the production of television and radio receivers to engineering consulting. General Electric, Zenith, SONY, Panasonic, RCA, Motorola, and others all vie for this lucrative broadcasting market. In addition, companies and governments actively produce and service satellite and microwave systems that span the globe. The industry also fosters its own technical service—the consulting engineer. When an antenna on a two-thousand-foot tower needs fixing, it is hardly the job for the local TV repair shop.

Audience-Measurement Services

An audience is the lifeblood of any mass medium. Measuring this audience uses the talent of a host of survey companies. Other such companies specialize in customized surveys, such as measuring the effectiveness of a station promotion, undertaking a station-image survey, or initiating a personality-recognition survey among the viewers.

Management Services

With the increasing complexity of electronic media, few broadcast managers have the skills necessary for handling all functions. They must therefore rely on management consultants. Among the most important of these are attorneys hired to help them process the mountain of governmental forms they now must file, and to give advice on complicated legal matters. Most of the major communication law firms are in Washington, D.C., close to the heart of government.

Promotion services and brokers are two other management services that are important to the industry. Media are becoming highly specialized where more competition evolves every day. Sophisticated advertising and promotion campaigns are necessary if a station is to thrive in the marketplace. Professional promotion consultants are available who handle such things as station public relations or special advertising campaigns. Brokers are the real-estate professionals of the industry. If we want to buy or sell a station or media property, we will probably use a broadcast broker.

Although we have discussed each of these allied organizations and services separately, keep in mind that they are interrelated. The production company is just as concerned about the FCC's stand on obscenity as the broadcaster is. The attorney's advice is just as valuable to the advertising agency producing a broadcast commercial as it is to the station manager. The organizations and interrelationships constitute the interactive process of broadcasting in our society.

DEFINING TELECOMMUNICATION

Now that we have examined definitions and processes of communication, and examined how mass communication and broadcasting fit into these definitions, we want to understand the other term that appears in the title of this book—*telecommunication. Telecommunication* is not a new term, but its use is somewhat more recent among teachers and researchers of broadcasting. Although we did not define it at the time, we have already discussed telecommunication. The microwave relay tower on Ocracoke Island sends and receives information that includes telephone conversations and computer data. Both *telephone* and *computer* (Figure 1–8) have traditionally played an important role in defining telecommunication. If we return to the dictionary and examine the definition of telecommunication, we find such words and phrases as "electronic communication," "transmission of impulses," "telegraphy," "telephone," "cable," "radio," "computer," "television," and "messages communicated electronically." We know from examining the Greek term *tele* that it means "at a distance" or "far off." Thus,

FIGURE 1–8 Personal computers are playing an increasingly important role in telecommunication. With the ability to remotely access data banks anywhere in the world, electronic publishing opportunities, and software sold much like books and magazines, the computer is taking on many of the characteristics of more traditional mass media. See also Chapter 5. (TRS 80 Pocket Computer. Used with permission of Radio Shack and Tandy Corporation. TRS 80 is a trademark of Tandy Corporation)

we can see in the juncture of *tele* and *communication* a meaning that includes "distant communication." At the same time, *telephone* is also derived from *tele,* and in its common usage *telecommunication* incorporates as much a sense of communication by telephone as it does the meaning of long-distance communication. Until the recent development of two-way cable-television systems, which we will discuss later, computer data and video communication traveled primarily through telephone lines or through microwave-relay systems that in many cases were owned by the telephone company.

The emergence of two-way interactive media, such as cable television systems that permit viewers to talk back electronically to their television sets and select information from central data banks, has enabled us to see how the differences between technologies are being diminished. *Telecommunication* has become a broad term that centers more and more in *electronic communication,* of which the computer, radio, television, cable, telegraph, and telephone are all a part. It encompasses *broadcasting* in its more traditional sense of a radio or television station sending signals to the masses as well as the electronic magazine in Montana accessed via a home computer. It encompasses the radio stations that broadcast weather reports to the fishing vessels off Ocracoke Island and the radar signals emanating from the antenna on top of the ferry leaving Cedar Island. Electronic signals may travel through the air and be *broad*cast to a wide region. The radio station on the mainland broadcasting weather reports uses radio waves, which we will later learn are part of the lower end of an electronic yardstick we call the electromagnetic spectrum. These waves are not relayed via telephone lines or other facilities but travel directly to the

listeners tuned to the station. Such stations are truly broadcasting in the traditional sense.

At the same time, however, a local radio station airing a newscast that originates in New York must first receive it via telephone lines through a satellite system. In addition, a local cable system may pick up the signal from the radio station and feed it to its subscribers on one of the cable channels. We can see from this that the term *broadcasting* is simply not broad enough to be accurately applied to all of the technologies that are now part of our world of electronic communication. Thus, we have adopted the broader term *telecommunication.* We will define telecommunication as *electronic communication involving both wired and unwired, one-way and two-way communications systems.* We can see that this definition includes broadcasting.

CONTEMPORARY APPLICATIONS OF TELECOMMUNICATION: WHERE THIS BOOK WILL TAKE US

The present chapter has helped us define key terms and understand some examples of them, but we have only scratched the surface of telecommunication. In the chapters that follow we will learn more about broadcasting and other fields in this important realm of technology.

The History and Development of Telecommunication

Although this is not a history book, Chapters 2–5 will examine some of the historical foundations of telecommunication. We will begin by examining the first technologies that could be called the ancestors of modern telecommunication, the telegraph and telephone. From the wires that stretched across Europe and the pony-express routes of the Great Plains to the first sound that emanated from Alexander Graham Bell's telephone, telegraph and telephone are part of our technological heritage. Today these two technologies stretch beyond the confines of any geographic region to satellites (Figure 1-9) traveling thousands of miles in space beaming telephone and telegraph signals across continents.

We will also see how the computer gradually integrated itself into these technologies and brought about a new frontier of communication. We will be introduced to terms such as *microprocessor,*

FIGURE 1-9 Satellite communication permits instantaneous transmission and reception of audio, video, and data signals anyplace in the world where ground stations are located. International and domestic satellite systems, aided by the space shuttle and proposed space docking and space stations, are continuing to revolutionize worldwide telecommunication in the 1980s. (See also Chapter 7) Shown is one of the INTELSAT satellites which is part of an international multi-nation satellite network. (Courtesy Aeronutronic Ford and Ford Aerospace & Communications Corporation)

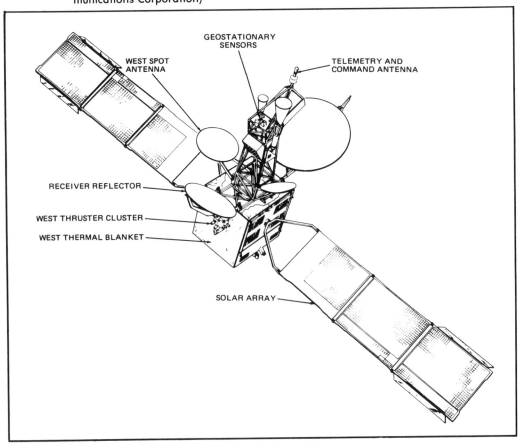

random-access memory, and *interactive video,* all of which we will learn more about in later chapters.

Broadcast and Information Technologies

In Chapters 6–10 we will look more closely at some of the technologies of broadcasting and telecommunication. As we learn about how radio waves bring us the morning weather and our favorite programs we will examine the electronic yardstick, or electromagnetic spectrum, that we referred to earlier. We will also learn about microwaves, which appear higher on our electronic yardstick and help carry telephone and data communication from microwave towers such as the one on Ocracoke Island. Microwaves can travel thousands of miles into space, bouncing back to earth thousands of miles from the point of origin and bringing us everything from our evening television programs to our long-distance telephone calls.

We will look at satellite communication, which has helped advance the technology and applications of telecommunication. From the navigation antenna on board a marine-research vessel to the rooftop antenna of a remote Alaskan village, satellites have challenged the boundaries of our minds and the boundaries of cultures.

We will discuss cable communication, which began as experimental antennas on mountaintops in the late 1940s and today is a billion-dollar industry that "wires" cities and greatly expands the number of television channels and other services we can receive. Two-way cable systems are capable of providing interactive video, whereby a small home terminal can activate services such as home banking, shopping, theater purchases, and airline reservations.

Of all the applications of new technology that are available to the public, teletext and videotex have perhaps received the most attention. Teletext is primarily a one-way system that operates much like a television signal but consists of textual information that may also be electronically illustrated. Videotex is a wired, two-way interactive textual system carrying information and electronic illustrations. Our example of the electronic magazine for the Montana rancher is an application of videotex. With a home terminal an individual can access a computer data bank. A "menu" of the information in this bank can be called up on a television screen, and the subscriber can then select from it.

Other communication technologies are also being developed. New cellular mobile radio systems permit many more mobile telephones to operate than ever before. Since mobile telephones, the kind we could use in our car, employ radio waves to transmit and receive messages, the number of these phones in each city, for example, used to be limited to prevent interference. But by dividing each city up into cells and using different frequencies for different cells, we have made it possible for more telephones to be licensed to the same geographic area.

The same satellites that carry data and other information into space carry the pictures and voices of businesspeople conducting meetings via a process known as teleconferencing. Using video and voice hookups between distant locations, a group of executives in, for example, Columbus, Ohio, can talk and see another group of executives in San Francisco, all via television monitors. The expense of a two-way audio-video link is much less than the travel costs and lost time of business executives who need to cross the country for a meeting. Teleconferencing is another of the technologies whose principles and applications we will investigate.

Systems and Programming

In Chapters 11–15 we will look at some of the telecommunication systems that are part of broadcasting and other technologies. The major networks and the public broadcasting services—for years, important parts of the distribution system for radio and television—are now being joined by distribution via syndication. Through syndication, programs are sold directly to stations. We'll examine both networks and syndication in Part 3. We will also look more closely at how telecommunication affects our educational system. What started in the late 1930s as a crude closed-circuit educational television program that ushered in the era of educational television (ETV) has expanded today into educational telecommunication whereby students may sit at their own personal-computer terminal and learn such subjects as statistics and accounting. At the same time, a group of managers in a nearby assembly plant may spend part of their lunch hour enrolled in a telecourse, a course taught by television. We will discuss the development of educational telecommunication and contemporary applications of telecommunication in business and industry, as well as broadcast programming. Much of Chapters 11–14 focus on telecommunication in North America. In Chapter 15 we will examine international broadcasting systems and how they differ from broadcasting systems in the United States and Canada.

Regulatory Control

As we have seen, control is one of the components of broadcasting's support structure. In Chapters 16–19 we will expand our knowledge of the controls that affect broadcasting and telecommunication. We will begin by examining the historical basis for the system of laws and regulations that affect telecommunication. We will then analyze the most prominent regulatory agency affecting telecommunication, the Federal Communications Commission. Looking more closely at the content of radio and television programming and the operation of broadcasting stations, we will study such regulations as the Fairness Doctrine and Section 315 of the Communications Act of 1934. We will also examine some of the steps one follows when seeking permission from the FCC to construct a new radio or television station. We will observe the regulatory structure affecting common carriers, such as telephones and other interstate communication systems. The provisions of a typical cable-television ordinance and how local governments deal with such ordinances will give us an insight into this emerging arena of municipal law. The increasing technological capacity to reproduce information has resulted in new issues in copyright law, ranging from cable-television systems to photocopying.

Economics and Evaluation

An inside look at any commercial radio or television station will uncover an economic base necessary to keep the station operating. In Chapters 20–23 we will examine some of the financial issues and procedures found in a typical station and study the important contribution of broadcast promotion to a successful operation. We will also take an inside look at broadcast ratings. Ratings in many markets are an indicator of station success, and a station's income is directly related to how well it does in the ratings—how many people are listening to or viewing the station.

From the station advertising director trying out a new promotional campaign to the college professor completing a study on television violence, research in telecommunication is necessary for intelligent decision making by everyone from legislators to station managers. In Chapter 22 we will examine the different types of research in telecommunication and some of the issues surrounding them. Much of this research focuses on the audience and users of telecommunication. Our study of broadcasting and telecommunication will conclude with an examination of the audience of radio and television programming and how it is affected by and reacts to it.

SUMMARY

The basis of the process of communication is intrapersonal communication—communication within ourselves. In intrapersonal communication our senses become the senders of communication, our brain processes the messages sent by our senses, and we react to feedback messages sent to our muscles.

The basic components of the communication process—sender, messages, medium, receiver, feedback, and noise—apply both to intrapersonal and interpersonal or face-to-face communication. Interpersonal communication encompasses intrapersonal communication. In interpersonal communication the sender of communication is one individual and the receiver another individual. The medium of communication is the human voice and messages are words. Feedback occurs when the receiver reacts to the message of the sender. Both physical and semantic noise may interrupt interpersonal communication as they do intrapersonal communication.

To understand better the process of communication we frequently use a communication model, a diagram that serves as a stop-action picture of the process. For effective interpersonal communication to take place, the sender and receiver must have certain things in common as they communicate. A high degree of homophily—the term for these overlapping fields of experience—can aid interaction.

Mass communication is somewhat different from intrapersonal and interpersonal communication. The term *mass* denotes the presence of a large number of people. Frequently, but not always, mass communication reaches millions of people. Moreover, mass communication involves the presence of a mass medium. Radio, television, and cable are examples of electronic mass media. We define mass communication as messages directed toward a group of people through a mass medium. Not all of our senses participate in the process of mass communication, as they do in interpersonal communication. We cannot touch the other person, we cannot smell the other person, and he or she cannot respond immediately to our sensory feedback.

Mass communication entails the presence of gatekeepers. A gatekeeper governs the flow of information in a communication system. Today gatekeepers can be individuals or institutions, a single reporter or a television-network news operation. Because they have access to more information than we do about a given topic, gatekeepers both expand our informational environment by giving us more information and restrict that environment.

In mass communication feedback is delayed, whereas in interpersonal or intrapersonal communication it is immediate. Writing a letter to a politician we see on television is a form of delayed feedback.

New technology is altering the way we present feedback via the mass media. Two-way interactive communication systems permit instant communication. From home shopping to public-opinion polling, today's emerging technologies allow us more opportunity for immediate feedback.

These same technologies are also changing the traditional definitions of the term *mass.* For example, a computer bank may store the contents of an electronic magazine from which a small number of subscribers may access a single article through their home-computer terminals. These smaller, highly specialized magazines reach a smaller, more specialized audience.

As with intrapersonal and interpersonal communication, noise can enter the process of mass communication. Physical noise ranging from interruptions in the living room of a viewer to static on the television screen can affect messages between sender and receiver. The inexactness of language increases the chances of semantic noise also being present.

Broadcasting—messages sent via radio or television—is a form of mass communication. Telecommunication—electronic communication involving wired and unwired, one-way and two-way communication systems—is a much broader concept that has come into use in the broadcasting industry as it begins to consider many new technologies. These new technologies range from teletext and videotex systems to home computers.

The support systems surrounding broadcasting include such areas as program suppliers, supporting industries, professional organizations, control mechanisms, technical services, audience-measurement services, and management services.

In the chapters to follow we will examine (1) the history and development of broadcasting and telecommunication; (2) broadcast and information technologies; (3) systems and programming; (4) regulatory control; (5) and economics and evaluation.

OPPORTUNITIES FOR FURTHER LEARNING

ADLER, R. P., ed., *Understanding Television: Essays on Television as a Social and Cultural Force.* New York: Praeger, 1981.

ARIES, S. J., *Dictionary of Telecommunications.* London: Butterworth, 1981.

AUSTIN-LETT, G. and J. SPRAGUE, *Talk to Yourself: Experiencing Intrapersonal Communication.* Boston: Houghton Mifflin, 1976.

BITTNER, J. R., *Each Other: An Introduction to Interpersonal Communication.* Englewood Cliffs, N.J.: Prentice Hall, Inc., 1983.

BITTNER, J. R., *Mass Communication: An Introduction* (3rd ed.). Englewood Cliffs, N.J.: Prentice-Hall, 1983.

CHANEY, D. *Processes of Mass Communication.* London: Macmillan, 1972.

CONNORS, T. D., *Dictionary of Mass Media and Communication.* Longman Series in Public Communication. New York: Longman, 1982.

CORNISH, E., ed., *Communications Tomorrow: The Coming of the Information Society.* Bethesda, Md.: World Future Society, 1982.

CZITROM, D. J., *Media and the American Mind: From Morse to McLuhan.* Chapel Hill: University of North Carolina Press, 1982.

DELOZIER, M. W., *The Marketing Communications Process.* New York: McGraw-Hill, 1976.

DEL POLITO, C. M., *Intrapersonal Communication.* Menlo Park, Calif.: Cummings, 1977.

ELLMORE, R. T., *The Illustrated Dictionary of Broadcast-CATV-Telecommunications.* Blue Ridge Summit, Pa.: TAB Books, 1977.

GUMPERT, G., and R. CATHCART, eds., *Inter/media: Interpersonal Communication in a Media World* (2nd ed). New York: Oxford University Press, 1982.

GUREVITCH, M., T. BENNETT, J. CURRAN, and J. WOOLLACOTT, eds., *Culture, Society and the Media.* London: Methuen, 1982.

HALL, S., ed., *Culture, Media, Language: Working Papers in Cultural Studies, 1972–79.* London: Centre for Contemporary Cultural Studies, University of Birmingham, 1980.

HOGGART, R., and J. MORGAN, eds., *The Future of Broadcasting: Essays on Authority, Style and Choice.* London: Macmillan, 1982.

HYDE, M. J., *Communication Philosophy and the Technological Age.* University: University of Alabama Press, 1982.

LEWIN, L., ed., *Telecommunications in the U.S.: Trends and Policies.* Dedham, Mass.: Artech, 1981.

LIPSET, S. M., ed., *The Third Century: America as a Post-Industrial Society.* Chicago: University of Chicago Press, 1980.

MCLAUGHLIN, J. F., and A. E. BIRINYI, *Mapping the Information Business.* Cambridge, Mass.: Harvard Program on Information Resources Policy, 1979.

MCQUAIL, D., *Mass Communication Theory: An Introduction.* Beverly Hill, Calif.: Sage, 1983.

MCQUAIL, D., and S. WINDAHL, *Communication Models for the Study of Mass Communications.* New York: Longman, 1981.

PELTON, J. N., *Global Communications Satellite Policy.* Mt. Airy, Md.: Lomond Books, 1974.

——, and M. S. SNOW, eds., *Economic and Policy Problems in Satellite Communications.* New York: Praeger, 1977.

ROLOFF, M. E., *Interpersonal Communication: The Social Exchange Approach.* Beverly Hills, Calif.: Sage, 1981.

SCHRAMM, W., *Men, Messages, and Media: A Look at Human Communication.* New York: Harper & Row, 1975.

SNOW, M. S., *International Commercial Satellite Communications.* New York: Praeger, 1976.

TAN, A. S., *Mass Communication Theories and Research.* Columbus, Ohio: Grid, 1981.

THOMLISON, T. D., with P. W. KELLER, *Toward Interpersonal Dialogue.* New York: Longman, 1982.

WILLIAMS, R., ed., *Contact: Human Communication and Its History.* New York: Thames & Hudson, 1981.

WOOD, J. T., *Human Communication: A Symbolic Interactionist Perspective.* New York: Holt, Rinehart & Winston, 1982.

WOODWARD, K., ed., *The Myths of Information: Technology and Postindustrial Culture.* Madison, Wisc.: Coda, 1980.

2

THE TELEGRAPH
AND TELEPHONE

When we flick the switch of our radio or turn the knob on our television, it is hard for us to imagine the hundreds of years of theory building and applied technology that paved the way for the modern era of electronic communication. Our dream of capturing electricity and applying it to the communicative process dates back centuries. As we gradually learned about electricity and began to apply its power, two inventions drastically changed the nineteenth century: the telegraph and the telephone. Both were responsible for whetting the appetites of the inventors who would bring mass communication in the form of radio and television into our homes, creating an electronic link with the other side of the world. This chapter introduces us to the beginnings of electronic communication, first the theoretical underpinnings and then the introduction of the telegraph and telephone.[1]

APPLYING THEORY TO PRACTICE

In 1791 Luigi Galvani, an Italian physician and professor of anatomy at the University of Bologna, published the results of his research on the nervous system of frogs.[2] Galvani sent an electrical current into the nerve of a dead frog and watched as the frog's leg contracted. Galvani discovered he could achieve a similar reaction by touching the nerve with different metals, such as copper and iron. Probably because of his background in anatomy, Galvani attributed the movement of the leg to the presence of "animal electricity" in the frog.

Greatly skeptical of Galvani's research, Alessandro Volta told the Royal Society in London in 1800 that Galvani's "electricity" wasn't to be credited to the frog but to the different metals, and that he, Volta, had proved the theory by constructing what was to become known as the *voltaic pile*. Volta first placed a zinc disk on top of a silver disk and then placed a cardboard or leather disk soaked in brine on top of the metals. On top of this he placed metal and then cardboard or leather disks in a series until he had formed a small pile of disks. What Volta had invented was the first practical energy cell. Now scientists had at their disposal a continuous source of electricity.

Hans Christian Oersted and André Marie Ampère

Research into the uses of Volta's battery continued, but not until twenty years later did a professor of physics in Copenhagen, Hans Christian Oersted, discover that an electrical current could cause a nearby compass needle to rotate. Oersted's discovery accomplished two things: (1) it provided proof of the relationship between electricity and magnetism, and (2) it joined the scholarly disciplines of electricity and magnetism. The same year, French physicist André Marie Ampère refined Oersted's discovery by applying mathematical formulas to electromagnetism.

Michael Faraday and Joseph Henry

Scientists had yet, however, to actually *observe* phenomena that would verify Oersted's and Ampère's theories. That task was left to the English chemist and physicist Michael Faraday (Figure 2–1) and the American physicist Joseph Henry. Henry did not manage to publish the results of his research until after Faraday's had achieved world recognition.

The son of a blacksmith, Faraday left school at thirteen and while working for a bookbinder read an article on electricity in one of the volumes he was stitching. He landed a job as an apprentice at the Royal Institution and eventually became one of the most respected scientists of his day, later to head the institution.

Faraday's work climaxed late in 1831. In his experiments in the late summer and fall of that year Faraday was attempting to discover whether magnetism could produce electricity. The discovery came on November 4, when he moved a copper wire near the poles of a large horseshoe magnet and produced a measurable electric current. Faraday said the phenomenon was caused by "lines of force," as can be illustrated by placing a magnet near small iron filings. Faraday continued research on lines of force for the next twenty years, and in a research paper prepared in 1852 he alluded to lines of force radiating into the atmosphere, thereby generating electricity.

James Clerk Maxwell

The next step in the development of Faraday's theory came shortly after his death in 1867. Industrial leaders were calling for an updating and modernization of science instruction in English universities. In 1874 the James Henry Cavendish Laboratory at Cambridge was established. James Clerk Maxwell (Figure 2–1), a respected Scottish physicist and mathematician, who had been appointed to an endowed chair of physics in 1871 became director of the laboratory. Having the luxury of devoting all his time to scientific research with no pressure for re-

FIGURE 2-1 Michael Faraday (top left), whose work with electromagnetism paved the way for James Clerk Maxwell's (top right) developing theory of electromagnetic waves that Henrich Hertz (left) proved actually existed. Later, Marconi (shown in Figure 3-1 in Chapter 3) used Hertz's discovery to develop wireless. (Photos courtesy of the Science Museum, South Kensington, London)

sults, Maxwell could work at his own speed, building theory upon theory. As a trained mathematician, he extended Faraday's theories into mathematical predictions. His Dynamical Theory of the Electromagnetic Field stated that electromagnetic action travels through the atmosphere in waves, and that the atmosphere has the capacity to carry these waves at the speed of light.

By the late 1800s the scientific community in Europe was experiencing support and growth. Whereas England's scientific movement was supported by lobbying in Parliament and endowments to universities, in Germany science was supported as a business. What had once been an agricultural region was now beginning to experience the profits of industrial growth. Raw materials and the technology to transform them into industrial products signaled changes in the economy and the labor force. Technology and industrial growth necessitated the support of scientific inquiry, and statesmen began to place their firm support behind research and instruction in the sciences at the universities. Moreover, government subsidies and national research organizations created an atmosphere that nurtured new knowledge and fostered experimentation with existing theories. German scientists found themselves treated with more respect than any other scientists in Europe, and the universities geared themselves to train and employ not only the brilliant but also the many people of average intelligence who had the necessary persistence and fortitude.

Heinrich Hertz

It was at the beginning of this era, in 1857, that Heinrich Rudolph Hertz (Figure 2–1) was born to a middle-class family in Hamburg, Germany. Taught an hour a day by tutors and obtaining the rest of his learning in his spare time, young Hertz developed a keen interest in science and outfitted himself with his own home laboratory. Engineering first whetted his appetite, but after a year of study at the University of Munich he moved to Berlin to study pure science under the well-known German scientist Hermann Ludwig Ferdinand von Helmholtz. It was there, under the lure of the Berlin prize of 1879, that von Helmholtz encouraged his twenty-two-year-old apprentice to further inquiry into electromagnetic forces. Their early experiments were not very fruitful, and for a while Hertz occupied his time with other experiments. However, he never ceased to be fascinated by the potential of proving the Faraday-Maxwell theory of the electromagnetic energy through space.

One day while lecturing, Hertz noticed that when a spark gap was introduced into a wire coil it produced a current in an adjacent wire coil. What Hertz had stumbled across were very high-frequency electromagnetic waves generated by the spark. From there the investigations proceeded systematically, and from 1886 through 1889 Hertz, using both transmitting and receiving spark gaps at high frequencies, was able to prove the hypotheses of Faraday and the predictions of Maxwell. Hertz had discovered electromagnetic waves—today we also call them radio waves—which catapult radio, television, and other communication around the world and into outer space.

Hertz's work carried him beyond radio waves and into light waves. He learned about both the penetrating qualities of electromagnetic waves and their reflective qualities at ultrahigh frequencies—frequencies approaching those of light. This electromagnetic theory of light gained as much attention from future researchers as Hertz's discovery of electromagnetic waves. Both von Helmholtz and Hertz died in 1894.

THE EARLY TELEGRAPH

Until now we have dealt with scientists who were concerned with inquiry for the sake of new knowledge and who did not necessarily apply that knowledge to some commercial principle. Pure scientific inquiry has an established place in history and continues to enjoy great esteem. Without new knowledge, the inventive minds of scientists may never have created new technology capable of grasping the attention of everyone from world leaders to the common people. We now examine how inventors applied new scientific knowledge to the field of communication.

Prior to the telegraph, many devices had been developed for signaling over long distances. The most familiar to us are the smoke signals used by Indians to signal the approach of warriors or the success of a hunt. The cannon volley from an early troop vessel sailing off Ocracoke would signal to Blackbeard and his pirates that they were about to encounter a fleet from the Crown governor. Flags on a mast and semaphores on the railroad were both early forms of telegraphic communication, and some are retained even today.

Early French Signaling

About 1790 Frenchman Claude Chappe developed a series of semaphores (mechanical flags) that relayed messages across land in France. A similar network later crossed southern England. Chappe based his system on the work of Englishman Robert Hooke, who more than one hundred years earlier had considered the use of a signaling system employing the newly invented telescope. The Chappe system consisted of a series of towers, each with a person standing on top with a movable wooden beam whose different configurations represented the different letters of the alphabet. Each of the people standing watch would read the signals from one tower and repeat them to the next tower. The system stretched more than 140 miles outside Paris, but was slow, cumbersome, and in bad weather subject to serious limitations. About the same time, the Spanish physicist Francisco Salva theorized that single-wire telegraph lines could be insulated and laid across the ocean, enabling water to act as the "return wire."

The Telegraph in Europe

The discovery of Volta's battery led the German scientist Samuel Thomas von Soemmerring to apply a steady current to sending and receiving units that were joined by a complex array of thirty-five wires. He tested his apparatus over relatively short distances of a few hundred feet and reported his findings on August 29, 1809, to the Munich Academy of Sciences. He incorporated an alarm whereby a spoon would fill with liquid and fall on a bell arrangement; this would alert the receiving operator that a signal was about to come down the lines. Soemmerring's telegraph (Figure 2–2) was improved by his friend and colleague, Paul von Schilling-Cannstadt (also spelled Shilling).

Another early application of electricity to telegraphic communication was made by Sir Francis Ronalds in 1816. To generate electricity, Ronalds used a friction machine that was much like an electric generator turned by a hand crank. The sending and receiving apparatus consisted of two round revolving discs, each with a small opening near its outer rim. Positioned behind the disc were the letters of the alphabet and the numbers 0 through 10. Power from the friction machine would make the discs rotate in sequence, and the position of the receiving disc would be the same as that of the sending disc. By reading the different positions of

FIGURE 2-2 The telegraph of Paul von Schilling-Cannstadt developed from a design by Soemmerring. While Samuel F.B. Morse is credited with the development of the telegraph in America, his work benefitted by developments in telegraph communication which originated in Europe. (Science Museum, South Kensington, London)

the receiving disc in sequence one could understand the message. The system lacked two important elements: (1) a steady power supply which was available in the form of Volta's pile but was not used by Ronalds, and (2) speed of transmission. The slow rotation of the discs did not even approach the rapid transmission of later systems. Ronalds tested the system by constructing two wooden frames twenty yards apart and stringing eight miles of wire between them. By connecting the sending and receiving apparatus to the two ends of the wire and placing the ends next to each other, he could watch how one disc reacted immediately to the other.

THE MODERN TELEGRAPH

Developments in England

The modern telegraph developed in England through the resourceful efforts of William F. Cooke. While traveling in Heidelberg, Germany, Cooke learned about the telegraph of Schilling-Cannstadt. Cooke knew that if the machine could be further developed, it would have practical application in England. He immediately began work on his own telegraph, copying the designs of Shilling but using magnetic needles that would point to different characters of the alphabet. He later refined Ronalds's telegraph by powering the rotating disc with a battery instead of Ronalds's friction machine. In consultation with Faraday, Cooke further refined the telegraph's power supply. He also made the acquaintance of Professor Charles Wheatstone of Kings College. Working together, the two men continued to develop the telegraph, increasing it to a four- and finally a five-needle system. Cooke and Wheatstone formed a legal partnership, and on June 12, 1837, a patent for their telegraph was issued.

The Cooke-Wheatstone telegraph had a keyboard with five keys, one for each of the needles on the telegraph. Each key would engage current into the circuit and thereby cause the corresponding needle to turn and point to a letter of the alphabet. The Cooke-Wheatstone telegraph became the major long-distance communication medium in England—so much so that Samuel F. B. Morse's first attempts to introduce his telegraph in England were unfruitful. The

FIGURE 2–3 Early telegraphic communication had its greatest importance to railroads where cumbersome mechanical signals were used. The Great Western Railway in England was one of the proving grounds of early telegraphs. The advertisement reads in part: "Despatches instantaneously sent to and fro with the most confiding secrecy. Post Horses and Conveyances of every description may be ordered by the ELECTRIC TELEGRAPH, to be in readiness on the arrival of a Train, at either Paddington or Slough Station." (Science Museum, South Kensington, London)

Under the Special Patronage of Her Majesty

And H. R. H.   Prince Albert

GALVANIC AND MAGNETO

ELECTRIC TELEGRAPH,
GT. WESTERN RAILWAY.

The Public are respectfully informed that this interesting & most extraordinary Apparatus, by which upwards of 50 SIGNALS can be transmitted to a Distance of 280,000 MILES in ONE MINUTE,

May be seen in operation, daily, (Sundays excepted,) from 9 till 8, at the
Telegraph Office, Paddington,
AND TELEGRAPH COTTAGE, SLOUGH.

ADMISSION 1s.

" *This Exhibition is well worthy a visit from all who love to see the wonders of science.*"—MORNING POST.

Despatches instantaneously sent to and fro with the most confiding secrecy. Post Horses and Conveyances of every description may be ordered by the ELECTRIC TELEGRAPH, to be in readiness on the arrival of a Train, at either Paddington or Slough Station.

The Terms for sending a Despatch, ordering Post Horses, &c., only One Shilling.

N.B. Messengers in constant attendance, so that communications received by Telegraph, would be forwarded, if required, to any part of London, Windsor, Eton, &c.

THOMAS HOME, *Licensee.*

G. NURTON, Printer, 48, Church Street, Portman Market.

Cooke-Wheatstone system received its first commercial test when it was installed on the Great Western Railway (Figure 2–3). Although their partnership was strained at times, Cooke and Wheatstone continued to develop their telegraph, and became more prosperous because of the railroad's use of it. The Cooke-Wheatstone system is important in that it differed from Morse's telegraph and was patented first.

DEVELOPMENTS IN AMERICA

The ship *Sully* was journeying home from England to the United States in the fall of 1832. On board, two gentlemen talked about the use of electricity for telegraphy in England and Europe. One of the men, Samuel F. B. Morse, was so enthralled listening to his companion, Dr. Charles T. Jackson of Boston, discuss electricity, that upon reaching America he began to work arduously on his own version of the telegraph (Figure 2–4). An artist by day, he spent his nights building the telegraph system that would simplify the transmission of messages over long distances. After considerable refinement, he demonstrated the Morse telegraph in 1837 and patented the system on June 20, 1840.

Experimenting With the Morse Telegraph

The system differed significantly from the Cooke-Wheatstone model in that Morse used a thin paper tape on which indentations were made as it slid across a wooden bar. Signals consisted of short and long marks, which became known as the Morse code although they were said to be the brain-child of Morse's partner, Alfred Vail, the son of a manufacturer who had invested some money in the new device. Similar aid was given

FIGURE 2-4 Samuel F.B. Morse's telegraph which used a paper tape to record the code. A more efficient way turned out to be the dot-dash clicks of the telegraph key which became the standard means of sending and receiving messages. (Science Museum, South Kensington, London)

Morse by Leonard D. Gale, a chemistry professor at the University of the City of New York, where Morse had been working as an art teacher. Morse, though blessed with an inquisitive brain and ingenuity, didn't know much about science. Art was his vocation.

Morse continued to work on the telegraph and mounted public displays in an attempt to garner support for widespread development of the device. An early demonstration came in the fall of 1842, when Morse tried to span a river with the telegraph only to have a ship hook the underwater wire and cut it. He then went abroad for financial backing, but was rebuffed. His chance arrived in 1843, when Congress appropriated $30,000 to build an experimental telegraph line between Washington, D.C., and Baltimore. In 1844 the system was completed, and using a greatly improved transmitting device Morse conducted a successful test whose famous message ''What hath God wrought'' signaled the telegraph's full-scale arrival in the United States. The Morse telegraph spread throughout the nation, linking western boom towns with eastern ports. Although he had to fight infringements upon his patent, Morse continued to develop the telegraph in America and later in Europe, where he was both honored and well compensated for the use of his system.

The Telegraph Expands: Western Union and the Atlantic Cable

It was in this setting that a Rochester, New York, businessman named Hiram Sibley established a telegraph line in 1851 from Buffalo to St. Louis. With other investors, Sibley formed the New York & Mississippi Valley Printing Telegraph Company. In 1856 the company changed its name to the Western Union Telegraph Company. The telegraph business, closely tied to the development of the railroads, began to expand. Telegrams were also expensive: Twenty dollars, a substantial sum in those days, was not uncommon. Through a variety of lease options, the company secured the rights to the Morse telegraph west of Buffalo. It then began immediately to buy up other smaller telegraph companies and established one large telegraph system.

By now Congress realized the need for a wireless connection of the West and East coasts. After all, gold had been discovered in California, ships were making regular passages from New York to California around the tip of South America, and the nation needed a communication link between eastern and western commerce. On September 20, 1860, Western Union was awarded a $40,000 contract to build a telegraph line connecting the eastern and western lines. Sibley hired Edward Creighton to survey the route. Creighton, who later helped establish Creighton University in Omaha, faced a great expanse of plains, rugged mountains, and unfriendly Indians. The Overland Telegraph Company, based in San Francisco and backed by California telegraph interests, and the Nebraska-based Pacific Telegraph Company began work on the line, one starting from each end on July 4, 1861. The eastern end of the line ran from Omaha to Salt Lake City and was surpervised by Creighton. The western end connected Sacramento and San Francisco with Salt Lake City and was supervised by James Gamble.

Construction was not uneventful. It wasn't until permission from the Shoshone Indians was obtained and Mormon leader Brigham Young gave his blessing to the project that the line could be completed. On October 24, 1861, three months and twenty days after ground had been broken and slightly less than ten years earlier than the experts predicted, the lines met. Shortly thereafter, work began on another telegraph line through the Pacific Northwest, Canada,

and across Alaska to Russia. The project was suspended in 1867, however, upon completion of the Atlantic Cable which bridged the communication gap between Europe and North America.

Now the telegraph sped news across the Atlantic. Stock-market quotations, shipping news, and economic fare dominated the transatlantic news flow. Yet despite all the popularity of the telegraph, it still could not operate without wires. And although the railroads were important to commerce, they were no less important than cargo ships, which were without communication once they had left sight of land. The wires simply couldn't follow them. So for the next thirty years, the telegraph would continue to function as it had originally been conceived.

ALEXANDER GRAHAM BELL AND THE IDEA BEHIND THE TELEPHONE

While the telegraph was making its impact on nineteenth-century communication, the telephone wasn't far behind.

Alexander Graham Bell was a product of European culture and refinement. His father was a well-known speech professor whose speciality was teaching the deaf and whose major contribution to his field was a system of "visible speech" whereby he taught the deaf to talk. When Alexander began studying at the University of London, it was natural that he would follow his father's profession. Tuberculosis struck the Bell family in the late 1860s, forcing them to Canada. There, Alexander Graham Bell himself had the opportunity to teach, and he became a respected practitioner of visible speech. He set up his own school for the deaf in Boston and was later appointed professor of vocal psychology at Boston University.

Bell had become captivated by the study of electricity while studying vocal resonance in London. He had read about experiments by von Helmholtz and the use of tuning forks to produce sounds. But Bell couldn't read German very well, and concluded mistakenly that the German scientist was transmitting sounds from one tuning fork to another by using a wire. That wasn't at all what von Helmholtz was doing, but the idea lit an experimenter's spark in Bell, and in Canada and America he began experiments on sound transfer. Bell envisioned a system whereby a transmitter would send different tones over a single wire to a "tuning fork" receiver. Bell therefore concentrated on designing a sending and receiving device based on a principle of vibrating metal reeds. The device would vibrate the way the human eardrum does in response to sound waves. Bell's idea was to invent a "harmonic telegraph" that would have direct and immediate application to the telegraph industry. Little did Bell know that that industry would later become a thorn in his side.

Bell's Association with Hubbard and Sanders

Bell's teaching gave him two important contacts that contributed both the financial and legal expertise he needed in order to continue his efforts. The first was Gardiner Greene Hubbard, a Boston lawyer who was president of the Clarke School for the Deaf. Hubbard provided Bell with money as well as legal advice on securing patents for Bell's inventions. He also gave him his daughter, Mable, in marriage. In her youth Mable had been stricken deaf with scarlet fever, and Bell used visible speech to teach her to speak. Also providing Bell with financial backing was Thomas Sanders. Sanders had a deaf son, and Bell taught him to speak as he had Mable. On February 27, 1875, the three men entered into an agreement to invent a harmonic telegraph. Bell would provide the inventive genius, Sanders the money, and Hubbard the legal advice and money.[3]

BASIC PATENTS OF THE TELEPHONE SYSTEM

One week later, Bell filed his first patent application in Washington, D.C. The patent, for "Improvement in Transmitters and Receivers for Electrical Telegraphs," was granted on April 6, 1875.

Bell set to work with Thomas A. Watson, an employee of a Boston electrical shop. The device developed by Bell and Watson was not the telephone, but it set the stage for the machine that would ultimately transmit speech over wires. What Bell and Watson did construct was an instrument that used the principle of *variable resistance*. It consisted of a membrane stretched over a small frame with a wire running from the center of the membrane perpendicularly into a small cup of acid water (Figure 2–5). When someone shouted at the membrane it would vibrate and the wire, correspondingly, would move up and down in the water, thereby varying the resistance between the wire and the liquid. The following year's experiments culminated in another patent (Figure 2–6). Filed on February 14, 1876, and granted on March 7, 1876, it was titled "Improvement in Telegraphy."[4] Nothing in the original agreement of the three men mentioned the telephone. For this reason, as the device being perfected by Bell and Watson turned more and more toward the telephone, Hubbard offered to relinquish his rights to that invention, since he saw the

FIGURE 2-5 Alexander Graham Bell's liquid telephone used variable resistance. A membrane was stretched over a small frame with a wire running to the center of a small cup of acid water. When words were shouted into the horn, it vibrated the membrane and changed the resistance. The concept can also be seen in Bell's patent illustrated in Figure 2–6. (AT&T)

FIGURE 2-6 Bell's patent granted March 7, 1876 was applied for on February 14, 1876. It was one of many patents credited to Bell, his associates, and the various companies which had their origin in Bell's work. (H.M. Boettinger, *The Telephone Book.* New York: Riverwood Publishers Ltd., 1977)

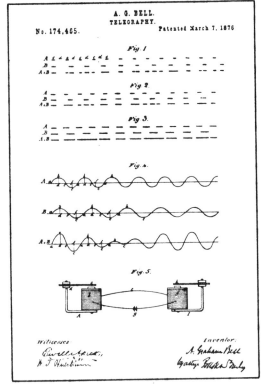

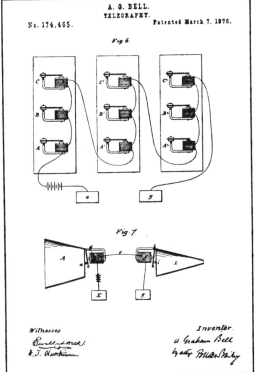

potential for substantial profit in the telegraph. Bell later wrote:

> My understanding always was that the speaking telephone was included in the inventions that belonged to the Messrs. Hubbard and Sanders from the autumn of 1874, but I found at a later period that they had not had this idea, which might account for the little encouragement I received to spend time on experiments relating to it. Even as late as 1876, when the telephone was an assured success, Mr. Hubbard generously offered to relinquish to me all right and title to that invention, as he was inclined to think it was outside our original understanding.[5]

Bell, however, consulted an attorney and agreed to include the telephone as part of the original agreement among the three men.

Experiments during the winter of 1875–1876 resulted in a third patent, "Telephonic Telegraph Receivers," filed on April 8, 1876, and issued on June 6, 1876.[6] Although the second and third patents were also originally issued in Bell's name only, he later assigned them to Hubbard and Sanders as well on September 15, 1876. On January 15, 1877 a fourth patent was filed—"Improvement in Electrical Telegraphy."[7] These four patents—the foundation of the modern Bell System—all referred to the "telegraph" instead of the "telephone."[8]

HUBBARD AND THE BELL SYSTEM

The original agreement among Bell, Hubbard, and Sanders provided that if something of commercial value were to arise from the work of Bell, a company should be formed to develop the product. Consequently, in 1877 Hubbard was put in charge of what was officially called the Bell Telephone Company, Gardiner G. Hubbard, Trustee.[9] Whereas it was Hubbard's

business sense that caused the company to grow, the scientific drive fell upon the shoulders of Watson.[10] Bell, meanwhile, had married Hubbard's daughter and traveled to England to help introduce the telephone there. Watson, under a contract dated September 1, 1876, received a beginning wage of three dollars per day.[11] Between 1877 and his resignation in 1881 he carried on the research and development of the company. Without scientific training he improved the device that Bell had left behind and molded it into a product suitable for a commercial enterprise. In 1877 Bell and Sanders assigned all of their rights to the telephone to Hubbard, who now became the person guiding the developing firm.

The Decision to Lease

Hubbard had to make a decision—to sell telephones or lease them. He decided on the latter, partly because of the example of one of his clients, the Gordon-McKay Shoe Machinery Company.[12] That company had leased its equipment to shoemakers and received a royalty for every pair of shoes sewn on the machines. This seemed an ideal arrangement to Hubbard, and was duly reflected in the Bell Company's declaration of trust: "The business of manufacturing telephones and licensing parties to use the same for a royalty, shall be carried on and managed by the Trustee, under the name of the Bell Telephone Company, under and in accordance with such general directions, rules and regulations as may be made for that purpose by the Board of Managers."[13] The declaration also provided for five thousand shares of stock to be divided among Hubbard, his wife, his brother, Watson, Sanders, Bell, and Bell's wife.

Hubbard's decision to lease and not sell telephones put one constraint on the company—a serious lack of funds. It was clear that even though Hubbard and Sanders had committed considerable money to the venture, still more resources were needed.

Expansion in New England

Sanders, who had ties with the New England financial world, interested a group of Massachusetts and Rhode Island business-people in investing in the development of the telephone in New England. The result was the incorporation of the New England Telephone Company on February 12, 1878. Headquartered in Boston, the new investors controlled a considerable share of the company. The articles of incorporation stated that the company was formed "for the purpose of carrying on the business of manufacturing and renting telephones and constructing lines of telegraph therefore in the New England States."[14] Hubbard assigned to the new company the rights of the four original patents. In return, Hubbard, Watson, and Sanders received half the stock in the New England Telephone Company and an agreement that the company would buy all of its equipment from the original Bell Telephone Company. The New England Company would in turn lease the equipment to individuals wanting telephone service.

Moreover, the two companies agreed to cooperate in the event that it became advantageous to expand their telephone system beyond New England. This agreement alluded to what is today the "long lines" concept of telephone interconnection. Specifically, the cooperative provision stated that

> insomuch as said parties and their successors and assigns may have a common interest in the working of continuous and connecting lines extending outside of New England, the said parties agree that they will endeavor to cooperate in the establishing of connecting lines and in the joint working of the same, and the division of the expense

> and the profits thereof pro rata upon some equally fair and equitable basis.[15]

Five days before the agreement was signed, the first commercial telephone exchange opened in New Haven, Connecticut.[16]

THE BELL TELEPHONE COMPANY

Prosperity came quickly (Figure 2–7). The projections for the development of a telephone system beyond New England caused a new company to be formed on June 29,

FIGURE 2–7 The early prosperity of the telephone industry is graphically illustrated in this picture of telephone wires strung in New York City in the 1880s. By the late 1880s, the Bell Telephone Company had been formed, lines were into New England, and substantial progress had been made linking telephone companies in the Midwest. (Photo Courtesy Western Electric Company)

1878, called simply the Bell Telephone Company. Hubbard, Sanders, Watson, and Bell (through his attorney) were all involved, as were principals from the New England Company. Hubbard received three thousand shares of stock and in turn awarded his interests, including patent rights, to the new company. Theodore N. Vail, a former Western Union employee, became the company's general manager, and the control and guidance of the company were invested in an Executive Committee of the Bell Telephone Company. The Bell Telephone Company, Gardiner G. Hubbard, Trustee, had come to an end.

WILLIAM H. FORBES AND THE NATIONAL BELL TELEPHONE COMPANY

On December 31, 1878, William H. Forbes was elected director of the Bell Telephone Company. Forbes immediately saw the advantage of consolidation. On March 20, 1879, the New England Telephone Company and the Bell Telephone Company assigned their rights under the first and third of the original Bell patents to the National Bell Telephone Company. The decision came none too soon. Thomas Edison had developed an improved carbon "transmitter" and patent litigation and challenges to the original Bell patents were filling the air.

The Era of Patent Challenge

One challenge came from Elisha Gray,[17] who had filed a *caveat* for a patent on a variable-resistance telephone just a few hours after Bell did. Although a caveat does not have the legal weight of a patent application, Gray went to court claiming credit for the concept of variable resistance and accusing Bell of looking first at the caveat and then altering his patent application. The court was sympathetic to Bell.

Another challenge came from a country tinkerer named Daniel Drawbaugh. His lawyers managed to persuade a contingent of farm folk to testify that they had used a device invented by Drawbaugh to talk to each other before Bell received his patent. The U.S. Supreme Court ruled in favor of Bell by a one-vote margin. A victory in either case might have resulted in fleets of telephone-company trucks roving the country today with the name of Gray or Drawbaugh printed on their cabs instead of the familiar Bell symbol.

We should remember that the harmonic telegraph was not the only device that Bell patented. He also developed a machine whereby the voice could be transmitted over light waves. Called the *photophone* (Figure 2–8), it was patented in 1880. Although it had no practical applications then, it was the forerunner of today's fiber-optics lightwave communication, which promises to revolutionize not only telephone communication but also data transmission and cable television.

The Battle with Western Union

Even with patents and public acceptance, the National Bell Telephone Company was not an instant commercial success. Western Union managed a nationwide system of telegraph lines and, with Gray's receiving device, the transmitter invented by Edison, and a handset created by Robert Brown it had made considerable inroads into the telephone industry.[18] Missing the chance a few years earlier to buy the Bell patents, Western Union was now pouring millions into its own telephone system. A showdown was inevitable. To let Western Union continue would be disastrous for the National Bell Telephone Company. Western Union

FIGURE 2-8   The photophone did not materialize as a commercial product the way Bell's telephone did. The device, which used light beams as a way of communicating between the sender and receiver, was based on the same idea that today is used for fiber optics, which are small strands of glass which carry light waves and thousands of channels of communication. (AT&T)

had the background, capital, expertise, and ambition to challenge its much smaller rival. What it did not have was the rights to the Bell equipment. After a long, involved court proceeding the two companies reached an agreement whereby Western Union would stay out of the telephone business if Bell would stay out of the telegraph business.

THE AMERICAN BELL
TELEPHONE COMPANY

The implementation of the settlement required a special session of the Massachusetts Legislature and the passage of an act that gave the telephone company the following rights: "manufacturing, owning, selling, using and licensing others to use electrical speaking telephones and other apparatus and appliances pertaining to the transmission of intelligence by electricity, and for that licenses purpose constructing and maintaining by itself and its public and private lines and district exchanges."[19] The act also resulted in the formation of the American Bell Telephone Company on March 20, 1880. The new company formally purchased the stock of the National Bell Telephone Company.

National Bell had served an important purpose beyond merely expanding telephone service: it had developed a system of telephone exchanges that permitted localized switching. The next hurdle in the development of the telephone system was to connect the various exchanges, and this became the hallmark of American Bell Telephone Company. The new company created the Long Lines System, which began with the construction of a telephone line between Boston and New York. Opened on March 27, 1884,[20] it was soon followed by lines linking Boston, New York, Philadelphia, and Washington and also New York and Albany. To finance long-lines development, the company issued $2 million in bonds.[21]

THE AMERICAN TELEPHONE & TELEGRAPH COMPANY

To develop the long-line system, American Bell formed a subsidiary called the American Telephone and Telegraph Company (AT&T). Incorporated in New York State because of its favorable legal and financial climate, the company was entrusted with constructing lines throughout the North American continent, including Mexico and Canada, and "by cable and other appropriate means with the rest of the known world."[22] (Figure 2–9) Theodore Vail became AT&T's first president and Edward J. Hall its first general manager.

Partly because of New York's importance and size and partly because of its business and legal climate, it became evident that AT&T would become the central organization of the telephone system. Although economic incentives by the Massachusetts Legislature attempted to favor American Bell, the enacted increases in capitalization were still not adequate. Thus, in 1900 the American Bell Telephone Company transferred all of its assets to AT&T through a somewhat involved trading procedure. AT&T now became the parent company, a coordinated federation that also included a number of associated companies'.

FIGURE 2–9 Expansion of the transcontinental telephone network progressed in the late 1800s. Scientific publications were heralding new achievements at about the same time that Marconi was beginning his experiments with wireless. In 1892, Alexander Graham Bell, pictured here, sits at the New York end of the circuit to Chicago. Looking down and standing directly behind Bell is Edward J. Hall, the first general manager of AT&T. (AT&T)

THE BREAKUP OF AT&T

AT&T's structure remained essentially the same until 1980, when the company entered into a consent decree with the Department of Justice.[23] The agreement ended a seven-year antitrust case against AT&T. The climate for change was prevalent in both regulatory circles and the marketplace (Figure 2–10). Originally, AT&T had been regulated as a monopoly, for the primary goal of the company and the government was to provide a unified system of low-cost telephone service throughout the United States. As that goal was achieved, however, new forces gradually began to appear. Technology was not confined to AT&T, and other companies with the requisite know-how and financial backing began to compete with it in long-distance communication. The customer who once was satisfied just with telephone service began to see new uses for the telephone, specifically the linking of the telephone with home information systems such as personal computers.

Under the consent decree, which was

MORE THAN A NEW LOOK, A NEW OUTLOOK.

AT&T

We're the new AT&T. A new company with a new symbol. But we're not exactly a newcomer. We have more than a hundred years' experience and a worldwide reputation. With the breakup of the Bell System, we know we must earn your confidence all over again—under new circumstances.

As we compete for your business, we'll stand out from the crowd by giving you better service than anyone. That's a commitment.

And we'll offer you the most advanced technology from our world-renowned Bell Laboratories. That's a guarantee.

We'll be the brand name that means dependable, state-of-the-art phones for your home, the best information systems for your business and the one and only long distance service that lets you reach out and touch anyone, any time –across the nation and around the world.

We'll use our research, development and marketing talents to keep American communications technology the best in the world.

We're the new AT&T. Our new outlook is also our competitive strategy and our goal: to give you every reason, every day, to choose us.

FIGURE 2–10 The breakup of AT&T occurred with the settlement of a long-standing antitrust suit brought by the U.S. government. The Bell companies were separated from AT&T, and long-distance communication was opened up to more competition. The 22 local operating companies regrouped into seven regional holding companies. Two of the companies, Southern New England Tel and Cincinnati Bell, were unaffected by the divestiture since AT&T owned a minority interest in them. The seven regional companies are Pacific Telesis Group which covers California and the lower Western states, US West which includes the Northwestern states as well as much of the upper Midwest and some of the lower Southwest, Southwestern Bell Corporation which covers Texas and the lower Midwest, BellSouth which covers the Southeastern states, Bell Atlantic which includes the Middle Atlantic States, and NYNEX which includes New England. AT&T now operates five principal subsidiaries: AT&T Information Systems (formerly American Bell), AT&T Communications, Western Electric, Bell Labs, and AT&T International. (Ad reproduced with permission of AT&T)

altered somewhat by the courts, AT&T divested itself of the local operations assigned to the twenty-two Bell telephone companies. The Bell companies could provide, but not manufacture, new equipment for use in the home. Equipment already installed at the time of the decree remained with AT&T, and AT&T could provide new equipment. Bell Laboratories and Western Electric—AT&T's research and manufacturing arms, respectively—remained a part of the parent company. AT&T shareholders retained stock in the parent company and were assigned a proportionate interest in the local companies. The competitors of AT&T were given access to the local exchanges. AT&T in turn was free to offer consumers equipment that could be rented or purchased and used in connection with local or long-distance telephone systems. In other words, AT&T was now in a position to sell virtually anything. But it concentrated on electronic equipment such as home information terminals—products that make the telephone one of the information technologies of the future.

The new subsidiary through which AT&T could now sell electronic equipment to the consumer was first called American Bell. But in 1983 it was renamed AT&T Information Systems as a result of further negotiations in which AT&T agreed to cease using the name Bell except for Bell Labs.

SUMMARY

In this chapter we traced the beginnings of electronic communication back to the eighteenth century and the experiments of Luigi Galvani. Subsequently, Alessandro Volta stored electricity in a stack of zinc and silver discs that came to be called the voltaic pile—the first storage cell. Oersted established the link between electricity and magnetism, and in doing so unified research and scholarship in these two areas. Ampère mathematically proved this relationship, and Faraday and Henry observed the phenomena. James Clerk Maxwell hypothesized the presence of electromagnetic energy, and Heinrich Hertz proved its existence by observing the presence of electromagnetic waves created by an electrical spark.

Our desire to communicate over long distances sparked the invention of two devices—the telegraph and telephone—that whetted the appetites of those who would later apply technology to wireless communication. The telegraph found wide acceptance in England and Europe and was developed in the United States by Samuel F. B. Morse. Morse conducted successful telegraph experiments between Washington and Baltimore in 1844, and through Western Union's efforts the telegraph later spanned the United States.

Closely intertwined with the history and development of the telegraph are those of the telephone. The telephone traces back to Alexander Graham Bell, who with the legal and financial support of Gardiner Greene Hubbard and Thomas Sanders developed a "telegraph" that became a wired system for communicating over long distances by voice. The telephone has its scientific and commercial foundation in four key patents issued to Bell between 1875 and 1877.

The association of Bell, Hubbard, and Sanders, accompanied by the scientific work of Thomas A. Watson, resulted in the first telephone company—the Bell Telephone Company, Gardiner G. Hubbard, Trustee. Using a strategy of leasing instead of selling telephone equipment, Hubbard sought to expand the company, and with a group of Massachusetts and Rhode Island investors he formed the New England Telephone

Company. Shortly thereafter the Bell Telephone Company replaced the original Bell Telephone Company, Gardiner G. Hubbard, Trustee.

When William H. Forbes was named director of the Bell Telephone Company he saw the advantages of consolidation, and he therefore joined with the New England Telephone Company in forming the National Bell Telephone Company. Through a series of patent challenges, some by Western Union, there resulted a settlement whereby Western Union would be concerned with telegraphic communication and National Bell with telephone communication. To implement the conditions of the settlement, the Massachusetts Legislature enacted the formation of the American Bell Telephone Company. The new company was instrumental in developing a series of local telephone exchanges and beginning a long-lines division, which eventually became American Telephone and Telegraph (AT&T). In time AT&T became the parent company of a coordinated federation that also included several associated companies.

In 1980 AT&T entered into a consent decree with the Justice Department whereby it was divested of its local companies but enabled to compete with other companies by providing electronic equipment to the consumer under a new subsidiary called AT&T Information Systems.

OPPORTUNITIES FOR FURTHER LEARNING

DE SOLA POOL, I., *Forecasting the Telephone: A Retrospective Technology Assessment.* Norwood, N.J.: Ablex, 1983.

———, ed., *The Social Impact of the Telephone.* Cambridge, Mass.: M.I.T. Press, 1981.

FINN, B. S., ed., *Development of Submarine Cable Communications.* New York: Arno Press, 1980.

KIEVE, J., *The Electric Telegraph in the U.K.* New York: Barnes & Nobel, 1973.

OGLE, E. B., *Long Distance, Please: The Story of the TransCanada Telephone System.* Toronto: Collins, 1979.

PIERCE, J. R., *Signals: The Telephone and Beyond.* San Francisco: W.H. Freeman, 1981.

SCHEIPS, P. J., ed., *Military Signal Communications.* New York: Arno Press, 1980.

SCHENCK, H. H., *1980 World's Submarine Telephone Cable Systems.* Washington, D.C.: Office of International Affairs, National Telecommunications and Information Administration, Department of Commerce, 1980.

SICHTER, J. W., *Separations Procedures in the Telephone Industry: The Historical Origins of a Public Policy.* Cambridge, Mass.: Harvard Program on Information Resources Policy, 1977.

SINGER, B. D., *Social Functions of the Telephone.* Palo Alto, Calif.: R & E Research Associates, 1981.

WILSON, G., *The Old Telegraphs.* London: Phillmore, 1976.

3

THE BEGINNING
OF WIRELESS

The work of the theorists would not be confined to the scientific curiosity of Morse and Bell,[1] to the corporate empires of AT&T and Western Union. It would not be confined to land-based communication systems or to cables running under oceans for thousands of miles. The lines of force that James Clerk Maxwell witnessed, the spark that Hertz saw, would become steps upon which another inventor would climb.

WIRELESS IS BORN:
MARCONI THE INVENTOR

The telegraph had captivated America and Europe. On April 25, 1874, two years after the death of Samuel Morse, the second son of Giuseppe and Anna Marconi was born.

By late-nineteenth-century standards, Guglielmo Marconi's (Figure 3–1) parents were quite well to do.[2] But the young, restless Guglielmo was not like the rest of his family, comfortable with gracious Italian living. Often he irritated his father by interrupting the quiet conversation at an evening meal with persistent, unrelated questions. There was no improvement when, after reading a scientific magazine, Guglielmo developed a keen interest in the work of Heinrich Hertz. Finally, having experienced his father's rancor and his mother's reinforcement, Guglielmo Marconi began to experiment in the top floor of the home. With crude tables, boards, hanging wires, and other paraphernalia he set about duplicating the experiments of Hertz.

FIGURE 3–1   Guglielmo Marconi seated at his receiving set at St. Johns, Newfoundland on December 12, 1901. (RCA)

Early Experiments in Italy

To the family, the work of the young son in his upstairs laboratory was intriguing but of questionable value. The boy's father felt that he was wasting the best years of his life, but he became more interested when Guglielmo asked him for money to advance his work beyond the experimental stage.[3] A stern and practical businessman, his father first wanted a demonstration. This was followed by a long discussion as to how he would get a return on his money. Little did he realize that the boy's corporate empire would eventually gross billions. Finally the two agreed to an initial investment, and Guglielmo began building his first transmitting device. Then, using a reflector sheet strung between two poles (Figure 3–2) he first managed to receive a signal across the room. His receiver utilized a *coherer*—a

small glass tube filled with metal filings and with wires in each end. The filings would collect between the two wires whenever electricity was applied.

Marconi, already familiar with the work of Samuel Morse, immediately realized the potential of his own device for long-distance communication.[4] He also had a sense of urgency, because to him the principle of his invention was extremely simple. Why had someone not thought of it before or, more important, applied it? His experiments became more and more frequent and the range of his signals more and more distant. On top of a hill twenty minutes from home, the experiments reached a threshold. Could the signal go beyond the hilltop? If the invention were to be a success, it would have to be able to leap over hills, mountains, buildings, and oceans. On the day of the

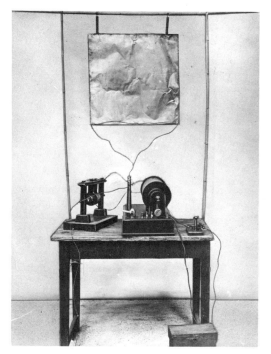

FIGURE 3–2 Marconi's first transmitter used in his early experiments in 1895. The large piece of tin suspended above the table served as the antenna. (The Marconi Company Limited, Marconi House, Chelmsford, Essex)

crucial test, his brother and two helpers carried the receiver and antenna over the hilltop out of sight of the family's villa. Guglielmo's brother also carried a gun with instructions to shoot to confirm the signal. No sooner had Guglielmo fed current to the transmitter than the shot rang out. Now the capital that his father had provided had to be increased before the experiments could progress. A letter was sent to the Italian Post Office Department in an attempt to obtain government backing for Guglielmo. The reply was negative. But if Italy were to say no, perhaps the great naval power of the day would say yes. Accompanied by his mother's encouragement, Marconi was off to England.

Experiments in England

The first stop was customs. Here the journey hit one of its low points, as ignorant customs inspectors ripped at the equipment until it was all but destroyed. Marconi managed to reconstruct the broken pieces, which had been crated so carefully in Italy. The next step was to be sure no one else captured the idea. For four months Marconi and his mother slaved over the papers that were to be presented to the London Patent Office.[5] The first specifications were filed on June 2, 1896. The complete diagrams and detailed specifications were filed on March 2, 1897, under the title "Improvements in Transmitting Electrical Impulses and Signals, and an Apparatus Therefor." On July 2, 1897, patent number 12,039 was granted to the twenty-three-year-old Italian inventor. The experiments could now be resumed, but it still was necessary to get from the government the capital with which to develop the invention to its full potential.

The help Marconi needed came first from the chief engineer of the British Post Office, William Henry Preece, who took a liking to the young inventor. With Preece's support Marconi began his experiments in England, first a transmission between two buildings and then a major demonstration across the Bristol Channel, a distance of about three miles (Figure 3–3). The press noticed Marconi's wireless and published the news to the world. More attention was bestowed on the device than the young inventor had ever dreamed of. Along with offers to buy the rights to his invention came offers of marriage from women who said Marconi's waves made their feet tickle.[6] The distance of his experiments increased from three to thirty-four miles. Publicity abounded again when Marconi was commissioned to install a wireless on a tugboat to report the sailing races at the Kingston regatta. He secured

FIGURE 3-3 Three officials of the British Post Office Department examine the equipment Marconi used to test the first successful wireless across the Bristol Channel in 1897. The British Post Office Department provided both encouragement and financial support for Marconi's early work. (The Marconi Company Limited, Marconi House, Chelmsford, Essex)

other patents. One of the most important, patent 7,777 for a selective tuning device, was granted in 1901.

Wireless Across the Atlantic

The year 1901 was also the year of the most convincing experiment of the power of wireless communication. Still to be hurdled was the vast expanse of the Atlantic Ocean. Marconi left England for America in February of that year and headed for Cape Cod, the point he felt was best suited to the test of his wireless. But as with any stretch of New England coastline, harsh winter winds on Cape Cod can play havoc with any structure not built for permanency. The same is true of the English coast. For Marconi, 1901 held a double disaster. News arrived that storms had toppled the antenna at his installation at Poldhu, England. Within weeks, the same fate befell the Cape Cod station. Marconi now decided to transfer operations to New-

foundland, then a British colony. Using a bit of intrigue, he told local officials he was attempting to communicate with ships at sea; he made no mention of the real purpose, transatlantic communication. Instead of antenna towers, he planned to use balloons, and packed six kites as a backup.[7]

The experiments in Newfoundland started on December 9, 1901. First, a balloon was tested, but a line broke and the balloon headed for open sea. The next decision was to try one of the large kites. Marconi's assistants, George Kemp and P. W. Paget, sent the kite soaring hundreds of feet up, stringing behind it the antenna wire connected to the essential receiving equipment on top of nearby Signal Hill. Serious monitoring started on December 12. There were no results in the morning; nothing was heard from Poldhu. Spirits were low as the men continued to listen for the tapping signal that would indicate that England was calling. At 12:30 P.M., Guglielmo Marconi listened intently as the tapping sound of three dots, signaling the letter *S,* crackled through the earphone. Marconi handed the earphone to Kemp, and the assistant verified the signal.

Reaction to Transatlantic Wireless

The world would spend the rest of December reading about it. The *New York Times* called it "the most wonderful scientific development of recent times" and headlined the story *WIRELESS SIGNALS ACROSS THE ATLANTIC.* Across the ocean, the *Times* of London headlined *WIRELESS TELEGRAPHY ACROSS THE ATLAN-TIC.*[8] The London paper described how Marconi had authorized Sir Cavendish Boyle, the governor of Newfoundland, to "apprise the British Cabinet of the discovery, the importance of which is impossible to overvalue." Not forgetting his beloved Italy, Marconi informed the Italian government himself. Magazines were equally enthusiastic about the feat. *Century Magazine* called Newfoundland "the theatre of this unequaled scientific development." *World's Work* labeled the transatlantic transmission "a red letter day in electrical history." *McClure's Magazine* demanded, "Think for a moment of sitting here on the edge of North America and listening to communications sent *through space* across nearly 2,000 miles of ocean from the edge of Europe!"[9]

Not all, however, was as happy as in Newfoundland. The apparent threat of competition between wireless and the cable telegraph surfaced immediately. Cable stocks declined shortly after the announcement of the transatlantic broadcast.[10] The Anglo-American Telegraph Company, which had a monopoly on telegraph communication in Newfoundland, was quick to threaten reprisals if Marconi did not stop the experiments. A few

days later, the inventor received a letter from the company stating:

> Unless we receive an intimation from you during the day that you will not proceed any further with the work you are engaged in and remove the appliances erected for the purpose of telegraphic communication, legal proceedings will be instituted to restrain you from further prosecution of your work and for any damages which our clients may sustain or have sustained; and we further give you notice that our clients will hold you responsible for any loss or damage sustained by reason of your trespass upon their rights.[11]

The Canadian government, however, obviously seeing the chance to emulate its neighbor, immediately offered Marconi its full cooperation. Public sentiment toward the action taken by the telegraph company was unfavorable on both sides of the Atlantic. The *New York Times* criticized the action, and letters to the editor of the London *Times* expressed similar sentiments. All of this soon became history as the world began to use the results of the December 1901 experiments.

WIRELESS EXPANDS: THE MARCONI COMPANIES

Marconi respected those who pursued pure science, but he was much more interested in applying results and harvesting financial rewards. Thus, it was only a short time after his patent had been issued in England that he began formulating a world corporate empire that would stretch over the seven continents and involve millions of dollars in capital.[12] The company that had the most direct effect on wireless development was the Marconi Wireless Telegraph Company, Limited, formed on July 20, 1897, as the Wireless

Telegraph and Signal Company, Limited.[13] It was Marconi's father who insisted that the family name be attached to the venture. The beginning capital amounted to 100,000 English pounds, of which 15,000 went to Marconi for his patents. It was from this 15,000 pounds that he paid the cost of organizing the company. He also received 60,000 of the 100,000 initial shares, valued at 1 pound each. The remaining 40,000 went on the open market.

England: The Marconi Wireless Telegraph Company, Ltd.

A year after the company's formation, its operating capital increased by another 100,000 pounds. Although wireless had captured the imagination of the British, there were warnings for unwary investors. *Investors World* remarked in 1898 that "from all we can gather, the public will be well advised to keep clear of this concern. . . . Marconi's ingenious ideas do not seem to have made much headway, and it would be interesting to learn what the government officials reported about them."[14] The warning had little effect, and although for years to come investments did not show much success in terms of dividends, the public was always ready to buy up new shares whenever they were placed on the market.

In March 1912 a contract between Marconi's company and the government became tainted with rumors of corruption. One rumor suggested that Marconi was treated favorably because of his close friends in Parliament. Some government officials had made a huge profit by selling their Marconi stock when it peaked after the news of the contract was signed. The second set of charges was of manipulation of stock by the American Marconi Company. A committee was appointed by Parliament to investigate the matter. After due deliberation, they came out strongly in favor of Marconi, but the matter was not over. Another committee investigated the role of middlemen and stockbrokers, and still another the role of the House of Lords. Libel actions were taken and the company stock tumbled. Because of the publicity from the scandal, the company enjoyed only briefly the prosperity for which Marconi had long hoped. The future development of Marconi in England would have to wait until the end of World War I. In North America, the story was much the same.

Marconi's Interests in Canada

Marconi's corporate interest in Canada dated from his experience with the cable-telegraph authorities in Newfoundland. He erected a station at Glace Bay, Nova Scotia, and began major attempts to achieve reliable transatlantic wireless communication. The first transatlantic service opened on the night of December 15, 1902, when the London *Times* correspondent at Glace Bay cabled a newspaper report across the Atlantic. Two nights later it was arranged that the American station at Cape Cod would send a message from the United States to the King of England. The signal would be relayed to Glace Bay and from there to Poldhu. As it turned out, the atmospheric conditions were so good that the station in England picked up the signal directly from America.

The *Times* was so infatuated with the prospects of transatlantic service that it convinced Marconi to open the station again so that its correspondent could send news flashes to England. But a little more than a week later an ice storm sent the Glace Bay antennas crashing to the ground. The station was later reconstructed, this time with a large umbrella antenna.

The American Marconi Wireless Telegraph Company

When Marconi came to the United States in 1899 to report the America's Cup races by wireless, he also began an American subsidiary of his English company so that he could utilize his patents in America. The American Marconi Wireless Telegraph Company was incorporated in the state of New Jersey in the fall of 1899. The first equipment installed by the company was on the Nantucket Light Ship and its shore station on the eastern shore of Nantucket Island, and was used to warn ships of bad weather and coastal conditions.

That same year, the American company ran into trouble over a proposed United States Navy contract for the installation of Marconi wireless on Navy ships. After a series of tests, the Navy recommended buying the Marconi equipment. But when it asked Marconi the cost, it received word that the company would not sell the equipment; the Navy would have to rent it. At that point the Navy backed out. Captain L. S. Howeth, writing later about the negotiations, said: "In light of future events, the Marconi leases and stipulations have proved a blessing in disguise. The foresight of the authorities in not permitting themselves to be shackled with its restrictions, which would have persisted for more than a decade, allowed the Navy a free hand in guiding and assisting in the development of radio in this country." [15]

Despite the loss of the Navy contract, American Marconi received a boost in its assets in 1912 when it won a patent suit against the United Wireless Company. Using a case in England as a legal precedent, the American company charged United Wireless with infringing upon patent 7,777, the Marconi tuner that could select different signals from a single aerial. United Wireless pleaded no defense, and Marconi assumed control of the company and all of its assets and contracts. It was an unusual way to obtain a corporate merger. The U. S. Navy ended up using Marconi equipment after all when World War I began, since it had either taken over or closed all commercial and amateur wireless stations, many of which used Marconi equipment.

A young boy named David Sarnoff had been hired by the American company in September of 1906. Shortly after World War I ended, American Marconi was purchased by the newly formed Radio Corporation of America (RCA). Sarnoff became part of RCA management, and later headed the company. We shall learn the reasons for the sale and discuss RCA's early development in Chapter 4.

IMPROVEMENTS IN WIRELESS RECEPTION

Marconi's success in transmitting signals across the Atlantic and developing a world corporate empire was greatly aided by subsequent developments in wireless communication. One of the most important needs was for a device that would more efficiently detect and receive electromagnetic waves. As it was, the receiving and sending antennas were the size of football fields. Yet the current that entered a radio antenna and received an electromagnetic wave was minute. The great challenge was how better to detect these tiny, almost indistinguishable currents of energy hitting the football-sized antenna of a radio receiver. For radio to become a household appliance, the huge receiving antennas had to be eliminated.

Edison's Contributions

Some of the first experiments leading to an improved detector came during the study not of radio but of electric light.[16] Thomas Edison, while in the process of inventing the light bulb, had experimented with a two-element bulb but had found it impractical. The bulb consisted of two metallic elements—a *plate* and a *filament*—in a vacuum. If a battery were attached to the bulb so that its positive connector attached to the plate and its negative connector to the filament, current would flow through the bulb. If the connectors were reversed, the current would stop. What Edison had invented but discarded was later to be called a *valve,* since it could "shut off" current running in one direction, much like a valve controls steam or water.

The Fleming Valve

One of the keys to unlocking future developments in wireless technology was to find some way to measure electromagnetic waves in order to understand better their behavior and frequencies. J. Ambrose Fleming, an employee of Marconi, determined that the best way to do this would be to invent a means of measuring the waves as they flowed in only one direction. The secret lay in Edison's two-element light bulb. Fleming went to work perfecting the device, which became known as the oscillation valve, or Fleming valve. He patented it in England in 1904 and, through the American Marconi Company, in the United States in 1905. One worked the device by attaching the plate to the antenna, attaching a wire from the filament to the ground, and then hooking a telephone receiver into this completed circuit. The receiver could then detect the presence of the electromagnetic waves. It was not long, however, before Fleming's device was greatly improved by the inventive hand of Lee de Forest.[17]

LEE DE FOREST AND THE AUDION

The work of de Forest ranks close in significance to that of Marconi in the development of radio. Born in Council Bluffs, Iowa, in 1873, de Forest was the son of a Congregational minister who was later to become president of Talladega College in Alabama. After attending Mt. Hermon School in Massachusetts, de Forest entered a mechanical engineering program at the Scheffield Scientific School at Yale University. Having completed a dissertation entitled "Reflection of Hertzian Waves From the Ends of Parallel Wires," he was granted a Ph.D. in 1899. The research done and knowledge gained at Yale and his desire to apply pure science, first to inventions, next to patents, and then to profits, led him to a remarkable career that spanned much of his more than eighty years. He died in 1961 in Hollywood, where he was closest to one of his most beloved works, talking motion pictures. Our emphasis here, however, is on his invention of the audion, a three-element vacuum tube that revolutionized radio.

Adding the Grid to the Vacuum Tube

Lee de Forest discovered that a third element—a tiny grid of iron wires—could be added to Fleming's two-element vacuum-tube valve. The result was characterized as follows in any early book on the radio:

> This may not seem much to the uninitiated, but that miniature gadget was the truest "little giant" in all history . . . that the brain of man ever created. It set unbelievable powerful currents in motion, magnifications of those which flicked up and down the antenna

wire, and thus produced voice amplification which made radio telephony a finished product. By adding another tube and another, the amplification was enormously increased.[18]

The vacuum tube now had a filament, plate, and grid. De Forest first announced the tube—named the audion by his assistant, C. D. Babcock—in a paper presented to the October 26, 1906, meeting of the American Institute of Electrical Engineers in New York (Figure 3–4). After the paper was reproduced in the November 3, 1906, issue of *Electrical World,*[19] it was not surprising that one of the first reactions to his discovery came from Fleming. In a letter to the editor of *Electrical World,* Fleming attempted to diminish some of the importance of de Forest's invention:

> There is a remarkable similarity between the appliance now christened by de Forest as an "audion" and a wireless telegraphic receiver I called an oscillation valve.... Dr. de Forest's method of using this appliance as an electric wave detector appears, so far as I can judge from published accounts, to be a little different from mine, but nevertheless the actual construction of the apparatus is the same.... Even if Dr. de Forest has discovered some other way of employing the same device as a receiver, I venture to think that my introduction and use of it should not be ignored, as I believe I was the first to apply this device . . . as a means of detecting electric oscillations and electric waves.[20]

De Forest did not let Fleming's suggestions go unchallenged. He replied with a letter to the same magazine, which was published two weeks later. In it de Forest credited German scientists Johann Elster and F. K. Geitel, not Fleming:

> Prof. Fleming has done me the injustice of expressing an opinion based on an extract only of my paper regarding the "audion." In a more complete abstract of that paper pub-

FIGURE 3–4 Lee de Forest's audion tube. Coming from a Yale engineering program, he added the grid to Fleming's two-element tube. The new vacuum tube was introduced in a paper presented to the October 26, 1906 meeting of the American Institute of Electrical Engineering in New York. Fleming reacted strongly to the paper when it was published in *Electrical World*, claiming the audion had a remarkable similarity to his own device. (AT&T)

lished in the *Electrician* of London, it is seen that I mention not only the device described by Prof. Fleming in 1904, but point out the real genesis of this device by Elster and Geitel in 1882, or eight years prior to its rediscovery by Prof. Fleming in 1890. . . . The difference which Prof. Fleming questions may be tersely stated as that between a few yards and a few hundreds of miles; between a laboratory curiosity and an astonishingly efficient wireless receiver employing the same medium but operating on a principle different in kind.[21]

The Feud With Fleming

The rift between Fleming and de Forest did not end in the pages of *Electrical World*. Lee de Forest went on to patent his audion, but as we have seen, the Fleming valve also had been patented, in both England and the United States. It was the United States patent that provoked a lawsuit by the American Marconi Company. The case went in favor of the company, which contended that Lee de Forest had read the paper presented by Fleming to the Royal Society of England in 1905 in which Fleming described the oscillation valve, and that de Forest had then used this knowledge to begin the experiments that resulted in the audion.[22] The case was appealed, and again the court ruled in favor of the Marconi Company and the Fleming patent. Two years passed between the lower court's decision and the appeal. In the meantime both de Forest and the Marconi Company continued to manufacture the tubes. To make matters more complex, the court held that although de Forest had infringed on the Fleming valve, the Marconi Company had infringed on the audion. The result was that neither company could manufacture the devices without the other's consent.[23] The situation was chaotic until the Fleming patent with Marconi expired in 1922. Incredibly, the United States Supreme Court ruled in 1943 that the Fleming patent had never been valid in the first place!

De Forest's account of the conclusion of his dispute with Fleming is worth reading, partly because of its humor. Most important, it captures a rivalry between two men that was typical in its intensity of feuds between companies and inventors during the early development of the radio:

[Shortly after the Supreme Court decision,] Sir John Fleming, still unregenerate at ninety-two, published an amazing article in which he ignored all the earlier work . . . claiming even the discovery of the so-called "Edison effect," but never mentioning Edison's name! For this omission I wrote him in righteous reproach, incidentally calling to his attention the recent Supreme Court decision. Fleming's reply evinced profound disdain for what a mere Yankee court might think of his best-loved child. Having married a young opera singer at 84, he lived to the ripe old age of 95, dying in 1945. He never yielded in his firm conviction that he was radio's true inventor! [24]

De Forest's modesty is not convincing when we remember that he entitled his autobiography *The Father of Radio*. He also had some choice words for a group of radio executives about what radio had become: "The radio was conceived as a potent instrumentality for culture, fine music, the uplifting of America's mass intelligence. You have debased this child, you have sent him out in the streets in rags of ragtime, tatters of jive and boogie-woogie, to collect money from all and sundry." [25]

BREAKING THE VOICE BARRIER: RADIO TELEPHONY

The second great development in the early history of the radio was the advance from the "dit-dahs" of Morse code and the "What hath God wrought" of the telegraph to the "O Holy Night" of Reginald Fessenden's Christmas Eve radio broadcast in 1906. The story of voice transmission starts long before 1906, back when early experimenters examined the capacity of the ground and water to act as a conductor for "wireless telephone" conversations.

The system had been used by telegraph operators in 1838.[26] It applied a process known as *conduction,* in which the ground or water provided the "second wire" in a telegraph hookup. Morse used it in his New

York experiments. It was not long before inventors discovered that they did not need any wire at all to communicate between the transmitter and receiver over short distances. Because a current in one antenna would produce a current in another one nearby, a process called *induction,* two antennas close to each other would make the system work. This was a different principle from that of electromagnetic waves traveling through space, which Marconi and others used. Induction created an electrical disturbance in the atmosphere that was detectable only in the immediate vicinity of the transmitter.

NATHAN B. STUBBLEFIELD AND HIS WIRELESS TELEPHONE

Before Marconi mastered the Atlantic and while de Forest was studying at Yale, a farmer and experimenter named Nathan B. Stubblefield developed a way to transmit the voice as much as three miles by means of induction.[27] Near his home in Murray, Kentucky (Figure 3–5), and later on the Potomac River in Washington, D.C., he successfully transmitted the voice without using wires. It was in Murray that he received his first publicity. Dr. Rainey T. Wells witnessed Stubblefield's experiments:

FIGURE 3–5 Nathan B. Stubblefield (left) and his wireless telephone. As early as 1892, Stubblefield is reported to have sent voice by wireless over short distances at his farm in Murray, Kentucky. His son, Bernard (right), later became an employee of Westinghouse. Stubblefield used a Bell-type transmitting device and formed his own Wireless Telephone Company of America. Although receiving a patent for his device, commercial development never materialized. (Murray, Kentucky Chamber of Commerce)

He [Stubblefield] had a shack about four feet square near his house from which he took an ordinary telephone receiver, but entirely without wires. Handing me these, he asked me to walk some distance away and listen. I had hardly reached my post, which happened to be an apple orchard, when I heard "Hello, Rainey" come booming out of the receiver. I jumped a foot and said to myself, "This fellow is fooling me. He has wires somewhere." So I moved to the side some 20 feet but all the while he kept talking to me. I talked back and he answered me as plainly as you please. I asked him to patent the thing but he refused, saying he wanted to continue his research and perfect it.[28]

The demonstration was reported to have taken place in 1892. A modified Bell-type transmitting device provided the signal, which emanated from a large, circular metal antenna. Other residents of the small town of Murray witnessed a similar demonstration in 1898. Claims of Stubblefield's accomplishments published in the *St. Louis Post Dispatch* generated so much interest that he was brought to Washington, D.C., for a public demonstration on March 20, 1902. Following the demonstration Stubblefield said, "As to the practicality of my invention—all I can claim for it now is that it is capable of sending simultaneous messages from a central distributing station over a wide territory.... Eventually, it will be used for the general transmission of news of every description."[29]

Commercial Exploitation

Commercial exploitation of the invention was not far behind, and in 1903 Stubblefield became director of the Wireless Telephone Company of America. Demonstrations in Philadelphia and Washington, D.C., created more interest in the device. Yet it is here that the rest of Stubblefield's life becomes somewhat obscure. There are various reports of what happened to him. One suggests that he became disillusioned with how the stock for the company was being handled and on one occasion even charged it with fraud.[30] Stubblefield returned to Kentucky and with the help of local citizens obtained a patent for the device on May 12, 1908. Obviously disenchanted with the commercial aspects of his wireless telephone, he went into seclusion and continued research in his workshop shack near Murray.

If you travel through the Kentucky countryside near Murray today you may pass the place where Stubblefield was found dead on March 30, 1928; the cause of death was listed as starvation. Or you might drive by Murray State College, where students perform a dramatization of Stubblefield's life, *The Stubblefield Story*. Then as you go downtown you can tune your car radio to 1340 kHz and hear a blend of rock, easy listening, and country, and the news "centrally distributed" from WNBS radio. At a certain time the announcer will tell you "You are tuned to WNBS 1340 on your radio dial in Murray, Kentucky, the birthplace of radio."

THE WORK OF FESSENDEN

Although Nathan Stubblefield had created a working wireless telephone, no one had yet mastered the ability to transmit the voice beyond very short distances. Some of the most productive experiments toward this goal were carried out in 1899 by Reginald A. Fessenden at Allegheny, Pennsylvania, at the Western University of Pennsylvania, later to become the University of Pittsburgh. Fessenden (Figure 3–6), a Canadian by birth and a professor at the University of Pittsburgh, worked to improve both the detection of electromagnetic waves and a means by which a human voice could be placed

FIGURE 3-6   Canadian Reginald Fessenden made advancements in voice broadcasting with experiments which started at what is now the University of Pittsburgh. Other work was accomplished at Cobb Island, Maryland; Roanoke Island, North Carolina; and Brant Rock, Massachusetts. (Archives of the University of Pittsburgh)

"piggyback" on electrical oscillations and sent into the atmosphere. Later he developed an improved detector, which would subsequently be called the *heterodyne circuit*. Fessenden applied for patent papers for the improved circuit in 1905. Simultaneously, he continued to improve the transmitting and antenna systems for wireless.

Experiments at Cobb Island, Maryland

Fessenden's early work was completed under government contracts, and was aimed more at improving wireless communication than at seeking out a new method of radiotelephony. An experimental "station" was established by Fessenden on Cobb Island, sixty miles south of Washington, D.C., in the Maryland section of the Potomac River. In a letter dated January 4, 1900, from Willis J. Moore, Chief of the U.S. Weather Bureau, Fessenden was informed of the terms of his agreement:

You will be employed for one year in the Weather Bureau at a salary of $3,000 per annum. The Bureau will pay your actual expenses while on the road to an amount not exceeding $4.00 per day. You will be allowed to remain in Allegheny and continue your local connections for not longer than 3 months. Two active young men of the Weather Bureau will be assigned to duty as your assistants, and if you are especially desirous of retaining the one you at present employ, he will also be employed in the Weather Bureau for one year, at a salary of $1200. Such apparatus as described in your letter of the 29th ultimo will be purchased at the expense of the Government, one of our own men making the purchases and auditing the accounts: the property to belong to the Government. At the end of the year, if your work is successful, your services may be continued at a salary not less than that paid the first year.[31]

Fessenden accepted the offer and, traveling partway by river steamer, transported his equipment to Cobb Island. There, Fessenden's emphasis was not on distance but on the exact measurement of signals, which could verify and expand on some of the theoretical applications of the work that Fessenden had first tested in the 1899 experiments.[32] Two fifty-foot masts were erected for antennas. In a report of the experiments published in *Popular Radio,* Fessenden described the Cobb Island system:

> The exact method of transmission of the waves was experimentally determined by means of ladders placed at varying distances from the antennas. The course of the waves in the air was fully mapped out up to distances of several hundred yards from and to the antennas, and by burying the receivers at different depths in the ground and immersing them in different depths in sea water, the rate of decay below the surface and the strength of the currents flowing in the surface were accurately determined.[33]

Although poor in quality, intelligible speech was transmitted between the two antennas.

Experiments at Roanoke Island, North Carolina

At the end of the year, both parties were satisfied with the arrangement and decided to renew the contract. This time Fessenden was to erect experimental stations in North Carolina at Roanoke Island, Cape Hatteras, and Cape Henry. These three stations formed a large triangle which enabled Fessenden to test the system over longer distances than were possible at Cobb Island. The new round of experiments were directed not as much toward perfecting speech as toward improving telegraphic communication, and especially the receiving circuit, the key for long-distance communication by voice or telegraph. Fessenden's letters to his

patent attorney reveal his early success with the improved circuitry. After overcoming the considerable frustration of equipment parts that did not meet specifications, Fessenden wrote from Roanoke Island:

> I could hear every click of the key at Hatteras, and got every dot and dash as plainly as could be and as fast as they could send.
>
> To do a little figuring. The resonator should increase the effect 10 times. The prolonged oscillations about 5 times. The vacuum about 20 times. Longer waves about 5 times. Salt water instead of insulating water about 5 times. Good coils about 4 times, i.e., the sensitiveness can be increased about 1,000,000 times over this crude apparatus. This would give about 1,000 times the distance or 50,000 miles.
>
> As it is perfectly selective, perfectly positive, i.e., can give no false dots and cannot omit dots or dashes, I think we are at the end of all our troubles.[34]

Later in a letter of April 3, 1902, from Roanoke Island he wrote:

> I have more good news for you. You remember I telephoned about a mile in 1900—but thought it would take too much power to telephone across the Atlantic. Well I can now telephone as far as I can telegraph, which is across the Pacific Ocean if desired. I have sent varying musical notes from Hatteras and received them here with but 3 watts of energy, and they were very loud and plain, i.e., as loud as in an ordinary telephone.—I enclose telegram which was received with less than 1/500 of the energy which it took to work the coherer. The new receiver is a wonder!!![35]

Experiments at Brant Rock, Massachusetts

Despite the success of the experiments, Fessenden's relationship with the Weather Bureau began to deteriorate and he left Roanoke in 1902 after beginning a series of business arrangements. First, Fessenden licensed Queen & Company, Instrument

Makers, of Philadelphia to fulfill contracts for his communication system.[36] Then, through an arrangement with his patent attorney two Pittsburgh financiers, Thomas H. Givens and Hay Walker, Jr., put $2 million behind Fessenden's work and the four of them formed the National Electric Signalling Company.[37] Besides $300 a month in salary, Fessenden also received stock in the new venture.

After conducting experiments on the Chesapeake Bay, Fessenden moved in 1905 to Brant Rock, Massachusetts. Here the next chapter in wireless history would be written. Trying continually to improve Marconi's invention, Fessenden constructed a high-power station at Brant Rock and radically altered his antenna design. Instead of the series of umbrella-like wires used in Marconi's experiments, Fessenden constructed an "antenna tower." It stood 420 feet high and consisted of a series of telescopic metal tubes 3 feet in diameter at the bottom, held in place by guy wires and insulated at all points from the ground. The result was a signal that penetrated the atmosphere, which Marconi's station could not reach. Signals were received in Puerto Rico and at a station in Scotland even during the summer months, when static normally interferes with transatlantic broadcasts. These first achievements at Brant Rock were shadowed by excitement as voice broadcasting moved out of the laboratory.

Alexanderson's Alternator

The problem that plagued Fessenden was how to increase the number of transmitted oscillations so that the human voice would be audible. A telephone-type receiving apparatus had already proved successful. Marconi had used it to hear the signals from England in his famous Newfoundland experiment, and wireless operators on ships used headphones to listen to messages in Morse code. The problem was to generate enough cycles so that the voice would travel with the signal and not be drowned out by the sound of the current passing through the headphones. To accomplish this, Fessenden enlisted the help of the General Electric Company in Schenectady, New York.

There in the GE laboratories, a young Swedish scientist named Ernst Alexanderson (Figure 3–7) was placed in charge of the engineering team assigned to produce the Fessenden alternator. Both trial and error and difficulties in meeting Fessenden's

FIGURE 3–7 Dr. Ernst F.W. Alexanderson, a General Electric engineer, developed the high-frequency alternator that gave America a big edge in early long-distance voice broadcasting. The alternator, shown here with Alexanderson, was one of many developed by him between 1905 and 1920. It was used to send transatlantic broadcasts from the RCA station at Rocky Point, Long Island. (General Electric Research and Development Center)

wishes slowed the project. Alexanderson first developed an alternator that utilized a revolving iron core called an *armature*. Fessenden, however, demanded a wooden core, and the work started over. Fortunately for Fessenden, his two Pittsburgh financial backers continued to pour money into the project. Fessenden tried another company, the Rivett Lathe Manufacturing Company in Boston, but their device failed when the bearings burned up at the high speeds necessary to produce 50,000 cycles, the amount Fessenden felt would be needed for voice transmittals. Finally, in September 1906, Alexanderson and the GE team delivered the wooden-armature alternator.

Within a few hundred miles of Brant Rock were ships filled with crews celebrating the mixed merriment and loneliness of Christmas at sea on that December night in 1906. In the wireless rooms the operators were on duty as scheduled, exchanging messages and receiving the food and good cheer of fellow officers, when the splitting sound of CQ,CQ came through their headphones. The universal call alerted them that a message would immediately follow. But instead of the dit-dah of Morse code came the sound of a human voice. Officers were called to the room to witness the phenomenon. The voice was that of Reginald Fessenden. "O Holy Night" rang out through the cabin, followed by the words "Glory to God in the highest, and on earth, peace to men of good will." Voice broadcasting had reached as far away as Norfolk, Virginia, and the West Indies, shouting the world of wireless into a new era.

The Canadian Controversy: The National Electric Signalling Company Is Bankrupt

Many of the early wireless experimenters managed to amass considerable fortunes from the new medium, and even those who at first had lost money later reaped a profit. For Reginald Fessenden, fate had the opposite in store.[38] With the Brant Rock experiments a success, Fessenden's backers wanted to develop some profit potential for the company, which until now had been devoted to pure research. But Fessenden was at odds with Givens and Walker over a proposal to open a Canadian subsidiary. The Canadian company had evolved from a plan by the three men to give Marconi competition in transatlantic broadcasts. Fessenden went to England and made an agreement with the British Post Office Department: if his station at Brant Rock could communicate with a station in New Orleans, a distance of about eighteen hundred miles, the British Post Office would approve a fifteen-year license for Fessenden's company to establish a reliable communication link between Canada and England.

Fessenden successfully completed the Brant Rock–New Orleans experiments, and then the trouble started. Fessenden, a Canadian by birth and the chief negotiator in the British contract, felt the Canadian subsidiary should be controlled mainly by himself, the Canadians, and the British. Despite providing the capital for the new venture, to say nothing of the millions they had already invested, Walker and Givens were not to serve in any position of authority. Naturally, both men objected strongly, whereupon Fessenden resigned and sued, collecting $460,000. The National Electric Signalling Company declared bankruptcy in 1912, and Marconi and his companies were once again the undisputed leaders in wireless communication.

de Forest Gains Publicity

After inventing the audion, Lee de Forest began to experiment with voice communication at the same time Fessenden was developing his hetrodyne circuit and conducting the Brant Rock experiments. Using a high-frequency arc to modulate the signal, de Forest succeeded in transmitting a voice across the length of a room during the same year Fessenden gained recognition for his Brant Rock experiments with ocean vessels. de Forest was quick to see the potential of voice broadcasting and felt that good publicity would bring investors to his own company. Although voice broadcasts were well known in the United States, they were unknown in Europe. So in the summer of 1908, de Forest traveled to France and conducted demonstrations of radiotelephony from atop the Eiffel Tower, communicating with stations about twenty-five miles away.

The European experience whetted de Forest's appetite for more publicity at home. Always an opera buff, the inventor contacted the Metropolitan Opera in New York. He arranged to place a transmitter in the attic of the music hall and connect it to the microphones on stage. Although not very clear by modern standards, the microphones were the new Acousticon models manufactured by the National Dictograph Company.[39] On January 13, 1910, Enrico Caruso and Ricardo Martin bellowed *Cavalleria Rusticana* and *Pagliacci* to a small audience listening to receiving sets in New York. A master at gaining publicity, de Forest could rival Buffalo Bill Cody in obtaining press coverage for a show. The opera broadcasts were no exception. "The newspapers had been tipped off in advance and reporters were listening in at the Terminal Building, 103 Park Row, the Metropolitan Tower station, at the Hotel Breslin, on one of the ships downstream, and at our factory in Newark."[40] Although World War I and patent squabbles would slow the growth of modern radio until the late teens, de Forest's

publicity helped set the stage and arouse the public's enthusiasm for what would occur in the decades ahead.

WIRELESS GAINS POPULARITY: CRYSTALS AND HAMS

Up to this time, the wireless had remained in the hands of the large companies, such as Marconi, and the major users—the Navy in the United States and the Post Office Department in England. All that changed in 1906 with the invention of the crystal radio receiver by General Henry C. Dunwoody. That same year, Greenleaf W. Pickard perfected a silicone-crystal detector. These two devices contributed two important words to the wireless vocabulary: *availability* and *inexpensive*. Remember, the audion was still being perfected, and vacuum tubes were expensive. As late as 1915, radio-receiving equipment ran anywhere from $20 to $125—prices that were beyond the reach of young experimenters attracted to the lure of wireless. But by using the silicone crystal and a long, outside antenna, the general public could listen in on everything from opera to Navy broadcasts.

These early experimenters were called *amateur radio operators,* better known today as *hams.*[41] They were primarily of two types: (1) those who were interested in using radio to test new equipment, and (2) those who wanted to use the new medium to communicate with others. In each type the spirit of the other was fostered. It was these early, home-town inventors who did much to see radio mature. Although the inventors and the big companies provided capital for international expansion, the ham operators were responsible for many of the early developments and experiments aimed at improving radio. In 1909, the first known amateur radio club was formed in New York City. The group started with five youngsters, and their advisor was Reginald Fessenden.

A second organization, the Wireless Association of America, was started by Hugo Gernsback, publisher of *Modern Electrics*. The membership roster jumped from 3,200 in 1909 to 10,000 in November 1910. The association published the first *Wireless Blue Book,* which listed ninety amateur stations as members. A second *Blue Book* followed a short time later, and by 1911 the circulation of *Modern Electrics* had soared to 52,000. Sensing a lucrative market, the D. Van Nostrand book publishing company put *Wireless Telegraph Construction for Amateurs* on the bookstore shelves. By now, other radio clubs were rapidly forming, including the Radio Club of Salt Lake City, the Wireless Association of Central California, and the Radio Club of Hartford.

Ham radio was also gaining stature because it could be relied upon when other communication systems failed. In March of 1913 a major storm hit the Midwest, knocking out power lines and telephone communication. Ham radio operators, including those at Ohio State University and the University of Michigan, carried on communication and relayed emergency messages for seven days following the storm. This sparked Hiram Percy Maxim, famous as an inventor of an automobile and an engine silencer, to form the American Radio Relay League in 1914, an outgrowth of the Hartford Radio Club of which he was a member.

Ham radio has continued to thrive as a hobby and has developed throughout the field of wireless communication. When radiotelephony replaced wireless, hams began to chat "in person," but the Morse code remains even today a cherished language of these amateur experimenters. They communicate worldwide, using teletype, teleprinters, video-display terminals, and television. In cooperation with NASA, relay satellites have been launched for use by hams in international communication.

SUMMARY

In this chapter we traced the beginnings of wireless, from the early work of Marconi to the successful transmission of voice broadcasting by Reginald Fessenden and Lee de Forest. Drawing on Hertz's discoveries, Guglielmo Marconi first transmitted wireless signals over a short distance near his home in Italy. When the Italian government showed little interest in his invention, he traveled to Great Britain, where he received financial support from the British Post Office Department. After tests near the Bristol Channel, he succeeded in receiving wireless signals from across the Atlantic in 1901.

Marconi continued his experiments while expanding his corporate interests. His companies began to spring up in many countries; they included the Marconi Wireless Telegraph Company Ltd. in England and the American Marconi Wireless Telegraph Company in the United States. Improvements in the wireless were also made by J. Ambrose Fleming, creator of the Fleming valve, and Lee de Forest, inventor of the audion.

It was not long before people started to transmit the voice over the airwaves. Using the devices that had been developed for telephone communication, scientists came closer and closer to quality voice transmission. A Kentucky farmer named Nathan B. Stubblefield performed short-distance wireless voice transmission. Then Reginald Fessenden developed the heterodyne circuit. With this improved detector of electromagnetic waves and with the help of a large alternator developed by GE and Ernst Alexanderson, Fessenden transmitted voice in December 1906. After disagreements with his financial backers, Fessenden was overtaken by de Forest and others in his quest for what was called radiotelephony. At the same time, radiotelephony became practical as inexpensive receiving sets using silicone-crystal detectors were manufactured and sold. The general public was becoming interested in what was now being called radio, and amateur ham operators talked across city blocks and eventually across continents.

OPPORTUNITIES
FOR FURTHER LEARNING

AITKEN, G. J., *Syntony and Spark—The Origins of Radio*. New York: John Wiley & Sons, Inc., 1976.

ARCHER, G. L., *History of Radio to 1926*. 1938. Reprinted by the Arno Press, 1971.

BAKER, W. J., *A History of the Marconi Company*. New York: St. Martin's Press, Inc., 1971.

BLAKE, G. G., *History of Radio Telegraphy and Telephony*. London: Chapman & Hall Ltd., 1928 (reprinted by the Arno Press, 1974).

DUNLAP, O. E., *Marconi: The Man and His Wireless*. New York: The Macmillan Company, 1937 (reprinted by the Arno Press, 1971).

FAHIE, J. J., *A History of Wireless Telegraphy*. New York: Dodd, Mead & Company, 1901 (reprinted by the Arno Press, 1971).

FLEMING, J. A., *The Principles of Electric Wave Telegraphy*. London: Longmans, Green, 1906, 1910, 1916, and 1919.

HANCOCK, H. E., *Wireless at Sea*. Chelmsford, England: Marconi International Marine Communication Company, Ltd., 1950 (reprinted by the Arno Press, 1974).

HAWKS, E., *Pioneers of Wireless*. London: Methuen, 1927 (reprinted by Arno Press, 1974).

JOLLY, W. P., *Marconi*. New York: Stein & Day Publishers, 1972.

LODGE, O. J., *Signalling Through Space Without Wires: The Work of Hertz and his Successors*. 3rd ed. New York: Van Nostrand, 1900 (reprinted by Arno Press, 1971).

MARCONI, D., *My Father Marconi*. New York: McGraw-Hill Book Company, 1962.

VYVYAN, R. N., *Marconi and Wireless*. Yorkshire, England: E P Publishing Limited, 1974.

4

THE DEVELOPMENT
OF RADIO
AND TELEVISION

The excitement of the first wireless signals, the thrill of the first voice broadcasts, and the world of the radio amateur—all came from an era of pioneer spirit and experimental technology. Radio was magic, and people welcomed it with open arms. They could set a black box on their kitchen table, stretch a wire into the evening sky, and pick voices and music right out of the air. There was no need to have it delivered by the paper carrier, no need to walk to the country store to get it. The sounds of presidents, operas, big bands, and sporting events were live and immediate. Needless to say, people wanted all the radio they could get, and the stations that gave it to them grew in stature and power. Some of the earliest stations are still household words, and by learning about them we can catch some of the spirit of early radio.

THE PIONEER STATIONS

Much like trying to identify the inventor of radio, it is hard to put a label on the town, place, or person responsible for the first broadcasting station.

Basic Criteria of a Broadcasting Station

R. Franklin Smith has established several basic criteria for modern broadcasting stations.[1] First, *a broadcasting station transmits by wireless*. The signals must travel through space as electromagnetic waves. Smith does not consider ETV a form of broadcasting, nor closed-circuit wired college stations. Second, *a broadcasting station transmits by telephony*. The sounds of the station should be intelligible to the general listener. Third, *a broadcasting station transmits to the public*. It is distinct from other types of communication, such as telephone or telegraph, and from such special services as safety, aviation, and marine use. Fourth, *a broadcasting station transmits a continuous program service*. Programming is interconnected and is recognizable as a program service. Last, *a broadcasting station is licensed by government*. In the United States, the government licensing arm is the Federal Communications Commission.

Although these criteria are too limited for our purposes, they are helpful in outlining the history of broadcasting. Merely finding the station that first met these five criteria is difficult, since definitions of broadcasting were changing even in the early 1920s. Ser-

vice, license, call letters, and ownership were often short-lived and sporadic.

Still, four stations are considered important to an understanding of the historical development of broadcasting. These are KCBS in San Francisco, which evolved over the years from an experimental station established in San Jose, California, in 1909; noncommercial WHA at the University of Wisconsin in Madison; WWJ in Detroit; and KDKA in Pittsburgh.

Charles David Herrold Begins in San Jose

Professor Charles David Herrold is credited with operating one of the first broadcasting stations in America (Figure 4-1). Others broke the airwave silence before him, but as

FIGURE 4-1 An early broadcasting station of Charles David Herrold located in the old Wells Fargo Building in San Jose, California. Left to right: Kenneth Saunders, E.A. Portal, Herrold (standing) and Frank G. Schmidt. (Courtesy KCBS Radio, Gordon B. Greb & the Sourisseau Academy of San Jose State University)

early as 1909, residents of San Jose could spend a Wednesday evening with their crystal sets tuned to news and music broadcast by Herrold. A classmate of Herbert Hoover at Stanford, Herrold had gone on to become owner of the School of Radio in San Jose.[2] The radio station was the school's medium of advertising—advertising that was aired more than ten years before KDKA in Pittsburgh and WWJ in Detroit began regular programming. Herrold had constructed a huge umbrellalike antenna in downtown San Jose and from the Garden City Bank Building the wire structure hung out in all directions for a city block. Although it was a far cry from the eastern giants that could carry football games and political speeches, the little San Jose wireless station became one of the famous firsts in the broadcasting industry.

After 1910, the station handled regularly scheduled programs with operators on regular shifts. Even Herrold's first wife, Sybil M. True, had an air shift, which made her one of the earliest female disk jockeys.[3] She would borrow records from a local store and play them as a form of advertising. When listeners went to the store to purchase the recordings they would register their name and address, thereby giving the station an indication of its extent and influence. The California station gained national recognition at the Panama Pacific Exposition in 1915, and when Lee de Forest spoke in San Francisco in 1940 he called it "the oldest broadcasting station in the entire world."[4]

WHA in Madison, Wisconsin

WHA traces its inception all the way back to 1904 in the physics laboratory at the University of Wisconsin, where Earle M. Terry was working his way toward a Ph.D.[5] Graduating in 1910, he stayed on as an assistant professor, and in 1917, with the help of colleagues and assistants, he began experimental broadcasting of voice and music. The equipment was makeshift, and the three-element tubes were not the sturdy successors of the 1920s. Instead, they were a mixture of creative craftsmanship, hand-blown glass, and immense frustration, especially when they burned out.

By 1922, station 9XM had been legitimized by the Department of Commerce with a license and the new call letters WHA. The same year, Professor William H. Lighty became WHA's program director. He developed the station into one of the first "extension" stations, responsible for bringing universities to the public with everything from news to college courses. WHA made other great strides in programming: broadcasts of the University of Wisconsin Glee Club, regular weather and road reports, farm and market reports, symphony broadcasts, and the famous Wisconsin School of the Air.

To aid listeners, Professor Terry taught them how to build their own radio sets. He even distributed some of the raw materials free of charge. The radio rage of the early twenties caught many of the large equipment manufacturers unprepared. Loudspeakers had not yet replaced the earphone, and Professor Terry first demonstrated amplified radio reception in the Wisconsin exposition hall.

Meanwhile, WHA's farm and market reports and weather broadcasts were being picked up by the newspapers, and weather-forecasting stations as far away as Chicago were using WHA data to aid prediction. Letters poured in from listeners as far away as Texas and Canada. WHA has since been joined by WHA–FM and WHA–TV. At the University of Wisconsin in Madison a historical marker reads: "The Oldest Station in the Nation . . . the University of Wisconsin station under the calls 9XM and WHA has been in existence longer than any other."

WWJ and the Detroit News

After leaving the historical marker at the University of Wisconsin, you can travel east around Chicago and the tip of Lake Michigan to another pioneer station still operating—WWJ in Detroit.[6] When broadcasting was still in its infancy, some forward-thinking newspaper publishers realized that it would be better to reap some of its profits rather than always compete against it. William E. Scripps of the *Detroit News* had such a vision. He presented the idea to his colleagues, and they responded by appropriating money for construction of a makeshift radiotelephone room on the second floor of the Detroit News Building.

At 8:15 P.M. on August 20, 1920, an Edison phonograph played two records into the mouthpiece of the de Forest transmitter; probably no more than one hundred amateur operators heard the signal. There was no advance warning of the trial broadcast; no publicity draped the pages of the *Detroit News*. Everything worked perfectly, and the staff began preparations for the next day's broadcast of a Michigan election. When the election returns began to trickle in, it was the radio, not the newspaper, that first brought them to the public. Like a proud parent doting on a child's accomplishments, the September 1 issue of the *News* reported: "The sending of the election returns by the Detroit *News* Radiotelephone Thursday night was fraught with romance, and must go down in the history of man's conquest of the elements as a gigantic step in his progress."

The early programming of WWJ, originally licensed under the call letters 8MK, reflects much of the same programming that other early stations experimented with and sometimes nurtured into long-running popular fare. The election returns were supplemented with a sportscast the following

day, a preview of the World Series on October 5, and reports of the Brooklyn-Cleveland match-up. Returns from the Harding-Cox election were heard on November 20, 1920, the same returns that later became KDKA's claim to the "first station" honor.

So important was music that WWJ organized the sixteen-piece *Detroit News* Orchestra expressly for broadcast. It also expanded its studios to auditorium proportions after which they were described as "magnificent," having perfect acoustics, two-tone blue walls, and a white ceiling with a silver border.

The latest equipment took WWJ's news microphone onto the road and into the air. A single-engine prop aircraft with NEWS painted in big letters on one wing was equipped for direct broadcast. Its news and photographic team thus became one of the first mobile units (Figure 4-2) now a common element of radio stations even in small communities.

With all of these early credits to its name, it is not surprising that on the front of an antique microphone illustrating the promotional literature of WWJ reads the inscription "WWJ RADIO ONE, WHERE IT ALL BEGAN, AUGUST 20, 1920."

KDKA in East Pittsburgh

Station KDKA also established its place in broadcasting history in 1920.[7] The story of KDKA begins with Dr. Frank Conrad (Figure 4-3). Assistant chief engineer at the Westinghouse Electric Plant in East Pittsburgh, Conrad had constructed a transmitter licensed in 1916 as 8XK. After the World War I ban on nonmilitary uses of radio was lifted, Conrad began his experimental programming. Through an arrangement with a record store in the nearby community of Wilkinsburg, Pennsylvania, he received records in exchange for mentioning the

FIGURE 4–2 WWJ's radio news truck which operated in conjunction with *The Detroit News*. WWJ was one of the early pioneer stations which claims some of the "firsts" of early broadcasting. It went on the air on August 20, 1920 and programmed two records over a de Forest transmitter. About one-hundred radio operators are estimated to have heard the signal. The sixteen-piece Detroit News orchestra was organized to provide music for the station's programming. (WWJ)

FIGURE 4–3 Dr. Frank Conrad of KDKA radio which began in East Pittsburgh, Pennsylvania. Originally licensed in 1916 as an experimental station under the call 8XK, KDKA broadcast under its new call letters beginning in November, 1920. The station carried continuous programming after the November, 1920 sign-on date and also makes claim to being the "first" station. (KDKA)

name of the store. The station's popularity grew so rapidly that Horne's Department Store in Pittsburgh ran an ad for inexpensive receiving sets.

To H. P. Davis, a Westinghouse vice-president, the ad was the inspiration for a license application including the call letters KDKA, granted on October 27, 1920. A month later, the new call letters identified the station as it sent Harding-Cox election returns to listeners with amateur receiving sets and to a crowd gathered around a set at a local club. The crowd called for more news and less music, and KDKA's mail reported reception of the signals even at sea. The success of the broadcast gained widespread publicity, overshadowing WWJ's similar effort. Moreover, the combination of a publicized event and a major effort to get receivers into the hands of the public made the KDKA broadcast a milestone.

Manufacturing receivers was Westinghouse's definition of "commercial" broadcasting. Addressing an audience at the Harvard Business School, H. P. Davis remarked, "A broadcasting station is a rather useless enterprise unless there is someone to listen to it. . . . To meet this situation we had a number of simple receiving outfits manufactured. These we distributed among friends and to several of the officers of the company."[8]

As the popularity of the station grew, so did the staff, and when one day a Westinghouse engineer walked into the transmitting shack, he became the first full-time announcer in radio. Harold W. Arlin's broadcasting experiences were quite a change from his duties as an electrical engineer. During his career he introduced to KDKA's listeners such famous names as William Jennings Bryan, Will Rogers, Herbert Hoover, and Babe Ruth.

Today, clear-channel, 50,000-watt KDKA can be heard over a wide area of the northern hemisphere late at night during good atmospheric conditions. If you are traveling in the Pittsburgh area, you might even pass the former home of Dr. Frank Conrad in the suburb of Wilkinsburg, where a plaque reads: "Here radio broadcasting was born. . . ."[9]

RCA IS FORMED

Although it may seem as though the pioneer stations and their owners were to become the corporate giants of broadcasting, by 1920 a new worldwide corporation was already operating with the blessing of the United States government. It would soon become a giant not only in broadcasting but in other communications areas as well. The company was the Radio Corporation of America (RCA). Its beginning was full of international intrigue, skilled corporate maneuvering, and presidential politics. Even the United States Navy played a role.

The play begins at the close of World War I, when the United States government still controlled all wireless communication. Turning a major share of the American wireless interests back to Marconi was more than President Woodrow Wilson wanted to do. After all, the Marconi Company was still substantially British in influence if not in stock ownership. Communication and transportation were now recognized as important keys to international power. Great Britain had a network of cable systems in Europe and the United States, and its shipping industry and strategic location gave it an edge in transportation. Although not necessarily a threat, the British were at least to be treated with caution. Moreover, President Wilson was a fan of radio in his own right, having seen the benefits of his famous Fourteen Points spread throughout Europe by an American station using the huge

General Electric alternator designed by Ernst Alexanderson.[10]

Government Attempts to Keep the Alternator

In 1918, two bills were introduced in Congress that were indirectly designed to bring wireless under control and to retain American control over Alexanderson's alternator. Seemingly harmless at the time, they suggested the use of technical-school radio stations for experiments but failed to mention anything about the ham stations. Although the legislation had the support of President Wilson and the Department of the Navy, neither counted on the lobbying efforts of the amateurs. In Chapter 3 we learned of the mushrooming popularity of radio and the growth of the amateur organizations. When World War I began and the government took control of broadcasting, the hams were silenced and their equipment did little more than collect dust. But now, because of their pent-up enthusiasm for going back on the air, a flood of war-trained operators wanting to continue their experiences as hobbyists, and their exciting tales of war escapades involving radio, the legislation did not have a chance. The scathing attacks on the bills even claimed that they would prohibit the youth of the country from participating in investigation and invention.[11] Finally, the bills were tabled permanently.

Bullard, Young, and Sarnoff

The next scene cast the General Electric Company, President Wilson, and Admiral William H. G. Bullard in leading roles. The war was a period of considerable government support for GE, especially for its Alexanderson alternator. When the war ended, the company faced substantial layoffs because of the lack of government contracts.

Although patriotism had taken precedence over trade during the hostilities, an end to the conflict meant GE was free to trade with any company it chose. By coincidence, that trading was about to begin with the British Marconi Company. But President Wilson wanted the new technology of radio to remain in American hands. Although the details of the conversation are unclear, we know President Wilson at least spoke to Admiral Bullard, who was chief of Naval Operations Service, about keeping the Alexanderson alternator on home ground.[12] Bullard then took it upon himself to speak to General Electric's general counsel, Owen T. Young. He managed to convince Young and GE to take the giant leap of forming a new, all-American company in the wireless business.

A man known for his significant corporate maneuvers, Young managed to coordinate international negotiations that not only formed the Radio Corporation of America but also facilitated the purchase by RCA of the American Marconi Company. GE also bought the American Marconi Company stock owned by the British Marconi Company. The new corporation had American directors and stipulated that no more than 20 percent of its stock could be held by foreign nationals. For American Marconi, becoming part of RCA was a necessity if it was to overcome its "British" image in the face of American patriotism. It also needed the alternator to succeed just as much as GE needed customers. As it turned out, the merger maintained the jobs of American Marconi employees and directors.

One of the more famous American Marconi directors was David Sarnoff (Figure 4-4). As a wireless operator he had "worked" the messages from the ships rescuing the survivors of the *Titanic*. In 1916, in a now famous letter, Sarnoff wrote his boss,

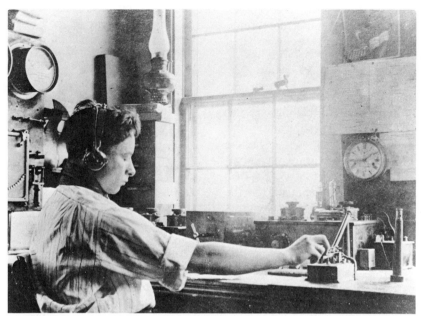

FIGURE 4-4 David Sarnoff taught himself Morse Code and began his career as a wireless operator with the American Marconi Company at Siasconset on Nantucket Island. (RCA)

Edward J. Nally, suggesting a commercial application of radio:

> I have in mind a plan of development which would make radio a "household utility" in the same sense as the piano or phonograph. The idea is to bring music into the house by wireless. . . . The receiver can be designed in the form of a simple "Radio Music Box"; . . . supplied with amplifying tubes and a loud-speaking telephone, all of which can be neatly mounted in one box.
>
> Aside from the profit to be derived from this proposition the possibilities for advertising for the company are tremendous, for its name would ultimately be brought into the household, and wireless would receive national and universal attention.[13]

Named commercial manager of RCA when the merger took place, Sarnoff later headed the corporation.[14]

PATENTS, CROSS-LICENSING, AND COMPETITION

KDKA's experiments and their accompanying publicity put the major corporations involved in wireless communication into a small turmoil. Corporate giants RCA, GE, and American Telephone and Telegraph had entrusted their futures to a joint enterprise that would effectively, if not completely, control the development of radio. But the vision of the triumvirate had been marine communication and radiotelephony, not the type of communication KDKA created with its November 1920 demonstration. Now Sarnoff's memo, which had originally gone politely unheeded, took on new significance. Perhaps there was money to be made from using broadcasting for mass appeal. The empire that Owen T. Young had built already had acquired allies in GE and AT&T—each had previously acquired important broadcasting patents, which the three now shared by agreement.

Sharing the Discoveries

Some of the earliest patents belonged to Lee de Forest. The audion, the forerunner of a series of improved vacuum tubes, was the most important link to the future of communication, at least to AT&T. In 1913 AT&T began buying de Forest's patents to the vacuum tube and having their own engineers improve the device. By 1915, using the latest equipment, including German-manufactured vacuum pumps that sucked the air out of the tubes, the company had perfected the first commercially successful vacuum tube.[15] AT&T used it for the first transatlantic telephone call.

As we learned in Chapter 3, the courts ruled that the audion infringed on the vacuum tube invented by Ambrose Fleming and that Fleming's patents belonged to the American Marconi Company. Yet war has its peculiar benefits, and breaking this AT&T–American Marconi conflict was one of them. The United States government stepped in and called for all companies to forge ahead as part of the war effort; thus, all became immune from patent-infringement suits.

The demand for vacuum tubes also involved GE and Westinghouse. Each had the capacity to manufacture light bulbs. The equipment that could suck air from a light bulb also could perform the same task in the manufacture of vacuum tubes.[16] General Electric, as we learned, also had the Alexanderson alternator.

So for the duration of World War I, everyone worked in harmony, but each with an important part of the pie that could be reheated after the war ended. When it did,

each had something the others needed. Thus, for the future of radio it was advantageous for RCA, GE, and AT&T to enter into a complex arrangement of cross-licensing agreements, which permitted each to share in the developments of the others but clearly divided the way in which radio would be marketed to the public.

Armstrong's Superheterodyne: Westinghouse Asset

Westinghouse, meanwhile, had been scrambling to compete with the RCA–GE–AT&T alliance. Just a month before KDKA's November 1920 broadcast, Westinghouse shrewdly bought the patents to a new type of circuitry invented by a graduate student at Columbia University, Edwin H. Armstrong. While Armstrong was serving in France in World War I, he became interested in finding a way for antiaircraft guidance systems to home in on the radio waves emitted by aircraft engines.[17] Although his invention never aided the war effort, it did spark the development of the *superheterodyne circuit,* an improvement on Fessenden's heterodyne circuit. The superheterodyne changed the frequency of incoming radio waves, amplified them, then changed them to an audible signal. Westinghouse also acquired some patents held by Michael Pupin, a Columbia professor who had worked with Armstrong, permitting him to use his laboratory and financing some of his work.[18]

When KDKA showed its stuff, Westinghouse was invited to become the fourth member of the RCA–GE–AT&T alliance. Still another company, United Fruit, joined because of its patents on crystal detectors. Under agreements among the big four, (1) GE and Westinghouse would manufacture radio parts and receivers; (2) RCA would market and sell them; and (3) AT&T would make, lease, and sell radio transmitters.[19] All of them were free to start their own broadcasting stations, and they did. But the agreements were concerned mostly with wireless telephony and telegraphy.[20]

When the stations did get under way they signed on fast and furiously. KDKA was only the beginning. More and more amateurs with number prefixed call signs applied and were granted licenses to operate broadcasting stations in the same fashion as KDKA. Westinghouse did not stop with that Pittsburgh station: before long it had signed on WBZ in Springfield, Massachusetts; WJZ in Newark; and KYW in Chicago (it was later assigned to Philadelphia). WJZ was sold to RCA in 1923.

RCA started its own station in 1921, WDY in New York. Although it stayed on the air only three months, the station tried some innovative programming, including a remote broadcast from the New York Electrical Show featuring Metropolitan Opera star Ann Case.

General Electric entered broadcasting by signing on WGY in Schenectady, New York. But of all the stations on the air in the early 1920s, the one to stir the attention of the public and the industry alike was AT&T's WEAF in New York.

TOLL BROADCASTING: WEAF, THE AT&T STATION

The idea of commercial broadcasting was realized at AT&T on June 1, 1922, with the licensing of WEAF. WEAF initiated the concept of toll broadcasting. This meant that anyone wishing to use the station could do so by paying a toll. Sponsoring a program meant buying the entire time segment and using it for whatever purpose desired. At first, the idea had few takers. To fill the programming void, the station used AT&T personnel as announcers. One of the earliest was Helen Hann, a member of AT&T's Long Lines Department. (Figure 4–5). The first sponsor to try the new toll concept was the Queensboro Corporation of New York, which on August 28, 1922, began a set of five short programs over five days to sell real estate.[21] At a cost of fifty dollars the Queensboro Corporation had begun the era of modern commercial broadcasting.

Criticism of Toll Broadcasting

Not everyone liked the idea. Arguments against commercial radio started surfacing in the trade press. The *American Radio Journal* suggested three alternatives: (1) have municipalities undertake programs on a civic-entertainment basis; (2) charge the public and collect revenues from a large number of "radio subscribers"; or (3) tax the manufacturers of radio equipment, the people who distribute it, and the people who sell it.[22] *Printer's Ink,* the trade journal of early advertising, concluded:

> Any attempt to make the radio an advertising medium, in the accepted sense of the term, would, we think, prove positively offensive to great numbers of people. The family circle is not a public place, and advertising has no business intruding there unless it is invited. . . . The man who does not want to read a paint ad in the newspaper, can turn the page and read something else. But the man on the end of the radio must listen, or shut off entirely. That is a big distinction that ought not be overlooked."[23]

But despite the skeptical reviews, advertising revenue gradually dribbled in to WEAF.

Through some political maneuvering with the Department of Commerce, the station managed to secure a more favorable frequency and extended hours. Both were important since stations then did not have the

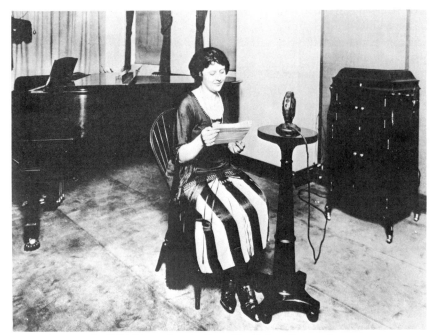

FIGURE 4–5 WEAF's early studio with Helen Hann, the announcer. WEAF is considered the first station to engage in commercial broadcasting, then called "toll" broadcasting. The first sponsor was the Queensboro Corporation of New York which used the station to sell real estate. (AT&T)

protection from interference that they do today. In fact, sometimes three or more stations had to share the same frequency and split up the broadcast day, each vying for the audience when another signed off.

As WEAF attracted more advertisers, AT&T began pouring money into the station, building new studios and obtaining the finest equipment that its manufacturing arm Western Electric could manufacture. That equipment became the envy of the broadcasting industry, and when other stations started to request it AT&T was reluctant to fill their orders. The short-term profit of a transmitter sale was less important to AT&T than the potential of a national advertising medium under its control. When AT&T increased WEAF's remote broadcasts the au-

dience clamored to listen, and when WEAF's competition made remote broadcasts AT&T responded financially.

Finally, AT&T concluded that it would be in its best interests to block remote hookups on AT&T lines by its old allies, RCA, GE, and Westinghouse. Resentment, fueled by profits, lit a spark that inflamed the industry. While its three competitors were scrambling to use Western Union lines for broadcasts, AT&T was arguing that it alone should be permitted to engage in toll broadcasting, based on nothing less than the 1920 cross-licensing agreements that spelled out the rights to manufacture and distribute radio equipment.

As time went on, the stakes grew higher. While WEAF's income from its toll venture continued to climb, hundreds of smaller companies ate away at the profits of RCA, GE, and Westinghouse by manufacturing radio receivers in defiance and sometimes in ignorance of patent rights. It was clear that the future lay in commercial broadcasting to a mass audience. AT&T even went so far as to collect license fees from some stations before permitting hookups into AT&T long lines. The company also strung together a group of stations on which an advertiser could buy time separately or all together. This *chain,* as early network broadcasting was to become known, was a prime example of how toll broadcasting could work.[24] Although AT&T was receiving some severe criticism in the press, it continued its toll concept.

Finally the accusations of infringement on the 1920 agreements escalated into open confrontation, and an arbiter—Boston lawyer Roland W. Boyden—was called in. The parties agreed to adhere to the verdict he would issue.[25] Simultaneously the Federal Trade Commission, apparently completely unaware of the arbitration action, issued a sobering report claiming the existence of a monopoly in the radio industry and placing the blame on none other than AT&T, RCA, GE, Westinghouse, and the United Fruit Company.

The Antitrust Issue

Taking his time in this delicate matter,[26] Boyden finally presented a draft opinion that effectively ended AT&T's claim to exclusivity in toll broadcasting. The opinion caused the telephone company to try an end run. First, the AT&T attorneys issued their reaction:

> We believe that the referee's unavoidably incomplete knowledge of the extremely intricate art involved in this arbitration (coupled

with) his effort to cooperate in the attempt of the parties to work out this situation, have misled him into a radical departure from the contract which the parties actually made, and into conclusions which amount to an attempt to make a new contract for them.[27]

They then got an opinion from none other than John W. Davis, who had helped draft the Clayton Act, that major piece of antitrust legislation passed the same year that the Federal Trade Commission was formed. Davis argued that if Boyden were correct, then the original cross-licensing agreements of 1920 were illegal and an infringement of antitrust laws. It was a crafty move on AT&T's part, effectively suggesting that it did not have to agree to the arbitration because the agreement was illegal in the first place.

Despite all the turmoil, AT&T was very conscious of public opinion. Waging open warfare to gain control of broadcasting was not an image it wanted to acquire. Consequently, the next scene would see the power structure of American broadcasting change dramatically.

NETWORK RADIO

Whether RCA realized AT&T did not want to begin battle, or decided it was time it went into toll broadcasting is open to speculation. Undoubtedly, both thoughts crossed the mind of David Sarnoff as he and other RCA officers watched AT&T organize its broadcasting interests into a separate corporation in May 1926 and call the new subsidiary the Broadcasting Company of America. At RCA a similar move was afoot: in September 1926 the RCA broadcasting interests were consolidated into a company called the National Broadcasting Company. Shortly thereafter, RCA bought WEAF for $1 million. WEAF was eventually consolidated into WJZ, which RCA had previously purchased from Westinghouse.

As for AT&T, the future forecast a healthy income from fees paid by broadcasters for the use of long lines for remote and network broadcasting. It also lifted the weight of negative public opinion from AT&T's shoulders. Although it might have won the court battles and the arbitration, and even survived the wrath of the Federal Trade Commission, AT&T felt comfortable with its network of "wires"; it would let NBC shoulder public opinion on the new "national network." In a major display of public pronouncement NBC advertised its new venture in newspapers, promising "better programs permanently assured by this important action of the Radio Corporation of America."

NBC's Red and Blue

NBC operated two basic networks as part of its nationwide coverage plan. The Blue network served some stations exclusively, as did the Red network, and a number of the stations had the option of drawing programming from both. Although still consolidated under NBC, the flagship station of the Red network was none other than WEAF. The Blue network chose its old rival WJZ. Not surprisingly the rivalry continued. In 1932, NBC executives began to consider giving a separate status to the Blue network and having it operate even more competitively with the Red. One of these executives was Mark Woods, later to play a key role in ABC's development. There was no change at the Blue until 1939, however, when a separate Blue sales department was established, followed by other departments separate from the Red network. Undoubtedly, an impetus for the changes was the Federal Communications Commission's announcement in 1938 that it was planning a full-scale inquiry into network broadcasting.

The FCC's Report on Chain Broadcasting

Out of the inquiry came the FCC's 1941 *Report on Chain Broadcasting*. Among other things, the report was critical of NBC's interest in talent management. This interest developed early in 1931, when, because of its need for talent, NBC acquired a 50-percent share of the Civic Concert Service, Inc., in order to complement an artist-management division of the company. Increasing its share in the Civic Concert Service until it owned it, the network became the target of conflict-of-interest charges by the FCC. The *Report* stated, "As an agent for artists, NBC is under a fiduciary [hold in trust] duty to procure the best terms possible for the artists. As employer of artists, NBC is interested in securing the best terms possible from the artists. NBC's dual role necessarily prevents arm's-length bargaining and constitutes a serious conflict of interest."[28] Scrutiny of the artists' service was only part of the investigation. The *Report* also examined NBC's growing interest in its transcription business, which included recordings for libraries and other services.

The FCC concluded that stations could not be bound by exclusive network contracts prohibiting them from airing programming from other networks; that network contracts were to be for a period of one year; and that stations were to be the sole determiner of programming, a right not to be delegated to the networks. The most important statement, however, hit at the very heart of NBC's dual-network concept: "No license shall be granted to a standard broadcast station affiliated with a network organization which maintains more than one network.[29] Seasoned veteran David Sarnoff, now president of RCA, set the wheels in motion to protect RCA's investment. He immediately organized the Blue network as a separate corporation. The action was an attempt (1) to pacify the FCC, at least temporarily and (2) to get an accurate reading of exactly how much the Blue network was worth by creating a separate accounting system. The handwriting was on the wall—Blue had to be sold.

Edward J. Noble Launches ABC

When it became clear that NBC's disposal of the Blue network was inevitable, major industrialists began to consider the jump into broadcasting. They included the Mellons in Pittsburgh, Marshall Field, Paramount Pictures, and Edward J. Noble, a former undersecretary of commerce who had amassed a sizable fortune making and selling Lifesavers candy. In the summer of 1943 Noble posted $1 million of Blue's purchase price and made arrangements to pay RCA the remainder from his own pocket and with loans from three New York banks.[30] The FCC, meanwhile, had delayed enforcing the 1941 *Report* in order to permit the sale of the Blue network in a calm atmosphere that wouldn't depress the price.

On October 12, 1943, the commission announced it was approving the sale of the Blue network to Edward J. Noble.[31] Mark Woods was retained as president. In approving the sale, the FCC stated that the transaction "should aid in the fuller use of the radio as a mechanism of free speech. The mechanism of free speech can operate freely only when controls of public access to the means of a dissemination of news and issues are in as many responsible ownerships as possible and each exercises its own independent judgment."[32]

For Edward J. Noble, the challenge to develop the Blue network was sizable.

World War II was raging, and American business, although geared up for war production, was in a state of uncertainty. A total of 168 stations and 715 employees were now Noble's responsibility. Already on the climb, however, were Blue's credits as an independent organization.

While still part of NBC, the Blue network showed promising opportunities as an investment. It instituted a special daytime-rate package permitting advertisers to buy at a discount over a series of daytime hours. Another discount package provided savings for advertisers who steadily bought programming time on more and more stations. Institutional advertising permitted companies to sponsor one-time programs publicizing important accomplishments. Typical were the famous "Victory Broadcasts" calling attention to the war effort. Noble also inherited the "strip" broadcasts, which permitted companies to sponsor programming over a strip of four to seven evenings per week. Some of the early takers included Metro-Goldwyn-Mayer, which sponsored the antics of Colonel Lemuel Q. Stoopnagle, heard five nights a week for five minutes a night over fifty-four stations.[33]

Despite all its recent accomplishments, the Blue network still had not made a profit. So Noble pulled together his own team of experts and named Adrian Samish, a New York advertising executive, vice-president of programs. Samish, in his mid thirties, had worked on the stage, and he realized the Blue network did not have the big-name talent that was pulling audiences to the other networks. He was also faced with a diehard group of female followers who lived for the tensions, intrigues, and love affairs of the soap operas aired on the other networks. To compete with these he instituted a series of game shows, and although they did not set the world on fire, they did provide the Blue with alternative programming.

Working with Samish was Robert Kinter, a former Washington correspondent. Vice-president in charge of special events, Kinter seemed like a public-relations trouble-shooter until he began showing everyone he had a head for management decisions. By the turn of the decade he was serving as executive vice-president, and he would later be named president of the network.

Noble had formed a separate corporation, the American Broadcasting System, Inc., in order to purchase the Blue network. On June 15, 1945, affiliate stations heard announcer James Gibbons say, "This is the American Broadcasting Company." The influence of the war effort and the patriotic mood of the country were reflected in Mark Woods's comments about the new name. The name was chosen, he said, "because 'American' so completely typifies all that we hope, and believe, this company will be and will represent to the people of the world. The tradition of independence and of free enterprise, liberality in social philosophy, belief in free education for all and in public service—all of this and much more is inherent in the name."[34]

To some today these words might seem overstated, but we must remember that Woods was appealing to the heart of a nation headed toward victory in global conflict. Patriotism was also present later that evening, when ABC officially retired the label *Blue* with an hour-long program. Entitled "Weapon for Tomorrow," it discussed the "importance to a democracy of a freely-informed people."[35]

CBS Is Born

When ABC began network broadcasting it had three formidable competitors—the Red network, which later became NBC; CBS; and Mutual. CBS can trace its beginnings to January 27, 1927, when a company called United Independent Broadcasters, Inc., was formed for the dual purpose of selling time to advertisers and furnishing programs for stations. Acting as the sales arm of United was another company and stockholder, the Columbia Phonograph Broadcasting System, Inc. Sixteen stations were included in the original United network. United had devised a plan by which it would pay them $500 per week to furnish it with ten specified hours of broadcasting. But the cost was simply too high, and it was not long before the venture became less than profitable. In the fall of 1927 the Columbia people withdrew from the venture and United bought the stock. United also changed the name of the organization to the Columbia Broadcasting System, Inc. The network revised its rate agreement with the affiliate stations, having suffered losses of over $220,000 in its first nine months of operation.[36] The new agreement cut the losses, but it was not until William S. Paley arrived that things began to look up.

Paley's father owned the Congress Cigar Company, one of the sponsors on the old United network. When cigar sales jumped from 400,000 to 1 million per day in six months, radio got the credit. Congress's advertising manager, the owner's son, went to New York with an eye on buying the faltering sixteen-station network. Taking control of 50.3 percent of the stock, the Paley family entered the broadcasting business.

The growth of CBS is somewhat legendary in broadcasting history. The very next year after Paley assumed control the network jumped into the black, and it continues to operate at a profit as one of the largest advertising media in the world. Ten years after Paley arrived, the network had grown from 16 to 113 affiliates. In its first year of operation it sank more than $1 million into programming and moved its facilities to new quarters.[37] Paley himself took an active interest in network programming, personally supervising CBS's coverage of the 1928 election returns. By 1930 CBS was holding its own against NBC and was actively participating in the era of "experimental" broadcasting that characterized early radio. We'll learn more about this later in the chapter.

The Mutual Broadcasting System

The Mutual Broadcasting System started in much the same way as the United network, except for two major differences.[38] First, Mutual did not enter into agreements to pay unmanageable sums of money to affiliate stations. Second, it started small. Mutual began with 4 stations—WOR in Newark; WXYZ in Detroit; WGN in Chicago; and WLW in Cincinnati. The 4 stations agreed that Mutual would become the "time broker" and pay them their regular advertising rate, first deducting a 5-percent sales commission and other expenses such as advertising-agency fees and line charges. Mutual expanded in 1936 by adding 13 stations in California and 10 in New England. In 1938 a regional network in Texas added 23 more stations to the chain. By 1940 Mutual had 160 outlets. Yet the network operated more like a co-op than a profit-making network like NBC or CBS. A special stock arrangement gave some stations a greater voice in the network's operation as well as in special sales commissions. But unlike United, which had to scramble to stay in business, Mutual grew slowly, becoming a formidable competitor in early network broadcasting.

A system of noncommercial radio stations also developed, and we shall learn more about them in Chapter 12.

FM BROADCASTING

Many stepping stones dot radio's path of development. Some are milestones, such as KDKA's first broadcast. Others mark decisions made in corporate boardrooms, decisions that charted the medium's course. Still others represent developments from inside the laboratory.

Armstrong Applies the Principle

Frequency modulation—changing the frequency of a wave in order to modulate a signal—was not new to Edwin Armstrong. He had studied it, and did not believe the words of his predecessors that FM had no meaningful application to broadcasting. Armstrong agreed with David Sarnoff on the need for a device that would clear the static from radio transmission.[39] To Armstrong that challenge came to mean years of research at Columbia. Finally, in 1933 RCA engineers accepted an invitation to witness his latest efforts. Although the equipment worked, RCA was not enthusiastic. Still, it gave Armstrong permission to continue the experiments at the Empire State Building. There, he conducted successful tests ranging up to sixty-five miles. Armstrong was sure FM held the key to revolutionizing radio.

But the vision in RCA's eye was television. Tests had already been successful, and the company was undoubtedly thinking a few years ahead to the public-relations splash a television demonstration would make at the 1939 New York World's Fair. Armstrong grew increasingly suspicious of the intentions of Sarnoff and RCA. Deciding not to wait, he launched a lecture tour and demonstrated FM to dozens of audiences across the United States.[40] Selling his RCA stock and receiving encouragement from the Yankee and Colonial networks in New England, Armstrong built his own FM station in Alpine, New Jersey. There, after battling the FCC for a license, he continued his experiments and managed successful broadcasts of up to three hundred miles while spending a personal fortune of between $700,000 and $800,000.[41] The World's Fair came and went, and Armstrong was left with his fledgling experiments. But even with the thrill of television, FM was beginning to catch on—so much so that on January 1, 1941, the FCC authorized commercial FM broadcasting. Although it might have seemed that Armstrong could look his old friend David Sarnoff in the eye with an "I told you so," that was not the case. In 1945, RCA won a victory when the FCC moved FM to a higher frequency in order to make room on the spectrum for television.[42]

In 1948, after seeing RCA get away without paying royalties on FM sound transmission for TV, Armstrong brought suit. The legal battle went on for five years, after which Armstrong finally agreed to a settlement. He died shortly thereafter, reportedly committing suicide. But in spite of setbacks, corporate lobbying, government tampering, and changed frequencies, FM has continued to develop and win audiences.

Factors Affecting FM Growth

The growth of FM broadcasting can be attributed to ten reasons. *First,* even though the development of FM was set back by World War II, the FCC gave its permission in 1941 for full-scale development of FM, which prospered during that brief prewar period. *Second,* the perfection of sound recording gave the public a new appreciation for quality reproduced music, which FM could provide better than AM. *Third,* FM was boosted by the development of stereo sound recording and the corresponding

public demand for stereo FM. *Fourth,* the June 1, 1961, decision by the FCC permitting FM to broadcast stereo signals gave FM the ability to supply that demand. *Fifth,* crowding on the AM frequencies prompted new broadcasters to enter the industry on the FM spectrum. *Sixth,* FCC requirements that gradually eliminated the once common practice of simulcasting the same program on combination AM/FM stations under the same licensee forced licensees to develop the FM stations. *Seventh,* more and more radio receivers are capable of receiving FM signals.

The *eighth* of the ten reasons is that FM stations are now presenting diverse programming that appeals to a wide range of tastes. Research on broadcast diversity conducted by Cox Broadcasting Corporation has found that 21 percent of FM stations programmed contemporary music, more than the corresponding proportion of AM stations. So the notion that FM is devoted mostly to classical music is already outdated. Cox found that "beautiful" music occupied only 6 percent of FM programming.[43] *Ninth,* although it is changing, FM has fewer commercials than AM. *Tenth,* automated programming equipment permits licensees with an AM/FM combination to program the FM station without increasing their staff.

FM's growth has been substantial. So, despite his frustrations, Edwin Armstrong opened a new era in radio, one that has had a profound effect not only on the industry but also on the radio programming we receive.[44]

THE TRANSISTOR

The story of the transistor begins in the Bell Laboratories in 1947, when Dr. William Shockley invited colleagues to observe an experiment he had conducted successfully by using crystals much like those in early radio receivers. What Dr. Shockley was experimenting with was the *transistor effect*. Using a small silicon crystal, scientists at Bell Labs discovered that the crystal could be made to react to electrical currents much the same as the vacuum tube did. Working with Walter H. Brattain and John Bardeen, Dr. Shockley perfected the transistor, early models of which were not much bigger than a grain of sand. Today, scientists have perfected the transistor to the point where thousands of them can fit onto a tiny chip smaller than the end of your finger.

Transistors function like a switch controlling an electrical current. The transistor in your portable radio consists of a wafer-thin crystal in three layers, with a wire attached to each. One wire detects the radio signal being sent through space. When it detects the signal the wire allows current to flow through the transistor in sequence with the incoming signal. By attaching a battery to the transistor, we can cause the radio signal to trigger a circuit and thereby release current from the battery. Because the current is released in exact sequence with the incoming signal, the transistor permits the signal to be amplified tens of thousands of times by the battery's current.

The small size of the transistor revolutionized radio. When the practical applications of the transistor were realized, radio receivers powered by nothing more than a tiny battery could be taken outside the home. Radio receivers were suddenly everywhere—on the beach, at the ball game, at picnics. There was a new gift-giving spree as transistor radios became *the thing* to own. We now take for granted the tiny pocket device that can put us in touch instantly with dozens of AM and FM radio stations. For William Shockley, Walter H. Brattain, and John Bardeen, their discovery won them the Nobel Prize in Physics.

REPRODUCING AN IMAGE

Even before Heinrich Hertz proved the existence of electromagnetic waves, scientists were working to find a way to reproduce images and send them from a transmitter to a receiver.

Early Mechanical Reproduction

In 1843 Alexander Bain developed in theory a system for sending pictures by wire.[45] In 1862 Abbe Caselli developed a facsimile transmission system that could send examples of handwriting and simple pictures over telegraph wires.[46] A somewhat more modern system was demonstrated four years later by Frederick Collier Bakewell.[47] During the 1880s Paul Nipkow experimented with a mechanical television system consisting of a scanning disc. The disc proved that images could be transmitted electrically and mechanically by means of a series of wires between the transmitter and receiver. By punching holes in the disc, arranging the holes in a spiral, and revolving the disc, one could scan a picture placed behind the disc. If a series of pictures replaced each other in rapid succession, the illusion of a moving image could be transmitted over wires. The system worked even in 1884, yet it lacked many of the components necessary for making television a reality. First, the system was mechanical, not electronic. Compared with today's television, it was slow and cumbersome. Second, the wires limited the distance that the image could be transmitted, because stringing wires to many different locations was impractical. Third, the image was unclear, because coordinating the scanning disc with the changing pictures still had not been perfected. Experimentation on the scanning disc continued. Ernst F. Alexanderson, inventor of the Alexanderson alternator, worked on mechanical television, experimenting with both small- and large-screen systems.

Philo Farnsworth: The Basic Electronic System

Although he lacked the publicity that some of his more famous contemporaries enjoyed, an inquisitive schoolboy from Buckhorn, Utah, made some of the most important contributions to the science of television.[48] Philo Farnsworth was born in 1906 into the Mormon family of Lewis Edwin and Serena Bastian Farnsworth. In 1918 the family was living in Rigby, Idaho, and Philo was becoming friends with his science teacher and school superintendent, Justin Tolman. Tolman provided the boy with science books in order to fuel a fire of intellect that Farnsworth had already exhibited in reading about the work of Einstein and other scientists. He was well acquainted with the experiments on electromagnetic energy and by 1922 had theoretically combined the components of the cathode-ray tube and the photoelectric cell into what he called a dissector tube. That year the family left Rigby, and after a short stint in the railroad yards at Glen's Ferry, Idaho, Farnsworth ended up in high school in Provo, Utah.[49] In Provo he had the run of the Brigham Young University laboratories and could continue his interest in science and in what would later become television.

After Provo, Farnsworth found brief employment at Feld Electric Company of Salt Lake City and then at the local Community Chest. At the Community Chest he encountered George Everson and Leslie Gorrell, who arranged $5,000 in funding for Farnsworth's research.[50] In partnership with one another, the three located a site for research near the California Institute of Technology. There Farnsworth developed a system consisting of an electro-light relay, a magnetic image dissector, a magnetic image builder, and a dissector-cell combination.[51] By 1926 the enterprise and the scientific developments had gained additional support, and preparations were made for patent applications. The system was found workable and moved to San Francisco in 1927. With trial and error modifications the first successful transmission of electronic television was achieved on September 7, 1927.[52] The following year demonstrations were made for the General Electric Company, and in 1930 the apparatus was seen by the Russian-born scientist V. K. Zworykin. On August 26, 1930, Farnsworth was awarded two patents: 1,773,980 for his television system and 1,773,981 for his receiving system.[53] Farnsworth continued his research and eventually moved east to the Chestnut Hill area of Philadelphia and an association with the Philco Company. The association later ended, and Farnsworth obtained independent support for his research.

Farnsworth and V. K. Zworykin

The visit of V. K. Zworykin to Farnsworth's San Francisco laboratory was not the only link between the two men (Figure 4-6). Throughout the 1930s they were entangled in major patent litigation. Zworykin had also been developing an electronic television system and had associated with such industry notables as Westinghouse and later RCA, whose Electronics Research Laboratory he directed. Zworykin is best noted for his "iconoscope" television pickup tube, which he began developing in the early 1920s and continued to perfect into the late 1930s. It became an early standard for television production and remained in use until it was gradually replaced by the more advanced orthicon tube in the mid 1940s.[54] He applied

FIGURE 4–6 Left to right: Philo Farnsworth and V.K. Zworykin. Both men were instrumental in the development of electronic television. Although there were disagreements over patent rights and some corporate legal battles, both men were individually successful in commercially advancing their inventions. Farnsworth eventually licensed some of his inventions to RCA, which tried unsuccessfully to buy outright Farnsworth's system. (Farnsworth photo © 1949, George Everson. From G. Everson, *The Story of Television: The Life of Philo T. Farnsworth.* New York: W.W. Norton & Co., Inc., New York. Zworykin photo from RCA)

for a patent for a television system on December 23, 1923, but it was not issued until fifteen years later.[55]

Two patent-interference suits developed during this time between Farnsworth and the Zworykin/RCA interests. Interference cases occur when there is a dispute over the priority between a patentee and a patent applicant or between two patent applicants.[56] In 1927 Farnsworth and four others brought a patent-interference case against Zworykin. After four and a half years of deliberation the priority of invention was awarded in 1932 to Zworykin. The same year, RCA in turn filed a patent-interference suit against Farnsworth. In the first suit Farnsworth and his colleagues had charged that Zworykin was "misdescriptive in his disclosure, his system was not operative, and the application was subject to change of new matter incorporated in the application after it was filed."[57] When RCA replied with its suit in May of 1932, it charged that patent 1,773,980 for Farnsworth's television system interfered with the Zworykin application filed in 1923. Testimony was heard from Farnsworth's old science teacher Justin Tolman, who re-created the original drawings the young Farnsworth had made for him in 1918. Others from the Farnsworth organization testified; Zworykin and members of the RCA staff testified on behalf of RCA. "The basis for the interference rested on a single claim in the Farnsworth patent. This was that the Farnsworth apparatus formed an electrical image, and means for scanning each elementary area of the electrical energy in accordance with the intensity of the elementary area of the electrical image being scanned.''[58] Testimony ended in a final hearing in the United States Patent Office in April of 1934. The examiner ruled in favor of Farnsworth. Zworykin and RCA appealed and lost. They did not pursue the matter in civil court.

Farnsworth Licenses RCA

Beyond the obvious issue of who owned the patent rights, RCA had a vested interest in the outcome of this case. Corporate policy at RCA was oriented toward purchasing and owning outright the emerging technology of television, not licensing it. Farnsworth, however, had no desire to sell his system, especially to RCA. For RCA to develop its television system, it had to enter into a licensing agreement with Farnsworth. For a fee of $1 million, RCA was licensed to use the devices Farnsworth had patented. Despite their patent dispute, both Farnsworth and Zworykin have been acknowledged for their contributions to the early development of television.

THE EXPERIMENTAL ERA

While the battles over patents took place, experiments (Figure 4–7) in the application of television technology continued. The first United States television station to sign on was W2XBS in 1930, owned by NBC in New York. The following year an experimental RCA–NBC transmitter and antenna were in operation atop the Empire State Building. At RCA $1 million was earmarked for field tests. From these tests came the forerunner of big-screen television: RCA's electron ''projection'' gun made history by producing television pictures on an 8-by-10-foot screen. RCA–NBC mobile television arrived in 1937. The following year, scenes from the

FIGURE 4–7 Felix the cat became the star of early experimental television which used a much smaller number of scanned lines than today's system. A model of Felix on a record turntable was placed in front of four spotlights and a television camera. (RCA)

play *Susan and God* were telecast from NBC studios in New York, and RCA president David Sarnoff announced that television sets would go on sale at the World's Fair in 1939.

President Roosevelt opened that World's Fair and became the first president ever seen on television by the general public. The fairgoing public flocked to look inside the special television-receiver prototype displayed by RCA (Figure 4–8). An 8-by-10-inch screen reflected on the lid kept fairgoers asking questions about how it worked and how they could buy one. The same year, AT&T lines linked an NBC camera at a Madison Square bicycle race to a broadcast transmitter, proving that both wires and airwaves could complement each other in aiding television's growth.

By 1941 the FCC had come to realize both

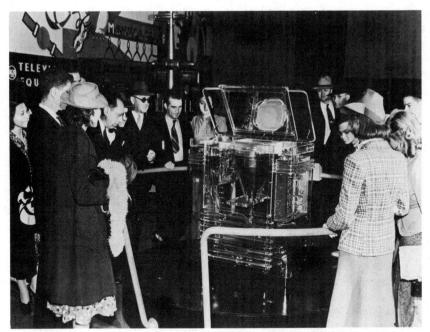

FIGURE 4-8 A crowd gathers in front of a clear glass model of an early television receiver on display at the 1939 New York World's Fair. The set contained an 8″ × 10″ screen reflected on a mirrored cabinet top. (RCA)

the potential and the demands of television and had authorized commercial licensing of television. But the glory was short-lived. War raged in Europe, and the United States needed skilled technicians to work in electronic plants and laboratories at home. There was little use for television. In fact, when the Japanese attacked Pearl Harbor, pushing the United States officially into World War II, it was radio, not television, that brought the sounds of bombs and gunfire into American living rooms. Television would have to wait for Vietnam in order to match that dubious distinction.

THE FREEZE, UHF, COLOR

Three events that occurred between 1948 and 1964 helped mold television's future.

Although not directly related, they occurred somewhat simultaneously and represent an era best described as one of decision and indecision. After World War II had ended, the broadcast industry once again began to gear up for television. At the FCC, concern was beginning to mount over the signal interference that would occur if all the stations wanting to begin broadcasting were licensed to do so. Bombarded by requests, the commission instituted the famous television freeze of 1948, placing a hold on all new licenses. In 1952 the freeze was lifted. The FCC assigned twelve channels in the very-high frequency (VHF) area (channels 2 through 13) of the electromagnetic spectrum, and seventy channels in the ultrahigh-frequency (UHF) area of the spectrum (14 through 83).

In theory UHF was on a par with VHF; in

practice they were far apart. One big reason was the lack of receiving sets having UHF tuners. UHF simply could not compete in the marketplace. If people did not watch UHF, the UHF stations would find it difficult to attract advertising dollars. Finally, in 1964 the FCC began requiring manufacturers to install both VHF and UHF tuners on all television sets. In 1976, the electronics firm of Sarkes Tarzian developed a device called a Uni-tuner that tunes both UHF and VHF channels with the same "click knob."

Although UHF still has a long way to go to reach its full potential, its future is beginning to brighten significantly. Many UHF stations are not network-affiliated, and expensive network advertising rates are sending many national advertisers to these independent stations. Moreover, a wider assortment of syndicated programming is permitting independent stations to capture a larger viewing audience once reserved for network affiliates.

At the same time the freeze was taking place and the FCC was deciding how to allocate frequencies, two giants were battling over the future of color television. RCA and CBS went to battle over what type of color television system should become the national standard. CBS won the first round when the FCC approved a noncompatible color system for commercial broadcasting.[59] This meant that color signals could not be received on sets built for black-and-white reception. Meanwhile RCA, which had been developing a compatible system, slapped CBS with a law suit. The appeals went all the way to the Supreme Court, which upheld the FCC's approval of the CBS system. Elated over the victory, CBS bought a company called Hytron Electronics and its subsidiary Air King. The new company manufactured receivers capable of picking up the CBS color telecasts. Unfortunately the joy was short-lived. Realizing the importance of compatible color, the FCC in 1952 reversed its decision, and CBS's venture into color television came to an abrupt halt.

TELEVISION TECHNOLOGY

The FCC eventually approved a 525-line resolution system for American television, meaning the picture would be scanned 525 times in rapid succession. It was a giant improvement over Zworykin's initial 60-line system and a considerable improvement over the 441-line system used in Europe before a 625-line system was adopted.

Iconoscopes to Plumbicons

Some of the most important improvements in television technology occurred in the area of camera-tube sensitivity. We learned earlier about Zworykin's iconoscope tube and the work of Philo Farnsworth. Although the iconoscope increased picture clarity, its need for high-intensity lights made it uncomfortable at best to work with. Scene illumination of at least 1,000 footcandles was necessary for even marginal quality.[60] In addition, the camera had problems in the way in which the image was scanned by the electron beam.

Gradually the orthicon tube replaced the iconoscope. Developed by the U.S. military, it overcame some of the shortcomings of the iconoscope. It permitted the use of conventional camera lenses but still needed an illumination of 1,000 footcandles. A better tube arrived in the form of the image orthicon, which reduced the needed light to 200 footcandles and improved the electron-beam scanning process.[61] After the new tube's successful debut in a telecast from New York's Yankee Stadium in 1947, stations quickly put it into operation.

While the image orthicon was being developed, educational and industrial broadcasters were using a smaller, low-cost pickup tube called the vidicon. With some adaptation, it was used in 1948 in the network television comedy "I Love Lucy."[62] Endorsed by the show's director of photography, Karl Freund, it achieved enough acceptance to become an important part of broadcasting.

Color television presented its own set of problems and a new generation of pickup tubes. The image orthicon started the color-television era, but the Plumbicon—the registered trademark of a tube developed by Philips in the Netherlands—was the first to be used in live color cameras, in 1965. The tube has been continually improved upon, with special attention given to its optical and scanning systems. The Plumbicon has the ability to capture color images with the sensitivity of the human eye. Two other tubes achieving acceptance since the Plumbicon are the Saticon—a registered trademark of NHK, the Japanese Broadcasting Corporation—and the Newvicon—a registered trademark of Matsushita Electronics Corporation. The circuitry and design of the latter two are derived from the vidicon family.[63]

Magnetic Recording

Capturing the live image was only part of television's progress. Recording that image for future playback would give the medium a new, flexible dimension. Thus, film and magnetic recording, later to be called videotape, developed side by side, each using the technology of the other.

Recording television fascinated John L. Baird, and as early as 1927 he conducted successful experiments using a magnetic disk.[64] Although the quality was too unsatisfactory for future television-recording purposes, Baird's research efforts ushered in a new era in video recording for everything from full-length movies to electronic news gathering

(ENG). Building on Baird's work, researchers spent the next twenty years trying to perfect a video-recording device by using such modes as a combination-television camera and standard 16mm film, and even large-screen television using 35mm film, the unsuccessful brainchild of Lee de Forest.

Early color television recording concentrated on combining color clarity with picture clarity. Although most of the early attempts were marginal, in 1948 Eastman Kodak introduced a 16-mm system developed in cooperation with NBC and the Allen B. DuMont studios. In February 1950 a Navy camera, Kodak film, and a CBS receiver were used in the first "completely successful" recording of color television.

The birth of videotape came a year later. The Electronic Division of Bing Crosby Enterprises demonstrated a videotape recorder in 1951 and improved the quality a year later. In 1953 RCA demonstrated its version of a videotape recorder. The big videotape breakthrough and attendant publicity, however, came in April 1956, when Ampex engineers demonstrated their videotape recording to a CBS–TV affiliates' meeting. RCA demonstrated a color videotape in 1957, but Ampex was to carry the banner for some years to come. Ampex engineer Charles P. Ginsburg is credited with much of Ampex's videotape success, although a team of engineers worked on videotape development.[65] In 1964 SONY Corporation of Japan introduced a system claiming improved recording-head design and simplified operation for black-and-white recording. Portable videotape units proved their worth in the mid 1960s as schools and businesses discovered the usefulness of the one-inch, reel-to-reel videotape, which could be easily stored and applied to instructional purposes. Next to arrive were the video cassettes. CBS introduced the first video-cassette system— EVR—in 1968. The following year, SONY

Corporation of America introduced the first color videotape-cassette recorder.

Further refinements in videotape storage were developed by CBS under the direction of Dr. Peter C. Goldmark. The CBS Rapid Transmission and Storage (RTS) system, which became operable in 1976, permits up to thirty hours of programming to be stored on one video cassette. Different programs can be played back from the tape simultaneously over different transmission systems, such as different cable channels.

The Role of Film in Video Recording

Although videotape is currently the center of attention because of its quick playback and reusable tape, film continues to be important. An intermediate film transmitter that "scanned" film was introduced at the Berlin Radio Exhibition in 1932. In 1933 an intermediate film receiver was demonstrated at the same exhibition. Kinescope recording, a quick-developing film-recording process, was used widely in the early 1950s. In fact, when a nationwide microwave link was completed in 1951, kinescope recording became popular for network transmissions until the conversion to videotape. Even after the conversion, the 16mm camera continued to be essential to the television news-production process and still remains a favorite of many television newsrooms.

Super-8 film has also become a favorite of some broadcasters. Less expensive than 16mm, super 8 uses one-third more area on the film and an improved camera, which make it adaptable to many broadcast uses. Professor Ron Whittaker has noted that super-8 film can serve broadcasting in several ways: (1) electronic image enhancers can increase image sharpness and provide clarity on television comparable with 16mm film; (2) advances in the film-emulsion pro-

cess have reduced graininess; (3) super 8 works well in low light conditions; (4) super-8 equipment is still more portable and lighter than ENG equipment; (5) at low light levels, a picture "lag" or "smear" can occur with many electronic cameras, whereas film can handle the greater brightness range; (6) film can be processed in as little as fifteen minutes; (7) the super-8 camera is small and inconspicuous compared with most ENG equipment, which can be especially important when news teams cover such things as civil unrest, in which the presence of television cameras can trigger crowd reaction; and (8) stringers can use super-8 cameras easily without much training and at less cost than an ENG setup.[66]

Electronic News Gathering

As refinements continued in videotape recording, bringing higher quality, lighter-weight cameras, and smaller microwave transmitting and receiving equipment, the stage was set for electronic news gathering (ENG). By the early 1970s, stations were beginning to jump on the ENG bandwagon, some disregarding film altogether. ENG changed much of the news and public-affairs programming as anchorpersons switched to live coverage of events in the midst of their local-news telecasts as easily as they switched to a commercial. Today we see live pictures from helicopters, boats, lettuce fields, and courthouse steps. We also have become accustomed to live aerial shots of a football stadium from one of the Goodyear blimps. The new technology has moved live television far beyond the confines of the television studio.

Changes in Receiver Design

Changes in television receiver design have been as dramatic as the rest of television's facelift. A comparison of the receiver displayed by RCA at the 1939 World's Fair with today's average home set illustrates the considerable difference in both size and design. The transistor's application to television permitted a vast reduction in size, and miniature computerlike processing devices called microprocessors constituted a further advance. Already, pocket televisions are rapidly becoming common. Scientists are experimenting with television screens the thickness of a standard picture frame, and predictions of three-dimensional television receivers using holography are more than mere science fiction. Dick Tracy's two-way wrist TV may someday be commonplace.

While some manufacturers are working to reduce the size of receivers, others are working to increase the size of the screen. Big-screen television, nothing new, is now becoming popular as a home medium and is especially attractive to restaurants as an inexpensive form of entertainment. The three primary colors of light are projected by three lenses onto a large screen that can be viewed from a distance with picture quality equal to that of a standard television receiver. The process is much the same as that of a set receiving a picture. We'll learn more about new advances in receiver design later in the text.

SUMMARY

Charles David Herrold's station in San Jose, California, started in 1909, was one of the earliest of a string of pioneer stations. Such names as WHA at the University of Wisconsin, WWJ in Detroit, and KDKA in Pittsburgh were added to the list. The stations expanded in power and in audience and were joined by thousands of others as radio matured.

One of the major developers was the Radio Corporation of America, formed in 1919 as part of a scheme to keep the Alexanderson alternator in the United States. RCA's direction was charted by former Marconi employee David Sarnoff.

The 1920s were marked by agreements and disagreements among the major radio powers. Although Westinghouse, GE, AT&T, and some smaller concerns joined together to share inventive efforts, they competed in developing commercial broadcasting. AT&T's WEAF attempted "toll broadcasting," and when it tried to monopolize stations' use of the long lines, matters went to court. A corporate agreement resulted, and AT&T went back to the telephone business while the others forged ahead with broadcasting.

NBC, CBS, and Mutual emerged as the major networks. When NBC was required to dispose of half of its dual-network system, the American Broadcasting Company was born.

New technology has been important in radio's development. Through the work of Edwin Armstrong, radio gained a sizable "sound" advantage in the form of FM. The FCC's support of FM, requiring separate programming from AM, and the development of stereo FM broadcasting opened up new possibilities for this area of the spectrum. And just when it was needed, the invention of the transistor by three Bell Lab scientists made radio a portable medium.

Early attempts to reproduce an image which used a mechanical process were soon replaced by electronic reproduction. The work of Vladimir Zworykin and Philo Farnsworth resulted in improved picture quality. The early experimental era of television saw station W2XBS sign on the air in New York, an event that was followed by a series of breakthroughs in television technology.

Television was introduced to the American public at the New York World's Fair in

1939. In 1941 the FCC approved commercial television. Then, during a television freeze that began in 1948, the commission spent five years deciding frequency assignments and standards for color.

Television cameras, meanwhile, improved from the iconoscope tube to the orthicon, the image orthicon, the vidicon, and the Plumbicon® tube, which is based on the vidicon concept but provides color clarity equivalent to that which can be detected by the naked eye. Magnetic recording of television programs progressed from the early kinescope methods to videotape. Film advanced to super-8 technology. Electronic news gathering allowed the live coverage of events which are being viewed on both pocket and big-screen television receivers.

OPPORTUNITIES FOR FURTHER LEARNING

BAKER, J. C., *Farm Broadcasting: The First Sixty Years*. Ames: Iowa State University Press, 1981.

BARNOUW, E., *A History of Broadcasting in the United States*. New York: Oxford University Press. Vol. I, *To 1933: A Tower in Babel*, 1966. Vol. II, *1933 to 1953: The Golden Web*, 1968. Vol. III, *From 1953: The Image Empire*, 1970.

———, *Tube of Plenty: The Evolution of American Television*. New York: Oxford University Press, 1975.

BITTNER, J. R., *Professional Broadcasting: A Brief Introduction*. Englewood Cliffs, N.J.: Prentice-Hall, 1981.

BLOCH, L. M., JR., *The Gas Pipe Networks: A History of College Radio 1936–1946*. Cleveland: Bloch, 1980.

DELUCA, S. M., *Television's Transformation: The Next 25 Years*. San Diego: A.S. Barnes, 1980.

DIAMOND, E., *Sign Off: The Last Days of Television*. Cambridge, Mass.: M.I.T. Press, 1982.

DUNNING, J., *Tune in Yesterday: The Ultimate Encyclopedia of Old-Time Radio 1925–1976*. Englewood Cliffs, N.J.: Prentice-Hall, 1976.

FREE, W. R. and others, *Program to Improve UHF Television Reception*. Atlanta: Georgia Institute of Technology, 1980.

GIANAKOS, L. J., *Television Drama Series Programming: A Comprehensive Chronicle, 1947–1959*. Metuchen, N.J.: Scarecrow Press, 1980.

———, *Television Drama Series Programming: A Comprehensive Chronicle, 1959–1975*. Metuchen, N.J.: Scarecrow Press, 1978.

LICHTY, L. W., and M. C. TOPPING, eds. *American Broadcasting: A Source Book on the History of Radio and Television*. New York: Hastings House, 1975.

MACDONALD, J. F., *Don't Touch That Dial! Radio Programming in American Life, 1920–1960*. Chicago: Nelson-Hall, 1979.

MCNEIL, A., *Total Television: A Comprehensive Guide to Programming from 1948 to 1980*. New York: Penguin, 1980.

ROPER ORGANIZATION, *Evolving Public Attitudes Toward Television and Other Mass Media 1959–1980*. New York: Television Information Office, 1981.

ROUTT, E., *The Business of Radio Broadcasting*. Blue Ridge Summit, Pa.: TAB Books, 1972.

SILVERSTONE, R., *The Message of Television: Myth and Narrative in Contemporary Culture*. London: Heinemann, 1981.

SLIDE, A., *Great Radio Personalities in Historic Photographs*. New York: Dover, 1982.

SUMMERS, H. B., ed., *A Thirty-Year History of Programs Carried on National Radio Networks in the United States, 1926–1956*. New York: Arno Press 1971.

TERRACE, V., *Radio's Golden Years: The Encyclopedia of Radio Programs, 1930–1960*. San Diego: A.S. Barnes, 1981.

———, *The Complete Encyclopedia of Television Programs, 1947–1979*, 2 vols. (2nd ed.) San Diego: A.S. Barnes, 1979.

UDELSON, J. H., *The Great Television Race: A History of the American Television Industry, 1925–1941*. University: University of Alabama Press, 1982.

5

COMPUTERS
AND
DATA PROCESSING

When Lee de Forest perfected the vacuum tube and the Bell Labs team of Shockley, Brattain, and Bardeen developed the transistor, they made contributions that far transcended the technology of the superheterodyne receiver and the transistor radio. The vacuum tube and the transistor would later transform the way machines would "think." The tiny transistor that won the Bell Labs team the Nobel Prize was the size of a thumbnail. Today, through the technology of integrated circuits and microprocessors, a single silicon chip tiny enough to slide through the eye of a needle can hold a million transistors. Those same silicon chips have revolutionized the entire electronics industry, from radios to radar, but nowhere has the impact been greater than with com-

puters. What once were cumbersome machines weighing tons and filling entire rooms today weigh but a few pounds and retain the computing power of their mammoth ancestors.

COMPUTERS AS MASS COMMUNICATION

Where once the computer was looked upon as a support system for mass media, today the computer has become a new medium of mass communication, a channel for which sophisticated software ranging from programs for accounting to asteroid games are available in the same stores that sell books, recordings, videotapes, and discs.[1] Moreover, personal computers, direct successors of the larger mainframe computers, can be linked together by telephone or cable and create data networks that can bring to the kitchen table an electronic newspaper from thousands of miles away or the latest edition of an electronic encyclopedia.

For an even more vivid link between computers and mass media we can turn to the field of book publishing. We naturally think of books as a form of mass communication, much like radio or television. But when a national convention of bookstore owners was held recently, the key topic of discussion was the sale of software for personal computers through bookstores. In other words, the software itself—the programs that make it possible for the computer to perform tasks —is marketed much like programs for videotape players or videodisc machines.

Even users of the traditional forms of telecommunication we have already discussed, such as the telegraph and telephone, will find the personal computer essential. While one executive is telephoning an associate in another city, a "computer conversation" between the two executives' personal computers will permit the conversation to be stored in a memory and then reproduced on a printer.

A marketing expert would consider the mail an important form of mass communication. In the future, mail may come more and more to take the form of "electronic letters" sent and received by personal computer. Getting up in the morning and walking to the mailbox could be replaced by the practice, already employed by many, of simply keying in the correct code and checking one's electronic mailbox through his or her personal computer to see if an electronic letter is waiting.

Peripheral Technology

Adding peripheral technology such as the videodisc has expanded personal computers beyond mathematical processing to the highest-quality color video. In the future you may buy this text not as a printed book but as a videodisc, the pages of which you would read on the display screen of your personal computer. As you read material on early television, for example, you would stop, key in the correct information on your keyboard, and then sit back and watch examples of early television programming— not still pictures but the actual programs the book is discussing. Other software will permit you to work management problems drawn from our discussion of economics (Chapter 20) or audience analysis (Chapter 21).

Computer Networks

The word *network,* which has traditionally meant a radio or television network, can also refer to a computer network. The evening edition of a national computer-based electronic newspaper is available through a computer network accessed via a personal computer just as the evening edition of the television news is available via a television network.

Growth of Personal Computers

How widespread will this personal use of computers become, this new medium of mass communication? In 1980 about 250,000 personal computers were sold. As you read this book, sales estimates are that more than 4 million personal computers will have been sold. Thousands of retail stores sell personal computers on the same shelves with radios and televisions. Dozens of computer magazines are in publication. In Chapter 9 we will discuss the use of personal computers to access videotex systems storing information on every conceivable subject from science to scallop recipes. Stretch your imagination only as far into the future as 1990, when experts predict that the personal computer will be as commonplace as high-quality color television sets. The same silicon chip that today holds one million transistors will hold ten million transistors.

Understanding the Historical Perspective

The impact of personal computers is even more startling when we view it in a historical perspective. In the previous chapters of this book we discussed such technologies as the telegraph, the telephone, radio, and television. Decades, even half centuries, are not uncommon time spans for tracing the development of these technologies. With personal computers, however, equivalent leaps can be measured in single years. Five years represents an entire era. In 1977 Apple Computer was being incorporated. Five years later it was a multimillion dollar business that was affecting our way of life.

As we begin to read about the history of computers we will start 2,500 years ago, much earlier than Marconi's experiments in the late 1800s or the birth of radio in the 1920s. Our discussion of the early scientific inquiry that became the foundation of computer technology will show how slowly we advanced from the abacus used thousands of years ago to the crude calculating machines of the 1900s.

We will also see that the advancements between 1900 and 1980 exceeded the combined technological advancements of thousands of years of scientific inquiry before 1900. Likewise, the advancement in personal computing just between 1975 and 1980 exceeded these in the entire history of computation. We need to keep this historical perspective in mind as we learn more about the computer's past and thus understand more of its future.

THE DEVELOPMENT OF COMPUTATION

Today, with the impact personal computers are having on society, it is hard to imagine that a time existed when people didn't even "think" in a manner that would have fostered the development of scientific knowledge analagous to what we have acquired in modern society.[2] Such was the case in the Greek society of some 2,500 years ago. New knowledge was looked upon as being acquired through observation, the sciences consisted primarily of astronomy and geometry, and the world was viewed as being composed of "living" organisms whereupon all other bases of scientific thought evolved.

Transforming Thought in the Scientific Revolution

It took approximately 2,000 years before we began to approach science in a different vein. Gradually, the changes from a rural to a more urban and industrial society evolved. In addition to geometry and astronomy with their sometimes mystical qualities, there evolved the disciplines of physics, chemistry, and biology. Machines began to be looked upon as an aid to society. More precision and care in the making of tools permitted people to develop new machines. The only computational device was the abacus, a crude instrument consisting of beads on rods mounted in a wooden frame. The abacus (Figure 5–1) is believed to have developed in India or China about 3500 B.C., and although it is basically a counting device, a skilled abacus user could speedily arrive at answers that would have taken much longer by longhand.

Mathematics began to take on new importance as ocean shipping became more widespread and navigation more sophisticated. Roman numerals were unsatisfactory for calculating a ship's position at sea; thus,

FIGURE 5-1 The abacus is believed to have developed in India or China about 3500 B.C. Skilled abacus operators were human calculators who achieved an important place in the carrying on of commerce. (Courtesy IBM)

new forms of mathematical theory were necessary. John Napier published a table of logarithms in 1614 and invented a device that would perform multiplication. Called Napier's Bones, it consisted of two strips of bones upon which numbers were painted. By 1620, Edmund Gunter had assembled and improved the device and, using two strips of wood, had fashioned an instrument resembling a slide rule. More and more the scientists, and the technologists, were combining forces in mathematical science. The Scientific Revolution, which began to emerge in the 1500s and 1600s, gradually produced the need, at least among mathematicians, for more sophisticated computational devices.

The Calculator

It was the work of a French mathematician, Blaise Pascal, that resulted in the first device that resembled the modern calculator—forerunner of the computer. Pascal developed a machine to assist in bookkeeping tasks (Figure 5-2). By 1645 he had constructed a device that could add and subtract. Attempts to market the device proved mostly unsuccessful. While conceptually sound, it was mechanically flawed. Although a simple gear-driven device by

modern standards, for the mid 1600s it was a complex machine that only Pascal could repair. Because the workings consisted of crude, imprecise parts, it needed a lot of repairing. We might speculate whether today's personal computers would have achieved the acceptance they have enjoyed if it weren't for the mass media telling us over and over again that personal computers are something we need and will eventually own.

A Prussian contemporary of Pascal, working independently, Gottfried von Leibniz, also began developing a calculator. In 1671, nine years after Pascal's death, Leibniz introduced an improved device that used the same mechanical principles to make the machine add and subtract that Pascal had used. He added other parts that made it capable of multiplication and division. Leibniz also tried to market his device, making it available to heads of state and scientists. Like Pascal, he met the same obstacles. The machine was ahead of its time.

It took a complete transformation of thought and science to produce the climate necessary for the development of an advanced computational device that could be programmed much like a modern computer. Such a machine first emerged from the French silk industry.

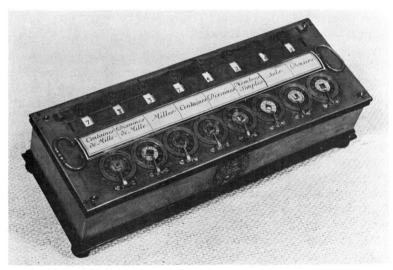

FIGURE 5-2 Pascal's calculator could add and subtract, but attempts to market the device proved largely unsuccessful. The lack of precision tool-making equipment caused the machine to falter, and it was so complex that only Pascal was skilled enough to repair it. (Courtesy IBM)

The Basis of Programming

Modern computers are *programmed*—that is, given a set of instructions on what functions they are to perform. The instructions can be in the form of punched cards, or can be entered directly into the computer by the user. Personal computers employ the latter method. The concept of a program being fed to a computer actually originated in the early 1800s in the form of a weaving-loom attachment invented by Joseph Marie Jacquard. During the emergence of the Industrial Revolution, roughly between the years 1760 and 1890, the textile industry in France underwent major changes in the way woven cloth was produced. Jacquard designed his attachment so that it would use punched cards, somewhat resembling modern data cards, which would automatically control the loom and produce pattern weaving. Wire hooks would protrude through the holes in the threads and produce the consistent pattern. The punched cards were a kind of program telling the loom what to weave. Unlike Pascal and Leibniz, Jacquard was successful in marketing his device—a case of having the right machine when it was needed by a large segment of industrial society. Thousands of the Jacquard looms were put into production throughout Europe.

Improved Mechanical Computation

If any individual stands out in the early history of computing it is Charles Babbage. By the time Babbage began making contributions to mathematical thought, inventors and applied science were taking on somewhat more respectability in British society. Babbage died in 1871, and thirty years later Marconi reaped the fruits of the support of the British Post Office in his work with wireless.

Babbage worked with the British astronomer John Herschel, who was trying to add exactness to astronomical tables. Because a significant number of human computations were necessary in developing the tables there was ample room for error. This is where Babbage tried to help. He conceptualized a gear-driven machine powered by steam, the new source of applied power, and received about $7,000 from the British government to build the device. Unfortunately, Babbage's conceptualizing didn't result in a workable product and the support was cut off in 1827. The *difference engine,* as Babbage called his super calculator, remained just a design, not a working model. Part of the problem was that the art of manufacturing precision instruments was not fully developed; thus, the intricate device could not be made to work properly.

Not giving up on the idea, Babbage continued to work to try to develop a workable product. While a professor at Cambridge he devised an advanced version of the difference engine called the *analytical engine.* The analytical engine incorporated the large, gear-based mechanisms of the difference engine and the programming features of Jacquard's loom. The analytical engine included a *store* area, where instructions and variables were to be maintained, and a *mill* area, where arithmetic operations were to be performed. Capable of storing a thousand numbers, the analytical engine was remarkably similar to the concept behind the modern computer. Babbage was not able to construct a working model of either the difference or analytical engine. However, a Swedish scientist, P. G. Scheutz, did construct a working device based on the difference engine, and an assistant to Babbage, Augusta Ada Lovelace, constructed a program for the analytical engine. Lovelace is credited with being the first programmer, and her scientific publications on Babbage's work further advanced his ideas.

Applied Processing

An engineer from Columbia University opened the next chapter in the history of computers. Herman Hollerith was working as an assistant to the director of the 1880 United States census when he was encouraged to explore the possibility of developing a machine that could automatically code census data. Using Jacquard's punch-card design he built a machine which could read an individual's vital statistics, such as age, sex, birth date, and citizenship, from a similarly punched card. The Hollerith Code became a key part of the system and was used to represent other types of data on punched cards. The code is still in use, and the machine remained in use through 1890, when another Census Bureau employee, James Powers, developed a machine that replaced it.

From the work of these two men were born two giants in the computer business, IBM and Sperry.[3] When Hollerith eventually left the Census Bureau he started his own company, the Tabulating Machine Company, which was later sold to the Computing-Tabulating-Recording Company. In 1924 that company, under the direction of Thomas J. Watson, became IBM. Powers also successfully marketed his own machine through his own company. Eventually bought by Remington Rand, the company later became Sperry Rand, and then Sperry Corporation.

THE EMERGENCE OF ELECTRONIC PROCESSING

Earlier in the text we discussed how Paul Nipkow's work in mechanical television produced the first television pictures, which were transmitted over wires connecting a sending and a receiving mechanism. With the work of Farnsworth and Zworykin, television moved out of the mechanical era and into the electronic era. Computers went through a similar transition. The work of Hollerith, Powers, and their predecessors belonged to the age of mechanics. It was an outgrowth of the American Industrial Revolution.

The Electromechanical Computer

The beginning of electronic computing is centered at Harvard, where in 1937 mathematician Howard Aiken began connecting separate components and controlling them with rolls of punched paper tape. Aiken's machine was named Mark I, short for Automatic Sequence Controlled Computer, and included both electronic and mechanical components. IBM backed the project. Other electromechanical computers evolved out of this era, which also saw government backing of computer projects in the United States, Germany, and Great Britain. Mark I arrived in 1944, in the midst of World War II. Other electromechanical computers were also being born, some under the direction of Bell Labs.

Along with its developments in telephone technology discussed in Chapter 2, Bell Telephone Laboratories, Inc., (Bell Labs) contributed to the development of computer technology.[4] The Complex Number Calculator built by G. R. Stibitz and S. B. Williams in 1939 contained relays and switches. It was accessed by three remote typewriters, which made it the first machine with remote multiple access. Remaining in operation until 1949, it was eventually called Model I. Model II was designed for the National Defense Research Council and became operational in 1943. It used a punched paper tape

and tested fire-control equipment for wartime antiaircraft units. Model II also had error-checking capability. Models III and IV were special-purpose computers designed to solve fire-control problems for land- and ship-mounted guns. Model IV (also called the Mark 22 Error Detector) was put into use by the Naval Research Laboratory in 1945 to calculate special ballistic problems for naval guns. Two versions of Model V existed. Both were general-purpose computers for the armed forces, and they went into use in 1946 and 1947. Model VI was a digital-relay computer that went into use in 1950.

The Electronic Computer

At the Moore School of Electrical Engineering at the University of Pennsylvania, J. P. Eckert and J. Mauchley began work on an all-electronic computer in 1943. Funded by a half-million-dollar grant from the Army Ordnance Department, the computer was built to aid calculations for artillery fire. In 1946 the Electronic Numerical Integrator and Computer (ENIAC) was born. With its 18,000 vacuum tubes ENIAC filled an entire room. A nonoperational design for an electronic general-purpose computer was generated about the same time by J. V. Atanasoff at Iowa State.

ENIAC lacked the ability to function with a stored program, so it had to be directed by a series of external switching arrangements. Stored programs arrived with EDVAC, also developed at the Moore school, by Eckert, Mauchley, John von Neumann, and others. Von Neumann was a mathematician who supplied the theory behind the design that incorporated punched cards as a means of storing a program in the machine.

Mauchly and Eckert later designed the Universal Automatic Computer (UNIVAC), the first commerical computer. The company they formed after leaving the Moore School, the Eckert-Mauchly Computer Corporation, was also acquired by Remington Rand, which as we just learned became Sperry Corporation.

By 1950 the first generation of computers, which were characterized by the vacuum tube, had begun to make way for the transistor.

TECHNICAL GENERATIONS
OF COMPUTER DEVELOPMENT

To understand today's personal computer, which belongs to the fourth generation of computers, it is necessary to briefly understand the generations that preceded it.[5]

Vacuum Tubes to Transistors

Vacuum tubes constituted the first generation of computers. The transistor ushered in the second generation. We have already learned how the transistor changed the face of electronics. The field of computers was no exception. The transistor permitted powerful computing power at a fraction of the size and cost of vacuum tubes. Less maintenance, greater computation speed, improved programming, larger storage capacity, and the ability of computers to interface with other computers, sometimes separated by great distances and linked by telephone lines, became possible. While teenagers were listening to the transistor radio, computer scientists were making big computers smaller and small computers stronger, also through the technology of the transistor.

Bell Labs again played a major role in this second generation of computers. Remember, it was Bell Labs where the transistor was invented. It was also Bell Labs where the first completely transistorized general-purpose computer, Transistorized Airborne Digital Computer (TRADIC), was built. As its name implies, TRADIC spent considerable time in aircraft. A transistor computer named Leprechaun also evolved from the TRADIC project. Leprechaun used a purer transistor circuitry than TRADIC and eventually found a home in the Air Force.

Integrated Circuits
and Microprocessors

The giant computer ENIAC filled an entire room. Such early computers, which laid the groundwork for the smaller personal computers that would follow, needed large internal cooling and external air-conditioning systems. Their components were vacuum tubes, which were hot, bulky, and not as reliable as today's components. Still, these larger components provided the vital on-off functions necessary for the computer to perform computations. The same size and wiring demands that were part of early radio and television equipment were also present, and every wire, every connection, every circuit needed to be assembled by hand and checked and rechecked at every stage of production. Along with being big, these early computers were very expensive.

Whereas the invention of the transistor helped to make these early computers smaller and less expensive, the next advance began the first step in a revolution of computing equipment. The size of the actual circuit necessary to perform the on-off work of a single relay consisting of two transistors and some support components was now reduced to the size of a small chip less than one-quarter inch square. On that single chip existed a "printed" circuit instead of the older and larger wired circuit. Thus, from the mechanical relays conceived by Babbage and others we evolved through mechanical equipment assisted by electronics, such as

Mark I; through all-electronic vacuum-tube computers, such as ENIAC; to all-electronic computers using transistors, such as TRADIC; and now to computers that could *integrate* the functions of multiple transistors on a single silicon wafer called a *chip*. Invented in 1958 by J. S. Kilby of Texas Instruments, they were appropriately named *integrated circuits*.

Gradually, the term *microcircuit* began to be used for the increasing number of circuits and transistor-type elements placed on a single chip. The function of the transistor was retained on these tiny microcircuits, although the transistor as it was first conceived by the Bell Labs team changed in size. So that we can make an easy comparison with the *function* of a transistor when discussing the number of elements and circuits that can be placed on a single chip, we still use the term *transistor* today. Thus, it is not uncommon to read that a single chip contains 100,000 transistors.

Along with the integrated circuit, programming changes highlighted the third generation of computers. The reduction of component size and the application of integrated circuits permitted multiple programs to be stored in a single computer and remote processing to take place. The latter is what makes possible computer networks in which a small personal computer can be used to access a central data bank. The electronic edition of a local newspaper, a magazine published thousands of miles away, and a stock-market report are all accessible in this manner.

A third characteristic of this third generation of computers was the development of both mainframe computers and minicomputers. Mainframe computers are used to store and process massive amounts of information and to be accessed by smaller remote computers. It is not the physical size of a mainframe computer that distinguishes it from minicomputers as much as its storage capacity.

Minicomputers, on the other hand, have a large storage capacity yet are much smaller in size than the mainframe computers. The technology that distinguished the minicomputer and mainframe computer of the 1960s, however, is today obsolete. Some mainframe computers of the 1960s did not possess the capacity of some of today's minicomputers, not to mention the microcomputers that made possible today's personal computer.

Another way to distinguish these two kinds of computers is to think of national and local applications. A computer that processes and stores all of the information found throughout the nation on a given subject, such as all the financial data on a class of corporate tax payers, would be a mainframe computer. A small to medium-size business, however, might find all of its computing needs served by a minicomputer. Keep in mind that these examples are applied to the third generation of computers. When we realize that a single silicon chip in 1990 will store as much computer power as a medium-size company used in the 1970s, we can see that even our terms and definitions can become obsolete. The mainframe computer of one generation becomes the minicomputer of another.

The fourth generation of computers took full advantage of the microcircuit, which had developed more fully in the 1960s. In the 1970s the microcircuit functioned as a processing unit in the computer.

The microcircuits constructed to function as processing units are called microprocessors (Figure 5-3) and are the most evident characteristic of the fourth generation of computers. These tiny devices significantly increased the capacity and power of computers, as we can see if we examine some of the developments of just one company, Bell

FIGURE 5-3 The microprocessor made possible the microcomputer. Smaller than the key on a telephone, these tiny devices can contain more than 100,000 transistor circuits and are capable of making over a million calculations every second. (Bell Labs)

Labs. In the late 1970s and early 1980s Bell Labs introduced a microprocessor under the trademark of BELLMAC—32. It contained 100,000 transistors. Installing these microprocessors in computers resulted in the development of the microcomputer. Lower prices made microcomputers available to the average consumer and resulted in small computers available for personal use.

THE FIFTH GENERATION: CONCEPTS IN ARTIFICIAL INTELLIGENCE

The fifth generation of computers consists of pushing technology and software into the frontier of artificial intelligence. In the 1980s, the government of Japan supported the development of this "fifth" generation of computers with initial grants of $850-million.

With the concept of artificial intelligence comes some philosophical and ethical questions to accompany ones about technology. Are computers already capable of artificial intelligence by their ability to perform complex mathematical tasks faster and with greater accuracy than the human mind? What will artificial intelligence bring to society? Will machines ever be able to perform all of the thinking functions of human beings? Probably not, but the way we process information, and how that information will affect our lives, are issues which demand our attention.

THE PERSONAL-COMPUTER ERA

Personal computers offer tremendous technical and social implications for society. As personal computers continue to become more and more commonplace, names such as Tandy, Apple, and IBM are becoming as familiar to the average consumer as Motorola, Zenith, and Sylvania. Computer networks such as CompuServe, The Source, and Dow Jones are becoming as familiar as NBC, ABC, or CBS.

Between the mid 1970s and the mid 1980s the early history of the personal-computer industry in the United States was written. Many companies played a part in this history. Some of the success stories are case studies of American business unequaled in any free industrial society. Four companies that made a particular contribution to this history are Apple, Tandy Corporation's Radio Shack, IBM, and Timex Corporation.

The Entrepreneur

The model for growth in the burgeoning field of personal computers is Apple.[6] It could be said that Apple invented the personal computer. It certainly was responsible for calling attention to the power and usefulness of personal computers and building a business that within five years of its start was international in scope and highly profitable.

Apple was a name derived from a last-minute decision of the corporate organizers to file a name for the company as part of the business-licensing procedure. The name turned out to be a marketing manager's dream. It was unthreatening, even friendly —something personal-computer manufacturers needed to consider when they began convincing the public to spend thousands of dollars on machines that had for years been equated with "big brother." Among the many office employees who were forced into the use of computers, Apple turned out to be a warm, unmenacing name. Who knows where Apple and the personal-computer industry would be if the first company to begin producing personal computers had been called Integrated Technology Computational Hardware?

The two individuals responsible for starting Apple were Steve Jobs and Steve Wozniak. Jobs was 21 and Wozniak 26. Working out of a Palo Alto, California garage, they built the first assembled personal computer, which became known as Apple I. The forerunner of the Apple computers to follow, Apple I consisted of a processing unit and a keyboard housed in a briefcase. Friends ordered fifty units and shortly sales reached $200,000.

The third person to leave an early mark on Apple was A. C. Markkula. Markkula, whose expertise was marketing, joined Jobs and Wozniak in incorporating Apple in January 1977. In May of 1977 the company introduced Apple II, a personal computer fully assembled and programmable. By the end of 1982 approximately 350,000 Apple IIs had been sold. Other models, including the popular Apple IIe followed. An Apple computer named Lisa was introduced in January 1983.[7] The product of four hundred human years of research and development effort, Lisa integrated word processing, graphics, and the many business forms typically utilized in general office procedures. Selling for just under $10,000, Lisa was designed to make Apple a strong force in the business market.

Lisa employed a pictorial approach to computer processing. Designed as a *very* friendly computer, it replaced codes and command language with small pictures on the screen that directed the user to different functions. Lisa permitted users to draw their own pictures, graphs, and charts to illustrate other material such as technical reports. Lisa's graphic system permitted a first-time user to work the machine in a fraction of the time it took to learn to operate other computers. Lisa also employed a separate, small desktop control module called the *mouse,* which contained the special function keys that other computers had placed on the keyboard.

Not neglecting the consumer market that had been the base of Apple's success, the company entered into an agreement to supply Drexel University in Philadelphia with a new personal computer to be used by students.[8] The new computer was designed to be more portable than previous models.

By the early 1980s the company that was just a dream in 1975 and wasn't incorporated until 1977 had grown to the multimillion dollar Fortune 500 company. A distribution system had been established that included more than half the retail computer stores in the United States, eight regional distribution centers in North America, and three in Europe. By the early 1980s a United States manufacturing site began operation near Dallas, Texas. Regional and district sales headquarters were located in key areas of the country. Apple Canada, Ltd., a wholly owned subsidiary, managed Apple's Canadian sales and distribution. Apple Computer International, headquartered in Paris, was responsible for European sales and marketing. Apple Computer Ltd. located in Ireland manufactured most of the Apple products distributed in Europe. Printed circuits were assembled and tested at a company site in Singapore and then sent to the assembly plants in Texas and Ireland.

The Large Corporation in the Marketplace

In 1976, when Apple's founders were conceptualizing its beginning, IBM was placing terminals and minicomputers in the homes of its employees. In 1981 the company again turned to its employees in developing software for its entry into the field of personal computers. With the announcement of its IBM Personal Computer came the notice that the company would "consider for publication" the programs of authors who write computer programs having an application to the IBM Personal Computer.[9] It may have been the first public announcement by a major corporation truly signifying the personal computer as an instrument of mass communication. IBM formed the Personal Computer Software Publishing Department to handle the program-publication effort. While generating an interest in the IBM Personal Computer among programmers, it was an important marketing move that alerted the industry and the public that IBM was going against tradition and turning outside the

company to make the IBM Personal Computer a machine with as wide an application as possible. Although still guarding its patent and copyrights, the company in uncharacteristic fashion provided somewhat detailed specifications of the new computer in order to help program writers develop usable software.

The thrust within the company for the development of the IBM Personal Computer came in July 1980, when IBM Chairman F.T. Cary and IBM President J. R. Opel requested a study on the requirements for a quality personal computer that would be easy to use and competitive with other computers on the market. Responding to the request was W. C. Lowe, then director of the development lab at Boca Raton, Florida. As Lowe noted, "IBM had been bringing down the cost of computing so rapidly it seemed inevitable that new technologies and lower costs would lead to a personal computer, presumably developed, made, sold, distributed and serviced within IBM's traditional divisional structure. But it soon became clear that a truly competitive microcomputer could emerge only through nontraditional ways."[10]

The nontraditional ways that Lowe referred to included going to outside suppliers for both hardware and software. Veterans of IBM's earlier computer studies contributed time and effort to the new venture, and teams of individuals are credited with the final product. IBM Japan located a vendor producing an advanced, low-cost printer. An IBM purchasing team located a quality display monitor made overseas. A Seattle software company, Microsoft, was contracted to do the software base for the personal computer.

Sales and servicing strategies were also nontraditional. For example, the computer was sold through retail outlets not originally affiliated with IBM. Employed to aid sales and distribution were Sears, Roebuck and Company's business-machine stores and ComputerLand. In addition, whereas in the past only IBM serviced IBM products, arrangements were made for servicing at these locations.

The small computer was marketed through a new National Marketing Organization of the Data Processing Division of IBM, in addition to the IBM Product Centers. In countries where it was marketed, employees of IBM were able to buy the computer at a discount. This internal effort also encouraged users to bring new ideas for application of the computer back to IBM.

The success of the first IBM Personal Computer quickly alerted the personal-computer industry that industry giants would not be taking a back seat while the upstart entrepreneurs such as Apple reaped all the profits. It also showed how a concerted effort within a large organization can produce a quality product quickly and that when competition looms, tradition must be set aside if a company is to compete in a volatile marketplace.

IBM's entry into the personal-computer field also spurred allied businesses. For example, a computer-maintenance company in Pennsylvania began offering on-site maintenance for the IBM Personal Computer in 160 locations. *PC Magazine,* devoted to the IBM Personal Computer but published outside IBM, was born, and accessory manufacturers began to produce hardware that could be used with the computer. Many of these ventures received IBM's blessing, since the more the attention that was paid to IBM the better its chances of spurring public interest in purchasing its product.

IBM also encouraged the use of already established software on its personal computer and made arrangements with other hard-ware companies for technology that would permit programs from competitors' personal computers to run on the IBM unit. IBM had realized that innovation was the key to continued acceptance among personal-computer users and potential buyers. IBM continued to offer new products. The next entry was a smaller personal computer called the PCjr. It was followed by the announcement of the IBM Portable Personal Computer. By 1984, IBM had passed Apple as the leader in personal computer sales.

A Retailing Strategy

Another company that made a major impact with various marketing strategies, hardware, and software was Tandy Corporation, which started as a Fort Worth, Texas, company dealing in leather.[11] Today its Radio Shack TRS-80 series of personal computers (Figure 5–4) are sold throughout Radio Shack outlets and provide the company with a major distribution force that can compete with Apple and IBM.

The first TRS-80, the Model I, was introduced at about the same time Apple was being incorporated. The TRS-80 Model II was introduced in August 1979, and aimed at the business market. In 1980, Radio Shack introduced three additions to its computer line: the TRS-80 Model III, the TRS-80 Color Computer, and the TRS-80 Pocket Computer.

Each of the three TRS-80 models introduced in 1980 showed how demand and competitors were contributing to market segmentation. Each had special features appealing to different segments of the market. The TRS-80 Model III was somewhat more streamlined than the Model I. Aimed at the business as well as the home market, the Model III sold in different configurations

FIGURE 5-4 Radio Shack's TRS 80 computer line has been a successful competitor to such brands as Apple and IBM. The firm still sees itself as a retailer. Its large network of retail electronic stores has been one of its strong points in competing in the personal computer market. (TRS 80 is a trademark of Tandy Corporation. Used with permission of Radio Shack and Tandy Corporation)

ranging in price from $699 to $2450. More memory, additional features such as disc storage, the opportunity to buy different components with which to expand the system to business use, and a high-resolution video display monitor were some of the distinguishing features of the Model III.

For the consumer market, the TRS-80 Color Computer offered a low-priced basic personal-computer system that included color graphics as well as many of the basic programs that appealed to the early consumer market. Base-priced at $399, it worked with a standard color television set and could be hooked up to a printer and modem (a device connecting to a telephone line that enables the computer to interface with other computers and data bases).

The TRS-80 Pocket Computer was the first of its kind and preceded by as much as five years what many people feel will be the growing trend in personal computers, the portable unit. Although originally viewed somewhat as a toy, the TRS-80 Pocket Computer went well beyond being a sophisticated calculator. Selling for $249, it measured 7 by $2\frac{3}{4}$ by $\frac{1}{2}$ inches. Instead of a video screen it contained a twenty-four-character liquid-crystal display. A scaled-down keyboard format was employed. Unlike other Radio Shack products, which are made in Fort Worth, the pocket model was manufactured for Radio Shack in Japan by Sharp Electronics.

Radio Shack continued to develop the TRS-80 computer line, giving it a firm hold on the early-burgeoning personal and business market. By 1983 it had introduced three additional pocket computers, the TRS–80 Model PC-1, Model PC-2, and Model PC-4.

Bridging the gap between the desk-top computer and the pocket computer was the TRS-80 Model 100 Portable Computer, introduced in 1983. For Tandy Corporation it signaled a move toward small computers with larger capacity.[12] The Model 100 snuggled into a market that other manufacturers had not yet captured: a demand for the portability of the pocket computer but some of the features of larger models. Weighing just over three pounds, it measured $11\frac{5}{8}$ by $8\frac{1}{4}$ by 2 inches and took up the space of a three-ring binder. A built-in liquid-crystal display could show eight lines of forty characters each. For business executives, the Model 100 was a more powerful personal computer that could be carried in a briefcase. A built-in modem gave it the ability to connect via telephone to other computers or data bases by means of an inexpensive adapter. Cassette storage was also available.

Radio Shack also turned out computers designed primarily for business purposes. Its Model 12 and Model 16 were early entries in this market.

A Pricing Strategy

At the same time a technology race was occurring in the late 1970s and early 1980s among personal-computer manufacturers, a price war was heating up. For some, the marketing strategy was to bring a personal computer to as many people as possible as inexpensively as possible. In 1982, during the early era of the desk-top units, Timex Corporation announced that it would offer a home computer priced under $100. The Timex Sinclair 1000 originally sold for $99.95, and was available in many of the locations where Timex sold its inexpensive

watches. The Timex Computer Corporation, the company responsible for the Timex Sinclair 1000, launched the machine in an advertising campaign costing between $25 and $30 million.[13] This commitment to marketing signaled the faith one company had in an inexpensive personal computer directed toward the masses.

The four companies we have just discussed were by no means alone in the early history of personal computers. Some of which succeeded, Texas Instruments, Zenith, SONY, and Data General were involved, among others. Atari, a division of Warner Communications, launched a major drive to capture part of the home market, spearheaded by home video games.[14] Xerox, famous for its office equipment, entered the market as a competitor of IBM. Xerox viewed the small computer as part of an office work station that could be hooked to other office equipment such as word processors and typewriters. Hewlett-Packard introduced a computer targeted to the scientific user. Commodore, which achieved early success with its PET personal computer, developed a large market overseas, where higher prices could be charged. Coleco introduced a personal computer named Adam, which included hardware and software that competitors were offering for much higher prices. It was a complete computer system—memory unit, keyboard, and printer.

Portability

Radio Shack's TRS-80 pocket models and its Model 100 were not the first machines to make the personal computer a *portable* computer. Panasonic introduced a hand-held computer with peripheral technology (Figure 5–5) in 1981. The same year, a much larger system was introduced at a West Coast trade fair: the Osborne 1, and the ex-

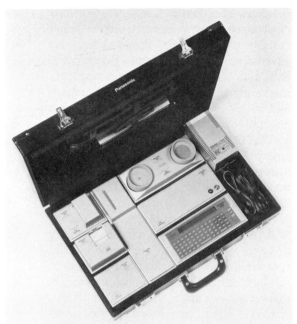

FIGURE 5-5 The move to portability resulted in many companies marketing personal computers which were easy to take to job sites, transport on trips, and included modems which could be used to access distant data banks. This component model designed for a briefcase was manufactured by Panasonic. (Panasonic)

ecutive models that followed it, included disk drives, screen, keyboard, and large amounts of software—all packaged at a cost lower than that of many desk-top computers alone.

The Shakeout Begins

Gradually the Osborne 1 underwent improvements and continued to grow in popularity, not seeing what was on the horizon. An optional monitor was available for users who wanted a larger screen.[15] A streamlined case was developed, and more storage capacity per disk was made available, along with the option to add a longer column-screen format that would display more data

and make the unit easier to use as a word processor. An instructional program consisting of an audio cassette, flip charts, and other materials made the Osborne an easy computer for the first-time user.

Then it happened. The financial analysts predicted it would. History indicated it was inevitable. Finally, as with all new technologies where there are more competitors than the marketplace will bear, a general shakeout takes place and only the strongest or those who offer a product or service that others do not, are left to survive. History will record that in the era of the personal computer, that shakeout began in 1983 when Osborne ran into financial trouble and filed for bankruptcy. By September of 1983 it had laid off as many as 80% of its workforce of approximately 350 employees. Unlike radio and television stations which base profits in advertising the personal computer industry is based on the number of units sold, be it hardware or software. Distributors can only display so many different brands and sooner or later they need to choose which brands will sit in the front of the store and which ones will be left to collect dust in the back room. Osborne was simply over producing for the marketplace and became the first major casualty of the industry. Just as the major names in radio remain today, the early years of the personal computer left such names as IBM, Apple, and others to chart the future of the industry.

FACTORS IN THE MARKETING AND ACCEPTANCE OF PERSONAL COMPUTERS

We may not know the full impact of personal computers on our lives, but no doubt exists that it will be substantial. What direction the growth of the industry will take will be determined by a number of factors.

Identification and Capture of Markets

To draw too many parallels between the development of radio and television and personal computers would be risky. With radio and television an immediate use was evident —entertainment. With personal computers growth is due more to utility than to entertainment value, although some manufacturers have touted the game-playing capabilities of their machines. For the most part, however, the growth of personal computers and their penetration of the mass market between now and the end of the decade will depend on their manufacturers' locating and then capturing different markets. The companies that are still major forces in the personal-computer field in 1990 will have had the ability to do both.

Some of the most visible markets in the early to mid-1980s were businesspeople and computer hobbyists. Consumers who purchased personal computers included affluent professionals and parents who desired an educational tool for their youngsters. Part of the reason personal computers did not achieve even more acceptance was the lack of the software needed to make the machines truly usable to wide segments of the population. Sophisticated accounting programs were certainly useful, but they didn't appeal to the average consumer. Convincing someone to spend hundreds or even thousands of dollars to store recipes wasn't the solution either. With improved software making the machines more useful and improvements in technology making them more powerful yet less expensive, the opportunities for growth could improve substantially.

As we have seen, some companies are investing in the development of portable personal computers. They feel there is a growth market for these computers—businesspeople and others who have become so reliant on computers that they will want the support of these machines, regardless of whether they are in the middle of a construction site, checking an electric meter, or stopping by a pay phone to check information stored in a central computer back at the office.

Other companies are directing their marketing efforts to specific users, such as scientists and educators. Believing that these individuals are less likely to need portable computers and do not suffer from "technophobia"—resistance to high technology— marketing people worry less about portability and concentrate more on the utility of the machines.

Distribution Channels

Regardless of how many computers a company can manufacture, and regardless of how many people are standing in line to purchase the machines, unless distribution channels are available, a company cannot succeed. Successful companies in the early era of personal computers enjoyed the advantage of distribution. Radio Shack, for example, had thousands of stores that could instantly stock the TRS-80 computers. Apple made arrangements with retail computer outlets that could both sell and service their machines. In fact, many of these outlets owe their success to the Apple computer. IBM entered the market with an already existing sales force selling IBM office equipment to businesses, and as we have seen, it made additional arrangements to sell the IBM Personal Computer through Sears, Roebuck and ComputerLand stores. Timex had an established distribution system in thousands of retail establishments where it sold its watches. Until competition arrived, it was for a time somewhat successful.

Whoever controls the distribution channels and the retail outlets will have a decisive advantage. The competition in this area is keen. Unlike a magazine stand, which can stock an infinite variety of publications, or a grocery store, which can stock a variety of merchandise and thousands of brands, a retail outlet selling computers is limited. Personal computers take up more space than other types of electronic merchandise. Thus, a retailer must select those products that can sell the most units and make the most profit. The popularity of the IBM Personal Computer, for example, pushed some competing brands off the shelf and narrowed the number of different brands being distributed through retail outlets. Major inroads such as this can drastically shift the balance of an entire industry.

Motivation to Purchase

Equally important factors are (1) the public's primary motivation for buying a personal computer and (2) what feature will cause them to purchase one brand over another. Computer manufacturers have used a variety of strategies to capture sales. Some have tried to keep attention on their products and ward off the continual influx of new machines from other companies by bringing out a stream of new models with new features. Since so much publicity and attention is paid to how fast computer technology becomes obsolete, this strategy is necessary for the company that wishes to keep up a corporate image of being always on the edge of the new technology.

Other companies have chosen pricing as a strategy. "The most hardware and software for the money"; "The least expensive computer on the market"—these are just two of the sales appeals to the cost-conscious consumer interested in buying. The technology strategy—focusing on memory size or computing power—has been another popular method of touting equipment. The first machines reaching a certain "storage thresh-old" within a given price range have also enjoyed some sales success.

Corporate Acquisition

Another determinant in the growth of personal computers will lie in which companies are acquired by other companies. When a company is acquired by a larger concern three things happen. First, the acquiring company gains a foothold in the other's market. Second, a competitor is eliminated. The marketing expertise and the technology are many times directed toward one entity, not two. Third, the resources of the acquiring company, which are usually substantial, are placed behind the other company. One small company may have identified and captured a market but simply didn't have the financial resources to take full advantage of it. The acquiring company has the resources with which to put financial muscle behind the smaller company.

The growth of personal computers has enabled a number of smaller companies to become highly successful. Some have emerged as major corporate powers able to aggressively go about acquiring other companies. Others are vulnerable to acquisition.

Friendly Technology

Few people will spend money on something they fear. Many people still fear computers. College and high school courses in computer literacy, telecommunication, and computer science are helping to lessen these fears, but those without access to such an experience can harbor technophobia.

Some companies have been successful in helping consumers overcome technophobia. Part of the marketing strategy of the Timex computer was to make a personal computer available at a low price, which permitted people to invest a small amount of money and learn computing at home at their own pace. The Osborne computers included an instructional program with cassette tape, designed to reduce technophobia. The Lisa model from Apple was touted as a "friendly" machine.

As competition continues, more emphasis is being placed on reaching buyers who have avoided buying a personal computer not because of utility or money but out of fear.

Adequate Software

The real power of the computer is not in hardware but in software—the programs that make the machine perform specific functions. Software has long lagged behind hardware. Some early entrants into the personal-computer market had excellent machines but did not own sufficient software to make the machines a success.

Software must continue to develop and be made available to the general public. Companies are realizing that without software they cannot survive. Some companies are openly advertising for software that can be published and distributed with or without a given product. Most early software was directed at business people and professional people. In the future, software must be developed that appeals to the average consumer. Only then can personal computers begin to achieve the widespread use that radio, television, and the telephone enjoy.

DATA PROCESSING

For individuals who have never been exposed to a computer, even a personal computer can be somewhat intimidating. Many of you will take classes in computer science, computer literacy, and computers in society. Such courses will help you understand and become comfortable with computers. Personal computers and larger computers operate in much the same way. Their basic functions include (1) input, (2) processing, and (3) output.

Theory and Input Hardware

Computers process data by means of a binary numbering system, which consists of two possible digits: 0 and 1. Think of 0 and 1 in terms of an on-off relay switch. The 0 represents the switch in the off position and the 1 represents the switch in the on position. As current flows through the computer it encounters these switches (called *relays* or *gates*), which are either open or closed. The combination of open and closed gates represents information, such as numbers and letters.

Input data can be fed directly into the computer in many forms—for example, from a keyboard or by a magnetic tape, a cassette tape, a small, flexible "floppy disc," an optical scanner, a punch card reader, a larger reel of magnetic tape, or a larger, rigid disc. Personal computers primarily use a keyboard terminal that looks much the same as a typewriter keyboard, a cassette tape, or a floppy disc. The cassette tape and disc permit information to be fed to the computer at speeds faster than a keyboard terminal will allow. Optical scanners read specially typed pages and can store the information on disc or tape.

Central Processing Unit

At the core of a computer is a central processing unit (CPU). The CPU contains a control unit that reads and interprets the instructions in a computer program. An arithmetic logic unit contained in the CPU performs the calculations required by the program. A memory unit in the computer stores information that can be fed to the

CPU. Two types of memory are important to the functioning of a computer: (1) read-only memory (ROM), which consists of pre-determined (prewired) functions stored permanently in the computer, and (2) random-access memory (RAM), which can be altered. When the power is shut off the RAM erases but the ROM does not. A computer contains a main memory and sometimes a secondary memory, such as a cassette tape or floppy disc. Output on a personal computer appears on a visual-display terminal or a printer. The memory capacity of a computer is described in *bits* of information. One binary digit is a bit. Data are represented in a series or pattern of bits called a *byte*. A typical byte consists of eight bits. Personal computers are frequently described in terms of their memory capacity. For example, a 256K computer can accommodate 256,000 bits of information.

The Modem

Some of the terms just introduced are examples of computer *hardware,* the physical equipment of the computer. The keyboard terminal, visual-display terminal, cassette tape, and floppy disc are all items of computer hardware, as are the silicon chips contained in a computer system.

The *Modem* is an important piece of hardware for a personal computer. The modem opens up new vistas for the user by connecting the personal computer with the telephone, which in turn can be used for communication with other computers. These may include other individuals' personal computers. Therefore, links among any number of individuals with personal computers are possible. Personal messages, electronic mail, and other information can be exchanged between users of this computer network. The modem may also be used to access a computer that stores a large amount of information and is the hub of a computer network. The network consists of thousands of other personal computer users who also have access to the central computer. It is these computer networks that truly make the personal computer a form of electronic mass communication.

Software and Firmware

Software is the information the computer processes, as opposed to the physical components, or hardware. A computer program that tells a computer what functions to perform is software. Software is of two types. The first, systems software, permits the computer to perform effectively and is necessary for the operation of the second type, applications software, which is designed to solve a specific problem or perform a specific task. For example, if you want to determine which radio station in a given market had the most listeners during a given period, you would employ systems software to tell the computer to utilize a computer program that we might call *Rating*. The Rating program is a type of applications software designed specifically to read and interpret data from audience-listening surveys.

The development of microprocessors that can store huge amounts of information has enabled manufacturers to preprogram software into the computer. The term *firmware* is commonly used for such software.

DEVELOPMENT
OF THE MEGABIT RAM

The key to developing more powerful, yet smaller, computers is the storage capacity of the RAM. The early memory chips were 64K RAMs which store 64,000 bits of information. A bit is a 0 or 1 and eight of them represent a byte. By 1985 an estimated half billion

64K RAMs will have been sold for a worth of about $1.5 billion. Also on the market is the 256K RAM. On the horizon is what is being called the megabit RAM which offers even more memory. How much more is still in the theoretical stages, but early experimental chips are capable of storing more than one million bits of information. That is equivalent to filling four newspaper pages with small type. As in the area of artificial intelligence, Japan is the country the world is watching and which some experts predict will take the lead in the megabit RAM market. Three key companies in the megabit RAM's development are Hitachi, NEC, and Nippon Telegraph and Telephone.

SUMMARY

Personal computers have become a new medium of mass communication. Through data bases ranging from electronic publishing to sophisticated computer programs distributed directly to consumers, the high-technology era of telecommunication will change the way we use the media of the future.

The growth of the personal-computer industry is fueled by both the profits to be made from smaller computing devices and the ways in which these devices aid us in solving problems and making decisions in both the work and home environment. Some experts predict that by 1990 the personal computer will be as commonplace as high-quality color television receivers. The same silicon chip that held one million transistor-like circuits in 1984 will hold ten million by the 1990s.

The growth of personal computers is but a speck in the yardstick of time. More advancement in technology has been made between the late 1970s and the early 1980s than in the entire history of computing.

The history of computing has its roots in the Scientific Revolution, when the changes from a rural to an urban society were accompanied by the development of physics, chemistry, and biology. Mathematics took on more importance, and various crude calculating devices emerged. The "Napier Bones," Blaise Pascal's calculator, Jacquard's "programmed" loom, and Babbage's engines are important milestones in this history. Major companies such as IBM and Sperry Rand played a part, as did major universities.

Electronic computers emerged at Harvard in 1937, when Howard Aiken conducted IBM-backed research into integrated components controlled by punched paper tape. Aiken's machine was named Mark I and included mechanical and electronic components. Other electronic computers evolved in Bell Labs, which produced six models from the late 1930s to the early 1950s. At the University of Pennsylvania two researchers, J. P. Eckert and J. Mauchley, began work on an all-electronic computer, which they completed in 1946 and named ENIAC. They later formed their own company, which produced the UNIVAC computer.

The history of modern computers is broken up into four generations. The first generation consisted of machines that relied on vacuum-tube technology. Transistor-based technology is represented in the second generation. The third generation is characterized by integrated circuits and stored programs. Mainframe and minicomputers were also characteristic of the third generation. The microcircuit and microprocessor represented the fourth generation of computers. A fifth generation on the horizon is the development of computers with artificial intelligence.

The era of the personal computer began in the early 1970s, when small computers were made available in kit form and later as factory-assembled machines ready for use. Different manufacturers are representative of the forces that charted the early era of personal computers. Apple, incorporated in 1977, is considered the earliest major manufacturer of personal computers. IBM entered the personal-computer market in 1981 and immediately became a major contender. Setting aside long-standing corporate policy such as not buying from outside suppliers and marketing only through IBM outlets, the IBM Personal Computer was matching its major competitors in sales within one year of its introduction.

Radio Shack, bolstered by its large distribution network of Radio Shack stores, became an early force in the personal-computer market. Launching its TRS-80 Model 1 at about the same time Apple was being incorporated, it brought out successive models of the TRS-80 series and found acceptance in both the home and business markets.

Using price as a marketing strategy, Timex marketed one of the first personal computers selling for under $100. Enjoying a distribution network that included retail outlets selling Timex watches, the Timex Sinclair 1000 appealed to those individuals who wanted to experiment with and learn about personal computing without investing much money.

Some industry analysts suggest that portable personal computers will see major growth in the late 1980s as people who rely on small computers begin to move them out of the restrictions of the office. Osborne was one of the first to base its manufacturing and marketing strategy exclusively on the portability of its personal computer. It was also

the first major casualty of the personal computer era.

The future growth and acceptance of personal computers depend on several factors. First, the ability to identify and capture key markets will distinguish some personal-computer manufacturers from others. Those that can grasp the public demand for both hardware and software, and time the release of machines and programs to meet that demand, will gain a substantial edge. The ability to control distribution channels will also be critical. With more and more machines being developed and only so much retail space available, some brands will be discontinued in favor of more profitable ones. Retailers will stock and sell the machines the public demands most and for which there is the most profit.

Understanding why people buy a personal computer and determining what feature will most appeal to the public will also separate the winners from the losers.

Some companies now in business will be acquired by others. Who remains independent and who gets swallowed up will be affected by such things as what resources are placed behind certain products, which products remain in the marketplace, and which companies standardize hardware and software.

Fear of computers and other high-technology hardware prevents some people from buying a personal computer, even if they realize its value. Manufacturers who can develop technology that appears friendly to the user will have an advantage in reaching potential buyers.

Perhaps no issue will affect the growth of personal computers more than that of adequate software. Much early software was directed at the business user and included electronic accounting, ledgers, inventory, planning, and similar functions. Software appealing to a wider range of users will be necessary in order for personal computers to reach the acceptance that radio and television enjoy.

Data processing in a computer is based on a binary numbering system. Input to the computer can be handled in many ways, including keyboard, tapes, discs, and punched cards. Software consists of the programs that tell a computer what functions to perform. Hardware consists of the actual physical components of a computer. A modem connects a computer to telephone lines that in turn link the computer with other computers and computer networks.

By the mid-1980s, Japan is predicted to market the megabit RAM capable of storing one million bits of information.

OPPORTUNITIES FOR FURTHER LEARNING

BADRE, A., and B. SHNEIDERMAN, *Directions in Human/Computer Interaction, Volume One.* Norwood, N.J.: Ablex, 1983.

COMPAINE, B. M., *Shifting Boundaries in the Information Marketplace.* Cambridge, Mass.: Harvard Program on Information Resources Policy, 1980.

CONDRY, J., and D. KEITH, *Educational and Recreational Uses of Computer Technology.* Beverly Hills, Calif.: Sage, 1983.

DIZARD, W. P., *The Coming Information Age: An Overview of Technology, Economics, and Politics.* New York: Longman, 1982.

——, with I. De Sola Pool, *The Coming Information Age.* New York: Longman, 1982.

FRANTZICH, S. E., *Computers in Congress.* Beverly Hills, Calif.: Sage, 1982.

HAIGH, R. W., G. GERBNER, and R. B. BYRNE, eds., *Communications in the Twenty-First Century.* New York: John Wiley, 1981.

HEISE, D. R., ed., *Microcomputers in Social Research.* Beverly Hills, Calif.: Sage, 1981.

KERR, E. E., and S. R. HOLTZ, EDS., *Computer-Mediated Communication Systems: Status and Evaluation.* New York: Academic, 1982.

KLIE, R. H., *Communications Network Management.* Cambridge, Mass.: Harvard Program on Information Resources Policy, 1981.

MARTIN, J., *The Telematic Society: A Challenge for Tomorrow.* Englewood Cliffs, N.J.: Prentice-Hall, 1981.

OETTINGER, A. G., K. BORCHARDT, and C. L. WEINHAUS, *Stakes in Telecommunications Cost and Prices.* Cambridge, Mass.: Harvard Program on Information Resources Policy, 1980.

OETTINGER, A. G., and C. L. WEINHAUS, *The Federal Side of Traditional Telecommunications Cost Allocations.* Cambridge: Harvard Program on Information Resources Policy, 1980.

——, *The Traditional State Side of Telecommunications Cost Allocations.* Cambridge, Mass.: Harvard Program on Information Resources Policy, 1980.

PAPERT, S., *Mindstorms: Children, Computers, and Powerful Ideas.* New York: Basic Books, 1980.

SCHNEIDERMAN, B., ed., *Human/Computer Interaction.* Norwood, N.J.: Ablex.

SLACK, J. D., *Communication Technologies and Society: Conceptions of Causality and the Politics of Technical Intervention.* Norwood, N.J.: Ablex, 1983.

TAYLOR, J. B., *Using Microcomputers in Social Agencies.* Beverly Hills, Calif.: Sage, 1981.

Telecommunications: Trends and Directions. Washington, D.C.: Electronic Industries, 1981.

VALLEE, J., *Computer Message Systems.* New York: McGraw-Hill, 1983.

WIIO, O., *Information and Communication Systems: An Introduction to the Concepts of Information, Communication, and Communication Research.* Norwood, N.J.: Ablex, 1983.

WILLIAMS, F., *The Communications Revolution.* Beverly Hills, Calif.: Sage, 1982.

6

RADIO WAVES
AND THE SPECTRUM

Heinrich Hertz probably never imagined that almost one hundred years after his discovery of electromagnetic waves, those same waves would carry information around the world and even to planets millions of miles away. In this chapter, we shall discover how radio waves travel and how radio and television signals and computer data travel between transmitters and receivers.

THE ELECTROMAGNETIC SPECTRUM

To understand how information such as data or broadcast signals are carried between transmitter and receiver, it is first necessary to understand the *electromagnetic*

spectrum. Consider the spectrum as a measuring stick for electromagnetic energy. (Figure 6–1) At the lower end of the measuring stick are radio waves. At the upper end of the spectrum we find visible light and X rays. For our purposes, we shall concentrate on radio waves.

DEFINING FREQUENCY

What differentiates radio waves from light waves or X rays? The answer is their *frequency.* You have heard the term used in reference to the dial on your standard radio. Two radio stations in the same community operate on different frequencies so that they will not interfere with each other. When cur-

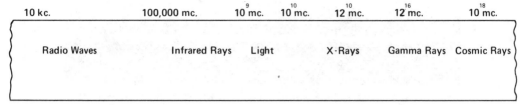

10 kc.	100,000 mc.	10⁹ mc.	10¹⁰ mc.	12¹⁰ mc.	12¹⁶ mc.	10¹⁸ mc.
Radio Waves	Infrared Rays	Light		X-Rays	Gamma Rays	Cosmic Rays

FIGURE 6–1 The electromagnetic spectrum. Notice that radio waves are at the lower end of the spectrum. Those which occur in the range of frequencies used by AM broadcasters tend to bounce off the ionosphere, whereas higher frequency waves adhere more to line-of-sight transmission paths.

rent is applied to the transmitter of a radio station the antenna emits electromagnetic radiation. This radiation is actually a series of electromagnetic waves, one after another. The next time you throw a rock into a pool of water, watch the series of waves that ripple one after the other in all directions from the point at which the rock entered the water. This is what happens when electromagnetic energy travels through the atmosphere or the vacuum of outer space. *The number of waves passing a certain point in a given interval of time* is the *frequency*. In broadcasting the waves are termed *electromagnetic waves,* but in this book we will sometimes call them simply *waves.*

FIGURE 6–2 When one complete wave passes a given point, it is called a "cycle." The term "kilocycle" (also called "kilohertz") is used to represent 1,000 cycles, and the term "megacycle" (also called "megahertz") is used to denote 1,000,000 cycles. Satellites and microwave transmission systems operate in the "gigahertz" (billions of cycles) range. (*FCC Broadcast Operators Handbook*)

DEFINING WAVELENGTH

The *distance between two waves* is called the *wavelength.* If we take a stop-action picture of the ripples (waves) in our pond and then figure the distance between two ripples, that would be the *wavelength.* Cycle is closely related to wavelength (Figure 6–2). When one complete wave passes our counting point, we have observed one cycle. The point can be any geographical location. If we were watching ripples in a pond, we might stand at a certain point on the edge of the pond. The same would apply to electromagnetic waves, except that they travel much too fast to count and cannot be seen.

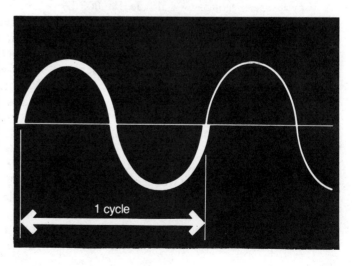

1 cycle

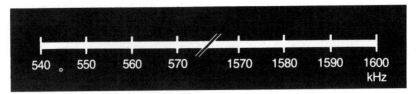

FIGURE 6–3 The typical AM radio dial reads from 540 kilohertz to 1600 kilohertz. (*FCC Broadcast Operators Handbook*)

We know that all electromagnetic waves travel at the speed of light, 186,000 miles per second. Since we measure the speed of light in miles per second or, using the metric system, in meters per second, the second becomes the commonly used time interval. The number of waves passing a certain point in one second is called *cycles per second*. One thousand cycles per second is called a *kilocycle,* one million a *megacycle.* With this in mind, we can determine the wavelength of radio waves by simple division. For example, given that electromagnetic waves travel at a speed of 186,000 miles per second, if 10,000 cycles (10,000 complete waves) pass a given point in one second, the wavelength of each wave would be 18.6 miles (186,000 ÷ 10,000). Now let's figure the wavelength of a higher frequency, 535 kilocycles (535,000 cycles per second). We divide 186,000 by 535,000. The answer is .3477 miles. Since there are 5,280 feet in one mile, we can convert our wavelength to feet by multiplying 5,280 by .3477. The answer is a wavelength of 1,836 feet.

COMPUTING FREQUENCY

Now that we understand cycles per second, we can easily compute frequency. If, for instance, 1,000 waves pass a given point in one second (1,000 cycles per second, or one kilocycle), the frequency, or location on the electromagnetic spectrum, is 1 kilocycle.

Similarly, 535,000 cycles per second is represented as 535 kilocycles. On your AM radio, that particular frequency would be at the lower end of the dial (Figure 6–3).

Do not be alarmed if you purchase an AM radio reading from 540 to 1600. Each radio station is assigned a 10-kilocycle range on the electromagnetic spectrum. Thus, the station assigned the lowest frequency is assigned 540 kilocycles, which permits it to operate between 535 and 545 kilocycles. Some radios, even though capable of receiving 540 kilocycles, begin numbering their dial at 550 kilocycles or abbreviate it as the number 55.

TUNING TO A WAVELENGTH

In simplified terms, a radio receiver "counts" the waves or cycles per second to determine a frequency. Your radio does this when you tune from one station to another. Your receiver is picking up only those waves that are being transmitted on the same frequency to which you tune. Thus, different frequencies on your radio dial correspond to different positions on the electromagnetic spectrum.

Figure 6–3 illustrates this concept. At one position on the spectrum is the frequency allocated to AM broadcasting. This represents that portion of the spectrum between 535 and 1605 kilocylces. Higher on the electromagnetic spectrum are citizens' band radio, television, and FM broadcasting. Later in this chapter we shall examine the even higher frequencies of microwaves.

COMMON TERMS: METERS AND HERTZ

Before going on to our discussion of AM and FM broadcasting we need to mention two terms: *meters* and *hertz*. In our discussion of wavelength we used miles and feet to compute the wavelength of 535 kilocycles. International wavelength, however, is based on the metric system. Thus, although you may find feet and miles easier to use, meters are the common international measure of wavelength employed in broadcasting. The speed of light is 300,000,000 meters per second (186,000 miles per second). A meter is equal to 3.3 feet. Also, we used the term *cycles* to denote a specific frequency on the electromagnetic spectrum. In recent years that term has been replaced by the word *hertz* (Hz), in honor of the man who discovered electromagnetic waves. Thus, 1,000 cycles per second becomes one kilohertz (1 kHz), and 1,000,000 cycles per second becomes 1 megahertz (1 mHz). Frequencies of 535,000 cycles per second

become 535 kilohertz (535 kHz), referred to simply as a frequency of 535 kilohertz.

AM BROADCASTING

Now that we understand the electromagnetic spectrum and how waves are radiated into space, we'll learn how voice and music use those waves to reach radio listeners. We'll begin with AM broadcasting, that portion of the electromagnetic spectrum falling between 535 and 1605 kHz.

AM stands for *amplitude modulation*. Amplitude is defined as breadth of range.[1] Modulation means to adjust or adapt to a certain proportion.[2] Now let's apply both of these words to radio waves. Figure 6–4 illustrates an unmodulated radio wave. Now examine Figure 6–5, a radio wave that has been altered by adjustment of the amplitude, or breadth of range," of the wave. The wave characteristics of music and the human voice are transformed into the wave, which in turn "carries" them between the transmitter and receiver. Notice that the wavelength, or frequency, remains constant. The change takes place in amplitude, not in frequency. When the wave is adjusted to carry changes in sound, it is said to be *modulated*.

FIGURE 6–4 Unmodulated wave. (*FCC Broadcast Operators Handbook*)

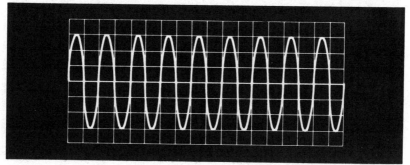

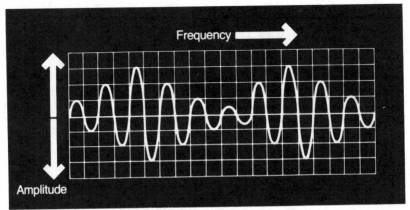

FIGURE 6-5 An amplitude modulated wave. Notice the frequency (width of the wave or distance between waves) remains the same, but the amplitude varies. (*FCC Broadcast Operators Handbook*)

FM BROADCASTING

From our discussion of AM broadcasting, you should have already started to figure out how FM (frequency-modulated) broadcasting works. Instead of changing the amplitude of the wave, we change the frequency, or wavelength. Figure 6-6 illustrates a frequency-modulated wave. Notice there is no change in the amplitude of the wave. In-stead, the frequency, or wavelength, varies. Different sounds indicate different wavelengths (cycles per second). FM broadcasting to the general public operates between 88 and 108 mHz (Figure 6-7). Each FM station is allocated a width of 200 kHz.[3]

The FCC has considered narrowing the space allocated to each FM station to 100 kHz to allow room for more stations. Major opposition to the proposal has been voiced

FIGURE 6-6 Frequency modulated wave. Notice the frequency varies, but the amplitude remains constant. (*FCC Broadcast Operators Hand-book*)

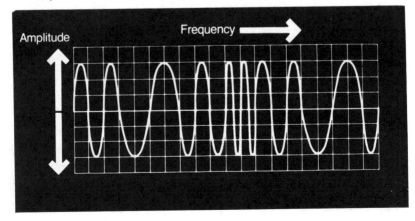

FIGURE 6–7 The FM radio band goes from 88.1 to 107.9 megahertz. Most FM radio dials are shown in whole numbers without the decimals and read from 88 to 107. (*FCC Broadcast Operators Handbook*)

by proponents of quadraphonic FM broadcasting, which uses four separate channels instead of the two channels common to FM stereo.[4]

FM STEREO

Throughout its history, radio broadcasting has taken three major strides to improve the quality of sound reproduction from the studio to the living room. One was the development of FM broadcasting. Another was the development of stereo FM broadcasting. A third, to be discussed in the next section, was the introduction of quadraphonic FM. AM stereo is also beginning to appear.

Within the 200-kHz space allocated to each FM station is ample room for the separation of broadcast signals, room that permits the same station to broadcast on *two* slightly different frequencies. There is also room for a tone that triggers specially equipped radios to receive this stereo signal. Radios equipped to receive stereo actually have *two* separate receiving systems, which, when triggered by the tone, separately receive the two frequencies being broadcast by the stereo station. When the tone is not transmitted, the radio still receives a monophonic signal. Many of us have seen a small light flip on in a stereo FM receiver when we tune it to a station broadcasting in stereo. This signals us that our radio is tuned to a

stereo station, that the station is broadcasting in stereo, and that our receiver is receiving both channels of the stereo system.

Stereo broadcasting has grown steadily in popularity. The reproduction of quality music with the added dimensions of space and depth—it is almost as if the orchestra were playing in your living room—has been the main distinction between stereo FM and standard FM and AM broadcasting.

QUADRAPHONIC FM

What added dimensions stereo broadcasting brought to FM, qaudraphonic doubled. In quadraphonic systems four instead of two frequencies are employed. Quadraphonic broadcasting is still in its experimental stages, and the FCC is currently evaluating various quadraphonic systems. Serious evaluation began in 1972 with the formation of the National Quadraphonic Radio Committee (NQRC) of the Electronic Industries Association. The problem in broadcasting four-channel sound is to develop systems that will provide distinct separation of the four frequencies and still allow radios not equipped for quadraphonic reception to receive stereo FM and monophonic FM. Without widespread standardization of equipment that can receive quadraphonic broadcasting, it is difficult to measure the potential demand for this system.

Experiments in Quadraphonic Broadcasting

Some attempts have been made, however, to educate the public in the potential benefits of quadraphonic broadcasting. In a promotional experiment on July 24, 1976, two San Francisco radio stations, both stereo, joined in a broadcast that permitted listeners with two radios, both capable of receiving stereo, to hear what quadraphonic broadcasting of high quality sounded like.[5] Two Sacramento, California, stations repeated the experiment by simultaneously rebroadcasting the signals of the two San Francisco stations.[6] Whether quadraphonic broadcasting assumes mass scale will depend on public demand, support from quadraphonic-equipment companies, and the FCC.

Dimensions of Quadraphonic FM

When there is true separation of the four quadraphonic channels, the listener is literally surrounded by sound. Assume you are listening to a live performance of a chamber orchestra. On stage is a violinist, a pianist, a trumpeter, and a flutist. As you listen to the music, all of the instruments are in front of you. If we placed microphones in front of the orchestra, one to the left and one to the right, and broadcast the music in stereo, you could hear the sound simultaneously from the same two directions in your living room.

Now assume we use four microphones. One is directed toward the violinist, the other toward the pianist, the third toward the trumpeter, and the fourth toward the flutist. We now broadcast the music on a quadraphonic four-channel system, and you listen to the music on a radio capable of receiving all four channels. A separate speaker is connected to each channel. If you place one speaker to the left front of you, a second to the right front, and the third and fourth speakers to your rear, the sound will be similar to what you would hear if you were sitting in the *middle* of the orchestra instead of in front of it. Now consider a radio commercial in quadraphonic sound. Close your eyes and imagine sitting in a new automobile as the salesperson walks around the car telling you about its features.[7]

Pros and Cons of Quad

Along with the "total" sound experience, proponents of quadraphonic broadcasting use the emergence of stereo AM as an argument for developing quadraphonic broadcasting. They claim that as AM stereo develops, FM broadcasters will need this added quadraphonic dimension to maintain FM's special attraction. More conservative watchers say there is a need to determine first where the software (records and tapes) will come from before leaping ahead with full-scale quad. Moreover, sales figures indicate that quadraphonic systems have not been overly popular for home use.[8] Somewhere among all of these arguments lies the future of quad.

AM STEREO

AM stereo is now emerging from the experimental stage. For many years, AM broadcasting did not seriously consider stereo beyond laboratory ventures, primarily for two reasons. The first was the narrow channel width of AM stations—10 kHz compared with 200 kHz for FM. Second, as long as FM was not a serious competitive threat to AM, there was no widespread interest in the system. However, with FM gradually cutting a wide swath through the AM audience, AM broadcasters began to search for something with which they could regain their competitive edge.

Active evaluation of all systems—undertaken by the National AM Stereo Committee (NASC) of the Electronics Industries Association—began in the mid 1970s. The collection of field performance data on AM stereo was completed in 1977.[9]

AM stereo could grow, for two reasons. First, there is considerable backing for it from the many AM broadcasters who have felt the competitive sting of FM.[10] Second, the technology is available and already in use by many stations. The future will depend on how quickly equipment can be standardized, and how the public accepts it, as demonstrated by the sale of AM stereo receivers.

TRANSMITTING TV SIGNALS

Our discussion would not be complete without mention of television transmission. Television stations broadcast on frequencies located both above and below the standard FM radio frequencies of 88 to 108 mHz. Radio waves carry the television picture. The width of the spectrum allocated for television transmission is established by the FCC at 6 mHz. Part of the frequency is used for transmission of the video portion of the signal, and part of it the audio portion.[11]

Processing the TV Picture

Earlier in this book we learned about Paul G. Nipkow's mechanical television, which consisted of a scanning disk in which holes were punched in the pattern of a spiral. When the disk turned, the holes would pass over a small opening through which could be seen a picture. In one complete revolution of the disk, the entire picture would be scanned and transmitted to another receiving unit, which would then reproduce the image. If the image were replaced with another in rapid succession, the illusion of motion would be created.

Further refinements changed the process, and with the work of Philo Farnsworth and the development of Vladimir Zworykin's iconoscope tube, electronics picked up where mechanics left off. Using electrons instead of a spiraling disk, one could scan the image with increasing clarity and speed. The result was the electron-scanning process as we know it today. For a simplified example, imagine a flag with a series of red and white stripes. The scanning process first scans the white stripes and then the red stripes. Now imagine this process taking place 525 times per second while the picture (flag) rapidly changes. The result is a series of rapidly scanned and broadcast pictures that appear on our television set as an illusion of motion.

Processing Color Television

Color television uses a similar process, except that the television camera separates the three primary colors of light: red, green, and blue.[12] All other colors are made up of a combination of these three. When the television camera scans an image, it separates the red, blue, and green hues. These are transmitted individually and then appear as tiny dots on our television screen. The dots are too small for us to see with our naked eye and thus tend to "run together," creating the color picture. This, plus the rapid scanning process, creates a picture in both color and motion.

THE PATH OF ELECTROMAGNETIC WAVES

Melinda drives in and out of the rush-hour traffic looking anxiously for the exit that will send her east on the interstate, over the Allegheny Mountains and on to the Atlantic coast. The sound of her favorite AM radio station makes the beltway seem a little less harassing. She decides to keep the station on as long as she receives clear reception. Here comes the exit sign; she is on her way. The station continues to provide clear signals, and Melinda listens attentively to weather reports. A major storm is ahead, but she will not reach it for at least an hour.

About ninety minutes from home the radio station begins to fade. Finally it is necessary to push another button on the car radio. This time she switches to the FM frequencies. As she turns the dial she hears another station from her home town. The signal is clear, and once again she settles back to enjoy the drive as she heads up the west side of the mountains. It is beginning to rain when she reaches the summit, and lightning flashes as she heads down the other side. Less than ten minutes after crossing the summit, she loses her home-town FM signal and switches back to the AM frequencies to pick up a nearby station. Heavy static garbles the receiver, but she finally finds a nearby signal and learns that the rain should stop in another hour. Sure enough, fifty miles later the moon breaks through the clouds and casts a soft glow on the open countryside.

Now she is beginning to feel the strain of the drive. The bright lights from the diner up ahead look inviting. She decides to stop for a sandwich. Walking through the door of the diner, she hears the familiar sound of her home-town AM station, the one she listened to when she started her trip more than three hours ago. Melinda tells the waitress not to hurry. She just wants to unwind and listen to the music.

Ground Waves

To understand how radio waves travel, let's retrace Melinda's route. When she was on the beltway and on the interstate approaching the climb over the mountains, she had lit-

tle difficulty listening to her home-town AM station. That station was on the lower end of the electromagnetic spectrum, and the signal from the transmitter was carried partially by *ground waves,* which are *electromagnetic waves that adhere to the contour of the earth.* As a result, Melinda was able to listen uninterrupted until the waves finally died out and she had to change stations. In radio terminology, the area covered by the ground wave is the *primary service area,* "the area in which the ground wave is not subject to objectionable interference or objectionable fading."[13] It is also the portion of the station's signal that is most protected by the FCC when it licenses other stations that could interfere.

Sky Waves

When Melinda arrived at the diner, she again heard her home-town AM station. The reason the radio at the diner was able to receive the station was because of *sky-wave propagation,* in which the *radio waves travel into the sky instead of along the earth's contour* (Figure 6–8). However, they do not all remain in the sky; some are reflected off various layers of the ionosphere back to the earth's surface. Nevertheless, there is a section of the earth's surface that neither ground nor sky waves reach (Figure 6–8). In Melinda's drive to the coast, this was the area just before the climb up the mountains. The diner, however, was in the path of the sky waves. This phenomenon is also referred to as *skip,* and the distance from the transmitter to where a sky wave touches the earth is the *skip distance.*

That area in which a station's signal is heard clearly because of sky-wave propagation is referred to as its *secondary service area.* It is defined as "the area served by the sky-wave and not subject to objectionable interference."[14]

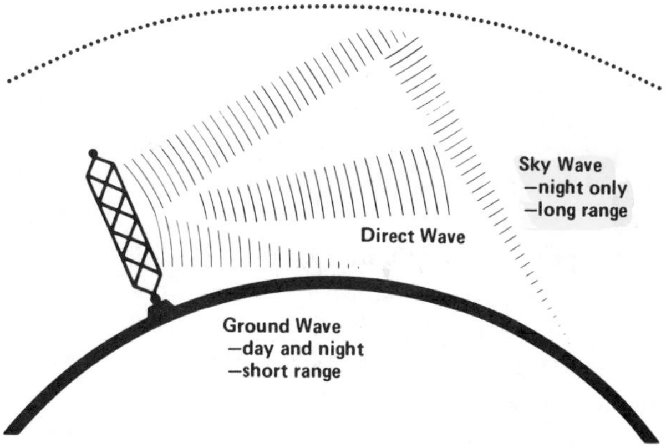

FIGURE 6-8 Radio waves travel in different patterns. Ground waves stay close to the earth's surface. Sky waves bounce off the upper layers of the atmosphere. Direct waves travel in straight lines, usually adhering to line-of-sight. (*FCC Broadcast Operators Handbook*)

Do you remember when the signal from Melinda's home-town AM station began to fade and she finally changed stations? At that point Melinda had reached the *intermittent service area* of the station, or that area "receiving service from the ground wave but beyond the primary service area and subject to some interference and fading."[15]

Melinda reached the diner at night. If she had reached it at noon, the AM station may not have been audible. The ionosphere has different reflective qualities at different times during the day. The sun warms it and decreases its ability to reflect sky waves.

Direct Waves

When Melinda reached the mountains and the ground waves died out, she changed frequencies on the car radio. She also switched to the FM band. Here she was again able to hear clearly a station from her home town, an FM station. At the higher frequency of FM (88 to 108 mHz) are radio waves called *direct waves,* which *travel in a straight line* (Figure 6-8). As Melinda began to climb the mountains, the antenna on her car was in a direct line of sight with the transmitter of the FM station. When she crossed the summit, the mountain blocked the waves and she could no longer hear the station.

Keep in mind that because the FM station was on a higher frequency, the signal traveled in a direct, "line-of-sight" path between the transmitter and the receiver. As a general rule, the higher the frequency, the more direct the wave propagation will be.

ALLOCATING TV CHANNELS

Through a long series of policy decisions, based partly on definite planning and implementation and partly on "squatters' rights," the FCC has developed a systematic allocation of the available frequencies on the electromagnetic spectrum. In the case of television, the allocations are based on the need to eliminate interference between channels. For channels 2 through 13, this means a separation of at least one channel between stations serving the same community. However, the development of more sophisticated transmitting and receiving equipment coupled with the demand for more channel utilization is beginning to change allocation of frequencies in some markets.

ALLOCATING AM

Between 535 and 1605 kHz on the broadcast band are 107 channels, or *frequency locations,* in which AM stations can operate. Each channel occupies 10 kHz of space;

thus, one is located at 540 kHz and others at every kHz thereafter until 1600 kHz. The characteristics of the frequency determine the ability of a station to reach a geographic region.

To provide maximum opportunity for AM stations to develop, to foster free-enterprise competition, and to protect the pioneer stations, which staked early claims to the airways, the FCC uses three major classifications and numerous subclassifications in assigning frequencies. The major classifications are clear channels, regional channels, and local channels.

Clear Channels

A clear channel is one "on which the dominant station or stations render service over wide areas and which are cleared of objectionable interference within their primary service areas and over all or a substantial portion of their secondary service areas."[16] From this definition, it is easy to see that clear channels operate at high power and have priority over a given frequency. Within the clear-channel allocations are Class I and Class II stations. Class I stations have more protection from interference. Class II stations can operate on clear-channel frequencies but must protect Class I stations by either using directional antennas, operating on reduced power, signing off at sunset, or a combination of all three. The maximum operating power of a clear-channel station is 50,000 watts; the minimum varies from 250 watts to 10,000 watts.

Regional Channels

Regional channels are assigned where several stations operate, none having a power of more than 5,000 watts.[17] There are many more regional channels than clear channels. The primary area serviced by stations operating on regional channels is the city or town in which the station is located and its adjacent areas. Regional channels are found over the entire range of the AM band, yet their specific channel assignments do not duplicate those of clear-channel stations. Their secondary coverage areas and sometimes portions of their primary coverage areas are not protected from interference, as are those of clear-channel stations.

Local Channels

Local channels are usually located at the upper end of the AM band and operate at a power no greater than 250 watts at night and 1,000 watts during the day. Some are required to sign off at sunset as a means of protecting other stations, which may include stations that also operate on local channels. Local-channel stations are the backbone of radio in small and medium-size towns. Many operate with a maximum power of 250 watts at all times, and their programming runs the gamut from automated country-western to want-ad radio.

ALLOCATING FM

The allocation of FM frequencies is similar to that of AM. However, the maximum range of an FM station, regardless of its power, is usually to the horizon or to a distance of about seventy miles. Generally, the lower end of the FM band—between 88.1 and 91.9 mHz—is allocated to noncommercial broadcasters.[18] The remaining portion of the band is allocated to commercially operated FM stations. Commercial FM stations also fall into station classes. As a rule of thumb, Class C FM stations serve the widest area and have the highest power, a maximum of 100,000 watts. Class B and Class B–C FM stations serve smaller communities. Noncommercial FM stations fall into the three classes assigned to commercial

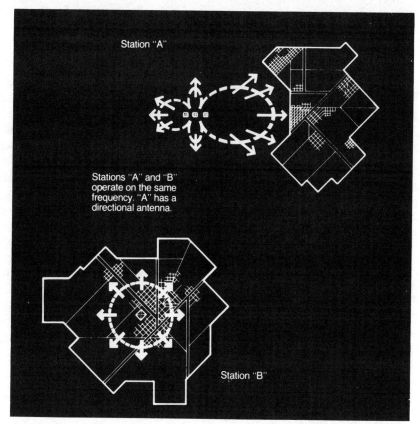

Station "A"

Stations "A" and "B" operate on the same frequency. "A" has a directional antenna.

Station "B"

FIGURE 6–9 Directional contours permit stations operating on the same frequency to avoid interfering with each other. (*FCC Broadcast Operators Handbook*)

FM stations but have an additional Class D category, consisting of noncommercial stations not exceeding 10 watts.

DIRECTIONAL AND NONDIRECTIONAL STATIONS

The importance of any station's frequency allocation is that it enables the station to serve a given population base without interference from other stations. The FCC is careful to require special antenna systems that prevent interference wherever possible. Although the problem is not yet critical in the FM band, spectrum space is at a premium. To avoid interfering with other stations, many AM stations operate as either directional or daytimer stations or as a combination of both. Daytimer stations are authorized to operate only between sunrise and sunset, local time. If they were allowed to operate past the sunset hour, their signals would travel great distances because of the reflective qualities of the ionosphere.

Directional-antenna systems are also designed to protect against interference. The next time you are out for a drive, scan the horizon for a cluster of antenna towers. That cluster has a purpose. The strategic location of the towers within the cluster permits the signal from one primary tower to be radiated among the other towers and create a specially shaped broadcast-coverage contour that does not interfere with the other stations' contours (Figure 6–9). Broadcast-coverage contours come in all shapes and sizes, all designated by the FCC as a means of maintaining relatively interference-free airwaves.

TELEPHONE COMMUNICATION

Although this chapter is concerned primarily with the use of the electromagnetic spectrum for radio and television transmission, the same concepts we have been discussing apply to the telephone. For example, telephone conversations can be examined in terms of their frequencies in much the same way we have been examining radio and television signals.

To reproduce the human voice in a telephone conversation a range of about 300 to 3000 Hz is necessary. Consequently, wired telephone communication takes place at certain frequencies, much like unwired radio communication. Many different telephone conversations can take place at the same time. When telephone conversations are sent over the air they are simply separated and each switched to its own space on the spectrum, much like airplanes "stacked" over an airport. Each plane occupies an available air space. Each telephone conversation occupies an available space within the larger space assigned to the telephone company.

DATA

With the increased use of computers and communication between computers there is an increasing demand for space on the electromagnetic spectrum in which to transmit data. Data communications require different standards than a typical radio station because they cannot tolerate interference and they need a considerable amount of

spectrum space. Our AM radio receiver may experience some static from a nearby electrical generator or a thunderstorm, but such interference would play havoc with sensitive computer data. As a result, computer data is transmitted at higher frequencies where line-of-sight transmission takes place, both because of the low noise ratios that exist there and because of the available spectrum space. Much data transmission occurs at frequencies from 1 to 10 gigahertz (GHz). (One GHz equals one billion cycles per second.) Frequencies between 1 and 10 GHz are referred to as *microwave frequencies,* the prefix *micro* indicating that the waves are very short. Long-distance telephone- and television-transmission relay takes place at microwave frequencies, as does satellite communication.

TELETEXT

Teletext—one-way transmission of textual information such as the electronic transmission of magazine copy—takes place where a certain amount of noise can be tolerated by the system but less spectrum space is available. Teletext operates in the UHF and VHF area of the spectrum and can be transmitted on cable. The data transmitted is in the textual form of a television video signal and does not require the standards that data transmission demands.

Teletext is frequently transmitted over the unused portion of the television signal, the *vertical blanking interval.* About one hundred frames, or full television screens, of textual information can be transmitted in this manner. When a station's assigned frequency is dedicated totally to teletext, as many as one thousand frames can be transmitted.

ANALOG VERSUS DIGITAL TRANSMISSION

Two types of transmission can exist in both wired and over-the-air communication systems: analog and digital. Think of analog transmission as an analogy, something like something else. For example, the voice of a radio announcer is modulated in a certain way, transmitted over the air, and received on a radio receiver. The transmission is *continuous* over a given frequency range, and unless the receiver or transmitter was turned off, the sound at the receiver is the same as the sound that was transmitted. A typical telephone conversation may consist of voice vibrations that are turned into analogous electrical vibrations. What a television camera sees is transformed into an analog signal, which creates in the television receiver a picture similar to what the television camera witnessed.

With digital transmission, however, the signal is not continuous; it is *broken up* into numbers. The signal consists of a series of on/off pulses transmitted in the same way that information flows in a computer circuit. The pulses are *bits* of information in a binary-number code. For all practical purposes digital transmission is noise-free. In current usage, the terms *digital* and *computer* are the same.

With the increased use of computers, digital transmission systems are gaining more and more importance. Since computer data are digital, analog systems that transmit them must convert them first to analog, then back to digital.[19] A *modem* serves this function by connecting a telephone with a computer. Overall, this is an inefficient way to move information. Yet because world telephone systems are primarily analog and considerable money has been spent on analog equipment, in many areas it is the only way to send information.

INTERNATIONAL SPECTRUM MANAGEMENT

The need for international agreements on sharing the available space on the electromagnetic spectrum is not new. When Marconi set up shop on Newfoundland's coast for a transatlantic broadcast, the Anglo-American Telegraph Company of Newfoundland promptly told him if he did not "remove his apparatus forthwith," he would face an injunction. Such rigidity has been softened over time by numerous agreements between nations not only on experiments but on allocation of frequencies.

The International Telecommunication Union

Some of these agreements are coordinated by the International Telecommunication Union (ITU), a United Nations organization responsible for worldwide coordination of frequency use.[20] We'll learn more about the ITU in Chapter 17.

The North American Regional Broadcasting Agreement

The United States entered into the North American Regional Broadcasting Agreement (NARBA) in 1937 at the Inter-American Radio Convention in Havana, Cuba. Although the NARBA contemplated working relationships for such broadcasting policies as standards for engineering practices, these relationships exist only between the United States and Canada.[21]

SUMMARY

Radio waves can be thought of as a point on the electromagnetic spectrum, a yardstick of electromagnetic energy that includes such forces as microwaves, light waves, and X rays. Radio waves travel at the speed of light at a frequency dependent on the length of each wave. They vary in amplitude and frequency. Variations in amplitude are used to modulate radio waves in the AM broadcast band, and variations in frequency are used to modulate radio waves in the FM broadcast band.

Because of the greater width allocated to FM stations, both stereo, (dual-channel) and quadraphonic (four-channel) broadcasting are becoming popular. In an effort to retain a competitive edge, proponents of AM are developing AM stereo.

Because of the increased demand for data communication, attention is being focused on the differences between analog and digital transmission systems. Analog transmission is a continuous process over a given range of frequencies, as illustrated by a radio or television signal or telephone communication. In digital transmission the signal is broken up into bits of information in the form of on-off pulses according to a binary-number code. Digital is more efficient, satisfactory, and economical than analog, especially where data are concerned.

In cooperation with other agencies of government and the International Telecommunication Union, the FCC participates in an international effort to avoid interference when assigning frequencies on the electromagnetic spectrum.

OPPORTUNITIES
FOR FURTHER LEARNING

AGNEW, C. E., *Alternative Licensing Arrangements and Spectrum Economics: The Case of Multipoint Distribution Service.* Stanford, Calif.: Stanford University, 1981.

BARTLETT, G., ed., *National Association of Broadcasters Engineering Handbook* (6th ed.). Washington, D.C.: National Association of Broadcasters, 1975.

BECK, A. H. W., *Words and Waves: An Introduction to Electrical Communication.* New York: McGraw-Hill, 1967.

CUNNINGHAM, J. E., *The Complete Broadcast Antenna Handbook: Design, Installation, Operation and Maintenance.* Blue Ridge Summit, Pa.: TAB Books, 1977.

ENNES, H. E., *AM–FM Broadcasting: Equipment, Operations, and Maintenance.* Indianapolis: Howard W. Sams, 1974.

———, *Television Broadcasting: Equipment, Systems, and Operating Fundamentals* (2nd ed.). Indianapolis: Howard W. Sams, 1979.

———, *Television Broadcasting: Systems Maintenance* (2nd ed.). Indianapolis: Howard W. Sams, 1978.

JONES, R. A., *Directional Antenna Handbook.* Overland Park, Kans.: Intertec, 1978.

KITTROSS, J. M., *Television Frequency Allocation Policy in the United States.* New York: Arno Press, 1979.

LAYTON, J., *Directional Broadcast Antennas: A Guide to Adjustment, Measurement, and Testing.* Blue Ridge Summit, Pa.: TAB Books, 1974.

LEVIN, H. J., *The Invisible Resource: Use and Regulation of the Radio Spectrum.* Baltimore: Johns Hopkins, 1971.

OVERMAN, M., *Understanding Sound, Video and Film Recording.* Blue Ridge Summit, Pa.: TAB Books, 1977.

PIERCE, J., *Electrons and Waves: An Introduction to the Science of Electronics and Communication.* New York: Doubleday, 1964.

Reference Data for Radio Engineers (6th ed.). Indianapolis: Howard W. Sams, 1975.

ROBERTS, R. S., *Dictionary of Audio, Radio, and Video.* London: Butterworth, 1981.

SMITH, C. E., ed., *Design and Operation of Directional Antennas.* Cleveland: Smith Electronics, 1969.

TREMAINE, H. M., *Audio Cyclopedia* (2nd ed.). Indianapolis: Howard W. Sams, 1969.

7

MICROWAVE
AND SATELLITE
TECHNOLOGY

The atmosphere and standard over-the-air broadcasting are both necessary in broadcasting to the public. Two other important parts of the worldwide system of broadcasting are (1) applications of microwave technology and (2) satellites.

MICROWAVES

In addition to standard AM, FM, and TV frequencies much higher frequencies of the electromagnetic spectrum—in the thousands-of-megahertz range—are used. It is in this area that *microwave* transmission is found. We have learned that the higher the frequency, the farther the electromagnetic waves will travel in a direct line-of-sight path between transmitter and receiver. Thus,

microwaves always travel by line-of-sight transmission.

Microwaves also allow many more channels of communication to operate because of their shorter wavelength. Because the waves are shorter, many more will fit into the same space on the electromagnetic spectrum. Many thousands of channels are possible. When we realize that an AM radio station is allocated a width of only 10 kHz, it is easy to see how much more information can be transmitted at higher frequencies. We need microwaves in order to view our evening television programs or to relay satellite pictures across oceans. However, the current microwave technology has barely scratched the potential of this multifaceted carrier of information, much of it affecting the broadcasting industry.

Microwave-Relay Systems

A network television program may travel thousands of miles before it reaches your local television station. The path it follows may very well use microwave-relay systems. Using high-frequency line-of-sight transmission, these systems can carry crystal-clear signals over long distances through a series of relay antennas approximately thirty miles apart. These dishlike antennas dot almost every kind of landscape, from the roofs of skyscrapers to the peaks of snowcapped mountains. The advantage of microwave-relay systems is their lower cost and increased efficiency of transmission compared with traditional land-line systems.

Consider, for example, a television station in the rugged Colorado mountains that receives its network signal from Denver. To string a cable over the Rocky Mountains would be far too costly. Instead, microwave towers on mountain tops (Figure 7-1), all within sight of each other, become the path over which the signal travels.

But mountain country is not the microwaves' only domain. Because flat areas are free from natural obstructions, microwave

FIGURE 7-1 Microwave antennas, such as these near Boulder, Colorado, provide long-distance communication without wires. Microwave systems are especially efficient in areas which are too remote to economically construct wired systems. (AT&T)

towers are also scattered over the plains of the farm belt and the deserts of the Southwest for an efficient transmission system.

Keep in mind that the program you receive in your home does not arrive directly by microwave. The local television station receives the signal by microwave and then retransmits it to your home receiver at a frequency regularly assigned to television transmission. You should also be aware that the television station probably does not own the microwave system but rather rents its frequency, just as it would rent a line from the telephone company. Many private companies, including major telephone companies, own microwave systems.

Satellite-Relay Systems

Ground-based microwave systems are not the only route for carrying television programming. Correspondents' reports are first fed by satellite to the network's headquarters, videotaped, and then played back as inserts in the evening news (Figure 7–2). Because space is a vacuum, microwaves travel over long distances unimpeded by the earth's heavy atmosphere near ground level.

This permits a transmitting station in London, for example, to transmit a television picture by microwave to a satellite thousands of miles in space, which relays it back to an earth-receiving station in the United States. Satellites are also used to bring television signals to many outlying regions in which even microwave links would be too costly. We shall learn more about satellites later in this chapter.

Cable and Pay (Subscription) TV

Although you may receive television programs through your local community antenna television system, often called CATV or *cable,* the original signal probably reached the local cable company through a microwave-relay link. A cable company often leases a microwave channel, receives the direct-broadcast signal from a television station, then restransmits by microwave to a cable system in a community hundreds of miles from that station. In fact, this use of microwave is one reason cable systems have come under FCC jurisdiction.

A newer use of microwave in certain metropolitan areas is to send special pro-

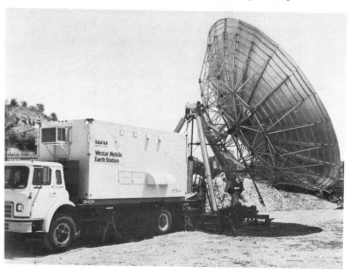

FIGURE 7–2 Satellite communication can be utilized wherever an earth station exists. Portable earth stations provide the communication links for a wide range of communication needs, ranging from data communication to transmitting pictures for a television news program. The antenna shown here connects to the Western Union Westar domestic satellite network. (Western Union)

gramming to pay-television subscribers. An example of this is the Chicago-based pay-TV channel.[1] From a studio control center a signal is sent by microwave to a receiving dish antenna on top of a Chicago skyscraper. From there it is restransmitted by microwave to other microwave-receiving antennas on top of high-rise apartment complexes and hotels. Hotel and apartment television sets are then connected by cable directly to the microwave-receiving antenna on top of the building. These systems can not only receive but also initiate live programming from a studio in the way a local television station can. The studio programs are then sent over the system to subscribers. Also called subscription television, the system is gaining popularity as an alternative to over-the-air broadcasting.

Electronic News Gathering

The application of microwave to electronic news gathering has given television the flexibility that only radio once enjoyed. A mobile van and portable camera can provide live programming from a community arts fair or live aerial scenes of a football stadium, and the unrehearsed moments of a newly elected politician's acceptance speech can give television news a dynamic dimension. New developments in microwave ENG systems now allow us to bounce the microwave beam off the side of a building to a relay antenna, permitting a live television camera to peer into almost every nook and cranny of the largest metropolitan areas.

Educational and Industrial Television

In Salt Lake City, Utah, a group of students watch an instructional television program sent from a classroom forty miles away at Brigham Young University in Provo.[2] The audio and video transmission between the two schools is made possible by a microwave link. Students in Salt Lake City can even answer the professor in Provo by microwave. In Indiana, all of the state-supported universities are connected by a microwave link and thus can exchange their instructional television programs.[3]

Businesses using television use similar microwave hookups. A plant with two locations in the same city can use microwave for an intracorporate television link. For example, special sales-training seminars can be broadcast from the main corporate television studio to a special seminar room on the other side of town. Or leasing the facilities of a national microwave system, a company can distribute a special videotaped management-training program to plants throughout the nation. Businesses and television stations alike can also use microwaves to transfer computer data and thereby connect studios hundreds and even thousands of miles apart.

When microwave systems were first developed, they opened up whole new frontiers for communication. Their wide channel width permitted users to send much more information than was possible with lower-frequency systems. Microwave systems were also relatively free from interference. In many ways they were superior to cable systems, especially for long-distance communication.

The existing, well-developed microwave systems will undoubtedly remain in service. Yet two words stand squarely in the way of microwave: *fiber optics*. These microscopic glasslike fibers through which light passes use laser beams to carry information equivalent to what can be transmitted on thousands of cable channels. In fact, fiber optics now permit telephone systems to compete with cable companies and microwave systems as major carriers of information.

The future interrelation of fiber-optics technology and our need and desire for its potential will determine the future of world-wide broadcasting systems. It will also determine how much regulatory control we exercise over its use and whether such multi-billion-dollar corporations as AT&T will be the "gatekeepers" of the future.

SATELLITES: THE TELSTAR EXPERIMENTS

The wedding between satellites and broadcasting took place on a warm New England evening in Andover, Maine. From this outpost the first television pictures were relayed by satellite across the Atlantic to Europe on July 10, 1962. The pictures were of Vice-President Lyndon B. Johnson and several AT&T officials gathered in the Carnegie Institute Auditorium in Washington, D.C. The event took up many columns in major newspapers in the United States and Europe as well as news bulletins on the television networks.

The hero of the evening was a 170-pound payload named Telstar, which had been launched into space in a cooperative effort by the National Aeronautics and Space Administration (NASA) and AT&T.[4] This beach-ball-sized satellite received television signals from earth-based antennas, amplified them ten million times, and retransmitted them to European receiving stations. Telstar (Figure 7–3) was powered by solar energy. On any given pass over the United States or one of the European receiving stations, the satellite was in viewing range for only about forty-five minutes. The highest point in Telstar's orbit, its apogee, was 3,502 miles from earth. The closet point to earth during its orbit, the perigee, was 593 miles away. Directing the project for AT&T was forty-four-year-old Eugene Frank O'Neill, a Columbia University engineering graduate.

FIGURE 7–3 Telstar was launched in 1962 and ushered in the era of live television, via satellite. Since it was not a synchronous-orbit satellite and therefore did not remain stationary above the earth's surface, it could only be used for a limited time during each orbit. (AT&T)

In return, the United States received signals from Europe the following evening. From France came a seven-minute taped program with an appearance by Jacques M. Marette, the French minister of Postal Services and Telecommunications, and musical entertainment by French performers. The British signal followed shortly thereafter, consisting of a test pattern and a live broadcast by Britain's Deputy Chief Engineer, Captain Charles Booth.

THE POLITICS OF TELSTAR

It is not surprising that the breakthrough of transoceanic broadcasting brought with it a series of political issues, some based on age-old rivalries, others on contemporary concerns. The most intense rivalries were between England and France, long-time economic and political sparring partners. Telstar merely set the scene for their combat. On the night of the first transoceanic broadcast, British pride was hurt when the British receiving station was not able to monitor clear audio and video signals from the United States. The French, meanwhile, using a station that was not supposed to be ready for tests, monitored signals so clear it was as though they came "from about twenty-five miles away." The British did achieve a victory that night when they relayed a live television program to the United States in contrast with France's taped program.

In the United States, the press was quick to report that AT&T had paid NASA to launch Telstar. This agreement also called for the free availability of any inventions arising from the Telstar project to any company that wanted them. President John F. Kennedy formally called for a national corporation to oversee all satellite-communica-tion developments in the United States. The Kennedy administration also emphasized the need for commercial broadcasters to participate in examining the potential of satellite communication. That bit of political rhetoric was meant to pull down the fence that FCC commissioner Newton Minow had put up a year earlier between the administration and commercial broadcasters with his famous "vast wasteland" speech before the National Association of Broadcasters convention.

ECONOMIC AND SOCIAL IMPLICATIONS OF TELSTAR

Telstar created much more than international television communication. The morning after Telstar's broadcast, AT&T became the most active stock on the New York Stock Exchange with 105,800 shares traded. Having opened at $109\frac{7}{8}$, it closed at $113\frac{1}{4}$, the day's high and a gain of $3\frac{1}{2}$ points. Less than a month later David Sarnoff, chairman of the board of RCA, proposed that a single company deal with international communication matters.[5] Western Union quickly supported Sarnoff's suggestion, saying it had proposed a similar concept before.[6] Having obtained the Kennedy administration's support, the concept was realized with the passage of the Communications Satellite Act of 1962 and the formation of the Communications Satellite Corporation (COMSAT).

The prospect of domestic television programming crossing national boundaries opened up a new arena for discussion and heated debate. The vast wasteland was one thing at home but something entirely different when it reached France and England. The initial Telstar broadcast itself caused some concern. The program was produced by AT&T, which provoked CBS to break away from the initial network-pool coverage and not carry the remarks of AT&T board chairman Frederick R. Kappel. Jack Gould, television critic of the *New York Times,* said of the event, "The sight of Government dignitaries serving as a passive gallery for private corporation executives was not very good staging, particularly for consumption in foreign countries." Gould went on to predict, "The crucial decision that will determine the lasting value of international television—a willingness of countries and broadcasters to clear the necessary time on their own screens to see and hear other peoples of the world—cannot be made in laboratories in the sky but in offices on the ground."[7]

PROGRAMMING BEYOND TELSTAR

The early 1960s brought many international satellite experiments. Perhaps the most vivid occurred eighteen months after the first Telstar broadcast when the funeral procession of President Kennedy in Washington, D.C., was seen in the halls of the Kremlin. By 1965 the Ecumenical conference in Rome was being seen on both sides of the Atlantic.[8] European viewers saw and heard Washington dignitaries react to the unveiling of the Mona Lisa in the National Gallery of Art. Special programming from the 1964 Olympic Games in Tokyo traveled far beyond Japan.

STOPPED IN SPACE: THE SYNCHRONOUS–ORBIT SATELLITES

A little more than a year after the launching of Telstar there was another breakthrough in satellite technology. At Lakehurst, New Jersey, in 1963 a technical crew waited for a satellite called Syncom II to "lock" into position for a transmission that would be heard halfway around the world on a ship stationed at Lagos, Nigeria. Out of a static-bearing receiver aboard the U.S. Navy's *Kingsport* were clearly heard the words "*Kingsport,* this is Lakehurst. *Kingsport,* this is Lakehurst. How do you hear me?" The words came from space, relayed back to earth from Syncom II, no ordinary satellite. This time the technical crew aboard the *Kingsport* did not have to adjust their receiving equipment just when the satellite passed within viewing range, because Syncom II was technically "stopped in space," the first successful synchronous-orbit satellite. Its baby sister, Syncom I, had failed six months earlier. So for Hughes Aircraft Company engineers Harold A. Rosen, Donald D. Williams, and Thomas Hudspeth, the team chiefly responsible for the satellite's development, Syncom II's success was especially welcome.[9] This is how it worked.

Before Syncom II, scientists could utilize the communication capabilities of a satellite only when it passed over a given region of the earth. This meant the satellite could be used for only about forty-five minutes at a time. However, scientists felt that if they could (1) position a satellite over the equator and (2) place it at a height (22,300 miles) at which it would travel at a speed similar to the earth's rotation, it would appear stationary above the earth. Syncom II's launchers achieved the desired position by placing the satellite in *synchronous* orbit (also called *geostationary* orbit) over the equator. Since Syncom II, major communication-satellite systems have used the synchronous-orbit positions to create so-called microwave towers in space, thereby permitting worldwide transmission of television signals, computer data, and telephone service.

COMSAT

By now the world was taking an active interest in satellite development. As we have seen, Congress enacted the quasi-governmental COMSAT in 1962. COMSAT became the early planner of satellite systems on an international scale when it evolved as the manager of the International Satellite Consortium, a cooperative effort to govern and develop world satellite systems. The consortium was established under two international agreements originally signed by fourteen countries and eventually ratified by fifty-four. In 1964 it became the International Telecommunications Satellite Organization (INTELSAT), having a membership of more than eighty nations and presided over by a secretary-general. Today its members are responsible for about 95 percent of the world's communication traffic.

INTELSAT

On April 6, 1965, Early Bird became the first of a long series of INTELSAT spacecraft to be launched. While orbiting the earth they have provided a worldwide system of communication, not only for broadcasting but also for computer data, telephone communication, two-way radio communication, weather monitoring, and other uses (Figure 7-4).

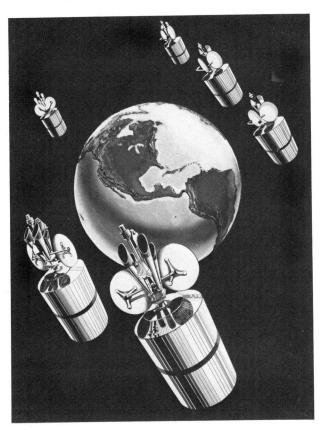

FIGURE 7-4 Synchronous orbit INTELSAT satellites form a ring around the earth, providing communication links from any location. Early Bird, launched in 1965, was the first INTELSAT satellite. The latest satellite in the series, the INTELSAT V-A, was launched in 1984 and has a capacity for 15,000 voice and two video circuits. (Courtesy, Hughes Aircraft Company)

Systems

The satellites that led up to the INTELSAT V system of the 1980s included the INTELSAT II series, launched in 1967 and positioned over the Atlantic and Pacific oceans. This series provided communication to two-thirds of the earth's surface. INTELSAT III satellites became operational between 1968 and 1970 and were positioned over the Atlantic and Indian oceans. With global communication now possible, the next step was to improve and increase the capabilities of satellite communication.

This step was realized with the four INTELSAT IV satellites, launched between 1971 and 1973. These were followed by the six INTELSAT IV-A satellites, which utilized an improved technology called beam separation. Beam separation allowed the same frequency to be used for transmitting a signal both to and from the satellite—a more efficient use of the frequency. Moreover, improved antenna systems permitted a more highly directed beam to an earth station, thereby improving the power efficiency of the system.

INTELSAT V is the most sophisticated satellite-communication system yet developed, one that will meet the communication needs of much of the world during the 1980s. It consists of seven satellites developed by AeroNutronic Ford. These satellites are twenty-two feet high and have a fifty-foot wing span when their solar panels are deployed. They consist of three primary modules: antenna, communications, and support subsystem. Since overcrowding is beginning to occur even at gigahertz frequencies—frequencies of billions of cycles per second—the INTELSAT V series has alternate-frequency capability and twice the circuit capacity of the INTELSAT IV-A series.

The INTELSAT V-A, launched in 1984, has an even larger capacity—15,000 voice circuits and 2 video circuits. The 1986 INTELSAT VI series will have 36,000 voice circuits and 2 video circuits.

To understand how INTELSAT is organized we will examine its membership, investment shares, and structure.[10]

Membership and Investment Shares

INTELSAT membership is open to any state that was a party to INTELSAT's Interim Agreements, and to any other state that is a member of the International Telecommunication Union (ITU). INTELSAT membership comprises over 100 countries.

To become a member of INTELSAT, a government accedes to the Agreement among Governments and it, or its designated public or private telecommunications entity, signs the companion Operating Agreement. These two agreements, known collectively as the Definitive Agreements, entered into force February 12, 1973, replacing the Interim Agreements, which established INTELSAT in August 1964.

Each signatory to the Operating Agreement has an investment share in INTELSAT equal to its percentage of the total use of the system, except when a signatory has requested a lesser share than its proportionate use and the difference between its use and the share requested has been assumed by other signatories. The required minimum share is 0.05 percent. The revenue of the system comes from utilization charges and is distributed to members after deduction of operating costs.

The investment share of each INTELSAT member is adjusted annually so that it approximates its proportionate use of the system.

Structure

The structure of INTELSAT consists of an Assembly of Parties, a Meeting of Signatories, a Board of Governors, and an Executive Organ.

The Assembly of Parties, comprising representatives of all states that are party to the Definitive Agreements, is required to meet every two years unless it decides otherwise. The assembly considers matters that are primarily of interest to its members as sovereign states. It also considers matters brought before it by other parties in the INTELSAT organization.

The Meeting of Signatories, composed of all signatories to the Operating Agreement, is required to convene at least once each calendar year. The meeting considers matters called to its attention by other bodies of INTELSAT as well as matters relating to financial, technical, and operational aspects of the system.

Representation on the Board of Governors is available automatically to any signatory to the Operation Agreement, or to any group of signatories. Representatives receive an investment share equal to the minimum established annually by the Meeting of Signatories. In addition, any five or more signatories from the same ITU region, regardless of investment shares, may combine to attain board representation. No more than two such groups, however, may represent any single region, and no more than five such groups may achieve representation.

Basically, the Board of Governors is responsible for all decisions concerning the design, development, construction, establishment, operation, and maintenance of the INTELSAT system's space segment.

The Executive Organ is headed by a Director General, who is responsible to the Board of Governors for the day-to-day management of INTELSAT. All operational tasks, except certain specialized tasks and technical functions, are performed by the Executive Organ.

Specialized tasks and technical functions, including fabrication of certain equipment, are carried out by COMSAT under contract with INTELSAT.

APPLICATION-TECHNOLOGY SATELLITES

COMSAT and INTELSAT were not the only organizations trying to develop satellite communication. NASA for its part developed the Application Technology Satellite (ATS) program. It launched six satellites in all, of which the sixth sent satellite signals to small earth stations. This was the key to important applications of satellite technology, from log-cabin schools in the mountains of Idaho to mud huts across the world in India.

In the United States, such towns as Gila Bend, Three Forks, Battle Mountain, Wagon Mound, Sundance, and Arapahoe all participated in the ATS experiments. The local schoolyards had a new visitor in the form of a microwave dish and its strange antenna of corkscrew wires around a long metal tube. With the help of their visitor, students could sit in a classroom in West Yellowstone and talk via satellite to a classroom in Denver. Where no land-line or microwave system had been developed, the ATS-6 satellite (Figure 7–5) would beam signals simultaneously across half a continent.

The program generated a cooperative, although somewhat reluctant, effort among state governments. For example, issues affecting the local autonomy of schools usually formed a political thicket. Nevertheless, the Federation of Rocky Mountain States, composed of Arizona, Colorado, Idaho, Montana, New Mexico, Utah, and Wyoming, joined together to bring two-way educa-

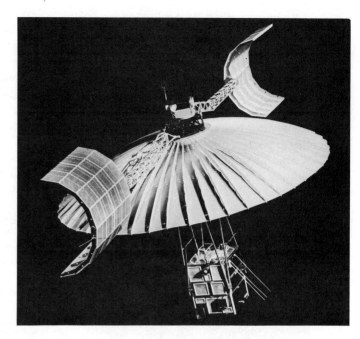

FIGURE 7–5 Application Technology Satellites offered in-school programming to schools in the Rocky Mountain and Middle Atlantic states. The satellite was then shifted and became part of educational demonstrations in India. (NASA)

tional television to the outlying communities in the region. In some areas, the satellite-receiving systems were hooked directly into the local cable systems or microwave translator systems, permitting the signals to be received at home. The ATS project provided similar educational-television programming for the eastern United States, especially Appalachia.

After the American experiments, earth-controlled rockets on the satellite shifted the ATS-6 from the Galapagos Islands to a new orbit over Kenya in Africa. From that position in 1976 the satellite was used for educational-television experiments in India, some of whose citizens had never even seen television or motion pictures. Programs on modern agriculture, health, and family planning were part of the fare. After the Indian experiments, the satellite traveled back into the Western Hemisphere, stopping along the way for demonstrations sponsored by the United States Agency for International Development (USAID).

WESTERN UNION SATELLITE SYSTEMS

Western Union entered the domestic satellite business with the launching of the first two satellites in its Westar series.

System Development

These two satellites were positioned in space in 1974 and a third satellite was launched in 1979. Placed in geostationary orbit over the equator and located on approximate lines with San Antonio, Texas; San Francisco; and Baton Rouge, Louisiana, the three satellites each had a capacity of twelve transponders, each transponder being capable of a send and receive channel.[12] The satellites were controlled from the Glenwood, New Jersey, earth station. Glenwood performed various tracking functions as well as periodic command adjustments that kept the satellites in a constant position relative to earth.

Because satellites have a limited life span due to component deterioration and because of the earth's gravitational pull, the first two Westars were scheduled to stop functioning and be replaced by two twenty-four-transponder satellites, Westar IV and V, in 1984 (Figure 7–6). A sixth Westar, also with a twenty-four-transponder capacity, is scheduled to become operational in the mid 1980s. Westar VI will provide continuous communication coverage for the continental United States as well as for Alaska and Hawaii.

Western Union is planning to supplement the current network with an Advanced Westar system in the late 1980s.[13] Advanced Westar is designed for commonly used satellite frequencies as well as K-band frequencies—those located between 10.9 and 36 GHz. K-band satellite systems can operate with smaller, lower-cost-per-channel equipment. Further research on these frequencies is necessary, however, before their full potential can be realized. They suffer from the disadvantage of interference from rain

FIGURE 7–6 Western Union's Westar series is one of the United States' domestic satellite systems. The latest in the Westar series, Westar VI, is scheduled to be operational in the mid 1980s and will provide continuous communication links for the continental United States, Alaska, and Hawaii. (Western Union)

and other atmospheric conditions.[14] When communication traffic can be rerouted and when transmission speed is not critical, the K-band system does have cost advantages.

Tracking Data Relay Satellite System

Western Union also operates a Tracking Data Relay Satellite System (TDRSS), which provides support services for the United States manned space missions, of which the space shuttle is a part (Figure 7–7). The TDRSS satellites supplement NASA's ground-tracking system, which has a limited coverage of about 15 percent for low-orbital vehicles. Depending on the altitude of the orbiting spacecraft, the Western Union system provides 85- to 100-percent coverage. The TDRSS satellites also serve as communication relays between the space vehicle and a White Sands, New Mexico, ground station, which receives data from other ground stations such as the Johnson Space Center in Houston and the Goddard Space Flight Center in Greenbelt, Maryland.

FIGURE 7–7 The Western Union Tracking Data Relay Satellite has been especially useful as a communication support system for the space shuttle. The satellite supplements NASA's ground-based tracking system. (Western Union and the TRW Defense and Space Systems Group)

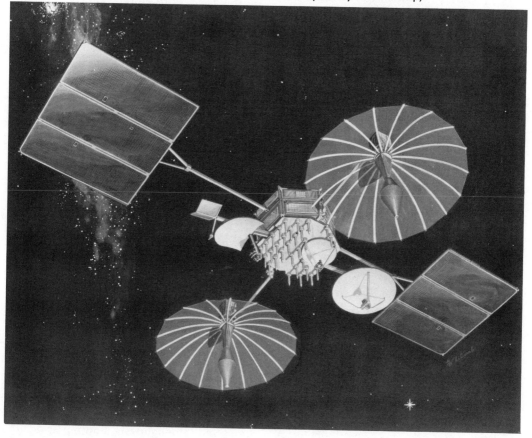

Earth Stations

Along with the satellites, the Westar system includes a network of earth stations and a ground-based microwave network. Major earth stations are located near New York, Chicago, Atlanta, Dallas, Los Angeles, San Francisco, and Seattle, providing coverage to twenty-six satellite-access cities.[15] Five smaller earth stations provide specialized data services to the United States government. An additional earth station is used exclusively for video service. In each of the seven major earth-station cities, a separate Television Operation Center (TOC) controls audio and video services for broadcasters.

Twenty percent of the Westar satellite system is owned by American Satellite Corporation, a jointly owned subsidiary of Fairchild Industries and Continental Telephone Corporation. Fairchild and Continental Telephone hold a twenty-five-percent interest in the Space Communications Company, the developer of the TDRSS system.

System Applications

Users of the Westar system are many and varied. Some of the more familiar have been the Corporation for Public Broadcasting, which distributes programming from National Public Radio and the Public Broadcasting Service; commercial networks such as ABC, NBC, and CBS; independent stations and syndicators; Associated Press; and the Westinghouse Broadcasting Company. Complete editions of the *Wall Street Journal* are transmitted via a facsimile process. Text and pictures for the *U.S. News & World Report* are transmitted over Westar by means of data-stream half-tone transmission techniques. For both publications the facsimile pages are sent from a central location to regional printing and distribution centers.

Private networks may be used for teleconferencing—video conferences over long distances—through a lease arrangement with Western Union. Harris Corporation, Martin Marietta, and Digital Communications Corporation are some of the users. VideoNet, Robert Wold Company, Hughes, and the Public Service Satellite Consortium lease frequencies and then provide teleconferencing for other users. Texas Instruments has used Westar to broadcast its annual stockholders' meeting from its Dallas headquarters to other company sites equipped with small receiving antennas. The Army Health Services Command uses the system for medical education. Programming is sent from Brooke Army Medical Center at Fort Sam Houston, Texas, to doctors at army hospitals at Fort Hood, Texas; Fort Sill, Oklahoma; and Fort Polk, Louisiana.

RCA SATCOMS

A domestic satellite system begun in December 1973, is operated by RCA. RCA formed a wholly owned subsidiary company, RCA American Communications (RCA Americom), to operate its domestic satellite system. The company became part of the RCA Communications group. A network of earth stations complements the RCA system. The RCA Satcom satellites are equipped with antennas that face the sun whenever it is in view, which makes the satellites more powerful than previous ones. When the sun is not in sight, the satellites are powered by nickel-cadmium batteries. In addition to this antenna design, Satcom employs three advances in satellite technology: (1) a high-capacity antenna that can carry up to twenty-four color television channels simultaneously; (2) the use of graphite fiber epoxy composition materials, which insure strength yet provide less weight in construction; and (3) a lightweight amplifier.

GENERAL TELEPHONE AND ELECTRONICS

General Telephone and Electronics (GTE) announced the development of a domestic satellite system in 1981. Initially the system will consist of three satellites, each having a sixteen-channel capacity, and will provide communication for all fifty states. The first launch is set for 1984.

COMSTAR

AT&T is planning a domestic satellite system, to become operational at the end of the 1980s. Currently it leases a system in cooperation with COMSAT. In 1976 COMSAT launched the first two of four satellites dedicated to AT&T. Each of the four is designed for a life span of seven years, but the fourth satellite, launched in 1981, accepted some of the traffic load of the two earliest satellites, thus saving their batteries and extending their life. COMSAT's investment in the COMSTAR program is $202 million. AT&T pays COMSAT a monthly fee for the use of the satellites.

MARISAT

The research vessel off the coast of Ocracoke Island (see Chapter 1) communicates with COMSAT's Marisat satellite. The satellite makes data, telex, and voice communications available with clear, interference-free service. Marisat has been especially helpful to the oil industry, which must maintain distant communication links among vessels, offshore oil rigs, and shore installations. For example, the captain of a vessel can keep in constant contact with the owner, and seismic-survey vessels can transmit data immediately to shore stations for analysis.

The primary user of the Marisat system has been the U.S. Navy, which, under contract with COMSAT, uses special ship-to-satellite and satellite-to-ship UHF communications.

SATNET

SATNET is an experimental system employed by COMSAT.[16] It typifies the constant search by users of satellite and other types of communication for the most efficient uses of satellite hardware and the electromagnetic spectrum.

Theory Behind SATNET

Supported by funds from the Defense Advanced Research Projects Agency, a Department of Defense agency, SATNET research is aimed toward much more efficient use of satellite channels. Under normal circumstances several satellite channels are used to carry multiple services. The theory behind the research being conducted through SATNET is that multiple services can be carried on a single satellite-communication channel through a process called Time-Division Multiple Access (TDMA). The TDMA process, already in use, lumps together many different messages on one satellite channel by converting all information to digital format and then sending different bundles or packets of information, each only part of a message. The parts of the messages are put back together at the receiving end and transposed into their original format.[17] Different earth terminals working at the different data rates of 64 and 16 kilobits per second can be linked together in the same network.

SATNET Operations

SATNET research uses a channel of the INTELSAT IV-A Atlantic Primary Satellite, which is linked to the ground-based network by antennas at Etam, West Virginia; Goonhilly, United Kingdom; Tanum, Sweden; and Clarksburg, Maryland. Basic to SATNET is equipment that converts messages to a digital format, breaks down the digital messages into bundles or packets, and then schedules the packets into different slots so that they remain separate and can be reassembled at the receiving end of the communication.

Various research support comes from such participants in SATNET as the University College in London; the Royal Signals and Radar Establishment in Malvern, England; the Norwegian Defense Research Establishment in Kjeller, Norway; Bolt, Beranek and Newman in Cambridge, Massachusetts; the University of Southern California at Los Angeles; Linkabit Corporation in San Diego; and COMSAT.

OSCAR: AMATEUR-RADIO SATELLITES

Although the major corporations and government consortiums receive most of the attention given to satellite communication, amateur-radio operators ("hams") are using the Oscar satellites to conduct their own experiments. Information gained from their experiments is being used to improve satellite communication among broadcasters and other users.

FIGURE 7-8 Direct broadcast satellites provide direct-to-home television programming. The system requires the subscriber to have a home antenna which captures the satellite signals and feeds them to a standard television set. (FCC)

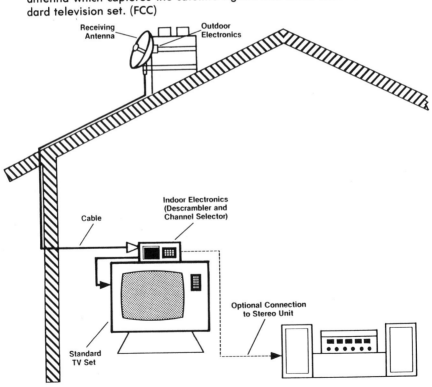

DIRECT–BROADCAST SATELLITES

Considerable attention has been given to the development of high-powered satellite systems designed primarily to beam signals directly to small home antennas. Canada produced a prototype of such a system in 1976—the CTS (Communications Technology Satellite). Japan and Germany followed. In the United States COMSAT, through its subsidiary the Satellite Television Corporation (STC), and numerous other firms have plans to begin a direct-broadcast satellite (DBS) system (Figure 7–8). In 1983 United Satellite Communications Inc. pushed ahead to offer DBS programming to counties of central Indiana. Plans included the expansion of the service to other states in the Northeast and Midwest. The United Satellite venture was backed by General Instrument and Prudential Insurance.

Pay-TV Service

STC has designed a DBS system that will offer pay TV without commercials directly to homes with small dish antennas.[18] If the system operates as planned, the service would be marketed on a competitive basis through different distributors. A small dish antenna would be affixed to a subscriber's rooftop and then connected by cable to the television set. A typical channel would feature general entertainment such as motion pictures, concerts, theater, and family entertainment. Another channel might carry children's programs, classic motion pictures, and public affairs. A third channel could carry sports, educational, and experimental programming. COMSAT believes that the service provides programming diversity at economical rates, offers new programming options, especially for rural areas, and promotes United States leadership in satellite technology.

High-Definition Service

Another DBS system, would offer high-definition television (HDTV) to consumers.[19] HDTV, which we will learn more about in Chapter 10, produces large-screen television without the usual grainy effect. The HDTV system would also connect with ground-based distribution systems such as cable television. The earliest HDTV systems were proposed by companies such as RCA, CBS, Western Union, the United States Satellite Broadcasting Company (Hubbard Broadcasting), the Direct Broadcast Satellite Corporation, the Graphic Scanning Company, Video Satellite Systems, and others.[20]

Master-Antenna Service

Still another DBS system would send signals to master antennas, which would then offer programming to hotels, motels, apartments, condominiums, and mobile-home parks. The system would provide programming for an installation charge and a monthly fee and would operate much like the subscriber-based systems just discussed.

SATELLITE BUSINESS NETWORKS

The increased use of computers, especially in business, accompanied by the increased costs of telephone and video communication, has prompted companies to use satellites for all types of business communication.

One of the first systems devoted to business use was the Satellite Business System, a cooperative project conceptualized in 1975 by COMSAT, IBM, and Aetna Life and Casualty. Becoming operational in the early 1980s, SBS is an all-digital network employing the TDMA process utilized in SATNET. Voice, data, and image communication are available to SBS users, with voice applications constituting the heaviest demand. Image transmission has special appeal, for document distribution in business has traditionally been slow and cumbersome. Charts, graphs, and other images must be sent through the mail, by overnight express, or through facsimile machines taking four to six minutes to send a single page. The SBS system of electronic document distribution can send seventy pages in one minute. In November 1982 an SBS satellite was launched from the *Columbia,* the first satellite to be put in orbit by space shuttle (Figure 7–9).

Despite some early optimism, however, SBS is approaching the mid 1980s with caution. It cost SBS six years and $600 million to plan and build the system, but the first year's (1981) revenues amounted to only $5 million.[21] The same year, it had to obtain a bank loan of $400 million. Early competitive strategies have turned to voice-only service, in competition with AT&T and other independent carriers. Highly touted high-speed data-communication services were being provided to only twenty-five companies by the early 1980s. If the system is to succeed it will need to generate significant income in a relatively short time. Competitors offering similar services are waiting in the wings, as evidenced by the proposed, but far from operational, Xerox system.

FIGURE 7–9 The Satellite Business Systems' satellite is ejected from the bay of the space shuttle, Columbia. The space shuttle's ability to launch payloads from space in addition to its reusable quality means that in the future, more economical launching of sensitive communication equipment will be possible. (NASA)

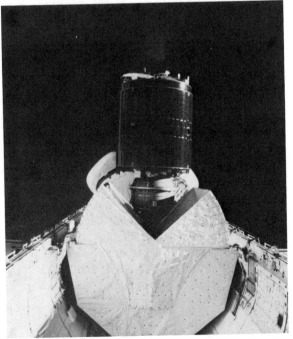

SUPERSTATIONS

With the advent of satellites some radio and television stations have expanded their listening and viewing areas by beaming their signals to satellite and then having the signals relayed to cable systems, which in turn send the signal to subscribers. Undoubtedly the most famous superstation, and the first to make the concept workable, is WTBS in Atlanta. Owned by Turner Broadcasting, WTBS (then WTCG) first beamed its signal to cable systems on December 16, 1976. Programming has tended to stress family-oriented fare complemented by movies and sports, including Atlanta Braves baseball and Atlanta Hawks basketball games. Original features are also presented. The station began with 24,000 households, and Turner Broadcasting predicts that it will reach over 80 million households by 1990. Turner also operates the satellite-fed Cable News Network (CNN) and the CNN Headline News.

Another superstation is the independent Chicago station WGN. Also oriented toward family programming, WGN carries original programming, its own news schedule and features, and syndicated features.

A radio superstation also operates out of Chicago: WFMT–FM stereo is a fine arts/classical station sent via satellite to cable systems. Programming includes the Boston Pops Orchestra, Boston Symphony Orchestra, Chicago Symphony Orchestra, Cleveland Orchestra, folk-music concerts, Houston Grand Opera, Library of Congress concerts, Lyric Opera of Chicago, New York City Opera, Milwaukee Symphony Orchestra, New York Philharmonic Orchestra, Philadelphia Orchestra, San Francisco Opera, and San Francisco Symphony Orchestra. Even without its cable audience, the station has managed to gain the respect of listeners and critics alike. The station's programming strategies include commissioning composers to create works for the station, forbidding commercial sponsors to use musical jingles, and limiting commercials to approximately four or five minutes per hour—much less than the normal eighteen minutes per hour found on many radio stations.

THE SPACE SHUTTLE

The space-shuttle missions of the early 1980s quickly showed the feasibility of using the shuttle as a satellite-launch vehicle. As we have seen, the first satellite to be launched from the shuttle was the Satellite Business Systems satellite in 1982. A Telesat Canada satellite was launched on the same mission.

In theory, the shuttle can be used not only for launching but also for repairing equipment in space. Plans for the shuttle involve a space-operations center (Figure 7–10) where

FIGURE 7–10 Future planning for the space shuttle involves in-space docking and repair facilities based in an unmanned space station. The space station concept is being developed by Douglas Astronautics under contract for NASA's Marshall Space Flight Center. (NASA)

the shuttle could dock and then assemble and repair space hardware, including satellites. The shuttle is capable of flying over one hundred missions, placing 65,000 pounds of equipment in space, and returning 32,000 pounds of payload to earth.

CULTURAL, POLITICAL, AND ECONOMIC ISSUES IN SATELLITE COMMUNICATION

At the heart of satellite communication are major issues of culture, politics, and economic development.

Intercultural Considerations

What will happen when world communication systems are developed to the point at which the dish antenna on the roof is as common as the television set in the living room or the radio in a car? American programs in foreign countries have become popular overnight, as have foreign programs broadcast in America. The evening news reports a president's visit to the Peoples' Republic of China, and major department stores immediately feature Chinese fashions. Stop and contemplate the cultural fusion of an evening of Russian lessons televised from Moscow, sports events from Germany and China, and a cooking demonstration from Egypt. What will happen when societies are bombarded with dozens of cross-cultural stimuli every day?

Communications attorney Leonard H. Marks asked similar questions in 1965:

> Will the man in the street in New Delhi be asked about the Hindu-Moslem problem so that the factory worker in Detroit will have a first-hand report? Will programs of this type be designed to encourage a common language and break down the barriers which currently exist for communications between peoples of different cultures? Is there any reason why we shouldn't feature international "town meetings of the air" with participants from Berlin, Rome, Cairo, or other distant points with their counterparts in Des Moines, Seattle and San Francisco?[22]

Such questions are at the heart of the direct-broadcast-satellite programming issue.

Political Implications

Direct-broadcast satellites are an example of technology advancing faster than legislation can deal with it. Today satellites provide a multitude of services, but the world does not have a governing body or regulatory structure to keep up with this rapidly changing technology. Back in 1960 Dallas Smythe, then head of the FCC's economics division, predicted that "the danger inherent in the development of space-satellite communications lies in the additional strain it will place upon international relations in the absence of international agreements on policy and organizations to control its use." Predicting more cold-war rivalry, he said, "The first power to begin extensive use of this new means of communication will initiate the deadly cycle. The second power will then try to outdo the first with a rival space-satellite communications system, and so on until international agreements are almost impossible to achieve."[23]

Problems are already developing, especially over the issue of what rights countries have in sending or receiving broadcasts across international boundaries. Mexico has banned certain American television programs it felt were too violent. Canada has taken economic steps to curtail American commercials. But these are only two countries. What happens when a Baptist church service in Alabama reaches a Buddhist monastery in Thailand? How can a dictatorship retain power with massive amounts of televised propaganda from a democracy? Conversely, can a democracy succeed in the wake of a dictator's propaganda? What happens when the FCC rules that certain films are too sexually explicit for American television yet every American living room has instant access to X-rated foreign television films?

Economic Implications

What will direct-satellite broadcasting do to the world economy? The local marketplace can literally become worldwide. A major department store having international branches can choose a popular world television program on which to advertise. A media buyer for an international ad agency may have to choose between purchasing time on a London channel or on one in Micronesia. Theoretically, a popular world program produced by a small, less-developed country could attract enough world advertising to significantly affect that country's balance of payments.

What happens when a television network moves its entire headquarters to a small country on the other side of the world where its labor costs are a fraction of what it was previously paying? Direct-broadcast satellites enable the network to reach the viewers back home with scarcely more effort or cost than it took to operate the domestic system. With this in mind, the research firm of Arthur D. Little, Inc., predicts that "the potential for competitive advantage afforded by the use of satellites might ultimately lead to the elimination of local TV broadcast stations." [24]

An Assessment

While these concerns are being debated by educators, government leaders, and corporate planners, we must not forget that the technology of satellite communication is still far ahead of public acceptance or accessibility. While heading the M.I.T. Research Program on Communications Policy, Ithiel De Sola Pool wrote:

The proposals for regulation of satellite communication have focused on one particular aspect of the topic, namely direct broadcast of television across borders. . . .

Now, 15 years later, the prospects of any country sending uninvited TV from a satellite direct to homes in any other country are as remote as ever. Forecasters overestimated the ease and speed with which satellites could be used for direct international broadcasting. The expensive high-powered satellites needed for direct broadcasting are only now ceasing to be experimental. Such satellites would have to transmit at a frequency which TV sets could receive, but which would not interfere with TV and other communications on the ground; there rarely are such frequencies. Furthermore, hundreds of thousands of TV owners in the receiving country would have to buy dish antennas and point them accurately at the transmitting satellite; otherwise, transmitting would be an expensive exercise in futility.

The direct satellite broadcast debate illustrated a typical overestimation by non-technicians of the ease of introduction of a new device, yet the debaters were groping at some genuine issues. Even if the fear of satellite broadcasts penetrating countries against their will was a hallucination, the long-run trend toward adoption of global direct communications unconstrained by national topographies is a powerful one. There is a powerful trend of modern communication in voice, data, and modes other than TV to become supranational. Just as one should not overestimate the imminence of direct satellite TV broadcasting without the cooperation of the receiving country, so equally one should not underestimate the pressure in the long run to use satellites efficiently, i.e., without respect to national frontiers. Political authorities, however, will try to resist that. [25]

COMMERCIAL ISSUES:
THE AT&T–COMSAT INTERFACE

Perhaps nowhere do economic issues surface faster than in the arena in which two corporations fight for the rights to operate future communication technology. Two companies with some of the biggest stakes are AT&T and COMSAT. The former is a private industry, the latter quasi-governmental.

COMSAT is responsible for overseeing satellite development in the United States. It even supplies AT&T with satellite circuits, which AT&T in turn leases to its users. Satellites are COMSAT's only business, but AT&T operates not only satellites but also ocean cables (Figure 7–11). Herein lies the crux of the problem. Will messages be sent by satellite or cable?

If satellites are used exclusively, then COMSAT benefits. If the government continues to permit a percentage of all messages to be sent by cable, then COMSAT could suffer. Of the two media, satellites have the greater number of circuits. AT&T's COMSTAR satellites have over 14,000 circuits each, but its transatlantic cable handles only about 4,000 circuits. To compound the issue, the life of a cable is much longer than that of a satellite, yet cables are much more costly to construct and operate. In the end, which is more economical?

Some writers have argued that AT&T is taking advantage of a regulation that permits it to set user rates according to the in-

FIGURE 7–11 An ocean cable-laying machine called the Sea Plow IV is used to install transatlantic cable. Such cables serve many of the functions of satellites, aggravating the discussion of the regulatory framework and cost-effectiveness of the two communication systems. (AT&T)

vestment necessary for developing the system.[26] COMSAT's position is succinctly stated in its report to its stockholders: "Any policy of the FCC which would permit COMSAT's carrier customers to bypass satellites in favor of new cables would have an adverse impact on the growth of COMSAT's international traffic."[27] The future of both carriers will depend on the future direction of telecommunication policy.

SUMMARY

Microwaves, which are found at very high frequencies on the electromagnetic spectrum, have many applications to broadcasting. They relay television programs between stations and networks. They are used by satellites to beam television signals around the globe, and by cable systems to import distant television signals for redistribution to cable subscribers. Microwave technology is also used in electronic news gathering and in educational and industrial broadcasting.

Satellites provide equally important functions. Telstar, launched in 1962, was the first satellite to broadcast international television signals. Since then, many satellites have been used in broadcasting. Synchronous-orbit satellites provide twenty-four-hour communication among almost any points on earth, making continuous, live television coverage of international events a reality.

In the United States much of the administration of international satellite communication is undertaken by the Communications Satellite Corporation (COMSAT). COMSAT manages the International Telecommunications Satellite Organization (INTELSAT), a cooperative effort of member countries using satellite communication and the network of INTELSAT satellites. Early Bird, launched in 1965, was the first INTEL-SAT satellite. It was followed by a series of more advanced INTELSAT satellites, the latest being the INTELSAT V series. Membership is open to any state that was a party to INTELSAT's Interim Agreements, and to any other state that is a member of the International Telecommunication Union (ITU).

Some of the first domestic satellites used for educational purposes were the Application Technology Satellites developed by NASA. School districts in outlying regions of the Rocky Mountains and in Appalachia were among the first to be served by the ATS system. Later, after being repositioned, the satellites served such areas as India and conducted demonstrations under the auspices of the United States Agency for International Development (USAID).

Domestic satellite systems are receiving attention as the amount of data communication and the preference for satellite over ground-based networks increase. Western Union's Westar system consists of five satellites, and more are planned. It also consists of a Tracking Data Relay Satellite System (TDRSS). A network of earth stations and a ground-based microwave network complement the Western Union satellite system. The system's users include major television networks and such customers as the *U.S. News & World Report* and the *Wall Street Journal,* which send facsimile pages from central locations to regional printing facilities.

The RCA Satcom series, the General Telephone & Electronics satellites, AT&T's Comstar system, the Marisat satellite used for marine communication, and the Satnet research and experimental program are some of the other domestic and international satellite programs in operation. Amateur-radio operators ("hams"), using the Oscar satellites, are also experimenting with communication links.

Proposals from a number of United States companies, following the lead of nations that already have operable systems, have applied for permission to operate direct-broadcast satellites (DBS). Services such as pay TV, high-definition television (HDTV), and master-antenna systems for apartments, motels, and similar dwellings would be offered through direct-broadcast satellites.

Satellite business networks provide video, voice, and data-communication services for companies. One of the first such networks was a cooperative arrangement conceived in 1975 by COMSAT, IBM, and Aetna Life and Casualty. It became operational in the early 1980s. One of its satellites was the first to be launched by the space shuttle *Columbia*.

Radio and television stations wanting to extend their coverage areas are beaming their signals to satellites and then back to earth stations owned by cable companies, which in turn distribute the signals to subscribers. The first of these superstations was Turner Broadcasting's WTBS (originally WTCG) in Atlanta. Other superstations are WGN–TV and radio station WFMT–FM, both in Chicago.

Rockets have traditionally been used to launch satellites, but in the future the space shuttle will provide an alternative launch vehicle. Moreover, the shuttle could theoretically be used to service space stations, where it could dock and repair communication hardware.

The growth of satellite communication opens up new political and economic issues. The transfer of information across international boundaries is one concern, although not as serious as once thought, because of the slow acceptance and insufficient accessibility of DBS systems. Competition between such industry participants as COMSAT and

AT&T has fostered debate over who, if anyone, should have preferential treatment in operating the developing satellite systems and has prompted discussion of the advantages and disadvantages of satellite systems compared with ground-based cable and microwave systems.

OPPORTUNITIES FOR FURTHER LEARNING

AYVAZIAN, B., and others, *Direct Broadcast Satellites: Preliminary Assessment of Prospects and Policy Issues.* Cambridge, Mass.: Kalba Bowen Associates, 1980.

Control of the Direct Broadcast Satellite: Values in Conflict. Palo Alto, Calif.: Aspen Institute Program on Communications and Society, 1974.

Direct Broadcast Satellite Communications: Proceedings of a Symposium. Washington, D.C.: National Academy of Sciences, 1980.

Direct Broadcasting From Satellites: Policies and Problems. Studies in Transnational Legal Policy No. 7. Washington, D.C.: American Society of International Law, 1975.

DIZARD, W. P., "Direct Broadcast Satellites (DBS): The U.S. Position," in *The Cable/ Broadband Communications Book, Vol. 2, 1980–81,* ed. Hollowell. Washington, D.C.: Communications Press, 1980.

KALBA BOWEN ASSOCIATES, *Direct Broadcast Satellites: Preliminary Assessment of Prospects and Policy Issues.* Washington, D.C.: National Association of Broadcasters, 1980.

MATTE, N. M., *Aerospace Law: Telecommunications Satellites.* Vancouver: Butterworth, 1982.

Policies for Regulation of Direct Broadcast Satellites. Washington, D.C.: Office of Plans and Policy, U.S. Federal Communications Commission, 1980.

Satellites and Broadcast Stations: A Guide to Present and Potential Satellite Technology, Uses, Regulation and Economic Impact. New York: Station Representatives Association, 1980.

SHOOK, F., *The Process of Electronic News Gathering.* Englewood, Colo.: Morton, 1982.

SIGNITZER, B., *Regulation of Direct Broadcasting From Satellites: The UN Involvement.* New York: Praeger, 1974.

SMITH, D. D., *Communication Via Satellite: A Vision in Retrospect.* Boston: A. W. Sijthoff, 1976.

TAYLOR, J. P., *Direct-to-Home Satellite Broadcasting.* New York: Television/Radio Age, 1980.

——, *What Broadcasters Should Know About Satellites.* New York: Television/Radio Age, 1981.

Technical Aspects Related to Direct Broadcasting Satellite Systems. Washington, D.C.: Office of Science and Technology, U.S. Federal Communications Commission, 1980.

YOAKUM, R. D., *ENG: Electronic News Gathering in Local Television Stations.* Bloomington: School of Journalism, University of Indiana, 1981.

8

CABLE

It is 1940, and television is in its infancy. Large, bulky home receiving sets strain to tune in to the preciously few television stations broadcasting the magic of pictures over the airwaves. If you live in a remote area, it takes a large, well-directed rooftop antenna even to focus on a picture. Rooftops are a maze of aluminum and steel.

Still, the excitement of this medium does not dampen your spirits. Instead you purchase numerous antennas. Newspapers are filled with ads claiming this or that make or model of antenna will give you clear reception. Stores even sell "rabbit ears," two telescopic rods about three feet long connected to a base that sits atop your television set. For the most part, though, rabbit ears cannot compete with outdoor antennas.

THE CABLE CONCEPT

Finally, someone realized there must be a better way. That way is *community antenna television,* commonly called *CATV* or *cable.* The concept is simple: Erect a single tower and antenna on a high elevation and then run cables from that tower to individual homes. The result is clear reception without the housetop clutter of antennas. Five hundred companies that owned the antennas and charged a fee to people who want a hookup were created. A new medium was born.

Cable was especially attractive to people in hilly or mountainous country. Because both television video and audio signals are broadcast at a relatively high frequency, they travel in an almost straight line from the transmitter. When there is a mountain between the television station's transmitting antenna and a home antenna, it blocks these signals (Figure 8–1).

Today, cable is advantageous to people other than those living in mountainous regions. Philadelphia cable subscribers, for example, can receive New York City's television channels. Although over-the-air reception necessitates one-channel spacing between stations so that spillover interference can be avoided, cable does not. Also, structures such as high-rise apartment houses, tightly spaced row houses, and clustered office buildings can obstruct even local televi-

sion signals. Consequently, cable has become popular for urban reception as well as for distant signals.

STARTS IN OREGON AND PENNSYLVANIA

There was a bit of friendly rivalry in the origin of cable television. Two individuals claim that famous first, one in Oregon and one in Pennsylvania. L. E. Parsons is credited with a working cable system in Astoria, Oregon, in 1948. John Walson is believed to have had a cable system operating in Mahoney City, Pennsylvania, that

FIGURE 8–1 Cable systems originally developed as a means to improve television reception of distant signals. Developing first in Oregon and Pennsylvania, cable is now found in virtually every major urban area, and its original function has been supplemented with two-way communication services ranging from public opinion polling to electronic banking. (NCTA)

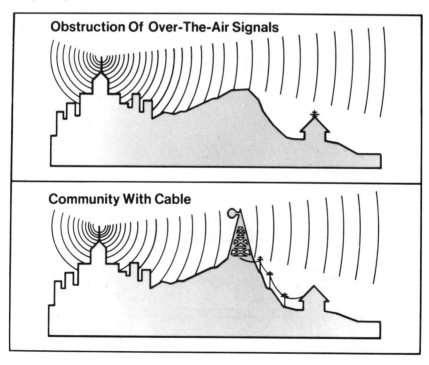

same year. Some of the discrepancy results from the definition of what is, or was, a true cable system. Parsons apparently did build a reception system but sold it to small cooperative groups. The system did not operate on a monthly-fee basis until sometime after August 1950. In 1952 fire destroyed Walson's records of his operations in Mahoney City. Research efforts have thus far failed to turn up bills, newspaper accounts, or other documentation. But Walson and others are unequivocal about the 1948 operation in Mahoney City.[1]

THE SIZE OF THE INDUSTRY

Since those beginnings in 1948, cable has grown considerably. Although it is still a long way from being connected to all of the television sets in use, it has developed to the point at which there are enough subscribers to make it profitable. In the United States there are approximately 5,600 systems serv-

ing about 10,500 communities. Pennsylvania has the most systems, and California has the most subscribers. About a fourth of the nation's television households are located in areas served by a cable system. Cable systems have as few as 100 or as many as 200,000 subscribers. Some companies operate more than one cable system. These multiple-system operators (MSOs) have as many as 1.5 million subscribers.[2] While early systems had from six to twelve channels, many recently constructed systems have as many as thirty channels and some go as high as one hundred channels. Many operators originate their own programming, and some sell advertising or lease channels to other services which pay a fee to the cable company.

COMPONENTS OF THE CABLE SYSTEM

To understand how a cable system operates, let's examine its parts (Figure 8–2). The

Basic Cable Television System

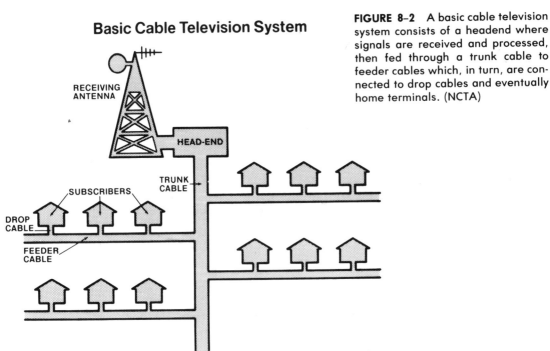

FIGURE 8–2 A basic cable television system consists of a headend where signals are received and processed, then fed through a trunk cable to feeder cables which, in turn, are connected to drop cables and eventually home terminals. (NCTA)

center of any cable system is the *headend,* a combination of human beings and technology. The human side includes the personnel who actually operate the system. The technical components include the *receiving antenna,* which receives the signals from a distant television station. The receiving-antenna system is usually a tall tower on which a number of smaller antennas are positioned for receiving the distant signals. The tower can be located on a hill outside of town or a mountain top far from a residential area. Installing the tower and antennas entails major construction and everything from lumber-cutting crews to giant helicopters (Figure 8–3).

The headend may also consist of television production facilities such as cameras, lights, and other studio hardware, depending on the size of the cable system and how much local programming originates in the studio. The facilities can range from a small black-and-white camera to full-scale color production equipment. With all of this in mind, we will define the headend as *the human and hardware combination responsible for originating, controlling, and processing signals over the cable system.*

Another important cable-system component is the *distribution system,* which disperses the programming. The main part of the distribution system is the cable itself. The coaxial cable (Figure 8–4) used in most cable systems consists of an inner metal conductor shielded by a plastic foam. The foam is covered with another metal conductor, which in turn is covered by plastic sheathing. This protected cable may either be strung on utility poles or buried underground. The primary cable, the main transmission line, is

FIGURE 8–3 Installing cable headend antennas can be a major task involving heavy equipment, expensive transport systems such as helicopters, and specially trained construction crews. (NCTA)

Coaxial Cable

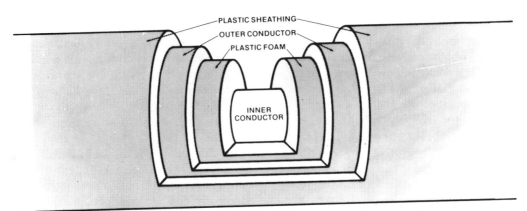

FIGURE 8–4 The basic distribution component of a cable system is coaxial cable. An inner conductor is shielded by a series of outer metal and plastic layers creating a system designed to be interference-free and capable of carrying numerous channels. The future will see more and more systems installed using optical fiber cable capable of carrying many more channels. (NCTA)

called the *trunk cable*. It usually follows the main traffic arteries of a city, branching off into a series of smaller feeder cables, or *subtrunks*. The feeder cables usually travel into side streets or apartment complexes.

The actual connection to the home is made with a *drop cable*. This coaxial cable goes directly into the house, where it connects with a *home terminal*. The home terminal, in turn, connects directly to the back of the television set. In most cable systems, the home terminal is simply a splicing con-

FIGURE 8–5 Hand-held two-way home terminals permit the subscriber to access many more services than are available with one-way systems. (Warner Amex)

nector that adapts the drop cable to a two-wire connector that fits onto the two screws on the back of every television set. In two-way cable, which we shall learn about next, the home terminal is more complex and may even include a small keyboard (Figure 8–5). Some cable systems install these more sophisticated home terminals even if two-way cable is not yet operative. When it does become operative, the system and the subscriber will be ready.

TWO-WAY CABLE TELEVISION

Two-way cable systems, sometimes called *two-way interactive television,* permit the subscriber to feed back information to the headend. They can bring a wide variety of services into the home, and are quickly becoming popular (Figure 8–6).

Programming reaches the two-way subscriber just as it would on one-way cable systems. The two-way subscriber, however, can communicate by means of a feedback loop. Feedback loops are generally of three types (Figure 8–7). One is a single cable used for both transmitting information to and receiving it from the subscriber. Another uses two separate cables. Incoming signals reach the subscriber through one cable, and signals from the subscriber return to the headend on the second cable. A third kind, the round-robin cable loop, is an adaption of the single cable but has separate drop cables.

FIGURE 8–6 Interactive emergency alarm services are just one of the ways in which two-way cable provides the subscriber with more than television programming. (Cable Television Business)

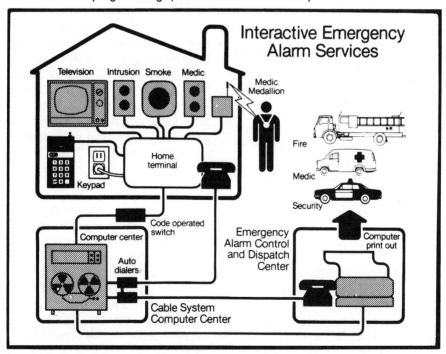

Two-Way Cable Transmission Techniques

| SINGLE CABLE | SEPARATE CABLE | ROUND ROBIN CABLE |
| TWO-WAY | TWO-WAY | LOOP |

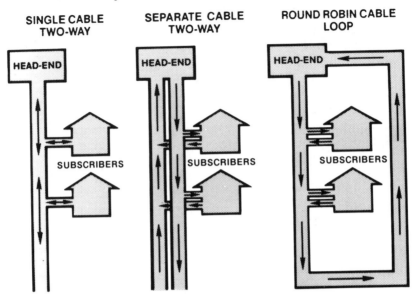

FIGURE 8-7 Different two-way cable installations can provide different system capabilities. (NCTA)

PAY CABLE

Pay cable is *the delivery of information and/or services to cable subscribers for a fee beyond the regular monthly rental fee.* Pay cable should not be confused with *subscription TV* or *pay TV*, terms defining an over-the-air TV-distribution system where the signal is scrambled as it leaves the transmitter and is descrambled by a special device on the home receiving set. The advantage of pay cable is the opportunity to see first-run movies, exclusive viewings of major sports events, and other special entertainment programs.

PAY-CABLE CONNECTION AND FEE ARRANGEMENTS

A number of different arrangements exist for providing pay-cable service to subscribers. The three that follow, or combinations of them, are the most common.

Simple Fee

The subscriber pays a monthly fee to receive a special channel not offered as part of the basic service (which usually consists of up to twelve channels). In some communities the basic service is free and all of the income is generated from pay services. In other cases, as we have seen, subscribers pay a fee for the basic service and then an additional fee for another channel.

Tiering

An adaptation of the simple-fee service is called *tiering.* Here the *cable operator lumps into tiers different channels or services and the subscriber pays an additional fee to receive the channels offered by a particular tier.* For example, a system may charge twelve dollars a month for the basic service and an additional five dollars a month for the first tier of service beyond basic service. This first tier might include some of the satellite superstations we discussed in

Chapter 7. It might also include an all-sports channel and a channel that shows first-run movies. Multiple tiers can exist where the programming is available. A second tier might include a channel showing adult movies and a local educational channel. A special rate may be available for those who want to buy everything the system offers.

Pay-per-View

A third pay-cable arrangement is pay-per-view. Pay-per-view charges the subscriber on a per-program basis. The system operates in most markets where two-way cable capacity exists, and the subscriber can automatically choose to watch or not watch a special program, such as a movie or sporting event. The subscriber enters a choice through the home terminal attached to the television set. The choice is automatically registered in the computer at the headend, which then channels the program to the subscriber, entering the additional charge on the subscriber's bill. Pay-per-view also operates in noninteractive one-way systems,[3] but subscribers must call in their choices in advance and then are billed for their selections.

CABLE RADIO

Radio is another medium that has been channeled by cable systems. The principle is the same as for television: distant station programming is cabled into a local community. As expected, commercial radio broadcasters have vehemently opposed cable radio. Radio is a very local medium. When a small community's cable system imports one or more stations from outside the local market, the local radio broadcaster feels the economic pinch. Importation usually translates into a reduced audience and

consequently reduced advertising dollars. The problem is not as serious for television, since many communities do not have local television. But few do not have local radio stations.

CABLE INTERCONNECTS

Cable systems serve individual communities, but many systems are connecting with one another in order to capture some of the advertising dollars that in the past have been spent exclusively on radio or television.

Types of Interconnects

Interconnects are of two kinds: "hard" and "soft."[4] Hard interconnects are cable systems physically connected by wires or microwave (Figure 8–8). Soft interconnects are associations of cable operators who work together to attract advertisers and air commercial programming but whose systems are not physically connected.

The Advertising Advantages

Interconnects developed as a way of attracting to cable systems the advertisers who were purchasing time on radio and television but who felt the accounting and mechanics of reaching audiences by buying time on many different small cable systems were simply not cost-effective. Moreover, independent cable operators working alone did not always have the ability or promotional and marketing expertise to attract major advertisers to their systems.

By working together, however, many cable operators have solved both of these problems. First, with one buy an advertiser can reach the audience of the combined systems, an audience total more in line with the large audience numbers that major-market

Microwave Interconnection Of Cable Television Systems

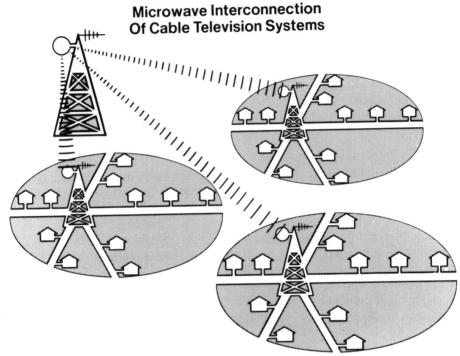

FIGURE 8-8 Microwave interconnections permit cable systems to link together and provide programming to larger audiences from a single headend installation. (NCTA)

television systems can deliver. Second, talents are shared in marketing and promotion. Furthermore, since advertisers are accustomed to purchasing an entire market area, such as that reached by television stations, fragmented buys of advertising time across different suburbs served by different cable systems was simply not practical. But with interconnects, advertisers can buy time on all of the systems serving a geographic area and thus receive blanket market coverage.

THE CABLE FRANCHISE

Whereas the headend is the hardware core of the cable system, the cable franchise is the political and economic core.[5] Unlike radio and television stations, which are awarded a license to operate by the Federal Communications Commission, an arm of the federal government, cable systems are awarded a franchise by local government.

Franchises differ from community to community, but most are for periods of fifteen years and specify certain requirements the cable operator must meet when the system is constructed and operating. The franchise is a valuable commodity and in major markets is hotly contested. Construction costs for a system are great, but the promise for revenue is even greater. Franchise fights sometimes result in lawsuits ranging from charges of antitrust violations to allegations of bribes of city officials.

The Operator's Promises

In any franchise the cable operator must enter into a contract with the grantor of the franchise. Theoretically, if the contract is broken the cable operator loses the franchise and another operator takes over the system. Under such circumstances it would seem that what a cable operator promises will be delivered and that what the city expects to get will in fact be provided. In most cases, however, it is not that simple. In a fiercely contested franchise area cable operators, in an effort to capture the franchise, may simply promise more than they can deliver.

Unfulfilled promises are not always intentional. Nevertheless, they happen. For example, an operator may not be able to meet a construction schedule. Running cables under streets and obtaining rights-of-way from utility companies are just two of the obstacles that confront an operator. Even after the system is built the projected number of subscribers may not be reached; this forces a cash-flow problem that prevents other services from being offered.

Since a sizable investment is made in the early stages of the cable system, simply throwing out one operator so another can take over cannot be accomplished without a major legal fight. Even then, there is no assurance that another operator could provide any better service. Moreover, the company that owns the system may have a sizable group of local investors who carry local political clout.

The Municipality

A second element of the cable franchise is the municipal pride that comes into play in franchise deliberations. Cable franchises tend to create emotional issues. First, politicians view the awarding of the franchise as more than a simple decision. Some view the franchise as a channel of communication for reaching voters. Second, because cable is a medium of communication that will compete with existing media, such as radio and television, it makes news. Third, local officials are sometimes less concerned with what their own community will receive than with what a neighboring community has already received. The desire to be "one better" shows up in cable franchising just as it does elsewhere in society. Unfortunately, in trying to obtain the best system some communities lose sight of what is a workable system.

The Uncertainty of Emerging Technologies

Added to the complexity of any cable franchise is the technological wonderland that is embodied in the communications industry. Today such emerging technologies as teletext, videotex, and interactive two-way cable, promise much but are untried. Communities deciding on a cable franchise must sort out what they want the system to do and what technology will deliver the service, and then try to answer some questions. Will the technology work? Will it become outmoded? Will the public accept and pay for it?

In the 1970s, two-way cable showed great potential but was a long way from being accepted on a mass scale. By the early 1980s we began to realize the power of personal computers and what they could do for us when they were connected to central data banks. Now two-way cable systems take on a new importance. If we change from passive receivers to active consumers of media, a one-way cable system may find the going tough against competitors such as the telephone company.

The Role of Consultants

In an effort to sort through the barrage of technical information received when a request-for-proposal is issued, many communities hire a consultant. Cable consultants were almost unheard of in the 1970s, but today they are competing for business much like the cable operators. Consultants can provide a valuable service, since most politicians know very little, if anything, about cable. Also, a consultant tends to isolate the city officials from what is still in reality a political selection process.

Some consultants are hired for window dressing by officials who wish to validate a political decision that has resulted in a behind-the-scene awarding of a franchise. Others are taken seriously and work closely with city officials from the time the community issues a request-for-proposal to the time the franchise is awarded. Some consultants find themselves in the dual role of adviser to the city and witness in lawsuits filed by operators whose proposals were rejected.

Some cable operators hire local public-relations consultants to help their company keep a favorable image in the community. In tough franchise fights play sometimes gets dirty, and more than one cable operator has pulled out unfavorable publicity against an opponent in order to sway public opinion and local officials. As professionals who can create a positive image as well as defend against smear tactics, public-relations consultants find their services in demand.

The Rent-a-Citizen Controversy

In the political atmosphere that surrounds the awarding of a cable franchise, few tactics have caused as much stir as the so-called rent-a-citizen strategy. Rent-a-citizen is a process by which a cable operator wanting to capture a local franchise provides a financial incentive to a well-known citizen who can make contacts and lobby for the operator. In one community a former mayor was se-

lected as one of the "local partners" in a company bidding for the franchise. The politician was given shares of stock in the company with the option of selling back the stock at a huge profit if the company was awarded the franchise. Such a payoff could amount to millions of dollars, a small price for the cable company to pay in a large market, which could generate that much income every month.

Unless the politician is holding office and votes on the franchise, there is nothing illegal about the practice. Nonetheless, it generates controversy. One opinion is that such tactics insult city officials. Another is that without such political clout a cable operator does not stand a chance of being awarded a franchise.

A variation of the rent-a-citizen strategy is rent-an-institution. The same principle applies except that a local institution, such as a citizens group, a nonprofit foundation, a college or university, or a library, is given a percentage of ownership in the cable company.

In either case, the operator has little to lose. The given-away stock is practically worthless if the franchise goes to another company, since any percentage of nothing is still nothing. On the other hand, if the operator wins the franchise, the shares can be bought back.

The Lure of Municipal Ownership

No political lobbying is more direct than the strategy that promises the municipality awarding the franchise a piece of the profits. For the local officials there is the lure of filling the city treasury with new income. Unfortunately some local officials fail to see beforehand the conflict of interest that will inevitably develop the first time they must vote on some aspect of the system. The regulator of the cable system (the municipality) ends up part owner and the public officials elected to look out for the best interests of the voters may find it hard to distinguish between the public's interest or the city's interest. Will they vote for more service for the public but less income for the city, or less service for the public and more income for the city?

The Franchise Area's Political and Economic Climate

The economic and political climate of a market can determine which operator gets a franchise, or even which operators bid for a franchise. Ideally a community should receive many proposals, at least enough to assure a wide selection and enough competition to keep costs at a minimum. Yet in some communities the perceived political climate can prevent operators from bidding in the first place. If, for example, there are rumors of inside deals, operators who feel they do not have a chance to win the franchise, even though they might be able to provide a superior cable system, simply do not bid.

The number of local groups who are perceived as placing demands on a cable operator may also influence who bids. For example, suburban franchises have traditionally been favored by cable operators because of the homogeneity of the community. Many suburbs consist primarily of one socioeconomic class and ethnic group. Thus, if a cable operator is wiring a middle-class suburb where no special ethnic interest groups reside, it is unlikely that these groups will demand ownership in the system or their own local-access channel. Suburbs are also residential, and thus the cable company that wires them does not need to construct lines through commercial areas where construction costs are high and subscribers few.

At some time in our lives we will live in a community that already receives cable or is considering the installation of a cable system. Knowing how to analyze the forces at work in the awarding of a cable franchise is a necessary step in becoming a responsible member of a community.

CABLE SERVICES

Cable systems today offer more than they did in the late 1940s, when the medium was in its infancy.

Improved Reception and Multiple Stations

The basic service is still to improve television reception and to increase the number of available channels. Especially in rural areas, the value of cable is not necessarily more channels or services but rather its ability to provide clear reception of distant stations.

Superstations

Without cable, superstations would not exist, much less have the national audience that some of them enjoy. Superstations provide the attractive, inexpensive programming that many cable systems need in order to round out a basic service and complement the local stations that are available.[6] Superstations, additional channels, and improved reception are often the programming choices that prompted a subscriber to order cable in the first place. Once successful contact is made between the subscriber and the cable company, there exists the opportunity for selling the subscriber additional tiers on the system.

Entertainment, News, Sports, Weather

Cable expands the entertainment and other programming choices provided by radio and television stations. For example, Home Box Office (HBO), the first pay-cable service, offers movies, features, and its own productions. The Movie Channel consists primarily of full-length feature films with sprinklings of star profiles and capsule features. Both services contend they help cable operators to prevent consumers from discontinuing service. HBO has also managed to become a major force in motion-picture distribution. For part of the Hollywood movie establishment this is an invasion of sacred ground. HBO's advance financing of movies, accompanied by its power to bid for first-run showings, makes it a formidable competitor to the motion-picture industy.[7] As a *Wall Street Journal* report noted,

> Since it ushered in the pay-television era precisely a decade ago, HBO has grown from a money-losing service with 365 subscribers to a significant bankroller of motion pictures—and a significant threat to big movie makers and distributors.
>
> Hollywood's major studies view HBO as a brash newcomer muscling in on their turf.[8]

Also available on cable are channels devoted primarily to children's programming. One such offering, Warner Amex Satellite Entertainment's Nickelodeon channel, utilizes sophisticated marketing techniques, such as addressing parents through print media such as *Woman's Day, People,* and *Parents Magazine.*[9] Both *Playboy* and *Penthouse* magazines have lent their name to cable formats oriented toward adult entertainment.

Expanded news and public-affairs programs are offered by a number of cable services. Uninterrupted coverage of Congress and twenty-four-hour news are available in many markets. Turner Broadcasting launched the Cable News Network (CNN) and has sold the service to some network affiliates for early-morning programming. Headline services, including Turner's CNN

Headline News, are available to many cable and broadcast subscribers. Cable news is available in textual format from such services as UPI Cable.

Instructional Television Through Cable

Cable companies often contract with a local university to fill one of its cable channels with instructional programming. Under such an agreement the university can offer a complete curriculum that can be taken in the living room instead of in the classroom. The continuing-education and outreach functions of colleges thus gain a whole new perspective through cable. Students can enroll in one college while taking courses by cable television from another. As we creep toward realization of the wired-nation concept, colleges could even become specialized in one type of instruction that is "syndicated" beyond the local campus. For instance, a school in New Mexico could use cable and national satellite hookups to teach Indian culture. Or a school in Wyoming could offer courses in mining economics.

Colleges and universities are not the only educational institutions involved in cable television. High schools have produced programs explaining school activities, which they then air over the local cable system for the parents' benefit.[10] Special programs for classroom use are also shown over cable systems, permitting taxpayers to see what is being done with their tax money. Schools even use the local cable system for such highly specialized programming as drug education. High-school sports programs are also broadcast on cable.

Cable is also becoming a means of communication between individuals and institutions that in the past have been distant and unable to communicate. The public that looks inside a school building, watches teacher-training programs, and hears school officials discuss issues learns more about and participates more in the institution. This social and political responsiveness in turn permits the school officials to be more accountable to those forces affecting policy.

Programming Local Arts

Another potential service of cable is fine arts programming. Commercial broadcasting has not been able to program the arts successfully, for two reasons. The first is the lack of viewers for such specialized programming. The second, caused by the first, is an inadequate profit foundation upon which to produce and program these arts. Although public broadcasting has inched toward this type of programming, it still must produce programs that appeal to a mass audience. Cable provides an alternative. Now local fine arts programming can be produced and funded on a local level.

Fine arts programming provides another benefit for cable. If a city has a good local symphony orchestra, for instance, it is not unusual for a group of local sponsors of the arts to contribute to its development with considerable zeal. This can spill over into the cable system. The local symphony can play to its audience over cable even during prime-time hours. On a commercial broadcasting station the only profitable time to air such programming might be in the wee hours of the morning.

PlayCable

The popularity of video games has spilled over into cable. Some two-way cable systems offer a video-game channel as a pay-TV option. Subscribers buy a master component similar to the control terminal sold with video games in retail stores. Intellivision equipment is available for the following PlayCable programs: Football, Baseball, Basketball, Soccer, Hockey, Auto Racing, Skiing, Tennis, Boxing, Golf, Armor Battle, Space Battle, Sea Battle, Poker, Roulette, Blackjack, Horse Racing, Backgammon, and Checkers.[11]

Shopping Services

The growth of catalogue sales has spurred merchants to look into other direct-marketing techniques, including the use of cable to deliver electronic catalogues of merchandise.[12] Shopping channels display goods and services that subscribers can purchase either by keying in their account information on two-way cable systems or by telephoning direct orders for merchandise seen on one-way systems. One company operates a satellite-delivered shoppers' channel that charges advertisers for a ten-minute product demonstration. Washing machines, encyclopedias, and cookies are just some of the products that have been advertised. In another system a cooperative arrangement exists among a department store, which supplies the merchandise; the cable company, which distributes the channel; and a credit card, which handles the billing.

Videotex and Teletext

Videotex, a two-way interactive wired system that provides textual information, can use cable just as it can use telephone lines. Although cable videotex is not widespread, it has been introduced in some markets served by two-way interactive systems.

Teletext, as we learned, is the one-way transmission of textual information by means of the unused scanning lines (the vertical blanking interval) of a television signal. Teletext can also take place over a cable system. A national teletext service is available to cable operators, and cable systems are beginning to use teletext at the local level. Special decoding equipment is necessary for teletext, and its cost has tended to impede the development of the technology. If advertising-supported teletext can generate enough income to help subsidize the cost of decoders, or if the cost of decoders decreases, then teletext may gain more of a foothold in the market.

Although cable has been available since the late 1940s, the great potential for cable programming is just now beginning to be felt. Technology that permits more channels, the increasing number of subscribers, who form a financial base for cable's development, and an industry that is beginning to mature—all have improved cable as a medium. At the same time, many ambitious cable ventures backed by big names in the entertainment industry have not succeeded. CBS's fine-arts cable programming was stopped when CBS management determined after a short experimental period that it would not be profitable. This and similar examples show that even though technology can offer multiple channels, only so many channels can find an audience large enough to make them profitable. A Nielsen survey found that "when viewers had an average of 3.6 channels available they watched an average of 2.6, or 72% of those possible, for 10 minutes a week or more. When the number rose to 12.4 channels, an average of 6.2 channels or 50% were watched, and when 29 channels were offered only 10 or 34% were viewed."[13]

NEWSPAPER–CABLE COOPERATIVES

Many cable systems lease channels to other parties. Local newspapers are leasing channels and competing with local television by using the resources of their reporters and editors and programming from the news-

room. One Omaha, Nebraska, newspaper produces approximately ninety live newscasts each week.[14] Other newspaper-originated cable news programs range from full-scale news roundups to news capsules.

Newspaper-cable relationships go beyond programming. Some newspaper salespersons also sell time on the advertiser-supported cable channels offering CNN and ESPN programming. Such arrangements open an interesting arena of competition, especially in an era of videotex and teletext. With these new technologies, the local radio or television station can offer an "electronic edition" of the news as easily as the newspaper can offer television news. The future may see more and more blurring of what constitutes print media and what constitutes electronic media.[15]

A New Hampshire company is developing a network of newspapers engaged in cable programming. The concept includes a central television production center that will produce a daily television newscast and then make it available to other newspaper cable channels, which can insert locally produced stories. National and international bureaus are planned, along with a marketing drive to sign up two hundred affiliate newspapers who will also feed news to the network.[16]

LOCAL POLITICAL PROGRAMMING

In addition to the services and cooperative arrangements just discussed, cable offers unique services to local politics.

Broadcasting Public Meetings

Cable gives the public access to even the smallest governmental body. Television cameras and microphones can be placed in the audience of a school-board meeting, a city-council meeting, or a zoning-commission meeting. Experience has shown that live cablecasting of such meetings can increase attendance. Those with an active interest attend the meetings, and those with a borderline interest watch from home.[17]

Candidate Access

Commercial broadcasting, and to some extent public broadcasting, is limited in the amount of advertising time that can be given to candidates for political office. It is just not economically feasible to turn all of a station's available advertising over to the politicians. The reason for this is that the FCC has decreed that political advertising be sold at the lowest rate the station charges to an advertiser. Although this helps politicians with scanty campaign coffers to obtain valuable television exposure, the procedure is not the favorite rule of commercial broadcasters. Some stations simply appropriate an amount of free time to candidates and dispense with selling political advertising altogether. In addition, election laws now restrict campaign financing, and thus the budgets that used to produce lucrative television campaigns.

Cable television provides a number of alternatives to these dilemmas. First, in small communities without a television station cable television permits candidates to reach the voters through a visual medium. Second, most local-access rates permit even the candidate running for dog catcher of Possum Hollow to campaign on the local cable channel. Third, when commercial access is not available, cable access may be. Fourth, cable permits the candidates to reach highly specialized audiences not normally reached by commercial television. In short, cable is helping our society recapture the old-fashioned town-meeting approach common to democracy yet difficult to attain in our modern age.

CABLE'S LOCAL-ACCESS CONCEPT

Most cable systems allow any member of the public access to a cable channel. Some larger cable systems also provide equipment at a nominal cost for people to produce local programming. Let's look at an example.

An Example of Applied Local Access

Local-access programming is not the glittering lights of Hollywood. Nor is it the elaborate production studios of a major network. It more than likely materializes as this program did, on an October day in a small community of 8,000 people and 1,500 local cable subscribers. It is evening, and on a drive in the country a local resident spots a poster tacked to a utility pole: "Halloween Parade—Everyone Welcome—6:30 P.M., October 31, The Fire House Parking Lot." The perfect opportunity for local-access programming. The next morning a call to the local cable company produces the name of the student at the nearby college who is in charge of cable equipment available for public use. The cost is minimal.

A second telephone call reveals that two small portable black-and-white cameras, a videotape recorder, and a switching unit are available.

"We can set them up in the alley behind the firehouse. That's where the parade starts."

"What about lights and electricity?"

"Whoops, I never thought of that."

Time to check with the fire department. Another telephone call . . .

At 6:30 P.M., the parking lot is filled with children. Costumes are everywhere. A hay wagon is in position, the parade's director and her megaphone atop it. The children line up to march around the block and back into the parking lot for an awards ceremony. Wait a minute. The light from the fire department isn't enough. Time to move some cars into position. Park some at the head of the alley and turn the headlights on high beam. It works; we're ready to go. Lights, cameras, action—the parade is on! A few hours later, the ninety-minute production of the parade and the awards ceremony is seen over the local cable channel. A full-scale television production? No, but to the parade participants it was just as exciting. The parents and children who participated will remember that Halloween for a long time to come.

This is what local-access television really is. It is the grass-roots side of mass media, one that is not possible to incorporate in standard broadcasting stations. Creative opportunities on many cable systems await not the seasoned professional but *the amateur citizen.*

Local Access and Specialized Audiences

One advantage of cable is its ability to reach specialized audiences. In Philadelphia, for example, cable-company hardware has made possible a series of "mini-hubs" that are creating new concepts in cable programming.[18] The mini-hubs are a series of local origination points along the cable route. A cable program can thus be limited to a few city blocks. Then, perhaps three blocks away, there is another program from another mini-hub. This highly localized access gives programming opportunities to small neighborhoods having similar ethnic or religious backgrounds or other common ties.

Another example of local-access programming to specialized audiences is programming for the elderly. Cable can be connected to living complexes for the elderly, such as nursing homes. It is popular with the elderly because of the added leisure time retirement permits. Local-access cable programming permits the elderly to communicate with one another, alleviate loneliness, and feel more a part of the community. Special programs about social security benefits, Medicare information, transportation, and shopping bargains for senior citizens, are all possible through local-access cable programming.

Problems Facing Local Access

Up to this point, our discussion of cable television has been positive. Instructional-television programming, fine-arts programming, the use of cable in the political process, and access to cable by specialized audiences are all beneficial. But not every aspect of cable is trouble-free, and the local-access concept is perhaps the least so.

The major problem of local-access television is that its viewing audience has been difficult to measure. Major commercial rating services do not usually include local-access channels in their survey measurements. When they do, the measurements have shown very few viewers. A study by the Institute for Communication Research at Indiana University sampled the television-viewing habits of the people of Columbus, Indiana.[19] Results showed that "the total public-access viewing time, for all persons in the sample, was two tenths of 1 percent (.2 percent) of the total of all television viewing for the week."[20] Explanations for this small audience were (1) a lack of promotion by the cable company, (2) "casual" scheduling, which included intermittent programming, (3) blacked-out periods, and perhaps (4) sampling error. However, a promotional campaign did slightly increase subsequent viewer levels.[21]

Another problem area for local-access

television is the programming itself. Pamela Doty, a researcher for the Center for Policy Research in New York, spent two months viewing local-access channels in New York.[22] Because local-access programmers did not expect a mass audience or need advertising revenue, she felt she would find a "higher percentage of hard-hitting social criticism and controversy" on local-access channels than on typical commercial television. This was not the case. She found that on local-access channels it was "rare to see a debate or dialogue between two persons who even mildly disagree, let alone have major differences."[23] Moreover, the bland format of people sitting around a coffee table talking to each other—the "talking heads" format—was rather boring.

Doty's recommendations for improving local-access programming include true debating of local issues, "explorational tours" of communities with "behind-the-scenes" glimpses, and programs showing the audience how to edit videotape. She also states that public-access users need to develop a clear sense of what they want their programs to accomplish and how to interest the audience they want to reach.[24] Done properly, local-access programming has great potential. We have already read about programming the local symphony. Other special events, such as Little League baseball, children's parades, community fairs, picnics, and church services, can fill a cable system's programming schedule.

CABLE VERSUS
THE BROADCASTER

Given cable's ability to carry broadcast messages beyond the coverage area of the over-the-air station, it would seem that broadcasters would support cable's efforts more. But the two have seldom coexisted harmoniously, and at times their opposition has been bitter.

The Broadcaster's Arguments

Place yourself in the position of a commercial broadcaster in a medium-sized community.

The importation of broadcast signals slashes your audience. You used to be able to offer a substantial audience to advertisers for a healthy profit. Second, as a broadcaster you are serving the viewing public's interest, convenience, and necessity and are providing that service free of charge. On the other hand, a large interconnection of cable systems can successfully negotiate exclusive programming with a college football team, for example, and charge viewers to see the games. You, in turn, because of the cable systems' exclusive contract, would not be permitted to carry the game. Third, economics usually dictates that cable, and especially pay TV, be installed only in densely populated areas, where most of the potential subscribers are. Yet you, while competing with cable, are also serving the rural public, regardless of the population density.

Your fourth argument—a more general one—is that cable has developed as a parasite industry of broadcasting and is now trying to compete with it. Fifth, you argue that cable has been favored by the FCC with a general relaxation of rules, which permits it to compete better with you. You compare this to fighting with one hand tied behind your back while your opponent's hands are free. Sixth, you claim that since cable companies have the ability to interconnect their systems, the theory of local accountability and service has been destroyed. Seventh, while you operate in a limited spectrum space, cable can carry large numbers of channels, many of them programmed by the local cable systems themselves.

Cable's Rebuttal

Now put yourself in the cable operator's position.

First, you contend that over-the-air broadcasters are severely restricted in serving their viewing audiences, since even in the largest markets only a few stations can operate within a limited spectrum space. You feel that cable serves its audiences far better with its variety of channels. Second, you point out that precisely because of their limited spectrum space, broadcasters have made giant profits. You state that those profits are sometimes at the expense of viewers, who long for more innovative, though perhaps more costly, programming. Third, when broadcasters criticize cable's exclusive contracts with program distributors, you remind them of their exclusive contract advantage with the major networks. Fourth, although commercial broadcasters answer to only one master, the FCC, you sometimes face regulatory control by three levels of government—local, state, and national.

All of these arguments, in varying detail and intensity, are used throughout the broadcasting and cable industries. They have been presented in cloakrooms to members of Congress, at special legislative hearings, and in public-relations literature. Meanwhile, mass consumers are living in both worlds, unaware that the future is bound to bring some dramatic changes in how they receive their daily television fare.

Healing the Split

Despite all the rivalry and rhetoric, broadcasters and cable operators must begin to consider how each can complement the other in working toward a common goal. In-

creasingly, new developments in telecommunication are drawing the two out of their warring camps. A television station broadcasting by satellite to a distant cable system operated by the same company will find it awkward to cut its partner's throat. Still, because of powerful lobbying groups the chasm will not be bridged overnight.

A call for unity has come from Clifford M. Kirtland, Jr., when serving as president of Cox Broadcasting Corporation, which has holdings in both cable and broadcasting stations. Kirtland argues that there needs to be "a recognition by all broadcasters, cable operators, and producers of programming that the viewer and listener in the home are *not* served by high-toned rhetoric lambasting the opposition and feeding the critics. What is needed is a recognition that—even after all the compromises, rule changes, technological changes, and criticism from all sides—the audience today is better served than ever before." He concludes that "perhaps a greater spirit of cooperation among all parties working toward balanced regulations in a positive way . . . a greater acceptance of technological change . . . and a greater reliance on the free enterprise system to work its wonders . . . (will) further enhance the total communication service of our country."[25]

It is difficult to predict a scenario that will bring cable operators and broadcasters together. Perhaps a regulatory issue demanding common lobbying efforts, or perhaps a foreign competitor beaming signals into North American living rooms. But for now, each side is working feverishly to protect its own economic domain.

REGULATORY ISSUES

Despite the respectable growth and impact of cable, it is in its infancy as a technological and social force. Standard broadcasting, both in size and influence, makes cable minute in comparison. Still, cable is a force with which to be reckoned. Let's briefly examine some of the regulatory issues pertaining to its future. A more detailed discussion of these issues is contained in chapter 19.

Levels of Control

As we have seen, cable and commercial broadcasting are subject to different levels of regulatory control. A cable system can find itself regulated by three systems—local, state and federal. Standard broadcasters answer only to the FCC. To make matters worse, some regulations conflict with each other, creating a maze of court cases ranging from rate structures to local-access programming. Directly related to these problems is the futility of trying to regulate, on the basis of state and local boundaries, a communications system that transcends boundaries. Indeed, communications attorney Anne W. Branscomb, using New York as an example, argues that the New York metropolitan area should coordinate its telecommunications planning and development with New Jersey and Connecticut, rather than with New York State.[26]

Cable's Interference With Legal Precedent

Another problem cable faces is its relationship with laws indirectly affecting its operation. Consider the case of local access. A local community group decides it wants to use the local-access channel to broadcast the school-board meeting live and in its entirety. The state's open-meetings law permits public access to all public meetings. But the school board says no. The school board's attorney contends that cable television cameras are not persons and can therefore be barred. The community group reminds the school board that it permits the local television station to film and videotape portions of its meetings. In fact, when major issues are being discussed the board even allows the station to broadcast live mini-cam reports. But the school board replies that cable is not considered a bona fide news-gathering organization and does not come under the protection given a free press.

This is just one of many gray areas cable faces. Many laws, such as open-meeting statutes and reporters'-shield laws, have yet to define their applicability to such situations. Until they do, cable has an uphill climb for its legal identity.

THE ECONOMICS OF CABLE CONSTRUCTION AND OPERATION

The future of cable and how we interact with and use it is tied directly to its economic aspects. It is important to understand them. You may find yourself voting in a local referendum on whether to raise the rates charged by your local cable system. Or your community may determine whether the local cable company should install its cable underground or, more economically, attach it to telephone poles. It may even decide what supplementary services, such as electronic funds transfer or bank-from-home, should be added to the local television fare. To make intelligent decisions, you will need to understand the economic forces affecting cable.

The Capital-Intensive Factor

Cable is a capital-intensive business. By capital-intensive we mean that maximum costs occur immediately. A standard radio or television station can go on the air with a minimum amount of equipment—some of it of marginal quality—and a skeleton staff.

Cable does not enjoy this luxury. Cable systems are designed for permanency, and the system must be taken to the total potential audience before it can even begin operation. Therefore, hiring skilled technicians, installing miles of cable, constructing elaborate antenna systems, and purchasing head-end equipment, must all be done before the first subscriber is hooked on.

Construction Costs

Starting a cable system requires construction of the headend and production facilities, the distribution plant, and subscriber equipment and involves preoperating expenses. Costs for underground construction of the distribution system can run as high as $100,000 per mile in crowded metropolitan centers. Radio stations have gone on the air for less. Even above-ground pole-attachment systems are expensive. The location and type of antenna can also raise the cost. An antenna that must be constructed on top of a mountain is going to cost much more than a tower built in a level field outside of town. A headend with production facilities for locally originated programming is going to cost more than one without local production capabilities. All of this determines how much the subscriber must be charged, how long it will be before the cable system makes a profit, where financing can be obtained, how high the interest rate will be, and whether it is economically feasible to construct the system at all.

Operating Costs

Construction costs are followed by the costs of operating the cable system. The main cost is system maintenance. Although cable operators usually install the best possible equipment for long life and maintenance-free service, nothing is infallible. Breaks due to storms and equipment repair at the headend are just part of the regular maintenance schedule. Second, a subscriber cannot simply turn on a television set and tune to the cable channel without first having the set connected to the cable. That requires a service call, and service calls are responsible for much of the cable company's personnel time.

A third expense is vehicle operation. Unlike a radio or television station, whose entire operation may be under one roof, the cable company can literally be spread all over town. In larger markets servicing this territory can require a fleet of trucks, many requiring aerial ladders. Because of the high price of gasoline, this is a spiraling cost for the cable system. Future developments in technology, however, will permit more and more switching and connecting functions to be done at the cable's headend.

Utility-pole and underground-duct rentals are a fourth large operating expense. If pole attachments are used, the cable company must rent them from the telephone company. When a major cable company like TelePrompTer rents more than 800,000 poles, the cost is considerable.

Fifth, local municipalities may charge franchise fees—money the cable company pays the local government for the privilege of operating. Sixth, cable companies are charged copyright fees by program distributors. Seventh, although construction of the antenna and other headend facilities is usually figured into the construction costs, the expense of bringing in distant signals may require separate lease agreements with telephone companies or private microwave carriers. Eighth, local origination costs can also be substantial. Here a local cable company can incur some of the same studio expenses that a small television station does. Although it can broadcast with black-and-white equipment, color capabilities help the operator to develop programming that can compete successfully for viewers of other channels. This does not mean that high-quality black-and-white programming with special local appeal cannot be successful. When local meetings, special seminars, and similar "individualized" programs are aired, interest will be high no matter what the quality of production is.

INCOME FOR THE CABLE SYSTEM

For the cable company to make a profit, it must receive income in the form of subscriber fees. The number of subscribers and the amount of the fee are the key components. Additional fees for pay-TV programs, such special services as electronic funds transfer, or even two-way interactive instructional-television programming are charged. As the variety of these services increases, the subscriber fee increases. At some point subscribers resist.

Another source of income is advertising. Cable companies have successfully sold advertising in the same way that standard broadcasting stations do. Moreover, the interconnection among cable systems through satellite and microwave makes the concept of a cable network a reality. In such a network a group of cable companies carry the same programming and derive income from sponsors who buy space for advertising that will be seen throughout the network. As cable networks develop, a larger percentage of cable's income will be from advertising.

In summary, income for the cable system can be classified into four broad categories: (1) subscriber's monthly rental fees for standard television services; (2) pay-cable fees for special programming, much of it exclu-sive, which usually consist either of a set charge above the regular monthly rental fee or a per-program assessment; (3) revenue from such special services as at-home banking; and (4) revenue from advertising.

APPROACHING THE PROFIT MARGIN

A cable system has no set formula for success. But the enterprising operator does follow some basic guidelines. Among them is the delicate balance between the amount of money that can be charged to a subscriber and the number of subscribers needed to make the system profitable.

Subscribers Versus Charges

For example, if a cable system has 1,000 subscribers, each of whom pays a $10 monthly subscription fee, the total income would be $10,000 per month (if there is no income from other revenue sources). Now assume that the cable operator decides to increase the subscription rate to $12 per month. Theoretically, this raise would net the company $12,000 per month. But what if the rate increase drove away 200 current subscribers? The income to the cable operator would then drop to $9,600 per month (12 times 800), a loss of $400 per month.

Another economic balance for the cable operator to determine is that between the original construction cost and the number of subscribers necessary to equalize that cost. The key here is subscriber cost, not to be confused with the subscription fee. Subscriber cost is what the "cable operator must obtain in revenues in order for the system to operate at a profit."[27] The more subscribers there are, the less the subscriber cost needs to be.

To understand this principle, consider the following example used by Rolland C. Johnson and Robert T. Blau in their report on a consulting project involving an Indiana cable company. A city of 40,000 people and 10,000 homes (100 homes per mile) grants a cable-television franchise. A cable operator is able to construct the entire system—100 miles of cable, the headend, and miscellaneous equipment—for $1 million. At the end of one year, 1,000 homes (10 percent of the total) are being served. At this point, the cost per subscriber is $1,000 ($1 million divided by 1,000)—drop costs are assumed to be covered by installation fees. During the second year an additional 1,500 homes subscribe; the cable operator now has 2,500 subscribers, or one-fourth of the market. Per-subscriber cost is now only $400. If at the end of ten years 80 percent (or 8,000 homes) of the community is served, per-subscriber costs drop to $125 (assuming the critical equipment is still in working order).[28]

The above example is hypothetical. *Actual situations include a number of variables.* Independent television stations that can beam clear signals into the areas served by the cable may be constructed. The potential for large subscriber blocks, such as apartment houses, may vanish when a landlord decides to prohibit the cable company from hooking up to his or her complex. Or a competing cable company may appear. Such competition would have been unlikely a few years ago; installing expensive lines along an existing cable route simply was not practical. But new technology has changed all that. A small satellite dish on the top of an apartment complex and the accompanying roof-to-residence cable hookups can turn the complex into an instant cable market. This comparatively inexpensive competitive system can upset the most solid projections for success.

Subscriber Penetration

Nevertheless, with the right marketing techniques cable systems can do a sizable business. A report by R. E. Park identifies the factors involved in subscriber penetration by cable:

> The more television stations of various types a cable system carries, the higher its saturation will be.
>
> The fewer of each type of station receivable locally over the air, the higher the system's saturation will be.
>
> The farther from the television transmitters the system is, the higher its saturation will be.
>
> The more stations that broadcast on UHF rather than on VHF channels, the higher the system's saturation will be, because of a variety of reception and tuning problems in UHF stations.
>
> The less the system charges for its services, the higher its saturation will be.
>
> The higher the average income of households in the community served by the system, the higher the system's saturation will be.
>
> The older a system is, the higher its saturation will be.[29]

Park bases his conclusions on data from cable systems already in operation. Constantly changing technology and our own changing media-use habits, however, require cautious optimism when we use such data to assess the chances of success for new cable systems.

Cable will certainly continue to grow as a viable medium. However, new technology may greatly change its current definition. Beaming broadcast signals directly to small satellite dish antennas positioned on rooftops may eliminate the physical wires used in current cable transmission. And if through regulatory protection the telephone companies gain primary development and use of fiber-optics technology, then they may become the cable companies of the future.

MANAGING A CABLE SYSTEM

For the manager of a cable system, key issues such as disconnects, reaching "untouchables," and program listings have a bearing on the ability of the system to operate effectively and profitably.

The Problem of Disconnects

In wiring the home of a subscriber a cable company incurs an expense. Vehicle and technician time, the time to contact the subscriber and sell the service, the time to set up the subscriber's account—all cost money. Thus, it is a serious matter when even one subscriber cancels service.[30] In many systems that lack automatic two-way connect and disconnect, cancellation means sending the technician and the truck back to the subscriber's home, disconnecting the service, and instituting another set of bookkeeping chores to take the subscriber off the account records.

Disconnects cut into the profits and up the operating costs of the system. Part of the problem stems from the cable company trying to sell too much. A customer may be enticed, cajoled, even pressured into buying as many services as possible. Some cable companies hire crews of professional straight-commission door-to-door salespersons to canvass neighborhoods and sign up subscribers. High-pressure tactics can close a sale but entail the risk that the subscriber will call and cancel upon realizing that he or she does not want or cannot afford the service.

To solve the disconnect problem cable companies are becoming more sophisticated in their sales and marketing techniques. By not trying to sell as many services, or by holding customers to fewer services so they do not feel they have "bought the store,"

they can reduce the number of eventual disconnects. Another method is to package services in such a way that buying a lesser number of services does not represent much savings. A more expensive basic fee with less expensive pay services is one way of accomplishing this. Thus, to realize a significant savings the subscriber would have to cancel the service altogether.

Redistributing the service is another method. The cable company arranges to have retail establishments sell cable service at the same place videodiscs, videotape recorders, home computers, and other consumer electronics products are sold. The atmosphere is different with a retail sales person than with a door-to-door salesperson. The buyer has usually decided to talk with the salesperson, and the salesperson is someone who understands electronic hardware and software.

Part of the solution will come from the cable-programming services themselves. To get a hold on the market many cable-programming services have been trying to be all things to all people. Although they are touted as having an exclusive programming identity, there are many similarities among them. Even the pay channels offering first-run movies have come under criticism for their duplicate programming of only the choice movies that everyone wants to watch. As more and more cable services find their identity in the marketplace and less and less duplication exists, subscribers may develop channel loyalty and be less likely to disconnect.

Changes in basic marketing strategies will also help. Cable is a new product that has yet to develop marketing strategies for attracting subscribers who will *stay* with a system. The right advertising message targeted to the right people is necessary for any product, and cable is no exception.

Reaching the Untouchables

In the cable business the *untouchables* are the potential subscribers who for some reason choose not to hook up to cable.[31] Estimates vary but industry sources claim that between 40 and 50 percent of the households that could be wired for cable are left unconnected because the subscriber simply chooses not to buy the service. A negative attitude toward watching television is one reason for the high proportion of unconnected households. Another is that families with small children sometimes worry about being able to control the viewing habits of youngsters who may be exposed to adult programming. Still another reason is lack of information about the cable offerings and fees. One company discovered that 90 percent of its customers did not know how much the installation and monthly fees were.

Clearly some of the problems associated with reaching the untouchables can be solved by better advertising and marketing techniques. But deep-seated resistance toward television will be more difficult to overcome.

Program Guides

Although cable operators have many services to offer subscribers, finding someplace to list those services accurately and consistently can be difficult.[32] Many newspapers find they do not have the space to list all of the available programming choices. Moreover, in some communities the cable operator and the local newspaper are bitter competitors. To find all of the cable offerings in a major market area it may be necessary to check as many as half a dozen different publications.[33] The problem goes beyond just the subscriber and operator. Advertising agencies are reluctant to buy commercial space on cable systems when they feel viewers will have a difficult time learning what programs are offered.

The problem is serious, but efforts are being made to solve it. Some newspapers realize that complete television listings appeal to the reader and are devoting the necessary space to them. Familiar publications such as *TV Guide* have expanded their cable listings in many markets. But because it maintains over one hundred regional editions, however, and because thousands of cable systems offer programs, a minimum penetration is necessary before *TV Guide* will list a channel.[34]

As the medium matures, as new printing and publishing technologies make regional editions easier to compose and print, and as cooperation develops among cable operators, local media, and programming services, program listings will be less of a problem for cable management.

Customer Service

Regardless of how successful a cable operator is in marketing, the business will suffer if customer service is not satisfactory.[35] Horror stories about customer service abound in the cable industry. It is cable management's nemesis.

Poor customer service has many origins. It can start at the level of the person who answers the telephone. Many cable operators hire untrained minimum-wage employees to handle customer inquiries. Such persons cannot articulate clearly, use improper grammar when answering the phones, are discourteous, lack adequate information, and in general are a disaster to the business. As one cable-industry executive stated, "Customer service in the cable industry is so pathetic it makes you want to cry."[36] He pointed out that "cable is an impulse buy but by the time the would-be customer gets through on the phone and talks with an office representative, that impulse might have vanished.''[37] Industry marketers admit that from ''the business office representative who describes HBO as 'a mature movie service with mostly R-rated films' to the cable installer who leaves [a] new subscriber a trail of mud and cigarette ashes along with a set-top converter, customer service is cable's Achilles' heel.''[38] The problem is compounded by the competition cable is receiving from other entertainment services besides newspaper, radio, and television. Pay and subscription television and the emerging videotex services offered through telephone companies mean that poor customer service will be met by disconnects and choices of other media.[39]

While the person who answers the phone can be a problem the telephone itself also contributes to customer dissatisfaction. Some systems installed a limited number of telephones when the system was being built and did not add phones as the service expanded. When the office is busy handling calls, an increasing number of customers and potential customers cannot reach the customer representative.

Dishonest installers who sell ''black market'' connections for a fee are still another sore point. Offering these illegal services to honest customers further taints the image of the cable company.

Cable companies are trying to correct the deficiencies. Some have contracted with training organizations to work with their customer representatives. Others have exchange programs whereby a customer representative works with an installer for a day and then the installer works with the customer representative. Each develops a total perspective on customer relations. Other companies are making random telephone checks with subscribers to gauge reaction to customer service.

IMPLICATIONS OF CABLE FOR THE HUMAN ENVIRONMENT

Before concluding our discussion of cable, it is appropriate to stop and ponder what this technology means to our human environment.

Civilization has developed and prospered partly because of its ability to originate and maintain systems of communication, not only between people but between cultures. Research has shown that we spend approximately seven hours per day watching television. Although we may not be silent during television viewing periods, we are not communicating with others as much as we would during periods of conversation. We do have opportunities during the day to participate in interpersonal relations. We may go to the grocery store, to the bank, or simply windowshop around our community or campus. In each instance, we are around other people. Walking between classes is a perfect time to greet others, and we love to converse with our friends in snack bars and coffee shops. In short, although many of us spend considerable time with television, we still spend a great deal of time communicating with other people.

Now project yourself into the future. The lure of television still attracts you, but it is joined by many more programming possibilities. Instead of taking a break between classes at the local coffee shop or walking across campus to attend another class, you spend the majority of the day in your room taking courses via cable television, from not one but four or five colleges around the country. Chemistry from the University of Washington, physics from the University of Notre Dame, English from the University of Texas, and sociology from the University of North Carolina are all part of your daily academic routine. The time you spend in a television screen can be as much as r more hours per day. Then there is shopping by cable, banking by cable, and endless other services by cable. What will be the psychological effect on people of this concentrated media interaction and human isolation?

As you learn about the economic, political, and technological developments in telecommunication, remember its effect upon the relationship between people and society.

SUMMARY

Cable began in the 1940s in Oregon and Pennsylvania as a means of bringing distant television signals to outlying communities. Antennas were installed on mountaintops and a cable led to the community. Individual households paid a fee to have their television connected to the cable. Today, the system still operates on the same principle.

A cable system contains a headend, the combination of people and hardware responsible for originating, controlling, and processing signals over the cable system. A trunk cable leads from the headend to main feeder streets in a community and subtrunks feed to smaller traffic arteries. A drop cable runs from the subtrunk to the household, where it is connected to the television set through a home terminal. Cable systems are of two types: one-way and two-way.

Pay cable is the delivery of information and/or services to cable subscribers for a fee beyond the regular monthly rental fee. Pay-cable connection arrangements include simple-fee, tiering, and pay-per-view.

Television is cable's primary programming, but radio stations are also carried by cable systems.

Many cable systems are joining together in cable interconnects. These permit broad coverage of a market and are especially appealing to advertisers, who by making one buy can reach a larger number of viewers, much the same way they would with television or radio time.

At the heart of the cable system is the cable franchise. Landing a franchise is an effort in political strategy, technical knowledge, and promises. In some communities the cable operator promises more than can be delivered in an effort to win the franchise. Surrounding any franchise is uncertainty as to how new technologies will affect the system's operation and profits. Consultants, local lobbying groups, and investors are all part of the franchising process.

Cable performs the same function of improved reception and increased channels as it did in its infancy. Since the 1940s, however, many new services have been added. These include entertainment, news, sports, and weather channels. Instructional television and local arts programming is available. PlayCable, shopping services, and videotex and teletext are also offered.

Some newspapers have established working relationships with cable companies and produce television news programming from their newsroom. Networks of newspapers who program cable channels are developing. These permit advertisers to make one media buy and reach a large number of viewers over a wide market area.

Local political programming and cable access are two additional services. Each finds a highly specialized audience. Although highly touted by cable operators, local-access programming is not widespread.

Fundamental issues still divide broadcasters and cable. Both economic and political, the split may be healing as more and more broadcasting stations and cable companies are owned by the same communication conglomerates. Moreover, both cable managers and broadcasters are realizing that they face similar problems, which can best be addressed through a cooperative instead of an adversary relationship.

Among the regulatory and economic issues facing cable are the different levels of control exercised by local, state, and federal government. Moreover, cable is a capital-intensive industry and therefore sustains formidable costs before it can deliver service to a community.

Managing a cable system means dealing with such problems as disconnects, "untouchables" who have negative feelings toward television or cable, the placing of program listings, and poor customer service.

As cable becomes a more and more important medium we should not forget to be sensitive to its impact on society and to the way it changes our media habits.

OPPORTUNITIES
FOR FURTHER LEARNING

A Cable Primer. Washington, D.C.: National Cable Television Association, 1981.

ADLER, R., and W. S. BAER, eds., *Cable and Continuing Education*. New York: Praeger, 1973.

———, *The Electronic Box Office Humanities and Arts on the Cable*. New York: Praeger, 1974.

BABE, R. E., *Cable Television and Telecommunications in Canada*. East Lansing: Graduate School of Business Administration, Michigan State University, 1975.

BAER, W. S., *Cable Television: A Handbook for Decision Making*. Santa Monica, Calif.: Rand Corporation, 1973.

BALDWIN, T. F., and D. S. McVOY, *Cable Communication*. Englewood Cliffs, N.J.: Prentice-Hall, 1983.

BRAUNSTEIN, Y. M., K. K. KALBA, and L. S. LEVINE, *The Economic Impact of State Cable TV Regulation*. Cambridge, Mass.: Harvard Program on Information Resources Policy, 1978.

GILLESPIE, G., *Public Access Cable Television in the United States and Canada*. New York: Praeger, 1975.

Glossary of Cable and TV Terms. Northbrook, Ill.: A. C. Nielsen, 1981.

KAATZ, R. B., *Cable: An Advertiser's Guide to the New Electronic Media*. Chicago: Crain Books, 1982.

KALBA, K. K., L. S. LEVINE, and A. E. BIRINYI, *Regulatory Politics: State Legislatures and the Cable Television Industry*. Cambridge, Mass.: Harvard Program on Information Resources Policy, 1978.

KLETTER, R. C., *Cable Television: Making Public Access Effective*. Santa Monica, Calif.: Rand Corporation, 1973.

KNECHT, K., *Designing and Maintaining the CATV and Small TV Studio* (2nd ed.). Blue Ridge Summit, Pa.: TAB Books, 1976.

LeDUC, D. R., *Cable Television and the FCC*. Philadelphia: Temple University Press, 1973.

MORGAN, M., and N. ROTHSCHILD, *Cable TV, Peers, and Sex-Role Cultivation in the Electronic Environment*. Beverly Hills, Calif.: Sage, 1983.

MUTH, T. A., *State Interest in Cable Communications*. New York: Arno Press, 1979.

PARK, R. E., *Audience Diversion Due to Cable Television*. Santa Monica, Calif.: Rand Corporation, 1979.

SCHILLER, D., *CATV Program Origination and Production*. Blue Ridge Summit, Pa.: TAB Books, 1979.

SCHINK, G. R., and S. THANAWALA, *The Impact of Cable TV on Local Station Audience*. Washington, D.C.: National Association of Broadcasters, 1978.

SMITH, R. L., and R. B. GALLAGHER, *The Emergence of Pay Cable Television*, 4 vols. Cambridge, Mass.: Technology and Economics, 1980.

VEITH, R., *Talk Back TV: Two-Way Cable Television*. Blue Ridge, Pa.: TV Books, 1976.

WEBSTER, J., *The Impact of Cable and Pay Cable Television on Local Station Audiences*. Washington, D.C.: National Association of Broadcasters, 1982.

9

TELETEXT AND VIDEOTEX

In many parts of the world a television viewer whose set is equipped with a special converter can turn the channel selector and read an electronic newspaper, learn of new products at the grocery store, check airline schedules, or learn what is playing at the local theater. Some experts predict that by 1990 the amount of such electronic textual information we consume will have increased dramatically, changing the way we use television and other media. Transmission of textual information by over-the-air signals is called teletext. Transmission by a wired two-way interactive system is called videotex. Both terms require explanation.

THE OPERATION OF TELETEXT

Transmission System

Teletext is primarily a one-way system (Figure 9–1) of transmitting textual information,

most commonly by means of the vertical blanking interval (VBI) of a television signal. The VBI is the thick black bar that appears on a television screen when the vertical-hold adjustment is manipulated. Teletext signals can also be transmitted over the entire television channel. FM-radio subcarrier signals, signals transmitted on unused portions of the assigned frequency, can also transmit a teletext signal, and some FM radio stations have experimented in sending teletext. The textual "frames," pages of text which fill the television screen, are transmitted in a rapidly repeated sequence, and the viewer "captures" a specific frame by means of the special converter and hand-held key pad attached to the television set.

System Capacity

The capacity of the system is limited by the number of frames that the viewer can wait through before frustration sets in and the

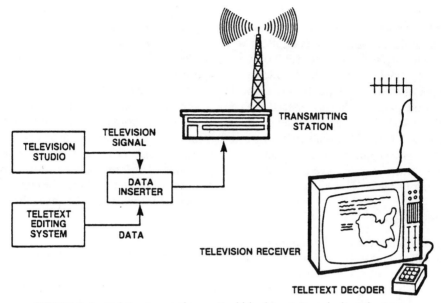

FIGURE 9-1 Teletext uses the vertical blanking interval of a television signal to carry textual information. (National Association of Broadcasters)

system goes unused. At a transmission rate of about five frames per second, a thousand frames can be stored and still make the system appealing to the user.

Graphic displays, though more appealing to the user, take longer to present than simple textual information. As a result, combination textual and graphic systems stressing news, sports, weather, and other popular information have become popular. In designing a system that will be profitable, one must take into account both the technical and content limitations of the system. To be appealing to an advertiser the information must be attractively packaged. To be appealing to a user it must be quickly accessible.

One of the earliest United States teletext systems belonged to KSL-TV in Salt Lake City. It consisted of a hand-held decoder control pad about the size of a small calculator along with a conventional television set. The decoder had three buttons on its right side for the functions TEXT, MIX, and PICTURE. With the TEXT button the user could access the teletext information exclusively. Pressing the PICTURE button resulted in the appearance of the standard television picture. The MIX button presents both text and picture. The decoder also contained a concealed button for displaying the answer to educational-quiz questions.[1]

Electronic Page Types

The KSL-TV system presented A-, B-, C- and D-type pages. Teletext systems use such page designations to describe page sequencing. A-type pages are single textual pages sent over the system and captured by users. When an A-type page is accessed and the user is finished reading it, he or she can command the decoder to call up another page. B-type pages are sequences of pages. A user can command the decoder to call up pages containing particular information, for example, grocery ads. The system then cycles through the grocery ads. C-type pages are accessed through a time code that can be keyed in on the decoder. For example, if we want to select a page transmitted at 9:00 A.M. then we key in 9:00 A.M. on the decoder control panel and at 9:00 A.M. the system will capture that page. Perhaps a special recipe for beef stew is being transmitted at 9:00 A.M. but we won't be home to capture it ourselves. By keying in the correct code when we return we can have the recipe displayed on our television screen.[2]

Two-Way Teletext

In two-way teletext the user commands the central teletext storage computer by telephone; the transmission back to the viewer is by standard over-the-air television signals or cable. Using a touch-tone telephone the user dials the telephone number displayed on the teletext page appearing on the television set. The computer answers the telephone and

transmits on a one-shot basis a D-type, or *decision* page. From the items on the decision page the user can select additional pages by keying in the correct numbers on the telephone.[3]

Touch-tone teletext operates on the theory that a station's teletext computer can store many more pages than the typical teletext cycle can accommodate and still have user appeal. The user wanting a small amount of information not normally being transmitted can telephone the computer and have the information sent over the system.

THE OPERATION OF VIDEOTEX

Unlike teletext, which uses television transmission, videotex is a two-way wired communication system (Figure 9–2) connecting the user with a central computer by telephone or cable. Videotex, like teletext, can

FIGURE 9–2   Videotex operates as a two-way wired transmission system. (FCC)

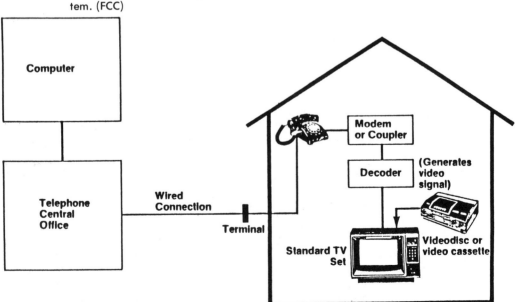

also be received on a home television set through the use of an interactive terminal or personal computer. The practical capacity of a videotex system is much larger than that of a teletext system. Tens of thousands of pages of text are easily stored by a small videotex system, and larger systems are confined only by the storage capacity of the computer. Although a teletext system could hold an equal amount of information, it would take too long to access it. Unlike teletext, where the user must wait until a frame rolls by and then capture it, the frame is immediately accessed with videotex.

INTERACTIVITY AND USER SATISFACTION

Important to an understanding of how teletext and videotex work is the concept of interactivity—the ratio of "user activity to system activity."[4]

The Range of Interactivity

Think of interactivity as two extremes. At one extreme is a one-way cable system that transmits textual news. The teletext concept is not even in use. The user simply tunes to the cable channel and reads the changing frames of news. The user has no control over what appears on the screen. At the other extreme is a two-way interactive videotex system. Perhaps it is used for an instant electronic-mail function in which two persons type messages to each other through a central computer. Both the cable and the videotex system use a central computer. With the cable system, interactivity is zero. In the electronic-mail function of the videotex system it is one to one. Neither is optimal for a general application of videotex or teletext. For example, if the only use of a teletext system was to send information one

way by over-the-air television signals and the user had no control over what was seen on the screen, the system would have little value. On the other hand, if a videotex system could merely access information sent to another user, the telephone or regular mail would be much more economical. In between is where teletext and videotex systems operate most efficiently. Theoretically, a teletext system containing only a few pages of information can be accessed just as fast and with as much user satisfaction as a videotex system having the same amount of information. When the information increases, however, the interactivity of the system becomes critical.

System Advantages and Disadvantages

Experts speculate that both systems will have an edge over other textual-transmission systems in the near future. The technologies are expected to grow considerably, especially in the United States, where they are still in their infancy. Although videotex systems hold more information and can be quickly accessed, not everyone owns a personal computer or the interactive terminal necessary to access the system. Moreover, accessing the system costs money. Charges are similar to economical long-distance telephone rates. With teletext the system can be practically free, the only cost being an original expenditure for a decoder or special television set equipped to receive teletext. Moreover, every television station and FM radio station could send teletext signals, as can one-way cable systems. Thus, teletext may have more senders and receivers of information than videotex.

An advantage of teletext is that additional decoders can be added to a system at no extra cost to the operator (unless, of course, the operator is buying the decoders). Nor will more television households having de-coders affect the responsiveness of the system. However, the more information that is sent over the system, the more space is necessary on the electromagnetic spectrum and the more time is necessary for the system to respond to a user's request. In other words, a user will have to wait longer to capture a page being sent in sequence.

At the same time, remember, videotex has some distinct advantages over teletext. Because the central computer handles the user interaction, much more information can be included in a videotex system without the responsiveness of the system being slowed. True interactive communication between a user and the central computer can take place with videotex.

EARLY BRITISH, FRENCH, AND CANADIAN TRIALS

Although KSL-TV was experimenting with teletext in the late 1970s, experiments in two-way interactive television had originated earlier, especially in the United Kingdom and France.

United Kingdom

The Prestel (Figure 9–3) videotex system operated by the British Post Office was developed in the United Kingdom in the early 1970s, pilot-tested in 1976, and phased into a public Test Service in 1978. A Public Service opened in London in 1979 and a Full Service was extended to other parts of the United

FIGURE 9-3 The British Prestel system was developed by the British Post Office and operates with information provided by more than 700 suppliers. (Prestel)

Kingdom in 1980. Two years after the Full Service was initiated Prestel claimed 16,000 subscribers who could access over 200,000 pages of information supplied by over 700 information sources.[5]

Teletext systems also became operational in the United Kingdom in the mid 1970s. The BBC developed its CEEFAX system and the Independent Broadcasting Authority developed ORACLE. CEEFAX was referred to as the "Magazine of the Air" and by the late 1970s was distributing through BBC-1 and BBC-2 about 200 pages of information. Both systems use the vertical blanking interval of lines 17, 18, 310, and 331 of the television signal.

France

The mid 1970s also saw the French, through their postal and telephone service begin a field trial of videotex service called Teletel. The first field trial involved approximately 3,000 users and 150 information suppliers.[6] At the same time an electronic telephone directory was field-tested: subscribers could choose between the printed or electronic directory. In the first field test, 2,000 users were able to access regional white and yellow pages containing 270,000 entries.

The Teletel system was part of France's Telematique program, the goal of which was to bring to all homes in France the combined advantages of computer and communications technology and services. Along with the telephone directories the early experiments included agricultural information made available to French farmers. Electronic mail, farm-management advice, agricultural market reports, and production advice were available in the system.[7]

Much of the publicity surrounding the French involvement in videotex and teletext services focused on the technical capabilities of the French-built Antiope system, which

was adaptable to both teletext and videotex. Antiope, unlike the British teletext system, was not limited to specific lines on the vertical blanking interval. Originally developed from a data-transmission service called Didon, Antiope dates back to 1972, when the Center for the Study of Television and Telecommunications started a research project on the system. Antiope was first displayed in 1974 and by the early 1980s was being marketed in the United States by the Washington, D.C., firm of Antiope Videotex Systems. Along with its teletext and videotex capability and its flexibility in not being tied to the VBI, the Antiope system is compatible with different television-transmission systems.[8]

Canada

In Canada videotex experiments began in the late 1970s with the Telidon system. The early experiments identified Telidon as being more flexible than the French and British systems, primarily because of its incorporation of a picture-coding device that produced high-quality graphics. Commercial services using both videotex and teletext were operating extensively in Canada by the early 1980s.[9]

Much of the Canadian development of teletext and videotex occurred because of the Canadian government's $9.5-million Telidon Industry Investment Stimulation Program. Project organizers agreed to match the government's contribution by buying an equal number of Telidon terminals. Early field tests of the Telidon system incorporated business systems and computer-assisted learning and health programs. Some of these systems used telephone lines while others used cable, microwave, and satellite communication.[10] Bell Canada operated an early Telidon system which included 491 terminals and permitted users access to information from government agencies, travel services, retail-store chains, and banks.[11] Other Telidon trials were conducted in Alberta, Manitoba, and British Columbia.

The first commercial Telidon project was designed for the agribusiness community. It was a joint project undertaken by the Manitoba Telephone System and Informart, a large supplier of Telidon systems and services.[12] The project was also tested in Bakersfield, California.

The Canadian Broadcasting Company conducted a $6-million teletext experiment funded by the Department of Communications. The three-year project started in September 1982 and included 700 terminals rotating among 1,400 homes in Montreal, Toronto, and Calgary.[13]

EARLY VIDEOTEX TRIALS IN THE UNITED STATES

Rediffusion, Sterling, Telecable, TelePrompTer, and Mitre

The first videotex trials in the United States took place in the early 1970s. Using two-way cable, Rediffusion, Inc.; Sterling Communications, Inc.; Telecable Corporation; TelePrompTer Corporation; and the Mitre Corporation all experimented with two-way interactive television.[14] Rediffusion focused on subscriber-originated programming, Sterling concentrated on experimental security alarm systems in New York, and Telecable developed a two-way pilot project for educational purposes. Telecable also tested alarm systems and retail sales services in Overland Park, Kansas, near Kansas City. TelePrompTer's experiments were conducted in Los Gatos, California, and the Mitre Corporation's project was based in

Reston, Virginia. The Mitre system used telegraph and telephone lines for the return communication.[15]

Warner Cable

Warner Cable Corporation, a subsidiary of Warner Communications, began developing a two-way interactive cable system in 1973 and introduced it in Columbus, Ohio, in 1977. The Columbus system, called QUBE, was originally designed around thirty channels. Warner has since expanded the system to other cities. Advertising and marketing efforts were included in the early Columbus QUBE system.[16]

The CompuServe/AP Newspaper Trial

A videotex trial of major newspapers began in 1980 through the time-sharing resources of CompuServe. Through the help of the Associated Press, CompuServe linked up with the Columbus (Ohio) *Dispatch.* Subscribers to QUBE as well as owners of personal computers anywhere were able to access directly the stories in the *Dispatch's* computer. Shortly after the *Dispatch* began its electronic editions, other major newspapers began participating in the experiment, including the *Washington Post,* the *Los Angeles Times,* the *St. Louis Post Dispatch,* the *New York Times,* the *Minneapolis Star and Tribune,* the *Atlanta Journal and Constitution,* the Norfolk (Va.) *Virginian-Pilot and Ledger-Star,* the *San Francisco Chronicle,* the *San Francisco Examiner,* and the *Middlesex News* of Framingham, Massachusetts. An electronic edition of *Better Homes and Gardens* could be accessed as well.

Knight-Ridder in Coral Gables

Other videotex trials, also involving communication companies, took place in the early

1980s. AT&T and Knight-Ridder Newspapers initiated a trial system called VIEW-TRON in July 1980. Approximately 15,000 pages of information were made available to users who had specially adapted home terminals attached to their television sets. Thirty terminals were rotated among 160 households in Coral Gables, Florida. The *Miami Herald,* the Universal Press Syndicate, and the Associated Press were among the original information providers.[17] Advertisers on the system included Eastern Airlines, Sears, Roebuck, and J. C. Penney.[18]

AT&T and CBS in Ridgewood, New Jersey

A trial undertaken by AT&T and CBS in Ridgewood, New Jersey, in the fall of 1982 involved 200 households. The two companies shared the expenses of the test and cooperated in designing the computer hardware. AT&T provided the home terminals and the adapters for the TV receivers. CBS was responsible for the information content of the system. The stated goals of the program were to "research consumer acceptance of potential CBS videotex products and services" and to "assemble, develop and test creative, editorial, artistic, and data base management skills."[19]

Cox Cable's Omaha INDAX Trial

In 1980 Cox Cable Communications, a subsidiary of Cox Broadcasting Corporation, developed a textual service for subscribers to their cable services. Called INDAX, the system utilized the technical capabilities of both teletext and videotex. Field testing of the system began in February 1981 and commercial operation at Cox Cable's Omaha system in March 1982. The INDAX system was also utilized in an educational test in cooperation

with the University of Nebraska's Division of Continuing Education, the Corporation for Public Broadcasting, and the Cox cable systems in Omaha and San Diego. Courses in modern government, marriage and the family, and business writing were tested.

Kentucky's Green Thumb Project

In the early 1980s two Kentucky counties, Shelby and Todd, participated in a videotex project named Green Thumb. Farmers were assigned interactive home videotex terminals with which they could access via telephone a computer at the University of Kentucky's Agricultural Data Center in Lexington.[20] The system provided an average of 250 frames of information per month. "Weather maps and forecasts, along with market prices, were displayed in 30 to 35 frames each, as was information about home economics and plant diseases. Horticulture, agronomy, and county affairs would usually be covered in 15 to 25 frames and such topics as 4-H activities, rural sociology, and community development would receive at least five frames each."[21]

The KPBS Interactive Videotex Project

In San Diego a videotex trial was conducted by KPBS (a public television station) and the Center for Communications at San Diego State University. The center evaluated the trial under a grant from the Corporation for Public Broadcasting, which also provided funds for the experiment. Becoming operational on July 10, 1982, "the KPBS Interactive Videotex project was composed of two components—a conventional television series, . . . delivered via open-air broadcast and cable repeats, and an accompanying videotex segment, which provided electronic course materials, delivered via Cox Cable's INDAX system.''[22]

The Dallas BISON System

At the local level BISON, a Texas firm, was offering the text of the *Dallas Morning News* plus news from AP, UPI and the UPI financial wire, Reuters news service, the *New York Times* News Service, and eight news syndicates. BISON, (Belo Information System, Online Network) was also providing an entertainment guide, a Dallas restaurant directory, and the schedules of major sports teams as well as airlines serving the Dallas/Fort Worth Regional Airport and Love Field.[23] History may show such services as BISON to be the forerunners of hundreds of electronic data banks operating at the local level and complementing the national and international services of systems such as Prestel. Linked together in a network, videotex users in Orono, Maine, would access news from major metropolitan centers such as Dallas or from smaller towns such as Bend, Oregon just as easily as news from New England.

EARLY TELETEXT TRIALS IN THE UNITED STATES

In 1983 the FCC officially approved teletext service, though it avoided specifying technical standards.[24] Prior to that date a number of experiments had been conducted on the feasibility of the service. One of the earliest, as we have seen, took place at KSL–TV in Salt Lake City.

KSL–TV, Salt Lake City

The KSL–TV teletext service began in earnest in 1977 and the first teletext signal was broadcast on June 15, 1978. Employing a modification of the British CEEFAX sys-

tem, the early KSL–TV system had a capacity of 800 pages, though it ran only 75. Newspaper ads, movie and airline schedules, and grocery specials were included. The station also worked with the Touch-tone teletext system discussed earlier, which permits users to access the teletext computer directly and have the information sent to the home terminal via the over-the-air television system. Later the system was adapted to permit access from home computers.

KCET's "Now" Magazine

In 1981 KCET in Los Angeles became the first public station to experiment with teletext. WETA in Washington, D.C., followed. KCET's *now!* magazine (Figure 9–4) premiered on April 1, 1981. It included a content page, which gave the viewer a selection from which to choose. An educational section included such subjects as children's history. Other material included a cultural-events section and an ''Inside L.A.'' section. National news was featured as well as special reports, weather, sports, and finance. Employing the Antiope system designed by the French, the KCET signal occupied two lines of the channel-28 vertical blanking interval.

FIGURE 9-4 The "now!" magazine of KCET–TV included national news as well as local cultural and educational information. (KCET)

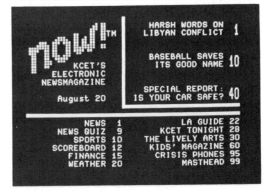

WETA, Washington, D.C.

In 1981 WETA undertook a cooperative test of teletext with New York University's Alternative Media Center. Using the Canadian Telidon system, the WETA system employed forty terminals in homes and another ten in public buildings, including the Smithsonian Institution. "Initially a menu of 135 pages was offered at an access rate of eight frames per second."[25] After a six-month review the number of pages was cut to 65 which resulted in an increasing viewing time of six seconds per page.[26]

WHA-TV, Madison, Wisconsin

In 1982 WHA-TV at the University of Wisconsin, a Duluth, Minnesota, station, and other stations began broadcasting a teletext service called Infortex. The service provided teletext programming to the hearing-impaired and farmers. Two channels were devoted to the service, both using the vertical blanking interval. The channel for the agricultural community included regional weather forecasts, storm warnings, and agricultural information. Reports on grain, livestock, and dairy markets were also included, as were special reports from the University of Wisconsin extension service and the United States Department of Agriculture Market News Service. The channel for the hearing-impaired provided UPI news headlines, health and consumer tips, and program listings for closed-caption programs (programs that present the dialogue textually alongside the picture so that viewers can read it).

KPIX-TV, San Francisco

In San Francisco KPIX-TV, a Group W station, developed a teletext service called DirectVision. Three teletext magazines were the heart of the service (Figure 9-5). Maga-

FIGURE 9-5 San Francisco's KPIX-TV DirectVision provided three teletext magazines with such information as local news, advertising, and classifieds. (KPIX-TV)

zine 1, *The Shopper,* included information on bargains in the stores of sponsors. Magazine 2 was called *Metro Mart* and included classified advertising produced in cooperation with a San Francisco publishing group, Sparks Newspapers. An index of alphabetical listings permitted the viewer to select the products advertised in the classifieds. For example, page 77 of the index listed advertisers whose names began with the letter *Y,* such as Yamaha motorcycle dealers. Magazine 3, *Newsline,* provided news features on the San Francisco area.

Trials in Chicago, Cincinnati, and Louisville

Chicago, Cincinnati, and Louisville were the sites of early teletext systems in the Midwest. A cooperative teletext experiment was begun in Chicago in 1982 by Centel Communications, Honeywell, and Field Electronic Services, a subsidiary of Field Enterprises. The system was an outgrowth of the Nite Owl teletext news service on Channel 32, a Field Enterprises station. About one hundred homes participated in the initial service.

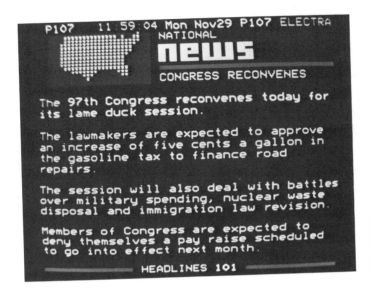

FIGURE 9-6 The experimental system operated by Taft Broadcasting's WKRC–TV in Cincinnati began with a one-hundred page teletext magazine serving approximately 50 homes. (Taft Broadcasting, WKRC–TV)

WKRC–TV in Cincinnati began a teletext trial in 1982 after placing teletext equipment in both homes and public places. Titled Electra, the service went on the air with a one-hundred-page teletext magazine (Figure 9–6) serving fifty homes. In early 1983 WKRC's parent company, Taft Broadcasting, announced an agreement with Zenith Radio Corporation whereby Zenith would produce the receiving equipment for the service.

A subsidiary of the *Louisville Courier-Journal* and the *Louisville Times* announced plans in 1981 for a teletext service using the Antiope system. In conjunction with a cable company, it inserted classified ads in teletext programming delivered through the cable system.[27]

The Dow Jones Trial in Danbury, Connecticut

Dow Jones, in cooperation with the Ottaway Newspapers Group, a Dow Jones subsidiary, conducted a teletext trial in Danbury, Connecticut. Using Antiope equipment, the system brought together the local Tele-

PromPTer cable system and the local Ottaway newspaper, the *Danbury News-Times.* Teletext decoders installed in about forty homes in Danbury and another ten in nearby Bethel made up the initial system design.

KTTV–TV and the Summer Olympics

During the Olympic Games in the summer of 1984, KTTV–TV in Los Angeles in cooperation with Zenith, Sanyo, Harris, Taft, the BBC, and Ameritext, operated a teletext service which served about 100 locations in the vicinity of the Games. The 100-page service included information about the Olympics and traffic reports provided by the California Department of Transportation.

Network Teletext Trials

CBS and NBC experimented with teletext in 1981. The CBS system was labeled EXTRAVISION and started as a cooperative experiment among the CBS Broadcast Group, KCET and KNXT in Los Angeles, and Telediffusion de France. Having begun as a one-way system with receivers located in public places such as shopping malls, EXTRAVI-SION later operated as a two-way teletext system and was expanded to private homes.[28] The system made available about eighty pages of information, which was drawn from such sources as CBS's own news-gathering organization and included such categories as "news updates, sports scores, smog conditions, airline flight schedules, a Los Angeles things-to-do-and-see calendar, stock prices and traffic conditions."[29]

In November 1981 NBC unveiled a teletext experiment called Tempo NBC Los Angeles, involving KNBC–TV in Los Angeles, and also KNXT and KCET. The information for the service was coded in the computer at the NBC Teletext Broadcast Center in Burbank and then transmitted to KNBC. The theater, biking and walking tours, restaurants, gallery and museum listings, and other items of local interest were included. The teletext *Tempo* magazine ran the same information on Monday through Friday and

special features such as ski reports and letters from viewers on the weekend.[30] The experiment also investigated the feasibility of incorporating advertising into a teletext service. Through the cooperation of a number of sponsors who received free time and space on the system, NBC was able to measure viewer reaction to a variety of advertising messages and formats. For example, Loews Hotels and Chief Auto Parts used an 800 number the viewer could call to make reservations or locate a nearby dealer. The Bermuda Tourist Development Authority and a real-estate company directed the viewer to other pages where detailed information was available. *Newsweek,* Dow Jones, the Lincoln Mercury Dealers of Southern California, PSA Airlines, and Pan American World Airways also participated.

Time Video Information Services

Time, through its subsidiary Time Video Information Services, Inc. launched a six-month teletext trial in 1982 (Figure 9–7).

FIGURE 9–7 Time operated its teletext trial through its subsidiary Time Video Information Services, reaching homes in San Diego and Orlando. (Time Video Information Services)

Homes in San Diego and Orlando, Florida, were involved in the trial, which was a satellite-distributed service to cable systems operated by the American Television and Communications Corporation, also a Time subsidiary. Local and regional information was provided by the *Orlando Sentinel* and the *Copley Press* in San Diego. Approximately 4,500 pages of information were made available to four hundred households. Research on the trial was contracted to A. C. Nielsen, and with the support of the Consumer Communications Center a laboratory was designed specifically to develop and test the teletext service. News, sports reports, weather forecasts, financial information, video games, and electronic television guides were included in the content.

Six advertising agencies, collectively called the Advertising Advisory Council, were also involved in the trial. The agencies, which received a retainer for providing content for the six-month test, were BBDO, Doyle Dane Bernbach, J. Walter Thompson, McCann-Erickson, Ogilvy and Mather, and Young and Rubicam.[31]

ISSUES IN CONSUMER ACCEPTANCE: RESULTS OF TELETEXT AND VIDEOTEX TRIALS

Whether teletext and videotex will become a major force in electronic communication will depend on how the information and hardware suppliers adapt to the needs of the consumer. Some results of the early field tests of these two technologies shed light on the direction that adaptation must take.

Graphic Presentation of Textual Material

Results from the Los Angeles KCET test of the teletext magazine *now!* showed the importance of tailoring the display of textual information to the consumer rather than asking the consumer to adapt to the text.[32] Since viewers have little experience in reading from a television screen, the layout and design of the textual information must be appealing. KCET discovered that the use of substantial black space helped keep the page clean and free from overcrowding.[33] Contrasting colors can be used to add emphasis to a page. For example, yellow is an effective color for information the reader must notice first.[34] Dates and times were found to be attractive when displayed in white. Sufficient margins were also found to be important.

A tight writing style is also necessary since the space limitations of a page of video textual information dictate that a great deal of information be presented without a great many words. "By writing in the present tense and using brief sentences of simple structure, the magazine's 40-word headline news stories seek to be as pointed and concise as possible."[35]

Appeal of Services

The Knight-Ridder VIEWTRON trial found news to have the greatest appeal. VIEWTRON users involved in the fourteen-month trial ranked the available categories of information in the following order of importance:[36]

1. news
2. bulletin board
3. local entertainment and events
4. food and dining
5. education
6. consumer information
7. shopping
8. games and quizzes
9. sports
10. health and medical information
11. travel
12. money management
13. home
14. auto

VIEWTRON viewers also listed the merchandise or services they would be most likely to purchase:[37]

46 percent said bargain and sale items from major retailers.

34 percent said services, such as those of plumbers, gardeners, and florists.

34 percent said hard-line merchandise, such as small appliances.

24 percent said soft-line items, such as groceries, clothing, and linens.

8 percent said major purchases, such as furniture and refrigerators.

Finally, VIEWTRON users preferred to use the system to *reduce* time spent on the following activities:[38]

64 percent said shopping for nongrocery items.

62 percent said shopping for groceries.

60 percent said looking up reference material at the library and other sources outside the home.

57 percent said getting information on shopping.

57 percent said paying bills and taking care of household finances.

53 percent said keeping up with local, national, and world news.

46 percent said keeping track of actual or potential investments.

Clearly the perceived advantage is convenience.

Demographic Characteristics of Users

Subscribers to videotex services show a generally high education and income level. For example, the CompuServe/AP newspaper trial showed that 45 percent of CompuServe subscribers had an average household income of $35,000+ and 62 percent were college graduates. This profile is changing, however. More and more younger people, including students, are subscribing to the service, as are people with lower education

levels. Moreover, individuals with children are more likely to subscribe than when the service began.[39] Earlier subscribers to CompuServe indicated they subscribed because it was something new. Later subscribers were less likely to cite this as a reason for subscribing and "more likely to indicate business or educational use."[40]

Relationship to the Use of Other Media

The VIEWTRON trial indicated that television use suffered when use of VIEWTRON increased. The percentages of VIEWTRON homes *using television and other media less* were as follows:[41]

television	45 percent
newspapers	33 percent
catalogues	24 percent
telephone yellow pages	22 percent
magazines	19 percent
radio	18 percent
books	13 percent

Television use among CompuServe users also showed a decline.

Part of the reason television took such a steep plunge is that in homes where a separate videotex terminal is not in use, it is the television set that is used to access the service. Use of the television set for videotex prohibits its simultaneous use for standard television viewing. As low-cost terminals are made available and households acquire more sets to compensate for increased videotex use, television viewing should not suffer the dropoff indicated in these early trials.

TELETEXT AND VIDEOTEX SERVICES

Just now emerging from their experimental era, interactive video systems offer a variety of services and conveniences.

Programming Flexibility

Two-way interactive video systems permit cable companies to offer pay-per-view programming. By keying in the correct information, the viewer is able to select specific programs. A subscriber might ask to see a special movie-preview channel and then choose one of the selections. If before the movie runs the subscriber wants to make another selection or cancel the order, he or she can accomplish this simply by keying in the correct information on the home terminal.

Another feature of interactive video is its ability to provide subscribers with control over television content. A subscriber might want to block out X-rated movies, for example. The cable-company computer would not activate such programming to a household that keyed in that restriction.[42]

Electronic Banking

Many of us take for granted the corner bank machine that permits us to insert a coded card and conduct transactions. Many of these same functions can be performed from our home or office through the use of video-tex (Figure 9–8). The same cable or telephone line that connects our home video terminal with the computer that brings us the evening newspaper can interface with our bank's computer. By keying in the correct information we can conduct a host of banking services. We can instantly check the balance in our accounts. We can transfer funds from one account to another. We can pay bills electronically. Moreover, information on bank services is available at any time.

If a printer is connected to our home terminal, we can produce a printed copy of any of the information on the video screen. Secrecy is maintained by subscriber codes. Multiple codes, such as a series of passwords, can add more security. Tampering with the system can cause the computer to block any additional transactions. For example, the bank's computer can be programmed so that if the passwords are not entered in the correct succession more than three times, it will alert bank officials to possible tampering.[43]

Detailed financial information and planning is available through various videotex services. For example, a user can access the latest business news and call up historical in-

FIGURE 9–8 Electronic banking is one of the services provided by videotex. One of the early systems was New York's Chemical Bank, which inaugurated the "Pronto" system. The system operated by using a special Atari personal computer. Balance inquiry, bill-paying, funds transfer, and electronic mail were some of the features announced at the introduction of the Pronto system. (Chemical Bank)

formation from business archives. If we call up a story about a company expanding into a new business, we can also call up earlier stories that tell us how successful previous business-expansion efforts were. If a new corporate board of directors is named, we can call up a story that will give us more information about who is chairing the board. Other financial services include international economic-planning guides, accounting guidance, tax information, corporate profiles, monetary exchange rates, stock trends and prices, prices of bonds, commodity news and information, money-market reports, information on mutual funds, financial planning and forecasting, and computer programs for financial problem solving.

Electronic Newspapers

The possibility of offering electronic editions of newspapers through videotex has encouraged a number of firms to make major investments in electronic publishing. The advantage of electronic newspapers is that they permit the publisher to reach *upscale* subscribers, those who have invested in home computers or special videotex terminals. The cost is smaller than that of publishing a newsprint edition, and the reporting staff—to be drawn from the staff producing the printed edition—is already in place.

Newspapers are accessed much the same as other data banks. For example, by keying in the proper code the subscriber can obtain a selection of newspapers from virtually anywhere. The subscriber then keys in a specific newspaper. He or she can select a particular section of the newspaper, and even a particular story. A printer can produce a hard copy in seconds. Advertisements can be programmed to appear with any story that is accessed, and can be selected so that they complement a particular story. For example, advertisements for flower seeds could be called up for stories on gardening.

Detailed information can be accessed, even from newspapers thousands of miles away. Assume you live in Ohio and are planning a trip to Oregon. You want to know whether to take along your skis. Using your videotex terminal, you can access the ski report in the sports section of an Oregon newspaper. The information will be up to date since it will be available as soon as it is placed in the Oregon paper's data base.

Want ads may turn out to be particularly attractive videotex information. Computer data banks are ideal for storing and calling up want ads, which need continual updating and deletion as items are sold. If we want to buy a car, we can call up the automobile index and find cars listed by year and make. We can then select a given year and find all of the advertised vehicles built in that year. We can read each want ad and select the car we want. The ad will have been placed in the computer as soon as it is called in to the newspaper. We will not need to wait for the newspaper to be physically printed and appear on our doorstep or the newsstand. As soon as the item sells, the seller notifies the newspaper, which can immediately delete the ad from the data bank.

Electronic Magazines

Interactive video permits readers to access magazines in much the same way they access newspapers. For example, the user can key in on the home terminal a code that produces a list of gardening magazines. From there the reader can select a particular magazine. Another code will produce a table of contents listing feature articles on anything from growing beans to building fences. The user then keys in the code for the article desired, which will be presented textually with illustrations.

Electronic teletext magazines, such as KCET's *now!* magazine, are also feasible. The BBC CEEFAX teletext system refers to its services as magazines. Different sections of a magazine provide information on news, weather, finance and business, and other services. Users can access additional information through subpages which exist in each section.

Magazines have traditionally been thought of as collections of articles, usually on a common subject, that are illustrated and bound together in pages smaller than those of a newspaper. However, any data bank containing information can be called a magazine if the information provider chooses to use the term. With the advent of electronic publishing, the physical characteristics which distinguish magazines from newspapers and other types of publications do not exist. Everything appears on a home video screen and the same technology is available to all information providers.

Encyclopedias

Assume we are writing a research paper and want general information. We might consult an encyclopedia. We could go to the library and look up the information. Another way to access an encyclopedia is through videotex. The well-known *World Book* encyclopedia also produces *Online World Book,* an electronic edition of the printed version. The *Online World Book* contains a menu with seven choices:

1. Online Encyclopedia
2. How to Use Online World Book
3. News Flashback
4. This Week in History
5. World Book Challenge
6. Product Information
7. World Book Talk-Back

By keying in choice # 1, we obtain directions on how to search for information in the en-cyclopedia. We will find, for example, that if we want to search for material on the subject *earth* we can key in EARTH. Articles dealing with earth include (1) "Earth," (2) "Earth Science," (3) "Earthenware," (4) "Earthquake," (5) "Earthshine," and (6) "Earthworm." If we want to learn more about earthquakes, we can press key 4 on our terminal and view the full text of the article on earthquakes. If we have a printer, we can obtain a hard copy of the article for future reference.[44]

Consumer- and Business-Information Services

When U.S. airlines underwent deregulation, many frequent travelers found themselves spending time calling travel agents in order to set up the best routes at the least expensive rates. Many used the publications of an Oak Brook, Illinois, firm called Official Airline Guides, Inc. A subsidiary of Dun and Bradstreet Corporation, this company publishes domestic and international airline schedules and travel guides. When it became clear that many business travelers were turning to personal computers and the accompanying videotex technology in order to improve efficiency in their office, the company launched the OAG Electronic Edition, a computerized airline-schedule and fare-information system designed to help businesses reduce their air-travel expenses.[45] This videotex service, which may be accessed from any interactive terminal, includes information on more than 640 airlines and hundreds of thousands of schedules (Figure 9–9).

The OAG Electronic Edition is only one of a number of business and consumer services that videotex makes available. Home shopping has been one of the most publicized. A videotex user can access electronic catalogues containing information on thousands of items of merchandise. By keying in

FIGURE 9-9 The OAG Electronic Edition is an automated version of the printed copies of the Official Airlines Guide. Included is schedule information for more than 640 airlines and data on more than 820,000 schedules for 115,000 city pairs. (Official Airlines Guides, Inc.)

our account number or bank-card number we can have merchandise automatically purchased and shipped and the charge placed on our monthly statement.

Additional consumer and business services available through videotex include information on personal computers, restaurant guides, hotel guides (Figure 9–10), college admissions and financial-aid information, grammar and spelling assistance, foreign-language instruction, career information, legal indexes and cases, automobile safety features and ratings, beauty tips, florist information and ordering, home decorating, recipes, health and medical information, real-estate listings, entertainment guides, and even information on wine tasting.

FIGURE 9-10 IBM developed an office videotex system for both internal and external communication. Accessing such things as hotel and restaurant reservations were some of the uses publicized by IBM. (Courtesy of International Business Machines Corporation)

Personal Communication

Interactive videotex permits users to converse with one another much as they would over the telephone, except with videotex the messages are typed and appear on the video-display terminal. Such deliberateness of communication may seem backward compared with the speed of the telephone. One advantage, though, is that with a printer a hard copy of the conversation can be kept for future reference.

Electronic Mail

Messages can be sent electronically from one user's terminal directly to another's. Electronic mail includes functions similar to sending and receiving printed mail. For example, by keying in the correct information a user can send an electronic letter to any other individual having access to an interactive terminal. Users can program an electronic mailbox and then check it to see if mail is waiting. If so they can access their letter, read it, and even store it for future reference.

INTERNATIONAL VIDEOTEX

With the growth in international relationships within the world social and economic order, current information has become an important part of international business. International videotex services are developing so that countries will have quick access to the data they need for carrying on their international business.

Multiple-Language Systems

Videotex systems such as the British Prestel system have available data banks in which information can be translated into different languages. This capability is especially use-ful in bilingual or multilingual areas, such as eastern Canada—where both English and French are commonly spoken—and in the international economy where people speaking different languages must have access to the same information.

Public-, Syndicated-, and Private-Access Capabilities

Different access capabilities exist for both domestic and international videotex information. Privacy of information, however, takes on a new importance where international competition is involved.

In the case of Prestel, for example, providers of information for international users can choose between three different access modes: public, syndicated, and private. *Public* information is available to any user of the Prestel system. Financial, marketing, travel, and consumer-oriented information is typical of this category.

Syndicated information is commercially valuable and has restricted access. To protect such information an international-information provider can form a syndicate of users, each assigned the syndicate's access code. The information is thereby restricted exclusively for use by syndicate members.

Private information—executive memoranda, sensitive corporate information, and other information of interest to a select group of users—can be handled best through a private-access mode. An internal-user group can be formed for this purpose.

THE FUTURE OF TELETEXT AND VIDEOTEX

If teletext and videotex are to reach their potential, a potential that some predict will translate into a billion-dollar industry by

1990, the industry and the consumers who pay for the services will both have to adapt to the technology.

Consumer Acceptance

Major marketing efforts will need to call attention to the services offered by teletext and videotex and also the utility of these services. Most consumers look at a television set more as a medium of entertainment than as a medium of information. The public will need to be educated as well as sold on the new services. This educational experience has already been started by interactive services such as the Warner QUBE system. Personal computers are also aiding the educational process. Having been exposed to an electronic keyboard and a video screen displaying data, users will be able to understand and accept a television that shows textual information.

Low-Cost Terminals

Any new medium that requires users to spend large sums of money to receive the service begins with a serious disadvantage. Teletext, for example, requires decoders that enable standard television receivers to convert signals carrying textual information. An outlay in the hundreds of dollars can create major consumer resistance. In the early days of teletext such prices were commonplace.

New television sets, such as those manufactured by Zenith, have built-in teletext decoders. Yet there is no indication that the public will run out and purchase new television sets just to receive teletext. For many people the separately purchased decoder will become the gate that opens into teletext. Teletext may come closer to achieving its full potential when television stations start providing the public with free decoders.

For videotex the problem is much the same as for teletext. Low-cost interactive terminals are necessary if one is to access data banks. Although any owner of a personal computer and a modem can access a videotex data bank, there is no indication that large numbers of people will buy a computer just to read an electronic newspaper.

Investment Capital

Another important factor in the success of teletext and videotex will be investment capital. Investment capital is money committed to a new venture in anticipation of a large return on the investment, which may, however, hold a sizable risk. Early in its development any new medium is a risk. The greater the risk the more difficult it is to attract investment capital. Thus, the growth of teletext and videotex will be determined by (1) the overall economy, which, when healthy, can provide investment capital, (2) the amount of risk involved, and (3) the potential for profit resulting from that investment. If the economy generates money, if the risk is low enough, and if the profit potential is high enough, then teletext and videotex systems will have a better chance of success.

Advertiser and Subscriber Support

The three factors just discussed—the economy, risk, and profit potential—are important, but getting advertisers and the public to pay for teletext and videotex will determine whether these media succeed. For example, advertisers are conditioned to spending money on such things as newspapers, the radio station, and television. Advertisers understand terms such as *full-page ad, sixty-second commercial,* and *prime-time scheduling.* With teletext a new vocabulary will be necessary. How effective are teletext advertisements versus television advertisements? Can an advertiser accustomed to sponsoring the evening television news be convinced she should invest money in an electronic textual page of advertising that doesn't move and will be seen only when a viewer elects to view the page instead of the entertainment of prime-time television?

Videotex, although it may be less dependent on advertising support, faces similar obstacles. A user must pay telephone charges in order to access data banks. Also, because videotex has an unlimited information capacity—as opposed to teletext, which is restricted to the amount of information that can be "rolled" to the public—the chances of any one piece of information being accessed are much less. Therefore, an information supplier must compete with thousands of pages of electronic information.

Only the future will tell us if teletext and videotex become mass media or turn out to be narrow in content and reach only a small group of users.

SUMMARY

In this chapter we have examined the developing media of teletext and videotex. Teletext is primarily a one-way transmission service. The vertical blanking interval of a standard television signal is commonly used to send teletext signals, although entire channels can be dedicated to the service. Some cable systems are involved in sending teletext, and some teletext systems, through the use of telephone connections to a central computer, enjoy two-way capability.

Videotex is a two-way wired service permitting the user to access a data bank containing pages of information that can be called up on a television screen or visual-display terminal. Because only so much information can be stored in a teletext system without slowing down a user's access time,

teletext cannot conveniently deliver large quantities of information. Videotex, which allows the user direct access to the data bank, can provide more information and enjoys faster access time. Both technologies are developing side by side.

Many teletext and videotex trials began in the 1970s. By the 1980s both systems were in operation in many parts of the world. Videotex systems included the British Prestel system, pilot-tested in 1976 and operational in 1978. The United Kingdom's CEEFAX teletext service also began in the 1970s and by the end of the decade was distributing about two hundred pages of information. In France the Antiope system offered technical advantages over CEEFAX. The French Teletel videotex service offered electronic mail and agricultural information. In Canada the Telidon system provided both teletext and videotex services.

In the United States Warner Cable, Mitre Corporation, Rediffusion, and Sterling Communications, were among the companies who participated in early videotex trials. KSL in Salt Lake City, KPBS in San Diego, KCET in Los Angeles, and WETA in Washington, D.C., were some of the television stations participating in early teletext experiments.

A wide range of services are available through teletext and videotex systems. Electronic mail, home banking and shopping, electronic publishing, electronic want ads, encyclopedia data banks, airline and hotel reservations, and restaurant and theater information are some examples.

Results of early teletext and videotex trials revealed a need to design textual information to fit the dimensions of a television screen and to adapt it to, rather than trying to change, the habits and preferences of users. The people who used teletext and videotex devoted less attention to other media. Television was the big loser. Early tests showed that older, more affluent users were attracted to the interactive media, but this trend began shifting in the early 1980s as more and more younger users, including college students, began to discover teletext and videotex.

The growth of teletext and videotex will depend on such factors as the graphic quality of the textual materials presented, the appeal of the services, the ability of companies to manufacture low-cost decoders and interactive terminals, the availability of investment capital, and advertiser and subscriber support.

OPPORTUNITIES
FOR FURTHER LEARNING

ALTERNATE MEDIA CENTER, *Teletext and Public Broadcasting*. Washington, D.C.: Corporation for Public Broadcasting, 1980.

BERGLER, P., *The Automated Citizen: Social and Political Impact of Interactive Broadcasting*. Montreal: Institute for Research on Public Policy, 1980.

BLOOM L. R., and others, *Videotex Systems and Services*. Boulder, Colo.: National Telecommunications and Information Administration, Institute for Telecommunication Sciences, 1980.

BRETZ, R., *Media for Interactive Communication*. Beverly Hills, Calif.: Sage, 1983.

BURKE, T. J. M, and M. LEHMAN, *Communication Technologies and Information Flow*. Elmsford, N.Y.: Pergamon Press, 1981.

CRANE, H. D., *The New Social Marketplace: Notes on Effecting Social Change in America's Third Century*. Norwood, N.J.: Ablex, 1980.

CRINER, K. M., "Videotex: Implications for Cable TV," in *The Cable/Broadband Communications Book,* Volume 2: 1980–81, ed. M. L. Hollowell. Washington, D.C.: Communications Press, 1980.

FEDIDA, S., and R. MALIK, *Viewdata Revolution*. New York: Halstead Press, 1979.

GAPPERT, G., and R. V. KNIGHT, eds., *Cities in the 21st Century*. Beverly Hills, Calif.: Sage, 1982.

GOODFRIEND, K. K., N. J. BAMBERGER, D. M. DOZIER, and J. P. WITHERSPOON, *KPBS Interactive Videotex Project: Final Report*. San Diego: KPBS-TV, 1982.

GRUNDFEST, J., and S. N. BROTMAN, *Teletext and Viewdata: The Issues of Policy, Service, and Technology*. New York: Aspen Institute for Humanistic Studies, 1979.

HAIGH, R. W., G. GERBNER, and R. B. BYRNE, eds., *Communications in the Twenty-First Century*. New York: John Wiley, 1981.

HILTZ, S. R., *Online Communities, Volume Two*. Norwood, N.J.: Ablex, 1983.

JOHNSON, A. W., *The Cultural Impact of Technological Change on Broadcasting*. Ottawa: Canadian Broadcasting Corporation, 1981.

LANCASTER, K. L., ed., *International Telecommunications: User Requirements and Supplier Strategies*. Lexington, Mass.: Lexington Books, 1982.

MONEY, S. A., *Teletext and Viewdata*. London: Newnes Technical Books, 1979.

MOSCO, V., *Pushbutton Fantasies: Critical Perspectives on Videotex and Information Technology*. Norwood, N.J.: Ablex, 1982.

NASH, D. C., and J. B. SMITH, *Interactive Home Media and Privacy*. Washington, D.C.: Collingwood, 1981.

NEUSTADT, R. M., *The Birth of Electronic Publishing: Legal and Economic Issues in Telephone, Cable and Over-the-Air Teletext and Videotext*. White Plains, N.Y.: Knowledge Industry, 1982.

OETTINGER, A. G., *Elements of Information Resources Policy: Library and Other Information Services*. Cambridge, Mass.: Harvard Program on Information Resources Policy, 1976.

ROSENBLOOM, R. S., *The Continuing Revolution in Communication Technology: Implications for the Broadcasting Business*. Cambridge, Mass.: Harvard Program on Information Resources Policy, 1981.

SIGEL, E., ed., *Videotext: The Coming Revolution in Home/Office Information Retrieval*. White Plains, N.Y.: Knowledge Industries, 1980.

Spigai, F., and P. Sommer, *Guide to Electronic Publishing: Opportunities in Online and Viewdata Services*. White Plains, N.Y.: Knowledge Industries, 1982.

Synthesis of Findings for AP/Newspaper/CompuServe Program of Marketing Research. Fair Lawn, N.J.: RMH Research, 1982.

Tydeman, J., H. Kipinski, R. P. Adler, M. Nyhan, and L. Zwimpfer, *Teletext and Videotex in the United States: Market Potential, Technology, Public Policy Issues*. New York: McGraw-Hill, 1982.

Videotex: Words on the TV Screen (*Viewdata, Teletext and the Rest*). Special issue of *Intermedia,* 7, no. 3 (May 1979). London: International Institute of Communications, 1979.

Webster, F., and R. Kevings, *Information Technology: Post-Industrial Society or Capitalist Control?* Norwood, N.J.: Ablex, 1983.

Wicklein, J., *Electronic Nightmare: The New Communications and Freedom*. New York: Viking, 1979.

Winsbury, R., *The Electronic Bookstall: Push-Button Publishing on Videotex*. London: International Institute on Communications, 1979.

Woolfe, R., *Videotex: The New Television/ Telephone Information Services*. London and Philadelphia: Heyden, 1980.

10

EMERGING TELECOMMUNICATIONS AND CONSUMER TECHNOLOGIES

Other technologies besides teletext and videotex are calling attention to the full potential of telecommunication. Investment capital is finding its way into these technologies, and terms such as *high-definition television, micro-TV,* and *cellular radio telephone* may someday become as familiar as the words *radio* and *television*. To better understand these varied technologies we may divide them, as this chapter does, into distribution systems, telephone systems, radio services, television receiving and transmitting technology, and consumer electronics.

DISTRIBUTION SYSTEMS

Radio waves provide one of the most common means of sending information from one point to another, but "wired" technologies are also becoming commonplace. One such technology is cable. Another is fiber optics.

Fiber Optics

Fiber optics utilizes thin strands of glass fiber through which light waves travel Figure 10-1. The concept can be seen in the department-store novelty lamps that transmit light from a lighted base to the ends of a spray of fibers. Fiber optics works by the same process except that light is transmitted through the fibers in the form of laser beams. Since laser beams are high-intensity coherent light waves, a form of electromagnetic energy, information can be sent over these waves from one point to another.

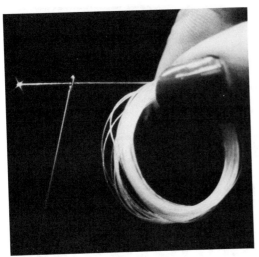

FIGURE 10-1 Fiber optic technology permits light waves to travel through strands of glass. A fiber optic system can carry thousands of channels of communication without distortion. (Western Electric)

Because light waves are extremely high on the electromagnetic spectrum—in the gigahertz range—considerable information can be packed into them. An optic cable with multiple strands of optic fibers, some thinner than human hairs, can carry thousands of television signals, while less than a hundred channels is standard for many coaxial cables. Since the light waves and the signals are kept in the glass fibers, fiber-optic communication is virtually free from the atmospheric and other interference that affects over-the-air distribution systems.

There are three main types of fiber-optic cables. The most common, *multi-mode graded-index fiber,* is used in some cable systems. It has broad bandwidths and a diameter of from fifty to sixty-three micrometers —less than the thickness of human hair. *Multi-mode step-index fibers* have less band-

FIGURE 10-2 AT&T's fiber optic communication link stretches from Washington, D.C. to Cambridge, Massachusetts. Thousands of telephone calls can be handled simultaneously through the link. (*Communications News*)

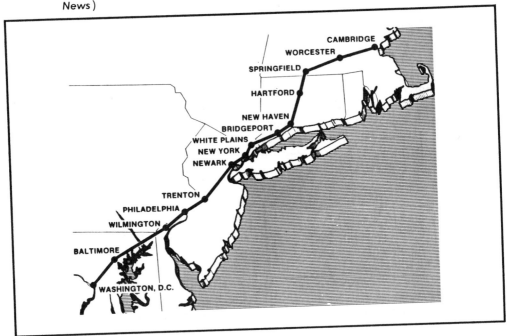

width—about 50 MHz—and are used for digital communication. *Single-mode fibers* are five micrometers thick (much less than the thickness of multi-mode graded-index fibers), and are mostly experimental, since their small diameter creates problems in installation and maintenance.[1]

The application of fiber-optic cables to communication is becoming widespread. A telephone application was reported in 1977 in Long Beach, California, where General Telephone and Electronics installed a fiber-optic link.[2] The first reported fiber-optic network-television link was in Tampa, Florida, in 1979. A CBS telecast of a National Football League game between the Tampa Bay Buccaneers and the New York Giants resulted in a 5.6-mile link between Tampa Stadium and downtown Tampa, where the signal was then distributed through non–fiber-optic channels to twenty other cities.[3] AT&T is scheduled to complete a New England link in the mid-1980s (Figure 10–2).

A typical fiber-optic installation in a cable system links a master antenna headend and a remote headend (Figure 10–3). Video inputs are fed into FM modulators. The output from the modulators is then fed into a *multiplexer,* which converts the signals to a frequency that fits into the frequency spectrum of the laser transmitter. From the transmitter the signal travels through a required number of optical repeaters to an optical receiver, where a demultiplexer reconverts the signal through FM demodulators to video outputs.[4]

Fiber-optic communication offers many advantages over over-the-air transmission and standard coaxial systems. It is particularly useful where interference-free communication is necessary, and a single fiber-optic cable has a large channel capacity and therefore permits multiple uses.

FIGURE 10–3 A fiber optic communication link for video includes equipment at a master headend and a remote headend. Video inputs are entered into the system through FM modulators (see FM transmission systems discussed in Chapter 6), are transmitted as laser beams by a laser transmitter, and eventually reach the remote headend where they are converted again to video outputs. (Times Fiber Communications, Inc.)

Point To Point Fiber Transport System

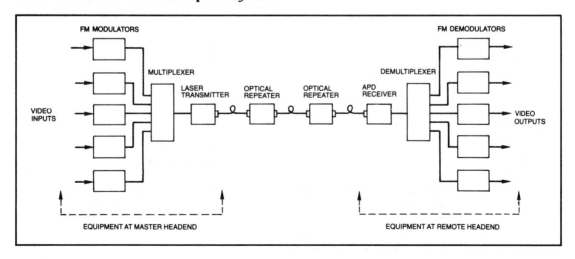

Multipoint Distribution Systems

In Chapter 7 we learned about microwave transmission systems. Microwaves are very short waves high on the electromagnetic spectrum. Multipoint distribution systems (MDS) (Figure 10–4) use microwaves to transmit television signals from a master omnidirectional microwave antenna to smaller microwave antennas, which are usually located on apartment houses and hotels, although some private homes are also attached to MDSs. The programming is similar to pay-cable programming, and the subscriber pays a fee to hook up to the sys-

tem. The advantage of the MDS is that it can operate without the installation of cables.

Multipoint distribution systems have considerable potential where cable systems are not operable, especially in high-density metropolitan areas. The cost of equipment has steadily declined, and most systems operate as common carriers, leasing channels to programmers who then buy programming from such sources as HBO and sell it to multi-unit dwellings. Construction of an MDS is not cheap, but the subscriber antenna need not be purchased until the subscriber requests service. With cable, the up-front investment of wiring a community is substantial and the cable-franchise require-

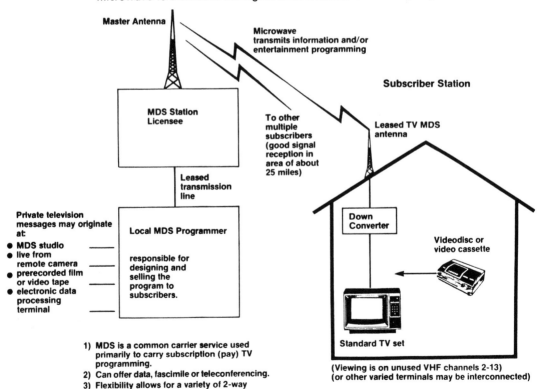

FIGURE 10–4 A multipoint distribution system uses point-to-point microwave to distribute the signal from a master antenna. (FCC)

Master Antenna

Microwave transmits information and/or entertainment programming

Subscriber Station

MDS Station Licensee

To other multiple subscribers (good signal reception in area of about 25 miles)

Leased TV MDS antenna

Leased transmission line

Private television messages may originate at:
- MDS studio
- live from remote camera
- prerecorded film or video tape
- electronic data processing terminal

Local MDS Programmer

responsible for designing and selling the program to subscribers.

Down Converter

Videodisc or video cassette

Standard TV set

1) MDS is a common carrier service used primarily to carry subscription (pay) TV programming.
2) Can offer data, fascimile or teleconferencing.
3) Flexibility allows for a variety of 2-way communications systems.

(Viewing is on unused VHF channels 2-13) (or other varied terminals may be interconnected)

ments can constitute a serious obstacle. A disadvantage of the MDS is that microwaves travel in line-of-sight paths. This can be a problem where numerous high-rise dwellings exist.[5]

Satellite Master-Antenna Television

Closely related to the MDS is satellite master-antenna television (SMATV). Whereas MDS antennas receive signals from a central ground-based microwave transmitter, SMATV antennas receive signals from satellites. The SMATV system operates entirely on private property. For example, a hotel might install an SMATV receiving antenna and then install cable from the antenna to each hotel room in much the same way an MDS system would be installed. Like the MDS, SMATV is particularly attractive in high-density population areas where cable service has not penetrated or is less than satisfactory.[6]

Problems arise when SMATV operators try to link buildings having different owners. Some form of connection is necessary, the most economical being cable. However, many municipalities believe that the stringing of cable brings the SMATV system under control of the local cable ordinance. Franchise fees, carriage requirements, and other restrictions immediately begin to apply. To get around such restrictions, SMATV operators sometimes resort to microwave hookups between buildings after obtaining from the FCC a cable-television relay-service (CARS) microwave license. The CARS license, while to some extent enabling the operator to avoid local control, brings the SMATV system under the FCC's cable-programming rules.

An SMATV system does not appear to need large numbers of channels in order to appeal to subscribers. One study found that a "well chosen four to five channel service can satisfy about 90 percent of the demand for nonbroadcast programming and gain a significant market share at the expense of cable.[7]

Subscription Television

Subscription television (STV) is a system whereby the signal from a television station is scrambled and the subscriber pays a monthly fee for a decoder that unscrambles the signal. Decoder rental fees provide revenues for the system, which can then offer special programming.

Four elements are important in a successful STV operation: (1) equipment manufacturers, (2) STV stations, (3) STV franchises, and (4) program suppliers.[8] Equipment manufacturers must produce reliable, tamper-proof equipment to decode the STV signal. When decoders are not secure unauthorized reception takes place, stripping the STV operator of revenue. Decoder prices vary, as does decoder reliability. Unsecured or less expensive decoders mean lost revenue and high maintenance costs. Expensive decoders mean high start-up costs. STV stations consist primarily of regular television stations that devote a portion of their programming day to STV. The STV franchisee runs the STV operation, leasing time from an STV station. Marketing, installation of decoders, warehousing and inventory control, billing and collections, and promotion are some of the functions a franchisee must undertake when operating an STV system.

Subscription television was given legitimacy in 1968, when the FCC established it as a broadcasting service. Its biggest competition has been pay cable, which had a distribution system in place before STV fully developed and a head start in developing relationships with program suppliers.

An STV system is much more costly than either an SMATV or MDS operation. Consequently, the investment capital has not been put forward to support STV the way it has cable television and other services. FCC restrictions on the number of STV stations and the amount of their programming have also had an effect on STV's development.

Low-Power TV

Low-power television (LPTV) stations are much like *translator stations,* which rebroadcast the signals of television stations to outlying areas (Figure 10–5). The difference between them is that the LPTV station can originate programming.

The procedure for obtaining an LPTV license is less complex than that for a full-service station, specifically in the areas of proposed programming, community needs, and ascertainment surveys. A full-service station, however, is more protected from interference. Should a full-service station decide to apply for the frequency used by a low-power station, it will be given priority even if an LPTV station is in operation.

Low-power television has its greatest potential in areas not fully served by existing full-service stations. LPTV stations are re-

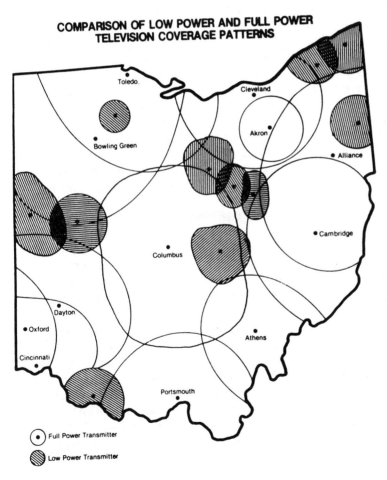

COMPARISON OF LOW POWER AND FULL POWER TELEVISION COVERAGE PATTERNS

Toledo.
Cleveland
Bowling Green
Akron
Alliance
Cambridge
Columbus
Dayton
Oxford
Athens
Cincinnati
Portsmouth

Full Power Transmitter

Low Power Transmitter

FIGURE 10–5 Low-power television consists of transmitters broadcasting with low power to relatively small geographic areas. It permits a larger number of stations to exist in the same geographic region and to serve smaller communities with individual television stations. (National Association of Broadcasters)

Overall Comparison between the Subjective Sharpness and Current and High Resolution Television and Film System

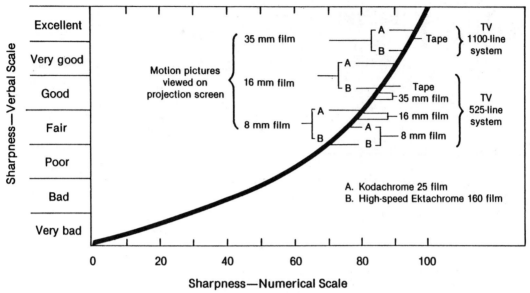

FIGURE 10–6 (Source: Donald G. Fink, "The Future of High Definition Television," *SMPTE Journal*, February, 1980, v. 89)

stricted in their coverage area by transmitter power ranging from one hundred to one thousand watts.

High-Definition Television

Imagine a television screen 8 inches by 8 inches with picture clarity equivalent to that produced by the best motion-picture studio and without the grainy effect seen on many large-screen televisions. High-definition television (HDTV) provides that level of picture quality (Figure 10–6). The standard United States transmission system of 525 lines cannot effectively be enlarged without distortion. HDTV, however, uses a system of 1,000+ lines and achieves the quality of 35mm film, the same quality found in a typical motion-picture theater.

The future of HDTV rests in consumer demand and the development of technology for receiving and transmitting HDTV signals.[9] Major motion pictures and televised spectaculars would be especially appealing on HDTV. HDTV does, however, take up more space on the electromagnetic spectrum than a standard television signal. Bandwidth-compression techniques (squeezing the signal into a smaller area of the spectrum) will need to be employed before the system can receive wide use. In addition, special receivers are necessary. Until these technical issues are dealt with by manufacturers and regulatory agencies, HDTV may initially be restricted to cable, theatre, or in-home systems (Figure 10–7) such as videocassette and videodisc players, where frequency allocation is not a critical issue.[10]

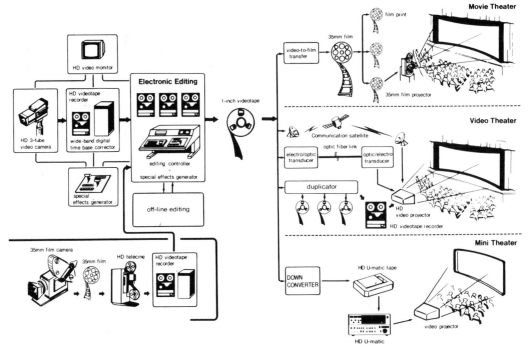

FIGURE 10-7 Because of the amount of space on the electromagnetic spectrum necessary to broadcast high-definition signals, HDTV's immediate future may turn out to be theatres and other public-viewing settings. (SONY)

VHF Drop-Ins

Limited spectrum space and the growing demand for television frequencies, have resulted in proposals that new television stations be "dropped in" between existing stations (Figure 10-8). The idea has not met with widespread approval, for a number of reasons.[11] First, additional stations could interfere with existing VHF stations, even if technical safeguards or directional transmission contours were used. Second, these directional contours could result in marginal reception in fringe areas and even curtail reception in outlying areas now in the contour of existing VHF drop-ins. Third, investment capital for developing the new stations may not be forthcoming. Although some experimental use of VHF drop-ins is feasible, the long-term development of this kind of television station seems unlikely.

FIGURE 10-8 The concept of VHF drop-ins have not met with major support because of the concern over interference and directional contours, resulting in marginal reception and low-audience ratings in fringe areas. (National Association of Broadcasters)

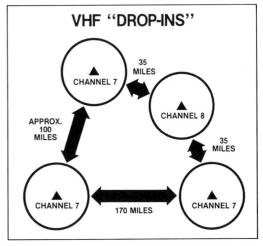

TELEPHONE SYSTEMS

When Alexander Graham Bell's telephone company was just starting, thoughts of telephone conversations initiated from luxury aircraft, business meetings conducted by video telephone systems, and thousands of mobile telephones utilized in cities throughout the world were fantasies. Today, as the technology of the telephone has steadily become more sophisticated and as consumer demand for telecommunication services has increased, the telephone, itself changing in concept and use, has become a vital link in human and electronic communication.

FIGURE 10–9 Cellular radio, with multiple transmitters and computer switching, permits a large number of mobile phones to be operated in the same geographic area. A person making a call from one cell and then traveling to another cell will have their call automatically switched to the next cell's transmitter. (Reprinted with permission from the January 17, 1983 issue of *Crain's Chicago Business.* Copyright 1983 by Crain Communications Inc.)

Cellular Radiotelephone Systems

By approving space on the spectrum for cellular radiotelephone systems, the FCC has made it possible for thousands of additional mobile telephones to become operational.[12] In the past, limited frequencies and less sophisticated technology severely restricted the number of mobile telephones that could be licensed to any one area. Today, cellular radiotelephone systems (Figure 10–9) have made it possible for a series of small transmitters with limited-coverage *cells* to make up the core of a mobile-tele-

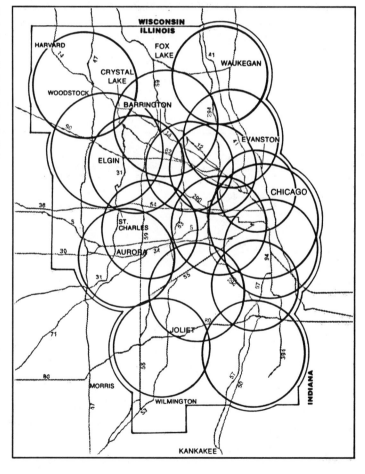

phone system. In earlier mobile-telephone systems, in comparison, a single transmitter served a much larger area.

With cellular radiotelephone service a person making a call from, say, an automobile automatically connects with the transmitter located in the same cell in which the automobile is traveling. The two-way radio transmission that carries the telephone call does not interfere with conversations in other cells. As the automobile moves closer to another cell, a computer automatically switches the call to an available frequency in the next cell. The central transmit-receive switching center in each cell links with telephone land lines to complete the connection. Along with the actual number of telephones, the cost to the consumer is also expected to decrease (Figure 10–10).

Plane-to-Ground Telephone Services

Imagine you are flying home for a holiday vacation and your flight is running late. You are airborne and will not have any time to call home when you change flights because the connection is too tight. Instead of having your friends spend two hours waiting for you at the airport, you call them from the airplane and inform them of the late arrival. The telephone call is automatically relayed to one of a series of ground stations. In your case it will be the ground station ahead of your flight path. Given the speed of the aircraft, your telephone conversation can last from fifteen to twenty minutes.[13]

Research suggests that approximately 20 percent of all people who travel through air-

FIGURE 10–10 As the number of cellular radio telephones increases, cost-per-phone will decrease. Estimated cost to subscribers drop substantially when use levels approach 30,000 units in a large metropolitan area. (National Association of Broadcasters)

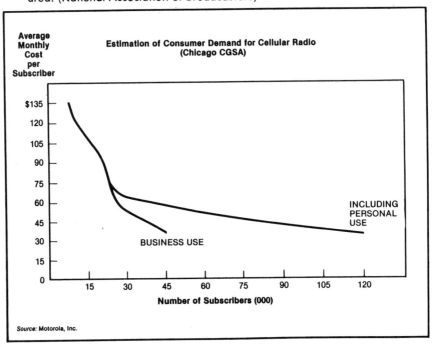

ports use the telephone. Consequently, the appeal of plane-to-ground calling is substantial.[14] For business travelers the service is particularly appealing since while flying they are out of touch with their office. Although you will not find plane-to-ground telephone service on every flight, more and more major airlines are including it on major routes and in large-capacity aircraft.

Teleconferencing

If a group of business executives wants to conduct a meeting, they have three choices: (1) to meet face to face, (2) to conduct a conference call, where everyone can talk to everyone else, or (3) to conduct a teleconference. The teleconference is the newest of the three formats and brings together the technologies of the telephone and television. AT&T's teleconferencing system utilizes full-color television facilities installed in major cities. Using strategically placed cameras and monitors, executives in different parts of the country can carry on discussions in full view of one another.

Modern teleconferencing facilities are equipped with graphic capabilites and devices such as electronic blackboards that permit participants to share sketches and other diagrams, computers capable of creating and transmitting data displays, distribution of documents to participants by means of facsimile transmission, random access and transmission of 35mm slides, and freeze-frame video (capturing a single frame of video and transmitting it to participants). Such services supplement standard teleconferencing and are called *audiographic teleconferencing services.*

The growth of teleconferencing will depend on such factors as (1) the cost of energy and therefore the cost of travel to remote meeting sites; (2) the cost of teleconferencing and therefore its availability to smaller

companies; and (3) whether users will really find that the system can replace the effectiveness and naturalness of good interpersonal communication in a face-to-face situation.[15]

RADIO SERVICES

Because of the dominant role television plays in our society, the application of radio technology sometimes takes a back seat. Still, research and development into radio communication continue. The medium plays an important role in mobile communication, especially in municipalities where police and fire services are critical. New uses of frequencies in the gigahertz range are becoming possible.

Satellite-Aided Land-Mobile Radio

Two-way radio is a vital communication link for government and business. Consider the oceangoing vessel we learned about at the beginning of this book. Ship-to-shore communication guards its very survival. The police officer on patrol, the firefighter on an emergency call, the dispatcher at the taxi company—all rely on two-way radio communication. For much of government and business, this radio communication takes place at high frequencies where line-of-sight transmission occurs. As we have learned, skyscrapers, hilltops, and other obstacles often block the path of these high-frequency radio waves. Even in flat terrain, moreover, line-of-sight communication is limited by the curvature of the earth and the height of the transmitter tower.

To help alleviate some of these interference problems, scientists and businesspeople are using satellites as an aid to land-mobile radio. Because of the satellite's position in space it can successfully relay radio communication and escape the interference that occurs at ground level. Pioneering tests by NASA in cooperation with such industries as shipping and trucking have illustrated the utility of satellites in aiding land-mobile radio. In addition, the truck dispatcher or shipping executive can instantly locate a vehicle or vessel by using the satellite to pinpoint the source of its radio transmission.[16]

Private-Frequency Business-News Service

Imagine you are a business executive who manages a large accounting firm. Your clients include a wide variety of companies. You need to know what is going on inside those companies, not only to understand their business but to develop and maintain satisfactory relationships with their executives. How do you receive news of these businesses? You can read daily newspapers and subscribe to monthly magazines. If you are a busy executive, however, time is at a premium and reading all of these sources of news takes up too much of it.

An alternative to the massive amount of printed material is to subscribe to a private radio news service tailored to the business community. To do so you rent a special radio receiver equipped with an audio-cassette recorder and a small keyboard with just enough keys to call in the individual codes of the companies you want to monitor.

Your receiver is automatically tuned to a single frequency that receives one signal, that of a special business-news service sent by FM radio. The signal arrives on the subcarrier of a local FM station by satellite from the network studios of the business-news service. Before each story is broadcast by the network it is assigned one or more codes, which are transmitted along with the story. The codes are inaudible, but trigger your receiver to tape-record those stories whose code matches one of the codes you have keyed into your receiver. Thus, if a story about AT&T is broadcast by the news service and you have keyed in AT&T's code on your receiver, the receiver will automatically tape-record that story. If you wish, you can also monitor it live.

The advantage of the system is that you do not have to continually monitor the receiver for the latest news about your clients. If you are out of the office or even away on vacation, the tape-recorded stories will be waiting for you when you return.[17] Instead of reading hundreds of pages of news articles you can be developing new business.

Increased Utility of the Spectrum

Although in theory the electromagnetic spectrum has space for many more radio services than are now available, the *usable* space on the spectrum is limited. Extremely high frequencies in the gigahertz range exist, but the technology to use them successfully has not been developed. The new "frequency frontier" is in the range of 30 to 300 GHz. If fully developed, such frequencies would provide more usable space on the spectrum than all of the current radio frequencies combined.

Millimeter waves, a generic term referring to waves between a centimeter and a millimeter long, have uses in space communication, where satellites can converse with each other in the 60-GHz range because there is no atmosphere to absorb the waves.[18] The signals can then be converted to more usable frequencies and sent back to earth. NASA is also developing millimeter-wave technology that will open up the 20-to-30-GHz area of the spectrum for satellite transmissions between earth stations and satellites.[19]

New Uses for Subcarriers

The frequencies assigned to FM radio stations can carry the signal of the standard FM-radio programming we hear in our home and also leave room for an additional signal, which can be used for supplementary purposes. This subcarrier signal is the same signal that broadcasts the private-frequency business-news service. And as we saw in the previous chapter, it can also carry teletext information.

FM stations are using frequency subcarriers for other purposes as well. In some paging services, for example, a small radio receiver is activated when a special code is transmitted. Each individual receiver has its own code. Messages are transmitted on the subcarrier frequency preceded by the code. Although a verbal message can be transmitted through the system, a simple tone suffices to alert the wearer of the receiver to call home or call the office. Other stations use the subcarrier for broadcasting commercial-free music to subscribers who pay a monthly fee to rent a special receiver capable of tuning in the subcarrier signal.

Future uses of FM subcarriers will be determined by consumer demand. For some marginally profitable FM stations such supplementary uses are particularly attractive as additional sources of income.

Digital Audio

The recording industry has continually striven to bring realistic reproductions of sound to the consumer. What started as the cylinder recording of the 1880s produced by Thomas Edison's early phonograph has evolved through such advances as the 45-rpm record, high fidelity, stereo, and quadraphonic sound. The most advanced form of electronic reproduction of sound, however, belongs to digital technology.

In Chapter 6 we learned about digital technology, the use of binary codes as a means of reproducing a signal. In digital recording this same computer technology is used to reproduce sound with a clarity unequaled in past recording technologies. The technology works like this. The sound to be reproduced—for example, a performance by an orchestra—is sampled as much as 50,000 times per second. Every detail of the sound, from the highest to the lowest notes, is captured and stored as a binary code. The sound that is captured at the performance of the orchestra can then be replayed with virtually perfect clarity, since each sampling is assigned a numerical value that is repeated exactly the way it was recorded. Moreover, since a recording usually goes through a series of editing and mixing steps before it is released to the public, any distortion that is detected during these steps is also eliminated.

The future will see more and more digital recordings and digital playback equipment. Along with records and tapes, recorded music will be available on digital audio discs.

What effect will all this have on radio? Radio's primary source of programming has traditionally been recorded music. But already radio finds competition in such devices as car stereos, portable stereos, and cassette tape decks. Part of the popularity of these new devices is their superior audio quality: certain distortions are inevitable when recordings must be transmitted over radio. Some industry executives predict that as the consumer demand grows for the high-quality sound that digital reproduces, radio will need to follow with digital transmitters and receivers.[20]

CHANGES IN TELEVISION RECEIVING AND TRANSMITTING TECHNOLOGY

At the 1939 World's Fair, RCA unveiled its new television receiver. The large console included a mirrored top that reflected the image appearing on the television receiving tube inside the set. Passers-by marveled at the exhibit and at the medium that could send pictures without wires. Those purchasing a "new" set had to truck it home and rearrange the furniture to make space for the large, cumbersome device. Today we can walk into a store and buy a miniature television receiver not much bigger than a few packs of cigarettes. We can carry it comfortably in one hand and slip it into a picnic basket or a handbag. Other changes are taking place in television technology, including stereo television, cable-ready television, component television, large-screen television, 3-D television, micro-television, flat-screen television, and digital television.

Stereo Television

Radio has had one distinct advantage over television—stereo sound. But the future may see more and more television stations broadcasting in stereo and more and more stereo television receivers appearing on the market. The sight of a rock concert, a major orchestra, even an automobile race will be complemented with stereo and create an audio panorama for the viewer. The FCC officially approved stereo for television in April, 1984. Prior to the approval, some television stations teamed up with local FM stations to simulcast concerts and other events.

Cable-Ready Television

Most viewers who want to subscribe to cable must rent a converter that transfers the channels of the cable system to the subscriber's television set. Some manufacturers, Zenith in particular, are now manufacturing sets that are "cable-ready": the cable company can connect the drop cable directly to the set without the converter. The future success of such sets will be determined by the willingness of the consumer to pay the additional price for cable-ready sets and the willingness of cable companies to permit subscribers to substitute their own television set for the company's converter.

Component Television

The more sophisticated uses of television, such as interactive video and stereo, have prompted manufacturers to examine the appeal of component television—monitor, tuner, speakers, video screens, and other attachment devices, each sold separately. Component television already exists to some degree, since anyone can purchase a television receiver and then hook such components as home computers, video-cassette recorders, and videodisc players to the set.

Large-Screen Television

We have already discussed high-definition television, which permits large-screen television to achieve the quality of 35mm motion-picture film. Still, high-definition television is a long way from being commonplace and those wishing to increase the size of their television screen must rely on some form of supplemental projection system. Though still not of the quality of HDTV, changes in large-screen projection systems have improved the brightness and lessened the grainy look of earlier large-screen systems.

For those who aren't satisfied with traditional large-screen projection systems there's Mitsubishi Electric's giant screen measuring $13\frac{1}{2}$ inches high and 18 feet wide.

This monster of the shopping-mall circuit consists of 27,000 high-brightness red, blue, and green electron tubes. Even larger versions exist in ball parks such as Dodger Stadium in Los Angeles, Shea Stadium in New York, and Comiskey Park in Chicago.

3-D Television

Still more novel and experimental than practical, three-dimensional (3-D) television has managed to interest a small group of people who continue to promote this technology. Three versions of 3-D television exist. The simplest is the broadcast of 3-D movies, which require the viewer to use a pair of special glasses to make the picture appear in three dimensions. If the glasses aren't worn, the picture appears blurry. A second system, DOTS (digital optical technology system), also uses glasses but the picture does not appear blurred when viewed without glasses. A third system is holography, which is not so much a form of television as a combination of photographic film and laser light that makes images appear to float in space.

Micro-Television

Television receivers as small as pocket calculators and weighing slightly more than one pound are available for those who want true portability in a television set. Although currently available only in black and white, color sets are predicted for the not too distant future. The questions arise, will micro-television sets be used in much the same way we now use portable radios, and will they siphon off the radio audience by enabling their owners to look as well as listen?

Flat-Screen Television

Imagine a television receiver with a diagonal measurement of fifty inches and flat enough to hang on the wall. Experts are predicting such a receiver will be available by 1990. In a research paper presented in 1980 at the Society of Information Display, RCA scientists said the screen would be about four inches thick. The advantages of such a screen include the size of a large-screen projection system but the clarity of a standard-size television receiver.[21]

Digital Television

While the recording industry develops digital recording techniques and radio considers a similar transmission system that would enhance audio quality, television engineers are developing digital circuitry for television that will permit the binary code of the computer to generate improved picture clarity and remove many of the interference problems now found in standard over-the-air television. Shadows, ghosts, and other distractions are eliminated with digital television.

CONSUMER ELECTRONICS

The technologies that have played a part in developing more traditional forms of telecommunication have also played a role in the burgeoning field of consumer electronics. From sophisticated computer-based media to simple novelty gadgets, the mass media are becoming more and more specialized and more and more personal. Cameras that once used silver-based technologies now capture still photographs on electronic discs. The mechanical pinball machine has been replaced with a sophisticated electronic flight simulator in a video-game parlor. Some of the more well known consumer-electronics devices include home video recorders, videodisc players, electronic still cameras, and video games.

Home Video Recorders

At the CBS affiliates meeting in Chicago in 1956, Ampex unveiled what stockholders were told was a practical way to record and reproduce TV pictures on magnetic tape. The new system brought wide acclaim and launched the era of the videotape. In 1957 RCA introduced its version, which could reproduce images in color as well as black and white. Then in June 1962 Machtronics introduced a portable videotape recorder, and many manufacturing companies, such as Sony, Memorex, Arvin Industries, and Panasonic, began manufacturing videotape components and systems.

The next revolution came in April 1969 with the introduction of the video cassette by Sony. The video cassette has entered every facet of television, from libraries and instructional resource centers to the newsroom.

A perspective on how we use home videocassette recorders was offered by researcher Mark Levy, who found they were used to complement and, not replace the use of broadcast television.[22] He also found that we use the video recorder to rearrange our viewing schedule to avoid viewing conflicts.[23]

The sufficient number of people owning video recorders in the home resulted in ABC announcing plans for a network of stations that would broadcast scrambled signals late at night to homes equipped with special decoders (Figure 10–11). The decoders would permit the television set to present a

FIGURE 10-11 ABC's HomeView network was designed to use existing television stations sending scrambled signals to subscribers who pay a fee for decoders. Subscribers then view or record programs on a standard television set. (American Broadcasting Companies, Inc.)

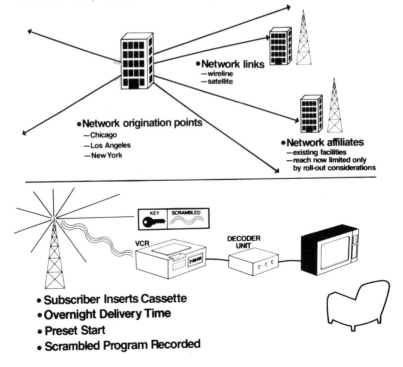

- **Network origination points**
  —Chicago
  —Los Angeles
  —New York
- **Network links**
  —wireline
  —satellite
- **Network affiliates**
  —existing facilities
  —reach now limited only by roll-out considerations

KEY SCRAMBLED

VCR DECODER UNIT

- **Subscriber Inserts Cassette**
- **Overnight Delivery Time**
- **Preset Start**
- **Scrambled Program Recorded**

clear picture which would in turn be recorded on the video recorder for viewing at the subscriber's convenience. The late-night programming would be sent from network origination points by both wired and satellite distribution systems to ABC affiliate stations which would broadcast the signals at times when commercial sponsorship was very low or the station had been signing off the air.

Videodiscs

Videodiscs are much like long-play records except they produce a television picture as well as sound. Using a laser-beam-based playback system, the discs are free from the distortion that can occur with videotape systems.

The potential of the videodisc lies with its ability to bypass television stations and distribute television programming directly to homes. Pushed to their full potential, videodiscs can be duplicated in mass quantities and shipped inexpensively anywhere in the world for playback on home players. They are particularly attractive when integrated with computer systems as educational tools.

These developments do not mean that television stations will start signing off the air, just as radio stations did not succumb when 45-rpm and $33\frac{1}{3}$-rpm records came on the market. However, viewers of the future will have many more choices of what to watch and when. As the technology develops for the consumer to record directly on disc (as they can with videotape), the disc should see more acceptance.

Electronic Still Cameras

Still-camera photography has merged with telecommunication to create electronic still cameras the size of 35mm cameras and able to produce instant electronic pictures on a video screen. The Sony Mavica system employs a single-lens reflex camera and records the image on a small spinning magnetic disc. The disc is then transferred to a player that reproduces the picture on a screen.

Since the quality of the Mavica approaches print standards, inherent advantages exist for its use in such fields as print journalism. For example, photographs can be developed instantly and sent electronically over telephone systems to an editor in a distant newsroom. The electronic photograph can be reproduced on a printing plate in fifteen minutes and be ready for the press run.

Video Games

In 1972 a computer designer who wanted to improve the mechanical version of pinball developed an electronic game called Pong. Instead of the metal ball and the spring-loaded plunger it employed circuitry, a video screen, and a set of hand controls. The game became popular and it wasn't long before the company that produced it was bought by a larger concern, Warner Communications. Through its Atari subsidiary, Warner began to plow money into the development of a series of electronic games, which in 1980 resulted in one-third of the total earnings of the Warner conglomerate. By the mid-1980s the video-game industry had surpassed the recording motion-picture industry in revenues.

Although Pong is considered the forerunner of video games, other companies in other countries have also contributed to their growth. The Japanese, long important in the electronics market, entered the international video-game market in 1978 when Taito marketed Space Invaders. In Japan the video-game explosion created a kind of financial culture shock, and the Bank of

Japan had to triple production of the hundred-yen piece used to feed the thirsty Space Invaders machines. In the first year of production Taito placed 100,000 Space Invaders in operation and the Japanese spent the equivalent of $600 million playing them. In the United States a company named Bally, through its Midway division, began licensing Space Invaders in 1978, and by 1980 it had 60,000 units in operation.

Game arcades began popping up in shopping malls, converted gas stations—anywhere operators could find space. Atari obtained the rights to offer Space Invaders through home video devices that could connect to television sets. The popularity of the arcade version whetted consumer appetites, and Space Invaders became the most successful of Atari's early home video-game offerings. Other early video-game classics were Galaxian, Asteroids, Missile Command, Pac Man, and Battlezone.

The burgeoning of video games leveled off in the early 1980s. Still, they remain a popular and profitable part of the consumer-electronics industry. One of the biggest challenges to maintaining this profit is developing new games to replace those that have lost their novelty. A new game's peak popularity, assuming it receives acceptance, is between six months and a year. A game may also have appeal in the home market, but even there it will diminish in popularity and must be replaced by another entry.

ADDITIONAL PERSPECTIVES ON TELECOMMUNICATIONS AND CONSUMER TECHNOLOGIES

Our discussion of broadcast and information technologies in this and the previous four chapters of this book shows some definite trends toward different uses and applications of these technologies.

We can see that the traditional use of the electromagnetic spectrum to broadcast standard over-the-air radio and television signals has already changed. Since Marconi performed his transatlantic-communication experiments at the turn of the century the use of the electromagnetic spectrum has expanded to such fields as satellite communication, high-definition television, millimeter-wave applications, and optical communication.

The use of fiber optics and cable points to the increased use, at least in the immediate future, of wired systems of communication as opposed to over-the-air or unwired systems. This does not suggest that we will stop using radio waves for communication, but just that the combination of spectrum crowding and new applications of wired technology has opened up other alternatives.

On the other hand, if the technology for using the millimeter-wave area of the spectrum continues to develop, we could find a transition back to over-the-air distribution as higher frequencies become useful.

The technologies of teletext and videotex offer a new, textual form of programming that may alter the way we use and even appreciate traditional visual media. The appeal of the printed newspaper page and the use of television primarily as an entertainment medium may both be affected by these alternative media.

As we learned in Chapter 1, the term *mass media* is changing to reflect what has become a plethora of specialized or personalized media. With the increase in the number of media choices—an increase in the channels of communication—media messages are being directed at narrower and narrower audiences. From the specialized formats of radio to the highly individualized messages of private videotex systems, the shift from mass to personalized media continues. Whether you are a responsible consumer of media or a practicing professional designing the messages and managing the telecommunication systems of the future, an awareness of these changes in broadcast and information technologies is important.

SUMMARY

Along with satellites, microwave technology, cable, and teletext and videotex, which we discussed in previous chapters, data processing and other technologies are playing a part in the development and uses of media.

Fiber optics promises some of the most radical changes in media-distribution systems. Glasslike fibers fed with laser light increase the amount of information that can be transmitted through either wired or unwired communication systems. Three main types of fiber-optic cables are multi-mode graded-index fiber, multi-mode step-index fiber, and single-mode fiber. The first is the most widely used.

Multipoint distribution systems (MDS) use microwave technology to transmit television signals from an omnidirectional master antenna to smaller microwave antennas usually located on multi-unit dwellings such as apartment complexes and hotels. Programming is similar to pay cable, and subscribers pay a monthly fee.

Satellite master-antenna television (SMATV) receives signals from a satellite and then redistributes them to subscribers. Since receive-only earth stations need not be licensed, the system can become operable as soon as it is installed. As long as the system does not connect by cable with dwellings under different ownership, it can operate generally free of regulatory control.

Subscription television (STV) is the use of a scrambled television signal to send programming to subscribers who pay a monthly fee for a descrambler. Most STV systems are leased by television stations who turn over part of their broadcasting day to the STV operator, who obtains programming, markets the service, and places the in-home decoders.

Low-power television (LPTV) operates much like television translator stations except that it can originate programming. Low-power TV has its greatest potential in remote areas not fully served by television or cable.

High-definition television (HDTV) uses a large portion of the electromagnetic spectrum but provides superior-quality large-screen images. Initial tests have been positive, but the system shows its greatest promise as a component of cable, where a large portion of the available frequency space can be allocated to it. Another alternative is to use satellite transmission, with which adequate spectrum space may become available at higher microwave frequencies.

The desire to gain the maximum use from the spectrum, especially in the range of frequencies used by television, has resulted in proposals to increase the number of VHF stations by ''dropping'' new stations in between already assigned frequencies. However, the VHF drop-in concept has not had widespread support among major industry groups.

Telephone systems are a key part of telecommunications. Cellular radiotelephones use a series of geographic cells, each containing a switching system that relays the radiotelephone call to the next cell as the mobile phone moves from one cell to another. Plane-to-ground telephone service is developing on the routes of major airlines, which use a system of larger ground-based geographic cells. High energy costs incurred in long-distance travel and the need to save time have resulted in the use of telephones for teleconferencing—a system of video and audio links between major cities permitting executives to meet in electronic face-to-face meetings.

While radio is continuing its traditional role as a broadcast medium, radio technology is being used in a number of other applications. Satellite-aided land-mobile radio permits the long-distance interference-free two-way radio service valued by such industries as shipping and long-haul trucking. Private-frequency business-news services and new uses of subcarrier frequencies offer radio services to the business and home consumer. The utilization of millimeter-wave frequencies is proving promising. Radio stations may begin investigating the feasibility of digital-transmission methods in order to meet what is expected to be consumer demand for high-quality sound reproduction, a demand resulting from the introduction of digital audio technology in the recording industry.

Changes in television receiving and transmitting technology are also taking place. Among the innovations are stereo television, cable-ready television, component television, large-screen television, 3-D television, micro-television, flat-screen television, and digital television.

Such consumer products as home video-tape recorders, videodisc players, electronic still cameras, and video games are offering alternatives to traditional media and providing examples of the application of micro-electronics and miniaturization to the field of telecommunication.

OPPORTUNITIES FOR FURTHER LEARNING

AGOSTINO, D., and J. ZENATY, *Home VCR Owner's Use of Television and Public Television: Viewing, Recording and Playback.* Washington, D.C.: Corporation for Public Broadcasting, 1980.

APAR, B., and H. B. COHEN, *The Home Video Book.* New York: Amphoto, 1982.

BENSINGER, C., *The Video Guide,* 3rd ed. Santa Fe: Video-Infor, 1982.

BODSON, D., *Fiber Optics and Lightwave Communications Vocabulary.* New York: McGraw-Hill, 1981.

CICCOLELLA, C., *A Buyer's Guide to Video Cassette Recorders: How to Buy, Install and Use Them.* New York: Sterling, 1979.

Consumer's Handbook of Video Software. New York: Van Nostrand Reinhold, 1981.

Digital Video, 3 vols. Scarsdale, N.Y.: Society of Motion Picture and Television Engineers, 1977–80.

ENNES, H. E., *Digitals in Broadcasting.* Indianapolis: Howard W. Sams, 1977.

GROSSWITH, M., *Home Video.* Garden City, N.Y.: Doubleday, 1981.

HELD, G., *Data Communications Procurement Manual.* New York: McGraw-Hill, 1979.

———, and R. SARCH, *Data Communications: A Comprehensive Approach.* New York: McGraw-Hill, 1983.

HOWARD, H. H., and S. L. CARROLL, *Subscription Television: History, Current Status, and Economic Projections.* Knoxville: College of Communications, University of Tennessee, 1980.

KARP, H., ed., *Practical Applications of Data Communications.* New York: McGraw-Hill, 1980.

KYBETT, H., *The Complete Handbook of Videocassette Recorders.* Blue Ridge Summit, Pa.: TAB Books, 1977.

———, and P. L. DEXNIS, *Complete Handbook of Home Video Systems.* Reston, Va.: Reston, 1982.

LACHENBRUCH, D., *Videocassette Recorders: The Complete Home Guide.* New York: Everest House, 1979.

LEHMAN, M., and T. J. M. BURKE, eds., *Communication Technologies and Information Flow.* New York: Pergamon Press, 1981.

The Low Power Television Guidebook: A Primer on the Low Power Service. Washington, D.C.: Corporation for Public Broadcasting, 1980.

McNITT, J., *The Home Video Sourcebook.* New York: Collier Books, 1982.

MDS Databook. Carmel, Calif.: Paul Kagan, 1981.

PANELAS, T., *Adolescents and Video Games: Consumption of Leisure and the Social Construction of the Peer Group.* Beverly Hills, Calif.: Sage, 1983.

PAULSON, C. R., *BM/E's ENG/EFP/EPP Handbook: Guide to Using Mini Video Equip-ment.* New York: Broadband Information Services, 1981.

SIGEL, E., and others, *Video Discs: The Technology, the Applications and the Future.* White Plains, N.Y.: Knowledge Industry, 1980.

SINGH, I., *Telecommunications in the Year 2000: National and International Perspectives.* Norwood, N.J.: Ablex, 1983.

11

NETWORKS

ABC, CBS, NBC, and PBS—those magical initials of living-room entertainment. We have all grown up with them, and they have shaped much of our lives. They still do. These are just the television networks. Radio has its own versions of national programming, as do the syndicated networks. Major broadcasting networks are the largest and most dominant systems of broadcasting, and most countries have them. In this chapter we shall view them as disseminators of information and as carriers of news and entertainment programming.[1]

THE NETWORK CONCEPT

Networks not only provide the public with broadcast programming but also serve the advertiser and the broadcaster. For the ad-vertiser, the networks provide a medium through which it can reach large numbers of people at economical rates. Even though the cost of a minute-long commercial on a major network can be staggering, the cost of reaching the same number of people through another medium, such as direct mail, would be far greater. Although direct mail can be used to reach a highly specialized audience, regional networks, a wide variety of programs, and selective scheduling of commercials help broadcasting remain competitive in reaching specialized audiences.

For the broadcaster, airing network programming is much more economical than producing and airing comparable local programming. In addition, affiliates usually receive compensation from the network for airing its programs.

Acquiring Programs

Within the networks, the news and public-affairs units are responsible for informational programming. Supported by major staffs of reporters, producers, directors, and technicians, these units produce daily newscasts seen and heard by millions. They also provide special coverage of such important events as elections, inaugurations, press conferences, and space flights. They offer special features and documentaries, which can range from a superficial look at a national fad to an investigative report of political corruption. Documentaries and reports produced in cooperation with network-owned-and-operated (O&O) stations are still another source of network news programming, as are reports contributed by local affiliates.

With entertainment programming the story is different. Here, various independent companies called *production houses* work closely with the networks and supply them with everything from detective thrillers to situation comedies. The ideas for programs come from the network, the production house, writers, or anyone else connected with the creative process. If a network is interested in an idea, both the network and the production house make a major investment and produce a pilot program. Audience reaction to the pilot program is then evaluated. If the ratings prove that it will be a hit, the production house moves into full-scale production. Usually a complete season of shows is produced only after the network tests the program during a new television season to see whether its popularity will last more than a few weeks. Conversely, if the pilot is disappointing, the program may never get on the air. Other factors determining an air date may include affiliate reaction to a program, scheduling availability, and competition from other shows.

Affiliate Relations and Clearance Ratios

How much attention do the networks really pay to their affiliates' wishes? On such major issues as clearing programming (agreeing to air a network program), the networks carefully heed them. The number of affiliates that agree to carry the program is called the *clearance ratio,* and this ratio is a form of direct feedback.

Clearance ratios are critical to networks. If a group of stations decides not to carry a program, then the network's audience suffers, the ratings go down, and the advertising dollar follows. The clearance aspect of the network-affiliate relationship has taken on considerably more importance because of the concern that has arisen over violent and sexually explicit television programming. Many local affiliate stations have simply refused to carry such programs. Others have rescheduled the programming to a later hour when children will not be watching. Although that idea may sound reasonable, to a network it can spell disaster, since the late-night viewing audience is only a fraction of the prime-time audience.

Affiliate Organizations

As a result of these continuing concerns, *affiliate organizations,* groups of affiliate stations that elect a representative to carry their concerns to the network, are becoming increasingly important. These organizations, some of which have grown out of advisory boards, have a set of bylaws and charge their members dues. There is no particular advantage of one over the other. Both provide feedback for the network. Affiliates that do not wish to become part of the organization or advisory board still have a voice in the network. No affiliate is overlooked. Each provides an audience for network programming and commercials. Some large-market affiliates purposely avoid belonging to the boards or organizations because they feel they have more impact as individual stations. On the other hand, some very small affiliates do not belong because they feel their voice is too small to be heard. These are the exceptions, not the rule. In theory, the affiliate organizations and advisory boards represent all of the affiliates.

The affiliates' organizations and advisory boards do not control the network directly, nor do they have any legal relationship beyond the contract between the network and the affiliate. The affiliates do, however, influence network decision making. Typically the organizations and boards elect representatives from their membership, although some are appointed by the network. It then becomes the responsibility of the elected representatives to be the voice of the affiliates.

Voicing Affiliate Concerns

Imagine yourself an elected representative of a network affiliates' organization serving a group of states in the West. About two months before the network-affiliate representatives' meeting, you circulate a questionnaire to all of the affiliates asking them what information they want communicated to the network executives. You ask if they are satisfied with the quality and scheduling of network programming, whether they want more news and less sports or vice versa, and other pertinent information about the operation of their station, which is affected by their network affiliation. You also ask them to respond in a letter to any points not covered in the questionnaire. About a month before the meeting, you forward to the network a summary of the results.

At the meeting, the discussion focuses on your summary and those provided by other representatives from around the country. One radio representative points out that many of the affiliates have a contemporary-music format, and ten minutes of network news on the hour is hurting their listenership. On the other hand, the news and information affiliates love the ten minutes. The network must make a decision. It decides to continue to air ten minutes of network news every hour but to permit the stations with contemporary formats to cut out of the news at five minutes past the hour. The network will, however, need to reduce the *local availability, that commercial slot in the network feed that is sold locally by the station.* The contemporary affiliates do not mind. They are willing to sacrifice the commercial availability in order to return to musical programming and please their audience.

Or perhaps you are at a television affiliates' meeting when a representative of affiliates in a conservative part of the country argues that the sex and violence in network programming have become too explicit for their audience. Complaints continually pour in to their stations from viewers and advertisers. The affiliates want something done to clean up the programming. A representative from a large city is not quite as upset over the programming. She says the affiliates she represents are aware of the sex and violence but also like the high ratings the network shows are receiving. Obviously the network must make some tough decisions based on this affiliate feedback. Should it cancel the shows with sex and violence, irritating the affiliates from the big cities, or should it keep the programs on the air and risk losing affiliate support in some conservative markets? Whatever decision the network makes, even in our hypothetical examples, it will want to know what the affiliates are thinking and how they will react to any changes in network programming.

Criticisms of the Network Concept

Any time an organization becomes a powerful conglomerate it attracts its share of criticism. Networks are no exception. Some of the criticism has been directed at the very concept of hugeness and the control it fosters. In a famous speech to a Republican political gathering in the late 1960s Vice-President Spiro Agnew lashed out at network control and claimed that network news coverage was permeated with an eastern liberal bias. His speech caused a stir among journalists and gave the public a target for widespread criticism.

More recent criticism of network news came in the 1970s when CBS paid a national political figure convicted of a felony for an exclusive interview. The incident launched a wave of discussion about "checkbook journalism," but CBS survived relatively unscathed. Similar criticism came when a one-time cooperative venture between the CIA and CBS became public knowledge. Criticism has been accompanied by satire. The movie *Network,* starring Faye Dunaway, went to the point of depicting a network having an anchorperson murdered on the air in order to gain top ratings. The movie was a farce, but not everyone saw it that way. More than one theater owner reported people leaving the lobby shaking their heads and commenting about how terrible it was inside the network decision rooms.

Let us turn our attention away from criticism and take a closer look at major-network operations. We shall begin with the commercial networks, leaving public broadcasting for the next chapter.

ABC

The youngest major commercial network is ABC. As we saw in Chapter 4, it was formed when NBC was forced to dispose of its dual-network operation. When ABC acquired its own identity in 1943, it began a concentrated effort to compete with its two closest rivals, CBS and NBC.[2] Because of some advantageous breaks, the late 1940s was a profitable time for ABC radio. One of its biggest breaks was singing star Bing Crosby. When Crosby wanted to produce a prerecorded show instead of meeting the demands of weekly radio appearances, ABC gave the innovative idea a try. The success of the program proved that even a prerecorded show could be a hit, and other stars followed Crosby's example. No longer plagued by the image of an unsteady toddler, ABC moved forward into television.

Launching Television Programming

In a special program originating from Broadway's famous Palace Theater, ABC launched its television ventures on Tuesday, August 10, 1948. ABC's flagship station, Channel 7 (call letters WJZ–TV), showed a documentary on the progress of New York City, narrated by Milton Cross. Cameras caught live the action of a parade outside the Palace, street dancing, music from Times Square, an eighty-piece combined police and fire-department band, majorettes, and horse-drawn fire engines and streetcars. Later that evening, viewers "watched" "Candid Microphone" with Allen Funt, a radio version of the future "Candid Camera." Shows in the coming weeks included "The Fitzgeralds," "Hollywood Screen Test," "Ethel and Albert," "You're Invited," "The Singing Lady," and "Quizzing the News."

A month later, ABC regional network programming began in Chicago with hook-ups between stations in Chicago, Milwaukee, Cleveland, and Toledo. A football game between the Chicago Cardinals and the Pittsburgh Steelers launched the regional network.

Merger with United Paramount

Not all of ABC's corporate maturity came from television. Needing capital to make inroads against its older competitors, ABC announced plans for a merger with United Paramount Theaters (UPT) in 1951. That year both the ABC and UPT boards of directors approved the merger, and in 1952 the FCC held hearings on it. By early 1953 the merger was complete, and cash reserves of $30 million were added to ABC's bank account. In a shrewd personnel move, Robert T. Weitman, a vice-president at UPT, was placed in charge of ABC talent. Weitman had previously been instrumental in advancing the careers of Frank Sinatra, Danny Kaye, Red Skelton, Betty Hutton, and Perry Como.

Changing Call Letters

The mid 1950s signaled changes in both station operations and corporate structure at ABC. New call letters were assigned to the network's O&O New York station, and WJZ became WABC. Within the company five new divisions were formed: the ABC Radio Network, the ABC Television Network, ABC Owned Radio Stations, ABC Owned Television Stations, and ABC Film Syndication. By the end of the decade ABC had become a formidable opponent of NBC and CBS.

Edging the Competition: ABC Sports

Unfortunately, the "formidable opponent" status was where ABC television remained. Although profitable and popular, moving out from under the dominance of NBC and CBS was no easy task. It took the combination of a greater number of television stations on the air and popular programming to bring ABC out of the cellar.

The magic formula started to work in the mid 1970s. The network had already managed to excel in one important area, sports programming, with its popular "ABC Wide World of Sports." The winner of major national programming awards, the popularity of "Wide World of Sports" was demonstrated by Johnny Carson's puns on NBC's "Tonight Show." Then, when weekends seemed saturated with football, ABC introduced "Monday Night Football." Featuring Howard Cosell, Frank Gifford, and Don Meredith, the show became the "in" pastime and parties huddled in front of the television set. Excellent Olympic coverage has added more gold to ABC's pot.

Entertainment and "Roots"

But sports could not manage by itself. Entertainment had to put in its share. ABC launched a talent raid that plucked comedian Redd Foxx and "Today" host Barbara Walters from NBC and programming executive Fred Silverman from CBS. Walters gained publicity for her reported one-million-dollar salary, and Silverman for making ABC stock jump upward the day he announced his resignation from CBS. Perhaps ABC's biggest push into dominant prime-time television occurred with its presentation "Roots." First aired in January 1977, this story of black struggle traced through the "roots" of author Alex Haley's family set new records in television viewing. The twelve-hour production included stars such as John Amos, Madge Sinclair (Figure 11–1), LeVar Burton, Lorne Greene, Ed Asner, and Cicely Tyson. A repeat showing of the series again brought ABC the lead over its competitors, and a second series titled *"Roots: The Next*

FIGURE 11-1 "Roots" did much to move ABC into a position of leadership in network programming. The twelve-hour presentation was based on Alex Haley's novel about a man who traces his ancestry back to Africa. A host of stars appeared in the program, including Madge Sinclair and John Amos (pictured). The first program ran in the fall of 1977 and was repeated in 1978. A sequel titled, "Roots, The Next Generations," first appeared in February, 1979. (Courtesy, ABC; Wolper Productions, Inc.; Warner Bros.; Phil Gersh Agency; Bresler, Wolff, Cota, and Livingston)

Generations'' topped another week of prime time for ABC in early 1979.

Meanwhile, Silverman had exited ABC in 1978 for a job at NBC. While he was attempting to get NBC out of the ratings cellar, ABC introduced new situation comedies, one of the most popular being "Mork and Mindy," the story of a Martian who lives with his girlfriend in Boulder, Colorado. Sports programming continued to be emphasized with coverage of the 1984 Olympic Games beginning a promotional theme to lead the network into the 1984–1985 season.

Improvements in morning programming, especially "Good Morning America," and another mini-series "The Winds of War," aired in February 1983, maintained ABC's strength in network programming. Although critical acclaim was somewhat lacking, "The Winds of War," which was over 18 hours long, captured approximately half of the United States television viewers the week it was aired.[3] The series was followed shortly by an adaptation of another novel, "The Thorn Birds," which managed to pick up advertising support on the heels of "Winds of War."[4] The film showing the horror of nuclear war, "The Day After," was another ratings success.

Daytime Profits

A strong daytime lineup contributes to ABC's profits. Programs such as "Ryan's Hope," "All My Children," "One Life to Live," "General Hospital," and "The Edge of Night" placed ABC in the top daytime spot for years running.[5] In the early 1980s its eighteen-to-forty-nine-year-old female viewers outnumbered those of NBC and CBS combined. Some of ABC's daytime programming consistently captures higher ratings than prime-time programming. The network controls more than half of all daytime advertising dollars, which is significant because daytime programming is the cheapest to produce.[6] Moreover, ABC produces a majority of its own soap operas, thereby keeping money inside the network that would normally be spent on production houses.[7]

"Nightline" and Documentaries

In 1980, when Americans were taken hostage in Iran, ABC decided to expand coverage of the hostage crisis by airing late-night news reports on most ABC affiliates after local evening-news programming. The audience that was found to exist for this late-night information programming resulted in the decision to air a late-night news program, "ABC News Nightline." ABC News "Nightline" began on March 24, 1980, with a Monday-through-Thursday run anchored by veteran ABC writer, producer, and chief diplomatic correspondent Ted Koppel. The experiment proved successful and the program expanded to Friday.

Besides giving "Nightline" a launching pad, the Iranian hostage crisis spawned a documentary on the hostage negotiations. Aired on January 22, 1981, and moderated by ABC Paris correspondent Pierre Salinger, the program examined the behind-the-scenes aspects of the international negotiations that eventually resulted in the hostages' release. Salinger put much of his own efforts and talents into researching the story. The program drew attention to ABC's journalistic excellence and praise to a degree that had been reserved mostly for its competitors.[8] A change in the format of the network's evening news to international, national, and regional anchorpersons and extended coverage of major events continued to advance public and critical acceptance of ABC's news and public-affairs programming.

The SNN Venture

In an attempt to gain a foothold in the growing field of cable programming, ABC and Westinghouse jointly introduced Satellite NewsChannels (SNN) in August 1981. The SNN concept was to provide twenty-four-hour news and information programming for cable systems, in head-on competition with Turner Broadcasting's Cable News Network and CNN Headline News. The original format called for ten minutes of network commercials per hour. Turner Broadcasting made an effort to stop the merger on antitrust grounds, and when SNN was announced the over-the-counter price of the Turner Broadcasting stock dropped $3.00 to $13.50 a share.[9] In 1983, however, Turner bought SNN, shut it down, and replaced its programming with its own CNN services.

CBS

CBS had both the resources and the personnel to be a formidable opponent of ABC. By the late 1940s William Paley (Figure 11–2) had established a track record as an excellent administrator and builder. He was joined at CBS by an exceptional management team.

FIGURE 11-2 William S. Paley guided the development of CBS after his father's cigar company purchased the floundering network in 1928. (CBS, Inc.)

Klauber, Kesten, and Stanton

The report card of Paley and his management team shows high marks for corporate growth. From net sales of $1.3 million in 1928, the network, exclusive of allied businesses, had climbed to an annual revenue of $1 billion by the late 1970s, which made it the largest single advertising medium in the world.

In addition to Paley, three individuals contributed greatly to CBS's early growth—Ed Klauber, Paul Kesten, and Frank Stanton. Klauber was a newspaper reporter until Paley coaxed him away from the night city-editor's desk of the *New York Times* in 1930. Klauber, hired as Paley's assistant, is credited with shaping the character of early journalism at CBS. Paul Kesten came from advertising. Recruited as head of sales promotion in 1930, he had earned his stripes with the New York ad agency of Lennen and Mitchell. One of his first decisions was to hire the accounting firm of Price, Waterhouse to "audit" NBC's claim to having the highest radio listenership. In the audit CBS came out on top.

Dr. Frank Stanton joined CBS in 1935. A psychology professor at Ohio State University, Stanton had an interest in measuring radio listenership. When CBS learned of his work it brought him to New York at a $55 weekly salary and gave him the number-three position in a three-person research department. Stanton continued to measure radio listenership and developed an electronic device that could measure immediate responses to radio programs in a closed laboratory setting. He later left the research department and by 1942 was an administrative vice-president. As much a statesman for the entire broadcasting industry as a CBS executive, Stanton rose to the top of CBS in 1946, giving the company what many said was a sense of character and responsibility.

Trial and Error in Corporate Expansion

CBS did not confine itself to the broadcasting business. Like ABC, it began to apply its profits to acquisitions that in some ways directly supported, yet were different from, network operations. As we learned in Chapter 4, a lucrative artist-management business gave the network ready access to top talent. However, the FCC questioned the propriety of the network's control of talent, so CBS sold its interests to the Music Corporation of America. The more profitable acquisitions, like those discovered by the other networks, turned out to be radio and television stations in large markets, which gave the network not only an affiliate station but also a share of the affiliate's profit.

CBS also ventured into sports, publishing, and the recording industry. The sports venture was not successful. After CBS bought the New York Yankees in 1964 the team promptly sank into the doldrums. Attendance dropped, and CBS sold the team in 1973.

In 1951, Frank Stanton asked CBS's creative director of advertising and sales promotion, William Golden, to design a corporate trademark for all these business ventures. Golden came up with the famous CBS "eye." Early depictions superimposed it on a clouded sky so as to lessen the fuzzy edges of the sharp lines that showed up poorly on some of the early black-and-white receiving

sets. Although the background has been dropped, the eye remains one of the few corporate trademarks that have not undergone radical change over the years and is consequently one of the most recognized corporate logos in the world.

Programming

For many years, until ABC began inching its way up the ratings ladder in the 1970s, CBS dominated television programming. Some of the early favorites were "I Remember Mama," an evening family drama about an immigrant family with three growing children. "I Love Lucy" set the stage for a generation of situation comedies. CBS Television City in Hollywood produced such

FIGURE 11-3 Edward R. Murrow was a major force in setting the goals, standards, and direction of both radio and television news. He was also skilled at producing and appearing in feature programs, such as "See It Now" and "Person to Person." One of his guests was motion picture star Marilyn Monroe. (WNET/13 and CBS, Inc.)

shows as "Playhouse 90." Led by the long-running "Captain Kangaroo," children's programming made a hit. Such adult variety programs as the "Ed Sullivan Show" continually capped the ratings. CBS News also had its share of successes with Edward R. Murrow (Figure 11–3) who became a classic in broadcast journalism. "Douglas Edwards and the News" and exclusive interviews with such notables as President John Kennedy and Soviet leader Nikita Khrushchev kept CBS News on top, and anchorman Walter Cronkite was found by polls to be the United States' most credible person. Cronkite retired in 1981 but was replaced by Dan Rather who kept CBS news on top.

While ABC was leading the daytime soap-opera race CBS continued to develop its prime-time programming, turning out successful shows such as "Dallas," "M*A*S*H" (which made its successful last run on the network in February 1983), "The Dukes of Hazzard," "The Jeffersons," "One Day at a Time," and "Archie Bunker's Place." Made-for-TV movies also improved CBS ratings.

CBS News

CBS News contributed some of CBS's highest-rated programming with its popular "60 Minutes" program. Walter Cronkite retired in 1981, and was replaced by Dan Rather as CBS anchor. Cronkite had been a familiar part of CBS for twenty years, and many CBS executives feared his departure would cause audiences to change their viewing habits and shift their loyalties. At first it appeared there was indeed some reason for concern, but Rather's reputation for broadcast journalism and some promotional help resulted in continued success.

Along with the successes came some embarrassments. A documentary titled "The Uncounted Enemy: A Vietnam Deception"

dealt with the alleged manipulations of statistics concerning enemy strength and casualties during the Vietnam War. The program was criticized for being biased and was attacked in such publications as the *Washington Journalism Review* and *TV Guide* which titled their piece "The Anatomy of a Smear." CBS responded with an internal investigation, which turned up five violations of its own news standards.[10]

Cable Ownership and the AT&T Venture

In 1981 CBS obtained the go-ahead to purchase cable properties, although in some ways it entered into competition with its own affiliates by doing so. The CBS move opened up the way for the other networks. Restrictions placed on such ownership were that the cable systems owned by the network could not reach more than 90,000 subscribers or more than 0.5 percent of the nation's cable subscribers, whichever was less.

In 1982 CBS also entered into an experimental videotex venture with AT&T. The system was designed to deliver textual information to homes having a special terminal that permits access to the data stored in a central computer (see chapter 9). Such experiments, also conducted by other communication companies, were also designed to obtain in-house research information for future development when videotex becomes a major home information medium.

NBC

The oldest of the three commercial networks is NBC. With its Red and Blue dual-network concept, it gained momentum early and was well entrenched when CBS arrived on the scene.

Sarnoff and Goodman

If we look at NBC's past and present, two individuals stand out—David Sarnoff (Figure 11-4) and Julian Goodman. Sarnoff's career bloomed at RCA, NBC's parent company. The shore-bound radio operator during the *Titanic* disaster, Sarnoff came to RCA from the American Marconi Company. His energies at RCA were directed to two areas—developing new broadcast technology and promoting television stars as a means of winning audiences. In the first area he encouraged the development of FM and committed millions of dollars to Zworykin so that he could continue his experiments

with an electronic television camera. Led by Sarnoff, RCA became a pioneer in color television, developing the system finally approved by the FCC for full-scale production (Figure 11-5).

Julian Goodman is a product more of NBC than of RCA. His career with the network started in 1945. Goodman was to NBC what Ed Klauber was to CBS. He had stints with NBC News as an editor in Washington and as head of news and special events for the NBC radio network. He attracted attention in top NBC echelons after holding key news directorships during both the 1952 and 1956 national political conventions. These were the years of television's golden age, a

FIGURE 11-4 David Sarnoff guided RCA and its subsidiary, NBC, through a strategy of new technologies and promoting television stars as a means of winning audiences. He is seen here holding magnetic tape which RCA demonstrated in 1953, ushering in the era of "electronic photography" for television. (RCA)

FIGURE 11-5 The first commerical RCA color television receivers came off the production line on March 25, 1954 at the company's plant in Bloomington, Indiana. (RCA)

time when the emerging dominance of the medium was watched closely by the public and industry alike. By the end of the 1950s Goodman was head of news and public affairs at NBC. In 1966 he became president of the network, and subsequently he advanced to the board chairmanship.

Strategy, Stars, Color, and Innovation

During Goodman's tenure the network continued to grow. Strategy was based on a three-pronged attack that Sarnoff had started and perpetuated: stars, color, and innovation.

Radio had been a medium of programs, but Sarnoff realized that television made people bigger than life. So people would be where NBC invested its efforts. Major moves were made to attract and sign top talent. Names like Milton Berle and the

"Texaco Star Theater" gave America a new night at home with the television set. Sid Caesar's "Your Show of Shows" and Eddie Cantor's "Comedy Hour" contributed to the "people" orientation.

Two other factors helped even more— color television and innovative programming. Following the FCC's approval of RCA's color system, it was only natural for NBC to move ahead full speed to air as many color programs as possible. Regardless of whether you were watching in color or in black and white, the famous NBC peacock spreading its tail feathers spelled credibility. The first network colorcast was the 1954 Tournament of Roses Parade. Ten years later, NBC was producing almost all of its programs in color.

NBC initiated a series of firsts in programming, many later copied by other networks. With host Dave Garroway, "Today" dawned in 1952, followed two years later by the "Tonight Show" with host Jack Paar, then Steve Allen, and finally Johnny Carson. By the 1970s insomniacs were watching the postmidnight "Tomorrow" program. Westerns were also NBC's glory. The Ponderosa swept the imagination of millions in "Bonanza." Then came the NBC "specials," such as "Satin and Spurs" with Betty Hutton and "Peter Pan" with Mary Martin. The network was a pioneer in the area of movies, producing "Saturday Night at the Movies" and later "World Premiere Movies." News and public-affairs programming included in-depth coverage of the political conventions, and the network capitalized on the popularity of two anchormen named Chet Huntley and David Brinkley.

By 1980 NBC's long-running "Today" program had been eclipsed by ABC's "Good Morning America." Fred Silverman left the network and was replaced by Grant Tinker, who had headed M–T–M productions, the creator of a number of highly successful shows including the long-running situation comedy "The Mary Tyler Moore Show." While CBS was regaining its foothold in the evening news, correspondent Roger Mudd jumped to NBC.

While NBC tried to regain a foothold in the ratings with such award-winning programs as "Hill Street Blues," it floundered badly in other programming and by 1984 was beginning to get tagged with the image as the "third-place" network.

NETWORKS AND ALLIED BUSINESSES

Although broadcasting contributes a major share of the network's income, it is interrelated with a wide range of other businesses, including publishing, recordings, amusement parks, and electronic supplies. For example, there are not only the ABC network and the ABC-owned-and-operated radio and television stations but also ABC Theaters. Located in eleven southern states, this theater division of ABC constructs multiscreen theaters in new urban areas. Having this large chain of movie houses, the network is able to negotiate profitable rental rates for first-run movies. Publications such as *Prairie Farmer, Wisconsin Agriculturist,* and *Modern Photography* are owned by ABC, as is the Historic Towne of Smithville, a tourist attraction near Atlantic City, New Jersey.

At CBS the organization chart shows a Broadcast Group, Records Group, Columbia Group, and Publishing Group. We have already learned about the Broadcast Group which consists of the network, the owned-and-operated stations, and CBS News. The CBS Records Group is the world's largest producer, manufacturer, and marketer of recorded music. Record and tape clubs, retail stores, Steinway pianos, and Creative Playthings toys are part of a company division called the Columbia Group. The publishing house of Holt, Rhinehart and Winston is part of the CBS Publishing Group.

For NBC, the umbrella of allied corporate interests is RCA. Electronic parts and equipment continue to be big business. Brand names such as the XL-100 television line are part of RCA's division of Electronics-Consumer products and Services. Commercial electronic products are manufactured and sold as part of RCA's Electronics-Commercial Products and Services. If you buy a Banquet frozen dinner, rent a Hertz Rent-A-Car, read a book published by Random House, or talk to Alaska through the Globcom satellite networks, you are contributing to RCA's income.

RADIO NETWORKS

When television reached its golden age, some predicted the demise of radio, especially the radio networks. This simply has not happened. Although they do not provide the same amount of programming they once did, radio networks are still a vital part of radio broadcasting. In fact, with the soaring costs of television advertising, radio networks, have been increasingly attractive to advertisers.

ABC's Demographic Networks

One of the more innovative ideas in modern radio was the decision by ABC in 1968 to break off into four separate radio networks. The split created the American Information, American Contemporary, American Entertainment, and American FM radio networks. These four networks are designed to serve affiliates reaching audiences with different demographic characteristics. For example, stations programming rock music and reaching a younger audience might affiliate with the American Contemporary Network, which has short, fast-paced newscasts. A station with news and information programming might affiliate with the ABC Information Network. Demographic characteristics are equally attractive to advertisers wishing to reach the audiences that display them.

The content of the news on the different networks also varies. Designed for younger audiences, the Contemporary Network has less emphasis on foreign news and more on consumer-oriented, "pocketbook" stories. The Information Network emphasizes foreign and domestic politics and political aspects of the economy. Many affiliates of the American FM Network program progressive rock music, reaching a college-age audience.

Thus, news stories on the FM Network emphasize such things as careers, young politicians, and information of interest to an audience ABC characterizes as "thoughtful and involved." American Entertainment Radio news serves affiliates that offer easy-listening, middle-of-the-road music to an older audience. Along with regularly scheduled newscasts, the Entertainment network features "Paul Harvey News."

ABC's Direction Network

The ABC Direction Network, billed as a "lifestyle-oriented" network targeted to the twenty-five-to-fifty-four age group, premiered on January 4, 1982. Direction features a three-minute newscast fifteen minutes before the hour. ABC promotional material states that "Direction Network newscasts report the who, what, when and where of the news and are more commonly referred to as the 'news people can use.' . . . Direction also has a strong commitment to mini-documentaries and commentaries showing how national and international events affect listeners."[11] In addition, "the network offers daily and weekend sports reports, and supplies 13 Newscalls of actuality material [recorded inserts such as the actual voices of newsmakers] and three Sportscalls daily to affiliated stations."[12]

ABC Talk Radio

ABC Talk Radio is a nationally distributed service that began broadcasting via satellite in May 1982. ABC literature notes that "a total of 18 hours of talk programming is broadcast to accommodate 12 hours of local time programming. The service is currently distributed via Westar satellite III, transponder 4 in all time zones between the hours of 10 A.M. and 4 P.M. and midnight and 6 A.M. local time, with additional programming hours available to stations at their option. Most programming originates from KABC Radio, ABC's AM radio station in Los Angeles."[13] Personalities on Talk Radio include Owen Spann, based in San Francisco on ABC's KGO radio, Southern California's Michael Jackson, and Ray Briem, originally with KABC radio.

ABC Rock Radio

ABC introduced its Rock Radio network in 1982. Features and news tailored to the network's eighteen-to-thirty-four audience are programmed. In addition, a number of full-length concerts and music series are offered. Rock Radio provides competition for some syndicators who had in the past distributed many of these features directly to individual stations. Included in the lineup are such programs as "The King Biscuit Flower Hour," "Supergroups," and "Rolling Stone's Continuous History of Rock and Roll." "The King Biscuit Flower Hour," produced by D.I.R. Broadcasting, is one of rock music's longest-running feature programs of its kind. Recorded live in clubs and arenas, "The King Biscuit Flower Hour" has featured Genesis, Men at Work, Rainbow, Pat Benatar, and Aldo Nova, among others.[14]

Mutual, NBC, CBS

Of the major networks, only the Mutual Broadcasting System (MBS) remains exclusively a radio network. Its identity has been shaped by regularly scheduled newscasts, including such familiar names as Fulton Lewis, Jr., and his son Fulton Lewis III airing regular commentaries on the network. Mutual affiliates also receive such major sports events as Notre Dame football, championship boxing, NFL football, PGA Golf, and the Sugar Bowl. Colorful commentaries are heard regularly from Jack Anderson and oddsmaker Jimmy the Greek.

In 1975 NBC launched its News and Information Service (NIS) in an attempt to capture some of the still unclaimed affiliates market. NIS fed approximately forty-five minutes of news per hour to all-news affiliate stations. The idea was good, but all-news stations, while reaching mainly an educated, affluent audience, incur major expenses. Costs for broadcast journalists can be high, especially in smaller markets. To affiliates, NIS was costly but less expensive than hiring local personnel to cover national news. Unfortunately, the number of affiliates needed to make NIS profitable did not materialize, and in 1977 NBC dropped the service. Some NIS affiliates scrambled to develop an alternative network, others switched to wire-service audio or other networks, and still others went back to programming music. For some affiliates, the dissolution of NIS was costly. They had publicized their all-news operations in major promotional campaigns, and suddenly had to change formats or else make major expenditures to hire local reporters to cover a full news schedule. Today the NBC Radio Network still serves affiliates nationwide, but NIS is a part of history. To reach the young-adult audience NBC programs The Source, a network heavy with concerts and specials much like those of ABC's Rock Radio.

The CBS Radio Network remains one of the more traditional radio networks, consisting of news and information programming and some feature material. It draws heavily on the news staff of CBS and features many of the personalities seen daily on CBS television. In 1981 CBS announced a new youth-network format that would compete with The Source and Rock Radio.[15] Called RADIORADIO, the network programs ninety-second features that include music-trivia quizzes. Its three-hour weekly countdown program is keyed to adult contemporary charts.

UPI AUDIO AND AP RADIO

Although wire-service audio is not a network in the traditional sense, many radio stations affiliate with these services. Local stations, paying a fee to subscribe, can then sell time within the wire-service newscasts to local advertisers—a more profitable arrangement in the opinion of many station managers.

United Press International first launched an audio service in 1956 by establishing state-news telephone feeds in North Carolina and California. By 1960 the wire service had established a New York audio headquarters, and three years later it added a Washington, D.C., audio bureau. The next year an audio bureau in London was opened, and by 1965 coast-to-coast hookups were operable. The 1970s brought hourly newscasts, expanded sports coverage, and experimental satellite transmission. In addition, UPI Audio feeds affiliates a daily set of audio actualities that stations can incorporate into locally produced newscasts.

Associated Press began an audio service in 1974 called AP Radio, basing it on the same principle as that of UPI Audio's national news service. Affiliates pay a fee to receive the service, then sell local advertising time within their regularly scheduled newscasts.

WIRE-SERVICE AND AUDIO ADVISORY BOARDS

Like the networks, the wire services use affiliate advisory boards. These can operate at either the state or national level. Typical of such organizations is the UPI Broadcast Advisory Board. The organization was conceived in 1976 at a steering-committee meeting of UPI executives and broadcasters. The committee formulated plans for the board and constructed a set of initial objectives:

1. to evaluate and improve UPI services
2. to foster a better understanding of UPI technology by subscribers and the public
3. to improve the general image of broadcast news
4. to encourage input, discussion, and recommendations at all levels
5. to serve as a forum for discussion of major complaints affecting the general performance of the services

These objectives were later incorporated into the board's bylaws.

The UPI Broadcast Advisory Board met for the first time in December 1976 in Chicago. To assure representative membership and orderly replacement of board members, the bylaws provide for a board "generally representative of geographical areas, large and small radio and television markets, independent and group ownership, management and working news people." Membership on the board consists of "a minimum of 13 and a maximum of 16 members, and the Board is empowered to expand its membership to include international members." The bylaws also provide for the election of officers, terms, and special committees. Evidence of the rapidly changing developments in broadcast journalism are found in a bylaw that appears under the heading "technology." It charges the board with encouraging "research and development of new methods and systems in broadcast news."[16]

ETHNIC, EDUCATIONAL, CABLE, AND MDS NETWORKS

Whereas ABC divides its listeners according to such demographic categories as age, education, and income, two other networks have been successful in directing programming to audiences on the basis of race and national origin. The National Black Network, a radio network formed in 1973 and headquartered in New York, serves affiliates covering black markets and reaching approximately 70 percent of the United States' black population. News on the network emphasizes events and issues of importance to black Americans. Owned and operated by blacks, the network produces approximately 120 hourly newscasts each week. Other programs heard on the network include the thirty-minute news forum "Black Issues and the Black Press," patterned after NBC's "Meet the Press." Commentators and entertainment programming supplement the regular newscasts. In 1981 the network announced a news and public-affairs service called the American Black Information Network.[17]

What the National Black Network offers to the black audience the Spanish International Network (SIN) provides for the Hispanic-American audience. Formed in 1961 to reach Spanish-speaking households, SIN is a television network that airs Spanish-language programming pertinent to Hispanic-American culture. Affiliated with television stations and cable, the SIN reaches a large percentage of Hispanic-Americans. There are SIN affiliates in Chicago, New York, Miami, and similar markets stretching from Texas across the Southwest and up the California coast to San Francisco.

Many noncommercial radio and television stations not only provide instructional programs for in-school use but also originate and transmit programming for state and regional networks. Often these networks are part of a state system of higher education. One of the pioneers is the Alabama ETV network. The Indiana Higher Education Telecommunication System (IHETS) links both state and private colleges and has two-way television capabilities. A professor can lecture from one campus to students on another, and the students can immediately ask the professor questions through a two-way talk-back system. The talk-back system is another example of the changing definition of mass communication that we discussed in Chapter 1—delayed feedback being replaced by immediate feedback.

Cable television's growth has spurred interest in networks linking cable systems. The technology already exists, in the form of satellite interconnection systems, to offer satellite-distributed programs to cable systems. Other cable networks operate more as an exchange, sharing programs or joining to purchase such special programming as sports events or first-run movies.

Multipoint distribution service—the use of microwave to distribute television signals over a small region—has enabled such organizations as schools and churches to enter the world of network television. For example, the Catholic Television Network of Chicago (CTNC) has its own television studios and distribution system and broadcasts educational television programs to Chicago's Catholic schools.

DECLINING AUDIENCES

While the networks venture into cable and pay TV, these same technologies are siphoning away the network audience. For example, the years 1976–81 saw the three major networks' share of the television audience decrease from 91 percent to 83 percent.[18] At the same time, pay-TV subscribers increased from .7 million to 10.1 million. Some estimate that by 1990 the networks could lose as much as one-third of their audience to pay TV and other technologies.[19]

Another factor in the decline in network audiences is the networks' scheduling practices, which have drawn criticism.[20] For example, because ratings are available two days after a show airs, and because a single rating point is worth millions of dollars, networks can quickly spot less successful shows. The practice of canceling shows and filling the slots with replacements in a never ending battle for ratings has resulted in television schedules that are, to some, confusing.[21] Some observers speculate that people are not watching television as much because they simply do not know what to expect. Regular shows are replaced with specials, reruns appear in place of new material, and shows are canceled before they have a chance to build viewer loyalty.

Although networks cannot stop the development of alternative technologies, they have made some efforts to stop using reruns. Attempts to develop fresh material, especially during the summer months, may prove helpful, but the trend toward network audience declines appears firm, and networks are adjusting by maximizing profits on the audience that does exist.[22]

DATA NETWORKS

In Chapter 9 we discussed the many services of videotex. Videotex is changing the traditional definition of network from a broadcasting system to a system of data services that provide information to subscribers. Subscribers have direct access to information networks such as Compuserve and The Source (not to be confused with the NBC radio network), through their personal computers, which they can interface with larger computers belonging to the data services. As more and more information networks become available they will begin to compete for subscribers just as the networks compete for audiences. Like advertisers who want to reach the largest audience, information suppliers will select among the information networks since their services will have a better

chance of being chosen where more subscribers exist. Many of the same considerations we now see with network radio and television will apply to these new networks. If, for instance, an information network supplies financial or business information, then it will be more appealing to, say, stockbrokers than a network oriented toward consumer goods.

The commercial television networks are already examining the new information networks. How far they venture into videotex will be determined by the number of subscribers videotex generates as well as its profitability.

SUMMARY

In this chapter we have discussed the major commercial radio and television networks. Networks give advertisers a means of reaching a mass national audience at economical rates. Their entertainment programs are usually bought from production companies, but their news and public-affairs programming is self-produced.

At the heart of the networks are the affiliate stations, which, along with the public, have strongly criticized network operation.

The three major commercial networks, ABC, CBS, and NBC, remain viable and profitable. ABC, formed when NBC sold its Blue Network, quickly acquired an identity and became a formidable competitor of NBC and CBS. CBS gained an early reputation as a leader in broadcast journalism under Ed Klauber and in sound management under William Paley and Dr. Frank Stanton. From little more than a million dollars in revenue in 1928, the network progressed to its first billion-dollar year in 1976. NBC, meanwhile, developed under the RCA umbrella and the guidance of David Sarnoff. NBC made its mark with big-name stars, color, and innovative programming, and continues to make profits. Although the networks themselves are big businesses, all are interconnected with other business ventures. These include such wide-ranging enterprises as publishing, amusement parks, rental cars, and frozen foods.

All three of the major commercial networks are involved in radio, as is the Mutual Broadcasting System. ABC, in attempting to satisfy the specialized audience of radio, split into four demographic networks in 1968.

Both UPI Audio and AP Radio provide alternatives for radio stations not affiliated with the commercial networks and for those that want to supplement their network programming.

Other types of radio and television networks include ethnic, educational, cable, and religious networks.

The growth of cable and pay TV is believed to have contributed to a decline in the networks' television audience, which has dropped as much as 7 percent, according to recent studies. Some predict that by 1990 the audience for network television will have been cut by one-third.

Data networks are continuing to grow. These information networks may prove profitable to the telephone companies, which make line charges to those who access the networks, or we may see the major television networks begin their own electronic newspapers.

OPPORTUNITIES
FOR FURTHER LEARNING

BEDELL, S., *Up the Tube: Prime-Time TV and the Silverman Years.* New York: Viking, 1981.

BOTEIN, M., and D. M. RICE, *Network Television and the Public Interest.* Lexington, Mass.: Heath, 1980.

Broadcasting the Next Ten Years. New York: NBC, 1977.

BURT, R. S., and M. J. MINOR and associates, *Applied Network Analysis: A Methodological Introduction.* Beverly Hills, Calif.: Sage, 1983.

BUXTON, F., and B. OWEN, *The Big Broadcast 1920–1950.* New York: Viking, 1972.

CANTER, M. G., *Prime-Time Television: Content and Control.* Beverly Hills, Calif.: Sage, 1980.

DAVIS, G. R., ed., *The Local Network Handbook.* New York: McGraw-Hill, 1982.

DORDICK, H. S., H. G. BRADLEY, and B. NANUS, *The Emerging Network Marketplace.* Norwood, N.J.: Ablex, 1981.

DREHER, C., *Sarnoff: An American Success.* New York: Quadrangle/New York Times Book Co., 1977.

FRANK, R. E., and M. G. GREENBERG, *Audiences for Public Television.* Beverly Hills, Calif.: Sage, 1982.

FRIENDLY, F. W., *Due to Circumstances Beyond Our Control . . .* New York: Random House, 1967.

GANS, H. J., *Deciding What's News: A Study of CBS Evening News, NBC Nightly News, Newsweek, and Time.* New York: Pantheon, 1979.

GERANI, G., and H. SCHULMAN, *Fantastic Television.* New York: Harmony Books/Crown, 1977.

HESS, G. N., *An Historical Study of the Dumont Television Network.* New York: Arno Press, 1979.

KIRKLEY, D. H., Jr., *A Descriptive Study of the Network Television Western During the Seasons 1955–1956 to 1962–1963.* New York: Arno Press, 1979.

LARSON, J. F., *Television's Window on the World: International Affairs Coverage on the U.S. Networks.* Norwood, N.J.: Ablex, 1983.

LEVINSON, R., and W. LINK, *Stay Tuned: An Inside Look at the Making of Prime-Time Television.* New York: St. Martin's, 1981.

LONG, S. L., *The Development of the Television Network Oligopoly.* New York: Arno Press, 1979.

MacKUEN, M. B., and S. L. COOMBS, *More Than News: Media Power in Public Affairs,* Beverly Hills, Calif.: Sage, 1981.

MARSDEN, P. V., and N. LIN, eds., *Social Structure and Network Analysis.* Beverly Hills, Calif.: Sage, 1982.

METZ, R., *The Today Show.* New York: Playboy Press, 1977.

MORRIS, J. A., *Deadline Every Minute: The Story of United Press.* Westport, Conn.: Greenwood Press, 1969.

NETWORK INQUIRY SPECIAL STAFF, FEDERAL COMMUNICATIONS COMMISSION, *New Television Networks: Entry, Jurisdiction, Ownership and Regulation,* 2 vols. (Vol. I: Final Report; Vol. II: Background Reports). Washington, D.C.: FCC, 1980.

PALEY, W., *As It Happened.* New York: Doubleday, 1979.

PEARCE, A., *NBC News Division: A Study of the Costs, the Revenues, and the Benefits of Broadcast News.* New York: Arno Press, 1979. The same volume includes *The Economics of Prime Time Access.*

QUINLAN, S., *The Hundred Million Dollar Lunch.* Chicago: J. Philip O'Hara, 1974.

REASONER, H., *Before the Colors Fade.* New York: Knopf, 1981.

RICE, D. M., "Direct Broadcast Satellites: Legal and Policy Options." In Federal Communications Commission, *Preliminary Report on Prospects for Additional Networks.* Washington, D.C.: FCC, 1980.

RIVERS, W. L., *The Other Government: Power and the Washington Media.* New York: Universe Books, 1982.

SARCH, R., ed., *Data Network Design Strategies.* McGraw-Hill, 1983.

SHANK, B. *The Cool Fire: How to Make It in Television.* New York: Norton, 1976.

SKLAR, R., *Prime-Time America: Life On and Behind the Television Screen.* New York: Oxford University Press, 1980.

TUROW, J., *Entertainment, Education, and the Hard Sell: Three Decades of Network Children's Television.* New York: Praeger, 1981.

12

EDUCATIONAL AND PUBLIC TELECOMMUNICATION

At 6:55 A.M., radio and television stations are keying up for another broadcasting day. For some, sign-on came in the predawn darkness with "Today," the "CBS Morning News," or "Good Morning America." In foreign countries, 7:00 A.M. ushers in news, special-feature programming, entertainment, and public affairs.

Sign-on preparations are also bustling at this hour in many school systems. A closed-circuit television system warms up for a "broadcast" of the daily calendar of events, students begin to produce a morning news program, and teachers preview instructional television lessons that they will incorporate into afternoon lectures. At a nearby college, a professor is preparing a lecture that will be aired over a statewide educational television network. In a famous medical school a television camera focuses on the operating table and broadcasts a color picture to interns in an observation room across campus. It is all part of the world of educational broadcasting.

ETV: THE BEGINNINGS

Although a closed-circuit television system was in use at the State University of Iowa as early as 1932, it was in 1938 that the first over-the-air experimental broadcast for educational purposes took place.[1] Undertaken in cooperation with NBC and the School of Commerce of New York University, the broadcast was arranged by Dr. James Rowland Angell, then educational director of NBC. Originating in a studio on the third floor of the RCA building, the program was broadcast from the transmitting tower on top of the Empire State Building. A class of 250 students seated in a large auditorium on the sixty-second floor of the RCA building viewed the program, which consisted of "an explanation and demonstration of television. A two-way radio hookup connected the studio with the auditorium. Capturing the flavor of the event, program instructor C. C. Clark asked a student in the auditorium to come to the studio to have a question answered. About ten minutes later, when the student arrived at the studio and appeared on the screen, the group in the auditorium broke into applause.

The Experimental Era

The early 1940s were years of continued experiments with the new medium. The Metropolitan Museum of Art in New York arranged with CBS to televise its painting collection. Francis Henry Taylor, director of the museum, predicted television would be "just as revolutionary for visual education as radio was for the symphony and the opera."[2] The following year saw such mass-oriented educational television programs as New York's WCBW broadcast of a series of first-aid programs in cooperation with the American Red Cross. Programs of a more informative and educational nature were aired during the height of World War II, including one from Schenectady, New York, on blood plasma.

Early enthusiasm for educational television was sidelined by World War II, but when the war ended the industry began to concentrate on it again. NBC announced the first "permanent" series in educational broadcasting, "Your World Tomorrow."[3] Some of the early program titles in the series included "The Mighty Atom," "Jet Propulsion," and "Huff-Duff, the Radio Detective." The network secured the cooperation of the New York City Board of Education in having students watch the programs in special "viewing rooms." The students then evaluated the programs. This was an early example, though on a very limited scale, of the systematic evaluation of educational programming.

Despite the encouragement from the networks and the willingness of certain school officials, educational television was a long way from widespread acceptance. As late as 1947, the *Journal* of the National Education Association reported the efforts of the state of Virginia to make the transition to what was termed *visual education*.[4] Although Virginia was known for its pioneering efforts in the field, the report never even mentioned educational television. The medium had not been able to rise above all the movie projectors, slide projectors, charts, models, and posters of the typical classroom. In 1946 two researchers studied the skills and knowledge elementary teachers needed in order to use audio-visual aids.[5] Out of the forty-two survey items that the study incorporated, which included mechanics, utilization, production, and facilities, none referred to television.

ETV Gains Acceptance

Finally, at the turn of the decade, educational television began to obtain recognition. In 1949 Crosley Broadcasting awarded a fellowship to a Kentucky high-school principal, Russel Helmick, to "carry on research of how education by television can best serve the needs of the general public." The broad charge assigned to Helmick illustrates the early survey approach to researching educational television:

1. Careful sifting of the literature of radio education to discover mistakes to be avoided and lessons helpful in investigating the educational possibilities of television.
2. Analysis of the television programs available for possible correlation with adult-education programs and the curriculum at university, high-school, and elementary-school levels.
3. Canvassing of school and home facilities and equipment for utilizing video programs.
4. Study of teacher interests and attitudes toward correlation of their school offerings in the curriculum with cultural and educational programs from television stations.
5. Investigation of pupil attitudes and interests in such cultural and educational areas as history, geography, English, science, and physical education and sports in relation to utilization of appropriate television programs.
6. Investigation of the educational levels at which television can be made most effective—adult education, colleges and universities, high schools, and elementary schools.[6]

Thirty years later, more narrowly defined and highly sophisticated research was still being conducted within the very broad parameters of Helmick's goals.

In 1950 public awareness of the importance and potential of educational television rose when Dr. Earl J. McGrath, U.S. Commissioner of Education, appeared at hearings before the FCC and called for at least one channel in every broadcasting area to be reserved for educational purposes. McGrath suggested "that it is vital to the continuous improvement of public education that every school system and college competent to produce educational television programs and financially able to construct and operate a station be assured that, when the time comes that it is ready to start construction of a television broadcast station, a suitable locally usable transmitting frequency will be available."[7] The FCC responded favorably.

Organized Support for ETV

Organized support for educational television came in the early fifties when the American Council on Education coordinated the formation of the Joint Committee on Educational Television (JCET). The committee brought together seven supporters of ETV, all of them organizations that had originally called upon the FCC to hold hearings on the subject. Financial commitment was also provided by a $90,000 grant from the Ford Foundation. One of the committee's main goals was to assist educational institutions in establishing stations. The first chairman of the JCET was Dr. Edgar Fuller, then executive secretary of the National Council of Chief State School Officers, one of the seven member organizations of JCET.

Other financial support for ETV went directly to colleges and universities. Syracuse University received a $150,000 gift earmarked for graduate programs in radio and television. In the fall of 1950 Syracuse announced it was conferring the new degree of Master of Science in Radio and Television.[8]

The medium even gained some artistic legitimacy when *Variety,* the show-business weekly, reviewed a "University Telecourse" program aired on the Cleveland station WEWS. *Variety* called the program a "preciously packaged mine of informational nuggets" and "a fast-moving, easily digested, highly accredited performance."[9] Few professors in the classroom could have been so enthusiastic.

When in 1952 the FCC lifted its freeze on new station licenses, it allocated 242 channels for educational use. The first to take advantage of the newly allocated frequencies was the University of Houston, whose station KUHT went on the air in 1953 (Figure 12-1). But the expensive facilities and televi-

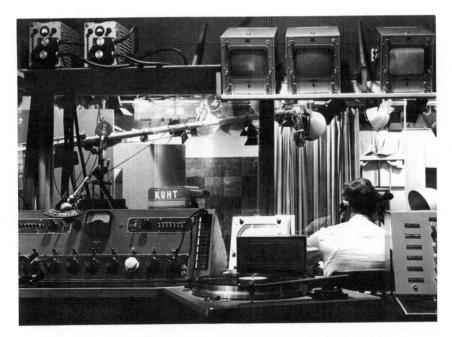

FIGURE 12–1 KUHT at the University of Houston was the first station to sign on the air after the FCC lifted its freeze and allocated 242 new channels for educational use. (Office of Information of the University of Houston)

sion equipment necessary for transmission prohibited the rush to the marketplace that the FCC had anticipated. Nevertheless, educational television had delivered its first-born.

As the decade progressed, forecasters saw educational television helping to teach the huge classroom enrollments predicted for the 1960s and 1970s. Educational television was used more widely, and state systems of educational television were created. But by the end of the decade the honeymoon was beginning to pall and educators were beginning to take a more critical look at teaching by television.

Evaluating the Effectiveness of ETV

Arguments both for and against ETV surfaced rapidly.[10] In some ways, the controversy was a compliment to the influence of the new teaching tool. Both sides did agree that more research was needed before educators could determine the true assets of ETV. Teachers, however, were beginning to object to administrators' requests that they allocate time for television teaching on top of their already crowded classroom schedules. They also wanted to participate from the very beginning in the formulation of instructional television programming. This is now a routine way of developing good instructional programming. The thought of television as a substitute teacher, understandably, received considerable resistance. Classroom teachers were fully aware that the interaction between student and teacher contributed much to the learning process. They appreciated television's particular abilities but wanted to protect their own role in the student-teacher interaction.

The Economics of ETV

The public's focus on the economics of educational television also concerned educators. The politicians' and taxpayers' misconception that the medium could eliminate personnel and save taxpayers' money was worrisome. Educators realized that they had to reemphasize the importance of the teacher in the classroom. They faced still another economic concern—the financing that educational television would receive. Television studios could easily incur bills in the hundreds of thousands of dollars. Money like that could not only pay several salaries but also provide many of the traditional classroom teaching aids.

AIRBORNE ETV: THE MPATI EXPERIMENTS

The DC-6 lumbered (Figure 12–2) down the runway, its motors roaring in unison. Inside, highly trained technicians waited with their sophisticated electronics gear until the big bird was airborne. It was early morning. The pilot climbed to 20,000 feet and leveled off. The plane's destination was northeastern Indiana and its target, thousands of schoolchildren waiting patiently below. The cargo was television programs on such subjects as Spanish, French, history, and science, broadcast to the outlying areas of Indiana, Illinois, Kentucky, Michigan, Wisconsin, and Ohio. Conceived in 1944, by a Westinghouse radar expert named Charles E. Nobles and his persistent colleague, Westinghouse engineer Ruben Lee, Midwest Program for Airborne Television Instruction (MPATI) was one of the most ambitious projects undertaken in the early years of educational television.[11]

The Theory Behind MPATI

The idea of taking a television station into the sky had been fixed in Nobles' mind. Doing so would theoretically raise the television tower to 23,000 feet. The distance then covered by this signal would expand to include a potential half-million pupils. Nobles reasoned that the plane must have a special gyroscope-controlled antenna that would always remain vertical, regardless of the position of the aircraft. Upon reaching its position over Indiana, the DC-6 would fly in a tight pattern of twenty miles, beaming its signals to the states below.

Funding and Programming

The project succeeded with support from a number of organizations. Purdue University agreed to furnish maintenance and other support personnel for the aircraft, which was based at the Purdue airport because of its proximity to the target area. Local school systems using MPATI contributed a nominal amount of money to buy equipment to receive the programs. Dr. J. A. Hutcheson, then Westinghouse vice-president in charge of engineering, aided the project by obtaining an initial $6-million grant from the Ford Foundation. Major national education organizations such as the National Education Association, the Parent-Teachers Association, and the U.S. Office of Education threw their support behind the experiment.

MPATI, despite its popularity, did not last. Satellite communication, with antennas 23,000 miles high and signals that could span large sections of continents, soon proved more useful. The MPATI plane that made its first broadcast in 1961 made its last in 1968, though the organization stayed in limited operation until 1971. This novel effort definitely pioneered research for future

FIGURE 12-2 Circling over the Midwest, the specially equipped plane of the Midwest Program for Airborne Television Instruction beamed educational television programs directly to classrooms in Indiana, Illinois, Kentucky, Michigan, Wisconsin, and Ohio. Based at the Purdue University airport in Lafayette, Indiana, the MPATI plane made its last television flights in 1971, and the concept of using an aircraft television transmission system was gradually replaced by the efficiency of satellites. (Purdue University Archives)

satellite experiments, when small communities would again receive educational television programs, this time from outer space.

EDUCATIONAL VERSUS INSTRUCTIONAL BROADCASTING

In television's formative years, experiments ranging from MPATI to televising art masterpieces for the public were all considered examples of educational television, or ETV. The programs were truly designed to educate. For our own purposes, we shall define ETV as *all noncommercial television programming and commercial programming produced especially for educational purposes, whether or not the program is used for direct classroom instruction.*

As educational television matured and more and more uses of in-school programming were developed, a second term—*in-structional television (ITV)*—evolved. Although both terms tend to be used interchangeably, instructional television refers to programming designed specifically for use in the classroom or in some other direct teaching role. Notice we did not use the words *in-school* in our definition. Both ETV and ITV are employed beyond the confines of the classroom.

Differentiating between the two terms is also important for economic and political reasons.[12] Remember that criticism of ETV reached full force in the 1960s. Part of this criticism went beyond the classroom to policy issues. Because much of the programming of ETV stations was designed for in-school use, and because major federal funding was emerging, some saw the potential threat of a national school system under federal control. Congressional advocates of ETV were charged with maintaining "a sinister conspiracy directed from the U.S.

Office of Education to homogenize the nation's moppets by a standardized curriculum spread from sea to shining sea."[13] The furor caused ETV stations to stop and seriously consider from where their future programming dollars would come.

During this time, smaller portable videotape equipment arrived in the marketplace. Such equipment permitted many educators to continue tinkering with television, but this time without the threat of outside controls. For school administrations this inexpensive portable television equipment was particularly satisfying since they could buy it with local money and thereby avoid the public criticism caused by large federal expenditures. Although new, the idea of airplanes and satellites beaming federally funded programming to local school systems was sold most easily to both school officials and taxpayers as something "strictly experimental." The portable equipment satisfied those who demanded new technology in the classroom. Instead of educational television for large numbers of students, something new appeared—instructional television used strictly in the classroom, the programs often produced by the teachers themselves.

THE QUEST FOR ACCOUNTABILITY: DEVELOPING QUALITY ITV PROGRAMMING

Almost anything significant that occurs in a local school system becomes the concern of the community. Students, parents, teachers, school-board members, and even the legislature are all involved. The educational process, in its simplest terms, attempts to provide the most for the taxpayers' dollars. This quest can reach extreme levels, as in Oregon, where taxpayers have refused to approve school budgets and thereby forced some

schools to close. It also prompts hard questions at PTA or school-board meetings. Thus, it is only natural that people are concerned about ITV. The public, parents, and policy makers want to know if ITV is worth the money. Are the expensive facilities paying for themselves in terms of student benefits? Does the programming really teach something, or is it just background entertainment?[14]

The result of this probing is a trend toward increased accountability in developing ITV programming.[15] Speaking before a congressional hearing, learning authority P. Kenneth Komoski noted that less than 1 percent of the instructional tapes now on the market are learner-verified. Komoski meant that although ITV programs are designed to teach something, students will not necessarily learn merely by viewing them. Most programs simply have not been tested, so program developers are beginning to ask questions. What do we really want to teach with this program? What are its objectives? What is the best way to present this material?[16] What techniques can we use to keep the student interested while learning? How much entertainment can we include without digressing from the basic subject matter? Such accountability affects people as well as programs. The person in charge of ITV program development is responsible for the overall effectiveness of ITV in the school setting. Also, the director of the ITV studio must justify to the school board budget increases resulting from ITV programming.

TRANSITION TO PUBLIC BROADCASTING: THE CARNEGIE COMMISSION

In the mid 1960s, as ITV programming switched to local production and distribution, educational television stations, their programming supplemented by locally produced videotape material, began to move toward a greater variety of programs beyond in-school programming. At about the same time, foundations and government agencies were supporting not only in-school production but also the development of state and national systems of noncommercial broadcasting. In 1962 the Educational TV Facilities Act provided over $30 million over a five-year period for the development of state systems of educational broadcasting. Today many of these systems are integral parts of a national system of noncommercial radio and television stations.

Full-scale planning for what would eventually become a national system of noncommercial radio and television stations began in 1965 with the Carnegie Commission for Educational Television. The commission, whose members were a broad range of industry leaders, was charged with conducting a "broadly conceived study of noncommercial television and to focus attention principally, although not exclusively, on community owned channels and their service to the general public." [17] The commission's report concluded that a "well financed, well directed educational television system, substantially larger and far more persuasive and effective than that which now exists in the United States, must be brought into being if the full needs of the American public are to be served." [18]

THE PUBLIC BROADCASTING ACT OF 1967

The commission's recommendations were the impetus for the passage of the Public Broadcasting Act of 1967, which allocated $38 million dollars to the improvement and construction of facilities for noncommercial radio and television in the United States.

Also formed by the act was the Corporation for Public Broadcasting, (CPB), a quasi-governmental company that would administer the funds appropriated for public broadcasting by Congress. The act authorized the CPB to

Facilitate the full development of educational broadcasting in which programs of high quality, obtained from diverse sources, will be made available to non-commercial educational television or radio broadcast stations, with strict adherence to objectivity and balance in all programs or series of programs of a controversial nature;

Assist in the establishment and development of one or more systems of interconnection to be used for the distribution of educational television or radio programs so that all non-commercial educational television or radio broadcast stations that wish to may broadcast the programs at times chosen by the stations;

Assist in the establishment and development of one or more systems of non-commercial educational television or radio broadcast stations throughout the United States;

Carry out its purposes and functions and engage in its activities in ways that will most effectively assure the maximum freedom of the non-commercial educational television or radio broadcast systems and local stations from interference with or control of program content or other activities.

With the passage of the act, noncommercial radio and television stations became known as "public" broadcasting stations, signifying their ability to secure income from the public as well as from corporations, foundations, and government agencies.

THE PUBLIC TELECOMMUNICATIONS FINANCING ACT

In 1978 Congress passed the Public Telecommunications Financing Act, which required CPB, in consultation with interested parties, to update a five-year plan for the development of public telecommunications. The planning funds supported three research projects.[19] The first, the Station Financial Model, is a computer model that uses information from the CPB annual surveys to describe how revenue changes influence the operations and services of public television stations. The other two projects investigate the uses of new technologies for delivering public telecommunications services. The Public Radio Extension Alternatives study examines options to traditional broadcasting for providing public radio service. It is an assessment of available technology alternatives, as well as a computer model for determining the most efficient means of radio distribution for unserved areas. The New Technologies Review is a critical examination, from a public-broadcasting perspective, of research on the use of new telecommunications technology. It evaluates a wide range of research, from field trials to market studies, and provides up-to-date projections on the availability and content of new services and the role of public telecommunications in the emerging media environment.

THE CPB PROGRAM FUND

The administrators of the CPB Program Fund, created in 1980, are charged with selecting and funding programs by a process that is protected from outside influences. A statement of priorities established by the fund lists:

Programs for children and the family.
Programs about the concerns of minorities and women, and opportunities for minorities and women to produce programs either for targeted groups or for a broader audience.
Drama.

Personal health, physical or spiritual; and
Public affairs programming—the development of public broadcasting as a source of "a regular and total account of the course of events presented in depth."[20]

PUBLIC BROADCASTING AMENDMENTS ACT OF 1981

The Omnibus Budget Reconciliation Act of 1981 contained the Public Broadcasting Amendments Act of 1981. It set authorization levels for CPB for fiscal years 1984–86. Appropriations were to be allocated for certain fixed costs and for CPB operations.

Public broadcasting stations that meet certain operating standards are eligible for financial support from the CPB. Such stations belong to National Public Radio (NPR), the radio network of public broadcasting, or the Public Broadcasting Service (PBS), the television network of public broadcasting.

THE PUBLIC BROADCASTING SERVICE

To help meet the goals of the Public Broadcasting Act of 1967, the CPB joined with many of the licensees of noncommercial television stations in the United States to form the Public Broadcasting Service (PBS) in 1970. Today the PBS is the primary distribution system for programs aired on public broadcasting stations. These programs are distributed through a four-channel satellite system that enables individual stations to choose programs that best suit their viewers. Although stations determine their own schedules and broadcast PBS-distributed programs at various times, 85 percent of the stations carry a core of programs fed by PBS during prime time on Sunday through Wednesday.[21]

PBS is similar to commercial television networks in that it distributes programs. Beyond that, however, most of the similarity stops. PBS is in many ways more sensitive to its affiliates, for the affiliates represent the public, which at least in theory, owns the PBS stations through its contributions and tax dollars. Part of this sensitivity is generated by the PBS board of directors. The board represents the general public and station managers and gains insights into the success and failure of its system. The board's communication with stations and the public makes it a good, broad-based indicator on which to base decisions.

THE ADVERTISING TEST

With the recession of the early 1980s came a series of decisions by PBS to try to provide a sound financial base for the future of public television in the United States. Some of these decisions were radical departures from past practices and philosophies. In a congressionally mandated advertising test representatives of ten stations met in New Orleans in 1982 and forged guidelines for incorporating advertising on an experimental basis into regular public television programming. Stations in New York, Chicago, Pittsburgh, Miami, New Orleans, Binghamton, Muncie (Indiana), Philadelphia, Erie (Pennsylvania), and Louisville participated. The guidelines developed for the experiment were as follows:

Advertising must be sensitive to the tastes and interests of the audience.

Advertising will respect the intelligence of the viewer.

Standards of quality that apply to regular programming will also apply to advertising.

Stations reserve the sole right to accept or reject advertisements on the basis of content or quality.

Stations will adhere to both the spirit and the letter of the National Association of Broadcasters TV code.

Stations will exercise particular caution in placement of advertising adjacent to programming intended for younger viewers, because such viewers and their programs deserve "a special sensitivity to the impact of advertising both in content and tone."[22]

In addition, the traditional taboos against tobacco, liquor, and personal-hygiene products were lifted. Stations wanting to develop programming could now request financial support from companies manufacturing these products. Corporate sponsors were given permission to display their logos and list their lines of business in the billboard credits at the beginning of a program.[23]

Another means of generating new income for PBS stations was the Public Subscriber Network, formed in 1981 to develop programming that could be sold to cable systems and distributed through the PBS satellite system. In addition, the network was given the go-ahead to investigate the feasibility of pay TV, which would use existing public television stations either directly or in cooperation with other pay-TV services in a market.[24]

THE NATIONAL ASSOCIATION OF PUBLIC TELEVISION STATIONS

In 1980 public television licensees formed a sister organization to PBS called the National Association of Public Television Stations (NAPTS). The NAPTS is designed as an organizational framework within which licensees can coordinate efforts in three non-programming areas: research, planning, and representation.[25]

Research, among other functions, includes maintaining up-to-date information on the public television system, making projections on the growth and income of the system, monitoring demographic trends that affect public television services, monitoring and analyzing key data, and providing advice on research projects. Planning includes assisting individual stations in their own planning efforts, performing long-range planning for public television services, and advising national organizations and government agencies in their planning of telecommunication services. Representation involves maintaining contact with Congress and government agencies on behalf of licensees, assisting licensees in their own direct representation, and preparing general information for and about public television stations.[26]

THE SCOPE OF PUBLIC TELEVISION PROGRAMMING

Public television has become a system of broadcasting whose wide variety of programs range from traditional in-school instructional programs to programming having a wide national and even international appeal. The appeal of "Sesame Street" (Figure 12-3) and "The Electric Company," for instance, went far beyond the preschool and elementary-school audiences they are designed to attract. "The Big Blue Marble," a program with similar appeal, sought to assure children that other children around the world have experiences similar to theirs. Still another program with national distribution and appeal was WNET-TV's "The

FIGURE 12-3 Big Bird of the popular PBS series "Sesame Street." "Sesame Street" was one of the early programs which showed the potential of educational and public broadcasting for mass audiences beyond the classroom. (Courtesy of the Children's Television Workshop)

Adams Chronicles,'' which depicted America's Adams family of presidential fame and its role in history from 1750 to 1900. Some programs, such as ''The Adams Chronicles,'' were accompanied by teacher and curriculum guides, which are especially helpful when the program is used in the classroom.

Regional programs have also reached a broad-based audience. ''Mr. Rogers,'' which started out as a regional program on WQED–TV in Pittsburgh, became popular nationally (Figure 12–4). This and other regional programs have made inroads into the cartoon fare so common to children's television.

Many colleges are taking advantage of the outreach programs that employ ITV to reach adults who may not want to take the trouble of coming to campus or, because of the distance and time, simply cannot come. As a result, television colleges are prospering. The Public Broadcasting Service has offered such ''nationwide'' courses as ''Classic Theater'' and ''The Ascent of Man.'' These programs were telecast over PBS stations, and many colleges offered students credit for viewing them and passing examinations on them. The colleges listed the television courses as part of their regular schedules, enabling students to enroll for them as they would for any other course.

In addition to the TV college, public television finds its way into classrooms as a supplement to lectures. A perusal of one ETV supplier's catalogue, the Great Plains National Instructional Television Library of

FIGURE 12–4 Fred Rogers of "Mr. Rogers' Neighborhood." The program began as a regional show broadcast over WQED television in Pittsburgh. Later it became a national favorite of pre-schoolers. Rogers' slow, quiet presentations and gentle manner are successful in holding the attention of young children and are in contrast to the fast-paced presentation of "Sesame Street." Rogers has achieved recognition as one of the pioneer educators in the field of public television and has been, along with the program, the recipient of numerous awards. (Copyright, Family Communications, Inc.)

Lincoln, Nebraska, reveals how broad the scope is. For example, under the heading of language arts, you can choose from "Language Corner" and "Ride the Reading Rocket," both for grade 1, "Word Magic" for grade 2, and eleven other language-arts possibilities. "Language Corner" consists of thirty fifteen-minute programs with such titles as "Listening," "Fairy Tales," "Story by the Teacher," "Letter Writing," and "Speech and Telephone." Approximately 150 different programming series are available. A given series may have two or three lessons or more than sixty. The program "Mathemagic," produced by Channel 33 in Huntington, West Virginia, features sixty-four lessons for second-grade youngsters. The goals of the program include improving computational skills through a better understanding of the numbering system and developing problem-solving ability through an interchange of mathematical and verbal language.

Some of the programs are designed especially for summer viewing so that they can help students retain the skills achieved during the academic year. One such program, a language-arts series entitled "Catch a Bubble," was produced by WNIN–TV of Evansville, Indiana, for a local school corporation and is now nationally syndicated. It consists of four thirty-minute lessons for students who have completed the second grade. The star of the show is a seahorse named Salty. The children share Salty's adventures while reinforcing their learning skills and maintaining their interest in reading during the summer vacation. They also work in the "Catch a Bubble" activity book.

Among programs offered by other suppliers is "Time-Life Multimedia," which explores the social sciences, language arts, the humanities, the sciences, business, and recreation. If you are interested in archeology,

you might want to view "How Old is Old?" which discusses the age of the Grand Canyon, explores the history of humans, and probes the longevity of the ice cover of Antarctica. Or if you are interested in dinosaurs, you might want to watch "The Dinosaur Hunters." This program studies how the dinosaurs reproduced. Then there is "Digging up the Past," which examines relics of ancient civilizations. Other archeological programs include "Cracking the Stone-Age Code," "Lost World of Maya," and "Ancient Egypt." Many of the programs are available in both English and Spanish and on film or videotape.

With the interest in metric conversion, mathematics programs that teach the metric system are becoming popular. Typical of these is "Metrify or Petrify," a series of eight thirty-minute programs produced by KLCS-TV in Los Angeles and distributed nationally. The programs include such topics as an introduction to the metric system, an overview of the metric units of linear, volume, temperature, and time measurement, and mass versus weight.

NATIONAL PUBLIC RADIO

Radio also benefited from the Public Broadcasting Act, and in 1971 many noncommercial radio stations became members of National Public Radio, the radio equivalent of PBS. NPR differs from PBS, however, in that it also produces programs, whereas PBS's chief responsibility is distribution. NPR affiliates also produce programs, which are often syndicated by NPR and made available to member stations. One of the most famous programs aired on NPR is the daily newsmagazine program "All Things Considered," acclaimed by both educators and the public for its informative, in-depth coverage of news and public affairs. NPR's growth has been closely aligned with the overall growth of noncommercial radio.

For a brief period of time in 1983, NPR found itself on shaky financial ground when an audit turned up a debit of approximately $9 million. The audit led to the resignation of some of the NPR administrative staff, not over charges of any wrongdoing, but in an atmosphere of alleged mismanagement. The result was a riff between NPR and many local NPR affiliates, who had to reconsider both their relationship with the network and their financial structure in the wake of possible funding shortfalls. By late 1983, Douglas J. Bennett, a former administrator of the Agency for International Development, had been appointed president of NPR. Bennett set about building bridges with Congress as well as with NPR affiliates. Congress ended its 1983 session by appropriating funds for CPB with some questioning of NPR's operations, but gave it a general vote of support to allow it time to rise above its financial difficulties.

NEW VENTURES FOR FISCAL STABILITY

Like public television stations, public radio stations and NPR have tried to develop new ventures that will provide income and supplement decreasing federal support. Some ventures have been more successful than others. Three examples of early attempts at profitability were digital delivery, pay-per-listen and a paging service.

Digital Delivery

In 1982 NPR announced INC Telecommunications, a twenty-four-hour digital-delivery system that uses the FM subcarrier frequency of public radio stations.[27] A joint venture of NPR and National Information Utilities of McLean, Virginia, the system is designed to transmit data over NPR member stations, where it is received by subscribers having a special home decoder. The information then appears on a computer terminal, where it can be stored; hard copy can be produced on another machine. Some of the service potential for the system includes electronic mail, financial services, and educational and training programs. The service is compatible with any home computer and is designed to be supported through subscriber fees.

Pay-Per-Listen

Another venture announced by NPR was a pay-per-listen service permitting subscribers with a special decoder to tape programs distributed during off hours by NPR.[28] The system operates late at night, when many NPR affiliates are not normally broadcasting. A recording device in the decoder is turned on automatically when a special signal is transmitted by the station. Subscribers were scheduled to order programs through a monthly catalogue and be billed for the programs they record.

Paging Service

Still another income venture was a telephone paging service called National Satellite Paging. A joint venture of NPR and Mobile Communications, the system is designed to utilize space on a satellite transponder leased to NPR.[29] Local paging companies would use up-link and down-link facilities already in use at NPR stations.

In order to seek out new directions for funding, the NPR board of directors created

NPR Ventures, a wholly owned profit-making subsidiary, in 1983.

AMERICAN PUBLIC RADIO

Despite some concern by NPR loyalists, certain public radio stations joined together in 1982 and formed American Public Radio. The organization is designed to assist public radio stations involved in producing their own programs. Marketing, scheduling, distribution, and cooperation were some of the initially stated goals of the organization.

PUBLIC RADIO AS INSTRUCTIONAL RADIO

Because of television's dominance, radio tends to be overshadowed as a medium of both educational and direct instructional value. This should not be, because in many places radio is as much a part of the educational scene as its visual counterpart, and sometimes more so. It certainly has been in use longer.

As we learned in Chapter 4, one of the first radio stations in the United States crackled on the air at the University of Wisconsin in 1919. Through the years, WHA radio served a wide spectrum of listeners with direct instructional programming. In fact, it was the flagship station of an entire state instructional radio network. What was WHA's effect? By the late 1950s, schools in Wisconsin had been listening to instructional radio for almost thirty years. The director of the Wisconsin State Broadcasting Service and former WHA director, Harold B. McCarty, told a Washington, D.C. conference on educational television that educational radio was alive and well.[30] He gave television enthusiasts some tough

goals to match: the Wisconsin school system had 100,000 pupils enrolled in creative-art classes by radio, 70,000 in music, and 43,000 in a social-studies class.

Today, educational and instructional radio programs are found at many colleges. WBAA at Purdue University has long had a viable instructional program and has not only been responsible for major research in the field but has also had a regularly scheduled offering of college courses taught exclusively by radio. The university charges a nominal fee for the courses, and students enroll just as they would for any other course. Lectures are broadcast mostly in the evenings and are repeated on Sundays. Tapes of the courses are available in Purdue's audio-visual center and can be checked out for review. The student receives credit by taking an examination at the end of the semester. Although credit is given, no final grade is assigned. Students must, however, maintain at least a *C* to obtain credit. The university maintains no record of those who fail the test and consequently receive no course credit.

Wisconsin is not the only state to operate a major instructional radio network. South Carolina, for example, simultaneously links four noncommercial FM stations, WEPR at Greenville, WLTR at Columbia, WMPR at Sumter, and WSCI at Charleston, into a special instructional network. The stations are located at strategic points in the state so that schools over a wide region will be within earshot of the broadcasts (Figure 12–5). The broadcasts are directed toward elementary grades through high school as supplements to regular classes, and teachers have found them effective in generating student interest. Each broadcast lesson is self-contained; if one is missed, it does not interrupt the regular classroom schedule. To facilitate reception, the state offers special radio receiv-

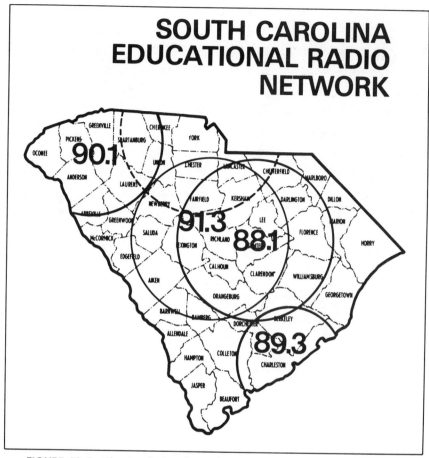

FIGURE 12-5 The South Carolina Educational Radio Network provides in-school services as well as public radio programming. (*Public Telecommunication Review*)

ers pretuned to the educational stations. A standard radio receiver also works (Figure 12-6). Each participating station designates a coordinator who helps teachers gain the maximum benefit from the broadcasts. Actual airings are scattered throughout the school day, and supplementary teaching materials are available for teachers who wish to plan lessons around the broadcasts.

Wisconsin and South Carolina are just two examples of states in which many instructional radio networks function at city and state levels. Radio is an especially effective medium for teaching the great works of literature and music, foreign languages, and other subjects that lend themselves particularly well to audio methods of instruction.

FIGURE 12-6   To facilitate reception, receivers pre-tuned to the South Carolina educational station are made available to schools. The stations designate an educational coordinator to help teachers gain the maximum benefit from the broadcasts. (South Carolina Educational Television and Radio Network and the South Carolina State Department of Education)

FUNDING AND THE FUTURE

The public broadcasting system in the United States has managed to survive criticism and erratic congressional support to mature into a viable and even competitive chain of stations serving most of the United States. Yet many issues need to be resolved before public broadcasting's future can be ensured. Perhaps the most vital one is funding. In theory, if not in practice, the support for long-range funding of the system came with the passage of the Public Broadcasting Financing Act of 1975. Signed into law by President Gerald Ford, it called for congres-

sional authorization of a five-year appropriation to the CPB. In fact, the money was tied to a separate appropriation measure, one that ran into trouble in the House Appropriations Committee.

In 1977 a second Carnegie Commission sponsored another inquiry into public broadcasting. These were the questions asked by the commission:

What is the mission of public broadcasting in American society, and how can Americans best be served by this important national resource?

How are quality programming and creativity to be fostered?

What should be the nature of citizen involvement in public broadcasting?

How can the local station cooperate with other community organizations—schools, churches, libraries, community groups, museums, and other institutions?

How adequately can public broadcasting meet the needs of the special audiences such as minorities, women, children, adults interested in life-long learning, the disabled, or groups with particular interests?

How will public broadcasting develop as a multichannel system and interact with growing technologies such as satellite, cable, and videodiscs?

Over the next ten to fifteen years, how should public broadcasting be funded and at what levels?

What should be the central and regional organizations and institutions in the system, and what should be their functions?[31]

Overall, the public broadcasting system is regarded as an important source of quality programming, much of which is not possible on commercial networks because of their need to garner audience ratings. The financial health of public broadcasting will be determined by how successful some of its new income ventures are and how much local subscribers are willing to contribute in order to offset the loss of government support.

SUMMARY

Educational television was used at Iowa State University as early as 1932. Support for educational television came in the early 1950s with the formation of the Joint Committee on Educational Television (JCET). With a grant from the Ford Foundation, the JCET became the early representative of educational television and assisted educational institutions both in getting stations on the air and in using educational television in the classroom.

One of the more novel early experiments was the Midwest Program for Airborne Television Instruction (MPATI), which sent television programs over a wide area of the Midwest via an airborne transmitter. Although with the introduction of satellites the system eventually became obsolete, it did prove that television could be integrated into the learning experience in many schools simultaneously.

With the increased use of portable equipment and educational television in the classroom, television became an important element in direct classroom instruction. At the same time, many stations that had been used mainly for instructional purposes began broadcasting to a more general audience.

After a series of foundation-supported evaluations of noncommercial broadcasting, Congress enacted the Public Broadcasting Act of 1967, which designated noncommercial and educational stations as public broadcasting stations. The act also created the Corporation for Public Broadcasting, a quasi-governmental body that would use congressional appropriation to help develop a national system of public broadcasting. The Public Broadcasting Service and National Public Radio were established as means of distributing programs to public stations. Public television programming ranges from nationally distributed programs such as "Sesame Street" and "The Electric Company" to locally produced specials and ITV programming for in-school use.

PBS has ventured into new income-producing services, such as pay TV and cable programming, in order to supplement government appropriations. National Public Radio and public radio stations have also launched new income-producing enterprises, including digital information services, pay-per-listen programming, and paging services.

American Public Radio was formed in 1982 by public stations wanting to provide cooperation and mutual support in the production and distribution of locally produced programs.

Instructional radio has proved an efficient educational medium in some sections of the country. South Carolina for example, uses a network of public radio stations for in-school instructional programming.

Public broadcasting's future will be determined by the degree of success of some of its new income ventures and the amount of money local subscribers are willing to contribute in order to offset the loss of government support.

OPPORTUNITIES
FOR FURTHER LEARNING

AVERY, R. K., and R. M. PEPPER, *The Politics of Interconnection: A History of Public Television at the National Level.* Washington, D.C.: National Association of Educational Broadcasters, 1979.

BARCUS, F. E., *Weekday, Daytime Commercial Television Programming for Children.* Newtonville, Mass.: Action for Children's Television, 1981.

BLAKELY, R. J., *To Serve the Public Interest: Educational Broadcasting in the United States.* Syracuse: Syracuse University Press, 1979.

BROWN, L., *In Search of Ways of Knowing the Impact of the Church's Use of the Communications Media.* Rochester, N.Y.: Diocese of Rochester, 1980.

BURKE, J. E., *An Historical-Analytical Study of the Legislative and Political Origins of the Public Broadcasting Act of 1967.* New York: Arno Press, 1979.

Carnegie Commission on the Future of Public Broadcasting. *A Public Trust.* New York: Bantam, 1979.

CBS Office of Social Research, *Communicating With Children Through Television.* New York: CBS, 1977.

DALE, E. *Audiovisual Methods in Teaching.* Hillsdale, Ill.: Dryden Press, 1969.

GERLACH, V. S., and D. P. ELY, *Teaching and Media* (2nd ed.). Englewood Cliffs, N.J.: Prentice-Hall, 1980.

GROSSMAN, G., *Saturday Morning TV.* New York: Dell, 1981.

HEDINSSON, E., *TV, Family and Society: The Social Origins and Effects of Adolescents' TV Use.* Stockholm: Almqvist & Wiksell, 1981.

HOLLISTER, B. C., *The Mass Media Workbook: Learning Activities Involving Today's Media.* Skokie, Ill.: National Textbook, 1981.

JOHNSTON, J. S., and J. S. ETTEMA, *Positive Images: Breaking Stereotypes With Children's Television.* Beverly Hills, Calif.: Sage, 1982.

KELLY, H., and H. GARDNER, eds., *Viewing Children Through Television.* San Francisco: Jossey-Bass, 1981.

KOSEKOFF, J., and A. FINK, *Evaluation Basics: A Practitioner's Manual.* Beverly Hills, Calif.: Sage, 1982.

LESSER, G. S., *Children and Television: Lessons From Sesame Street.* New York: Random House, 1974.

LIEBERT, R. M., J. N. SPRAFKIN, and E. S. DAVIDSON, *Effects of Television on Children and Youth* (2nd ed.). Elmsford N.Y.: Pergamon Press, 1982.

MAHONY, S., and others, *Keeping PACE With the New Television: Public Television and Changing Technology.* New York: Carnegie, 1980.

MOIR, G. ed., *Teaching and Television.* London: Pergamon Press, 1967.

PEPPER, R. M., *The Formation of the Public Broadcasting Service.* New York: Arno Press, 1979.

Public Broadcasting Industry Responses to Minority Task Force Report: A Formula for Change. Washington, D.C.: Corporation for Public Broadcasting, 1981.

Public Radio and State Governments. Washington, D.C.: National Public Radio, 1981.

ROGERS, R., ed., *Television and the Family.* London: UK Association for the International Year of the Child, 1980.

SALOMON, G., *Communication and Education: Social and Psychological Interactions.* Beverly Hills, Calif.: Sage, 1981.

SCHRAMM, W., *Big Media, Little Media: Tools and Technologies for Instruction.* Beverly Hills, Calif.: Sage, 1977.

SCHRAMM, W. ed., *Quality in Instructional Television.* Honolulu: University of Hawaii Press, 1972.

SCHULTZ, J. M., with T. BERKOVITZ, *A Teacher's Guide to Television Evaluation for Children.* Springfield, Ill.: Charles C. Thomas, 1981.

SMITH, N. L., ed., *Communication Strategies in Evaluation.* Beverly Hills, Calif.: Sage, 1982.

STAMBERG, S., *Every Night at Five: Susan Stamberg's All Things Considered Book.* New York: Pantheon, 1982.

STURM, H., and S. JORG, *Information Processing by Young Children: Piaget's Theory of Intellectual Development Applied to Radio and Television.* Munich: K. G. Saur, 1981.

Television Programming for Children: A Report of the Children's Television Task Force, 5 vols. Washington, D.C.: Federal Communications Commission, 1979.

U.S., Congress, House, Committee on Energy and Commerce, Subcommittee on Telecommunications, Consumer Protection, and Finance, *Alternative Financing Options for Public Broadcasting.* Washington, D.C.: Government Printing Office, 1982.

WILKINSON, G., *Media in Instruction: 60 Years of Research.* Washington, D.C.: Association for Educational Communications and Technology, 1980.

WINICK, M. and C. WINICK, *The Television Experience: What Children See.* Beverly Hills, Calif.: Sage, 1979.

WITHEY, S. B., and R. P. ABELES, eds., *Television and Social Behavior: Beyond Violence and Children.* Hillsdale, N.J.: Lawrence Erlbaum, 1980.

13

CORPORATE TELECOMMUNICATION

Across town at the manufacturing plant, the nine-o'clock whistle is about to blow. Inside, a television crew has just received an urgent message. "Contact the air mobile units! Alert the camera crews! We have a breakdown at Arctic Station One. They want us there by tonight." Telephone calls, checks with management, notification to the crew of the company jet—it all sets in motion a chain of events that by nightfall will lead to the arrival of a complete television crew thousands of miles away at a power station in northern Canada. A generator manufactured by the company has broken down. When the repair crews start their job, television cameras will be there to record it. Later, back at the manufacturing plant, the videotape will be edited into an instructional television program that the company will use to train future repair crews. It is all just one example of corporate telecommunication in action, a growing area of mass media far removed from the typical commercial television station.

GROWTH AND IMPACT

The purpose of this chapter is to acquaint you with telecommunication in business and industry. It is an expanding field with many applications. More companies use television than there are commercial television stations in the United States.[1] In addition, a variety of corporate television networks are developing. Communication consultant Judith M. Brush of D/J Brush Associates in New York City classifies a corporate television network as "an organization which distributes programming at least once a month to six or more locations away from the point of origin." [2] She notes that "more than 40 of these networks have more than 50 viewing locations with at least half that number distributing programs to 100-plus locations. For example, Pepsico has more than 300 locations in its network, IBM has some 1,300 locations in 400 countries, and Bank of America has 1,100 locations." [3] What kinds of firms use television? One survey of the top 500 companies listed in *Forbes* magazine indicated "just over half were engaged in manufacturing, followed in order by financial institutions, utilities, retailers, natural resources, and transportation companies." [4]

IN-HOUSE PROGRAMMING OF CORPORATE NEWS AND INFORMATION

Most of us think of television as the network prime-time programs or daily newscasts broadcast in our area. These programs are the result of decisions on what stories to use, how to edit them, what the audience wants and what it should have, what graphics to use, which audio cuts to include, and many more matters. Those same decisions are also made every day in places far from the network and newsrooms. They're made at corporations, where television production crews and corporate newscasters are preparing the daily newscast that will be sent to employees at the downstate plant or through corporate networks to international offices.

Applications of Corporate Newscasts

Dow Chemical Corporation is one company that televises daily newscasts for its employees. When Dow president Paul F. Oreffice wanted better communications with Dow's 10,000 employees, he thought that television would be the medium to do the job. [5] Produced at Dow headquarters in Midland, Michigan, the Dow corporate newscast is five to seven minutes long and is broadcast through closed-circuit television systems to lunch-hour viewers. Topics such as company news, stock-market reports, and safety procedures are featured. Other companies follow a similar process. Some even produce commentaries. Union Carbide Corporation produced a twenty-nine-minute tape reporting on its gases, metals, and carbon divisions. [6]

To diversified companies spread over wide areas, corporate news programming is especially valuable. An oil company may consist of oil exploration, refineries, and gas stations, as well as the corporate office. How is it possible to link the people and activities of these varied enterprises? The main instrument for many companies has been, and still is, the corporate magazine or newsletter. Filled with pictures and articles about the corporation's activities, it is sent to all employees. Different parts of the company have their own reporters or stringers who contribute to the magazine. Now, although continuing the corporate magazine, corporations are turning to television. A gas-station owner wins a community award; an oil-rig worker is promoted; a pipeline crew starts a new project (Figure 13–1); a secretary is married—they all appear on the lunch-hour news program. The corporate news cameras catch it all.

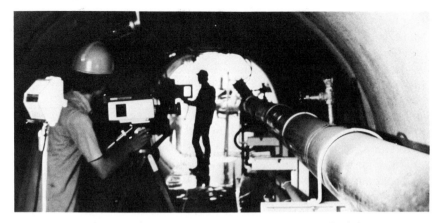

FIGURE 13-1 The portability of television makes it ideal for many remote production projects. (Phillips Petroleum Company)

Content of Corporate News Programming

The scope of corporate news programming can be seen in one company, First National City Bank in New York. Consultant Eugene Marlow describes a daily news program called "Channel 6" seen by approximately 10,000 bank employees scattered throughout three buildings in New York City.[7] The show runs about fifteen minutes and has three segments—news, a feature on some aspect of the bank, and an entertainment feature. Content ranges from an interview with a bank employee to a report on the opening of a new regional headquarters a continent away. Features might be a report on computer programming, an interview with a professional magician, or a conversation with a nationally famous artist.

Unique approaches are often used to communicate somewhat dry topics. First National City Bank had to inform employees of company benefits but wanted to do so in an interesting manner. The solution was to use a puppet called Professor Wienerschnitzel on "Channel 6." The professor finds himself in various settings, all designed around a company benefit. On one occasion he runs for mayor of New York, his platform being the program of scholarship benefits for the bank's employees. On another occasion he practices his voice and diction for a speech he is to deliver on employees insurance benefits.

Not all of what appears on "Channel 6" is limited to internal programming. "Channel 6" cameras also venture into New York City to capture the after-hours activities of the bank's employees. For example, when a group of employees purchased group tickets to a hockey game, "Channel 6" interviewed some of them on their reactions to the game. When the Ringling Brothers Circus came to town, "Channel 6" cameras had ringside seats. The bank's involvement in community affairs is also part of corporate news programming. Corporate programming's combination of features and news has two effects: the programming is entertaining and it is informative—and in this sense not much different from the prime-time network news program.

Not all corporate news programming is as elaborate as that of First National City Bank. Dana Corporation's Reading Frame

Division, for example, places news and information on a motor-driven wheel that revolves slowly in front of a fixed-position camera.[8] Each message or news story remains in view for fifteen seconds. The messages are broadcast around the clock, and television monitors are scattered throughout the plant's facilities. For Dana Corporation, the problem is reaching workers while they circulate through the plant, not when they are gathered at a centralized lunch location. Consequently, the monitors have become a substitute for many of the bulletin boards. At Dana, the concept of more elaborate corporate news is secondary to that of brief messages sent quickly to employees by television.

General Information Programming

Corporate newscasts are not the only way to communicate with employees. Many companies produce special television programs to inform employees of their concerns. For instance, a company's public-relations efforts may be just as interesting to the employees as they are to the general public. How do the employees learn of these activities? The company produces special television programs on such topics as how the company is volunteering executives to help with the local United Way drive, how volunteers are canvassing the city for the March of Dimes, or how children are being taught to swim and play sports at the corporation's summer camp in the mountains. Such programs may also fill the slots of public-service programming on many commercial television stations.

Corporate Policy

Corporate policy can be disseminated effectively through television. New employees in large companies need to know such things as how to file insurance claims, where claims offices are located, and how they are staffed. The company can produce a television program spelling this out in detail, and the employee can view it at his or her convenience. At first a booklet might seem just as effective. It would contain the same information. But the voice and gestures of a courteous claims officer can set a positive example for the new employee, reducing tension and making it easier for him or her to file a claim. In addition, a welcoming statement from the president of a large corporation might mean much more when the president can be seen and heard.

Executive Reports

Another programming concept is the "state of the corporation" address. Although we are familiar with the State of the State and the State of the Union addresses, we do not usually hear chief executives speak on the health of their corporations. Such information, accompanied by statistics, charts, and accounting jargon, is usually given in the annual report. However, many chief executives are learning that speaking to employees by television in an understandable language about how well the corporation is doing and its prognosis for the future can be an extremely effective way to communicate.

Information About Regulations

Many companies have had to scramble just to keep up with the increasing number of federal regulations. This has been especially true with safety regulations. A new governmental safety regulation may require educating thousands of employees and gaining their compliance. To help solve this problem, companies have produced television programs on safety procedures in their own particular plant. A manufacturing firm produced an on-location program detailing its fast-moving equipment and areas of danger. An oil company took a television crew to a drilling rig to produce a series of programs on the protective measures necessary for preventing on-the-job accidents. Before new employees are assigned to one of the many drilling operations, they watch these safety programs. Such a series is much more efficient and effective than a foreman educating each new employee individually.

USING TELEVISION FOR MARKETING AND SALES

Video cassettes (Figure 13–2) have opened up a whole new world for many companies in the area of marketing and sales. Assume you are one of the nation's major automobile manufacturers. Your showrooms are full of new models, styles, colors, special performance features, and sales personnel who want to communicate all of this wonderful information to all of their potential car buyers. How do you secure the edge in this vastly competitive business? First, you amass the best sales tips and techniques from all of the dealers. Then you have the central office use the methods in preparing a special video-cassette tape showing a test driver effortlessly maneuvering the cars through their paces to the accompaniment of a narrator who would rival a network radio newscaster. It is simple electronic persuasion. Placed in the showroom playback unit, the video-cassette tape entertains the customer with a professional television presentation. The local salesperson is still there to answer questions, add the personal touch, and sign the contracts.

FIGURE 13–2 The Xerox training facility makes extensive use of corporate television production. (Xerox)

FIGURE 13-3 Many corporations are equipped with full-scale television production facilities which provide the opportunity for programming which ranges from in-house corporate newscasts to training tapes. (Deere & Company)

Training Sales Personnel

Deere and Company, manufacturers of the famous John Deere tractors and farm equipment, uses television to train its sales personnel and dealers. The company maintains a full-scale television production facility at Moline, Illinois, site of Deere headquarters.[9] Replete with sophisticated computer editing equipment, the facility produces programs for all corporate activities, including videotapes that can explain to a dealer the advantages of using John Deere equipment (Figure 13-3). The company started to use television in 1968. At that time the television facility was part of Deere's audio-visual department and consisted of black-and-white equipment and two persons to operate it. In 1973 the company equipped a mobile van for color-television production. A year later television became a separate department in the company, outgrew its space in corporate headquarters, and moved to an office building in Moline. The facility now includes a forty-by-forty-foot studio and a twenty-by-thirty-two-foot control room besides the mobile van and storage and office space.

The programs for dealers are only a few of the more than seventy-five programs produced each year by the facility. The Industrial Equipment Division alone uses two or three new programs every month as sales training aids. Programs are distributed to about 250 John Deere dealers in the United States and Canada, each of whom has a playback unit. They are also distributed to each of the Deere factories, which are also equipped with playback units. The company has even enlarged its television production capabilities. Its Dubuque, Iowa, Industrial Training Center now has television facilities and produces an average of eighteen programs each year, which help inform both salespersons and customers about John Deere products.

Reliance Electric also uses television to help train sales personnel. The company produced its first videotape in 1975 and since then has been expanding the use of television throughout the company. Jerry Wilson, employee supervisor for the Electric Group of Reliance Electric points out, "We have all the normal channels of communication between our main offices and the far plants and offices but, unfortunately, we have had no way to show motion. Motion is important to Reliance because that's what we sell ...motors, drives, power transmission equipment and so forth. We build hard and softwear that cause things to move." [10]

Sales Meetings and Salesperson Updates

Television can also benefit a typical sales meeting and communicate the motion of which Wilson speaks. Capturing on television the emotion and content of these brainstorming pep talks has many advantages. First, it provides a record of what happens. The videotape takes notes, thereby eliminating many procedural and secretarial burdens. Second, the tape can be given to sales personnel unable to attend. Perhaps the meeting is regional. If so, it can be videotaped and distributed to other regional offices for other sales personnel. In this way, moreover, the meeting is not slowed down by too many participants. With professional editing, the highlights of the meeting can be condensed into a half-hour program of high-intensity sales training to be viewed by sales personnel throughout the company.

Consider another use. A company is having difficulty selling one of its products. Perhaps it is a special attachment for garden tractors. The problem is not company-wide, however: five sales outlets have had very high sales. Management decides to fly in the five sales representatives who have tallied

the highest sales. For over an hour they discuss how they sell the attachment, why customers find it useful, and what special technique they use to convince customers that it is worth the money. The session is videotaped and edited into a fifteen-minute training program on that one product. The company then distributes the program to all of its retail sales outlets. As soon as the sales representatives view the program, sales begin to climb and the program is hailed a success.

Customer Information

A related use of the medium is keeping customers informed. When Owen-Corning Fiberglass® found certain raw materials in short supply, it needed to tell its customers of this problem, clearly and openly. So the company produced a television program in which its purchasing managers discussed the problem. Ben Coe, Architectural and Home Building Products branch manager in Los Angeles, said the customers "could see what we were doing in our own mind to minimize the adverse effects. And since the program showed our own purchasing people in frank, candid discussion, the information came across very believably." [11]

Customers need to know how to use the products they buy. This may seem unnecessary for items like clothespins and detergent, but consider the computer. Many businesses are integrating computers into their overall operations. Minicomputers permit even the smallest companies to use this new technology. However, just because the computer is small does not mean that it is simple to operate. Even some small electronic calculators are difficult for the uninitiated to use. Although some manual training is normally included with many major computer purchases, it is time-consuming and does not solve the problem of training the employee hired after the computer is installed.

To help solve this problem, many computer-manufacturing companies are developing their own training videotapes. These help instruct employees in the use of the new equipment without tying up the time of company personnel. For example, Honeywell has produced videotapes that instruct not only its own customers but also anyone else who needs to learn the basis of computer language. Honeywell's curriculum of video programs covers such topics as FORTRAN, BASIC, Decision Tables, PERT, and DATA Base.[12] Its Video-Assisted Learning program uses a multimedia approach, combining video lecture material with readings and examinations. The courses are designed by educators, writers, and computer experts who develop, test, and review the courses.

IN-SERVICE TRAINING

Besides being used to increase sales and train customers, television is used to teach employees new skills. Company X has just converted its order and shipping departments to computer technology. Before the conversion, every order received was checked and verified, and separate slips were made out for every item on it. The slips were then distributed to the various warehouses at which the items were assembled. Finally, the shipping department received the individual slips and the master order from which to package the goods and prepare the mailing label. But the conversion ended all of this. Even typewriters have been replaced, by visual-display terminals. Now comes the task of training two entire divisions of the company to use the new equipment, as well as the personnel of the company's branch

plants located throughout the world. Company X accomplishes this through special television training programs. It could just as easily have trained its personnel in the uses of a new telephone system or any other device. Television is especially useful in being able to go places where people cannot. Hazardous locations, off limits to many, become readily accessible to the television camera. The inside of a factory, the welder in a steel plant (Figure 13–4), the equipment operator of a coal mine—all can be captured on videotape by portable equipment.

One of the most difficult training assignments any company faces is educating equipment-maintenance personnel. Every year new models are produced, new parts are required, and refinements are made. What about the person who must repair this equipment when it breaks down? How can he or she keep abreast of the latest developments? Again, television comes to the rescue. When a company introduces a new piece of equipment it automatically produces a new television training program along with it. Company service representatives can thus learn how to fix the new equipment at their home locations scattered throughout the world. This is much less expensive than bringing together all the repair personnel each year for a new training program.

Along with management and employee-training services, television gives corporations a way to offer college-credit classes to employees. For example, in the Chicago area employees at such companies as Illinois Bell, Western Electric, Motorola, and Standard Oil receive college credit from the Illinois Institute of Technology. The programs are made in the IIT classrooms and sent by a special microwave frequency to the plants, where they are received on standard television sets. Without the corporate link with IIT, students would either have to miss work or attend IIT night classes.

FIGURE 13-4 Television can be used in areas which would be dangerous to bystanders. Here a portable television camera and recorder are used to record a welding demonstration at the Inland Steel Company. (Inland Steel Company)

MANAGEMENT DEVELOPMENT

High- and middle-level management people are constantly learning. Let's examine how corporate television helps.

The Executive Communicator

One area in which television is used effectively and frequently is in teaching managers communication skills. Public speaking is a regular part of executive life. Speaking effectively is an important asset. Communication specialists conducting speaker-training sessions can use television to videotape an executive's speech and then play it back for criticism. In some cases the speech is delivered before an executive panel, which criticizes the playback. Portable equipment enables the executive to use television after hours in the privacy of his or her office without worrying about technicians. Many companies also offer short videotaped courses that help executives learn essential writing skills. In addition, principles of organizational communication can be taught through videotape. New executives can learn the organization of the company as well as its rules and procedures in this way.

More and more often, companies are using television settings to train their executives in press relations. The business community frequently finds itself the subject of inquiry from the press, and few public-relations directors can substitute for the chief executive when news such as a gas shortage surfaces. Many corporate executives have not been effective or convincing in such encounters. As a result, they are now receiving training in how to act and what to say in front of live television cameras while being pumped by reporters. Dress rehearsals involving interrogation by corporate personnel under the lights of a corporate television studio help the executives gain skills in handling public encounters with the press.

Training Management Decision Makers

Television is also used in training management in everyday decision making, and especially in dealing with personnel. Videotaped models simulate such situations as firing employees, reprimanding them, or counseling them about a personal problem. After studying the tapes, a group of executives usually act out the different roles in these situations. Their role playing is also videotaped, then played back and compared with the models. This type of training often includes trained professionals who criticize the executives' performances.

Communicating with middle-level management can be aided by television, especially in highly technical industries in which the company is spread over a large geographic area. Suppose a supervisor in Mexico must train a group of assembly-line workers to construct a new product. This will mean changing many workers' jobs. Since such changes can cause serious personnel problems, the manager in Mexico watches a videotaped lecture by the supervisor at another plant at which the product has already been introduced. The supervisor tells what problems to watch for, how to solve them, and how their solutions will af-

fect other workers. The entire program is in Spanish. In other parts of the world, supervisors can view the same lecture in French, German, or Italian. Produced in the corporate headquarters, the program is an alternative to having executives fly all over the world with interpreters in order to start a new product down the assembly line.

One company that communicates with management by television is Holiday Inns.[13] With more than 1,600 motels around the world, the company has many managers to reach. It keeps them abreast of new corporate developments by equipping each Holiday Inn with a videotape playback system. The company also offers over twenty-four hours of video-based training programs.

Earlier in this chapter we learned about Dana Corporation's Reading Frame Division. However, that is just one phase of Dana's use of corporate television. Much of the rest of it helps management make quick decisions with a minimum of paperwork.[14] At the desk of key executives is a television monitor equipped for multichannel reception. The executive can tune in an almost limitless amount of information, including charts and graphs of the day's production. In addition, at a given time each day the company broadcasts investment and stock reports on closed-circuit television for any Dana manager who wants to watch. These reports can also be seen on the monitor in an executive's office.

IN-HOUSE ADVERTISING

Although many companies hire advertising agencies to produce their television and radio commercials, some companies produce their own. After hiring skilled advertising professionals away from the agencies, the companies furnish them with creative facilities and establish in-house advertising agencies having most of the responsibilities and rights of a regular agency. One of these rights is the lucrative media commission paid to agencies by the stations for providing them with advertising business. Since this commission is usually 15 percent of the advertising budget for a station, in-house agencies can even make a profit for the company. At least they can make a return on their investment. One argument against such a system is that in-house agencies cannot view the company objectively and therefore often overlook the most creative approach. Another is that a company should stick to what it knows best—manufacturing the product—and leave its broadcast advertising to the ad-agency professionals. Still another argument is that not all media recognize in-house agencies and allow them the media commission. Somewhere among all of these pros and cons is the best arrangement for each company.

PERSPECTIVES ON THE FUTURE OF CORPORATE TELEVISION

How will technology and the relationship between employees and corporate media affect the future of television in business and industry? Already there has been much research on communication within organizations, but the study of television's position in this organizational setting is still not complete. We need to know what happens when a television screen replaces face-to-face interaction. To what extent can a corporation employ television without decreasing the company's sensitivity to people, or can television help increase this sensitivity?

Despite these questions, corporate television is expanding. With the development of inexpensive and compact satellite receiving equipment, the 1980s will see larger companies produce a corporate newscast and send it simultaneously into offices and plants throughout the world. The public-relations coordinator once trained in print journalism and skilled in editing the company magazine will be producing a video magazine and a television newscast. All of this will necessitate a broader understanding of broadcasting and how it can be used effectively for communication in a corporate atmosphere. We must not forget that the generation currently moving up the corporate ladder is the "television generation." When these younger executives reach top management positions, what decisions will they make about corporate television?

Smaller components and more sophisticated delivery systems also promise to change television. For example, the night watchman of the future will approach a troubled area of the plant with a tiny television camera strapped to his belt, constantly monitoring and videotaping the path before him. Confronting a thief will mean simultaneously taking his picture.

Another perspective on the future of corporate television was offered by Will Lewis, while vice-president of communication at International Paper, a major user of television for corporate communication: "When the contribution of employees is not principally physical strength or physical speed but, in fact, the ability to think and make rational decisions, the Company has an obligation to extend the vision of employees so that they become better informed." Lewis goes on to argue that "as the need for more timely information increases, we must seek new and better ways to provide access to information."[15] Lewis's prescriptions are based on more companies realizing the potential of television as a medium for both internal and external corporate communication.

CORPORATE VIDEOTEX

More and more offices are finding that a personal computer equipped for videotex is as important a component of an office communication system as the telephone. That same computer may be connected with personal computers at the desks of other employees, and all may feed into a central mainframe computer with a large storage capacity. These corporate videotex systems are equipped with graphic capability that permits data to appear as pictorial representations. Printers can make a hard copy of anything seen on the desk-top display terminal.

Interoffice Communication

A corporate videotex system permits electronic mail to be delivered between personal computers as easily as it can be delivered between post offices. Instead of writing a letter or memo and having it typed, placed in an envelope, and delayed while traveling through the interoffice mail system, an employee can type the letter into the videotex system and send it instantaneously to the intended receiver. Either the sender or receiver can then electronically discard the letter or store it in the computer for future reference.

Employees who want to electronically mail a letter outside the company can easily do so by interfacing personal computers at one location with those at a distant location. A branch office across town or around the world can be connected through telephone lines and microwave links. Security against tampering is achieved by personal and access codes assigned to individuals and the system.

If the memo is intended for anyone in the company it is keyed into the corporate electronic bulletin board. Employees starting their day first access the bulletin board to check for messages which have been posted electronically. An alert system built into the videotex system activates a light or beeper alarm when priority information is waiting on the board.

Information Retrieval and Electronic Filing

Retrieving a letter is one form of information retrieval, but other information is also retrievable, everything from the latest inventory to airline schedules. Any information entered in the central data bank or accessible elsewhere can be called up on each videotex terminal. The graphic capabilities of the system enable employees not only to know what's in inventory but to look at the screen and see a computer-displayed illustration of each item.

An executive's assistant is planning a trip for his boss. From the videotex terminal he calls up a map of the United States featuring color-coded weather zones and temperatures. He then accesses the airline schedule and keys in the flight information, the corporate account number, and his boss's name. Within minutes the trip is planned. The executive knows what plane to catch and what to wear when she arrives. All of the information, all of the planning and decision making, was done from the videotex terminal located on the assistant's desk. The same system that checked the weather and made the plane reservations can also show a diagram of the plane's seating arrangements, the dinner menu, and a computer-generated picture of the food served on the flight.

If the executive wants to consult with one of the sales managers before leaving for her trip, she telephones and asks her to check her videotex terminal for the sales projections for the coming month. Viewed by both the executive and the sales manager on their respective videotex terminals, the sales projections appear as computer-generated bar graphs. As the two of them talk about the monthly quota they discuss how a change in inventories would affect sales. They key in the pertinent information, and the screen displays a new bar graph showing different projections.

Both the executive and the sales manager like the new projections and decide to change inventories. So that they can refer back to their discussion later they electronically file the projections. Without the computer-based videotex system the same information would not have been available or simply would have taken too much time to retrieve to be practical. Companies in which it *is* practical to retrieve such information may very well put their competitors out of business. The old adage time is money takes on new importance in our computer society.

In addition to the information in our example, such things as telephone numbers, stock quotations, credit authorizations, accounting information, financial notices, job openings, and reference guides are among the thousands of pages of information that can be accessed through a videotex system.

Retail-Sales Support

Earlier in this chapter we discussed how a television program can facilitate showroom sales. Videotex can be used for similar functions. For example, a retail sales clerk can take orders at a central catalogue location and call up on a videotex screen a description of the catalogue item, its price, and a computer-generated picture of the item. The customer and the clerk can both view the article in order to verify its specifications and make sure the order is correctly entered.

At another videotex terminal the customer searches through an electronic catalogue for the item he wants. There on the screen he sees a picture of the item and its price and specifications. He also spots a notice on the screen that that particular item is on display and on sale in the hardware department. If he wishes, he can go there and see the merchandise firsthand. The same videotex system that showed him the merchandise can take his order. By keying in his credit-card number he can charge the item to his account and then pick it up at the warehouse or have it delivered to his home.

Employee Training

The same employee who in the past sat at her desk with a training manual can now sit at a videotex terminal and use the electronic manual accessible through the videotex system. If she needs additional information she can check other pages right on the screen. Illustrations appear along with instructions. If the employee wants to jump ahead to the advanced section of the manual she simply keys in the correct information and there on the screen appears the instructions and graphics at an advanced level. The employee's office is not piled up with volumes of seldom used books, paperwork, manuals, printouts, and other space-consuming information. All of this clutter is stored neatly in a computer accessible by any employee with a videotex terminal.

The Corporate War Room

As corporations move more and more toward videotex and other individually accessible data bases, the central decision-making processing center of a large corporation becomes much like a command control center. Researcher, writer, and scientist

James Martin succinctly describes this scene of the 1980s:

> A "war room" in business is now conventional. It takes many forms and is given many different names. Sometimes it is a showpiece of a firm's data processing. Many offices of top management have video links to a firm's information center. There is now (after some bitter failures) a general recognition that the *human element* in the information center is as important as the machine element. Experienced and highly professional staffs operate with an array of terminals and wall screens that often rivals a NASA Mission Control Center in appearance. Although some managers like to demonstrate their prowess at operating their own terminal, many have an assistant for this task, or else they use their video link to a local information room, which in turn may route some questions to a remote or central information room.[16]

Whether a person sits at a desk with our videotex terminal or commands the war room, a knowledge of corporate telecommunication in all of its facets is indispensable. The competent employees or managers of the future will need to know much more than how to crunch numbers or plot graphs. They will need to understand both the human and hardware components of an organization's communication system and be competent in practicing both interpersonal communication and telecommunication.

This use includes producing and disseminating corporate newscasts, developing information programming for employees, training sales personnel, and informing customers.

In-service training of employees in new skills is also a function of corporate television. Another is helping managers to acquire effective communication skills, deal with employees, and communicate with other managers.

Televised surveillance can be used not only for security but also for production control. Some companies are even trying to cut costs by using corporate television in their in-house advertising agencies to produce their own commercials.

Corporations using videotex systems send, receive, and process information on employees' personal computers. Graphically enhanced information is shared, accessed, and transmitted between locations. Interoffice communication, information retrieval and electronic filing, retail-sales support, and employee training are just some of the services a corporate videotex system can provide.

The large corporation of the 1980s will develop central processing and decision-making centers that are much like military war rooms. The competent employee or manager of the 1980s will need skills in both interpersonal communication and telecommunication.

SUMMARY

The use of television in business and industry is growing. In the United States in the 1980s there are more companies using television than there are commercial television stations.

OPPORTUNITIES FOR FURTHER LEARNING

BRUSH, J. M., and D. P. BRUSH, *Private Television Communications: Into the Eighties.* Berkeley Heights, N.J.: International Television Association, 1981.

BUNYAN, J. A., and others, *Practical Video:*

The Manager's Guide to Applications. White Plains, N.Y.: Knowledge Industry, 1979.

JOHANSEN, R., and others, *Teleconferencing and Beyond: An Exploration of Communications in the Office of the Future.* New York: McGraw-Hill, 1983.

LANDAU, R. M., J. H. BAIR, and J. H. SIEGMAN, eds., *Emerging Office Systems.* Norwood, N.J.: Ablex, 1979.

NORMAN, A., and A. D. LITTLE, *Electronic Document Delivery: The ARTEMIS Concept for Document-Digitalisation and Teletransmission.* White Plains, N.Y.: Knowledge Industry, 1982.

SAMBUL, N.J., ed., *The Handbook of Private Television: A Complete Guide for Video Facilities and Networks Within Corporations, Nonprofit Institutions, and Government Agencies.* New York: McGraw-Hill, 1982.

SCHILLER, H. I., *Who Knows: Information in the Age of the Fortune 500.* Norwood, N.J.: Ablex, 1981.

14

BROADCAST PROGRAMMING AND SYNDICATION

We often take for granted the programming available to us on radio and television. Over-the-air broadcasting is mostly free. Programming ranges all the way from a network television spectacular to a local radio station's swap-shop program. We may watch an art exhibit from Italy, a news report from Iran, or a bicycle race from Indiana. Despite the seemingly effortless way in which programming reaches our living room, behind the scenes are talented strategists who must combine creative decisions with economics, technical reality, and political constraints. The purpose of this chapter is to look more deeply into the field of radio and television programming and to learn more about the decision making that results in what we as consumers of broadcast communication receive.[1]

THE CONTEXT OF BROADCAST PROGRAMMING

Programming is the *product* of broadcasting. Just as a store sells goods or a law firm sells advice, broadcasting sells programming. And just as store owners set prices for their goods and lawyers set fees for their services, broadcasters set rates for the commercials that will share time with their programming. Even public broadcasting solicits contributions on the basis of the type of programming it can offer. But if programming on either commercial or public broadcasting should be irresponsible or not meet the public's needs, then, like the lawyer who gives bad advice or the store owner who sells inferior goods, broadcasting will be out of business.

But not all broadcast programming is produced and disseminated in a democratic society. And where it is not, the competitive or noncompetitive marketplace it operates in and the associations and government that control it will have a profound effect on the end product. Keep in mind that competition in our society is a great determinant of broadcast programming. And although such competition can evoke outcries over programming quality, the alternative to our system could be total government control, as is common in authoritarian governments. Thus, even though we may not like everything we hear or see on broadcast media, if the programming is preferred by the majority of the viewing or listening public, and if the competitive marketplace will support it, then it will likely stay on the air.

This does not mean that programming cannot be improved. The critical question for commercial broadcasters, rather, is this: How can we effectively program a station to serve the needs of the public while making a profit? If this dual responsibility can become the foundation of broadcast programming, then program planners and broadcast management can work cooperatively with the public.

UNDERSTANDING RADIO FORMATS

Radio programming evolved from the theatrical elements of radio drama to the music and news formats of today. Decreasing its reliance on network programming, radio became a specialist in locally produced programming. It even specialized in different formats in order to compete not only with other stations but also with television.

Today radio enjoys an almost endless number of formats and combinations of formats, each designed to reach specific audiences. One of the earliest specialized formats was Top 40 radio, which developed in the 1950s and concentrated on rock-and-roll. Top 40 radio has now become more of a middle-of-the-road format, still catering to rock-and-roll fans but mild in tempo compared with the progressive- and acid-rock formats that developed in the late 1960s.

When the ABC radio network split into demographic networks in 1968, it brought news programming into a specialized format. It wasn't long before all-news stations and those with an information format settled into competition with the many musical formats. NBC launched its News and Information Service Network in 1975, but the projected number of affiliates this all-news network needed in order to be profitable wasn't reached, and it folded two years later. Yet despite this well-publicized failure, all-news radio continues to be a strong force in many markets.

Music played the major role in the specialized formats of still other stations: beautiful music, classical, jazz, and country-western. Still other stations catered to the needs of various population groups— blacks, Hispanics, speakers of other foreign languages, and religious groups. Public and educational broadcasting stations filled an additional programming niche.

For program directors, trying to reach a specific audience has become a very challenging task. This is due to the vast number of stations, closely overlapping formats, considerable variance in station power, and a wide variety of on-air personalities. Reaching an audience has become a select art that combines musical tastes, demographics, an understanding of popular music, and the skill to put them all together.

SMALL-MARKET RADIO: PROGRAM FLEXIBILITY

Imagine you're the general manager of the only radio station in a small market. How would you plan your programming? First, you would consider the characteristics of your community. What type of people reside there? Since your market has no other stations, you would not have to base your programming decisions on local competition. That in itself gives you greater flexibility. Since your community is small, you could include programs that would appeal to a small-town audience. For example, you might include a swap-shop program, where people call the station and list things they want to sell. Such programming might be entirely out of place in a large city, but in the small community, where church suppers, bazaars, and auctions are a way of life, it could very well be popular.

Or you could automate your programming, using a syndicated programming package. The syndicate would plan your musical programming, but you would still be responsible for providing service to your community through locally produced programming. Such programming could include play-by-play coverage of local high-school or college sports events, live coverage of community-sponsored events, and a community call-in or talk-show program.

Because your station will operate with a small staff, their duties will be many and varied. The person responsible for the morning air shift may double as the afternoon talk-show host. The station news director may also broadcast the football play-by-play. As general manager, you may be responsible for producing commercials, taking an afternoon air shift, and selling advertising time. Your station's programming will reflect these multiple roles as your staff becomes well known for its community involvement.

As general manager of the small-market station, you will have a challenging and exciting job. It will give you the freedom to program your station on the basis of the needs of your community. Your colleague at a large-market station is faced with all of these concerns and more—how to handle the competition.

PROGRAMMING STRATEGIES IN COMPETITIVE MARKETS

General managers of large-market stations usually delegate programming responsibilities to a specialist, a program director, while retaining overall station responsibilities.

Analyzing the Competition

As the program director for a large-market station, you would be concerned not only with the needs of your audience but with competing stations. Which stations are the leaders? What do they program? In addition, you need to realize that long-cherished listening habits are very hard to break, and that the reputation of being the leading station and having seniority in the community is a powerful advantage. A friend of mine passed up buying a radio station in a large market because an old, established station was capturing over 50 percent of the listenership. Even though the station for sale was a good buy, programming a sound that would cut into the leader's market appeared very difficult. The time and talent that would have been necessary made the investment too risky and expensive. Interestingly, the formats used at many established stations would fall flat on their faces in any other market. But in their case, twenty years of the same radio personality, programs heard in the same time slots, and familiar newscasters can be tough to beat.

Adjusting to Formats

Assuming that no station completely dominates the market and that sharp programming decisions can be made, careful planning can significantly improve your station's position. A good way to start is to examine the other stations' formats. You may discover a format that is not covered by the competition, perhaps country-western. Another possibility: formats that seem to be already covered may lend themselves to alteration. For example, there are many varieties of rock-and-roll. Even though a competing station may be programming a tight playlist (few songs but each song repeated often) with the top twenty hard-rock songs, the market may have room for a soft-rock format—more mellow rock songs with a slower tempo.

The Radio Personality

Still another strategy is to examine the radio personalities in your area. You may find that although a popular personality gives a station an identity, when that personality signs off the air the other personalities do not retain his or her listenership. At this point you can make one of two decisions. You can develop and promote a personality at your own station and then place that person on the air head-on with the competing personality. Or you can schedule your personality's show so that it avoids such a confrontation. If you have the money, you can sometimes hire the popular personality away from the competing station. This practice is risky, however, especially if the personality is linked with a certain format. For instance, a per-

sonality who has achieved popularity with a rock-and-roll format may be disastrous with country-western music. Remember, popularity may have been achieved because of a *combination* of personality and music. Having one without the other may simply prompt the listeners to turn the dial.

Bringing in a personality who has been a big hit in another city may also spell disaster. Listeners develop habits and tastes based on a variety of factors. Perhaps the previous popularity was achieved by a series of successful promotions. But the listeners in the new city have not been exposed to the same promotions, so they simply view the newcomer as a rank amateur and give their loyalty to another station. A famous Chicago station once brought a top disc jockey out of the South to run a popular morning show. Although his southern humor had made the announcer popular in his home state, he immediately turned off Chicago listeners who weren't attuned to southern speech patterns.

You may discover that your market simply has no dominant personality, and that by adding and promoting one of your own you can bring your station a loyal following. If you're successful at this, you will probably find your idea becoming very expensive as other stations try to hire the person away. If and when the person leaves, the popularity vacuum may be filled by another station. But it's all part of large-market programming.

What constitutes a good on-air radio personality? Program directors have their own ideas about this. For beginning announcers, however, one radio station's guidelines are worth considering:

Don't be NAME–HAPPY. That is, don't use your own name all the time. Listeners are quick to notice anything that hints of personal ego. Sell your K–COUNTRY Station first!

Do not give your opinions about records, programs or newscasts on the air.

When on the air, remember . . . do not have private jokes between you and another staff member. Always include the listener in on your joke, or leave it off the air.

Do not make editorial comment on any subject whatsoever. The General Manager is the only person authorized to editorialize . . . when AND if it is deemed necessary.

Be yourself. Do your job by being natural, genuine and sincere. Don't try to sound like someone else whose air work you may admire. Radio listeners are quick to spot . . . and reject . . . a phony.

Respect your listeners. A DJ will sometimes privately express a low regard for the intelligence and good taste of his audience. As a result of this attitude, he deliberately lowers the caliber of his music and chatter. This is sometimes offensive to listeners. On the other hand, they are usually complimented when you give them credit for intelligence and understanding. Don't downgrade your vocabulary to a 12-year-old's level. You're a mature adult . . . don't be afraid to sound like one.

Be humorous if you can . . . but if you can't, please don't try. Many *successful* DJ's never tell a joke or try to be clever. If you want to try humor, go ahead. Your manager will tell you if it isn't right.

Think about your job. Millions of people find companionship in radio. Many of them are lonely. Many feel worried and insecure. You have an enormous power to bring them a sense of belonging . . . a contact with things that seem familiar and real.[2]

The Jingle Package

In addition to considering personalities and formats, you will also want to obtain a good set of jingles. Jingles are a set of short musical recordings, all designed around a common musical theme and usually related to the station's call letters. Consider an upbeat combination of musical notes behind the call letters WABC. Each letter of the call would have a musical identity, as would the set of call letters as a whole. The same musical identity would be woven into a musical background for a thirty-second commercial or public-service announcement, a ten-second musical background for a station identification or a promotional announcement, and most likely a news bulletin in a fast tempo combined with a teletype sound. A good jingle package, although costing many thousands of dollars, is not only a good investment but a must in large-market programming.

TELEVISION PROGRAMMING

The versatile Steve Allen, in discussing a PBS television program in which he interviewed celebrities from history, commented in the publication *Bookviews* on the audience he wanted to reach. "I want it all," Allen said. "I want the intellectuals to be pleased because we're discussing ideas, but I want the ordinary people at the gas stations to be able to enjoy it too." The author of the *Bookviews* article, John Firth, wrote that "Allen is the first to admit that finding an audience for such a program is a problem, and that he has to steer a course between making it absurdly simplistic, and thus not getting across the ideas adequately, or aiming it above the heads of the large audience he hopes to reach."

The comments of Allen and Firth illustrate what television programmers face every day. Unlike the specialized medium of radio, television must program to a mass audience. Even PBS realizes its impact will be greater if its high-quality programming can appeal to a large segment of the population. Reaching this mass audience amid the morass of competing stations and networks is a big job.

Network Strategies

Television programming differs from radio programming in two ways. First, radio is primarily music. Television, on the other hand, includes everything from cartoon shows to coverage of major news events. Second, although independent stations and cable are certainly factors to be contended with, the real competition in any market is usually found among the affiliates of the three commercial networks. Networks play a powerful role in determining the position of their affiliates in local ratings. The investor wanting to buy a television station or the program director programming it inherit the merits and demerits of the network, and each has only a limited amount of flexibility in instituting programming changes.

For the network the audience is national, and the programs that make the networks are those that appeal to the largest segment of the population. After all, the network is in the business of convincing advertisers that buying its commercial time will enable them to reach the largest national audience. Any program that weakens that audience base has little chance for survival. The result has been what critics call programming to the lowest common denominator, or trying to reach the largest mass audience.

If television advertisers wish to reach a more specialized audience, they select different types of programming rather than changing stations or networks the way a radio advertiser can. Television has not yet become a specialized medium, although new technology and competition are rapidly changing this. It is only a matter of time before all-news television stations, sports television, stations programming nothing but motion pictures, and other specialized stations become commonplace.

Affiliate Goals

In the meantime, local stations that want an alternative to network programming are finding an increasing variety of syndicated programs available. Affiliates are also exercising their right to have a say in network programming. And the networks, facing competition from syndication, independent stations, cable, and stations implementing their own satellite distribution system, are taking the time to listen.

Despite the powerful position of the network, it could not exist without its affiliates. Unless its affiliates agree to carry its programming, the network will have no market for its advertisers. If a network program does not receive affiliate clearance, its national ratings can suffer. Advertising dollars aren't spent on network programs that show up poorly in the ratings. In a sense, a station imposes economic sanctions on a network when it refuses to carry a network program.

Instead of refusing to clear network shows, some affiliates record the programs and air them at a different time. A violent or sexually explicit program may be rescheduled late at night. The show is still broadcast, but the new time slot may give a much smaller audience than it would have reached during prime time. The audience may also have a different makeup, perhaps a different income level. The program shown opposite the rescheduled program may seriously cut into its viewership; if the program had appeared in its regularly scheduled time slot, it would have faced weak competition. Even more important, there is no way to successfully measure this new audience, for each station rescheduling the program may show it at a different time. So a rescheduled program can spell the same economic disaster as a preempted one.

Now that we have acquired an overview of radio and television programming, we will examine the competitive environment (Figure 14-1) in which a station operates. Many of the concepts we have just discussed

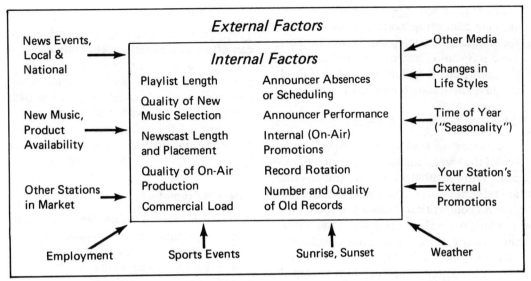

FIGURE 14–1 Many different factors operate to determine a station's programming. Internal factors, many within control of the station, and external factors over which the station has little control play a part in programming decisions. (© The Arbitron Ratings Company)

apply to this environment. The competitive environment is made up of both internal and external factors. The key to effective station operations is to integrate them so that they produce the most favorable competitive climate. External factors are largely beyond the control of station management. Internal factors, on the other hand, are under the complete control of station management. First, we'll examine the *external* factors.

THE STATION'S COMPETITIVE ENVIRONMENT: EXTERNAL FACTORS

News Events

Every news director has finished a day saying, "It's been a slow news day." In other words, very little has happened in the community. This doesn't mean every broadcast journalist is interested in sensationalism, but if nothing happens, nothing can be communicated to the public. News programming tends to draw more listeners or viewers on a day when things *are* happening than on "slow news days." If the mayor announces an investigation of alleged corruption in the police department, if a flood wipes out a portion of the city, if a plane crashes, if a new school bond passes, or if a local citizen wins a national award, people want to know about it. Essentially, a station and its news programming are at the mercy of news events.

New Music

While the news department is spending time covering events, the programming department is concerned with the latest music or syndicated features. For example, when the disco craze hit, stations that could adjust their formats accordingly could reap the rewards of the disco appeal. Conversely, some stations competing against a disco station found their listenership dwindling. In short, the disco station had a new product to sell the public and the sponsors, and that product gave the station a competitive edge.

Other Stations in the Market

The number of stations in a market can be one of the biggest factors in determining success. Many small markets have stations that are extremely successful, partly because they face no competition. Stations in these markets are not overly worried about the format they employ, since there is no competition to take away the advertising dollar. But consider the station competing with fifteen or twenty other radio stations. Finding a niche is tough, and wooing a particular audience with a particular format can be a very difficult job.

Employment

Employment conditions can affect a station in two ways. First, the level of employment in a community will be related to the overall economy. If people are working, they are buying. If they are buying, the merchants are making money and in turn can afford to advertise. Second, if there's a large employment pool, the station can find ample talent. Typically, good talent is scarcer in small markets than in larger ones.

Sports Events

How can sports events affect a station? Coverage of the local high-school sports schedule and—if a market includes a college town—the college sports schedule is an excellent way to attract advertisers. And naturally, a winning team can attract a larger audience and consequently more advertisers than a losing team.

Sunrise-Sunset

The type of license a radio station is issued can affect its competitive environment. If a station is a *daytimer,* then the number of hours it can operate (and air commercials) depends on when the sun sets. If the daytimer is competing with stations able to operate around the clock, then it must hustle in the morning in order to regain an audience that might have been lost the night before.

External Promotions

An external factor a station can control is its external promotions. Billboards, community-sponsored events, and such special activities as Easter-egg hunts or Christmas-present drives all contribute to a station's visibility. Most stations in highly competitive markets utilize external promotions to their fullest.

Seasonality

For any advertising medium, the season of the year can change the competitive environment. Christmas is a period of heavy advertising as stores prepare for the onslaught of shoppers. Primaries and general elections bring politicians flocking to buy advertising. August is perfect for back-to-school specials, and gardening shops are ideal spring sponsors.

Changes in Lifestyle

Closely tied to the season of the year are changes in life style. The opening of a new factory can signal the arrival of a "blue-collar prime time" and create an opportunity for an all-night format that keeps company with the assembly line. Smart station managers keep close tabs on the life styles of their communities. When a radio or television station can coordinate programming with a given life style and target audience, then advertisers have a ready-made medium through which to reach that audience.

Other Media

Just as other stations in a market are important external factors, so are other media. The most common competitor of broadcasting is the local newspaper, and in some communities the economic rivalry between radio and newspaper is fierce. City magazines or weekly newspapers for shoppers also contribute to the competition. Station managers must be alert to the advertising that local businesses buy in nonbroadcast media. Why does an advertiser prefer the local newspaper to radio or television? What can the station do to lure money away from print advertising? These are questions management must answer in order to survive in the competitive environment.

All of the factors we've discussed fluctuate from market to market. The key to broadcasting's success as a business lies in the station manager's ability to understand how each of these external factors relates to a given community and how the station can adapt to it.

INTERNAL FACTORS AFFECTING PROGRAMMING DECISIONS

A station's ability to adapt to the competitive environment is partly determined by internal factors.

Playlist Length

In radio, *playlist length* is the number of different songs played with regularity. Some stations have rather long playlists, which means that in any given week they'll play a large number of songs, but each one only once or twice. Stations with short playlists usually play twenty or so songs with regularity. A short playlist can catch a large number of listeners but will not necessarily hold them for any length of time. After all, hearing the same songs over and over can become monotonous. These stations aren't too concerned with the "dial hoppers." Rather, their objective is to reach a large number of *different* listeners. On the other hand, a station with a long playlist and more diversified programming may not capture as many different listeners, but those they do have are more loyal and will listen to the station longer. It then becomes the job of each station to convince the advertiser that it is the better buy.

Record Rotation

By *record rotation* we mean how often records are changed on the playlist *plus* how frequently they are played on the air. Stations with longer playlists, naturally, have a less frequent rotation.

Quality of New-Music Selection

In many markets, good program directors are hard to find. Such a person must not only be able to supervise people, make out schedules, and publish a playlist but also intimately understand the music business. In demand is the program director who understands trends in music *before* they reach the listener, and who has an ear for interpreting this trend by selecting for air play those few songs, from the hundreds released, that will appeal to a wide segment of the listening audience. Talent such as this is rare. The ability to choose music well can strengthen the competitive position of any station.

Newscasts

Depending on the amount of news and information programming a station airs, newscasts can run from less than a minute to twenty-four hours a day. News is an important commodity to sponsors, and in multistation markets where each station places heavy emphasis on local news coverage the competition can be fierce.

In addition to length, placement of a newscast is also important. Most stations have a regular newscast time slot with which the listeners or viewers and sponsors can identify. For a new station, scheduling a newscast at this same time is usually less satisfactory than airing news at a noncompeting time, at least until the station can get a foothold in the market.

Quality of On-Air Production

Almost anyone can sit in front of a radio control board and play records, talk over the microphone, and punch a few buttons to play jingles. The skilled announcer, however, works those controls like an artist. Every word, every song, and every jingle is finely tuned to the second. For the listener, such skill creates a sound that massages rather than irritates. The professional announcer who is creative and can understand on-air production stands out in the competitive environment.

Commercial Load

Some stations have been known to sign on the air and operate for months without commercials just so they can bring themselves up in the ratings and then use the data on their increased listenership to sell advertising. Other stations pump their commercial load up so high that little time is left for music. The balance between these extremes is where the station's optimum income and listenership meet. A heavy commercial load will lose listeners. A light commercial load will lose money.

Announcers

The human factor is what makes any station run. Good announcers identify with their audience, and knowing this, good program directors try to match the two as closely as possible. For example, a Top 40 morning disc jockey may be a complete disaster at midnight, and a soft-talking, easy-listening personality may put listeners to sleep at morning drive time. For a station to be successful, the match between audience and on-air personality must be a good one. And once that match is made, loyalty grows between the two. Similarly, on-air personalities who care only about collecting a paycheck will usually collect listeners who care little about the station.

Internal On-Air Promotions

Promotions—contests, exhibits, call-ins, giveaways—especially when well planned and carried out, can generate more listeners and more income for a station. In recent years, broadcast promotion has been recognized as a vital element in a station's overall performance. In fact, the Broadcast Promotion Association was created especially for this cause. Many stations are even forming in-house promotion departments, either to take the place of outside advertising agencies or to work in conjunction with them.

In concluding our discussion of a typical competitive environment, in this case for radio, keep in mind that every station and every market is different. A unique combination of economic and human factors act upon each other.

THE RELATIONSHIP OF PROGRAMMING TO STATION INCOME

Now that we understand the forces that affect the competitive environment, let's apply them to programming and sales, two important aspects of the broadcasting business. Once again we'll use radio as our example. We'll want to examine four advertising strategies used in broadcasting. At the same time we'll draw a parallel between the advertising strategy and the programming strategy.

Keep in mind that while the station airs commercials that sell sponsors' products, the station's programming is itself a product being sold to the listener or viewer. Thus, programming against competing stations in the competitive environment and planning a broadcast advertising campaign for a client have many similarities. Using the four advertising strategies employed in *Arbitron Radio's Research Guidelines for Programming Decision Makers,*[3] we can draw parallel programming strategies for selling the station to the listener. The four strategies are as follows.

Saturation Schedule

This involves a heavy load of commercials aired over a short period of time. This strategy is used by an advertiser to make a strong impression for a short-lived event, such as a weekend sale.

Programming parallel: an extraordinarily heavy play of a new release by a very popular artist.

Spectrum Plan

This strategy consists of a medium level of commercials distributed equally throughout the broadcast day. It is designed to give product exposure to a great number of different people, but each listener may only hear the commercial once or twice a week. This strategy is appropriate for a consistent advertiser who is reminding the listener that he or she is still around.

Programming parallel: playing a familiar

hit that was hot on the charts a few weeks ago and is still liked by listeners, but that may have already peaked in sales at record stores.

Spot Schedule

This entails a series of commercials aired in one or two day-parts only, so that they will reach a particular target audience that is most available during that time.

Programming parallel: gearing programming to appeal to a particular audience which tends to listen in great numbers during certain time periods.

Fixed Position

This strategy involves placing a commercial at the same time every day. Listeners then become accustomed to hearing the commercial daily in this time slot. Fixed-position commercials are sometimes associated with particular programs, such as a morning sports show or a daily drama.

Programming parallel: airing a feature vignette at the same time every day as part of a personality's regular show. As an example, the morning show may air that day's lunch menu for the public schools.

Just as we were able to make a parallel between sales and programming, we could also make sales parallels for the frequency with which news stories are aired, the placement of newscasts, the record rotation for oldies, and how many times internal on-air promotions are played. Remember, the station's product is its programming.

SYNDICATED PROGRAMMING

So far we have learned about general radio and television programming, a station's external and internal environment, and how programming is related to station income. We have also discussed a major source of programming, the radio and television networks. Another important source of programming is syndication. Syndicated programming is distributed directly to stations, not through a network, although it may have first appeared on a network. With more and more independent stations, the development of cable, and alternative delivery systems such as pay TV and multipoint distribution, the demand for syndicated programming continues to grow.

Breaking the Ice: "Mary Hartman, Mary Hartman"

In order to go into syndication, most programs first started as network material, proved they could attract a loyal following, then made the break with the network and wooed individual stations. The first program to go directly into syndication on a mass national scale and achieve popularity was Norman Lear's somewhat controversial "Mary Hartman, Mary Hartman." Having been turned down by the television networks, Lear resorted to direct syndication for the show. It drew large audiences, and some bold metropolitan stations even put the program up against their competitors' late-evening news programs, scoring rating points that gave news consultants a headache.

"Mary Hartman, Mary Hartman" started a chain of events that may do more than merely attract television viewers. Local affiliates have become increasingly dissatisfied with the type of programming coming out of network hoppers. With the success of "Mary Hartman, Mary Hartman," station managers realized that there were alternatives to the network distribution system. What is popular in one city may be unpopular in another, and syndication gives managers a freedom of choice that network television does not.

The Deer Hunter and Other Early Syndicated Programs

Another successful syndication effort that caught the eye of the networks was MCA's decision to release the motion picture *The Deer Hunter* directly to independent stations instead of to the networks. Many of these stations ran the movie against the 1980 election-night coverage and scored impressive results. *The Deer Hunter* gave WOR–TV in New York one of the highest ratings in its history and KCOP–TV the highest metered rating ever for a televised movie in Los Angeles. Many stations ran the film with almost all of its violence and strong language intact. Nineteen stations purchased the film immediately before or after its initial television release.

Many network programs are familiar favorites in syndication. "M*A*S*H," for example, became a popular syndicated feature long before it concluded its original network run in 1983. The "Mary Tyler Moore Show" aired as one of the nation's most popular and longest running situation comedies before it made a successful syndication appearance. Even such early favorites as "The Lone Ranger" are seen regularly in syndication. Contemporary artists such as Barbara Mandrell have achieved syndication success with original musical variety programs. Rock-and-roll radio authority Dick Clark has been syndicated on both radio and television. Major novels such as John Jakes's *The Bastard* have appeared in syndication through release to independent stations.

Direct Syndication

The success of syndicated programs has lured more syndicators into the marketplace and thereby increased programming variety and kept costs competitive. Direct syndication eliminates the need to "fit" the network audience. For example, if you own a production company that produces a weekly series on skiing techniques, the network probably will not be interested. Although its affiliates in New England and the Northwest would consider the show, stations in the Deep South would very likely preempt the program with something more popular in their local areas. Yet by going into direct syndication you can create your own network of stations. In fact, you might find enough stations in New England and the Northwest that are interested in airing your series to make your venture profitable.

The same principle applies to the expanding enterprise of regional syndication. Perhaps your area hosts a salt-water fishing tournament. A documentary of the tournament would be of interest to other stations located near the ocean. Conversely, generating wide acceptance for the show in Nebraska and Iowa would be difficult.

Major events are becoming attractive to syndicators. Tying up rights to special productions can make a long-term syndication package very lucrative. Take, for example, the Miss Rodeo America Pageant, held in the Southwest in conjunction with the National Finals Rodeo. Contestants from the fifty states and Canada compete for the title of Miss Rodeo America. Although the networks (which broadcast the Miss America Pageant internationally) shied away from the pageant, syndicators saw major audience appeal, especially with pretty girls, colorful western outfits, and such hard-fought competition as barrel racing and horse showing. These all spell color, action, and entertainment—three appealing ingredients to a television syndicator. Public broadcasting saw the potential first and gave the pageant regional television syndication. This event is just one more example of the growing variety and potential of direct syndication.

Many syndicated programs find their way out of the broadcasting station and into an educational institution, corporation, library, or church. A syndicated religious documentary that first airs on television can find additional audiences at a Sunday morning Bible class or at a convention of lay preachers. As you can see, the market possibilities for syndicated material are turning it into a booming business.

SYNDICATED RADIO

So far we have been talking about television syndication. But syndication is also alive and well in radio, especially since the networks take up so little of the station's programming schedule. Syndication has found a ready market in the increased number of automated stations. Such stations still program commercials and local newscasts, but much of their remaining programming comes from syndication. Automated stations can choose from a wide variety of syndicated radio programming—anything from music to interviews and talk programs. In addition, both nonautomated and automated stations use syndicated jingles between records, as an introduction to newscasts and weather reports, and as a musical background for commercial and public-service messages.

Why Syndicate?

Syndication is an economical way to operate a station while providing a competitive sound. But before deciding to use syndicated programming you first should evaluate the competition. Is there a programming need not being met or an audience not being reached by the competing stations? Second, you must decide that when your station does air locally produced programming it will be of the highest quality. Commercials, local newscasts, weather reports, and supplemental entertainment by the local disc jockey must be able to blend professionally with the syndicated music. Poor quality in local production is only accentuated by high-quality syndicated programming.

Formats

A wide variety of syndicated formats are available, but not every syndicator defines the same format in the same way. Thus, managers must preview the syndicated "sounds" to make sure they fit the needs of their market. Most syndicators offer a limited number of formats, keeping to a reasonable minimum the size and range of their own musical libraries. Syndicators specializing in contemporary music might syndicate progressive-rock, country-rock, and soft-rock formats. These formats tend to overlap, and hit songs appearing on more than one chart, such as *Billboard,* can be inserted in more than one syndicated format.

Other syndicated packages can be even more specialized, offering "middle-of-the-road string orchestras" or "up-beat string orchestras." Still another may contain "middle-of-the-road orchestras and bands." To offer these specialties, the syndicator purchases mostly albums and interchanges the different cuts on the albums to fit the different formats.

Talk radio is a specialized format in which a talk-show host interviews listeners who call in to the station. The original program can be taped in one market and aired in another. The host is careful not to make any reference to the city in which the show originates, and the topics do not have a highly localized emphasis. If the show does become localized, local references can be deleted before the program is syndicated.

The Consultant as Syndicator

In television syndication, the syndicator has little involvement with the station except to sell the program. In radio, however, the association is much closer. Radio formats are a more "finely tuned" type of programming than television formats. First, they last longer, in some cases for the entire twenty-four-hour broadcast schedule. Second, the competition may be much greater. Instead of three or four television stations the market may consist of twenty or more radio stations. Third, the local radio station directly participates in the programming because of its locally produced and inserted commercials and newscasts.

As a result, the radio syndicator often doubles as a broadcast consultant, recommending how the programs should be utilized. Judging whether the local commercial production is up to par or if the musical background of the commercials matches the syndicated format becomes the consultant's major concern. If the station is going to continue to use syndication, it must see an increase in its audience and ultimately its profits. Moreover, the reputation of the syndicator is at stake. A station at the bottom of the ratings is not good publicity for the syndicator. But a station on top can be a valuable asset in selling other stations. Thus, management's willingness to work closely with the consultant once the syndicated programming has been acquired can determine the difference between success and failure.

FORMAT CONTROL IN SYNDICATED PROGRAMMING

With the increase in both the number of automated stations and the reliance on syndicated musical programming, the issue of format control has become important to the field of syndicated programming. The FCC feels the licensee should be responsible for its format in order to serve the public interest. As a result of some binding contracts offered to broadcasters by syndication companies, the FCC has adopted guidelines for broadcasters to follow when agreeing to carry syndicated programming. The commission suggests stations should not enter into contracts that

1. Fix the number of broadcast hours;
2. Prohibit AM–FM duplication;
3. Prohibit sub–carrier authorizations;
4. Require the exclusive use of any music format service, or prohibits other sources;
5. Fix the amount of format service company music broadcast;
6. Prohibit any announcement by the station;
7. Fix the number of commercials broadcast;
8. Limit the content or source of any non-musical programming;
9. Fix the amount of air time for news, music, or other programming;
10. Prohibit automatic gain control of company-supplied material; or
11. Allow termination in the event of program format changes by a licensee exercising his responsibility for the public interest.[4]

The key to making contracts is to retain flexibility. This is especially important in long-term contracts. The FCC does not want the licensee obligated to the degree that programming "in the public interest" might not air because of restrictions placed upon the station by the syndicator.

THE ECONOMICS OF SYNDICATED PROGRAMMING

Before you run out and rent a television camera, enlist your friends as actors, and find a ski slope or a fishing tournament, it's important to understand the economics of syndication. Although profits can be made with good syndicated material, the investments, the competition, and the gamble are all big business.

The Financial Commitment

Regardless of how popular an event may be or how good a script looks, networks and station managers make commitments only to finished products. More than one show that looked good on paper turned out to be a flop once it was produced. The star of the show might not pull it off, what seems like a good idea to New York program executives may fall flat in Peoria, and it can rain on the day of the ski tournament. Networks and stations have been through it all before. The cost of producing a pilot program in the hope of getting it syndicated can run into many thousands of dollars. Many foreign countries with developing television systems purchased syndicated features, then decided they could produce the programs cheaper themselves. After about two years they went back to buying syndicated features—what had seemed like a two- or three-thousand-dollar savings turned into a fifty-thousand-dollar investment that flopped.

Before syndication comes a pilot show. The pilot—which requires writers, producers, directors, talent, sets, and equipment—can cost as much as a quarter of a million dollars for the quality that will appeal to management and meet the competition. Perhaps more than one pilot will be necessary. But even if the pilot looks good, the investment can go down the drain if the audience rejects it. It's a gamble.

For major one-time events there is the cost of securing the rights to the event. If more than one company is bidding, the cost can escalate out of reach. Major sports events are one example. Minor sporting events can't compete with the audience-drawing power of major events, even though the cost of production might be less. A million-dollar investment can mean a million-dollar profit. It can also mean a million-dollar loss.

Promoting the Commitment

After key stations have made the commitment to air your program and the program is ready for syndication, you must advertise and promote it. You'll need to buy advertisements in trade magazines, produce promotional brochures for a direct-mail campaign aimed at station managers, and exhibit your program at major conventions where program executives gather.

In some cases, you may decide to sell your program at a reduced rate to large-market or prestigious stations so that their acceptance can be publicized in your advertising. Seeing that a major Los Angeles station has purchased your program may reassure a Cheyenne, Wyoming, station that the program will draw an audience. You can create a bandwagon effect: the more stations that buy your program, the more others will want to buy it.

Promotion can be especially difficult if the program is a single event, if it's a bit unusual, or if the syndicator or production company is untried. Managers understand football and situation comedy. But the Minnesota Canoe Championship or the White Water Raft Races will be tougher to sell. A well-known syndicator can deal with credibility. But a new company must prove its stripes. It must promote not only its product but its reputation as a company as well.

SELLING SYNDICATION

The selling of syndicated programming is much like a farmers' market. There are more deals, more contractual arrangements, more variety, and more companies than there are fresh vegetables and homemade pies. Many syndicators sell on a market-to-market basis. Others try for contracts with groups of stations, such as network-owned-and-operated stations. The syndicator who can, for example, say that the ABC-owned-and-operated stations have already purchased one of his programs is in a strong position to deal with other stations. This is especially true when the syndicator is marketing pilot programs. If too few stations buy the program, production for the series is cancelled. But by the time it's cancelled the stations have lost the opportunity to buy alternative programming, which might then be in the hands of their competition.

Bidding

The syndicator who wants to let the marketplace determine the selling price may decide to auction a program, an increasingly common practice. On a given day a syndicator will send telegrams to all the station managers in a market, announcing the availability of a program. Each manager is given a certain amount of time to bid on the program, and the highest bid buys the show. Variations include open bidding, where each manager knows at any time what the highest bid is, and sequence bidding, where each manager is told the bid of the previous manager contacted. First practiced in the book-publishing trade, auctioneering has produced record prices for syndicated programs.

Barter Arrangements

Bartering, or trading advertising time on a station for the opportunity to air a program for free, is still being used to sell syndicated shows, but even here there are pitfalls. Some large-market managers shy away from bartering, feeling that if the program was of top quality it would have been sold outright. In some cases that's true, but there are many exceptions. For example, major advertisers who want barter time may place a large financial commitment behind the program. A major corporation that has a reputation for sponsoring quality programs can use that reputation to make both a syndicated program and the accompanying public-relations efforts a success. Also, some programs are available only through barter. Many advertising agencies are actively involved in barter because the station supplying the advertising time airs not only the program but also their client's commercial. Other agencies provide barter programs as long as their clients receive "commercial credit" in return. For instance, an ad agency may provide a program series in exchange for one hundred minutes of commercial time to be used in whatever way the agency wants.

SUMMARY

Programming is the product of broadcasting. It can be compared to the goods and services sold by other businesses. Even in public broadcasting, which solicits contributions for programming, programs are the "goods" that people want to continue to hear and view.

In radio, the format is the heart of programming. Formats vary among stations and range from foreign-language broadcasts to hard-rock music. Specialized formats are the key to modern radio programming. They reach specialized audiences, and accordingly permit advertisers to target their commercials and messages. The person responsible for programming a station is the program director, who combines an awareness of musical tastes, an understanding of demographics, and the ability to put them together.

The key to small-market radio is program flexibility. Because stations in small markets operate with limited staffs and a diversified audience, station personnel must be aware of all facets of station operations, including programming.

A number of programming strategies exist in competitive markets. It is first necessary to analyze the competition and determine how other stations are programming for the market. Assuming that no station dominates the market, it is necessary for a program director to adjust to the formats that will fit into the competitive marketplace. The radio personality will play a large part in this adjustment. Jingle packages complement air personalities and help create a unified sound for the station.

Programming strategies also exist for television programming. Some of these strategies are dictated by the network, which control the majority of programming for network-affiliated stations. But the goals of affiliates must be taken into consideration by the networks, which after all depend on affiliates to carry network programming to a mass audience.

A station's competitive environment consists of a number of external and internal factors. External factors include news events, new music, other stations in the market, employment, sports events, sunrise–sunset limits on broadcasting, external promotions, seasonality, changes in life style, and other media. Internal factors include playlist length, record rotation, quality of new-music selection, newscasts, quality of on-air production, commercial load, and internal on-air promotions.

A close relationship exists between programming and station income. There are a number of strategies for purchasing time on broadcast media, and these strategies parallel station programming. Strategies available to advertisers include the saturation schedule, the spectrum plan, the spot schedule, and the fixed-position plan.

An alternative to network programming is syndicated programming, which bypasses the major commercial networks and is distributed directly to stations. Syndicated programming is available for both radio and television. Many successful network programs have been released in syndication.

Syndication companies that deal with broadcasters are subject to controls. So that local stations can retain the authority to determine programming for their markets, syndication companies are prohibited from specifying such things as broadcast hours, the amount of syndicated programming the station airs, commercial loads, or time devoted to news.

To be successful, syndicated programming must receive a financial commitment and skillful promotion. The sale of syndicated programming includes both bidding and barter arrangements.

OPPORTUNITIES
FOR FURTHER LEARNING

BALDWIN, H., *Creating Effective TV Commercials*. Chicago: Crain Books, 1982.

BITTNER, J. R., and D. A. BITTNER, *Radio Journalism*. Englewood Cliffs, N.J.: Prentice-Hall, 1977.

BLISS, E., JR., and J. M. PATTERSON. *Writing News for Broadcast* (2nd ed.). New York: Columbia University Press, 1978.

BRANDT, B. G., *The College Radio Handbook*. Blue Ridge Summit, Pa.: TAB Books, 1981.

BURROWS, T. D., and D. N. WOOD, *Television Production: Disciplines and Techniques* (2nd ed.). Dubuque, Iowa: William C. Brown, 1982.

CANTOR, M. and S. PINGREE, *The Soap Opera*. Beverly Hills, Calif.: Sage, 1983.

CARROLL, J. K., and R. E. SHERRIFFS, *TV Lighting Handbook*. Blue Ridge Summit, Pa.: TAB Books, 1977.

CLIFT, C., III, and A. GREER, eds., *Broadcast Programming: The Current Perspective,* 7th ed. Lanham, Md.: University Press of America, 1981.

COLEMAN, H. W., *Case Studies in Broadcast Management: Radio and Television,* (2nd ed.). New York: Hastings House, 1978.

DUBEK, L. J., *Professional Broadcast Announcing*. Boston: Allyn & Bacon, 1982.

EASTMAN, S. T., S. W. HEAD, and L. KLEIN, *Broadcast Programming: Strategies for Winning Television and Radio Audiences*. Belmont, Calif.: Wadsworth, 1981.

EASTMAN, S. T., and R. A. KLEIN, *Strategies in Broadcast and Cable Promotion*. Belmont, Calif.: Wadsworth, 1982.

ELLIS, E. I., *Opportunities in Broadcasting* (2nd ed.). Skokie, Ill.: National Textbook, 1981.

ETTEMA, J. S., and D. C. WHITNEY, eds., *Individuals in Mass Media Organization: Creativity and Constraint*. Beverly Hills, Calif.: Sage, 1982.

GARVEY, D. E., and W. L. RIVERS, *Broadcast Writing*. New York: Longman, 1982.

———, *Newswriting for the Electronic Media*. Belmont, Calif.: Wadsworth, 1982.

GRADUS, B., *Directing: The Television Commercial*. New York: Hastings House, 1981.

GREENBERG, B. S., ed., *Life on Television: Content Analyses of U.S. TV Drama*. Norwood, N.J.: Ablex, 1980.

HALL, C., and B. HALL, *This Business of Radio Programming*. New York: Billboard, 1977.

HAMMOND, C. M., Jr., *The Image Decade: Television Documentary, 1965–1975*. New York: Hastings House, 1981.

HAWES, W., *The Performer in Mass Media. . . in Media Professions and in the Community*. New York: Hastings House, 1978.

HIMMELSTEIN, H., *On the Small Screen: New Approaches in Television and Video Criticism*. New York: Praeger, 1981.

HOWARD, H. H., and M. S. KIEVMAN, *Radio and TV Programming*. Columbus, Ohio: Grid, 1983.

KEIRSTEAD, P. O., *All-News Radio*. Blue Ridge Summit, Pa.: TAB Books, 1980.

———, *Modern Public Affairs Programming*. Blue Ridge Summit, Pa.: TAB Books, 1979.

MacFARLAND, D. R., *The Development of the Top 40 Radio Format*. New York: Arno Press, 1979.

McLEISH, R., *The Technique of Radio Production: A Manual for Local Broadcasters*. New York: Focal/Hastings House, 1979.

National Association of Broadcasters and the Radio-Television News Directors Association, *Radio News Handbook for the Small Market Station*. Washington, D.C.: National Association of Broadcasters, 1978.

QUAAL, W. L., and J. A. BROWN, *Broadcast Management: Radio-Television* (2nd ed.). New York: Hastings House, 1976.

Radio Program Department Handbook: A Basic Guide for the Program Director of a Smaller Operation. Washington, D.C.: National Association of Broadcasters, 1975.

REED, M. K., and R. M. REED, *Career Oppor-*tunities in Television and Video. New York: Facts on File, 1982.

RICHARDSON, D., *Puget Sounds: A Nostalgic Review of Radio and TV in the Great Northwest*. Seattle: Superior, 1981.

SHANKS, B., *The Cool Fire: How to Make It in Television*. New York: Norton, 1976.

SMITH, V. J., *Programming for Radio and Television*. Lanham, Md.: University Press of America, 1980.

WHITE, H., *How to Produce an Effective TV Commercial*. Chicago: Crain Books, 1981.

WILKIE, B., *The Technique of Special Effects in Television*. Woburn, Mass.: Focal Press, 1971.

WILLIS, E. E., and C. D'ARIENZO, *Writing Scripts for Television, Radio and Film*. New York: Holt, Rinehart & Winston, 1981.

WINTERS, A. A., and S. F. MILTON, *The Creative Connection: Advertising Copywriting and Idea Visualization*. New York: Fairchild, 1982.

15

INTERNATIONAL BROADCASTING

To confine the study of broadcasting today to one country is to restrict oneself to a very narrow view of both the world and the broadcast media. The international flow of broadcast programming, direct-broadcast satellites beaming signals across national boundaries, the growing importance of World Administrative Radio Conferences, and the expanding role of the International Telecommunication Union all demand a universal perspective of these electronic media.

We learned in chapter 4 that broadcasting developed simultaneously in many different parts of the world, especially after World War I. Some countries progressed more rapidly, others introduced broadcasting as late as the 1970s. The different political, economic, and social conditions in which broadcasting operates are as varied as the countries themselves. Not every country permits commercial advertising, has a free press, or allows private ownership of broadcasting. Each country has its own system serving both domestic and international audiences.

We will not examine every country, nor will we view each country from the same perspective. What we will do on our world tour is acquaint ourselves with many different elements of international broadcasting.

THE SCOPE OF INTERNATIONAL BROADCASTING

As we visit different countries, remember that the United States represents only one model of broadcasting. Our commercial radio and television stations are supported by advertising, and our public broadcasting is supported by government funds, the public, corporations, and institutions. In other countries, advertising also supports some systems of broadcasting, as do public contributions. We can also find systems totally supported by the government. We can find systems supported in part by a tax paid on radio and television receivers. We can find systems supported by license fees that the public pays in order to listen to radio or watch television. In many countries, different methods of financial support are found side by side.

Also keep in mind that not every country has the freedom of expression found in the United States; some countries are even freer. And the content of radio and television programming abroad, like that in the United States, is determined by many things, such as the ratings, the government, and advertising. Some countries operate very large systems and some, very small ones. In some parts of the world you can watch television only a few hours a day. In other parts of the world you can watch television beamed in from many different countries. Do not view any country from a narrow perspective. Compare and contrast the different systems and ask yourself questions about the advantages and disadvantages of each.

The term *international broadcasting,* as we use it in this chapter, refers to various systems of broadcasting outside the United States. For example, we will view the external services of the BBC, Switzerland's Short Wave Service, the USSR, Radio Australia, and NHK's Radio Japan. We will examine two different regulatory frameworks, countries that exhibit a mixture of government and commercial broadcasting, France's highly diversified system, and the open-door

system of the Netherlands. We will observe the regional diversity of Scandinavian broadcasting, the authoritarian system of the USSR, and the contrasting systems of West Germany and East Germany. We will discuss attempts by Canadian broadcasting to preserve cultural integrity and look at a broadcasting system that exists in an atmosphere of cultural and racial contrast—that of South Africa. Our discussion of international broadcasting will conclude with an examination of educational broadcasting in developing nations.

EXTERNAL SERVICES

Many countries operate external broadcasting systems designed to reach audiences in other countries. Some of these systems, such as the BBC, have gained world respect for the quality of their offerings. Others, such as the USSR system, carry mostly propaganda. Most offer a wide variety of foreign-language programs that reach people of diverse cultures and political perspectives.

The BBC

The BBC started in 1922 as the British Broadcasting Company and was made a nonprofit, public corporation by royal charter in 1927. Today it is an independent broadcasting organization, although it receives its budget for overseas broadcasting from Parliament. The fees it collects from licenses are also determined by Parliament. Directed by a twelve-person board of governors appointed by the queen, the corporation operates under the advice of a series of advisory boards. These include the General Advisory Council, the National Broadcasting councils of Scotland and Wales, and advisory bodies in such areas as religion, education, and local radio. The BBC does not receive income from advertising. Over one hundred countries use BBC productions, and on the average five hundred programs are seen per week in various parts of the world. The BBC has a policy of not relinquishing editorial control over any of its programs and does not tailor its programs to any specific region.

Radio is also "exported," not only through direct broadcasting but also through a transcription service that permits selected BBC radio programs to be played back in other countries. At the heart of both transcription and direct broadcasting is the BBC External Service. The BBC receives respect and attention from a global audience. "This is London" uses thirty-nine different languages to broadcast news, information, cultural, and entertainment programming. As the BBC has stated, the Ex-

ternal Service transmits values "of a society governed by laws voted democratically, yet willing to listen to dissidents, both within its own frontiers and outside them. It mirrors a national community retooling itself economically and ideologically for the 21st century."[1] Three major services constitute the External Service: the European Service and the World Service, (Figure 15-1) which broadcast twenty-four hours a day in English, and the Overseas Service. Complementing the External Service are BBC radio and television regional services transmitting to Northern Ireland, Scotland, Wales, and the English regions served by television.

Switzerland:
SBC Short Wave Service

The Swiss Short Wave Service also operates an extensive program of European and over-

FIGURE 15-1 The BBC has an extensive broadcasting system with radio programs beamed to many different parts of the world in many different languages. Shown here is one of the control consoles of the BBC World Service. (BBC)

FIGURE 15–2 Radio Moscow operates from the USSR and provides programs overseas through short-wave and transcription services. The content closely follows the governmental political philosophy and is controlled by the state under the Union Republic State Committee of the USSR's Council of Ministers. (Radio Moscow)

seas broadcasting. Its high-powered transmitters beam news, information, and cultural programs to all the continents of the world. The Swiss, because of their reputation for neutrality in international affairs, have substantial credibility among many nations, whereas other countries may be perceived as having vested interests in the content of their programming. The Swiss service is well accepted, especially in third-world countries and developing nations.

The Short Wave Service has two goals—providing timely information to Swiss citizens living in other countries and spreading Swiss culture. Special care is taken in news programming: no report of world sig-

nificance is broadcast until it is verified by at least two other sources. Entertainment programs are also part of the worldwide service, and recorded programs are mailed to over three hundred stations throughout the world.

The USSR

The USSR's external and overseas service is the responsibility of Radio Moscow. Broadcasted in sixty-four languages, Radio Moscow (Figure 15-2) programs focus mostly on life in the USSR, the Soviet view of international issues, and Russian drama and entertainment. Programs are distributed free of charge to stations in other parts of the world. Weekly programs include "Soviet Press Review," an editorial and commentary program, and "Moscow Meridian," a short commentary. Other biweekly and monthly programs are available on such topics as politics, science, and art.

The Radio and Television Committee cooperates with other countries wishing to produce programs about Soviet life. One such program is "Pravda," a documentary produced by Finnish broadcasters showing the inside workings of the Soviet Union and *Pravda,* a newspaper with one of the world's largest circulations.

Radio Australia

In Australia overseas broadcasting is the responsibility of Radio Australia. Its twenty-four-hour service concentrates on news and information interspersed with music and entertainment programs. Radio Australia broadcasts in eight languages and several dialects, approximately 54 percent of which is in English, 17 percent Indonesian, 7 percent Chinese, 7 percent French, 4 percent Vietnamese, 4 percent Japanese, 2 percent Thai, and 6 percent a combination of simple English and Neo-Melanesian.[2] The fate of Chinese refugees has been an important part of the Chinese broadcasts. Reports to relatives, messages from students studying in Australia, and songs and interviews with children of Chinese refugees are typical broadcast fare.

Voice of America and USICA Film and Television

Under the auspices of the United States International Communication Agency (USICA), the Voice of America (VOA) broadcasts over nine hundred hours of programming per week in English and thirty-eight other languages. Short and medium-wave transmitters reach an estimated 67 million listeners and perhaps tens of millions more listening in China. News and news analysis are the basic programming formats, supplemented with information on American society and American popular-music programming, notably jazz. The 101 domestic and overseas transmitters have a combined power in excess of 20.5 million watts. Radio programs from VOA are made available to local stations in many countries.

In addition to overseeing the Voice of America, USICA acquires and produces videotape programs and films. These are shown by USICA posts to audiences overseas and are sometimes distributed through foreign television stations and commercial theaters. USICA also provides foreign television stations with newsclips of events in the United States.

REGULATORY FRAMEWORKS

In the United States, broadcasting falls under the jurisdiction of the Federal Communications Commission. Compare the Canadian Radio–Television Commission with the FCC, which we will learn more about in Chapter 17, and then notice how Mexico diversifies its broadcasting under different government bodies.

Canada

Canada's place in the history of international telecommunication began when Marconi selected Newfoundland to test his transatlantic wireless. Those dots and dashes started a chain of events that eventually gave birth to the Canadian Marconi Company. Today Canada is the home of a broadcasting system that stretches from Eskimo villages in the north to the United States in the south.

It is a country in which the evening news can be delivered by satellite, yet in which television can be a strange phenomenon to an inhabitant of the northern tundra. Canada is also a country whose fierce pride and loyalty are reflected in everything from broadcast regulations to television programming.

Canadian broadcasting is regulated by the Canadian Radio–Television Commission (CRTC) created by the Broadcasting Act of 1968. The CRTC is composed of fifteen members. The five full-time members form the CRTC's Executive Committee. They are appointed for seven-year terms and can be reappointed. The ten part-time appointees are the key to CRTC's operation. Appointed for up to five years, they are drawn from throughout the country and must be consulted before any major decisions can be made, such as issuing, renewing, revoking, or amending the license of a radio, television, or cable company.

Canada's broadcasting policy is stated in the 1968 act:

(a) Broadcasting undertakings in Canada make use of radio frequencies that are public property, and such undertakings constitute a single system, herein referred to as the Canadian broadcasting system, comprising public and private elements;

(b) The Canadian broadcasting system should be effectively owned and controlled by Canadians so as to safeguard, enrich and strengthen the cultural, political, social and economic fabric of Canada;

(c) all persons licensed to carry on broadcasting undertakings have a responsibility for programs they broadcast, but the right to freedom of expression and the right of persons to receive programs, subject only to generally applicable statutes and regulations, is unquestioned;

(d) the programming provided by the Canadian broadcasting system should be varied and comprehensive and should provide reasonably balanced opportunity for the expression of differing views on matters of public concern, and the programming provided by each broadcaster should be of high standard, using predominantly Canadian creative and other resources.[3]

The "balanced opportunity for expression" is equivalent in intent to the Fairness Doctrine in the United States. Enforcement is not taken lightly. For example, station CFCF–AM was called to task after broadcasting what the CRTC felt was one-sided coverage of the Official Language Act of the Province of Quebec. The CRTC charged that the station had "failed to provide adequately in its own programming for a reasoned and responsible discussion of the subject."[4]

Mexico

The government takes an active part in Mexican broadcasting. It owns and programs its own stations and requires privately owned stations to provide 12.5 percent of their air time for government use (Figure 15–3). The government also owns educational-television production studios and produces and distributes programs through a nationwide microwave link. Three government agencies participate in Mexican radio and television: the Ministry of Transport and Communications, which deals directly with station regulations; the Ministry of Internal Affairs, which oversees government-supported programming; and the Ministry of Education, which coordinates educational programming.

MIXED GOVERNMENT AND PRIVATE OPERATING SYSTEMS

Along with diverse regulatory frameworks, international broadcasting exhibits diverse combinations of government and private interests.

FIGURE 15-3 Televised block parties are a popular part of some Mexican programming. Artists and award-winning international films are also popular. While some American programming also appears, the country has been firm in controlling the amount of violent programming it imports from the United States. (TELEVISA, S.A.)

Canada

Canada is just one example of such a mixed system. The private sector has a well-established system of commercial broadcasting stations serving the entire country. The main commercial television network is the CTV Television Network, which is owned by broadcasters. Inaugurated in 1961, CTV reaches about 95 percent of Canadian television households and transmits over sixty-six hours of programming per week. One popular program is "A.M. Canada," an early-morning information show. CTV entertainment features such shows as "Stars on Ice," which reflects the popularity of ice skating in Canada and the appetite of the Canadian viewer for everything from hockey to ice ballet.

Comparable in many ways to PBS in the U.S., the Canadian Broadcasting Corporation (CBC) is Canada's government-owned public broadcasting service. Although the CBC reports to Parliament through a designated cabinet minister, the responsibility for its programs and policies lies with its own directors and officers. CBC is financed by public funds and by advertising. Several national services are operated by the CBC, including French-language and English-language television, AM, and FM-stereo networks and radio broadcasts to the Indian and Inuit peoples of the north. Programs represent a wide range of tastes and can be received by 99 percent of the Canadian population. Typical of CBC cultural presentations is the all-Canadian production of *Madame Butterfly* seen on the French-language network. Radio Canada International is CBC's overseas service. Headquartered in Montreal, it broadcasts in eleven languages and distributes programs throughout the world.

In addition to the CTV and CBC networks, the Canadian Association of Broadcasters has a program-exchange service for its members. Despite its huge land mass, Canada has managed a coordinated policy of broadcast development that uses the latest technology to reach the diverse Canadian population.

Mexico

Along with Mexico's government stations and government-supported television networks, privately owned radio and television networks crisscross the country. A federation of four coordinated television channels 2, 4, 5, and 8 called Televisa serves most of Mexico. To some degree the channels represent an attempt to reach more specialized audiences in Mexico. Channel 2's signals, for example, cover most of Mexico and are received by a predominantly middle-class viewing audience. Its programming includes state-produced programs for young children, such as a Mexican version of "Sesame Street" titled "Plaza Sesamo," soap operas, the Mexican version of "Today," weekend sports events, and family entertainment programs. Channel 4 covers metropolitan Mexico City and the immediately surrounding area. Aimed at the mass urban public, it programs specials on Mexico City's neighborhoods and regularly televises block parties. Evening programs feature films, amateur hours, and variety artists.

Channels 5 and 8 are geared to younger, better-educated Mexicans. Channel 5's signals reach about half the population of the country via a series of repeater stations, which receive and retransmit the signal. Channel 5's target audience is the youthful middle class, including university students. Programs on current issues are featured, as are American, British, and Japanese programs. Approximately thirty hours of national productions are also seen. Reaching about ten million viewers in the urban valley of Mexico, channel 8 produces many cultural programs. Academic groups and people with differing political beliefs make up its target audience. Much of Mexico's programming consists of performances by recognized artists, award-winning international films, and international productions.

The United Kingdom

Although North America enjoyed the fruits of Marconi's labor, Europe saw the seeds of his achievements in communication germinate much earlier. Perhaps nowhere was the impact of the new medium felt more than in the United Kingdom, whose naval vessels, merchant fleet, Post Office Department, high-powered stations linking continents, and British Marconi Company all used it from its inception. Two systems of broadcasting have grown out of the wireless in the U.K.: The BBC and the Independent Broadcasting Authority (IBA). Whereas the BBC is a government supported public system of broadcasting, the IBA is the United Kingdom's commercial service.

The BBC Radio programming is disseminated throughout the United Kingdom by four domestic networks. BBC-1 and BBC-2 are the popular formats. BBC-1 is more progressive and BBC-2 attracts a more general audience. Together they capture about 80 percent of Britain's listening audience. They provide news and information, and BBC-2 presents shipping forecasts. BBC-3, on the other hand, programs more classical music as well as dramatic and cultural programs. Live concerts, both in Britain and in other countries, are emphasized. Masterpieces of world theater and discussions of scientific and philosophical subjects round out BBC-3's programs. BBC-4 is devoted to speeches, news and information programming, dramatic entertainment, and current events. "Today," "The World at One," PM Reports," "The World in Focus," and "The World Tonight" are typical of its extended magazine-type news programs. Phone-in programs, panel games, plays, and readings are also heard on BBC-4. Together these four national networks complement the local radio stations, which serve small geographic areas.

Although radio continues to be the foundation of the BBC, television does not take a back seat. Experimental television was launched in 1936. Suspended during the Second World War, it went back on the air in 1946. Today, two BBC television networks serve nearly the entire United Kingdom. Over 80 percent of the programs are produced by the BBC; the remainder come from independent producers and other countries. As in the domestic radio system, television is financed by license fees collected from owners of receiving sets. Although the licensing-fee system brings in income, economic difficulties can cause severe inflation and cutbacks in the overall operation of BBC television.

The IBA The IBA operates Independent Television (ITV) and Independent Local Radio (ILR) (Figure 15–4). A commercial broadcasting system, IBA was created by Parliament in 1954 to broadcast side by side with the BBC. Its sole income is from advertising. Commercials are aired between programs, not in the middle of them. IBA's structure was amended by the Independent Broadcasting Authority Act of 1973. IBA supervises a developing system of local radio outlets and fifteen television production companies. Operating much like American television stations, the production companies serve different regions of the United Kingdom. IBA also monitors the quality of the programs carried by its radio and television stations.

The production companies, although supporting themselves by regional advertising, receive their assignments from the IBA, which also operates their transmitters and receives a percentage of their income in return. Like the BBC, the IBA is free to sell its programs to other countries. At home, it has the authority to assign time to such specific programs as education, news, religious broadcasts, and documentaries. The nature and amount of advertising are controlled by the IBA in keeping with the mandate of the 1973 legislation. Other guidelines are provided by the IBA's Code of Advertising Standards and Practice. Television advertising is limited to an average of six minutes an hour, and radio advertising approximately nine minutes each hour. Like the BBC, the IBA is advised by a group of quasi-citizen-quasi-governmental committees on advertising, medicine, religion, education, local radio, and other operations.

The Broadcasting Act of 1980 added a new channel to British television, Channel 4. Channel 4 is operated under the authority of the IBA and is specifically designed to provide an alternative to British television programming seen on ITV stations. Its revenue comes from the IBA in a somewhat unusual shared arrangement with ITV. In effect, Channel 4 and ITN share revenue generated by both channels. Channel 4's charge under

FIGURE 15-4 Independent Local Radio operates throughout the United Kingdom. It operates under the auspices of the Independent Broadcasting Authority created by Parliament in 1954. (IBA)

the 1980 Act is to provide programming with "innovation in form and content." Channel 4 does not produce its own programs but instead chooses them from other suppliers both in and out of the United Kingdom. Emphasis on educational and international programming brings programs which could be likened to American continuing education programs and foreign programming addressing multi-national audiences in Britain.

Subjects such as psychology, history, gardening, sex, and retirement are part of Channel 4's programming as are foreign films in their original language presentations. The cultural heritage of the Irish, Cypriots, Poles, and other nationalities living in the United Kingdom are reflected in the mission of Channel 4. The service operates under a Channel 4 board picked by the IBA. In addition, a Welsh Fourth Channel Authority oversees a Welsh-language television service in Wales.

Australia

Radio Services The Australian radio system is a battle for audience listenership. The Australian Broadcasting Commission operates the government radio system, which is called the National System. Responsible to Parliament, the ABC controls fifty transmitters scattered throughout the continent. The National System consists of two major networks. One services local and regional areas and the other is nationwide. License fees, supplemented by government subsidies, help finance the system. Programming has emphasized cultural entertainment and classical music. Concerts by world-recognized musicians have been popular. Since these concerts are often held in large Australian cities, an admission charge helps defray their cost.

Australia also has a comprehensive commercial broadcasting system. Its service areas are more limited, but it can sell advertising throughout Australia. Commercial stations, partly because they must depend on local advertisers, orient their programming to their own locale. As in the United States, commercial stations compete directly with each other as well as with the government stations. A voluntary code of ethics, similar to the code of the National Association of Broadcasters in the United States, helps control the content of Australian broadcasting and acts as a buffer to increased government control. Australia also has public stations, similar to those in the United States, that are supported by subscription, universities, and organizations.

Television As with radio, there are two systems of television in Australia: the government-supported system and the private commercial system. More than fifty government stations are in operation compared with just under fifty commercial stations. Government stations come under the ABC jurisdiction; commercial stations are part of the Federation of Commercial Television Stations (FACTS). Drama, public-interest programs, and sports make up the majority of government television programs. About 60 percent of the government programs are produced by the ABC, 12 percent by the BBC, 7 percent by other United Kingdom and Commonwealth countries, and 21 percent by the United States and other overseas countries. The most popular programs on commercial television include "Number 96," an adult serial drama; news and weather; theater; "Disneyland"; and "Matlock Police," a drama series.

Japan

Nippon Hōsō Kyōkai Correspondent, critic, and network executive Sander Vanocur has called Japan's governmental broadcasting service, Nippon Hōsō Kyōkai (NHK), the best he has ever seen, and ranks it above the BBC. To many Japanese, NHK means television. Financed by license fees, the system provides a blend of information and both Japanese and Western cultural programming (Figure 15–5). Operating two television channels, one for education and the other for information and entertainment, and three radio networks, NHK reaches every corner of the country.

FIGURE 15–5 NHK is financed by license fees and includes both Japanese and Western cultural programming. (NHK)

Commercial Service Following the end of World War II, the democratization of Japan, and the introduction of television technology, the important 1950 Broadcast Law recognized private commercial broadcasting as a competitor of NHK. NHK (Figure 15–6) and the commercial companies operate over six thousand radio and televi-

FIGURE 15–6 One of the control centers of NHK television. (NHK)

sion stations covering even Japan's mountainous terrain. The public has a wide choice of programming. Tokyo, for example, has the two NHK television networks, five commercial television stations, four commercial radio stations, and the three NHK radio networks.[5] There are approximately fifty commercial companies in radio and eighty-five in television programming. With Japan's interest in high technology and with a well-supported government broadcasting system competing with a commercial system, the future for broadcasting in this nation is particularly bright.

FRANCE'S DIVERSIFIED SYSTEM

France has one of the most diversified broadcasting systems in the world.[6] Ranging from government-controlled to citizen-access channels, the seven-part system consists of four independent program societies and three support societies, all formed by the reorganization of French broadcasting in 1974. The first of the program societies is Télévision Français 1 (TF1), which has been operating since 1948. It most closely resembles pre-1974 French broadcasting when the Office de Radiodiffusion-Television Française (ORTF) operated it. The second program society is Antenna 2 (A2), created in 1964; it has a UHF color channel. Third is the French regional radio and television service, France-Regions 3 (FR3), which allows the public considerable access and fosters the widest latitude of public opinion. Fourth is Radio France, under whose auspices all of French broadcasting is organized. The three support societies are the Société Française de Production et de Creation Audiovisuelles (SFP), which is responsible for program production; Télédiffusion de France (TDG), responsible for transmis-

sion services; and the Institute Nationale de l'Audiovisuel (INA), responsible for auxiliary services such as research, technical training, and archives. The system is supported mainly by listener fees and, on TF1 and A2, by advertising.

Because the reorganization was greatly influenced by French politics, it is only natural that there are varying opinions of the system's effectiveness. Critics generally agree, however, that there is less government control of the system now than before and that there are more opportunities to present diverse programming and political views.

THE OPEN-DOOR SYSTEM OF THE NETHERLANDS

The four domestic radio services and two television services of the Netherlands are almost unique in the world of broadcasting. The radio services—Hilversum 1, 2, 3, and 4—program everything from news to radio drama, and mostly in stereo. The television services—Netherland 1 and 2—broadcast about eighty hours a week, mostly in color and mostly at night. What is unique about these services is that they will give organizations air time if they qualify for it by proving they have substantial membership and support. Approximately thirty organizations have qualified for broadcasting time on the radio and television services. Some 70 percent of all programming is used by these qualified organizations; the remaining time is devoted to programs jointly produced by the television service and the organizations as well as educational services.

To be granted air time, Dutch citizens must fulfill certain requirements defined in the Broadcasting Act. An organization must claim at least 40,000 Dutch citizens who are its members or who support its aims. The organization is then given the status of *candidate broadcasting organization* by the Ministry of Culture, Recreation, and Social Welfare, the body governing broadcasting. The candidacy period is used mostly to recruit new members, since the organization's membership must reach 100,000 within two years, or it loses permission to broadcast. There are three categories of qualified organizations—A, B, and C—each permitted different amounts of air time. Which category an organization falls into is determined by the size of its membership. Along with air time comes the right to publish program guides. Despite exercising what may seem like arbitrary controls, the Dutch government cannot censor any of a qualified organization's programming, whose content is determined solely by the organization.

The system is financed both by advertising and receiver license fees. Every Dutch citizen who owns a radio or television must pay an annual fee. Joint programming is permitted and even encouraged between organizations. The Netherlands Broadcasting Foundation (NOS) coordinates the activities of the approximately thirty qualified organizations.

REGIONAL DIVERSITY: SCANDINAVIA

In Northwest Europe lies the land of the midnight sun—Scandinavia, which comprises Iceland, Sweden, Denmark, Finland, and Norway. Their proximity to one another illustrates how in some cases countries that share borders may still have diverse political backgrounds within which broadcasting developed.

Icelandic broadcasting is controlled by the Icelandic State Broadcasting Service, which derives its income from receiver-

license fees and advertising. Television was introduced into the country in 1966. The U.S. Armed Services Radio and Television Service also provides programming for Iceland.

Sweden's broadcasting is controlled exclusively by a national broadcasting corporation, Sveriges Radio. Although the government has ultimate control over the size of the radio and television budget assigned to the corporation, it does not control programming. The Radio Act of 1967 forbids public authorities and agencies to examine programs before they are aired. But the government does have indirect control, as it appoints the chairman of a board of governors that has final authority over the operation of Sveriges Radio.

There are three radio networks in Sweden, the earliest dating from 1925. The second and third networks began service in 1955 and 1962. All three share a variety of programming: Program 1 (P1) airs mostly talk and informational programs; Program 2 (P2) broadcasts classical music; and Program 3 (P3) broadcasts mostly light music interspersed with regional and national news. All are financed by receiver-license fees, as is Swedish television.

Television and overseas broadcasting also come under the jurisdiction of Sveriges Radio. Introduced in 1957, two television networks currently serve the country—TV1 and TV2. In a somewhat unusual arrangement, the two, even though part of the same system of broadcasting, compete with each other. Overseas broadcasts are conducted by Radio Sweden and reach four continents via short-wave transmissions. Programs are broadcast in English, German, French, Spanish, Portuguese, Russian, and Swedish.

The chief regulatory body in Sweden, comparable in some ways to the FCC, is the Swedish Radio Council. This seven-member body has the authority to examine programs already broadcast and to resolve complaints made by organizations and individuals. At the same time, a group of chief program editors have final authority over all programs and can be held personally responsible for any libel action that might be taken. Sveriges Radio, on the other hand, cannot be prosecuted for libel.

Denmark's broadcasting system is somewhat similar to Sweden's. Danmarks Radio is a public corporation funded entirely by receiver-license fees. Advertising is prohibited. Through a series of transmitters located across the country, the corporation operates three radio program services. Danmarks Radio also has a television service. A radio council comprising twenty-seven members represents the listeners and viewers. Reporting to the Minister of Cultural Affairs, the council is responsible for carrying out the provisions of the Radio and Television Broadcasting Act of 1973, the most recent major broadcast legislation. The Voice of Denmark has a regularly scheduled overseas broadcast.

Experimental broadcasting began in Finland in 1923. In 1926 regular service began with the formation of a public radio company. A year later, legislation placed broadcasting under the Ministry of Communications. Today, all radio and television is controlled by a state monopoly called Yleisradio (YLE). Two networks cover the country's heartland, and a third covers the coastal regions. Radio broadcasting, which is conducted in Swedish and Finnish, is financed entirely by receiver-license fees. The External Service aims its programs at three groups: English-language listeners, Finns living in North America, and Finns at sea.

Finnish television started in 1955 at the Technical University and began limited service on January 1, 1958, with a dedication broadcast by former president Urho Kekkonen (Figure 15-7). A second channel was added in 1964. Revenue is gained from license fees and from advertising, which is sold by Mainos-TV (MTV), a private company that rents time from YLE. Founded in 1957, MTV transmits its own programs on

FIGURE 15-7 President Urho Kekkonen's New Year's speech on January 1, 1958 initiated YLE's regular TV broadcasts in Finland. (YLE)

both television channels. Commercials are transmitted in groups of two to three minutes at the end of and at natural breaks in the programs. The agreement between YLE and MTV has certain restrictions, such as the prohibition of political programs and the unnecessary use of children in commercials.[7]

In Norway, radio and television are operated by a government-owned company, the Norwegian Broadcasting Corporation. Advertising is prohibited and the system is financed by license fees paid by registered listeners. Started in 1923, the Norwegian broadcasting system consists of a single radio and television network, the programming of which consists largely of educational and cultural fare.

AN AUTHORITARIAN SYSTEM: THE USSR

Soviet broadcasting is controlled by an arm of the state—the Union Republic State Committee of the USSR Council of Ministers.[8] Income is derived from the state budget and from the sale of programs, announcements, and public concerts. Approximately 60 million television sets are in use, or about 98 for every 100 families. The Molina satellites help relay programming to the Pacific coast and Central Asia. Central operations are housed in the Moscow TV Center Tower Building, which is higher than the Empire State Building and has full production facilities for everything from small-studio to large-auditorium productions. Color television using the Soviet-French SECAM system is seen in many areas of the USSR.

The government operates four television networks. Channel 1 serves all of the Soviet Union. Moscow and the immediate area are served by Channel II. Channel III is an edu-

cational channel, and Channel IV carries drama, music, film, and literary programs. Typical programs seen on Soviet television are "Time," a half-hour news program; "The 13 Chairs Tavern," a musical satire; and "Come on, Boys," an audience-participation show for boxers, wrestlers, weightlifters, and motorcycle racers. Programs are broadcast in the sixty-six different languages of the various Soviet nationalities.

Soviet radio broadcasts are heard in sixty different languages and received by approximately 65 million radio sets. The Home Service of Radio Moscow has four networks. Channel I, like its television counterpart, is heard throughout the country and broadcasts news, commentary, drama, music, and children's programming. News and music are heard on Channel II, the former every half hour. Literary programs and drama are presented on Channel III, and Channel IV concentrates on FM musical broadcasting. FM stereo can currently be heard in twenty-six major Soviet cities. Furthermore, there are three different channels of cable radio, which reach about four hundred Soviet communities.

PROXIMITY AND POLITICAL CONTRAST: WEST GERMANY AND EAST GERMANY

Both proximity, as illustrated by the Scandinavian countries, and authoritarianism, as exemplified by broadcasting in the USSR are considerations in a comparison of West German and East German broadcasting. West German broadcasting includes radio, television, and a highly developed cable system. Radio broadcasting is coordinated by the ARD, a federal organization made up of nine members of the Land public broadcasting corporations. Two radio organizations, DLF and DW, are operated by the government and engage mainly in international broadcasting. The Land broadcasting stations all exchange programs with one another. They also engage in television broadcasting, as does the ZDF, which broadcasts both separately and jointly with ARD's Land stations. Receiver-license fees, government grants, and advertising provide income for broadcasting in West Germany.

East German radio is controlled by the State Broadcasting Committee of the Council of Ministers. Four radio networks are in operation. Television is controlled by the State Television Committee of the Council of Ministers. Broadcast income is obtained from receiver-license fees. Interestingly, although East Germany has banned most West German printed media, it cannot ban West German television. Thus, instead of watching East German television, which many consider rather dull, East Germans often watch West German signals, which are easily received across the border.[9]

MAINTAINING CULTURAL INTEGRITY: THE CANADIAN EXAMPLE

Broadcast signals can strain friendly relations between nations when they cross national boundaries and impose upon the viewers and listeners of one country the culture of another. Add to this the economic issues inherent in a commercial broadcasting system and we can see why a policy to "safeguard, enrich, and strengthen the cultural, political, social and economic fabric of Canada" has opened up a series of electronic confrontations between the United States and Canada, some involving high-ranking diplomats from the two countries.[10] For example, Canada has clamped down not only on American advertising that reaches Canadian audiences but also on Canadian firms buying advertising on American media. When Canada decided to stop permitting Canadian businesses to claim tax deductions for expenditures on advertising in American media, the National Association of Broadcasters in the U.S. protested vigorously, and then Secretary of State Henry Kissinger became involved. Both Canadian and American cable companies import the other country's signals, and Canada has moved further to delete American commercials from Canadian cable. Although these actions may seem arbitrary, the problems lie in preserving national interests. Nevertheless, Canadians have no control over what American media send into Canada and vice versa. Broadcasting signals simply do not honor national boundaries.

Programs containing violence that are imported from the United States are a major worry to Canadians. Some Canadians have claimed that American program suppliers dump violence-filled cartoons on Canada that cannot be aired in the United States. Citing French, Mexican, and Swedish limitations on the importation of programs containing violence, some Canadian politicians suggest that Canada follow the same course. As a start, the American detective program "Cannon" was struck from the CBC television lineup. Violence in television is a popular topic of the politically and socially aware in Canada. Much of their attention has been focused on the Ontario Royal Commission on Violence which amassed from throughout the world approximately 2,500 studies of violence in the communications industry that purport to show a relationship between crime and the portrayal of violence in the media. Whatever the results of the Canadian debate, violence in the media will remain as important an issue in Canada as it is in the United States.

RACIAL AND CULTURAL DIVERSITY: THE REPUBLIC OF SOUTH AFRICA

The Republic of South Africa has a fully developed broadcasting system. Controlled by the South African Broadcasting Corporation (SABC), the system currently provides both radio and color-television services programmed in two languages for the white population and seven African languages for the Bantu peoples. The South African Railways launched the first broadcast transmissions in July 1924, and these signaled the beginning of three separate broadcasting services. Three years later the three services were consolidated into the African Broadcasting Company (ABC).

Financial problems beset the consolidated service, which limped along until 1936, when legislation responding to a study group's recommendations formed the SABC. The English-speaking descendants of the British and the Afrikaans-speaking descendants of the Dutch—the Afrikaners (once known as the Boers)—shared equal control of the SABC until World War II, when they split along political and philosophical lines. The Afrikaners had been a rural minority having virtually no representation in early broadcasting save for an-hour-per-week service provided by the heavily British ABC. Their resentment lasted until the legislation creating the SABC called for an equal number of programs in English and in Afrikaans. However, equal numbers did not always mean equal political content, and the Afrikaners began to complain about the political bias of programs, about being forced to report statements issued by the ruling English, and about the required oath of loyalty to the SABC.

World War II brought two important changes. First, many of the English-speaking staff of the SABC went abroad to fight for the Allied cause, leaving behind a majority of Afrikaners. Second, the Afrikaner Nationalist party won the 1948 elections and an opportunity to regain a strong voice in the affairs of the SABC. In any event, because control of the SABC has traditionally been restricted to the English and the Afrikaners, the black-white struggle is publicized more from the standpoint of the whites. Moreover, that struggle is influenced heavily by the political issues embodied in the earlier struggles between the two groups.

The SABC retains control of South Africa's broadcasting, including private radio which represents both white factions. The SABC is headquartered in Johannesburg in one of the most lavish broadcasting complexes in the world. A huge office complex and production facilities overlook a giant broadcasting tower nearby, which houses the SABC antennas. Radio is heard throughout the country over the English service, the Afrikaans service, regional commercial services, Radio Bantu, and the Voice of South Africa, which is beamed to twenty-three different areas of the world.

Because of the country's mountainous terrain and sparse population, television arrived late in South Africa. Approved by the government in 1971, a one-channel service devoting equal time to English and Afrikaans broadcasts began in 1976. Four mobile units—one in Cape Town, one in Durban, and two in Johannesburg—provide supplementary programs.

EDUCATIONAL RADIO IN DEVELOPING NATIONS

Many developing nations are reassessing the importance of education to their systematic growth. Understanding a common language, participating in political processes, and providing local government leadership all require a literate populace. For most countries, however, this renewed emphasis on education has been a painful and deliberate process. Many nations lack the funds to train a national teacher corps. Others find it difficult to find qualified personnel who are both sensitive to their cultural heritage and acceptable to local communities. As a result, these nations have turned to the media for help, often using foreign-aid dollars to defray the cost. To understand how broadcasting has helped the growth of education in these developing nations, we shall examine radio.

Emile G. McAnany has categorized radio's role in development into five strategies.[11] The first is open broadcasting to the unorganized audience—in other words, broadcasts to the general population. For example, the people of Zaire hear the voice of "Dr. Massikita" bringing them information on feeding newborn children or on nutrition. Other African countries have instituted similar health and agricultural programs, which are usually repeated in different languages. Latin American programming strategies also follow this broadcasting pattern.

A second strategy is the use of instructional radio with organized learning groups. Here radio is used as a substitute teacher. Australian children often receive broadcast lessons in remote rural settings, far from a traditional classroom. In Tanzania, instructional radio teaches basic skills by correspondence. Around the globe in Thailand, radio beams music, social studies, and English courses to the populace. In Sudan, instructional radio teaches Arabic, tribal history, and etiquette.

A third strategy is the use of rural forums broadcast to decision groups. These programs offer information on rural news, answers to listeners' questions, or a discus-sion or lecture topic. Listeners get together in groups, listen to the broadcasts, and then are guided through a dialogue on the subject by a discussion leader. Countries using this approach, among others, are Ghana and India. McAnany uses Benin, a small country in western Africa, to illustrate this strategy. There, ten to thirty villagers gather to listen and discuss the programs, which are broadcast in ten native languages at different times during the week. A group discussion leader called an *animateur* is chosen from the village to lead the dialogue. This person then sends a monthly report to the production center, which may be used as feedback in the production of future programs. A second person called an *encadreur* serves as a technical resource for the village, providing guidance for any projects that result from the discussions.

Another strategy is the use of radio schools with nonformal learning groups. These audiences are made up mostly of illiterate rural adults, so the programming consists of basic training in reading, writing, and figuring. Nations adopting this strategy often use a multimedia approach that combines radio, newspapers, filmstrips, booklets, and charts.

McAnany's fifth strategy is the use of radio animation with a participating group. Although participation may at first seem like a rural forum or a radio school, it is not. Radio's chief contribution here is to identify and define community problems rather than to provide solutions. Discussion leaders then promote dialogue among community members that is geared to solving these problems.

The future of educational radio in developing nations is brighter than that of educational television. A television receiver can in some ways be more intrusive than a radio receiver, especially in areas unaccustomed to new technology. Moreover, many mountainous areas cannot receive television signals, and radio is the only alternative. Radio also lets local discussion leaders maintain their identity, unchallenged by a visual commentator.

SUMMARY

This chapter has examined the structure and programming of broadcasting systems outside the United States.

External services reach different international audiences with multi-language broadcasts. The BBC reaches over one hundred countries with an average of five hundred television programs per week. BBC radio is exported through both direct-broadcast and transcription services. Switzerland operates an extensive European and overseas service through direct-broadcast and transcription systems that mail programs to over three hundred stations throughout the world. Radio Moscow programs in sixty-four languages on such subjects as life in the USSR and Soviet views on international issues. Radio Austrialia's overseas broadcasting pays special attention to Southeast Asia and Chinese refugees. The United States reaches overseas audiences through Voice of America and the USICA.

Regulatory frameworks are not the same from country to country. In Canada broadcasting falls under the jurisdiction of the Canadian Radio and Television Commission. In Mexico regulation of broadcasting is diversified among several government agencies.

Many countries operate a mixture of government and private broadcasting systems. Canada's CTV Television Network competes for the same audience as Canadian Broadcasting Corporation stations. Other mixed systems are found in Mexico; the United Kingdom, where the BBC and the Independent Broadcasting Authority compete; and Australia, where the stations o. ... Australian Broadcasting System share the audience with the Federation of Commercial Television Stations. Japan also operates both commercial and government-owned stations.

France operates a diversified broadcasting system. In the open-door system of the Netherlands, qualified organizations are permitted air time without the threat of censorship. Regional diversity is found among the Scandinavian countries of Iceland, Sweden, Denmark, Finland, and Norway.

The USSR maintains an authoritarian system of broadcasting: all programming is controlled by the state. A similar system operates in East Germany. West German broadcasting is coordinated by the ARD, a federal organization consisting of nine members of the *Land* public broadcasting corporations.

Canada's desire to retain cultural integrity in its programming has resulted in a communication policy designed to "safeguard, enrich, and strengthen the cultural, political, social and economic fabric of Canada." The Republic of South Africa's broadcasting system must be sensitive to both cultural and racial differences.

Radio plays an important part in developing nations. Strategies for using radio in developing nations include open broadcasts to unorganized audiences, instructional radio beamed to organized learning groups, rural forums broadcast to decision groups, radio schools serving nonformal learning groups, and radio animation involving participating groups.

OPPORTUNITIES
FOR FURTHER LEARNING

ADAMS, W. C., ed., *Television Coverage of the Middle East*. Norwood, N.J.: Ablex, 1981.

ALISKY, M., *Latin American Media: Guidance and Censorship.* Ames: Iowa State University Press, 1981.

ATWOOD, L. E., S. J. BULLION, and S. M. MURPHY, *International Perspectives on News.* Carbondale: Southern Illinois University Press, 1982.

BOKONGA, B. E., *Communication Policies in Zaire.* Paris: Unesco, 1980.

BOYD, D. A., *Broadcasting in the Arab World: A Survey of Radio and Television in the Middle East.* Philadelphia: Temple University Press, 1982.

BROWNE, D. R., *International Radio Broadcasting: The Limits of the Limitless Medium.* New York: Praeger, 1982.

BURCHFIELD, R., *The Spoken Word: A BBC Guide.* New York: Oxford University Press, 1982.

CLIPPINGER, J. H., *Who Gains by Communications Development? Studies of Information Technologies in Developing Countries.* Cambridge, Mass.: Harvard Program on Information Resources Policy, 1976.

CRANE, R. J., *The Politics of International Standards: France and the Color TV War.* Norwood, N.J.: Ablex, 1979.

DUA, M. R., *Programming Potential of Indian Television: With Special Reference to Education, Economic Growth, and Social Change.* New Delhi: Communication Publications, 1979.

EDELSTEIN, A. S., ed., *Information: Comparing the Japanese and American Experiences.* Seattle: International Communication Center, School of Communication, University of Washington, 1979.

GALNOOR, I., *Steering the Polity: Communications and Politics in Israel.* Beverly Hills, Calif.: Sage, 1982.

GANLEY, O. H., *The Role of Communications and Information Resources in Canada.* Cambridge, Mass.: Harvard Program on Information Resources Policy, 1979.

——, *The United States-Canadian Communications and Information Resources Relationship and Its Possible Significance for Worldwide Diplomacy.* Cambridge, Mass.: Harvard University Program on Information Resources Policy, 1980.

HARTIKAINEN, R., *Local Radio: An Examination of the Concept of Local Radio.* Helsinki: Finnish Broadcasting Company, 1981.

HEDEBRO, G., *Communications and Social Change in Developing Nations: A Critical View.* Ames: Iowa State University Press, 1982.

HINDLEY, P., G. McMARTIN, and J. McNULTY, *The Tangled Net: Basic Issues in Canadian Communications.* Vancouver: J. J. Douglas, 1977.

HOWKINS, J., with A. BRIGGS, *Mass Communication in China.* New York: Longman, 1982.

HUGHES, P., *British Broadcasting: Programmes and Power.* Bromley, Kent: Chartwell-Bratt, 1981.

KATZ, E., and G. WEDELL, *Broadcasting in the Third World: Promise and Performance.* Cambridge, Mass.: Harvard University Press, 1977.

LENDVAI, P., *The Bureaucracy of Truth: How Communist Governments Manage the Russian Public.* New York: Praeger, 1981.

MATTOS, S., *The Impact of the 1964 Revolution on Brazilian Television.* San Antonio: V. Klingensmith, 1982.

McANYNY, E. G., *Radio's Role in Development: Five Strategies of Use.* Washington, D.C.: Academy for Educational Development, 1973.

——, ed., *Communications in the Rural Third World: The Role of Information in Development.* New York: Praeger, 1980.

McCAVITT, W. E., *Broadcasting Around the World.* Blue Ridge Summit, Pa.: Tab Books, 1981.

McPHAIL, T. L., *Electronic Colonialism: The Future of International Broadcasting and Communication.* Beverly Hills, Calif.: Sage, 1981.

NORDENSTRENG, K., and H. I. SCHILLER, eds., *National Sovereignty and International Communication.* Norwood, N.J.: Ablex, 1979.

PAULU, B., *Television and Radio in the United Kingdom.* Minneapolis: University of Minnesota Press, 1981.

ROBINSON, G. J., *News Agencies and World News in Canada, the United States and Yugoslavia: Methods and Data.* Fribourg, Switzerland: University Press of Fribourg, 1981.

SANFORD, J., *The Mass Media of the German Speaking Countries*. Ames: Iowa State University Press, 1976.

SCHRAMM, W., and E. ATWOOD, *Circulation of News in the Third World: A Study of Asia*. Seattle: University of Washington Press, 1981.

SCHRAMM, W., L. M. NELSON, and M. T. BETHAM, *Bold Experiment: The Story of Educational Television in American Samoa*. Stanford, Calif.: Stanford University Press, 1981.

SMYTHE, D. W., *Dependency Road: Communications, Capitalism, Consciousness, and Canada*. Norwood, N.J.: Ablex, 1981.

SORAMAKI, M., *New Communications Technology, Households and Finland: An Overview*. Helsinki: Planning and Research Department, Yleisradio, 1982.

TAN, A., ed., *Mass Communications in the Third World*. Norwood, N.J.: Ablex, 1983.

Television and Artistic Patrimony. Rome: Edizioni RAI Radiotelevisione Italina, 1982.

THOMAS, R., *Broadcasting and Democracy in France*. Philadelphia: Temple University Press, 1976.

TROYER, W., *The Sound and the Fury: An Anecdotal History of Canadian Broadcasting*. Rexdale, Ont.: John Wiley, 1980.

TRUEMAN, P., *Smoke and Mirrors: The Inside Story of Television News in Canada*. Toronto: McClelland & Stewart, 1980.

TURBAYNE, D., eds., *The Media and Politics in Australia*. Tasmania: University of Tasmania, 1980.

UNESCO, *World Communications*. New York: Unipub, 1975.

WILLIAMS, A., *Broadcasting and Democracy in Western Germany*. Philadelphia: Temple University Press, 1976.

ZARRY, P. T., and R. D. WILSON, eds., *Advertising in Canada: Its Theory and Practice*. Toronto: McGray-Hill Ryerson, 1981.

16

EARLY ATTEMPTS AT GOVERNMENT CONTROL

By the second decade of the twentieth century, the British Marconi Company had built a well-developed worldwide corporate empire. Ships were comfortable with wireless and had demonstrated its effectiveness in numerous cruises. Experimental radio stations were popping up everywhere, and ham-radio operators were toying with a hobby that would soon became a major social influence. As we learned in Chapter 4, in the 1920s some of the historical giants of broadcasting took to the air—WHA at the University of Wisconsin, KDKA in Pittsburgh, WBZ in Springfield/Boston, Chicago's WGN, and WWJ in Detroit. The public was being entertained with Big Ten football, live orchestras, election-night fervor, and presidential speeches, but its enjoy-

ment of radio was being inhibited by higher-powered stations, interference, and rampant competition. There simply was not enough room on the electromagnetic spectrum for everyone to jump on without someone being pushed off.

The government first became concerned about radio's impact when Marconi started prohibiting ships and shore stations from communicating with each other unless they were equipped with Marconi equipment. This may seem incredible by today's standards, but Marconi managed to get away with it for some time. Germany was especially affected by Marconi's antics, since it housed the competing Slaby-Arco system. The Germans finally took the initiative and called a conference in Berlin in 1903, at which a protocol agreement was reached on international cooperation in wireless communication. Three years later Berlin hosted the first International Radiotelegraph Convention, at which an agreement was signed by twenty-seven nations. In the United States the stage was now set for domestic legislation that would embody the spirit of the Berlin agreement and foster safety and cooperation among American shipping interests. It is with this 1910 legislation that we'll begin a study of the development of government involvement in broadcasting.

THE WIRELESS SHIP ACT OF 1910

In 1910 there were few visions of commercial broadcasting stations as we know them today. Transatlantic experiments were less than a decade old, and Congress was think-

ing only about the safety applications of the new medium, especially to ships at sea. Some ships, although by no means all, had installed wireless apparatus (Figure 16–1). It was in this atmosphere that the Wireless Ship Act of 1910 was passed.[1] Containing only four paragraphs, it set the stage for maritime communication. Among other provisions, the act made it illegal for a ship carrying more than fifty persons not to be equipped with radio communication. The equipment had to be in good working order and under the direction of a skilled operator. The range of the radio had to be at least one hundred miles, day or night. Exempted from the provisions were steamers traveling between ports less than two hundred miles apart.

The act also specified that the "master of the vessel" see that the apparatus could communicate with both shore stations and other

FIGURE 16–1   Early wireless room showing Marconi equipment aboard the Lusitania. (The Marconi Company Limited, Marconi House, Chelmsford, Essex)

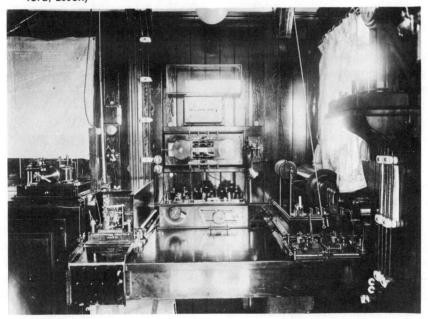

ships. Violations meant a $5,000 fine, and a vessel could be fined for every infraction of the law and cited in the district court having jurisdiction over the port where the ship arrived or departed. Enforcement of the law was clear: "The Secretary of Commerce and Labor shall make such regulations as may be necessary to secure the proper execution of this Act by collectors of customs and other officers of government."

THE RADIO ACT OF 1912

By 1912 wireless had achieved international recognition and cooperation. Yet the United States had been lax in participating in agreements with other nations to control wireless, partially because in the United States wireless was not under total government control as it was in some other countries. That all changed on an April night in 1912 when an iceberg took the American ship *Titanic* to the bottom of the North Atlantic. The following days and months were filled with news of the sinking and of the role of wireless in the event. Reports focused on everything from how shipboard wireless operators might have prevented the sinking to the brilliant performance of the medium in relaying news of survivors. Ironically, four months before the tragedy the provisions of the 1906 Berlin treaty had been taken out of congressional mothballs for discussion in Senate committees. Those discussions, hastened by the sinking of the *Titanic,* led to the passage in August 1912 of a second Radio Act.

The Radio Act of 1912 was much more comprehensive than the 1910 legislation. It defined authority between federal and state governments and established call letters for government stations. The law did not claim to regulate intrastate communication: "No-

thing in this Act shall be construed to apply to the transmission and exchange of radiograms or signals between points situated in the same State." Along with providing clauses for revocation of licenses and fines for violators, it established the assignment of frequencies: the license of each station would "state the wave length or the wave lengths authorized for use by the station for the prevention of interference and the hours for which the station is licensed to work." In addition to these specified wavelengths, however, stations could still use "other sending wave lengths." Licenses were to be granted by the secretary of commerce and labor "upon application thereof." The president of the United States was given the power to control stations during wartime but had to compensate the station's owners when doing so. The act also established the famous SOS distress signal and allowed it to be broadcast with a maximum of interference and radiation. It was required to reach at least one hundred miles. Moreover, it was the first time an act of Congress had defined *radio communications:* "any system of electrical communication by telegraphy or telephony without the aid of any wire connecting the points from and at which the radiograms, signals, or other communications are sent or received." Other provisions of the act included secrecy-of-message restrictions designed to protect government stations' signals, rules for ship-to-shore communication, and a ban on any station refusing to receive messages from stations not equipped with apparatus manufactured by a certain company.[2]

Even though it was passed specifically in reaction to the sinking of the *Titanic,* the 1912 act was a valiant effort to control wireless communication. But few legislators could have foreseen the huge popularity of wireless, and even if they had, legislative processes could not have begun to keep up with the new technology. It was not long before the regulatory framework began to crumble.

The National Radio Conferences: The 1912 Law in Trouble

By 1917 both the United States and radio were involved in World War I. For the U.S. Navy, this meant hurried construction of wireless towers on board warships (Figure 16–2). Having taken over the country's radio stations, the government stopped all radio developments except those designed for wartime service. But the end of the war was like the uncapping of a bottle. All the

FIGURE 16–2 Wireless tower aboard a U.S. Navy ship passing near New York City's Manhattan Bridge prior to World War I. (U.S. Navy)

pent-up enthusiasm for the new technology of radio was released, and experimenters flocked eagerly to their equipment. Although the Radio Act of 1912 survived the war, it was headed for rough sailing in a radio industry exploding with popularity and technology. By the 1920s chaos reigned. In 1922 alone, receiving-set sales climbed 1,200 percent. The airwaves were flooded with everything from marine military operations to thousands of amateur-radio experimenters. Added to this was the advent of commercial radio and its powerful stations booming onto the air.

On February 27, 1922, groups of government officials, amateur-radio operators, and commercial-radio representatives met for the First National Radio Conference in Washington, D.C.[3] The conference was addressed by representatives of all the opposing factions. Amateur-radio operators were afraid their privileges were going to be curtailed under the influence of such large commerical firms as General Electric and Westinghouse. The large commercial firms were afraid their privileges were going to be delegated to the military. After the rhetoric subsided the conference split into three committees: amateur, technical, and legislative. Since interference was still the biggest problem, it was not surprising that the technical committee's recommendations received the most attention. Based on that report, legislation was introduced in Congress in 1923, but it never emerged from a Senate committee.

The second conference began on March 20, 1923. This one reaffirmed the problems of interference and recommended discretion in frequency allocations. Taking into account the commercial interests of the new medium, the conference suggested that allowing more stations on the air would only aggravate the young industry's already shaky financial condition. By today's standards of competition among almost eight thousand stations, that proposal seems inappropriate. Realizing that different geographical areas had different problems, the second conference suggested splitting up the country into zones, each of which would tackle its own problems locally. As he had after the first conference, Congressman Wallace White of Maine introduced legislation, but again it did not budge from committee.

Deafening interference still characterized the airwaves when the Third National Radio Conference convened on October 6, 1924. Two major developments captured the attention of the delegates. Network broadcasting had become a reality. AT&T's wire system and Westinghouse's short-wave system were proving interstation connection was not only possible but also potentially successful. Almost simultaneously, David Sarnoff announced RCA was going to experiment with the concept of superpower stations crisscrossing the country. It is little wonder that the third conference recommended resolutions opposing monopoly and even encouraged government intervention. Nevertheless, the conference supported the development of network broadcasting. But although it agreed to let the superpower experiments proceed, it warned that they "should only be permitted under strict government scrutiny."[4] At the request of Secretary Hoover, (Figure 16–3), Congressman White refrained from introducing legislation. A third defeat would have been bad

FIGURE 16–3 Herbert Hoover served as the Secretary of Commerce and Labor and later as President of the United States. Perhaps more than any other government official, he was responsible for dealing with the regulatory issues surrounding radio's growth during the late teens and 1920s. (AT&T)

politically, and so the decision was made to wait until still another conference was called.

Convening on November 11, 1925, the Fourth National Radio Conference ended with proposals that became the foundation of the Radio Act of 1927. This conference suggested a system of station classifications and admonished Congress to pass some workable broadcasting legislation. The delegates recommended preventing monopoly, installing five-year terms for licenses, requiring stations to operate in the public interest, providing for licenses to be revoked, and giving the secretary of commerce the power to enforce regulations. They also wanted to guard against government censorship of programming, provide for due process of law, give the president control of stations in wartime, and prevent broadcasting from being considered a public utility. But the good intentions were too late.

Judicial Setbacks for the Radio Act of 1912

Despite the radio conferences' valiant efforts to make the Radio Act of 1912 workable, two lawsuits and an opinion from the United States attorney general made it clear that the law was in serious trouble. Highlighting the problem in 1923 was *Hoover* v. *Intercity Radio Co., Inc.* Intercity had been engaged in telegraph communication between New York and other points under a license issued by the secretary of commerce and labor. Upon its expiration, Intercity applied for a renewal but was denied because there was no space available on the spectrum for a frequency assignment that would not interfere with government and private stations.

The issue went to court, and the judges ruled that the secretary had overstepped his bounds in refusing to renew Intercity's license. Cited as justification was a statement by the chairman of the Committee on Commerce when the bill was passed that "it is compulsory with the Secretary of Commerce and Labor that upon application, these licenses shall be issued." The court ruling meant that the secretary of commerce and labor, although having the power to place restrictions on licenses and to prevent interference, could not refuse to issue a license as a means of reducing that interference. The court stated that "in the present case, the duty of naming a wavelength is mandatory upon the Secretary. The only discretionary act is in selecting a wavelength within the limitations prescribed in the statute, which, in his judgment, will result in the least possible interference." The court went on to define the relationship between the restrictions and the license: "The issuing of a license is not dependent upon the fixing of a wavelength. It is a restriction entering into the license. The wavelength named by the Secretary merely measures the extent of the privilege granted to the licensee."[5]

For Secretary of Commerce Hoover the ruling was extremely frustrating. Broadcasting had progressed beyond the experimental and military stages. The secretary was faced with regulating a limited resource, and the court was telling him that he had to give some to everyone who wanted it. The 1912 act had given the secretary broad responsibilities, but not the power to implement them.

This was only the first of Hoover's setbacks. Three years later came the case of *United States* v. *Zenith Radio Corporation et al.* Zenith had received a license authorizing it to operate on a "wavelength of 332.4 meters on Thursday night from 10 to 12 P.M. when the use of this period is not desired by the General Electric Company's Denver station.'' Zenith clashed with the secretary when it operated at other times and on another, unauthorized frequency. Yet the court ruled in favor of Zenith. The legal catch was a section of the 1912 law reading: ''In addition to the normal sending wavelength, all stations may use other sending wavelengths.''[6]

The crowning blow came when Acting Secretary of Commerce Stephen Davis denied a request from the Chicago Federation of Labor for a license.[7] Before the application even reached Washington Davis wrote the federation telling it that all the wavelengths were in use, and that even if the federation constructed a station there would be no license forthcoming. Davis put the blame on the Fourth National Radio Conference, but it did not belong there since the conference did not have the power to dictate policy.

Some politicians became concerned over the deterioration of the radio industry and the stations continued to interfere with each other. Finally, the Office of the Secretary of Commerce sought an opinion from the attorney general. In a letter dated June 4, 1926, the secretary asked the attorney general for a definition of the secretary's power. The questions in the letter, as restated by the attorney general, were these:

1. Does the 1912 Act require broadcasting stations to obtain licenses, and is the operation of such a station without a license an offense under that Act?
2. Has the Secretary of Commerce authority under the 1912 Act to assign wavelengths and times of operation and limit the power of stations?
3. Has a station, whose license stipulates a wavelength for its use, the right to use any other wavelength, and if it does operate on a different wavelength, is it in violation of the law and does it become subject to the penalties of the Act?

4. If a station, whose license stipulates a period during which only the station may operate and limits its power, transmits at different times, or with excessive power, is it in violation of the Act and does it become subject to the penalties of the Act?
5. Has the Secretary of Commerce power to fix the duration of the licenses which he issues or should they be indeterminate, continuing in effect until revoked or until Congress otherwise provides?[8]

The attorney general's answers made it clear that the problems were going to get worse, not better. The answer to the first question was affirmative. The act definitely provided for stations to be licensed, and stations operating without a license were clearly in violation. To the second question the attorney general replied that the secretary of commerce had the right to assign a wavelength to each station under one provision of the act, but for the most part the stations could use whatever other frequency they desired, whenever they wanted. The attorney general also stated that with the exception of two minor provisions, the secretary had no power to designate hours of operation. Also lost was the contention that a station's license limited its power. The act stated that stations should use ''the minimum amount of energy necessary to carry out any communication desired.'' The attorney general said, ''It does not appear that the Secretary is given power to determine in advance what this minimum amount shall be for every case; and I therefore conclude that you have no authority to insert such a determination as a part of any license.''

The third answer was obvious: stations could use any other wavelength they desired. The act and the courts had confirmed that. That answer in turn settled question four. Since the secretary could not limit a station only to the power and operating time stipulated in its license, stations were free to use other wavelengths, power outputs, and times. Finally the attorney general replied to the fifth question that he could "find no authority in the Act for the issuance of licenses of limited duration."

Clearly a law that only a decade earlier had seemed firmly in control of the new medium was now almost worthless. Four months later, on December 7, 1926, President Coolidge called on Congress for legislation that would remedy the chaos that threatened to destroy radio broadcasting.[9] The next day he signed a joint resolution of Congress placing a freeze on broadcasting until more specific legislation could be passed.

THE RADIO ACT OF 1927

Congress had been working on the Radio Act of 1927 before Coolidge's message. The act passed both houses and received the president's signature on February 23, 1927. The Radio Act of 1927 was administered by the secretary of commerce and provided for the formation of a Federal Radio Commission (FRC) that would oversee broadcasting. The act was intended to remain in force for only a year, but was subsequently extended until 1934. With court decisions to guide them, Congress did an admirable job of plugging the holes left by the 1912 law.

The formation of the FRC was the most important provision of the 1927 act. It was to be "composed of five commissioners appointed by the President, by and with the advice and consent of the Senate, and one of whom the President shall designate as chairman."[10] The law specified that each commissioner be a citizen of the United States and receive compensation of $10,000 for the first year of service. The commissioner system, as

well as many other provisions of the 1927 legislation, became part of the Communications Act of 1934.

Other provisions in the 1927 act divided the United States into zones represented by individual commissioners. No more than one commissioner could be appointed from any one zone. One zone covered New England and the upper tip of the Middle Atlantic states and included the District of Columbia, Puerto Rico, and the Virgin Islands. The second zone included the upper Middle Atlantic states west to Michigan and Kentucky. The third zone covered the South, and the fourth and fifth zones the Great Plains and the West, respectively.

The act provided for the licensing of stations, but only for a specified time, and gave the government considerable control over the electromagnetic spectrum. The act also set out to define states' rights in regard to communication. Keep in mind that federal regulation of intrastate commerce, for which wireless was used, was not popular. So it was not surprising that the Radio Act of 1927 tried to avoid direct control of intrastate communication while retaining control of communication crossing state borders. The act stated that the law's jurisdiction would extend "within any State when the effects of such use extend beyond the borders of said State." The most quoted provision was the statement in Section 4 that stations should operate "as public convenience, interest, or necessity requires."

Section 4 also prescribed "the nature of the service to be rendered by each class of licensed station and each station within any class." Control over frequency, power, and times of operation was covered by the act, which gave the FRC the power to "assign bands or frequencies or wavelengths to the various classes of stations, and assign frequencies or wavelengths for each individual station and determine the power which each station shall use and the time during which it may operate.'' Coverage areas for stations were to be fixed by the FRC, and the commission was to have power over ''chain'' or network broadcasting. Stations were also required to keep operating logs.

In addition to regulating the industry, the 1927 act gave the commission ''the authority to hold hearings, summon witnesses, administer oaths, compel the production of books, documents, and papers and to make such investigations as may be necessary in the performance of its duties.'' The secretary of commerce was empowered ''to prescribe the qualifications of station operators, to classify them according to the duties to be performed, to fix the forms of such licenses, and to issue them to such persons as he finds qualified.'' He was also given the authority to issue call letters to all stations and to ''publish'' the call letters. But before issuing a license, the government made certain that the prospective licensee gave up all rights ''to the use of any particular frequency or wavelength.'' Once granted, station licenses were limited to three years.

To close the wavelength loophole of the 1912 legislation, the 1927 law stated that ''the station license shall not vest in the licensee any right to operate the station nor any right in the use of the frequencies or wavelength designated in the license beyond the term thereof nor in any other manner than authorized therein.'' The act also discouraged monopolies and prohibited the transfer of licenses without the commission's approval. Furthermore, it empowered the commission to revoke the licenses of stations that ''issue[d] false statements or fail[ed] to operate substantially as set forth in the license.''

The wording of the famous Section 315 of the Communications Act of 1934 came from the 1927 legislation: ''If any licensee shall permit any person who is a legally qualified candidate for any public office to use a broadcasting station, he shall afford equal opportunities to all other such candidates for that office.'' Commercial broadcasting for its part gained instant recognition and regulation with the requirement that paid commercials were to be announced as having been paid or furnished by the sponsor.

Putting a station on the air was governed by another important provision of the act. Specifically, the act stated that ''no license shall be issued under the authority of this Act for the operation of any station, the construction of which is begun or is continued after this Act takes effect, unless a permit for its construction has been granted by the licensing authority upon written application thereof.'' The law acknowledged that construction permits for stations would specify ''the earliest and latest dates between which the actual operation of such station is expected to begin, and shall provide that said permit will be automatically forfeited if the station is not ready for operation within the time specified.''

An anticensorship provision, later to become incorporated into Section 326 of the Communications Act of 1934, was also included. Ironically, that provision was immediately followed by the statement that ''no person within the jurisdiction of the United States shall utter any obscene, indecent, or profane language by means of radio communication.''

We can see immediately the conflicts that could develop not only between these two provisions but also in the ''convenience, interest, and necessity'' clause. It was not long before the broadcasters and the government were indeed arguing. Yet keep in mind that the 1927 law was the very foundation of contemporary regulation of broadcasting. It was simple and straightforward, and the courts gave it strong support.

From 1927 to 1934 the Radio Act of 1927 withstood challenges from all sides. It achieved the ability to regulate effectively the expanding medium of "wireless," which now blanketed the nation with entertainment and news programming envisioned by few of the 1910 pioneer regulators. It is little surprise that the 1927 law was liberally quoted in the Communications Act of 1934, the law governing contemporary broadcasting.

THE COMMUNICATIONS ACT OF 1934

This law removed broadcasting from the supervision of the department of commerce and gave it separate status under an independent agency of government. It had become clear that broadcasting needed a new, more comprehensive regulatory agency. The FRC was still limited in scope, having to share responsibilities with the department of commerce. Although the department had at one time been an appropriate home, public consumption of radio was now tending to overshadow radio's commercial uses. Although commercial stations would still far outnumber those directing their signals to the public, guarding the public's convenience, interest, and necessity was no small task.

After examining a number of proposals to coordinate regulation, President Franklin D. Roosevelt sent to Congress on February 26, 1934, a proposal for a separate agency known as the Federal Communications Commission. Roosevelt told Congress that the FCC should be invested with the authority "now lying in the Federal Radio Commission and with such authority over communications as now lies with the Interstate Commerce Commission—the services affected to be all of those which rely on wires, cables, or radio as a medium of transmission."[11]

Congress responded within five months by passing the Communications Act of 1934. With it came the Federal Communications Commission, which was eventually to reign over everything from citizen's-band radios to satellite communication, from intrastate to international communication. The scope of the FCC had already been hammered out in court challenges to the 1927 law. In fact, much of the 1927 law was left intact in the act of 1934, including the guiding phrase "public convenience, interest, or necessity," which was retained as a nebulous but very powerful concept.[12] There were a few minor changes in wording. "Wavelength" was changed to "frequency," and whereas the 1927 law was concerned with "wireless communication," the FCC was to govern both wire and wireless.

As with most laws, the 1934 legislation has been amended many times.

SUMMARY

This chapter traces the government's role in early broadcasting. The Wireless Ship Act of 1910 was an outgrowth of the international radio conferences held in Berlin in 1903 and 1906. It provided early safeguards for ships at sea, requiring them to be equipped with radio apparatus that could communicate with other ships and shore stations. Violations meant possible fines and court proceedings. The Radio Act of 1912 expanded the 1910 legislation but could not even begin to deal with radio's explosive growth in the 1920s. Four National Radio Conferences discussed how to bring the new medium under government control in a way that was acceptable to the industry yet permitted the orderly use of the spectrum. The combination of these conferences and two landmark court cases that threatened the legality of the 1912 legislation generated enough support in Congress for passage of the Radio Act of 1927. This act created the Federal Radio Commission, which was renewed on a year-to-year basis while it fought a series of court battles to affirm its control over radio. The Communications Act of 1934 established the Federal Communications Commission, an independent government agency.

OPPORTUNITIES
FOR FURTHER LEARNING

BENSMAN, M. R., "Regulation of Broadcasting by the Department of Commerce, 1921–1927," in *American Broadcasting: A Source Book on the History of Radio and Television,* ed. Lawrence W. Lichty and Malachi C. Topping, pp. 544–55. New York: Hastings House, Publishers, 1975.

DAVIS, W. J., "The Radio Act of 1927," *Virginia Law Review,* (June 1927), 616–618.

GEOFFREY, M., *The Maiden Voyage.* New York: Viking, 1969.

JAMESON, K. C., *The Influence of the United States Court of Appeals for the District of Columbia on Federal Policy in Broadcast Regulation, 1929–1971.* New York: Arno Press, 1979.

KAHN, F. J., ed., *Documents of American Broadcasting.* Englewood Cliffs, N.J.: Prentice-Hall, Inc., 1984.

LE DUC, D. R., and T. A. McCAIN, "The Federal Radio Commission in Federal Court: Origins of Broadcasting Regulatory Doctrines," *Journal of Broadcasting,* 14(Fall 1970), 393–410.

McMAHON, R. S., *Federal Regulation of the Radio and Television Broadcast Industry in the United States, 1927–1959.* New York: Arno Press, 1979.

MIDDLETON, K. and R. M. MERSKY, compilers, *Freedom of Expression: A Collection of Best Writings.* Buffalo, N.Y.: William S. Hein & Co., 1981.

MUELLER, M., *Property Rights in Radio Communication: The Key to the Reform of Telecommunications Regulation.* Washington, D.C.: Cato Institute, 1982.

SARNO, E. F., Jr., "The National Radio Conferences," *Journal of Broadcasting,* 13(Spring 1969), 189–202.

STERN, R. H., "Regulatory Influences Upon Television's Development: Early Years Under the Federal Radio Commission,"

The Radio Act of 1912, Public Law 264, 62d Congress, August 13, 1912.

The Radio Act of 1927, Public Law 632, 69th Congress, February 23, 1927.

The Wireless Ship Act of 1910, Public Law 262, 61st Congress, June 24, 1910.

WALTER, L., *A Night to Remember.* New York: Henry Holt & Company, 1955.

THE FEDERAL COMMUNICATIONS COMMISSION AND ALLIED AGENCIES

Few government agencies have had such a direct effect on the public as the Federal Communications Commission. Nearly everything we watch on television and hear on radio is in some way touched by the FCC's control over broadcasting stations, cable, satellites, even the telephone systems. A descendant of the Federal Radio Commission, the FCC is an independent agency accountable directly to Congress. In this chapter we'll learn about the jurisdiction of the FCC, how it conducts business, its organization, its enforcement powers, and current criticism of its actions.

We will also examine other agencies of government which affect broadcasting and telecommunication. Included in our discussion will be the Federal Trade Commission (FTC), the National Telecommunications and Information Administration (NTIA), the Office of Technology Assessment (OTA), and the United Nations-based International Telecommunication Union (ITU).

PRIMARY RESPONSIBILITIES

The FCC's thirteen areas of responsibility are:

1. The orderly development and operation of broadcast services and the providing of rapid, efficient nationwide and worldwide telephone and telegraph service at reasonable rates.
2. The promoting of safety of life and property through radio, and the use of radio and

television facilities to strengthen national defense.

3. Consultation with other Government agencies and departments on national and international matters involving wire and radio communications, and with State regulatory commissions on telephone and telegraph matters.

4. Regulation of all broadcast services—commercial and educational AM, FM, and TV. This includes approval of all applications for construction permits and licenses for these services, assignment of frequencies, establishment of operating power, designation of call signs, and inspection and regulation of the use of transmitting equipment.

5. Review of station performance to assure that promises made when a license is issued have been carried out.

6. Evaluation of stations' performance in meeting the requirement that they operate in the public interest, convenience, and necessity.

7. Approval of changes in ownership and major technical alterations.

8. Regulation of cable television. . . .

9. Action on requests for mergers and on applications for construction of facilities and changes in service.

10. The prescribing and reviewing of accounting practices.

11. Issuance of licenses to, and regulation of, all forms of two-way radio, including ship and aviation communications, a wide range of public safety and business services, and amateur and citizens radio services.

12. Responsibility for domestic administration of the telecommunications provisions of treaties and international agreements. Under the auspices of the State Department, the Commission takes part in international communications conferences.

13. Supervision of the Emergency Broadcast System (EBS), which is designed to alert and instruct the public in matters of national and civil defense.[1]

As we can see, the commission's functions cover much more than just radio and television. Telephone, telegraph, and cable are all within the FCC's jurisdiction, as are applications of communication to public safety, transportation, industry, amateur radio, and citizen service. The regulation of some of these services is shared with other government agencies, such as local municipalities in the case of cable. A television station in New York City and a CB radio in Wyoming are both within the FCC's domain. This domain stretches beyond the fifty states into Guam, Puerto Rico, and the Virgin Islands.

WHAT THE FCC DOES NOT CONTROL

It is equally important to understand what the FCC *does not* have jurisdiction over.[2] Many people—especially consumers unhappy about something they have seen or heard on local radio or television—perceive the FCC as having broad powers of regulation. In fact, we have learned that the commission has very little control over the content of broadcasts. With the exception of obscene and indecent programming—and even that is vaguely defined—lotteries and deceptive advertising are the only areas the FCC can regulate without infringing on First Amendment rights. Even when it does act in these areas, a court battle over those rights is bound to arise.

Nor can the FCC tell a station when to air a program or when to run commercials or public-service announcements. The FCC will not substitute its judgment for that of the local broadcaster in those areas. Although some network contracts prohibit editing of certain programs, that is a matter solely between the network and the station. Despite the nonediting clauses, the licensee retains control over local programming and the right to delete the network's entire offering if it feels that it would not be in the local public interest to air it.

Although lotteries are forbidden, the FCC has little jurisdiction over legitimate contests, and especially the awarding of prizes. If a station has a contest and you win a prize that for some reason does not satisfy you, the best recourse would be to deal directly with the station or the manufacturer of the prize. The FCC would not have the authority to tell the manufacturer to give you a different prize or to help you obtain repairs for a defective item. Similarly, although stations broadcast a variety of sporting events, the FCC has no jurisdiction over the promoters or organizers of those events. If your favorite boxer fails to appear on the local televised Golden Gloves championship, you can write the boxing commission, but the FCC will not be able to help you.

The commission does not have any jurisdiction over countries whose radio or television signals cross into the United States. Although there are reciprocal international agreements on the use of the electromagnetic spectrum, the consumer in Michigan who complains to the FCC about a Canadian radio station would receive little satisfaction. A listener in southern California complaining to the FCC about a station in Mexico would experience similar frustration. An exception would be if the Canadian or Mexican station were operating off its frequency and interfering with American stations, but even in this case the FCC would go through the regulatory agencies in Canada and Mexico in order to solve the problem.

The FCC also has no jurisdiction over news-gathering organizations, either local or national.[3] Press associations, such as United Press International, Associated Press, and Reuters, are independent of the broadcast stations they serve and are not regulated by the FCC. To the extent that such organizations use radio frequencies or satellites to transmit information, the FCC does have jurisdiction, but only over technical operations. The commission does not directly control the networks but does control network-owned broadcasting stations. Music-rights organizations, such as ASCAP, BMI, and SESAC, are independent bodies not involved in activities that the commission controls. They directly serve stations and collect royalties from them for airing performers' works. Audience-measurement firms such as Nielsen and Arbitron are also independent of the FCC, although a station's fraudulent use of audience ratings would reflect on the licensee's commitment to serve the public interest and could consequently draw the attention of the commission.

The commission has instituted rules governing the simulcasting of programs on AM and FM stations owned by the same company, but it has no authority to tell a radio station to broadcast in stereo or quadraphonic sound or a television station to broadcast a program in color. Although the FCC can act in the public interest to question overcommercialization of radio and television, it does not have the specific authority to tell a station to air so many commercials per hour. Likewise, the commission views public-service programming as a condition for renewing a station's license, but it has no authority to tell the station what public-service programming to air. If a licensee chooses to air public service announcements for the Red Cross instead of for the American Cancer Society, that is its prerogative. The exception to this would be if the announcement concerned a controversial issue. Then, because of the Fairness Doctrine (see Chapter 18), the commission would want to ensure that the station aired a balanced presentation of the issue through whatever type of programming it chose.

The occurrence of libel or slander during a radio or television broadcast is another area over which the FCC has no jurisdiction. If you feel you have been libeled or slandered (both terms sometimes apply to a speech that is broadcast, and therefore considered published), your best recourse would be to consult an attorney, not the FCC. The FCC even shies away from this matter in renewing licenses. In fact, when defamation did become an issue in a license renewal, the FCC stated that

> it is the judgment of the Commission, as it has been the judgment of those who drafted our Constitution and of the overwhelming majority of our legislators and judges over the years, that the public interest is best served by permitting the expression of any views that do not involve, quoting from Supreme Court decisions, "a clear and present danger of serious substantive evil that rises far above public inconvenience, annoyance or unrest.". . . This principle insures that the most diverse and opposing opinions will be expressed, many of which may be even highly offensive to those officials who thus protect the rights of others to free speech. If there is to be free speech, it must be free for speech that we abhor and hate as well as for speech that we find tolerable or congenial.[4]

Once again we see the First Amendment rising to protect free speech, even when that free speech is unpopular. Programs containing derogatory comments about sex, race, or religious beliefs also enjoy the protection of the First Amendment. Ethnic humor on such shows as "Sanford and Son" and "All in the Family" may offend some people, but any attempt to control this area of programming would clearly fall outside the FCC's jurisdiction.

DECISION MAKING AT THE FCC

The commissioners hold weekly meetings and executive sessions in which they oversee commission activities. Their meetings are open to the public, a procedure started in 1977 under a congressional mandate.[5] Closed meetings can be called by a majority vote of the commission. They may also be scheduled when the parties involved in an FCC decision request that the meeting be closed. Closed meetings usually deal with matters of national defense, manufacturer's trade secrets, or criminal matters.

Meeting Agenda

A typical FCC agenda is classified so as to reflect the organization of the commission.[6] The various items on the agenda are grouped into general categories such as *hearing, general, safety and special, common carrier, personnel, classified, CATV, assignment and transfer, renewals, aural, television, broadcast,* and *complaints and compliance.* The commission deals with these agenda items usually after it has heard a series of briefings by the appropriate FCC bureaus and offices.

In a *hearing,* the FCC acts as the final tribunal when someone appeals a decision made by an FCC administrative law judge or, in some cases, by the FCC Review Board. The *general* category covers items not included in the other categories. For example, a representative from another federal agency might discuss the FCC's compliance with that agency's rules. *Safety and special* deals with the application of broadcast communication to such areas as fire-department, taxicab, and police-department radios. Other industrial applications would be the business use of mobile radios, citizens-band radio, and amateur (ham) services. The next category on the agenda, *common carrier,* concerns the FCC's regulation of telephone and telegraph systems. Here, the commission acts as a quasi-public utility on issues concerning microwave and satellite systems, among others. Next comes *personnel.* FCC staffing matters and promotion and appointments come under this category. Promotions are generally routine, since three other FCC officers—the bureau chief, personnel chief, and executive director—have usually approved the promotions before they reach the seven commissioners.[7]

National security, manufacturer's trade secrets, and other classified matters fall into the *classified* category. *Cable* is next on the agenda. Approval of a new linkup between two cable systems, mergers of cable companies, difficulties a community might be having with a franchise or rate structure, and matters concerning a public-access channel can be taken up here. If you buy or sell a radio station, the transaction will be approved or rejected during the next order of business, *assignment and transfer.* The commission's deliberations may dwell upon previous inquiries into the transaction, which may have arisen in a hearing or in recommendations made by the administrative law judge. If a group of stations is seeking to acquire more broadcasting properties, the discussion might focus on the possibly powerful influence of a single owner of multiple broadcast properties and whether the public interest would be served by approval of such a sale.[8] The transfer of licenses would first have to be approved during this order of business.[9] If you already own a station, the process of renewing it will be acted upon during the next agenda category, *renewal.* Most of the renewals reaching the commissioner level are contested renewals. Uncontested renewals are usually approved at the staff level.

If you are applying for permission to start a new radio or television station, a decision will be made on your application during either the *aural* or *television* agenda categories. Altering the service your station is already licensed to provide will also be acted upon at this time. If your station is on the air and for some reason wishes to seek a waiver of FCC rules, your request will be considered during the next category on the agenda, *broadcast.* For example, a network may request a waiver of the prime-time-access rule so that it can offer a special sports program. Or a station operating in an area in which there is already one network affiliate may request permission to affiliate with the same network.[10] Rule violations are considered during the *complaints and compliance* category. A station that has seriously violated FCC rules, complaints about the Fairness Doctrine, and fraudulent operating practices would all be considered at this time. It goes without saying that not every violation is discussed by the entire commission. However, when an alleged violator feels there has been an injustice, then the case could reach this level.

Commissioner Influence on Regulatory Policy

As researchers Lawrence Lichty and Wenmouth Williams, Jr.,[11] have noted, individual commissioners can help shape regulatory policy. It is not surprising that during the early years of the Federal Radio Commission the commissioners, four of whom were trained in law, were comfortable in the atmosphere of the frequent court challenges to the FRC's early decisions. That the FRC added a legal division one year after it was formed demonstrates the importance that the commissioners placed on not only fighting but also winning those challenges.

The FCC carried on this tradition when it began its six-year trust-busting campaign in 1939, breaking up networks and setting up rules for chain broadcasting. Two FCC chairmen, Frank R. McNich and James L. Fly, led the fight and weathered appeals that claimed the regulations were unconstitutional. McNich had served on the Federal Power Commission and was a lawyer; Fly had headed the legal department of the Tennessee Valley Authority and taken charge of judicial proceedings defending TVA's constitutionality.

The growth of television was also influenced by the attitudes of the FCC. Williams found that during the Kennedy administration the commission advocated strict regulation. Newton Minow set the pace with his "vast wasteland" speech and was joined by liberal Democrats E. William Henry and Kenneth A. Cox. The Kennedy years also saw the FCC pass nonduplication rules governing simulcasting on AM and FM and bring cable under its regulatory um-

brella. President Nixon's appointment of Benjamin Hooks emphasized the importance of minorities to broadcasting. The chairmanship of Richard Wiley under presidents Nixon, Ford, and Carter was characterized by attempts, many of them successful, to streamline FCC decision making. Chairman Charles Ferris tended to support deregulation of radio and criticize children's television programming. In February 1981 Ferris was replaced by veteran commissioner Robert E. Lee, who served as interim chairman until an official appointment was made by the Reagan administration. The new chairman was Mark Fowler, a Washington, D.C., communications attorney who also supported deregulation.

COMMISSIONERS

Now that we have a basic understanding of how the FCC functions, we will examine its organization. At the top of the commission

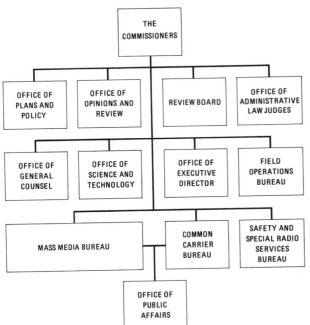

FIGURE 17-1 Organization chart of the Federal Communications Commission. The Commission is headed by five commissioners appointed by the President of the United States.

(Figure 17–1) hierarchy are five commissioners, one of whom is a chairperson. Appointed by the president of the United States and confirmed by the Senate, commissioners are prohibited from having a financial interest in any of the industries they regulate. This prohibition applies even to industries that are only partially FCC-regulated businesses, such as parent corporations which may own broadcasting stations in addition to publishing companies. Appointees who fill the unexpired term of a commissioner may or may not be reappointed when that term expires.

FCC OFFICES

Directly under the commissioners are seven offices. Let's examine each in turn.[12]

Office of Plans and Policy

This office is responsible for developing long-range policy decisions for industries coming under FCC jurisdiction. It also assesses the policy implications of FCC decisions, providing policy analyses and recommendations to the commission staff and coordinating policy research. The chief of the Office of Plans and Policy recommends budgets and priorities to the commission policy-research program and functions as the central account manager for all contractual research studies funded by the FCC.

Office of Opinions and Review

When the FCC makes a major decision, the document outlining that decision is written with the assistance of the Office of Opinions and Reviews. This office serves as the commission's legal staff, advising it on procedural matters, researching judicial precedent, and overseeing hearings ordered by the commission. The office then recommends action to the commission based on the evidence presented by the parties involved.

Office of Administrative Law Judges

This office is the first ladder in the appeals process. The administrative law judges preside over hearings and make initial decisions. It is not unusual for their decisions to be appealed. When there are two applicants for a broadcast license, both have a major investment at stake and a ruling in favor of one will prompt the other to continue the appeals process.

Review Board

The Review Board is the second step in the FCC appellate process, above the administrative law judges and below the commissioners. It is made up of senior-level employees of the commission. In some cases, the decisions of the administrative law judges are reversed by the Review Board and then restored by the five commissioners. This is a reflection not so much on the ability of the judges to adhere to judicial procedure as on the desire of the offended to exhaust every administrative possibility. In special cases, initial decisions can even be reviewed directly by the commissioners. If, for example, a renewal decision goes against a licensee, the licensee can appeal to the Review Board. Individual FCC bureaus can also appeal to the Review Board. If, for instance, a bureau rules against a licensee and an administrative law judge rules in the licensee's favor, then the bureau can appeal to the Review Board. If the ruling still goes against the bureau, or the licensee for that matter, that party can appeal the ruling to the commissioners, who as a body choose which cases to accept for review. The five commissioners are the last appeals step before the matter goes to a federal court of appeals.

Office of the General Counsel

This office contains the commission's attorney, who represents it before the courts. The office helps prepare legislative programs supported by the commission and works closely with the attorney general and the Justice Department in cases that entail prosecution or in which jurisdiction extends beyond FCC boundaries. For example, if a person steals radio equipment and then uses it to broadcast illegally, both the Justice Department and the FCC would become involved. The Office of the General Counsel also works closely with the Office of Opinions and Review, since the decisions written by the latter may be the basis for the former's defense of the commission in court.

Office of the Chief Scientist

This is the top "technical" office within the commission. All of the policies associated with administering the electromagnetic spectrum are developed here. The staff of the office, about half of whom are engineers, consider such matters as the appropriate number of stations in a given market, equipment testing and certification, frequency allocations and modifications, and requests for increases in power output. The Office of the Chief Scientist operates a Laboratory Division in Laurel, Maryland. Here, new equipment is tested against FCC specifications. For example, manufacturers of radio and television transmitters must first receive authorization before they can sell them for broadcast use. The commission usually uses the technical data submitted by the manufacturer as a basis for its authorization, but on occasion it spot-checks equipment in order to verify the test data. Citizens-band radios, for example, are tested at the laboratory.[13] With the help of this testing, the FCC issues approximately one thousand authorizations per year for a wide range of equipment. The office also works with other organizations that test new equipment and its applicability to broadcasting.

Office of Executive Director

Although the commissioners are the highest-ranking officers of the FCC, the FCC executive director coordinates the overall operation of the commission. The position is somewhat analogous to that of a city manager, who runs a municipality even though the city council is the highest level in the administrative hierarchy. The executive director coordinates the activities of the different staff units, including the personnel division, the internal review and security division, the financial management division, and the public information officer.[14]

FCC BUREAUS

The decisions made by the FCC offices are implemented by the FCC bureaus, which perform the day-to-day administration of the thousands of broadcast stations and licensees. There are four bureaus: the Safety and Special Radio Services Bureau, the Field Operations Bureau, the Mass Media Bureau created in 1982 by a merger of the Broadcast and Cable Television Bureaus, and the Common Carrier Bureau. The bureaus concerned most directly with broadcasting are the Mass Media and Field Operations bureaus.

Assuming control over radio and television stations and cable systems is the Mass Media Bureau. The bureau comprises four divisions. The audio service division consists of three branches, which are responsible for AM, auxiliary services, and FM. A data-management staff and the public reference room are assigned to this division. The video services division has four branches, responsible for cable, distribution services, low-power television, and standard television. The division processes applications for new television services and for modifications of existing facilities. Such technologies as low-power TV, direct-broadcast satellites, and cable antenna-relay systems are authorized to operate by this division. The enforcement division consists of a complaints branch; an equal-opportunity-employment branch; a fairness/political-broadcast branch, which considers issues related to the Fairness Doctrine and Section 315 of the Communications Act of 1934; and an investigations branch. The policy and rules division consists of an allocations branch, a legal branch, a policy-analysis branch, and a technical and international branch. The division was formerly part of the Broadcast Bureau.

The Field Operations Bureau maintains a number of field offices in the larger cities across the United States, as well as mobile monitoring stations in specially equipped vans. Special investigative teams are assigned to make on-location inspections of stations, and a separate unit concentrates solely on CB-radio violators. The field offices are also placed where the public can get information about the FCC and the communications industry. In addition, this bureau is responsible for administering FCC license examinations.

The Field Operations Bureau maintains sophisticated equipment that can trace a signal and pinpoint its location. It can thus catch illegal CB transmitters and amateur stations and even "pirate" broadcasting stations operating on frequencies assigned to commercial AM and FM radio stations. Those detected operating an illegal station will be raided by the FCC and U.S. marshals, and their equipment seized as evidence.

The Field Operations Bureau has four divisions. The Field Enforcement Division directs field-enforcement programs, including the monitoring and inspecting of stations. It also conducts investigations. The Regional Services Division directs the FCC's public-service programs, such as radio-operator licensing. Responsibility for receiving and processing enforcement reports, such as violation files and investigations, lies with the Violations Division. The Engineering Division is responsible for constructing the field facilities and providing engineering support and equipment specifications for them.[15]

The Common Carrier Bureau oversees such areas as telephone and telegraph, and the Safety and Special Radio Services Bureau supervises such areas as aviation and marine communication. In addition to the FCC's seven offices and four bureaus, an Office of Public Affairs directs liaison between the commission and the public.

ENFORCEMENT POWER

The Communications Act of 1934 specified that violators of its provisions would be penalized, and the commission has at its disposal a number of enforcement measures. Depending on the type of violation, the commission may take one of the following actions: a simple letter, a cease-and-desist order, a forfeiture (fine), a short-term license renewal, a license revocation, or a denial of renewal.

Letters

Letters are usually used in less serious matters or in cases in which the FCC accepts assurance the violation will stop instead of imposing a forfeiture. Letters can be used to reprimand stations for incomplete community-needs and ascertainment surveys, failures of programming to meet Fairness Doctrine requirements, or improper submission or failure to submit required FCC documents, such as employment reports or exhibits for a license-renewal application. The letters are not always a reprimand. In the case of license renewal, for example, they state that renewal is being withheld pending receipt of the required exhibit, and that after a certain date the license will be forfeited.

Cease-and-Desist Orders

Cease-and-desist orders are rare, partly because of the effectiveness of the commission's forfeitures and other sanctions. In one case a minister asked the FCC to issue a cease-and-desist order prohibiting a station from dropping a religious program. The FCC declined to issue the order, citing the anticensorship provision of the Communications Act, although it confirmed it had the authority to do so.[16] On the other hand, the commission issued a cease-and-desist order to an AM station for broadcasting off-color remarks.[17]

Forfeitures

The most common sanction imposed on a station is a forfeiture, usually for a technical-rule violation or the more serious offense of fraudulent billing (the latter can also set the stage for a license revocation). The forfeitures vary, not only with the violation but also with the ability of the station to pay. They can rise as high as $10,000 for serious violations by major-market stations. The following partial list of liabilities, announced during a single week of commission activity, contains typical forfeiture notices for alleged violations:

Broadcast Bureau ordered licensee to forfeit $250 for failing to calibrate remote ammeters to indicate within 2% of regular meter.

Broadcast Bureau ordered licensee to forfeit $1,000 for failing to maintain actual antenna input power as near as practical to authorized power.

Broadcast Bureau ordered licensee to forfeit $500 for failing to keep proper log as required.

Broadcast Bureau ordered licensee to forfeit $500 for operating with antenna input power greater than 105% of authorized power during daytime operation.

Broadcast Bureau notified licensee that it had incurred apparent liability for $1,300 for failing to maintain receiver capable of receiving Emergency Broadcast System tests or emergency action notifications and terminations at nighttime control point.

Broadcast Bureau ordered licensee to forfeit $2,000 for operating with modes of power other than those specified in basic instrument of authorization.[18]

Notice that with the exception of logging violations and the lack of equipment for monitoring the Emergency Broadcast System, these alleged violations are infractions of technical rules. Now consider the following list of more sizable apparent liabilities:

$10,000 for logging violations and for fraudulent billing practices.

$5,000 for failure to make time available to political candidates at the lowest unit charge, charging different rates for political announcements of the same class and duration to legally qualified candidates for the same office, and failure to comply with logging requirements.

$8,000 for failure to comply with logging requirements (program-length commercial).

$10,000 for falsification of operating logs.

$10,000 for fraudulent billing practices.

$8,000 for broadcasting information concerning a lottery.[19]

Notice the increased importance the commission assigns to alleged commercial violations. This is one area in which a maximum fine is not uncommon, and even stations in smaller communities can incur substantial liabilities from these violations. These listings *do not* necessarily imply that the stations were guilty, but only that forfeiture notices were served.

A station being investigated by the FCC has certain rights. First, the FCC cannot simply impose a fine on the station. Procedures outlined in the Communications Act state that a written notice of the apparent liability must first be sent by certified mail to the "last known address" of the licensee or permittee. The permittee then has thirty days in which to pay the fine or to submit in writing the reason why it should not be held liable. The notice sent by the commission also must include the date, facts, and nature of the act or omission and must identify the "particular provision or provisions of the law, rule, or regulation or the license, permit, or cease and desist order involved." The fine is payable to the United States Treasury and can be collected in a civil suit if the violator refuses to pay. Of course, the station can appeal the commission's action through the usual administrative processes. In many cases, however, logs are powerful evidence as documents, and the excuse that an unsupervised or unqualified employee is to blame is no defense.

The commission issued its first letter of apparent liability in March 1961, one month after it outlined its policy and procedures regarding forfeitures. The authority to issue forfeitures had been granted to it in September 1960.[20] Three researchers who studied the pattern of FCC forfeitures over the decade immediately after the law was enacted found the highest percentage (87.1 percent) of forfeitures occurred because of a failure to observe a provision of the act or a rule or regulation of the commission. Included in this category were such infractions as logging violations, fraudulent billing, unlicensed or underlicensed operators, improper station identifications, and failure to conduct equipment-performance measurements. The second highest category (8.0 percent) of forfeiture notices were delivered for failure to operate the station as set forth in the license. Violations of broadcasting hours, power specifications, and presunrise authorization accounted for 3.4 percent of all forfeiture notices. Rigged contests and violations concerning sponsorship identification also fell into this category. The fourth category—violations of lottery, fraud, or obscene-language sections of Title 18 of the United States Code—accounted for 1.4 percent of the notices. The researchers found no forfeiture notices resulting from failure to observe an FCC cease-and-desist order.[21]

Short-Term Renewals

Next to renewal denials and revocation, the most severe sanction that can be imposed on a station is a short-term license renewal.[22] The purpose of these renewals, which range from six months to two years, is to give the commission an early opportunity to review alleged past deficiencies. Typical of short-term license renewals are those issued for the following infractions:

1. Station's equal employment. (Not meeting its affirmative action requirements.)
2. Utilization of broadcast facility to gain competitive advantage in nonbroadcast business activities; fradulent billing.
3. Fraudulent billing; inadvertent misrepresentations to the commission; falsification of logs; violation of logging rules; nonfulfillment of prior proposals concerning public service an-

nouncements; lack of supervision and control over station operations.

4. Broadcast of false, misleading, or deceptive advertising in connection with the promotion of a contest.

5. Predetermining the outcome of a contest.

6. Fraudulent billing.

7. Conducting contests during audience survey periods (hypoing).[23]

Notice again that alleged violations concerning commercial matters were responsible for most of the renewals, indicating the seriousness with which the FCC views such actions.

An investigation of 156 short-term license renewals granted by the commission showed that 113 (72 percent) of the stations received one-year renewals, 29 (19 percent) received renewals for more than one year but less than three, and 14 (9 percent) were licensed for less than a year.[24] Three reasons accounted for the majority of the renewals: (1) improper control over station operation, which generally means that the owner was not adequately supervising the employees; (2) repeated rule violations, both technical and programming; and (3) performance versus promise—in other words, the licensee was not living up to the promises made in the previous license renewal.[25]

Renewal Denials and Revocation

The most serious penalty the FCC can impose on a licensee is to deny it the right to operate, by either revoking or denying renewal of its license. In 1975 the FCC revoked the licenses of the entire Alabama Educational Television Commission. This sweeping action was a precedent demonstrating that the commission was not going to tolerate what it considered lack of service to an audience—in this case, the black audience. The action came before public broadcasting stations were required even to

conduct community-needs and ascertainment surveys. Nevertheless, the FCC acted on the premise that the licensee has the responsibility to determine the needs of its audience and to program in accordance with those needs.

Two years later, an administrative law judge denied renewal of a noncommercial station licensed to the board of trustees of the University of Pennsylvania. The FCC upheld the decision, charging among other things that the licensee had delegated and subdelegated authority to students. Although the FCC accepted the station's application for a new license, the renewal denial awoke many boards of trustees to the fact that even they had the responsibility to see that a broadcasting station is operated in the public interest. If it is not, their university can be held responsible.

CRITICISM OF THE COMMISSION

Perhaps because it regulates a very visible industry, and perhaps because that industry directly affects all of us every day, the FCC has received criticism from the public, from Congress, and even from commissioners within its ranks.

Conflict With Judicial Precedent

One criticism is that the FCC has issued rulings that conflict with judicial precedent. Nicholas Johnson and John Dystel cite a case in which AT&T applied for permission to build a 350-foot tower near a residential area of Finksburg, Maryland.[26] Despite opposition from citizen's groups, the commission granted the request, partly because AT&T had conducted an environmental-impact study and found that the tower would not harm the environment. As Johnson and Dystel note, however, the courts had previously ruled that federal agencies cannot rely on interested parties' environmental-impact statements.[27]

Frequency-Allocation Matters

Not everyone feels that the way in which the FCC allocates frequencies on the electromagnetic spectrum is in the public's best interest. For example, the designation of certain frequencies for marine use means that there are wide areas of the country in which these frequencies go unused, simply because there is no demand in these areas for marine communication.[28] Moreover, because this policy has been perpetuated for years, trying to change it now would entail major capital expenditures for the industries affected.

The commission's local-station concept, whereby it allocates certain frequencies to lower-powered stations serving small communities, has drawbacks in that it ties up a sizable portion of the spectrum for local-station use. One way of reducing crowding on the spectrum is to switch to regional allocations, the result of which would be fewer but higher-powered stations serving large regions. But this idea, although technologically sound, seems somewhat impractical when we think of the local service that would be lost.[29] A regional station in Chicago serving a small town in Illinois would be hard pressed to include that community's local news in its regional programming.

EEO Policies

Several criticisms have landed squarely on the FCC's equal-employment-opportunity (EEO) policies. A report by the Citizen's Communications Center claims the criteria for stations' compliance with FCC–EEO requirements are vague and can be met even by broadcasters who discriminate.[30] The report also asserts that the commission requires an unrealistically high standard of proof of discriminatory practices before designating a hearing in a renewal case. Another report critical of the Commission's EEO policies was issued by the U.S. Commission on Civil Rights.[31] This report suggests that the FCC should improve the image of women and minorities in television programming, an area many would argue is clearly outside the commission's jurisdiction and would violate the First Amendment.

Citizen Participation

The effect of citizens' groups on FCC decision making has also been criticized. A report by the Rand Corporation suggests that the commission do more to encourage citizen participation, one effort being to support legislation that would provide financial assistance to citizens' groups participating in commission proceedings.[32] Giving citizens' groups access to evidence that might support their cause is also high on the list of recommendations. In judicial processes today, a person or group enjoys the *right of discovery*—that is, access to information—only after proceedings have begun in the courts or, in the case of the FCC, after a hearing has been designated. The FCC has started an Actions Alert program designed to solicit advice on FCC rule making. Written in plain English, the Actions Alerts are issued to citizens' groups and other interested parties, who can then give written opinions to the FCC.

Decision-Making Processes

One of the most serious shortcomings of the FCC according to critics, is its sluggishness in making important decisions. Observers have stated that the FCC is "incapable of policy planning, of disposing within a reasonable period of time the business before it, of fashioning procedures that are effective to deal with its problems."[33] A classic case is the assignment of WHDH–TV in Boston. The case started in 1947, when WHDH filed an application for a license to operate Channel 5. This channel allocation was the subject of competing applications and the FCC decrees for 25 years. It was one of the longest proceedings ever to come before the FCC. Two scholars who reviewed the chronology of the case concluded that if there was no clear winner in the proceedings, "one party was a significant loser: the public."[34] In a lighter account of the case, a former FCC commissioner was quoted as saying, "Let's face it. This was the 'Whorehouse Era' of the commission. When matters were arranged, not adjudicated."[35]

Conflicts of Interest

The commission has often been called to task for potential conflict of interest because of its staff-owned stocks of corporations it regulates. For example, a staff report by the House Oversight and Investigations Subcommittee criticized FCC members for transferring shares of stock in communications-related industries to members of their immediate families (The law as it now stands does not prohibit that practice.). The stock in question included shares of General Electric owned by the spouse of a staff member in the Office of the Chief Scientist, shares of AT&T owned by the spouse of a staff member in the Common Carrier Bureau, and shares of AT&T owned by the spouse of an engineer in charge of an FCC field office.[36]

Johnson and Dystel divide their criticism of the FCC into seven areas. They contend that (1) the FCC delves into areas beyond its expertise and issues beyond its ken; (2) it takes years to resolve important cases; (3) the FCC is manipulated by its own staff and the industries it is supposed to regulate, the

results of which are precedents that return to haunt the commission; (4) principled decision making does not exist because the FCC no longer approves of its own rules and precedents, and instead ignores them—by either waiving them or evading them; (5) the commission ignores its own administrative principles and those established by the judiciary; (6) the commissioners decide cases they do not understand; and (7) the FCC has yet to develop rational policies for governing its day-to-day decisions.[37]

The Need for In-Depth Evaluation

Criticism of the FCC will undoubtedly continue, regardless of future changes. However, it is time for an in-depth evaluation of the entire commission. It is operating under the procedures of 1934, a time when cable, satellites, microwaves, and fiber optics were only a dream. Today, it is very possible that the communications industry is simply becoming unmanageable. The commission has established bureaus responsible for specific areas of the industry, but because so much is at stake when two competing corporations seek allocations or permission to develop technology, a ruling against one sends the matter through an appeals process that eventually reaches the five commissioners. Those individuals may very well be forced into a decision they are not qualified to make. As a result, the numerous reversals between the administrative law judges and the courts play havoc with anything that resembles judicial precedent.

THE FEDERAL TRADE COMMISSION

As noted earlier, in addition to the FCC, other agencies can play a part in the regulation of broadcasting and telecommunication. The Federal Trade Commission was formed in 1914 by the FTC Act. The act succinctly stated its purpose: "unfair methods of competition in commerce are hereby declared unlawful." Closely related to the FTC Act was the Clayton Act, also passed in 1914, which guarded against corporate mergers that would lessen competition. Since 1914 the FTC Act has been amended many times. Some of the most familiar pieces of legislation that have amended it are the 1966 Fair Packaging and Labeling Act and the 1969 Truth in Lending Act, which requires full disclosure of credit terms. The FTC has five commissioners, who are appointed, like those of the FCC, by the president with the advice and consent of the Senate for seven-year staggered terms. No more than three commissioners can be from the same political party. The president designates one of them as chairperson.

Organization

The primary components of the FTC are the commissioners and the various departments. The Office of Public Information acts as a liaison between the FTC and the public and is charged with three primary functions: (1) informing the public about the enforcement activities of the FTC; (2) keeping the commission advised on public-information policy; and (3) coordinating the public-information programs of the FTC regional offices.[38] Working under the direction of the FTC chairperson, the executive director is the chief administrative officer of the FTC. The administrative law judges conduct trials in cases in which the FTC has issued a complaint. They serve as the initial fact finders and have tenure much like federal judges.[39] Advising the FTC on questions of law and policy is the general counsel, the FTC's chief law officer. The general counsel represents

the commission in federal courts. The secretary is responsible for keeping the minutes of FTC proceedings and is the custodian of the FTC's records. The signature of the secretary appears on all FTC orders. This person also handles requests for information made by the public under the Freedom of Information and Privacy acts. Planning the activities of the FTC is the Office of Policy Planning and Evaluation. This office has three functions: (1) to evaluate the commission's programs every six months and suggest new ones for it to undertake; (2) to develop questions that will elicit information the commission needs in order to assess where the public's interest lies in a given matter; and (3) to determine the effect of previous FTC decisions on the public.[40]

Three key bureaus handle most of the tasks that affect both consumers and practitioners of broadcast advertising. The Bureau of Competition is responsible for enforcing the antitrust laws. The Bureau of Economics advises the commission on the economic impact of its decisions. The Bureau of Consumer Protection is charged with investigating trade practices alleged to be unfair to consumers. The Bureau of Consumer Protection is one of the closest allies of the public, helping to guard it against deceptive advertising. Formed in 1971, the bureau brought under one roof all of the various consumer-related activities that had been performed by the FTC.[41]

Processing an FTC Complaint

To better understand the enforcement procedures used by the FTC, let's imagine that you are about to receive a complaint from the FTC alleging that you are airing false and deceptive commercials (see Figure 17-2).[42] The first notice you would probably receive from the FTC would be a letter. You would then have the opportunity to reply to

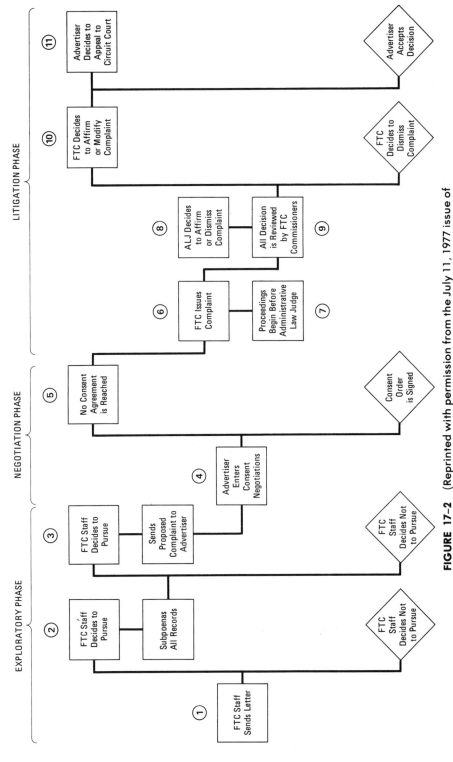

FIGURE 17-2 (Reprinted with permission from the July 11, 1977 issue of *Advertising Age*. Copyright 1977 by Crain Communications, Inc.)

that letter and explain your position. The FTC at this point may decide that your arguments have merit and simply decide not to pursue the matter further. But if it is not satisfied with your arguments, it may proceed to subpoena all pertinent records, such as the details of any product testing you may have undertaken.

Examining the records takes us to step 3 in the process. If the records clearly show your claims not to be deceptive, then the FTC may consider your case closed. If, on the other hand, it is not content with your test results and still feels the advertising to be deceptive, enter step 4, the beginning of negotiation. Two developments will normally take place during this phase. First, you may offer a consent order, stating that you will agree to remedy the problem, perhaps by taking your commercials off the air. The FTC then has an opportunity either to accept or to reject your consent agreement. If the commission accepts your agreement, it will be placed on the public record for sixty days. During that time, other parties can file pro or con comments on the agreement. And if the evidence builds up against you, the FTC can actually withdraw from the consent agreement and begin formal proceedings.[43] Second, if the consent order is approved by both the FCC and the advertiser, that usually ends the matter.

Let us assume that the evidence built up against you during the sixty-day period was substantial, and that the FTC decides to proceed to step 6 and issue a complaint. Then, in step 7 an administrative law judge rules on that complaint. In step 8 the law judge issues a decision, which is reviewed by the FTC commissioners in step 9. In step 10 there are again two options. The FTC can decide either (1) to affirm or modify the decision of the law judge or (2) to dismiss the complaint. We'll assume that it was not your lucky day,

and that the FTC decided to uphold the decision of the administrative law judge, which was to prohibit you from using the commercials in any future advertising. You have two choices in step 11. You can either accept the FTC decision and tell your ad agency to move on to some new commercials, or you can tell your lawyers to appeal the FTC decision to the circuit court.

Regardless of which decision you make at step 11, one thing is certain: the road to the court has been both long and rough. You undoubtedly spent large sums of money fighting the case through the commission, and you will now face additional expenses in the appeals process. Although you may feel you have been overwhelmed by the power of a high federal agency, the FTC would contend that such safeguards are for the benefit of the public. For the commission, enforcement powers are a stern warning to advertisers to see that their advertising meets the standards of truth and accuracy. A broadcasting station hypoing a rating, misrepresenting a coverage map, or participating in unfair competition faces not only the wrath of the FCC but an equally ardous battle with the Federal Trade Commission.

THE NATIONAL TELECOMMUNICATIONS AND INFORMATION ADMINISTRATION

Although much of the telecommunications industry is under the FCC's jurisdiction, the growth in the industry has prompted other government bodies to take an active interest in it. The newest agency to directly concern itself with telecommunications, including radio and television, is the National Telecommunications and Information Administration. Formed under a reorganization plan sponsored by President Jimmy Carter, the NTIA consolidated the functions of the Office of Telecommunications Policy (OTP) in the Office of the President and the Office of Telecommunications (OT) in the Department of Commerce. The plan specifically provided for five actions:

1. It transferred all functions of the Office of Telecommunications Policy to the Department of Commerce.
2. It abolished the Office of Telecommunications Policy.
3. It abolished the Office of Telecommunications.
4. It established the Office of Assistant Secretary for Communications and Information in the Department of Commerce.
5. It formed the National Telecommunications and Information Administration, to be directed by the assistant secretary for communications and information.

President Carter appointed Henry Geller as the first head of the agency. Geller had been a former deputy general counsel and also general counsel of the FCC under two presidents and had served with the Rand Corporation and later the Aspen Institute Program on Communications and Society.

Although the NTIA is still charged with advising the president, and although it is still an executive-branch agency, its removal from the Office of the President has at least presented the appearance of detachment and created the potential for better cooperation with other agencies of government.

Similar in many ways to the old Office of Telecommunications, the NTIA sees itself as having four primary functions, or *program elements.* The first is *policy analysis and development,* which includes analyzing the issues surrounding common-carrier industries, such as telephone communication; developing options for deregulating cable

and broadcasting; analyzing issues in international telecommunication; and assessing the issue of protecting privacy in data communications. A second program element is *telecommunications applications,* which involve such concerns as improving telecommunication in rural areas; stimulating minority ownership of broadcasting and cable-TV stations; coordinating local and state telecommunications policy; and promoting user-industry cooperation in the development of satellite systems for public-service activities. A third program element, *federal-systems spectrum management,* is concerned with assessing the federal use of the electromagnetic spectrum and evaluating the procurement plans of other federal agencies. The fourth program element is *telecommunication sciences,* the research arm of NTIA. Studying the effects of climate on radio waves, examining various direct-broadcast systems for public-service use, and developing user-oriented standards for federal data-communication systems are some of its functions. These four program elements are just *some* of what the NTIA at its inception perceived as its appropriate functions.

OFFICE OF TECHNOLOGY ASSESSMENT

Created in 1972, the Office of Technology Assessment (OTA) provides Congress with forecasts on the impact of technology on society. The issues tackled by the OTA range from technology used to measure water supplies to solar-powered satellites. Specifically, the OTA is charged with bringing "a long-term global and comprehensive perspective to bear and to provide Congress with independent, authoritative, even-handed assessments."[44] For Congress, the

OTA is a ready source of digestible information on long-range goals that are separate from the more narrow issues taken up in the daily routine of lawmaking. Projects for the OTA are initiated after being approved by a Technology Assessment Board composed of six senators and six representatives. Initial requests for studies by the OTA can originate from the OTA director, members of the Technology Assessment Board, or chairpersons of congressional committees.[45]

THE INTERNATIONAL
TELECOMMUNICATION UNION

The International Telecommunication Union is a United Nations organization responsible for coordinating the use of telecommunications among nations.[46] It does not have the enforcement powers of the Federal Communications Commission or of the Radio and Television Commission in Canada. Rather, it is a collective body of sovereign states and is only as strong as the willingness of those states to abide by its treaties. In other words, if a country violates an ITU agreement, no field office will revoke licenses or impose forfeitures. ITU's sovereign states view it not so much as an independent agency but as an arena in which to negotiate the uses of telecommunications,[47] and it has been effective in that role.

Background and Functions

The history of the International Telecommunication Union (ITU) dates back to 1849, when the impact of the telegraph was dawning on Europe. In that year, Austria and Prussia signed a treaty whereby they joined their telegraph lines. The treaties that were subsequently signed and the technology that was developed prompted twenty European states to meet in Paris in 1865 to approve an agreement titled the International Telegraph Convention (Figure 17-3). Included in that agreement was a set of telegraph regulations. A series of Telegraph Conferences grew out of the Paris agreement, and at the Vienna Conference in 1868, the International Bureau of Telegraph Administrations was formed. Located in Berne, Switzerland, it became known as the Berne Bureau and was staffed and funded mostly by the Swiss. It was charged with a variety of administrative functions. The 1865 Convention, the periodic conferences, and the Berne Bureau collectively became known as the International Telegraph Union in 1875. The International Telegraph Convention was its charter. By 1885 the union was involved with the telephone as well as the telegraph.

At this time, Marconi was tinkering with the new technology that would soon revolutionize the world's concepts of communication. The rapid corporate development of the British Marconi Wireless Company created a worldwide monopoly. As we saw in the last chapter, the German government convened a conference in 1903 to resolve some of the problems resulting from the monopoly, specifically the failure of ships equipped with Marconi apparatus to communicate with ships equipped with apparatus manufactured by other companies. Six of the eight sovereign states in attendance signed an agreement, which, although mostly protocol, became the foundation for international radio regulations. The agreement called for wireless stations to "operate, as far as possible, in such a manner as not to interfere with the working of other stations."[48] Further international cooperation emerged from the first International Radiotelegraph Conference in 1906. There, twenty-seven nations adopted the Radiotelegraph Convention and specific

FIGURE 17-3 Representatives of European states met in Paris in 1865 and approved an agreement titled the "International Telegraph Convention." Over the years, the various agreements and the administrative bodies responsible for administering those agreements have evolved into the International Telecommunication Union.

Radiotelegraph Regulations. Realizing that radio was a rapidly changing technology, the nations also made provisions to meet at periodic administrative conferences. The Berne Bureau, already serving the telegraph and telephone interests, was designated to handle the administrative duties which concerned radio.

Gradually the Radiotelegraph Convention and the periodic conferences together came to be called the Radiotelegraph Union. Except for the fact that they shared the Berne Bureau, the International Telegraph Union and the Radiotelegraph Union operated independently until 1932. In that year the International Telegraph Convention and the Radiotelegraph Convention were combined into a unified agreement called the International Telecommunication Convention. The International Telegraph Union and the Radiotelegraph Union also merged, becoming the International Telecommunication Union. The International Telecommunication Convention was its charter. The respective radio, telegraph, and telephone regulations of the previous organizations were welded into three sets of international regulations—radio, telegraph, and telephone—and annexed to the International Telecommunication Convention.

The primary functions of the ITU include:

1. Effective allocations of the radio frequency spectrum and registration of radio frequency assignments;

2. Coordinating efforts to eliminate harmful interference between radio stations of different countries and to improve the use made of the radio frequency spectrum;

3. Fostering collaboration with respect to the establishment of the lowest possible rates;

4. Fostering the creation, development, and improvement of telecommunication equipment and networks in new or developing countries by every means at its disposal, especially its participation in the appropriate programs of the United Nations;

5. Promoting the adoption of measures for ensuring the safety of life through the cooperation of telecommunication services;

6. Undertaking studies, making regulations, adopting resolutions, formulating recommendations and opinions, and collecting and publishing information concerning telecommunications matters benefiting all Members and Associate Members.[49]

At any given time, the ITU may send cooperative teams of experts to help developing nations establish modern communications systems. Every year upward of three hundred experts are out on field missions and four hundred more are undergoing training in telecommunication services. The ITU's technical-cooperation activity continues to focus on "(1) promoting the development of regional telecommunication networks in Africa, Asia, and Latin America; (2) strengthening the telecommunication technical and administrative services in developing countries; and (3) developing the human resources required for telecommunications."[50] The ITU also sponsors numerous feasibility studies for new systems of communication. In addition, it is directly involved in negotiations on securing funding sources for new telecommunications systems. These sources include the International Bank for Reconstruction and Development, the African Development Bank, the Asian Development Bank, and regional banks.

Organization

The machinery for carrying out the functions of the ITU is housed in six areas, which have evolved out of various conferences and mergers over the years.[51]

Plenipotentiary Conference This conference is the supreme body of the ITU. It is composed of all of the ITU member nations, and it meets approximately every seven years to revise the International Telecommunication Convention. It differs somewhat from other U.N. conferences in that it tackles a complete, not a partial, revision of the convention, and compared with other conferences it meets infrequently.

Administrative Council The Administrative Council is composed of twenty-nine members elected on a regional basis. It meets for about a month each year to conduct business in the interim between the Plenipotentiary Conferences.

Administrative Conferences These are called periodically to revise the regulations annexed to the convention. The radio conferences, called World Administrative Radio Conferences, examine such issues as international allocation of the electromagnetic spectrum.

International Consultative Committees These consist of the International Radio Consultative Committee (CCIR) and the International Telephone and Telegraph Consultative Committee (CCITT). Each comprises plenary assemblies that meet every three to five years, periodically convened study groups, and full-time specialized secretariats. The committees make recommendations on such developments as technical specifications for equipment. The CCITT dates back to a 1955 merger of two committees, one dealing with the telephone (the CCIF) and the other representing telegraph interests (the CCIT). The CCIT and CCIF were formed at the 1926 Paris Conference of the International Telegraph Union. The CCIR traces its founding to the 1927 Washington Radiotelegraph Conference.

International Frequency Registration Board (IFRB) The IFRB is composed of five elected members—reduced from nine in 1965 as a compromise with those who wanted it abolished altogether. It is responsible for adopting technical standards for international telecommunication, and it maintains a master register of international-frequency use. When a country desires to use a certain frequency it notifies the IFRB, which then determines if the use will meet ITU regulations and not interfere with other registrants.

General Secretariat This office carries out the administrative duties of the ITU. It consists of an elected Secretary General and a Deputy Secretary General. The General Secretariat does not have the authority to establish policy.

World Administrative Radio Conferences

The World Administrative Radio Conferences (WARC) that are called by the ITU leave an indelible impression on international radio regulation. These conferences meet periodically to consider either limited or general topics of importance to member nations and the world use of communications. A limited WARC was held in 1977 to deal with satellite communication. Five weeks of negotiations produced a treaty providing for direct-to-home and conventional satellite communications in the 11.7-to-12.2 GHz area of the electromagnetic spectrum. A more general conference, WARC 1979, was held in Geneva, Switzerland. This conference reviewed the entire international use of the electromagnetic spectrum and established policy for that use for much of the remainder of the twentieth century.

Since each WARC country has one vote, the superpowers do not necessarily control policy the way they do in other international negotiations. The conferences examine frequency use in different regions of the world and strive for the greatest latitude of spectrum use without interference.

SUMMARY

In this chapter we discussed the operation of the Federal Communications Commission and allied agencies. We learned that the FCC has thirteen areas of responsibility, among them the orderly development and operation of broadcast services; control over AM, FM, TV, telephone, common-carrier, cable, and satellite communications; new stations and transfer of ownership of those already operating; domestic administration of the telecommunications provisions of treaties and international agreements; and supervision of the Emergency Broadcast System. The FCC does not have jurisdiction over such things as program scheduling, awarding of prizes in contests, broadcasting outside the United States and its possessions, news-gathering organizations, and libel and slander.

The typical agenda of an FCC meeting includes the following categories, which correspond in many ways to the functions and organization of the commission: hearing, general, safety and special, common carrier, personnel, classified, cable television, assignment and transfer, renewals, aural, television, broadcast, and complaints and compliance. Research has taught us that although the commissioners are selected as a bipartisan group, individual commissioners can have considerable influence over the policy directions the FCC takes. The organization of the FCC includes, along with the commissioners, the Office of Plans and Policy, the Office of Opinions and Review, the Office of Administrative Law Judges, the Review Board, the Office of General Counsel, the Office of Chief Scientist, and the Office of Executive Director. Among the four bureaus of the commission, those most responsible for broadcasting are the Mass Media Bureau and the Field Operations Bureau.

No government agency can function effectively as a regulator without enforcement powers. The FCC is no exception. At its disposal are such measures as letters, cease-and-desist orders, forfeitures, short-term renewals, renewal denials, and revocations.

Criticism of the FCC has surfaced in recent years. Critics have focused on such issues as FCC decisions that conflict with judicial precedent, the commissioners' influence on and separation from the middle staff, the FCC's allocation of frequencies, its affirmative-action policies, citizen participation in commission decisions, and the decision-making processes of the FCC.

The Federal Trade Commission is organized much like its communication counterpart, the FCC. The executive director is the chief administrator. Administrative law judges conduct trials in complaint cases. The general counsel acts as the FTC's attorney. The secretary keeps minutes in FTC meetings and keeps the FTC's records. The Office of Policy Planning and Evaluation is charged with evaluating programs, developing questions that will elicit information, and determining the effects of FTC decisions on the public. The three FTC bureaus concerned most directly with broadcasting are the Bureau of Competition, the Bureau of Economics, and the Bureau of Consumer Protection.

The origins of the National Telecommunications and Information Administration date back to the Nixon administration's establishment of the Office of Telecommunications Policy (OTP) in the Office of the President and the Office of Telecommunications (OT) in the Department of Commerce. The OTP was beset with political issues that limited its effectiveness. President Carter reduced the executive branch's involvement in telecommunications policy by abolishing the OTP and the OT and creating the NTIA in the Department of Commerce. The Office of Technology Assessment (OTA) gives support to Congress on policy matters and issues evenhanded reports on the probable effects of new technology on society.

The International Telecommunication Union (ITU) establishes and administers agreements among countries on the use of the electromagnetic spectrum. A United Nations agency, the ITU is an outgrowth of the telegraph era of the mid 1800s. It has gradually evolved through a series of telegraph and radiotelegraph conventions into its current role as a coordinator of telecommunication policies and applications throughout the world.

OPPORTUNITIES FOR FURTHER LEARNING

BENSMAN, M. R., *Broadcast Regulation: Selected Cases and Decisions.* Washington, D.C.: University Press of America, 1983.

BITTNER, J. R., *Broadcast Law and Regulation.* Englewood Cliffs, N.J.: Prentice-Hall, 1982.

BRIEF, K. H., ed., *The Media and the Law.* Long Island, N.Y.: Newsday, 1981.

BROWN, J. A., JR., AND K. GORDON, *Economics and Telecommunications Privacy: A Framework for Analysis.* Washington, D.C.: Office of Plans and Policy, Federal Communications Commission, 1980.

COMPAINE, B. M., ed., *Who Owns the Media? Concentration of Ownership in the Mass Communications Industry.* White Plains, N.Y.: Knowledge Industry, 1979.

"Electronic Journalism and First Amendment Problems," *Federal Communications Bar Journal,* 29, no. 1 (1976), 1–61.

The FCC in Brief. Loose-leaf. Washington, D.C.: Federal Communications Commission, 1977.

GINSBURG, D. H., *Regulation of Broadcasting: Law and Policy Toward Radio, Television and Cable Communications.* St. Paul: West, 1979.

Legislative and Regulatory Actions Needed to Deal With a Changing Domestic Telecommunications Industry. Washington, D.C.: General Accounting Office, 1981.

LEVIN, H. J., *Fact and Fancy in Television Regulation: An Economic Study of Policy Alternatives.* New York: Russell Sage Foundation, 1980.

MURRAY, J., *The Media Law Dictionary.* Washington, D.C.: University Press of America, 1978.

NOLL, R. G., and others, *Economic Aspects of Television Regulation.* Washington, D.C.: Brookings Institution, 1973.

ULLOTH, D. R., *The Supreme Court: A Judicial Review of the Federal Communications Commission.* New York: Arno Press, 1979.

18

POLITICAL BROADCASTING, PROGRAMMING, AND OPERATIONS

In the last two chapters we have examined the historical foundations of regulatory control of broadcasting and looked at such regulatory agencies as the Federal Communications Commission and the Federal Trade Commission. We now turn to rules and regulations that affect the programming decisions made at radio and television stations and in some cases the content of programming. Our discussion in this chapter focuses on over-the-air broadcasting. In the next chapter we will examine wired systems and such issues as common-carrier and cable regulations.

THE RATIONALE FOR REGULATORY CONTROL

The control of broadcasting is a function of supply and demand. We know that if there is a great demand for a product in short supply, people will write certain rules for obtaining it in order to avoid chaos. Imagine that a group of children all want a piece of candy but there are only half as many pieces of candy as there are children. Who gets the candy? Perhaps the children who have perfect behavior records. Perhaps only those who agree to share their candy with others.

Perhaps those who eat responsibly and do not gobble. Or perhaps only those who can afford to buy it. Our example illustrates the need for controls that will both regulate the allocation of the product and maintain order.

Limited Spectrum and Mass Influence

Now transpose our example to the allocation of frequencies on the electromagnetic spectrum. The spectrum has only so much space within which radio and television stations can operate. Consequently, certain rules governing the allocation and operation of stations are necessary. This limited-resource concept is the reason behind much broadcast regulation.

The second important reason is that broadcasting influences a great number of people. The citizens-band radio that sends out a five-watt signal to a passing motorist has little impact on a mass audience. If the operator decides to sing songs into the microphone, chances are the FCC will not be overly concerned. On the other hand, if a local television station decides to forego all its regular programming for a steady diet of jokes and traffic reports, it will have a difficult time justifying its privilege to operate. Messages that are broadcast to the public have a considerable effect on it. Thus, to assure that society is protected from abuse, we make certain rules.

At this point you may say, "Fine, we set up certain rules, people follow the rules, and the system functions." Unfortunately it is not that simple. Everyone from FCC commissioners to citizens' groups to broadcasters argue the legitimacy of the regulatory process. Part of the discussion focuses on the legal philosophy upon which our society operates. America is considered a free country. Harold Nelson and Dwight Teeter have written that "Seventeenth and Eighteenth

Century thought in much of Western Europe and America turned to faith in man's reason as the safest basis for government." Lee Loevinger describes the practical application of this philosophy as negative or proscriptive rather than positive or prescriptive. Law in America, for example, forbids behavior that might harm society, but it does not require behavior that society has determined to be beneficial.[1] Nor does it require the best behavior of which one is capable, or even behavior that is socially desirable. At first, it might seem that this attitude would undermine the good of society. Not so, Loevinger assures us, for "when the law prohibits antisocial conduct, it leaves an extremely wide area of personal choice and individual liberty to the citizen."[2]

Control Versus Noncontrol

From the standpoint of broadcasting, we can see the head of regulatory conflict beginning to protrude. Although we must control the allocation of frequencies on the electromagnetic spectrum, to control programming on those frequencies is to go against traditional American legal philosophy.

The arguments concerning control of broadcasting run between two extremes. One point of view suggests a total lack of control; its supporters point out that the First Amendment assures free press and free speech. Some legal scholars even suggest that one freedom embodies the other.[3] The other point of view supports total control of broadcasting. Its advocates base their case on four assumptions: (1) there is a reliable and authoritative basis for determining program quality; (2) the public interest can be determined in one broadcast without reference to all other broadcasts; (3) there are programs that meet the assumed authoritative government standards; and (4) if the government commands it, then quality programs will be produced.[4] The debate over all these arguments has led to a regulatory system that greatly affects what radio and television stations will program.

POLITICAL BROADCASTING: SECTION 315 OF THE COMMUNICATIONS ACT

Section 315 regulates political broadcasting. Part of the Communications Act of 1934, it instructs the broadcaster and the candidate for office in how the electronic media are to be used as part of our political system. Along with the Fairness Doctrine, to which we will turn next, it affects how we, the consumers of broadcast communication, are informed of our electoral process.

Definitions Guiding the Equal-Time Provision

Section 315's "equal-time" provision states that "if any licensee shall permit any person who is a legally qualified candidate for public office to use a broadcasting station, he shall afford equal opportunities to all other such candidates for that office in the use of such broadcasting station." The Communications Act defines a legally qualified candidate as

> any person who has publicly announced that he is a candidate for nomination by a convention of a political party or for nomination or election in a primary, special, or general election, municipal, county, state or national, and who meets the qualifications prescribed by the applicable laws to hold the office for which he is a candidate, so that he may be voted for by the electorate directly or by means of delegates or electors, and who:
>
> (1) has qualified for a place on the ballot or
> (2) is eligible under the applicable law to be voted for by sticker, by writing in his name on the ballot, or by other method, and
>> (i) has been duly nominated by a political party which is commonly known and regarded as such, or
>> (ii) makes a substantial showing that he is a bona fide candidate for nomination or office, as the case may be.[5]

Hundreds of state and local statutes further clarify political eligibility. Broadcasters are prohibited from deciding themselves who is legally qualified. It makes little difference whether the candidate has a chance of winning. If he or she is qualified under the law and has publicly announced his or her candidacy, then the equal-time provision will apply. That provision also applies to cable-television systems.

The Anticensorhip Provision

As a further safeguard against unfair treatment of political candidates, Section 315 expressly prohibits the broadcaster from censoring the content of any political message: the licensee "shall have no power of censorship over the material broadcast under provisions of this section." Broadcasters were confused by the noncensorship rule, fearing it was only a matter of time until some candidate blatantly libeled an opponent and the station was sued for damages. The dreaded event occurred in 1959 in North Dakota, when U.S. senatorial candidate A. C. Townley charged on the air that the North Dakota Farmers' Union was Communist-controlled. The Farmers' Union sued the station and Townley for $100,000. But the North Dakota Supreme Court ruled that the station was not liable and that the suit should have been brought against Townley alone. Undoubtedly the Farmers' Union had thought about that, but since Townley made only $98.50 a month, the prospect for recovering damages was not bright.[6] The union then appealed to the Supreme Court. Justice Hugo Black, in delivering the opinion of the Court, stated, "Quite possibly, if a station were held responsible for the broadcast of libelous material, all remarks even faintly objectionable would be excluded out of an excess of caution . . . if any censorship were permissible, a station so inclined could intentionally inhibit a candidate's legitimate presentation under the guise of lawful censorship of libelous matter."[7]

Exemptions from the Equal-Time Provision

Exempt from the equal-time provision are appearances by candidates on these types of news programming:

1. bona fide newscast,
2. bona fide news interview,
3. bona fide news documentary (if the appearance of the candidate is incidental to the presentation of the subject or subjects covered by the news documentary), or
4. on-the-spot coverage of bona fide news events (including but not limited to political conventions and activities incidental thereto).

In the fall of 1975 the FCC added to the exemption list political debates and news conferences that were broadcast in their entirety and whose broadcaster made a good-faith judgment that they constituted a bona fide news event. In the spring of 1976 a three-judge panel of the U.S. Court of Appeals in Washington, D.C., ruled two to one that the FCC had the right to do this. The court noted that Congress could correct the FCC if it overstepped its authority in issuing the added exemption.[8]

The exemption itself is a hot political issue, since party loyalty as well as congressional autonomy tends to surface during an election year. For example, an FCC exemption permitted Gerald Ford and Jimmy Carter to participate in nationally televised debates in 1976. For John F. Kennedy and Richard Nixon to debate in 1960, Congress had to suspend Section 315.[9] If these measures had not been taken, networks and local stations would have been faced with a plethora of minority-party candidates demanding equal time.

Selling Time: The Lowest Unit Charge

Besides granting equal time to candidates, Section 315 spells out how much they are to be charged for the use of broadcast facilities:

> The charges made for the use of any broadcasting station by any person who is a legally qualified candidate for any public office in connection with his campaign for nomination for election, or election, to such office shall not exceed—
>
> (1) during the forty-five days preceding the date of a primary or primary runoff election and during the sixty days preceding the date of a general or special election in which such person is a candidate, the lowest unit charge of the station for the same class and amount of time for the same period, and
>
> (2) at any time, the charges made for comparable use of such station by other users thereof.

This is known as the "lowest unit charge" rule. To understand it more clearly, assume that you are the sales manager for a television station. The station's rate card charges an advertiser $1,000 to buy a single one-minute commercial in prime time. An advertiser purchasing two commercials receives a discount and is charged only $850 per commercial. We'll assume that the rate card permits an advertiser purchasing twenty-five commercials to receive an even bigger discount: each commercial will cost $500. Along comes John Doe, who is running for municipal judge. Doe wants to buy just one commercial to remind his friends that he is running for office. He wants it to run in prime time. What will you charge him for the cost of his one commercial? You will charge him $500. Even though he is buying only one commercial, the law states that you must charge him the "lowest unit charge." If he wanted to purchase a commercial in a fringe-time period during which the rates are lower, then you would charge him the "lowest unit charge" for that time period.

Access: The Relationship of Section 312 to Section 315

Our discussion of Section 315 would not be complete without mentioning another section of the Communications Act of 1934, Section 312, and how it relates to Section 315. Section 312 is a prerequisite to 315, since 312 succinctly states that stations must not deny access to any candidate for federal office, regardless of what form that access takes. Section 312 cautions the broadcaster that a station license may be revoked "for willful or repeated failure to allow reasonable access to or to permit purchase of reasonable amounts of time for the use of a broadcasting station by a legally qualified candidate for Federal elective office on behalf of his candidacy."

The Issue of "Federal Office"

Notice that the law reads "Federal elective office." This clause has been a bone of contention and a source of confusion to those interpreting Section 315, especially when candidates below the federal level are involved. Some stations have used Section 312 as grounds for refusing to sell commercial time to such candidates. The advantages of such a policy are mainly economic. First, there are fewer federal candidates than local

candidates, which translates into fewer political commercials. You may ask whether the station is not in business to sell commercials. Yes, but remember the lowest unit charge. If a department store pays a nondiscounted rate for commercials but cannot get on the air because of the many political commercials sold at the lowest unit charge, then the station will lose money. Second, federal candidates often place their advertising through advertising agencies. Although the station must still give a discount to the agency, the number of commercials purchased is usually more than what candidates would purchase on their own. Thus, the total amount spent by the agencies results in a profit to the station that is closer to that obtained from typical business advertising. Third, the commercials from the agency are usually prerecorded, which eliminates the need for the station to tie up its staff and facilities helping a local candidate produce a commercial that may run only one time at the lowest unit charge.

By inserting the term *Federal,* Section 312 left no definition of "reasonable access" for candidates for state and local offices. Historically, stations have been flexible in such cases. In its guidelines for political candidates, the commission says, "The licensee in its own good-faith judgment in serving the public interest may determine which political races are of greatest interest and significance to its service area, and therefore may refuse to sell time to candidates for less important offices, provided it treats all candidates for such offices equally.[10]

THE FAIRNESS DOCTRINE

The Fairness Doctrine was first issued in 1949 as an FCC report to broadcasters on handling controversial issues with fairness to all sides.[11] The FCC reexamined the doctrine in policy statements issued in 1964, 1974, and 1976.

The Mayflower Decision

The Federal Radio Commission, in discussing the limited spectrum space, noted that if issues "are of sufficient importance to the listening public, the microphone will undoubtedly be available. If not, a well-founded complaint will receive the careful consideration of the commission."[12] Attention to the fairness issue crystallized in 1941 in the Mayflower decision, which involved station WAAB in Boston. The Mayflower Broadcasting Corporation petitioned the FCC to give it the facilities of WAAB, which were up for renewal. Although the FCC ruled in favor of WAAB, it strongly criticized it for its practice of "editorializing." The FCC stated that it was "clear that with the limitations in frequencies inherent in the nature of radio, the public interest can never be served by a dedication of any broadcast facility to the support of his own partisan ends."[13] Therefore, the FCC argued, "a truly free radio cannot be used to advocate the causes of the licensee. . . . In brief, the broadcaster cannot be an advocate."[14] The Mayflower decision successfully discouraged other stations from jumping on the editorial bandwagon.

The WHKC Decision

While the Mayflower decision was stifling editorials, the Code of the National Association of Broadcasters was stifling discussion of controversial issues by prohibiting the purchase of commercials airing those issues. It was not long before a station was caught in the triangle formed by the FCC, the NAB Code, and the First Amendment. Station WHKC in Columbus, Ohio, had adhered to the NAB Code, believing it was operating in the public interest by doing so, and promptly found itself in a dispute with a labor union. Claiming the station had refused to sell it time and had censored the scripts it submitted, the union filed a petition against WHKC's license renewal. The FCC held a hearing on the matter between August 16 and 24, 1944, and heard the argument about the NAB Code. By October the union and the station had agreed to a compromise. The agreement broke with the code by prohibiting any further censorship of scripts, requiring the station to drop its policy of banning selling time for controversial issues. The FCC stated the station must be "sensitive to the problems of public concern in the community and . . . make sufficient time available on a nondiscriminatory basis, for full discussion thereof, without any type of censorship which would undertake to impose the views of the licensee upon the material to be broadcast."[15]

The Scott Decision

Further support for airing controversial issues came in 1946, when Robert Harold Scott of Palo Alto, California, filed a petition asking the FCC to revoke the licenses of radio stations KQW, KPO, and KFRC. Scott claimed that he wanted time to expound his views on atheism and thereby balance the station's "direct statements and arguments against atheism as well as . . . indirect arguments, such as church services, prayers, Bible reading and other kinds of religious programs."[16] Scott did not get the stations' licenses revoked, but in its decision the FCC stated,

> The fact that a licensee's duty to make time available for the presentation of opposing views on current controversial issues of public importance may not extend to all possible

differences of opinion within the ambit of human contemplation cannot serve as the basis for any rigid policy that time shall be denied for the presentation of views which may have a high degree of unpopularity.[17]

Issuing the Doctrine

The commission began to tackle the issue of editorialization in March and April of 1948. In eight days of hearings on the subject, it heard from forty-nine witnesses; twenty-one other persons filed written motions. From the hearings came a statement issued by the FCC on June 1, 1949, under the heading *In the Matter of Editorializing by Broadcast Licensees*. It was to become known as the Fairness Doctrine. The statement reasserted the commission's commitment to free expression of controversial issues of public importance, as stated in the WHKC and Scott decisions. It also reversed the Mayflower decision by supporting broadcast editorials. The commission came "to the conclusion that overt licensee editorialization, within reasonable limits and subject to the general requirements of fairness . . . is not contrary to the public interest.[18]

The Fairness Primer

As expected, a series of court cases and complaints about abuse of the Fairness Doctrine ensued. Finally, it became necessary in 1964 for the FCC to issue some clarifying guidelines. Commonly called the Fairness Primer, these guidelines consisted of representative FCC rulings from the period 1949–64.[19] The document gave people an opportunity to study the FCC's decisions, and it shed light on other stations' practices and policies, showed when complaints might be warranted, and guided stations on how to meet Fairness Doctrine requirements.

Still waiting, however, was a major test of the constitutionality of the Fairness Doc-

trine. It came in a 1967 appeals-court case that reached the Supreme Court in 1969. In what came to be called the Red Lion decision, the Court affirmed the constitutionality of the Fairness Doctrine. We'll examine this landmark case in more detail.

The Red Lion Decision

The Red Lion decision involved the Red Lion Broadcasting Company of Red Lion, Pennsylvania. In November 1964 the Reverend Billy James Hargis lashed out on Red Lion's radio station against the author of a book about Barry Goldwater. The author, Fred J. Cook, was held in low esteem by Hargis, who spelled out what he felt to be the less favorable aspects of Cook's career as a writer. When Cook asked the station for a chance to reply to Hargis it claimed it did not have to offer free time to Cook unless he could prove that there was no commercial sponsorship available for the presentation of his views. Cook went to the FCC, which ruled in his favor, citing the Fairness Doctrine. The appeals court upheld the FCC's decision.[20]

Appealing Red Lion

At that point the Radio-Television News Directors Association appealed the case to the United States Court of Appeals for the Seventh Circuit in Chicago. The court ruled that the Fairness Doctrine's personal-attack and editorial rules would "contravene the First Amendment."[21] But the RTNDA's victory was short-lived. The FCC took the case to the Supreme Court, which ruled that "in view of the prevalence of scarcity of broadcast frequencies, the Government's role in allocating those frequencies, and the legitimate claims of those unable without governmental assistance to gain access to those frequencies for expression of their views, we hold the regulations and ruling at issue here are both authorized by statute and constitutional.''[22] With this the Court upheld the FCC and reversed the decision in the RTNDA case. The Fairness Doctrine was now not only a broadcast regulation but a judicial precedent affirmed by the highest court in the land.

The Personal-Attack Rule

One area of the Fairness Doctrine that remained somewhat nebulous was the broadcast of direct personal attacks on individuals or organizations. When the Red Lion issue came to the FCC's attention, the commission decided that this was the time for a ruling. Becoming effective on August 14, 1967, the FCC's rules regarding personal attack read,

> When, during the presentation of views on a controversial issue of public importance, an attack is made upon the honesty, character, integrity or like personal qualities of an identified person or group, the licensee shall, within a reasonable time and in no event later than one week after the attack, transmit to the person or group attacked (1) notification of the date, time and identification of the broadcast; (2) a script or tape (or accurate summary if a script or tape is not available) of the attack and (3) an offer of a responsible opportunity to respond over licensee's facilities.[23]

The rules exempted foreign groups or foreign public figures, certain types of attacks made by political candidates during campaigns, and the same bona fide news events exempted from the equal-time provision of Section 315.

At the same time, the FCC spelled out new rules covering editorials:

> Where a licensee in an editorial, (i) endorses or (ii) opposes a legally qualified candidate or candidates, the licensee shall, within 24 hours after the editorial, transmit to respectively (i) the other qualified candidate or candidates for the same office or (ii) the candidate opposed in the editorial (1) notification of the date and the time of the editorial; (2) a script or tape of the editorial; and (3) an offer of a reasonable opportunity for the candidate or a spokesman of the candidate to respond over the licensee's facilities: Provided, however, that where such editorials are broadcast within 72 hours prior to the day of the election, the licensee shall comply with the provisions of this paragraph sufficiently far in advance of the broadcast to enable the candidate or candidates to have a reasonable opportunity to prepare a response and to present it in a timely fashion.[24]

Broadcasters now know exactly what is expected of them when personal attacks are aired by their stations. They do, however, have the discretion to determine what constitutes a personal attack. Here the FCC has permitted broadcast management to remain in charge of its local programming, somewhat unimpeded by a federal agency.

Broadcast Advertising

The FCC's position on the fairness issue is that the overall programming of a station, and not just a single program, should reflect its commitment to fairness. The status of advertising in this programming became an issue when New York lawyer John W. Banzhaf requested equal time from WCBS–TV to reply to cigarette commercials. The station refused, but the FCC agreed with Banzhaf. Its decision was upheld by an appeals court, which tried, however, to confine it to cigarette advertising. But that was too much to hope for, and over the years the Fairness Doctrine has been applied to many areas of advertising. (Cigarette advertising, meanwhile, was banned on radio and television after 1971 by the Public Health Cigarette Smoking Act of 1969.)

In 1974 eight California stations became caught in a Fairness Doctrine controversy over programming on nuclear power plants. At a time when people in California were being asked to sign a petition calling for a referendum on nuclear power plants, the stations aired commercials sponsored by the Pacific Gas and Electric Company promoting nuclear power and power plants. Citizen-action groups brought the matter to the FCC's attention and in 1974 filed an action against thirteen stations. The commission found that five stations had presented the issue fairly by also programming commercials advocating the antinuclear stand. In a sweeping order, it required the other eight to show the FCC how they intended to comply with the Fairness Doctrine. The commission felt that the issue was controversial and of public importance and investigated to the minute the amount of time the stations had devoted to different sides of the issue.[25]

The 1974 Report

In 1974 the FCC reopened hearings on the Fairness Doctrine. It concluded the hearings by issuing an updated report on the applicability of the doctrine. More important, the report also attempted to create an atmosphere of flexibility for interpreting the doctrine. What the FCC, the broadcasters, and the public had been worrying about was the absence of guidelines defining such sensitive concepts as "controversial issue" or "reasonable opportunities for contrasting viewpoints." The commission summed up its feelings on these matters as follows:

> The Fairness Doctrine will not ensure perfect balance and debate, and each station is not required to provide an "equal" opportunity for opposing views. Furthermore, since the Fairness Doctrine does not require balance

in individual programs or a series of programs, but only in a station's overall programming, there is no assurance that a listener who hears an initial presentation will also hear a rebuttal. However, if all stations presenting programming relating to a controversial issue of public importance make an effort to round out their coverage with contrasting viewpoints, these various points of view will receive a much wider public dissemination.[26]

The 1974 report, however, did not diminish debate over the Fairness Doctrine.

Reconsidering the Fairness Doctrine

In 1976 the FCC decided to reconsider the Fairness Doctrine in response to citizens' groups who wanted more access to broadcasting. The commission generally reaffirmed the decisions in its 1974 report. It felt that the doctrine should continue to be applied to advertisements of public issues, not of specific products. It reiterated that broadcast editorials should come under the aegis of the doctrine and reaffirmed the right of the broadcaster to decide how the doctrine should be applied locally. If the FCC did have to intervene, the probable action would simply be to require that the station provide time for opposing viewpoints.

REGULATING OBSCENE, INDECENT, AND PROFANE MATERIAL

One of the most complex areas of broadcast regulation is obscene and indecent programming. The statutes governing such programming have evolved from both the Radio Act of 1927 and the Communications Act of 1934. The former provided for penalties of up to $5,000 and imprisonment for five years for anyone convicted of violating the act, including its obscenity provisions. The

Communications Act changed this to $10,000 and two years in jail, and stated that the violator's license could be suspended for up to two years. In 1937 the penal provisions covering obscenity were amended to include license suspension for those transmitting communications containing profane or obscene "words, language, or meaning." The license suspension was no longer limited to two years, and the word *meaning* became even more appropriate as television became more popular.[27]

The U.S. Criminal Code

In 1948 Congress took the obscenity provisions from the Communications Act of 1934 and put them into the United States Criminal Code. Section 1464 of the code states that "whoever utters any obscene, indecent, or profane language by means of radio communication shall be fined not more than $10,000 or imprisoned not more than two years or both."[28] "Radio communication" includes television. Both the Department of Justice and the FCC have the power to enforce Section 1464. Penalties include forfeiture of a license or construction permit and fines of $1,000 for each day the offense occurs, not to exceed a total of $10,000. The Justice Department can also prosecute under Section 1464 and send a licensee to jail.

Topless Radio and Seven Dirty Words

Among the cases in which the FCC has acted against stations that have broadcast obscene, indecent, or profane material, two stand out. One concerned an Illinois station's "topless" format and the other a New York station's broadcast of a monologue by comedian George Carlin.

On February 23, 1973, a station in Oak Park, Illinois, broadcast a call-in program on oral sex. Female listeners called modera-

tor Morgan Moore with graphic descriptions of their experiences. The format, also employed at other stations, was known as topless radio. Female listeners were not the only ones to contact the station. The FCC notified it of an apparent liability of $2,000 for violating *both* the indecency and obscenity clauses of the criminal code.[29]

Two groups, the Illinois Citizens Committee for Broadcasting and the Illinois Division of the American Civil Liberties Union, asked the FCC to reconsider the ruling. When the commission declined, the Illinois Citizens Committee for Broadcasting went to court. On November 20, 1974, the circuit court upheld the FCC's action and in effect ruled that the commission was acting constitutionally.

On the afternoon of October 30, 1973, WBAI–FM warned its listeners that the broadcast to follow included language that might be offensive. What they heard was an excerpt from George Carlin's album *George Carlin: Occupation Foole*. Carlin's monologue satirized seven four-letter words that could not be used on radio or television because they depicted sexual or excretory organs and activities. A month later the FCC received a complaint from a man who said he had heard the broadcast while driving with his son. It was the only complaint received about the broadcast, which had been aired as part of a discussion on contemporary societies' attitudes toward language.

The FCC issued a declaratory ruling against WBAI–FM, stating that such language "describes, in terms patently offensive as measured by contemporary community standards for the broadcast medium, sexual or excretory activities and organs, at times of the day where there is a reasonable risk that children may be in the audience."[30] The commission also argued that broadcast media should be treated differently from print media in the regulation of indecent material, because broadcast media are intrusive. The argument was based on four considerations:

(1) children have access to radio and in some cases are unsupervised by parents; (2) radio receivers are in the home, a place where people's privacy interest is entitled to extra deference; (3) unconsenting adults may tune in a station without any warning that offensive language is being or will be broadcast; and (4) there is a scarcity of spectrum space, the use of which the government must therefore license in the public interest.[31]

The commission reiterated that it was not in the business of censorship but that it did have a statutory obligation to enforce those provisions of the criminal code that regulated obscene, indecent, or profane language.

Whatever good intentions the commission had in issuing its declaratory order, the U.S. Court of Appeals for the District of Columbia did little to uphold it. Striking down most of the commission's major arguments, the court gave the FCC a judicial setback bordering on embarrassment. It found first that the commission's order was in direct violation of Section 326 of the Communications Act of 1934, which prohibits the FCC from censoring programming. Although the FCC clearly stated that it was not censoring, the appeals court felt it was doing just that simply by issuing the order. The issue did not stop there, however. The case went to the United States Supreme Court, where the FCC found itself back in favor. The single complaint from a father about what his son heard on radio had set a strong precedent for future FCC action against questionable material on the air. It was now clear that there were at least seven words that would cause broadcasters much trouble if they decided to use them on the air.

CONTROLLING RADIO-STATION FORMATS

Although the FCC has tried valiantly to regulate offensive language, it has not tried to dictate radio formats. In fact, the courts have tried to force regulatory power over this area onto the commission—power it does not want, feels to be unconstitutional, and believes to be contrary to the intended purpose of the Communications Act.

Precedent for Format Control

Traditionally, the kind of format a radio station provides for its audience has been the prerogative solely of the licensee. And over the years, stations have shifted formats to meet the pace of competition, not only from other radio stations but also from television. As television grew in popularity, radio decided to compete by incorporating specialized formats. The rock-and-roll of the 1950s thus became soft rock, top-forty rock, progressive rock, oldie rock, and country rock. The diversity succeeded as radio stations were able to capture a specialized audience and attract advertisers wanting to reach that audience. But the marketplace dictated the diversity, not the FCC.

Then, government intervention arrived on the doorsteps of the broadcasting industry.[32] It started in 1970 in Georgia, where in a U.S. Court of Appeals case the Citizens' Committee to Preserve the Voice of the Arts in Atlanta was able to preserve a classical-music format on a local radio station.[33] But the case that set the commission back on its heels involved station WEFM–FM in Chicago. Owned by the Zenith Radio Corporation and having programmed classical music since 1940, the station went up for sale. The prospective buyer, GCC Communications of Chicago, announced that it would change

WEFM–FM's format to contemporary music. Despite citizen uproar, the FCC approved the sale of the station. It reasoned that the Communications Act prohibited it from making decisions based on formats—and in a sense from depriving the licensee of the freedom to operate in the public interest. But the decision was appealed, and in 1974 the Washington, D.C., District Court said that the FCC had erred and should have held a hearing prior to making a decision on the sale.[34]

At this point, the FCC decided to take a closer look at its role in deciding station formats. It asked for opinions on the issue, and broadcasters responded, aided by powerful lobbying from the National Association of Broadcasters. After considering the evidence, the FCC took the unprecedented stance of direct opposition to the court and said that it saw no reason to become involved in determining station formats.[35]

FCC Support for the Licensee's Right to Choose a Format

The FCC's first argument in defense of its stance was that it was unconstitutional for it to become involved in such decisions, and that opening up hearings every time a citizen's group complained about a change in format would create an administrative nightmare. Furthermore, the FCC felt that the marketplace was the arena in which formats should be decided. Audiences and advertisers could determine what best served the public interest. After all, broadcasting was still a business.

Another argument concentrated on the format itself. How could the FCC determine when format changes actually took place? The difference between classical and rock music was one thing, but differentiating between different types of rock music could be extremely difficult, let alone inappropriate,

for a government agency. Furthermore, if the FCC were to rule on one format, then to be equitable it should examine every format of every station in every market. The commission would soon be telling each community what format was best and what radio station should program what format.

Nevertheless, to completely wash its hands of any further consideration of format selection did not seem appropriate. There was still the matter of making sure that stations served the public interest. FCC Commissioner Benjamin Hooks believed that the FCC should still "take an extra hard look at the reasonableness of any proposal which would deprive a community of its only source of a particular type of programming."[36] Commissioner Hooks also felt that minorities should be served with programming, even if the marketplace did not inherently provide it. Those sentiments were echoed by citizens' groups. The Action Alliance of Senior Citizens of Greater Philadelphia, for example, protested that broadcasters direct their programming to groups whom the advertisers pay the most to reach, and thus discriminate against senior citizens. Spanish-American groups also felt that Spanish-culture formats might be eliminated without any recourse for the Spanish-American audience.

Supreme Court Review

Arguments supporting the holding of hearings on formats during licensing proceedings returned to the forefront in the summer of 1979, when the U.S. Court of Appeals reaffirmed its 1974 position and criticized the commission for being lax in its responsibility.[37] The U.S. Supreme Court agreed to hear the case, and in 1981 ruled in favor of the FCC.[38] After a decade of wrestling over the issue of who could have final control over a format, the FCC's choice of the licensee gained the high court's approval. Specifically, the marketplace would become the regulator. Although the Supreme Court's decision would not stop a challenge to a format change, it did give the local broadcaster strong protection against such challenges.

PRIME-TIME ACCESS

Concern over the dominance of network programming prompted the FCC in 1971 to take measures assuring that alternative programming would be aired during the evening hours. Out of these measures came the prime-time access rules. The latest of these, the 1975 Prime Time Access Rule III (PTAR III), charges stations in the top fifty markets that are either network-affiliated or network-owned to clear an hour from network prime-time programming (programming from 7:00 P.M. to 11:00 P.M. in the Eastern and Pacific time zones and from 6:00 P.M. to 10:00 P.M. in the Central and Mountain time zones).[39] In 1975 PTAR III was "refined" by order of the United States Second Circuit Court of Appeals.[40] The rule is designed (1) to give independent producers and syndicators a market for their programming and (2) to encourage local stations to develop creative programming. By applying the rule to the top fifty markets, the FCC has successfully covered the nation. Yet the rule has been more successful in providing time for syndicated programming than in stimulating local creativity. The result has been a plethora of quiz and game shows in the 6:00-to-8:00 P.M. time period across the country.

General Exemptions

PTAR III allows a variety of exemptions. Stations *can* broadcast network or off-network documentary, public-affairs, and children's programming. Public-affairs programming is defined in the same terms as it is in the FCC logging rules, as "talks, commentaries, discussions, speeches, editorials, political programs, documentaries, forums, panels, roundtables, and similar programs primarily concerning local, national, and international public affairs." Feature films can also be broadcast, as can fast-breaking news that would be of interest to the viewing audience. In other words, if a network provides its affiliates with coverage of a major news event, such as an assassination or a natural disaster, the local affiliates can carry the program and have it count as prime-time access. If a television station produces an hour of local news (for example, from 6:00 to 7:00 P.M.) immediately before the prime-time access hour, then it can carry network news up to one-half hour into the access period, or until 7:30 P.M.

Sports Exemptions

Sports programming is also exempt. If a sports event is scheduled to end at the beginning of prime-time access but lasts longer, stations are permitted to continue covering it. Major sports events whose coverage requires all of prime time, such as a New Year's Day football game or an Olympic contest, receive the same exemption.

BROADCAST ADVERTISING

Advertising provides the economic lifeblood for the American system of broadcasting; this is not the case with the government-financed systems existing in many other parts of the world. But federal, state, and even municipal regulations can oversee this lifeblood. We will now concern ourselves primarily with state and federal jurisdiction over commercial radio and television.

State and Federal Jurisdiction

Although we tend to think of radio and television as being governed by federal law, as expressed in the Communications Act of 1934, state laws play an important part when advertising is involved. In a landmark case that applied state jurisdiction to broadcast advertising, a court upheld a New Mexico statute that prohibited a New Mexico radio station from accepting advertising from Texas optometrists. The Texas advertising violated a New Mexico law regulating optometric advertising. The U.S. Supreme Court upheld the New Mexico law, rejecting the contention that it interfered with interstate commerce and was thus preempted by federal law. In a concurring opinion Justice Brennan said, "Rather than mandate ouster of state regulations, several provisions of the Communications Act suggest a congressional design to leave standing various forms of state regulation, including the form embodied in the New Mexico statute."[41]

Robert Sadowski has found advertising to be second only to individual rights in the attention given it by state laws. Forty-three states have passed laws governing over thirty-one different areas of advertising that affect broadcasters.[42] The laws fall into two primary areas: (1) "general regulations, which govern fraudulent advertising, deceptive trade and consumer fraud practices," and (2) more specific regulations, covering "controls over foods, drugs, cosmetics, political advertising, and various other commodities such as insurance, loans, and real estate."[43] Eleven states have given protection to broadcasters who in good faith broadcast an advertisement that turns out to be deceptive. Although we do not hear much about prosecution being conducted under these state laws, they are more than just window dressing. In Mississippi, the attorney general's office moved to stop an individual from advertising paintings supposedly painted by local "starving artists." The office concluded that the paintings were mass-produced in Asia and that all the profits went to the promoter.[44]

The two principal federal agencies affecting broadcast advertising are the Federal Communications Commission and the Federal Trade Commission. The FCC can call upon its blanket "public interest" clause to move in on an unscrupulous broadcaster involved in a deceptive advertising scheme. And move it does, right into a possible license revocation. We have already learned that the commission is directly involved in regulating political advertising through Section 315 of the Communications Act.

Federal Trade Commission Controls

The most pervasive of the agencies that control advertising is the Federal Trade Commission. Through its Bureau of Consumer Protection, the FTC keeps watch on advertising practices affecting both the broadcasting and print media. The quickest way for an advertiser to get into trouble with the FTC is to violate one of its six "basic ground rules":

1. Tendency to deceive. The Commission is empowered to act when representations have only a tendency to mislead or deceive. Proof of actual deception is not essential, although evidence of actual deception is apparently conclusive as to the deceptive quality of the advertisement in question.

2. Immateriality of knowledge of falsity. Since the purpose of the FTC Act is consumer protection, the Government does not have to prove knowledge of falsity on the part of the advertiser; the businessman acts at his own peril.

3. Immateriality of intent. The intent of the advertiser is also entirely immaterial. An advertiser may have a wholly innocent intent and still violate the law.

4. *General public's understanding of controls.* Since the purpose of the Act is to protect the consumers, and since some consumers are "ignorant, unthinking and credulous," nothing less than "the most literal truthfulness" is tolerated. As the Supreme Court has stated, "laws are made to protect the trusting as well as the suspicious." Thus it is immaterial that an expert reader might be able to decipher the advertisement in question so as to avoid being misled.

5. *Literal truth sometimes insufficient.* Advertisements are not intended to be carefully dissected with a dictionary at hand, but rather are intended to produce an overall impression on the ordinary purchaser. An advertiser cannot present one overall impression and yet protect himself by pointing to a contrary impression which appears in a small and inconspicuous portion of the advertisement. Even though every sentence considered separately is true, the advertisement as a whole may be misleading because the message is composed in such a way as to mislead.

6. *Ambiguous advertisements interpreted to effect purposes of the law.* Since the purpose of the FTC Act is the prohibition of advertising which has a tendency and capacity to mislead, an advertisement which can be read to have two meanings is illegal if one of them is false or misleading.[45]

One famous example of FTC action is the "sandpaper shave" case. A commercial for Rapid Shave shaving cream attempted to show the cream's merits in a demonstration with a piece of heavy sandpaper. While an announcer praised the product, it was applied to what appeared to be sandpaper. The next thing you knew, a razor was shaving the sandpaper right before your eyes. As it turned out, the razor did not *immediately* shave the sandpaper, and what was supposed to be sandpaper was really a type of plexiglass with sand affixed to it. After a series of decisions—including those of an FTC examiner, the FTC, and the Supreme Court—the Rapid Shave commercial was stopped.[46] There were, however, convincing arguments that the public was not really harmed by the commercial and that Rapid Shave could in fact shave sandpaper after the sandpaper was soaked for a while. Although the commercial was amended, the FTC action did not prohibit the use of artificial props in television commercials.

The FTC and Corrective Advertising

Corrective advertising is another area overseen by the FTC. For example, the ITT Continental Baking Company, distributors of Profile Bread, was required to run corrective advertising to clarify earlier commercials that, according to the FTC, misled people into thinking Profile Bread could help them lose weight. In another case, Firestone Tire and Rubber Company agreed to pay $50,000 in penalties and $750,000 for a tire-safety campaign to settle an FTC claim that the company had aired misleading advertisements.[47] A substantial $550,000 of the settlement was appropriated for television commercials to be aired in major-network news and sports programming. The FTC had pursued the company through the federal courts under provisions of the FTC Act. In a third case, the J. B. Williams Company of New York agreed to an out-of-court settlement in a suit brought by the FTC concerning ads for Geritol. The FTC claimed the commercials violated an FTC order prohibiting statements that the products "helped relieve tiredness, loss of strength, run-down feeling, nervousness or irritability without also saying that these symptoms usually result from iron deficiency and that Geritol could not help in these cases."[48]

Guarding Against Fraudulent Billing

One of the most serious infractions a broadcaster can commit is fraudulent billing, sometimes called double billing.[49] The FCC rules are definitive in this area: Section 73.1205 warns that

> no licensee of a standard, FM, or television broadcast station shall knowingly issue or knowingly cause to be issued to any local, regional or national advertiser, advertising agency, station representative, manufacturer, distributor, jobber, or any other party, any bill, invoice, affidavit or other document which contains false information concerning the amount actually charged by the licensee for the broadcast advertising for which such bill, invoice, affidavit or other document is issued, or which misrepresents the nature or content of such advertising, or which misrepresents the quantity of advertising actually broadcast (number or length of advertising messages) or which substantially and/or materially misrepresents the time of day at which it was broadcast, or which misrepresents the date on which it was broadcast.

Fraudulent billing can occur in a variety of situations, the most common being co-op advertising. Here, the manufacturer or major distributor of a product pays part of the cost of the advertising. To better understand this concept, let's assume that the Ordinary Appliance Store sells a toaster manufactured by Tommy Toasters. Ordinary enters into an agreement with Tommy Toasters to split the cost of one hundred commercials on station WXXX, but instead of mentioning Tommy Toasters the Ordinary commercials talk about stoves and refrigerators. The cost of the commercials is $500. WXXX sends a bill for $250 to Ordinary and another $250 bill to Tommy Toasters for co-op advertising. The station is thus guilty of fraudulent billing practices and is in danger of having its license revoked.

Another variation of fraudulent billing occurs if WXXX sends a bill to Tommy Toasters for more than the amount of the co-op advertising, such as $500 instead of $250, in the hope that Tommy will pay the bill without realizing the overcharge. If Tommy does recognize it, WXXX could claim it expected Tommy to pay only half the bill and Ordinary the remainder. A more direct form of fraudulent billing is to charge an advertiser for commercials that did not air, or to overbill an ad agency in order to recoup the 15-percent discount normally given agency orders. A subtle fraudulent-billing practice would be for WXXX to take the Ordinary portion of the bill in trade-out, such as having Ordinary furnish WXXX's lunchroom with a new stove at a wholesale price. Since at that price the stove would cost Ordinary less than $250, Tommy Toasters would be paying more than half of the bill.

Network Clipping

Network clipping is also considered fraudulent billing. Network clipping is *the practice of certifying to a network that a network commercial has been aired when in fact it has not.* Local affiliates provide networks with an accounting of all the network commercials that they air locally. Failing to air a commercial may cut the amount of compensation a station receives from the network. Nevertheless, when a station fails to air a commercial, either deliberately or inadvertently, the network is notified of that as part of the special certification report. Listing a network commercial as having been aired when it was not is considered a violation of the FCC's Section 73.1205. The roster of commercial credits shown at the end of a game show is also considered commercial matter, and deleting this content without reporting that it was deleted is also a violation. The FCC *does not prohibit* local stations from deleting network programming. What it prohibits is deleting the programming *without notifying* the network and thereby receiving compensation for services *not* rendered.

Fraudulent billing not only reflects directly on a broadcaster's character but also sheds negative light on the entire broadcasting industry. As a result, the FCC has shown few qualms about revoking a station's license over this issue.

EQUAL-EMPLOYMENT OPPORTUNITY

The federal government's insistence on increasing the proportion of women and minorities in the work force has been translated into action by the Equal Employment Opportunity Commission and the requirement that affirmative-action measures be taken by business and industry throughout the United States. Although the Federal Communications Commission is not directly responsible for enforcing affirmative-action programs, it has taken steps to assure that broadcasting stations do not fall behind in their commitments to affirmative action. An extensive explanation of how a station administers its affirmative-action program is required at the time of license renewal. And when considering a license renewal, the FCC will compare the current affirmative-action program with the one in the previous license renewal. By using the "public interest" clause of the Communications Act, the FCC is able to put some teeth into its requirements. Its power is based on the rationale that a "broadcaster who refuses to hire minority and women employees will face a difficult, if not insurmountable obstacle to the presentation of programming to meet the problems, needs and interests of minorities and women."[50]

Model Affirmative-Action Plan

The FCC has outlined a model affirmative-action program for all stations.[51] Let's assume we are operating a station and examine the steps we could take to conform with this program. Keep in mind that our commitment would be communicated in writing to the FCC as part of our station's license renewal. (The discussion that follows is a highly abbreviated version of the full FCC text.)

1. Statement of General Policy The first part of our program would consist of a statement committing the station to affirmative action in all areas of station business, which would include not only hiring employees but also promoting, compensating, and terminating them. Take note of the word *terminating*—if we aren't going to discriminate in hiring, then we can't do so in firing. Overall, the program must be a positive effort, assuring equal opportunity without regard to sex, race, national origin, color, or religion.

2. Responsibility for Implementation Our next responsibility would be to implement our commitment. We would want to appoint someone at the station as our affirmative-action administrator. If we have delegated the responsibility for firing and hiring to another administrator, such as a sales manager or news director, then we will want to make sure that person adheres to our commitment.

3. Policy Dissemination But it is not enough merely to have an affirmative-action program. We need to publicize it through such means as posters, which tell applicants or employees where to write if they feel they have been discriminated against. The Department of Labor makes available posters containing such warnings. We could also put an affirmative-action statement on the station's employment application.

4. Recruitment Hiring is usually the easiest task in an affirmative-action program. What takes work is obtaining a pool of applicants from which to choose. We will need to recruit people by advertising our job openings. And in each ad we will want to include a statement identifying our station as an equal-opportunity employer. Potential women applicants can be reached through ads in newsletters such as *Matrix,* published by Women in Communications, Inc., and *News and Views,* from American Women in Radio and Television. Minorities can be reached through similar publications. Employment agencies and the placement services at local colleges are two additional avenues. Keep in mind that we will need to provide the FCC with a list of the organizations we contacted and the number of applicants received from each one.

5. Training If our station is small, developing a full-scale minority-training program may be difficult. On the other hand, an internship program initiated with a local college can at least show a good-faith effort within our means. If we set up such a program, or if we are large enough to have a minority-training program, we will want to describe these efforts to the FCC.

6. Availability Survey In order for the FCC to compare the success of our program with the work force in our local area, we will need to supply them with a recent availability survey. Such a survey discusses such factors as the percentages of women and minorities in the work force from which we can directly recruit—usually the metropolitan area in which the station is licensed, or in some cases the county in which it is located.

7. Current Employment Survey In addition to the FCC's model EEO program, our station should file an annual employment report. To become part of the public file, this report details the number of women and members of minority groups who are employed by the station and notes how many occupy top management positions. We may even want to supplement the employment report with a description of women and minority employees in all job classifications within the station.

8. Job Hires Section 8 of our EEO program will note the number of women and minority employees hired in the past twelve months. If in our opinion not enough minority applicants are applying for positions, we will want to explain how we are going to beef up our recruiting practices in the future.

9. Promotion A responsible affirmative-action program deals not only with hiring but also with promotion. When openings develop within our organization we should always scan our current personnel to see who might be qualified for the jobs. If we find them, let's reward them. Visible opportunities for upward mobility increase station morale. Let's encourage women and minority employees to apply for advancement within the organization, and be sure to report the number of those affirmative-action promotions to the FCC.

10. Effectiveness of the Affirmative-Action Plan In reporting the results of our affirmative-action program to the FCC, we will want to include an objective evaluation of our program's effectiveness. Honesty is important, even if our program is deficient. And as in Section 8, we will want to examine how our program can be improved if it is not meeting our expectations. For example, we might try to improve self-imposed or FCC standards.

FCC Evaluation

What does the commission look for when it evaluates a station's affirmative-action program? The FCC suggests that at the very least it will see whether the station follows its ten-point model program. The commission will then examine the percentage of minority and female employees, both overall and in the top four job categories. As a general rule, full-time minority and women employees must constitute 50 percent of the work-force availability overall in the upper four job categories. If not, the station could be headed for a review.

SEXUAL HARASSMENT

Broadcasters are becoming increasingly aware of the effects of sexual harassment both on individuals and on the overall operation of stations. Recent court rulings consider sexual harassment a form of sexual discrimination under Title VII of the 1964 Civil Rights Act. What exactly constitutes sexual harassment is something that must be determined by the circumstances surrounding each incident. Moreover, because such incidents often occur in private, the testimony of the plaintiff and the defendant without the benefit of other witnesses makes the sexual-harassment area of discrimination law particularly difficult to rule on.

Specifically, the Equal Employment Opportunity Commission considers unlawful sexual harassment to occur:

(1) When submission to such sexual conduct is "explicitly or implicitly" a condition of an individual's employment;

(2) When submission to or rejection of such sexual conduct becomes the basis of employment decisions "affecting" an employee; or

(3) When such sexual conduct has the pur-

pose or effect of substantially interfering with an individual's job performance or creating an intimidating, hostile or offensive working atmosphere.[52]

Because sexual harassment can be treated as a violation of a station's affirmative-action policy, communications attorneys advise stations to try to make employees aware of what constitutes sexual harassment, what the penalties are for those engaging in sexual harassment, and how to file complaints of sexual harassment.

STARTING A NEW STATION

Even though in many communities frequencies are getting harder and harder to find, enterprising entrepreneurs have not been deterred from seeking out locations for new stations. Let's briefly review the steps that one must go through to start a new station.

Preliminary Steps

The first step in starting a new station is to find an area where a frequency is available. For an AM radio station, the search will involve not only consulting the engineering data of stations already in the market but also having a qualified engineer conduct a *frequency search*. The frequency search entails checking the exact broadcast contours of stations presently serving the area and determining what type of signal will not interfere with those currently operating. Thus, researching possible wattage, contour patterns, and available frequencies must all precede the application process.

Starting an FM radio or TV station is a bit different. An applicant for an FM radio license must select either an available frequency already assigned by the FCC to the area where the applicant wants to operate or a place within a specified radius where no FM frequency has been assigned. TV applicants must request a UHF or VHF channel, assigned either to the community or to a place where there is no channel assignment within fifteen miles of the community.

Once the frequency search has been completed, the next step is a community-needs and ascertainment survey.

From Construction Permit to License

Once the community-needs and ascertainment survey is completed, the applicant applies to the FCC for a *construction permit*. The applicant must also possess the wherewithal to operate the station for at least one year after construction. Notice of the pending application must be made in the local newspaper, and a public-inspection file must be kept in the locality where the station will be built. After the applicant has filed with the FCC, others have the opportunity to comment on the application or, in the case of competing applicants, file against it. If necessary, the FCC will schedule a hearing on the application. Following the hearing the FCC administrative law judge will issue a decision, which can be appealed.

If everything in the application is found satisfactory and there are no objections, the FCC then issues the construction permit. Construction on the station must begin within sixty days of the date the construction permit is issued. Depending on the type of station, a period of up to eighteen months from that date is given for construction. If the applicant cannot build the station in the time allotted, then he or she must apply for an extension.

After the station is constructed the applicant applies for the *license*. At this time the applicant can also request authority to conduct program tests. These tests will usually be permitted if nothing has come to the attention of the FCC that would indicate that the operation of the station would be contrary to the public interest. When the license is issued the station can go on the air and begin regular programming.

Although the procedure is somewhat systematic, putting the station on the air is anything but simple. Completing the paperwork, dealing with engineers and communication attorneys, and securing the financing necessary not only to buy land and equipment but also to keep the station running for a year can all be difficult and time-consuming obstacles to overcome. If objections or competing applications become an issue, the court costs involved can discourage an applicant from completing the application process. Still, for those who succeed the rewards can be substantial, both in personal satisfaction and in income.

SUMMARY

Government control of over-the-air programming is a major concern of the broadcasting industry. It is based on the fact that the electromagnetic spectrum over which radio and television waves travel is a limited resource that must have safeguards if it is to be responsibly used. Coupled with this is the tremendous influence of radio and television, an influence that with the aid of satellites can cross international boundaries.

The regulations that have arisen from Section 315 of the Communications Act and from the Fairness Doctrine are of concern to both broadcasters and the public. Section 315 is concerned mainly with political broadcasting and assures that candidates for the same public office will have the same opportunity to gain access to the broadcast media. Key parts of Section 315 include its definitions of equal time, its anticensorship provisions, and its lowest-unit-charge rule.

The Fairness Doctrine traces its roots to the 1940s, when the FCC prohibited editorializing. The FCC reversed itself in 1949, and since then the doctrine has been revised considerably, mostly through FCC policies and court decisions. It now covers all areas of radio and television broadcasting, including advertising and news programming.

The FCC has found one of its strongest footholds in the control of obscene, indecent, and profane material. Supported by the U.S. Criminal Code, the FCC has levied sanctions against numerous stations for violations in this area. Two of the most famous cases were the frank discussions of sex found in "topless radio" formats and the broadcasting of comedian George Carlin's monologue on words prohibited on radio and television.

The FCC and the courts have wrestled over control of radio-station formats. Until 1981 most of the pressure for control came from the courts. But in that year the United States Supreme Court ruled in favor of the FCC and stations were permitted to let the marketplace determine the format.

The Prime-Time Access Rule (PTAR) is designed to encourage alternatives to network programming during certain hours preceding prime-time programming. Although PTAR makes available certain exemptions, it has created a market for syndicated programming and some nonnetwork programs produced by local stations.

Broadcast advertising is controlled mostly by the Federal Trade Commission, though in some areas it falls under both state and federal jurisdiction. Six areas in which violations can quickly draw FTC scrutiny are the tendency to deceive, the immateriality of knowledge of falsity, the immateriality of intent, the general public's understanding of controls, the insufficiency of literal truth, and ambiguous advertisements interpreted to effect purposes of the law. Fraudulent billing and network clipping are illegal and can result in severe penalties administered by the FCC.

Of all the federal agencies, the FCC has been one of the most vigorous in enforcing affirmative-action programs. A typical affirmative-action program consists of a statement of general policy, responsibility for implementation, policy dissemination, recruitment, training, an availability survey, a current employment survey, a job-hires summary, promotion, and an evaluation of the effectiveness of the program.

Allied to a station's affirmative-action plan is its policy statement on sexual harassment. Because sexual harassment can be regarded as a violation of a station's affirmative-action policy, communications attorneys advise stations to make employees aware of what constitutes sexual harassment.

Starting a new station is a systematic process. The owner must first obtain a construction permit and then a license to operate.

OPPORTUNITIES FOR FURTHER LEARNING

Applicability of the Fairness Doctrine in the Handling of Controversial Issues of Public Importance FCC 64-611. Washington, D.C.: Federal Communications Commission, 1964.

BOSMAJIAN, H. A., ed., *Obscenity and Freedom of Expression*. New York: Burt Franklin, 1976.

CHAMBERLIN, B., and C. J. BROWN, eds., *The First Amendment Reconsidered*. New York: Longman, 1982.

Cox, A., *Freedom of Expression*. Cambridge, Mass.: Harvard University Press, 1981.

CULLEN, M. R., Jr., *Mass Media and the First Amendment: An Introduction to the Issues, Problems, and Practices*. Dubuque, Iowa: William C. Brown, 1981.

DEVOL, K. S., ed., *Mass Media and the Supreme Court: The Legacy of the Warren Years*. New York: Hastings House, 1976.

Fairness Doctrine and Public Standards. Docket 19260. Washington, D.C.: Federal Communications Commission, 1974.

FRANKLIN, M. A., *The First Amendment and the Fourth Estate*. Mineola, N.Y.: Foundation Press, 1977.

FRENCH, C. W., E. A. POWELL, and H. ANGIONE, eds., *The Associated Press Stylebook and Libel Manual*. Reading, Mass: Addison-Wesley, 1982.

FRIENDLY, F. W., *The Good Guys, the Bad Guys and the First Amendment: Free Speech vs. Fairness in Broadcasting*. New York: Random House, 1976.

GULLEN, M. R., Jr., *Mass Media and the First Amendment*. Dubuque, Iowa: William C. Brown, 1981.

HAIMAN, F. S., *Speech and Law in a Free Society*. Chicago: University of Chicago Press, 1981.

KURLAND, P. B., ed., *Free Speech and Association: The Supreme Court and the First Amendment*. Chicago: University of Chicago Press, 1976.

LABUNSKI, R. E., *The First Amendment Under Siege: The Politics of Broadcast Regulation*. Westport, Conn: Greenwood Press, 1981.

LAWHORNE, C. O., *The Supreme Court and Libel*. Carbondale: Southern Illinois University Press, 1981.

LEWIS, F. F., *Literature, Obscenity, and Law*. Carbondale: Southern Illinois University Press, 1976.

National Association of Broadcasters, *Purchasing a Broadcast Station: A Buyer's Guide*. Washington, D.C.: National Association of Broadcasting, 1978.

National Association of Broadcasters and National Broadcast Editorial Association, *The Editorial Director's Desk Book*. Washington, D.C.: National Association of Broadcasters, 1980.

OWEN, B. M., *Economics and Freedom of Expression: Media Structure and the First Amendment*. Cambridge, Mass.: Ballinger, 1975.

PALETZ, D. L., R. E. PEARSON, and D. L. WILLIS, *Politics in Public Service Advertising on Television*. New York: Praeger, 1977.

Political Broadcast Catechism. Washington, D.C.: Legal Department, National Association of Broadcasters, 1976.

READ, W. H., *The First Amendment Meets the Second Revolution*. Cambridge, Mass.: Harvard Program on Information Resources Policy, 1981.

ROBERTSON, S. M., *Courts and the Media*. Toronto: Butterworths, 1981.

RUCKELSHAUS, W., and E. ABEL, eds., *Freedom of the Press*. Washington, D.C.: American Enterprise Institute for Public Policy Research, 1976.

SADOWSKI, R. P., *An Analysis of Statutory Laws Governing Commercial and Educational Broadcasting in the Fifty States*. New York: Arno Press, 1979.

SANFORD, B. W., *Synopsis of the Law of Libel and the Right of Privacy* (rev. ed.). New York: World Almanac, 1981.

SCHILLER, D., *Objectivity and the News: The Public and the Rise of Commercial Journalism*. Philadelphia: University of Pennsylvania Press, 1981.

SIMMONS, S. J., *The Fairness Doctrine and the Media*. Berkeley: University of California Press, 1978.

STEVENS, J. D., *Shaping the First Amendment*. Beverly Hills, Calif.: Sage, 1982.

19

REGULATORY ISSUES INVOLVING COMMON CARRIERS, CABLE, COPYRIGHT, AND COMPUTERS

The microwave link between the island of Ocracoke and the mainland and the satellite relaying data from an ocean research vessel both operate on regulated channels of communication. These channels, which are leased to the public, are called common carriers. Under the law, a communications common carrier is defined as "one whose services are open to the public for hire for handling interstate and foreign communications by electrical means."[1] An over-the-air radio or television station that sends us the evening news is not a common carrier. The services of the station are not open to the public for hire. On the other hand, the telephone lines that come into our home are common carriers since anyone can "lease" these lines from the telephone company, and

in fact we use these leased lines every time we make a telephone call. We pay a monthly fee for this service, and the Federal Communications Commission regulates the telephone company just as it does the radio or television station.

With the advent of information technologies, a knowledge of common carriers has become important to a total understanding of telecommunication regulation. When we interface our personal computer with a central data bank through our telephone and call up information on a videotex terminal, we are using a common carrier. When we purchase a machine that automatically answers our telephone calls when we are not at home, we become subject to the regulations that guarantee us the freedom to purchase and connect to our telephone any answering machine we like as long as it meets certain technical standards prescribed by the FCC.

THE COMMON-CARRIER CONCEPT: HISTORICAL BASIS OF CONTROL

Two pieces of legislation regulated interstate communication long before modern applications of telecommunication—the Post Roads Act of 1866 and the Mann-Elkins Act of 1910.

The Post Roads Act of 1866

The system of telephone lines and cables that intertwine across vast stretches of landscape was encouraged by the Post Roads Act of 1866. At the time of its passage, however, the telegraph was the new electrical device being introduced to long-distance communication. The act granted the government the right-of-way over public land, thereby permitting it to install telegraph lines over the most accessible routes. The legal basis for this system was inherited by the telephone companies and even the railroads. Essential to a nationwide system of electrical communication was this capacity to install lines uninhibited by private property.

The Mann-Elkins Act of 1910

The authority of the FCC, and state utility commissions, to set the rates common carriers charge for their services is based in the Mann-Elkins Act of 1910. The act extended certain provisions of the Interstate Commerce Act to cover common carriers using both wire and radio communication.

Today, through a series of amendments to the Communications Act of 1934, com-mon carriers are regulated by the FCC. Internationally they are regulated by treaties administered through the International Telecommunication Union in cooperation with various government bodies such as the United States Department of State.

STATE VERSUS FEDERAL CONTROL OF COMMON CARRIERS

The FCC does not have exclusive control over common carriers. Much control is shared by state governments. To understand this division of regulatory responsibility it is necessary to understand the differences between *fully subject* and *partially subject* carriers.

Partially Subject Common Carriers

These are carriers that are only partially subject to the controls of the FCC and the Communications Act. Partially subject carriers do not engage in "interstate or foreign communication except through connection with the wire, cable, or radio facilities of non-affiliated carriers."[2] An intrastate common carrier (one that is entirely within a state's boundaries) is generally subject not to FCC jurisdiction but to the state utility commission.

Fully Subject Common Carriers

These carriers are engaged in interstate and international communication and come under FCC jurisdiction. Before constructing, acquiring, or operating common-carrier facilities for such communication they must receive FCC approval. In addition, they cannot discontinue or curtail service without FCC approval. Charges and practices must be reasonable, and the carriers must file rate schedules with the FCC, which reviews and has final authority over them.

AREAS OF FCC JURISDICTION OVER COMMON CARRIERS

The areas where the FCC has jurisdiction over common carriers can be divided into (1) operations and (2) licensing and facilities.

Operations

Fully subject carriers are subject to FCC control over their basic operating practices. For example, the FCC determines the forms, records, and accounts that fully subject carriers employ. This uniform system of accounts includes establishing and maintaining uniform records for cost accounting, property records, pension-cost records, and depreciation records. Much like radio and television stations, common carriers must keep certain records over time.

The FCC also has the authority to determine the depreciation rates the larger carriers use for equipment and facilities. Monthly and annual reports required of the carriers provide the FCC with operating and financial information. The FCC, moreover, "regulates the interlocking of officers and directors of carriers fully subject to the Act, it being unlawful for any person to hold office in more than one such carrier unless authorized by the FCC."[3]

Licensing and Facilities

Common carriers that use radio waves, including microwave and satellite communication, must obtain a license. The FCC guards against interference of these radio signals just as it does the signals of standard broadcast stations. Licenses are limited to citizens of the United States and denied to corporations in which any officer or director is an alien or of which more than one-fifth of the capital stock is owned by aliens or foreign interests. The FCC is charged with seeing that facilities are adequate but not excessive and that rates are "reasonable and prudent."

REGULATING COMMON-CARRIER INTERCONNECTION DEVICES

With the increased use of videotex devices, more and more companies are becoming involved in marketing equipment that connects to a telephone in the home. The opening up of this market, once primarily the domain of the telephone companies, has been made possible by key court and FCC decisions. In *Hush-a-Phone* v. *United States* the courts overruled the FCC, claiming that the public should be protected against "unwarranted interference with the telephone subscriber's right to use his telephone in ways which are privately beneficial without being publically detrimental."[4] In another case the FCC ruled that prohibiting the use of interconnection devices that do not adversely affect the telephone system was unreasonable and unlawful.[5] In litigation over General Telephone's acquisition of the Hawaiian Telephone Company a court held that a telephone company could not limit purchase of equipment from the company's subsidiary.[6] Such action was an unreasonable restraint of trade.

THE BASIS FOR REGULATING CABLE

Originally the FCC exercised considerable control over cable systems.[7] Its authority over cable began as early as 1962, and established rules for regulating cable were approved by the commission in 1965. FCC control was based on cable's use of microwave systems: since the FCC had control over microwave, it gradually acquired control over cable systems as well. In 1966 the FCC passed rules controlling cable systems that did not employ microwave links.

United States v. Southwestern Cable Co.

Knowing that a court case would soon test its jurisdiction over cable, the FCC decided to prepare for the inevitable when it issued a decision limiting the signals that a San Diego cable system could import from Los Angeles. The test case came in *United States* v. *Southwestern Cable Co.*, in which the Supreme Court upheld the FCC's right to regulate cable as part of its mandate under the Communications Act to regulate "interstate commerce by wire or radio."[8] By 1968 the FCC had started developing comprehensive regulations for cable, which it finally issued in 1972.[9]

Gradually, however, local government began to exercise control over local cable systems. It became clear that this new medium was much better controlled at the local level than by the federal government. Regulatory conflicts between agencies of federal and local control (and in some cases of state control) began to develop, and today the FCC has delegated much of its authority to local communities.

Registration Requirements for Cable Systems

Before a cable system can begin operation or add any television broadcast signals to existing operations, the cable operator must register each "system community unit" with the FCC. A system community unit is defined as "a cable TV system, or portion of a cable system, operating within a separate and distinct community or municipal entity, including unincorporated areas and separate unincorporated areas within them."[10] Moreover, "if a cable television facility serves fewer than 50 subscribers but is part of a larger system which, taken as a whole, serves 50 or more subscribers, the smaller facility is considered a community unit and is required to register."[11]

To register a cable facility, the cable operator must file with the secretary of the FCC

(1) The legal name of the operator, Entity Identification or Social Security number, and whether the operator is an individual, private association, partnership or corporation; if the operator is a partnership, the legal name of the partner responsible for communications with the Commission;

(2) The assumed name (if any) used for doing business in the community;

(3) The mail address, including zip code, and the telephone number to which all communications are to be directed;

(4) The date the system provided service to 50 subscribers;

(5) The name of the community or area served and the county in which it is located;

(6) The television broadcast signals to be carried which previously have not been certified or registered; and

(7) For a cable system (or an employment unit) with five or more full-time employees, a statement of the proposed community unit's equal employment opportunity program, unless such program has previously been filed for the community unit or is not required to be filed based on an anticipated number of fewer than five full-time employees during January, February and March of the year following commencement of operation; an explanation must be submitted if no program statement is filed.[12]

Cable systems serving fewer than one thousand subscribers are mostly exempt from the FCC rules governing cable. In general these smaller systems must merely

(1) Comply with the registration requirements described above;

(2) Comply with requests from local television stations for carriage on the cable system;

(3) Comply with the Commission's technical standards for cable television systems, including the frequency use requirements (except that annual proof of performance tests are not required);

(4) Correct and/or furnish information in response to the following forms sent to the cable operator annually by the Commission:

—Form 325: "Annual Report of Cable Television System" (Schedules 1 and 2 only)

—Form 326: "Cable Television Annual Financial Report"

—Form 395A: "Annual Employment Report" (including the annual report of complaints)[13]

CABLE'S LOCAL REGULATORY FRAMEWORKS

The concepts that regulate cable are based at the local level. Unlike over-the-air broadcasting, cable can be regulated by its local community, which has the authority to place certain service and operational requirements upon it, to levy fees, and to determine community-access channels. The types of local control vary considerably. Vernone Sparkes studied these different types and classified them into five agency organizations.[14] The first is an *administrative office*, where the local government establishes a regulatory agency much like the FCC. It might be found in the mayor's office or in the city planner's office. A second type is the *advisory committee* which can be appointed by the mayor or the city council to "advise" city government on cable regulation. Closely related to the advisory committee is an *advisory committee, with administrative office*, which "combines an appointed advisory committee with a full-time salaried executive office." Sparkes points out that the executive usually works independently of the advisory committee, which advises the city council on policy matters. A fourth organization calls for the creation of an *independent regulatory commission*, which administrates and participates in rule making. A fifth plan provides for an *elected board*, which answers to the electorate on cable regulations rather than to another elected body.

RECOMMENDED FRANCHISE STANDARDS FOR CABLE SYSTEMS

The franchise is the contractual agreement between the local governmental unit and the cable company. Although the FCC has kept a regulatory distance between itself and the local authorities who govern cable systems, it has recommended standards that communities can follow in dealing with local cable systems. The FCC suggests that any cable franchise contain the following provisions:

1. The franchising authority should approve a franchisee's qualifications only after a full public proceeding affording due process;

2. Neither the initial franchise period nor the renewal period should exceed 15 years, and any renewal should be granted only after a public proceeding affording due process;

3. The franchise should accomplish significant construction within one year after registering with the Commission and make

service available to a substantial portion of the franchise area each following year, as determined by the franchising authority;

4. A franchise policy requiring less than complete wiring of the franchise area should be adopted only after a full public proceeding, preceded by specific notice of such policy; and

5. The franchise should specify that the franchisee and franchisor have adopted local procedures for investigating and resolving complaints.[15]

The FCC also recommends that local franchisees adopt a local complaint procedure, identify a local person who will handle complaints, and specify how complaints can be reported and resolved. The FCC recommends further that the franchisee identify, by title, the office or person who is responsible for the continuing administration of the franchise and the implementation of complaint procedures.[16]

STATE REGULATION OF CABLE

State government also plays a major role in controlling cable.[17] However, state control is not widespread and varies in degree. State laws can be classified into three categories.

Preempt Statutes

These are the strongest laws, and they take precedent over local regulations. If subject to preempt statutes, cable will fall under the jurisdiction of the public utility commission or public service commission in some states. Preempt statutes give considerable clout to a state commission, permitting it to issue and enforce a separate set of state cable regulations. These rules can govern everything from the day-to-day operation of the cable system to collecting fees on gross revenue to demanding financial collateral before allowing construction.

Appellate Statutes

Here, local municipalities retain some control over franchising, but the state has the power to review local agreements and be the final arbiter of disputes. Everything works fine until the state and a municipality disagree. Then the municipality stands a less than even chance against the state.

Advisory Statutes

These are more popular with cable systems and municipalities, since they do not have either the clout or the enforcement power of a state commission. Some serve as general guidelines for local government.

Arguments for State Control

Proponents of state control argue the need for consistency among cable systems within a state. Such arguments gain support when two municipalities cannot resolve their jurisdictional differences over a cable system or when significantly different fee structures provoke public outcry. Control of cable can also be a political plum for legislators, since it means control of a communication system, and communication influences public opinion. Since cable commissions can have a significant effect on cable growth within a state, appointment to the commission can be a sweet political reward for a member of the party in power.

Arguments Against State Control

Opponents of state control are equally vociferous, asserting that it presents an unnecessary duplication of law. States are sometimes caught between local and federal control, and meeting the requirements of one can violate those of the other. Opponents claim that state control throws local interests into a political arena with representatives who are looking out for their own interests, not for those of the local community. The Big Brother argument also pops up: when a state becomes involved in direct programming it will be oriented more toward propaganda than toward the public interest.

Despite the existence of state statutes, local municipalities seem to continue to have fairly firm control over local cable systems. Moreover, with the tremendous diversity among the systems and the communities they serve, governance at the municipal level appears to have significant advantage over state control.

COPYRIGHT LEGISLATION

In 1976 Congress completely overhauled copyright legislation for the first time since 1909. Of interest to broadcasters were sections of the new copyright law on the length of copyright works, provisions covering cable television, and rules governing reproduction of programming for educational purposes.

Most of the content of broadcast programming can be copyrighted. For example, a local commercial that was prepared by an ad agency or by someone at the station can fall under copyright.[18] Even a disc jockey's afternoon radio show can be copyrighted.[19] The original script of a television drama, the local or network evening news, and a sports documentary can all be copyrighted. Copyright law is designed to protect all of these works from infringement by other parties who may want to use the material for personal gain.

Most of us think of copyrighted material as books, magazine articles, or pictures. But these only scratch the copyright surface. Even an idea can be copyrighted if an aural or visual recording can be retained as evidence of its origin. Network news programs have been copyrighted for years as a protection against someone recording and selling them as either entertainment or source material. And we are all familiar with the careful protection that copyright gives to musical recordings in an industry where pirated tapes and records are a constant concern.

Length of Copyright

The 1976 copyright law extended the length of copyright from a maximum of fifty-six years (two twenty-eight-year terms) to the length of the author's life plus fifty years. Especially meaningful to heirs, the extended term permits the "estate of the deceased to benefit from profits obtained from the copyrighted work.[20]

Reproduction for Educational Purposes

The fair-use provisions of the law provide for certain kinds of reproduction of broadcast programs by teachers and libraries. However, this area of the law is nebulous, and *fair use* is a very flexible term, applicable in different ways under different conditions. No one can unlawfully record a program without the possibility of incurring the charge of copyright infringement.

COPYRIGHT GUIDELINES ON FAIR USE OF VIDEOTAPES FOR EDUCATIONAL PURPOSES

Considerable confusion exists over what constitutes fair use. In 1979 the House Subcommittee on Courts, Civil Liberties and Administration of Justice charged a committee of representatives of educational organizations, copyright proprietors, and creative guilds and unions with determining a set of guidelines for fair use of television programs for educational purposes. Here is the nine-point program that resulted.

1. The guidelines were developed to apply only to off-air recording by non-profit educational institutions.

2. A broadcast program may be recorded off-air simultaneously with broadcast transmission (including simultaneous cable retransmission) and retained by a non-profit educational institution for a period not to exceed the first forty-five (45) consecutive calendar days after date of recording.

Upon conclusion of such retention period, all off-air recordings must be erased or destroyed immediately. "Broadcast programs" are television programs transmitted by television stations for reception by the general public without charge.

3. Off-air recordings may be used once by individual teachers in the course of relevant teaching activities, and repeated once only when instructional reinforcement is necessary, in classrooms and similar places devoted to instruction within a single building, cluster or campus, as well as in the homes of students receiving formalized home instruction, during the first ten (10) consecutive school days in the forty-five (45) calendar day retention period.

4. Off-air recordings may be made only at the request of and used by individual teachers, and may not be regularly recorded in anticipation of requests. No broadcast program may be recorded off-air more than once at the request of the same teacher, regardless of the number of times the program may be broadcast.

5. A limited number of copies may be reproduced from each off-air recording to meet the legitimate needs of teachers under these guidelines. Each such additional copy shall be subject to all provisions governing the original recording.

6. After the first ten (10) consecutive school days, off-air recordings may be used up to the end of the forty-five (45) calendar day retention period only for teacher evaluation purposes, i.e., to determine whether or not to include the broadcast program in the teaching curriculum, and may not be used in the recording institution for student exhibi-

tion or any other nonevaluation purpose without authorization.

7. Off-air recordings need not be used in their entirety, but the recorded programs may not be altered from their original content. Off-air recordings may not be physically or electronically combined or merged to constitute teaching anthologies or compilations.

8. All copies of off-air recordings must include the copyright notice on the broadcast program as recorded.

9. Educational institutions are expected to establish appropriate control procedures to maintain the integrity of these guidelines.[21]

COPYRIGHT AND CABLE: THE COMPULSORY LICENSE

Under the new copyright law cable systems must obtain a *compulsory license,* which permits them to carry over-the-air signals pursuant to FCC rules. This license should not be confused with the contracts or other agreements instituted by local or state governments with cable systems, which govern the actual operations and fee schedules of the systems.

Structure of Compulsory Licensing

The new copyright law views cable systems as commercial entities involved in the "performance" of copyrighted works, and as such they must pay copyright fees under the compulsory-licensing system. For example, under the new law and compulsory licensing, commercial broadcasters receive protection from infringement by cable systems, which might carry the over-the-air system's programming but delete its commercials. As another example, assume a cable company carries Channel 2 television from Anytown, U.S.A. Channel 2 sells advertising to sponsors with the understanding that the station's signal reaches not only Anytown but also outlying communities via cable. The cable company, on the other hand, decides to delete Channel 2's commercials and insert either its own commercials or public-service announcements. This action by the cable company could now be considered illegal. The law gives a television or radio station the right to take a cable company to court not only to stop the practice of commercial substitution but also to receive damages.

Obtaining and Renewing the Compulsory License

To obtain and keep its compulsory license, a cable company must meet four requirements.

> **Initial Notice of Identity and Signal Carriage Complement.** The cable system obtains its compulsory license by filing an Initial Notice in the Copyright Office. The statute requires that the filing take place at least one month before the date when the cable system begins operations.
> **Notice of Change of Identity or Signal Carriage Complement.** If the owner of the cable system changes, or if there is a change in the list of television and radio stations that the system is carrying regularly, the system is required to send a notice of the change to the Copyright Office within thirty days.
> **Statement of Account for Secondary Transmissions by Cable Systems.** Every six months the cable system must send the Copyright Office a Statement of Account Form, depending on the amount of "gross receipts" [in the very simplest terms, think of "receipts" as income the cable system earns] for the accounting period.
> **Royalty Fee.** Each semiannual Statement of Account must be accompanied by the deposit of a royalty fee covering retransmissions during the preceding six months.[22]

Primary- and Secondary-Transmission Services

An important distinction made by the compulsory license for copyright liability is be-

tween primary- and secondary-transmission services.

Primary-Transmission Service This service consists of *broadcasts by radio and television stations to the public.*

Secondary-Transmission Service This is *the basic service of retransmitting television and radio broadcasts to subscribers.* Under the old law, as interpreted by the courts, secondary-transmission services were free from copyright control. This is no longer true. The new statute requires all U.S. cable systems, regardless of how many subscribers they have or whether they are carrying any distant signals, to pay some copyright royalties. However, instead of obliging cable systems to bargain individually for each copyrighted program they retransmit, the law offers them the opportunity to obtain a compulsory license for secondary transmissions.[23] The secondary-transmission service *does not* include "transmission originated by a cable system (including local origination cablecasting, pay-cable, background music services, and originations on leased or access channels)."[24]

Restrictions Contained in the Compulsory License

While many benefits are granted by the compulsory license, such as not having to negotiate individual copyright licenses for retransmission of television and radio broadcasts, there are also certain things the license *does not* permit, among them:

> **Originations.** . . . a cable system's compulsory license extends only to secondary transmission (retransmissions). It does not permit the system to make any originations of copyrighted material without a negotiated license covering that material.

Nonsimultaneous Retransmissions. In general, to be subject to compulsory licensing under the copyright law, a cable retransmission must be simultaneous with the broadcast being carried. As a rule, taping or other recording of the program is not permitted. Taping for delayed retransmission is permissible only for some (not all) cable systems located outside the 48 contiguous States; and, even in these exceptional cases, there are further limitations and conditions that the cable system must meet.

FCC Violations. The broadcast signals that a cable system can carry under a compulsory license are limited to those that it is permitted to carry under FCC rules, regulations, and authorizations. If signal carriage is in violation of FCC requirements, the cable system may be subject under the Copyright Act to a separate action for copyright infringement for each unauthorized retransmission.

Foreign Signals. In general, the copyright law does not permit a cable system to retransmit signals of foreign television and radio stations under a compulsory license. The only exceptions have to do with the signals of certain Mexican and Canadian stations. Unless foreign signals fall within these exceptions, their carriage would not be authorized under a compulsory license, even if permissible under FCC rules.

Program Alteration or Commercial Substitution. Cable systems are not permitted to alter the content of retransmitted programs, or to change, delete, or substitute commercials or station announcements in or adjacent to programs being carried. There is only one exception: under certain circumstances, substitutions involving "commercial advertising market research" may be permitted.[25]

Forfeiture of the Compulsory License

Somewhat like a station license, a cable system's compulsory license can be revoked. For example, failure to file the required Initial Notice of Identity or Notice of Change can result in loss of the Compulsory License.[26] Other violations can include failing to file the "Statements of Account or

royalty fees; taping for delayed transmission; carrying signals in violation of FCC requirements; carrying certain foreign stations; and altering programs or substituting commercials."[27]

If a cable system goes so far as to disregard the copyright laws and not obtain a license, it can be sued by a copyright owner. In the case of willful infringement the owner can attempt to collect actual damages and profits, or statutory damages up to $50,000. Moreover, civil and criminal penalties as well as injunctions can be served on the cable system.[28]

REGULATING COMPUTER TECHNOLOGY

With the growth of the computer industry the FCC has become involved in monitoring technical standards for commercial and home computing devices. Such monitoring is authorized and necessary since computers are capable of emitting radio-frequency signals that can interfere with standard radio and television receiving devices. Although static caused by a personal computer on a nearby television set may not seem serious, interference with police radios may be.

Radio-Frequency Interference

Title III of the Communications Act of 1934 gives the FCC the power to control anything that might interfere with the operation of radio and television systems and other hardware licensed by the commission. Computers are classified into two groups by the FCC: Class A, which includes computing devices used primarily in commercial environments, and Class B, which includes computing devices used in the home environment. Class B devices are regulated more heavily than Class A devices, for they are usually located closer to radio and television receivers. Many of them are housed in plastic cases that do little to stop radio-frequency interference. Furthermore, manufacturing standards may be less strict for less expensive consumer devices, and preventive maintenance is less than with commercial computers, or nonexistent.[29]

There are differences in how Class A and Class B computing devices are regulated. Manufacturers of Class A devices are required to *verify* through testing that their equipment is free of radio-frequency interference.[30] But although the test results must be kept on file, the FCC does not require the *certification* of these results, as it does for Class B devices.[31] When the certification of a Class B device is approved by the FCC, a certification number is assigned to it and must be affixed to each item of that model that is produced.[32]

Patent Law

Outside the realm of administrative agencies, the courts continue to interpret the law as it applies to computer technology. Patent law has been one of the most visible areas of litigation. Early decisions involving the patenting of computer software did not support that concept. Indeed, from long ago the courts have given narrow interpretations of patent law. In the mid eighteenth century a man named Tatham tried to patent and at the same time monopolize the use of conventional machinery to manufacture seamless lead pipe. The patent was rejected by the U.S. Supreme Court, since although Tatham had invented the process he had not invented the machinery.[33] In a case involving Samuel Morse and his telegraph, the Supreme Court rejected a patent that would have controlled "electromagnetism developed for making or printing intelligible characters . . . at a distance."[34] The Court

reasoned that the entire physical process of electromagnetism would be at issue if the patent were approved. In 1948 the Supreme Court refused to approve a patent involving the use of strains of bacteria as an agricultural inoculant.[35] The Court considered the bacteria "works of nature" and not subject to patent.

One of the most far-reaching decisions concerning computers occurred in 1972 in *Gottschalk* v. *Benson.* Here the Supreme Court rejected a patent claim based on a technique for converting decimal numbers into binary numbers. The process involved what mathematicians call an *algorithm,* a technique for "performing simple arithmetic using digits."[36] The Court claimed the patent was too broad, since it would "monopolize all present and future uses of the algorithm." The decision was broadly interpreted to mean that computer programs could not be patented. Some observers have claimed that the ruling has in fact stifled the development of software, since instead of filing patents and thereby disclosing advances in computer software, programmers have felt compelled to operate within trade-secrecy law.[37]

A shift in precedent, however, occurred in 1981. The Supreme Court ruled that a computer program could in fact be patented when it showed a specific application, in this case an improvement in a rubber-cutting process. The Court reasoned that there was more to the invention than a mathematical formula, and thus the *Benson* rule did not apply.[38]

Copyright Law

Copyright law does provide some protection for computer software.[39] For example, anything that is "authored" on a word processor takes on the same qualities of something authored on a typewriter. A book, for *mple*, may be produced on a word pro-*ssor*, which is in fact a computer. The *book* still enjoys copyright protection as soon as the idea is formed. Computer programs are also subject to copyright law, although both the law and the manner of registering computer programs are changing. Under copyright law, copying a computer program can incur the same penalties as copying a book. Fair use for educational purposes is a vague area in computer software, and guidelines like those that exist for videotape recordings are yet to be formulated.

Some of the larger data-processing companies, especially those involved primarily in software, are not as concerned about copyright and do not take much care in trying to protect software. They reason that the availability of inexpensive software means that much more potential demand for hardware. Other companies, such as those devoted to producing, marketing, and selling software, and individuals who write software are more cautious and concerned. As copyright law develops more fully and incorporates court decisions dealing with computer software, guidelines on registering and protecting software will emerge, as will penalties for copying it.

SUMMARY

Increased emphasis on information technologies has made common carriers, cable, copyright, and computers important areas in the study of telecommunication regulation.

The basis for the development of common carriers can be found in two early pieces of legislation, the Post Roads Act of 1866 and the Mann-Elkins Act of 1910. The Post Roads Act established right-of-way over public lands and the Mann-Elkins Act authorized the establishment of rate structures for common carriers that are involved in interstate communication.

Common carriers are subject to state and federal control. Carriers engaged only in intrastate communication are regulated by state public utility commissions and are classified as partially subject. Fully subject carriers are "fully" covered by the Communications Act of 1934 and are regulated by the federal government through the FCC. Fully subject carriers are involved in interstate and international communication.

Both the operation and the facilities and licensing of common carriers are regulated by government.

Court decisions have assured manufacturers that devices connecting to telephone equipment in the home can be produced, marketed, and sold in a competitive marketplace.

Since *United States* v. *Southwestern Cable Co.* the FCC has gradually shifted control of cable systems to local communities. Registration requirements exist for cable systems. Local regulatory frameworks for cable vary.

State regulation of cable takes place within three frameworks: preempt statutes, appellate statutes, and advisory statutes.

The Copyright Act of 1976 overhauled the measures that protect authors' and performers' works. Length of copyright and reproduction for educational purposes are two areas of the act that have received special attention from broadcasters.

A committee appointed by the House Subcommittee on Courts, Civil Liberties and Administration of Justice has adopted guidelines for the fair use of videotapes for educational purposes.

Cable systems must meet copyright statutes by obtaining a compulsory license. The license can be revoked if the terms of the license are not met and the payment of copyright royalty fees are not made.

The regulation of computer technology emphasizes the areas of radio-frequency interference, patent law, and copyright law. A clearer picture of how patent and copyright law affect computer technology will emerge as more cases are filed and the courts establish legal precedents.

OPPORTUNITIES
FOR FURTHER LEARNING

Decisions of the United States Courts Involving Copyright and Literary Property, 1789–1909. Washington, D.C.: Copyright Office, Library of Congress, 1980.

DIAMOND, S. A., *Trademark Problems and How To Avoid Them* (rev. ed.). Chicago: Crain Communications, 1981.

HENN, H. G., *Copyright Primer*. New York: Practicing Law Institute, 1979.

JOHNSTON, D. F., *Copyright Handbook* (2nd ed.). New York: Bowker, 1982.

LAWRENCE, J. S., and B. TIMBERG, eds., *Fair Use and Free Inquiry: Copyright Law and the New Media*. Norwood, N.J.: Ablex, 1980.

PRESTON, E., comp., *Writer's Guide to Copyright*. Boston: The Writer, 1982.

STRONG, W. S., *The Copyright Book: A Practical Guide*. Cambridge, Mass.: M.I.T. Press, 1981.

VIAN, K., *Communication Technologies and Political Control*. Norwood, N.J.: Ablex, 1983.

20

ADVERTISING, ACCOUNTING, AND ACQUISITIONS

H. P. Davis was a vice-president at Westinghouse in 1928 when in a lecture delivered to the Harvard University Graduate School of Business Administration he said,

> In seeking a revenue returning service, the thought occurred to broadcast a news service regularly from ship-to-shore stations to the ships. This thought was followed up, but nothing was accomplished because of the negative reaction obtained from those organizations whom we desired to furnish with this news material service. However, the thought of accomplishing something which would realize the service referred to, still persisted in our minds.[1]

Davis's persisting thoughts turned out to be the foundation of American commercial broadcasting. The purpose of this chapter is to examine the different aspects of that foundation: building station revenues, managing station finances, buying and selling stations, starting new stations, and promoting the station.

BUILDING STATION REVENUE

In the United States, advertisers pay stations to broadcast their ads during a certain time to the listening or viewing public. That elusive commodity, time, is the product stations offer. Some times are better and more expensive than others, and a great deal of time is cheaper than a small amount.

The Local Rate Card

The rates a station charges for its time are listed on two types of rate cards—the local one for businesses in the local community and the national one for advertisers who buy large amounts of time on many different stations. Figure 20–1 presents one station's local rates for two time classifications, AA and A. Class AA time runs from 6:00 A.M. to 10:00 A.M. and from 3:00 P.M. to 7:00 P.M., Monday through Saturday. These times— the most expensive on the local rate card—represent drive time, those heavy radio-listening hours when radio captures not only the home audience but also the people driving to and from work. All other times are class A times, and are less expensive than drive time since they traditionally do not attract as large an audience.

THE NATIONAL RATE CARD: REPS AND AD AGENCIES

Now compare the rates listed in Figure 20–2 with those in Figure 20–1. You will notice a difference of approximately 17.65 percent. The higher rates in Figure 20–2 are from the same station's national rate card. To eliminate all the paperwork and negotiations involved in placing advertising with every individual station, advertisers purchase their advertising time through either station representatives, called *reps,* or advertising agencies. Station representatives, as their name implies, represent the station to large advertisers. They also represent more than one station and contract to buy time on many different stations in order to reach the audience the advertiser requests. Advertis-

FIGURE 20–1 Local Rate Card

ANNOUNCEMENTS

(AA)   6:00 to 10:00 a.m., Mon./Sat.
3:00 to 7:00 p.m., Mon./Sat.

	60 Sec.	**30 Sec.**
1	19.00	15.20
52	16.00	12.80
156	13.00	10.40
312	11.00	8.80
624	9.50	7.60
1040	8.50	6.80

(A)   All other days and times

	60 Sec.	**30 Sec.**
1	16.00	12.80
52	13.00	10.40
156	11.00	8.80
312	9.00	7.20
624	7.50	6.00
1040	6.50	5.20

FIGURE 20–2 National Rate Card

ANNOUNCEMENTS

(AA)   6:00 to 10:00 a.m., Mon./Sat.
3:00 to 7:00 p.m., Mon./Sat.

	60 Sec.	**30 Sec.**
1	22.40	17.90
52	18.90	15.10
156	15.30	12.20
312	13.00	10.40
624	11.20	9.00
1040	10.00	8.00

(A)   All other days and times

	60 Sec.	**30 Sec.**
1	18.80	15.10
52	15.30	12.20
156	13.00	10.40
312	10.60	8.50
624	8.80	7.00
1040	7.70	6.10

ing agencies, on the other hand, represent the advertiser but buy time in the same way reps do.

A company using a rep or agency typically pays a rate 17.65 percent higher than the rate on the local rate card. Of this increase, the rep or agency takes a commission of 15 percent. The remainder goes to the station. This 2.65-percent increase is considered compensation to the station for the long-distance account, promotion of itself to and through the rep and the ad agencies, the extra bookkeeping, and related costs. The advertiser, in turn, saves the time and cost of placing each individual advertising order, a cost that on large buys would run much more than the 15-percent commission paid to the rep or agency.

Despite the rate cards, stations in highly competitive markets wheel and deal to entice advertisers to buy time on their station. This usually happens when an advertising agency tries to buy the most time for the least money and pits stations against each other to see which one can offer the best price. Sometimes it is successful. There is considerable price slashing: discounts of 35 percent below the rate card are not unusual, and some stations discount 50 percent.

Time for announcements or commercials can be purchased in two lengths—sixty seconds and thirty seconds. Some stations divide their time into twenty- or ten-second lengths. The shorter time periods are common in television, whose rates are higher than radio's, and make it possible for smaller businesses to buy television time; forcing them to buy longer commercials might price them out of the market.

Commercial time is less expensive when bought in quantity. For example, on the local rate card one sixty-second announcement costs $19.00 in AA time (Figure 20–1). If you purchase 52 announcements, the cost

drops to $16.00 per announcement. If you purchase 1,040 sixty-second announcements, the cost drops to $8.50. Similarly graduated discounts are available for thirty-second announcements, and for all announcements made in A time as well.

Stations periodically revise their rate cards just as supermarkets revise prices of meat and eggs. Successful stations revise theirs upwards in response to inflation and to increases in their audience. The more viewers or listeners a station has, the more people an advertiser can reach and the more the station can charge for its commercial time. Another factor in rate changes is the station's market. If there are no other broadcast outlets in the market, the station's rate may be higher than if there were other stations offering competing rates. It is the old rule of supply and demand. The cost of local newspaper advertising can also influence the rate charged by the broadcast media. All media compete for those advertising dollars.

Other time buys are available on most stations. These include time for remote broadcasts, such as live coverage of a store opening, and larger time blocks in which to air entire programs.

Trade-out Arrangements

Trade-out arrangements are another way in which stations receive income. Here the station provides advertising time in exchange for goods or services offered by the advertiser. These goods and services—anything from appliances to world cruises—may be used by the station at its discretion. Many stations give them away as prizes; others award them to their top account executives.

Most prizes awarded on television game shows are supplied by manufacturers who pay a small fee for on-air announcements in return for their products' publicity. National television exposure of this kind is a relatively inexpensive way of obtaining advertising time, compared with the usual national television rate. For the game show, the prizes are for all practical purposes free merchandise, and beyond the salary of an announcer there is almost no cost involved in announcing the products on the air. Incorporated into the programming, the announcements add the elements of excitement and dream fulfillment to the description of the "fabulous prize" the contestant has a chance to win.

Many companies engage in trade-out advertising. Windjammer "Barefoot" Cruises Ltd. trades on a dollar-for-dollar basis. The cruise can be a powerful incentive to the station's account executives to "beat the bushes" for advertising. Or a station contest with a Windjammer cruise as a prize can entice listeners to stay tuned for their chance to bask in the sun on the open sea. For the station, the cost of airing the commercials is minimal since the announcements are usually scheduled in unsold time that would otherwise go unused. Moreover, it is profitable for both the advertiser and the station to trade on a dollar-for-dollar basis, since each is getting something at a less expensive rate than if they had to buy it outright.

The easiest way to understand the advantage of the dollar-for-dollar trade-out is to consider the example of a new car. Assume station WAAA furnishes its sales manager with a new car for business travel, such as calling on sponsors. In order to do this, the station enters into a trade-out agreement with a local car dealer. The car costs $8,000. In return for the car, the station will air $8,000 worth of commercial announcements for the dealer. For the station, the cost of providing these announcements is less than $8,000, since the commercials are scheduled

at unsold times when other commercials would not air anyway. Without the trade-out, the time would simply go unsold. Since the station must stay on the air in any case, the cost of operating the station remains the same. For the dealer, since it bought the car wholesale, say for $6,000, that would be the total cost of $8,000 worth of advertising.

Although trade-out advertising is common, stations try to avoid it, especially when the advertiser can be persuaded to pay cash instead. Cash looks better than merchandise when the station prepares its annual financial statement. Furthermore, when stations are sold, trade-out advertising is usually not considered part of the station's annual income, since the merchandise supplied by the advertiser usually cannot be used to pay the station's bills.

Co-op Advertising

Co-op advertising is an arrangement by which a local store splits part of the cost of advertising with the company whose products are mentioned in that advertising. Let's assume a radio announcement of a sale of Westinghouse appliances at the Ace Appliance Store costs $19.00. In a 10/90 co-op advertising arrangement between Westinghouse and the store, Westinghouse would pay 10 percent of the cost of the announcement, or $1.90, and the store would pay $17.10. The radio station receives the rate-card price for the announcement, Ace airs the commercial at a 10-percent discount, and Westinghouse receives local advertising exposure.

Not all companies use co-op advertising, and the amount paid by the manufacturer and the local store varies considerably. Newspapers continue to receive the majority of co-op advertising dollars, about 75 percent, since co-op advertising began with newspapers before broadcast advertising was widespread.[2] Some companies employ full-time co-op managers whose responsibility is to keep track of co-op advertising by retail outlets and to show retailers how to coordinate their advertising with the manufacturer's co-op program.

Barter Arrangements

Stations sometimes receive programming in return for providing advertising time. Such barter arrangements are widespread in syndicated programming: a station receives a free program and in return airs certain commercials that are built into the program and sold through the syndication company. The station also has an availability within the program and can insert commercials sold locally.

Combination Sales Agreements

Although not a common practice, some account executives are employed by more than one station. Their activities are regulated by strict FCC guidelines that guard against rate fixing or the selling of time on more than one station for a single rate.[3] Although representing two stations is not illegal, selling time for two competing stations is. *Competing stations* are defined as any two stations whose signals overlap, regardless of which market they serve. Moreover, the combining of a radio station and a television station for the purpose of offering a single rate is illegal, even if the two stations are jointly owned. Because other radio stations might not be able to team up with a television station, the FCC feels such arrangements are counter-competitive.

A single rate for an AM station and an FM station engaged in simulcasting is permissible. But if a combination rate is offered by two stations that are commonly owned

but not engaged in simulcasting, management must be careful not to use the combination rate to "carry along" the weaker of the two stations. Stations not engaged in simulcasting may not force an advertiser to buy a combination rate. If the advertiser wants to buy advertising on only one station, then that opportunity must be available.

THE ROLE OF PROMOTION IN BUILDING STATION REVENUES

For both new stations and those with long records of operation, station promotion is an important part of the broadcasting business. Perhaps more than other businesses, broadcasting as an entertainment industry entails promotion. Successful station promotion involves much more than a few announcements promoting a program or personality: it is a well-planned and systematically executed campaign. More and more stations are realizing the importance of station promotion. Many have rested on the laurels of their programming without learning from the example of other businesses that competition requires promotion to convince the public that they should patronize your business or listen to your station. In fact, broadcast promotional campaigns are becoming a necessity in many markets.

Promoting Assets

The most important commodity for any station is its listenership or viewership. Thus, how the station fares in the ratings is the central theme of many promotional campaigns. Although only one station can be first overall, many stations can find their own niche in the ratings data. A certain station, for example, may be first among women, another first among eighteen- to thirty-four-year-olds, another first among men thirty-four to forty-nine, another first during morning drive time, and still another first in late-evening news viewership. Each placement in the audience surveys can provide opportunities to promote the station's accomplishments.

Another consideration for every station is the cost-per-thousand (CPM) of reaching the station's audience—that is, what it will cost an advertiser to reach each one thousand viewers. Perhaps the station does not have a first-place showing but does have a lower CPM than any of its competition. Pointing this out to cost-conscious advertisers in a sales presentation can make ratings a moot issue. Naturally, the station with both an audience and a low CPM is in an especially competitive position.

Other promotional campaigns can focus on new call letters and format changes. If a station changes hands and subsequently call letters, calling attention to the new identity is important. Similarly, a change in format often results in a new audience. Telling that audience about the new sound and telling advertisers about that new audience are equally important.

Everyone understands awards, and some of the most familiar belong to broadcast journalism. Although publicizing a journalism award promotes only one department—the news department—it can boost other areas of the station as well. Such promotion is especially critical to television, in which the local news can be the single most important determinant of the audience's perception of the station. More than one television station has had its local news pull to the top in the ratings while its network programming was running a poor third in other markets and nationwide.

Planning Successful Promotion

To be successful, a promotional campaign must have certain qualities. One of the most important is simplicity (Figure 20–3). Al-

FIGURE 20–3 Promotional campaigns involving billboards, television, and newspaper advertising as well as specially staged promotional events are part of the process of marketing a station. (Turner Advertising Company. Atlanta)

though contests and giveaways can be effective audience builders, successful long-term promotions have a central theme. Such slogans as "Musicradio," "Candlelight and Gold," "Radio Indiana," and "Happy Radio" can be woven throughout the station's programming. If ratings are being publicized, a single concise statement that the station is first is much better than many sentences about the station's share of the audience.

Simplicity also belongs in station logos. Effective designs are uncluttered; come out well in black and white, which is essential to newspaper advertising; look good on letterheads; and can be easily recognized and understood.

An audio identity is as basic as a visual identity, especially in radio. Most radio stations have a particular "sound" in addition to their musical format. These sounds are usually reproduced in a *jingle package*—a collection of sounds designed around a four-to-eight-note sequence fitting the call letters. Variations in the jingle package are then incorporated into news introductions, bulletins, musical bridges between records, and backgrounds for commercial and public-service announcements.

As important as simplicity is consistency. Too many stations make the mistake of constantly changing their promotional theme. Many mediocre promotional efforts have been successful simply because they have continued unchanged long enough for the audience to accept them as household words. To schedule even the very best promotional effort for six months and then disappear is to defeat the purpose of a promotional campaign. Contests and giveaways will change from season to season, but there needs to be a consistent theme that represents the station over time, be it the logo, the jingle package, or a combination of both.

Done effectively, a promotional campaign can elevate listener awareness of the station, and fostering awareness of the station is the first step in building an audience.

FINANCIAL ACCOUNTING

Once earned, a station's advertising revenue is translated into a series of numbers that managers, bookkeepers, accountants, investors, and bankers spend many hours studying in order to answer some complex questions. How can we improve daytime sales? How can we cut expenses? How much money will we need to borrow? How much money should we invest? These and countless other queries plague station executives as they mull over their charts of accounts and financial statements.

Chart of Accounts

The basic ledger for recording all station finances, both income and disbursements (expenses), is the chart of accounts.[4] Although charts of accounts vary, many in broadcasting use a system of numbers whose first two digits (commonly starting with 10 and going up) represent various account classifications. Assume the numbers 100 to 199 represent assets. A specific two-digit prefix is assigned to each type of asset. Here, for example, are cash accounts, which are designated by the 10 prefix:

101 Cash in banks—regular
102 Petty cash
103 Cash in banks—payroll
104 Cash in banks—other

The prefix 14 might represent advances and prepayments:

141 Prepaid insurance
142 Prepaid rent

143 Prepaid taxes and payments of estimated taxes

144 Expense advance to officers and employees

Three-digit accounting systems provide about as much flexibility as the average broadcaster needs, but additional digits can be added wherever appropriate. For instance, a group owner might want a different prefix for each station in the group. WAAA might have the prefix 5. Thus, if we wanted to know the petty cash at WAAA, we would look under account number 5–102, 5 representing the station and 102 petty cash. WBBB might be assigned the number 6, and so on. Some computer programs use additional digits to facilitate more complex data analyses of a station's financial status.

Using the chart of accounts, management can periodically check the station's financial structure as well as pinpoint and plot its activity over time. Such information is critical if management is to ensure the station's profit structure. A station's information and accounting systems are equally important to the broadcaster selling the station, the banker lending the station money, or the accountant preparing its tax returns.

FINANCIAL STATEMENTS

The chart of accounts is the basic accounting tool of the station, but the money recorded on it is translated into many different financial statements. The balance sheet (Figure 20–4) is a stop-action picture of the station on any given day, usually the last day of the year. Notice that assets ($90,000) equal liabilities and equity. Balance sheets must always balance. Why? Because all assets have a claim on ownership, which is equal to those assets. Suppose you drive a car worth $5,000 (a $5,000 asset). The title is in your name, and for all practical purposes it is your car. But what about claims of ownership on your car? We shall assume you still owe the bank $1,000 on the car. In accounting terms, the bank owns $1,000 worth of your car, and you own $4,000 worth. The claims on ownership of your car are $1,000 (the bank's claim) plus $4,000 (your claim),

FIGURE 20–4 (National Association of Broadcasters)

WBPE, Inc.
BALANCE SHEET
January 31, Year 1

Cash	4 000
Accounts receivable	2 000
Depreciable assets	50 610
Land	10 000
Intangibles	23 390
ASSETS	90 000
Accounts payable	5 000
Notes payable—sellers	38 000
Notes payable—stockholder	50 000
Liabilities	93 000
Contributed capital	1 000
Loss since inception	(4 000)
Stockholders' Equity (Deficit)	(3 000)
LIABILITIES AND EQUITY	90 000

which total the exact value of the car—$5,000.

A comparative balance sheet compares assets and liabilities between two points in time. An income statement shows the amount of income remaining after the debits are subtracted from the credits—in other words, how much money is left after all the bills are paid.

A comparative income statement compares income between two points in time. Figure 20-5 is a comparative income statement comparing two years of broadcast operation. Notice that the revenues are listed first, then the separate expenses (indented), and then the total expense. We can see that in year 8 the station's income before taxes was $11,500, on which a federal income tax of $2,530 was paid, leaving an income of $8,970.

If you were the treasurer of a broadcasting station, you would find the cash-flow statement especially important. This statement would tell you the amount of money the station needs in order to keep running smoothly. It would also tell you if you needed to borrow money to pay the bills or to invest excess income. A cash-flow statement is looked upon as a statement of the station's health and can help management find where changes in operations may have to be made.

Figure 20-6 is a cash-flow statement comparing one year of operation with the projected cash flow for the coming year. Notice year 9. If projections hold true, year 9 will see the station spend more money than it makes, resulting in a cash overdraft of $29,795. As treasurer, you will need to inform management of the necessity to borrow at least $34,795 to make ends meet and still have the desired $5,000 minimum cash balance. If management does not want to borrow the money, it must change that year's projected operating procedures. It might decide to make do with the equipment on hand and save the $20,000 budgeted for purchase of equipment. But as treasurer you point out that never in the station's history has that been done, that the equipment is old, and that the station's transmitter cannot last even through this year. Can you suggest cutting other disbursements? What recommendations can you make, and what will be the consequences? For the individuals who run a broadcasting station these are the questions that financial statements both pose and help answer.

FIGURE 20-5 (National Association of Broadcasters)

WBPE, INC.
COMPARATIVE INCOME STATEMENT
Year Ending December 31

	Year 8	Year 7
Revenues	168 900	162 200
Technical expense	12 300	12 100
Program expense	48 200	47 600
Selling expense	29 400	28 100
General & administrative	67 500	63 900
Expense	157 400	151 700
Income before tax	11 500	10 500
Federal Income Tax	2 530	
INCOME	8 970	8 190

	Projected Year 9	Year 8
CASH BALANCE AT JANUARY 1	8 505	9 113
Collections from advertisers	190 000	173 460
Cash Available	198 505	182 573
Technical disbursements	15 000	8 229
Program disbursements	50 000	45 861
Selling disbursements	52 000	39 400
Administrative disbursements	74 000	70 825
Agency commission payments	8 000	6 100
Repayment of stockholders loan		886
Dividend payments	200	200
Federal income tax payments	9 100	2 567
Purchase of equipment	20 000	
Total Disbursements	228 300	174 068
CASH BALANCE AT DECEMBER 31, YEAR 8		8 505
PROJECTED CASH AT DECEMBER 31, YEAR 9—overdraft	(29 795)	
DESIRED MINIMUM CASH BALANCE	5 000	
REQUIRED ADDITIONAL FUNDS	34 795	

FIGURE 20-6 (National Association of Broadcasters)

BUYING AND SELLING BROADCAST PROPERTIES

Financial statements are also especially important when a station changes hands. Buying and selling broadcast properties, including CATV, is big business, involving everyone from small-town entrepreneurs to corporate conglomerates. Buying a station requires knowledge of the broadcasting business and considerable money, not only for the purchase itself but for operating the station until it builds an income. The sale of a station must be approved by the FCC, which scrutinizes the buyer's and stockholders' character, their financial worth, their other media investments, their history in managing other enterprises, and more. A record of bankruptcy can quickly close the door to owning a broadcasting property.

The Broadcast Broker

At the heart of over 70 percent of broadcast-property sales is the broadcast broker—the real-estate person of the broadcasting business. Most are professionals with years of experience in station transactions. Many people wanting to sell or purchase a broadcast property begin by contacting the broker.[5] On the basis of personal contacts, referrals, advertisements, and in some cases direct solicitation, the broker knows what properties are for sale at what price, and who the buyers are. Since the sale of a broadcasting property can run into millions of dollars, good brokers are highly paid, but most industry professionals would agree that they are well worth their commission.

Commissions

Although commissions vary among brokers, typical fees for a station sale are 5 percent of the first million dollars, 4 percent of the second million, 3 percent of the third million, and 2 percent of the balance.[6] Brokers also perform property appraisals, typically charging $500 to $1000 a day.

A BUYER'S CHECKLIST

Still, the primary business of the broker is handling the sale of broadcast properties. For the buyer, there are many factors to consider before the final transaction. These considerations are summarized in the concise fourteen-point checklist prepared by Richard A. Shaheen, and reprinted below with modifications. The prospective buyer of a broadcast property should examine them carefully.

Financial Checks

GROSS SALES

1. Review gross-sales record for the three previous years.
2. Determine if any receipts represent "trade" dollars.
3. Check any undue use of promotions to inflate gross.
4. Determine what share of the total market revenue the station enjoys.

OPERATING PROFIT

1. Is it before or after all taxes?
2. Does it come after depreciation?

CASH FLOW

The most accepted method of determining a true cash flow calls for it to be a total of the following ingredients:

1. net profit before taxes
2. depreciation
3. interest paid
4. officer's salaries
5. director's fees

To this can be added any true nonrecurring expenses. A buyer should also consider the effect a new, higher base of depreciation will have with respect to the net profit after taxes. An owner-operator's salary and that of others should also merit consideration as part of cash flow.

FIXED ASSETS

1. Age and condition of major pieces of equipment?
2. Do they meet FCC specifications?
3. Does the sale include all fixed assets?
4. Anything on a lease basis?

LEASES, LICENSES, AND CONTRACTS

Determine beginning and end date and all details of:

1. land and building rentals
2. personnel contracts
3. news service
4. transcription or jingle services
5. film contracts
6. station-purchased advertising contracts
7. music-copyright services
8. trade-association memberships
9. equipment purchased or leased
10. time-sale contracts
11. representative-firm arrangement
12. union contracts
13. network agreements
14. music-format contracts

Legal and Operations Checks

LEGAL ACTIONS

1. Are there any legal actions pending against the station?
2. Are there any complaints filed with the FCC?

PERSONNEL

1. salary and position of all employees
2. commission arrangements for sales representatives
3. bonus or percentage plans
4. vacation policy
5. status of station's affirmative-action program

ADVERTISING RATES

Obtain a copy of all current rate cards and determine both when these rates went into effect and how they compare with those of the competition.

STATION COVERAGE

1. Is it sufficient to cover the market?
2. How does it compare with that of the competition?
3. Can the signal be improved?

PROGRAM FORMAT

Determine:

1. rating and demographic position for past two years
2. definitive explanation of present format
3. type of programming on competitive stations
4. promotions in the market—type and extent

FCC RECORD

Ascertain if the license is presently in effect and also whether there are any actions pending in the FCC that directly involve the facility. This could include engineering, programming, EEO policies, and minority-hiring status.

MARKET FREQUENCIES AVAILABLE

See if there are any applications filed or construction permits granted for additional facilities servicing the market.

COMPETITION

Compare ratings, rates, and program formats of competitive stations. Also, determine circulation and advertising strength of daily or weekly newspapers.

MARKET

As much care should be spent in investigating the market as the physical facility of the station itself. Carefully review:

1. population growth—past and anticipated
2. retail sales
3. major sources of employment
4. consumer spending power

If a buyer finds positive information after reviewing the items in the checklist, then the buy is probably a good one, provided the price is right. A fair price is a very difficult thing to pinpoint, but for radio and television stations, it is usually about two and a half times the gross annual billing. Cable companies are appraised at about $500 per connection. Today, however, with the scarcity of space on the electromagnetic spectrum, inflation, the potential of AM stereo, the growth of FM, and the effects of other media, the formula for determining what a property is worth can vary considerably.[6]

SUMMARY

At the basis of building station income is the rate card. Local rate cards illustrate the rates charged to local advertisers. The national rate card, whose rates are approximately 17.65 percent higher than local rates, is used for national advertisers placing orders through station representatives or advertising agencies. Tradeout advertising, co-op advertising, and barter arrangements are two other sources of station revenue. The FCC has certain guidelines guarding against monopolistic practices and prohibits certain revenue-building schemes that involve combination advertising rates among competing stations.

Promoting a station is becoming essential as more stations sign on the air and competition increases. An effective promotional campaign contains two major qualities—simplicity and consistency.

In the managing of station finances, the chart of accounts is the numerical and descriptive list used to classify income and expenditures. Financial statements usually include the balance sheet, comparative balance statement, income statement, comparative income statement, and cash-flow statement.

People who invest in broadcasting buy stations or start new ones. The broadcast broker is the real-estate person of the broadcasting business and is responsible for arranging many of the transactions. A prospective buyer should examine fourteen key areas of a station before buying it: gross sales; operating profit; cash flow; fixed assets; leases, licenses, and contracts; legal actions; personnel; advertising rates; station coverage; program format; FCC record; market frequencies available; competition; and market.

OPPORTUNITIES
FOR FURTHER LEARNING

Application for Authority to Construct a New Broadcast Station or Make Change in an Existing Broadcast Station. FCC Form 301. Washington, D.C.: Federal Communications Commission, 1977.

ATWAN, R., B. ORTON, and W. VESTERMAN, *American Mass Media: Industries and Issues* (2nd ed.). New York: Random House, 1982.

BARNOUW, E., *The Sponsor: Notes on a Modern Potentate.* New York: Oxford University Press, 1978.

BESEN, S. M., *The Value of Television Time and the Prospects for New Stations.* Santa Barbara, Calif.: Rand Corporation, 1973.

BROCK, G. W., *The Telecommunications Industry: The Dynamics of Market Structure.* Cambridge, Mass.: Harvard University Press, 1981.

BUNCE, R., *Television in the Corporate Interest.* New York: Praeger, 1976.

BUNYAN, J. A., and JAMES C. CRIMMINS. *Television and Management.* White Plains, N.Y.: Knowledge Industry, 1977.

CHARLES RIVER ASSOCIATES INC., *The Audience-Revenue Relationship for Local Television Stations.* Washington, D.C.: National Association of Broadcasters, 1978.

COUGHLAN, J., *Accounting Manual for Radio Stations.* Washington, D.C.: National Association of Broadcasters, 1975.

FLETCHER, J. E., ed., *Handbook of Radio and TV Broadcasting: Research Procedures in Audience, Program, and Revenues.* New York: Van Nostrand Reinhold, 1981.

GEIS, M. L., *The Language of Television Advertising.* New York: Academic, 1982.

HEIGHTON, E. J., and D. R. CUNNINGHAM, *Advertising in the Broadcast Media.* Belmont, Calif.: Wadsworth, 1976.

HOFFER, J., and J. MCRAE, *The Complete Broadcast Sales Guide for Stations, Reps, and Ad Agencies.* Blue Ridge Summit, Pa.: Tab Books, 1981.

How to Apply for a Broadcast Station. Washington, D.C.: Federal Communications Commission, 1977. Periodically updated.

HOWARD, H. H., *Multiple Ownership in Television Broadcasting: Historical Development and Selected Case Studies.* New York: Arno Press, 1979.

How to Read a Financial Report. New York: Merrill Lynch Pierce Fenner & Smith, 1975.

LARSON, T. L., *Aspects of Market Structure in the Broadcast Brokerage Industry.* Salt Lake City: Media Research Center, Department of Communication, University of Utah, 1979.

LITMAN, B. R., *The Vertical Structure of the Television Broadcasting Industry: The Coalescence of Power.* East Lansing: Graduate School of Business Administration, Michigan State University, 1979.

MEYER, J. R., R. W. WILSON, M. A. BAUGHCUM, E. BURTON, and L. CAOUETTE, *The Economics of Competition in the Telecommunications Industry.* Cambridge, Mass.: Oelgeschlager, Gunn & Hain, 1980.

MURPHY, J., *Handbook of Radio Advertising.* Radnor, Pa.: Chilton, 1980.

Office of Public Affairs, Federal Communications Commission, *Minority Ownership of Broadcast Facilities: A Report.* Washington, D.C.: Government Printing Office, 1980.

OWEN, B. M., JACK H. BEEBE, and WILLARD G. MANNING, JR., *Television Economics.* Lexington, Mass.: Lexington Books, Heath, 1974.

ROBINSON, S., *Radio Advertising: How to Sell It and Write It.* Blue Ridge Summit, Pa.: Tab Books, 1974.

THOMAS, D. L., *The Media Moguls.* New York: Putnam's, 1981.

21

THE RATINGS

To be truly effective, any communication system must have an efficient means of gathering and evaluating data. We have learned how intrapersonal communication sends electrochemical impulses from our senses through our nervous system, triggering our muscles to react. We have also learned how in interpersonal communication we use direct feedback to evaluate what people are saying and how other people react to this communication. Such feedback is also vital to mass communication and is found in many forms in broadcasting.

A disgruntled viewer writes a letter to the television station or network complaining about programming. Every day a sophisticated computer analyzes viewing-habit data from meters attached to home television sets, from viewers' diaries, from an assortment of answers to questions by interviewers, and from viewing questionnaires returned through the mails. A network pollster gathers data on election day. A radio program director examines data while preparing the weekly playlist. Management listens to its employees' opinions. All are examples of the feedback necessary for the successful maintenance and operation of a broadcasting system. The present chapter deals with this feedback.

THE BACKGROUND OF BROADCAST RATINGS

The first rating of a broadcast may have taken place in 1929, when an interviewer for the Crosley Radio Company called a randomly selected number from the telephone directory. The person who answered was asked, "What radio stations did you listen to yesterday?"[1] Since that time, broadcast ratings have been criticized as being inaccurate, unreliable, and arbitrary. They have been accused of canceling quality programs, determining network policy, and influencing everything we see and hear on the broadcast media. They have also been perceived as a subsidiary of the television networks and a partner of sponsors. These are all misconceptions. Broadcast ratings are services that tell how many people are viewing or listening to what, when they do it, and how often. Some of the most familiar are the A. C. Nielsen Television Index, Arbitron, and Pulse. The rating services have nothing to do with the networks and are not responsible for canceling programs. They are separate corporations, not part of the network structure. However, stations and networks use the data from rating surveys to make decisions on what programs to cancel or keep on the air. As a result, the rating services get blamed for canceling programs when it is the stations and networks that make the decisions.

Despite sustaining serious criticism, the ratings have for the most part proved to be very reliable, producing some of the most accurate and sophisticated audience research data available. But they are by no means perfect. Along with the major ratings services, which are controlled and professionally responsible, are minor ratings services that do use some of the methodologies that legitimize criticism of broadcast ratings. It is important from both a consumer and a professional standpoint to learn how ratings work, what function they have, and how reliable they actually are.

THE FUNCTION OF BROADCAST RATINGS

Media subscribe to broadcast rating services in much the same way they subscribe to syndicated material. But in the case of the rating services the product is feedback—feedback on the size and composition of the medium's audience. For instance, if you were operating a commercial television station in a major city, you would want to know how many people watched your station and how many watched other stations. You would also be interested in detailed demographic information on those viewers, such as their age, sex, education, and income. This information is essential to your advertisers. Similarly, you would want to know when these audiences tune to your station. You would also want to know whether a particular program commanded a larger share of the audience than some other programs. What share of the audience did your newscast capture, compared with those of competing television stations? Your advertisers need all of this information in order to purchase air time—your station's air time—wisely.

Determining the Cost of Reaching the Audience

Advertisers also want to compare the cost of attracting viewers. By combining the information found in ratings with the price schedule on your station's rate card, an advertiser might discover that the cost of reaching one thousand people (the cost-per-thousand) over your television station is less than the cost-per-thousand of another television station. If it can prove that your television station reaches more potential customers than your competition does, the advertiser will probably realize that buying commercials on your station is a wise investment. Rating services provide the necessary proof.

With this proof in hand, you may find that certain programs need to be rearranged or even canceled because of limited viewership. It simply is not profitable to air them, at least in their current time slot. Notice the word *you*. As a media executive it is you, and not the rating service, who make the decision to cancel or reschedule a program. Many viewers who do not realize this have complained to the rating services about the cancellation of their favorite television program or the dismissal of their favorite radio personality.

Data Versus Decisions

Rating services provide station management with information on how many viewers or listeners a station has, compared with other stations in the same community or, on a national scale, other networks. If a station is not attracting the number of listeners or viewers that management feels it should, and if management feels a change in personnel or programming will improve the ratings, then the result may be a change in staff or programs. But keep in mind the many aspects of ratings. A station may be perfectly comfortable with a relatively few viewers if they have high incomes and considerable buying power. Public broadcasting stations, knowing their ratings' position among commercial stations, direct quality programming to an audience with a higher than average educational level. Such a station may be completely satisfied with less than first place.

The entertainment industry is also interested in ratings because they specify the kinds of programs that will be hits. If the public demands situation comedies, then

producing science fiction for prime-time television might not be a wise decision. Similarly, producers of television series are interested in what share of the audience their program has in cities across the country or around the world.

Although broadcast management and the entertainment industry generally believe that the larger rating services are accurate and reliable, the public does not. A lack of understanding of the methodologies used creates much of this skepticism. Personal preference is also powerful, and all the mathematical formulas in the world will not convince a devoted viewer that a favorite television program has been canceled because too few people watched. "That's impossible; all my friends watch that program every week!" This enthusiastic conclusion may be mistaken. Among your friends, perhaps everyone does watch the program. But perhaps because your friends watch the program and talk about it in the dormitory their friends do not want to be left out, and so they also watch. Neither "standard" is an accurate indication of how the rest of the viewing audience feels about the program. Just how, then, is a broadcast rating determined?

JUDGING ACCURACY: THE SAMPLING PROCESS

A typical ratings skeptic will claim there is absolutely no way a small group of people selected to tell what television programs they watch or what radio stations they listen to can possibly determine the viewing or listening habits of thousands or millions of other people. To some extent they are correct, but only if the group of people polled is extremely small.

Defining Sampling

At the heart of broadcast ratings is a process called *sampling*. Sampling means examining a small portion of some larger portion to see what the larger portion is like. A chef in a large restaurant tastes a tiny teaspoon of soup from a five-gallon kettle to determine if the soup is ready for serving. A doctor can examine a small blood sample from your arm to ascertain the characteristics of the rest of the blood in your body. Obviously, sampling is a much better way of determining your blood characteristics than draining you dry!

Random Sampling

The essence of the sampling process is called *random sampling*—sampling such that *each unit of the larger portion has an equal chance of being selected*. If the population of Toronto is being randomly sampled, then each person in Toronto has an equal chance of being selected. If households are being sampled, *each household* in Toronto has an equal chance of being selected. There are even different types of random sampling. If you picked numbers out of a hat, you would be conducting a simple random sample. But let's assume you wanted to draw a sample of a hundred names from a voting list of a thousand names. So you chose every tenth name on the list to obtain your sample of one hundred. By doing this you conducted a systematic random sample.

Sampling Error

You may say, "Okay, I'll get on the phone, randomly select ten people from my hometown telephone directory, ask them what radio station they're listening to, and find out what the rest of the town is listening to." If you do this and your prediction turns out to be true, you would merely be lucky. Be-cause the random sample you selected was so small, its sampling error was too *large* for you to make an accurate prediction. *Sampling error* is determined by the size of the sample. The larger the sample, the smaller the sampling error.

Centuries ago mathematicians proved that a truly random sample is all one needs to tell the characteristics of a larger population. Moreover, once a certain number of people are chosen for the random sample, increasing that number will not significantly change the outcome. You may be surprised to find out how small that random sample needs to be. For example, a truly random sample of six hundred persons is sufficient to make a prediction about the entire city of New York with only a ± 4-percent sampling error.[2] That means that if 75 percent of the six hundred you sampled were listening to a certain radio station, then you could predict that somewhere between 71 percent (75 percent − 4 percent) and 79 percent (75 percent + 4 percent) of the entire city of New York were listening to the same station. Increasing your sample size to one thousand would decrease the sampling error only to ± 3.1 percent. Moreover, increasing the size of the population to include the entire United States would not significantly change that error. With these figures, it is easy to see that a rating service can predict within a few percentage points the viewing or listening habits of an entire city or nation by sampling about twelve hundred persons. Although there will always be skeptics, those who understand sampling and the other factors in the ratings process rely on that process in making their programming decisions.

DATA COLLECTION

Some of the most critical steps in determining a broadcast rating take place in the data-gathering process. After the random sample has been selected, the rating service must next find people who are willing to provide the information it is trying to collect.

Gaining Cooperation

For a number of reasons, people may be hesitant to cooperate with a rating service. Perhaps they are apprehensive about the stranger at the door or on the telephone who is requesting their help. Other prospective candidates may not be at home or may have moved. To overcome these obstacles, the major rating services employ field representatives who are highly trained in everything from persistence to interpersonal relations. This training has paid off in a cooperation rate of approximately 80 percent. One interesting research finding is that those who watch educational television are more inclined to cooperate with a rating service than those who seldom watch educational television.[3] Thus, a rating service that interviewed only "easy cooperators" could find its results leaning toward educational television programs. Therefore, although a high cooperation rate is important in securing fairly accurate ratings, the rating service needs to persevere if it encounters resistant candidates for its survey.

Interviews

The rating services use three different methods of gathering information: interviews, diaries, and meters. Interviews are either personal or by telephone. Different studies have come to different conclusions as to which is more effective.[4] Some rating services use both. Regardless of which type a service uses it must consider certain variables in determining its outcome. For example, differences in question presentation among interviewers can affect how you answer them. You know that you react differently to the same question asked by different people. Tone of voice, articulation, and inflection all influence your interpretation of an interviewer's question. Dress can be another variable. A neatly dressed interviewer can communicate a sense of importance to the interview. Showing up at the front door unshaven or with hair set in rollers would communicate something entirely different. When many different individuals gather data, these same variables can distort the results of the survey. Even a slight rewording of a question can change the results. Rating services, therefore, conduct sophisticated training sessions to make sure their interviewers are asking the same questions in the same way.

Diaries

Besides personal and telephone interviews, rating services frequently utilize the diary method of collecting data. Here, the viewer or listener keeps a record of the programs and stations he or she tunes in to during a given week. This diary is then mailed back to the company, which tabulates the results of all diaries submitted. In some cases a small monetary incentive is included with the diary.

Meters

The third of the rating services' methods of data collection is the meter. This method is used by both A. C. Nielsen and Arbitron. The rating service enlists the cooperation of a household in installing on the television set a small, inconspicuous, monitoring device which is connected through a telephone system to a central computer. The computer automatically dials each monitoring device at specific intervals and records the readings. The monitoring not only reveals what channel is on at any time of the day but also tells if more than one set is in use in the household. Diaries in other homes supplement and help verify the meters.

Although each of these three methods has its advantages and disadvantages, research has shown little difference among them in the reliability of their data.[5] When the data reach the rating-service headquarters, banks of computers process the information and provide printouts in the form of ready-to-publish sheets that are bound in booklet form and made available to the local stations and networks. Sometimes the computer data are also given to advertising agencies and station sales representatives as an aid in making time buys. If a media buyer for an ad agency in New York wants to know on which stations to buy commercial time in order to reach the female audience eighteen to thirty-four years of age in Seattle, the computer will provide the information. Similar information can be supplied for national time buys when an advertiser wants to reach a certain type of audience.

INTERPRETING THE RATINGS

Now that we have talked about some of the methods of collecting data for broadcast ratings we're going to learn how these ratings are interpreted, some of the formulas used to interpret them, and the meaning of the terms commonly used in reporting them. This material is not difficult, and you do not need to know much math. But read carefully. The terms we'll encounter sometimes have different meanings to different rating services.[6] With this in mind, let's begin.

Rating

The first term we'll tackle is *rating*. You may say, "But we've already been talking about ratings." That is correct. The term has become a cliché for all the processes employed in predicting viewing and listening habits. But that is a more general definition of the term. More precisely, a rating is the *percentage of the people in a given population who are tuned to a radio or television station during a given time period*. For example, the formula for determining a rating for a radio station is the population divided into the number of people who are listening.[7]

$$\frac{\text{Station's Listeners}}{\text{Population}} = \text{Rating}$$

(In the case of television, households with at least one television set are used in place of population.) Let's assume that the town of Elmsville has a population of 10,000 and supports three radio stations. Using a random sample of the Elmsville population, we have projected that 1,000 persons are listening to WAAA radio. Dividing 1,000 by 10,000, we find that WAAA radio has a rating of 10 percent.

$$\frac{1,000}{10,000} = 10\%$$

Share

Share is also expressed as a percentage—the number of a station's listeners divided by the number of *all listeners during a given time period*:

$$\frac{\text{Station's Listeners}}{\text{Total Listeners}} = \text{Share}$$

In determining share we do not use the entire population of Elmsville, only those in Elmsville listening to radio during a certain period. Suppose we find through sampling that between 3:00 P.M. and 7:00 P.M., only

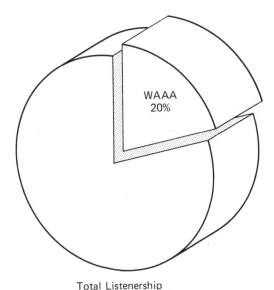

Total Listenership

FIGURE 21-1 *The circle represents the total number of listeners tuned to radio. WAAA's share of those listeners is 20%.*

half, or 5,000, of the Elmsville residents had their radios on. Thus, although we found that WAAA had a rating of 10 percent, its share is higher—in fact, twice as high. We determine this as follows:

$$\frac{1,000}{5,000} = 20\%$$

Another way to understand share is to consider it as part of the listening pie.[8] Figure 21-1 represents all of the Elmsville radio stations' listeners. Notice that WAAA occupies only 20 percent of the pie; the other two stations have the remaining 80 percent.

Average Quarter-Hour Persons

Now let's examine *average quarter-hour persons,* which is *an estimate of the number of persons listening to a station during any quarter-hour in a specified time period.* Many ratings are based on four-hour time

blocks, such as 6:00 A.M. to 10:00 A.M. or 3:00 P.M. to 7:00 P.M. In the case of radio, the morning time block of 6:00 A.M. to 10:00 A.M. is called morning drive time and the evening time block of 3:00 P.M. to 7:00 P.M. is called evening drive time. Time blocks can *vary* from market to market and from rating service to rating service. For television, time blocks as small as fifteen minutes are necessary since television programming changes much more frequently than radio programming.

To define average quarter-hour persons, we'll use radio and as our example the evening drive time of 3:00 P.M. to 7:00 P.M. Between 3:00 P.M. and 7:00 P.M. there are 16 quarter-hours (4 hours consisting of 4 quarter-hours each). Let's assume that our random sample of Elmsville revealed that only 100 persons were listening to station WAAA, and that they *only listened* from 3:00 P.M. until 4:00 P.M. (later we discovered the station had been knocked off the air at precisely 4:00 P.M. by a storm). That means that they listened during only 4 quarter-hours (four quarter-hours between 3:00 P.M. and 4:00 P.M.). We also know that each person in our sample represents 20 residents of Elmsville, since there are 10,000 persons in Elmsville and our sample is 500 (10,000 ÷ 500 = 20). Since our sample showed that 100 persons were listening to WAAA, we can predict that between 3:00 P.M. and 4:00 P.M., 2,000 persons were listening to WAAA (the 100 persons from the sample multiplied by 20, the number of persons represented by each person in the sample). Now to find WAAA's average quarter-hour persons between 3:00 P.M. and 7:00 P.M., we take 2,000 and divide it by 16 (the number of quarter-hours between 3:00 P.M. and 7:00 P.M.). The answer is 125. Notice that our survey discovered that people were listening to WAAA only during the 3:00 P.M. to 4:00 P.M. time block, and so we projected those figures beyond 4:00 P.M. to the end of the evening drive time block which is 7:00 P.M. We did this because when the ratings for Elmsville are published, all of the stations will compete in that same evening drive-time block. The published ratings might also note that WAAA was off the air after 4:00 P.M.

Cume Persons

In determining the average quarter-hour persons, we also determined the number of *cume (cumulative-audience) persons,* which was 2,000. Cume persons are *the number of different persons listening to a station at least once during a given time period.* The term refers only to a specific time period and only to people listening *at least once* during that period. We never count a person more than once when we are figuring cume. For example, if our sample discovered that of the 100 persons who were listening to WAAA between 3:00 P.M. and 4:00 P.M., 10 of them turned their radio back on and listened again between 6:00 P.M. and 7:00 P.M., we would not count those 10 a second time during that evening-drive-time block.

The easiest way to understand cume is to compare it to a magazine subscription. Those who figure the circulation of a magazine count the subscriber only once, regardless of how many times that person reads the magazine. After picking up the magazine in the afternoon mail at 3:00 P.M., the subscriber might read it until 4:00 P.M., fix dinner, and finish the magazine between 6:00 P.M. and 7:00 P.M.. Although he or she reads the magazine twice before finishing it, he or she is counted as only one subscriber. The same applies to cume persons.

Subdivisions of Data

An actual rating entails many more subdivisions of data than those we have encoun-

tered above. You might compare women between the ages of twenty-five and forty-nine who listen between 3:00 P.M. and 7:00 P.M., or men between twenty-five and sixty-four who listen during that period. A portion of an actual rating from an Arbitron survey of radio listening in Dayton, Ohio, shows how a listener survey is displayed for broadcast clients. The survey represents radio listening during the 3:00-P.M.-to-7:00-P.M. time block on Sunday. Notice how women are broken down into categories of twenty-five to forty-nine and twenty-five to sixty-four years of age. Other age-category breakdowns for both men and women are included in the complete survey.

Not all of the stations listed are actually in the Dayton area. Some are in outlying areas; others, such as WKRQ and WSAI, are in Cincinnati, southwest of Dayton. The survey focused on radio-listening habits in the Dayton area, and since some residents of that area listen to radio stations broadcasting from other communities, those stations are listed in the survey data.

Survey Area

A rating report lists categories for both the total survey area (TSA) and the metro survey area (MSA)—the geographic areas from which the random samples were drawn. The TSA and MSA (Figure 21–2) are determined by a combination of data, including the signal contours of the stations, audience listening habits, and government census data. The TSA is larger than the MSA, encompassing outlying areas. The MSA corresponds more closely to the metropolitan district of a city. Look closely at the white area and the area containing horizontal lines. The area in white is the TSA. The area of the map in which horizontal lines appear is the MSA. The diagonal lines in the map represent the Area of Dominant Influence (ADI), which applies primarily to television viewing. It is

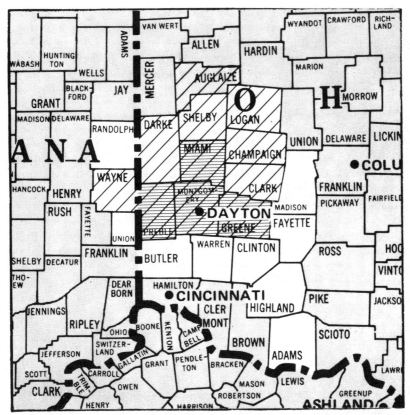

FIGURE 21–2 The area in white represents the TSA, the area covered by horizontal lines represents the MSA, and the area covered by diagonal lines (which includes the MSA) represents the ADI. (Arbitron Radio)

an exclusively defined market area (no two ADIs overlap) of measurable viewing patterns.

There are many more terms and formulas than we have covered here. If you are interested in learning more about ratings, consult the reference list at the end of the chapter.

APPLYING RATINGS TO MANAGEMENT DECISIONS

Ratings by themselves are not valuable. Their importance lies in how broadcast management uses them to make decisions.

If you were a television station manager and the ratings showed that your station was second in the local news ratings, you would have a number of alternatives. First, you could do nothing, leaving everything as it is. Your station might be profitable, and you would see little need to change. Or you could replace your news department with different personnel. A third alternative would be to replace the news with another type of programming you feel would be more profitable. Whatever your decision, it could not be made without a careful analysis of the ratings.

You might find that although your station was second in the category of all adults eighteen years and older, you had some other strength to offset this. You discover that among adults between eighteen and thirty-four your station was first. The other station was reaching mainly adults forty-nine and older. You are very satisfied with your station's showing in the younger group. It is an acquisitive group that still is forming buying habits and is making such major purchases as homes, home appliances, and automobiles.

Looking more closely at the ratings, you discover that for the time slot immediately preceding the local news, the other station is far ahead of yours. What does this mean? Perhaps the news department is not to blame for the second-place showing as much as the program that precedes the news is. Some viewers simply would rather stay in their comfy chairs than get up to change channels. So changing the program leading into the news may be all that is needed for your station to capture first place.

Ratings determine something else that your station's sponsors and advertising agencies will want to know—how expensive it is to reach an audience on your station, compared with the competing station. The answer lies in the *cost-per-thousand* (CPM), which, as we saw in the last chapter, is *the cost of reaching one thousand people*. Let's assume that your station's rate card lists the cost of a one-minute commercial as $100. That same commercial on the competing station costs $150. Now let us assume that the Ace Garden Supply Company wants to advertise topsoil to people twenty-five to forty-nine years of age. You examine your station's latest ratings and find that between 9:00 and 10:00 A.M., you are reaching about 12,000 viewers in the twenty-five-to-forty-nine age bracket. But your competition reaches 14,000 viewers and has convinced the Ace people that they should buy advertising on their station. Now you compare the

CPM of your station with that of the competition. First you figure your station's CPM by dividing the cost of your one-minute commercial by the thousands of people reached by that commercial.

$$\frac{\text{Cost}}{\text{Thousands of Viewers}} = \text{CPM}$$

Before reading further, substitute the figures from our sample rate card and ratings and figure the CPM. The correct answer is $8.33 ($100 ÷ 12). If you did not get $8.33, it was probably because you divided the $100 by 12,000. That would tell you how much it cost to reach just one person. But remember, CPM is the cost of reaching 1,000 persons, and since there are 12 of those (12,000) we divide the $100 by 12.

Now you need to figure the CPM for your competition. To do this, divide $150 (the cost of the competition's one-minute commercial) by 14 (the thousands of persons viewing). The answer is $10.71. Clearly the most economical way to reach the viewers is on your station. It is now up to you to convince Ace Garden Supply of that.

As a consumer of broadcast communication, you will immediately recognize that what you see on your television screen is the result of management's statistical scrutiny. A legitimate criticism of this decision making is that it creates bland programming that will please the general public. That is true. Commercial broadcasting is a business, and nowhere does this become more evident than in the use of broadcast ratings.

CRITICISM OF BROADCAST RATINGS AND IMPROVEMENT OF ACCURACY

Despite mathematical formulas and efforts toward accuracy, the broadcast ratings receive considerable criticism. Some is warranted; some comes from ignorance.

Sampling Error

One criticism of ratings focuses on the actual sample. Statistics tell us that although there may be a given sampling error for a random sample of an entire population, that sampling error increases as the population shrinks. For example, if you have an error of ± 4 percent for the total sample, that sampling error grows as you divide the sample into smaller units, such as those of sex or age. Although your total sample may have been 600 persons, it may include 100 teenagers. Thus the sampling error for teenagers is based on 100, not 600.

Minority Audiences

There is some criticism of ratings of the minority audience. Since it is usually necessary for a station to reach a certain percentage of the total audience before it can even be listed in the ratings books, those that reach small, specialized audiences can suffer. When a station's ratings do not show any listeners, an advertiser's reluctance to spend dollars on that station is understandable. Some rating services use 10-percent listenership or viewership as the cutoff, below which a station is not reported. In a large city such as New York, where there are approximately half a million Spanish households, if each of these were tuned in to the Spanish station, that station still would not be reported.[9]

Some criticism has made a difference. Arbitron withdrew a market report for McAllen-Brownsville, Texas, after receiving complaints that the sample was not adequate. The rating service attributed the problem to field staff members who helped viewers fill out diaries.[10] Elsewhere, Rene Anselmo, president of the Spanish International Network, charged that "both the Spanish and Black communities have been deprived of the variety and diversity of media to which they are entitled because rating practices have adversely affected the economics of minority-owned broadcasting."[11] There have been efforts to correct these alleged deficiencies, which include having diaries printed in Spanish and compensating more accurately for minority audiences.

Broadcasters have their own brand of criticism of the rating services. In a letter to one of the major services an Austin, Texas, broadcaster complained about surveys of the Austin market. Having examined the diaries used by one service, he said he was "particularly disturbed" that the people who were heads of households tended to be people over fifty years of age: "In one county, the average head-of-household age in the diaries was 60, in another county 65, and in still another county 62." He felt that "an accurate rating couldn't be taken from people in that age group when the over-all average is so much younger."[12] He went on to cite instances in which two different surveys of the Austin market differed substantially for the same period.

In 1975 the ratings received widespread attention when Nielsen reported a significant drop in television use.[13] When the decline continued, finding out why a decline had taken place became more important than blaming the ratings for creating an artificial decline.[14]

The press has also leveled its share of criticism. The Associated Press reported that a man in Manhattan became part of the Nielsen sample by not telling the rating service that his grandfather, the man it had asked to complete the diary, had been dead for eleven years.[15] On another front, the Radio Advertising Bureau launched a task force designed to stimulate competition between services. The task force concentrated on improving the methods used in measuring radio audiences.

Attempts to Improve Broadcast Ratings

Because of the developments in cable television, people's changing life-styles, and the sophisticated needs of clients, there are continual efforts to improve the accuracy of broadcast ratings. Some of these efforts are credited to the services themselves, others to networks and broadcast associations. In the case of the latter, for example, a state broadcasters' association complained to the Federal Trade Commission about a station that engaged in heavy promotion, or *hypoing,* during a rating period. Because of this complaint, the major rating services now include special notations within their reports that alert readers to any special promotions during the rating period that may have artificially increased the size of the viewing or listening audience.

In 1975, the three major commercial networks began developing systems for monitoring their affiliate stations' use of network programming. Remember that although a network program may be fed to affiliates, there is no guarantee that every affiliate will air it. Instead, the affiliates may substitute something else. And although a meter attached to a viewer's television may record that a channel is being watched, it does not record the program being watched. Thus, although ratings may show that homes were tuned to a network-affiliate channel, the viewers may instead have been watching a local basketball game that preempted network programming. Meters equipped with the automatic monitoring system can tell the rating service's computer if the station is airing network programming.

Cable has been a particular problem for the ratings. Not only are channels from distant markets often preempted for local programming, as with over-the-air broadcasting, but some cable operators also supply different stations at different times on the same channel. Such procedures keep the rating services hopping, and they continually attempt to distinguish the viewing habits of cable and noncable subscribers in their reports.

Rating services are attempting to give their clients more demographic information. For example, Arbitron's Information on Demand Zip Codes gives clients such demographic breakdowns as income, education, occupation, and additional characteristics. Such specialized target-audience measurement may revolutionize the station rate cards of the future. We may even see specialized rate cards for different sections of town. For example, if you own a neighborhood store in a high-income residential area, you may be able to purchase commercials based on your clientele's viewing habits. A television account executive may show you a ratings book indicating that a certain weekend sports program has a large viewing audience in your clientele's zip-code area. You thus could receive a special advertising rate based on that program's "broadcast circulation." It would be cheaper than the rate for reaching the entire viewing audience but perhaps more than you might pay for reaching a low-income audience. This specialized sales approach may become more common as cable television brings a multitude of specialized channels into our living rooms.

Some radio networks have arranged for rating services to base their radio surveys on the areas of dominant influence used in television ratings.[16] The problem in using a metro service area and a total survey area is to accurately rate the many smaller radio

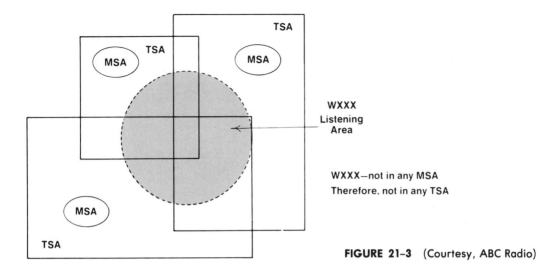

WXXX
Listening
Area

WXXX—not in any MSA
Therefore, not in any TSA

FIGURE 21-3 (Courtesy, ABC Radio)

stations that are not located in one of the larger metropolitan areas. Remember, for a station to be listed in a ratings report it must have a certain minimum number of the listeners in a metro survey area. Thus, a station in an outlying community that does not have the minimum MSA audience may be left out of the rating (Figure 21–3). Even if an outlying station manages to reach one or more

MSAs, most of its listeners would be outside the MSA. Thus, to report the MSA audience for that station would be to report a much smaller audience than there actually is. Even adding together that station's TSA audiences would not give a true audience measurement, since some of the audience would be counted twice and some three times (Figure 21-4). Using the ADI to measure the

FIGURE 21-4 (Courtesy, ABC Radio)

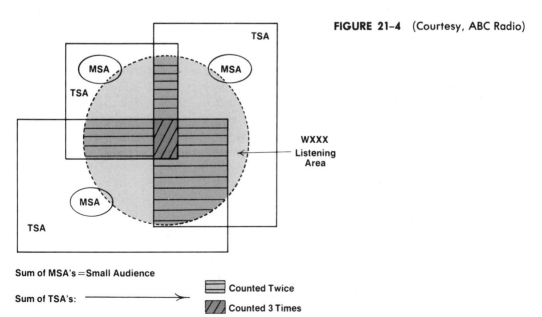

WXXX
Listening
Area

Sum of MSA's = Small Audience

Sum of TSA's: ⟶

Counted Twice

Counted 3 Times

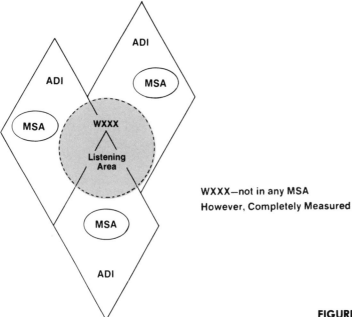

WXXX—not in any MSA
However, Completely Measured

FIGURE 21-5 (Courtesy, ABC Radio)

listenership solves all of these problems. Since ADIs do not overlap, the station that spills over into three different ADIs can add the listenership from each one to find out its total audience (Figure 21-5).

MONITORING QUALITY: THE ELECTRONIC MEDIA RATING COUNCIL

Concern over the accuracy of the ratings and their influence on national programming prompted congressional hearings on these issues in 1963. The publicity generated by the hearings focused on the industry's need for a systematic, self-regulatory body that would assure confidence in broadcast ratings. Thus, in 1963 the National Association of Broadcasters, with the blessings of the American Association of Advertising Agencies and the Association of National Advertisers, joined with ABC, CBS, NBC, and

Mutual to form the Broadcast Rating Council. In 1982 the name of the organization was changed to the Electronic Media Rating Council. The council's main duty is to give the industry and the rating services credibility, assuring advertisers that radio and television are indeed reaching the audiences they say they are reaching.

Since its inception the council has policed the rating services, granting or revoking the seal of approval it gives them and their surveys. The council coordinates a major audit of rating-service practices, paid for by the services themselves. These audits cover all phases of the rating process—the development of sample design, the gathering of data, data processing, and the published report. The audits are unannounced and cover various market areas selected by the auditors. In return for the council's accreditation, the accredited services agree to (1) provide information to the council; (2) operate under substantial compliance with council criteria; and (3) conduct their services as they represent them to their subscribers and to the council.

Technological advances will undoubtedly affect the rating services' future operations. In the experimental stages are an exterior monitoring device that records a household's television-viewing habits from outside the home, and a device that monitors the radio listening habits of passing motorists.

Although they continue to receive criticism, the rating services are still the only source of reliable, economical broadcast-audience data. And rating is done quickly. A network executive can walk into the office on Tuesday morning and find Monday night's ratings on the desk. A local broadcaster can obtain data on local listeners without having to conduct the ratings or to hire, train, and supervise someone else to do it. Continual efforts are being made by broadcasters, networks, and rating services alike to improve the quality of this important area of feedback for the industry.[17]

THE FUTURE OF RATINGS

The entire realm of mass communication is undergoing rapid change. This change will become even more pronounced as audiences become more specialized, as the number of media increases, and as new transmission techniques such as fiber optics transform the broadcasting spectrum from a limited to an almost unlimited resource. Speculating on the future of the ratings, Robert E. Balon developed a scenario predicting that in the year 2016 as many as twenty-six networks will be in operation. Those networks will be trying to gain a mandatory 3-percent share of the audience and will be programming reruns of "Bionic Grandson." Viewers will have thirty to forty shows to watch every

half-hour on multi-screen television, developed back in 1996. Prime time will extend from 4:00 P.M. until 2:00 A.M. and from 6:00 A.M. until 10:00 A.M. Minute populations will be the target audiences, and advertisers will be trying to reach eighteen-to-twenty-one-year-olds. Balon predicts that almost "nothing short of a total, daily sensory monitoring of hundreds of selected subpopulations will be acceptable.[18]

Ask yourself how our current as well as our future society fits into the rating scheme. Do you feel, after learning about random sampling, that the ratings are an accurate gauge of national preference in television and radio? Would there be a better way to analyze the audience and make decisions affecting the content of broadcast messages? If we actually do reach a point at which daily sensory monitoring becomes necessary, would you volunteer to walk around with a minicomputer strapped to your wrist sending data about your viewing and listening habits to a central data-processing unit? What would be the ethical considerations of such a system? Should there be government control over such a system? Discuss these questions with your friends and begin thinking about your own philosophy of broadcasting in the future.

SUMMARY

This chapter examined broadcast ratings. We learned that they are a controversial subject and that the public does not always believe them. Ratings are only as good as the sampling procedure employed. Random sampling, in which each person or household has an equal chance of being surveyed, is an important element of accurate ratings. The larger the sample, the smaller the margin of sampling error. A sample of six hundred persons is sufficient to create a margin of error of about ± 4 percent. Once the sample is drawn, the interviewers should make every attempt to gain the cooperation of as many people in the sample as possible. Data for broadcast ratings are collected by three methods: interviews, diaries, and meters.

We also learned some of the terminology employed in ratings, including *rating, share, average quarter-hour person,* and *cume persons.* We examined the different survey areas—the total survey area (TSA), the metro survey area (MSA), and the area of dominant influence (ADI). Some radio networks have used the ADI, a survey area usually reserved for television, to measure network-radio audiences.

When accurate and reliable ratings are available, management can use them to make programming, personnel, and marketing decisions. Nevertheless, the ratings services have been criticized for such things as the adequacy of their samples and their neglect of minority audiences. For the most part, however, the major rating services continually try to provide more reliable and accurate data for their clients. The quality of the major services and their samples is monitored by the Electronic Media Rating Council.

OPPORTUNITIES
FOR FURTHER LEARNING

Committee on Nationwide Television Audience Measurement (CONTAM), *How Good are Television Ratings?* New York: New York Television Information Office, 1969.

Committee on Nationwide Television Audience Measurement (CONTAM), and MARTIN MAYER, *How Good are Television Ratings?* New York: New York Television Information Office, 1966.

Committee on Nationwide Television Audience Measurement (CONTAM), *Television Ratings Revisited.* New York: New York Television Information Office, 1969, 1970.

Demonstration Report and User's Manual: Nielsen Station Index. Northbrook, Ill.: A. C. Nielsen Co., 1975.

Description of Methodology: Arbitron Television Market Reports. Beltsville, Md.: Arbitron (American Research Bureau), Inc., 1975.

FRANK, R. E., and M. G. GREENBERG, *The Public's Use of Television: Who Watches and Why.* Beverly Hills, Calif.: Sage, 1980.

GOLDMAN, R. J., and R. LA ROSE, *Assessment of Audience Feedback Systems for Research and Programming.* Washington, D.C.: Corporation for Public Broadcasting, 1981.

How Arbitron Measures Radio. Beltsville, Md.: Arbitron (American Research Bureau), Inc., 1974.

MYRICK, H., and C. KEEGAN, *Boston (WGBH) Field Testing of a Qualitative Television Rating System for Public Broadcasting.* Washington, D.C.: Corporation for Public Broadcasting, 1981.

NIELSEN, A. C., *Greater Prosperity through Marketing Research: The First 40 Years of A. C. Nielsen Company.* New York: Newcommen Society in North America, 1964.

Reference Supplement: NSI Methodology, Techniques and Data Interpretation. Northbrook, Ill.: A. C. Nielsen Company, 1974.

Understanding Broadcast Ratings. New York: Broadcast Rating Council. 1978.

Additional readings dealing with research methodologies, many of which can be applied to procedures employed by the rating services, can be found at the conclusion of Chapter 22.

22

THE RESEARCH PROCESS

To the average undergraduate student, the word *research* is about as exciting as a flu epidemic. The word conjures up images of bloodshot eyes pouring over unsolved problems, stuffy laboratories with bubbling flasks, incomprehensible calculations, and all-night study sessions for impossible exams. Even related words can cause the research jitters—words such as *theory, numbers, experiments, statistics,* and *computers.*

The jitters would subside quickly if we stopped long enough to realize that we use research every day. We conduct research, we make decisions based on research, and we are affected by research. Turning to the radio-television section of the evening news-paper is a form of research. You survey the available programs and decide which ones to watch or not to watch. When you decided to enroll in college you may have examined college catalogues, looked at college guides, written letters to different college admissions counselors, and even had on-campus interviews. In each case you were performing research.

The professional researcher in a major television network does the same sort of thing every day. He or she may look through back issues of annual reports in order to establish the image of the company, much the way you examined college catalogues. The researcher might send letters to affiliate stations asking local managers to write back and describe network service. Just as you wrote to the admission counselors and studied their responses, the researcher will examine the managers' responses. If the researcher needs additional information, he or she may interview the manager over the telephone or even visit the station and talk to the manager in person.

Certainly broadcasting has much more complex and sophisticated research projects than these. However, with some training and the opportunity to conduct research projects of your own, you will be able to direct the same type of research undertaken by many local broadcasting stations. So the next time the word *research* pops up, don't be afraid of it. By learning more about how research takes place in the field of telecommunication, you can open up a whole new frontier of exciting knowledge and experience.

TYPES OF RESEARCH

We first should become acquainted with the different types of research—historical, descriptive, experimental, and developmental.

Historical Research

As the name implies, this kind of research focuses on the past. For example, you might trace the history of one of the radio stations in your community. Perhaps a local broadcaster is nationally famous as an industry pioneer. A study of his or her professional career would be a historical study. Historical studies are not necessarily studies of something ancient. A research study of the first five years of WAAA radio would be considered historical even if WAAA signed on the air in 1975.

Descriptive Research

Descriptive research describes a current condition. The most common type of descriptive research is the survey. A survey of local listenership and a survey of television sets in use are examples of descriptive research. Descriptive research is one of the most common types in the broadcasting industry.

Experimental Research

Experimental research is sophisticated research that entails a "controlled" experiment. For example, we might compare children's aggressive behavior before and after they watched television programs containing violence. We would select two groups of children. One group would watch a television program containing violence while another watched the same program but with the violence deleted. We would then compare the behavior of the two groups. Two terms used frequently in experimental research are *independent variable* and *dependent variable*. An independent variable is the factor that is manipulated in the research study. In our example, it is the episodes of violence in the television program. The dependent variable refers to the phenomenon of change, which in our example is the children's behavior.

Developmental Research

Developmental research is conducted mostly in the field of instructional television. Continually perfecting an ITV program on teaching tennis is an example of developmental research. The researchers first establish certain objectives. Then they develop an instructional radio or television program, producing, testing, revising, and retesting it until it meets the stated objectives (Figure 22-1).

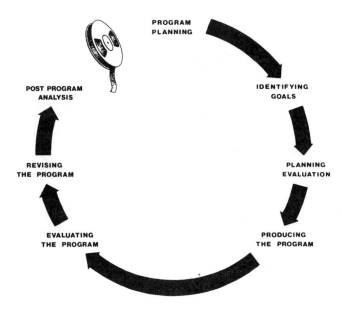

PROGRAM
PLANNING

IDENTIFYING
GOALS

POST PROGRAM
ANALYSIS

PLANNING
EVALUATION

REVISING
THE PROGRAM

EVALUATING
THE PROGRAM

PRODUCING
THE PROGRAM

FIGURE 22-1 Developmental research involves a systematic process of determining what will be the objectives of a program and then producing a program to meet those objectives. Program development research has its most common application in educational and instructional television.

THE SCOPE OF TELECOMMUNICATION RESEARCH

Telecommunication research reaches nearly every facet of the industry. Aside from government research studies and those conducted by such research corporations as A. C. Nielsen, telecommunication research extends from colleges and universities to local stations.

Research in Colleges and Universities

Some of the most sophisticated research on every aspect of broadcasting is done in an academic setting. Many colleges have major research centers that concentrate on radio and television. Among these centers are the Communication Research Center, Broadcast Research Center, Division of Communication Research, Center for Media Research, and Institute for Communication Research. These centers range from depositories for current studies and scholarly research papers to institutes that administer

major research contracts examining everything from the social effects of broadcasting to technical problems associated with fiber-optic transmission. Doctoral dissertations provide another opportunity for research, as do research projects undertaken by students and faculty. Many individual studies appear in scholarly journals.

Research in academia is funded by a multitude of sources. Major foundations are active in funding broadcasting research, including the Ford Foundation, the Rockefeller Foundation, the Lilly Endowment, and the John and Mary Markle Foundation. The networks, corporations, and the federal government contract with institutions of higher learning to do the research for projects of special interest to the funding organization.

The Networks and the CPB

Although we are more attuned to the networks' prime-time programming, their research arms are an integral part of their total operation. Perhaps the most famous network research project was the one on radio listenership started in the early days of CBS by an Ohio State University professor named Frank Stanton. Stanton, who had been hired by the network, went on to become a CBS executive.

Even in the networks' early years, research was clearly defined. Duties assigned to NBC's research department in 1948 were broken down into five areas, which were to be developed under a Master Plan for Television Research:

1. The audience: its size, characteristics, and viewing habits.
2. TV stations and their coverage.
3. Programs: the contribution of research to their better selection and presentation.
4. Advertising: measuring TV's advertising effectiveness.
5. The social impact of TV: its effect on the family and children, the psychological effects of TV, public attitudes toward TV, and TV as an educational medium.[1]

NBC's Thomas E. Coffin believes that some of the recent changes in NBC research have included the more effective communication between researchers and creative people—news and program executives, personnel in program development, producers, and NBC's advertisers.[2] In turn, creative people are finding new ways in which research can help them, the result being that more and more research is devoted to on-the-job problems.

Noncommercial broadcasters also undertake much research. The Research Office of the Public Broadcasting Service conducts research in the areas of system information, system finance, and audience evaluation. The office, moreover, offers six services: it (1) provides information to stations and other PBS departments using federal monies distributed by the Corporation for Public Broadcasting to public stations; (2) coordinates information on program funding and calculates such information as PBS broadcast hours, hours of programming produced by independents, programming acquired from foreign producers, programming sold to foreign countries, and programming hours intended for or dealing with minorities and women; (3) answers requests for information from such places as other PBS departments, Congress, the White House, the public, the press, and book publishers; (4) measures the extent of usable signals transmitted by public television stations and the demographic breakdown of the population in each signal area; (5) provides prompt accounting of each affiliate station's use of PBS programs; and (6) publishes reports on PBS activities.[3]

Although it is not a network, the Office of Communication Research at the Corporation for Public Broadcasting both conducts research itself and contracts for research studies that benefit noncommercial public stations. The office keeps abreast of current research, both in and out of public broadcasting, and disseminates and interprets this research for public broadcasting stations.

Local Stations

Although we usually do not think of local stations as conducting research, virtually all do in some way or other, from community-needs-and-ascertainment surveys to advertising-effectiveness studies. Some of the areas of applied research that can be conducted by local broadcasters who have had some research training are: (1) how many radio or television sets are in the market served by the station; (2) the size of the station's audience; (3) what share of the total listening or viewing audience the station has; (4) the demographic characteristics of the audience; (5) the buying habits of the audience; (6) the use of products and services, such as how many people who use a certain product also listen to or watch the station; (7) how the station's coverage compares with the coverage provided by competing media; (8) audience reaction to station programming; (9) the effectiveness of air personalities; (10) the image of the station (which in many ways includes example 8); and (11) public-opinion polls.[4]

RESEARCH COMMON TO STATION OPERATIONS

The research areas listed above are mostly examples of descriptive survey research. Partly because survey research is more easily interpreted and applied than other types, it is the type most often used by local stations. Let's now look more closely at the methodology of two of the most common types of broadcast surveys: the FCC-required community-needs and ascertainment survey and the station-image survey.

Community-Needs and Ascertainment Surveys

Let's assume you are starting a television station and are about to conduct a community needs and ascertainment survey, as required by the FCC. You could select representatives from the groups in your community and interview them about the community. In doing so, however, you might very well miss some of your most important listeners, groups that are not part of the mainstream of society. Let's look at one such group, the "voiceless."

Researchers Orville G. Walker, Jr., and William Rudelius examined the procedure

for reaching the voiceless. They defined them as "people with a common problem who were not formally organized and who had no widely recognized leaders or spokesperson in the community"[5] and classified them into three categories.

The first category is the *past-in, future-out* group. These people were once in the mainstream of society but now watch from the sidelines. They include such people as the elderly, mental patients, and the deaf. But Walker and Rudelius found that others were equally concerned about medical facilities for the mentally ill or special captioned subtitles on television programs for the hard of hearing, yet did not voice these concerns. No one had asked them.

The second category is the *past-in, future-in* group—such people as "runaway teenagers, unwed mothers, VD victims, and prisoners."[6] This group was in the mainstream in the past and intends to return in the future, once physical or personal problems are overcome. The researchers found that although not all these people needed communication from broadcasters, the unwed mothers wished for information on single-parent child care and the prisoners wanted educational programs.

The third category is the *past-out, future-out* people, those who are minorities because of race or disabilities. They felt "more or less permanently removed from the mainstream of American life because of a lack of understanding or outright discrimination."[7] The FCC ascertainment guidelines provide for reaching racial minorities and women, but ends there. The two researchers discovered that the principal desires of these groups were to have their story told, and for broadcasters to communicate the truth about the negative misconceptions and stereotypes that had been attached to them in the past. Consistent with the past-out, future-out groups' ''desire for a more realistic and truthful portrayal of their cultures and lifestyles, most of these groups expressed a very strong desire for greater influence over the creation and execution of television programs about themselves.''[8] In other words, they were not satisfied with the type of messages being directed toward them. To these groups, media access was important. ''Consequently, they see creative control and active participation—both in front of and behind the cameras—as the only guarantee that a television program or series would accurately reflect their viewpoint.''[9]

Station-Image Surveys

Besides discovering what people think of their community, broadcasters are also interested in finding out what people think of broadcasters and programming. One way of determining this is to conduct station-image surveys. These surveys can be combined with ratings to yield an in-depth look at how the audience perceives a station's programming.

Imagine you are managing a television station and discover that certain programs are not getting a satisfactory share of the viewing audience. But you do not know why. Ratings tell only who is viewing what and when. They do not tell why a person likes or dislikes a certain program. A station-image survey seeks to find out why people do or do not watch or listen to a station. It explores such nebulous areas as attitudes toward and opinions about programming and personalities, and it helps management make decisions. For example, if you discover that a program is being watched by a large share of your audience but find in a station-image survey that the audience actually rates the program very

low, then you could have a problem. The audience may be watching that program only because the competition is airing even more dismal programming. If the competition were to change their offerings and insert a popular program instead, you could have your audience swept away overnight.

Now let's consider an example from radio. Assume you are the program director of a radio station in a large market. You discover that although you seem to be capturing a large share of the audience for most of the broadcasting day, that share tends to dip during the local news. Why? You have already conducted research comparing the number of stories your news department produces with the number produced by the rest of the stations in your market. You know your station has been consistently ahead of the others. So you decide to design a station-image survey (Figure 22–2).

First you decide to determine if the audience even recognizes the name of your station's news director. Then you include in the survey a series of open-ended questions on why people listen or do not listen to your station's local news. From these questions, you will try to isolate those factors that are hurting the ratings of your news.

You discover that the public perceives your news director as being the only local correspondent employed by your station. Although you have a full staff of reporters, the audience is not aware of it. Second, you discover that the public thinks the competing stations cover national news much better than your station does. Finally, you find out that when there is fast-breaking news, the audience consistently turns to other stations.

A bit shocked by the results, you swallow your ego and go to work. Fortunately, you are too smart to fire the news director. If you did, you might lose the audience you already have. Besides, your budget does not have

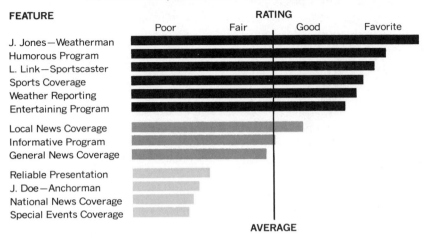

STRENGTHS AND WEAKNESSES
HOW WAAA NEWS VIEWERS RATE WAAA EARLY NEWS REPORT
MONDAY-FRIDAY, 6:00-6:30 PM   TOTAL ADULTS 18 +

FIGURE 22-2   Station image surveys are compliments to other audience data. (Arbitron)

enough funds for the publicity campaign you would have to initiate in announcing the hiring of another director. You decide to develop the talent that is there.

Actually, your problem is not serious. You already have a fine staff of reporters. You just have not been using their voices on the air. When they cover a story they telephone the facts back to the news director, who then writes and airs the story. That will change. You will now have the field reporters phone in and record their reports, which will then be played back in the local news.

The national news programming is another problem. You cannot afford to hire additional reporters to cover national news. But your station does subscribe to one of the wire-service audio networks. Each day the network feeds to its subscribers a series of correspondents' reports from around the nation over its telephone hookup. You have not been paying much attention to these reports since you air the regularly scheduled network newscast at the top of each hour. That also will change. You now will have the news director record those feeds and insert one or two of them in each local newscast.

Finally, to overcome the fast-breaking-news problem, you will try to include a live report from one of your reporters in every local newscast. For example, in the middle of the local news the news director will switch live to the reporter at city hall, or to the one covering a fire. You will also have your news staff call the station and interrupt the regularly scheduled programming whenever important news breaks in the city.

Six months later you begin to see the fruits of your labor. Your share of the audience for your local news now equals that for the rest of your programming. You even see signs of an increase in that share, which would mean that people are tuning in especially to hear the news on your station. Without the station-image survey your station's news might still be in the cellar.

Methods of collecting data for image surveys are as varied as the surveys themselves. Remember, however, that most station-image surveys are designed to dig deeper than the ratings do. Figure 22–3 is a portion of a questionnaire used by WFIU in Bloomington, Indiana. Notice that for each program the respondent has five different rankings to choose from. This format is much more detailed than one that merely asks if that person does or does not listen to the program. Sophisticated computer analysis of this type of questionnaire can tell which programs are popular and how they compare with other programs.[10] Similar questionnaires can reveal how an audience feels about the station's hours of operation, overall selection of programs, news coverage, and scheduling.

The semantic-differential scale is another sophisticated instrument often used in station-image surveys.[11] These scales use pairs of bipolar adjectives, such as *bad* and *good* or *like* and *dislike*. Each pair of adjectives are separated by an odd number of "semantic spaces," usually from five to eleven, and the respondent marks an X in the one he or she feels is appropriate:

Qualified__: X :__:__:__:__:__Unqualified
Inexpert __:__:__:__: X :__:__Expert

Numerical values then are assigned to each space. If this scale measured an audience's reaction to a television newscaster, the newscaster's score would be 11. We got this score by adding the numbers corresponding to the appropriate spaces between the bipolar adjectives:

Qualified 7: 6: 5: 4: 3: 2: 1 Unqualified
Inexpert 1: 2: 3: 4: 5: 6: 7 Expert

The highest number, in this case 7, corresponds to the positive adjectives *qualified* and *expert*. Notice that we placed the positive adjectives at opposite ends of the scale, *qualified* on the left and *expert* on the right. By randomly alternating the position of the adjectives in longer questionnaires, we prevent someone from carelessly marking Xs down one side of all the scales.

FIGURE 22–3 Local stations can rate programs on audience appeal and make programming and scheduling decisions based on those ratings. (WFIU)

In order to assist us in evaluating how effectively we are serving our audience's needs, would you please take a few minutes to rate our programs. Any comments you wish to make will also be welcome.

PROGRAM TITLE	Ranking				
	Low				High
Afterglow	1	2	3	4	5
Afternoon Concert	1	2	3	4	5
Alec Wilder & Friends	1	2	3	4	5
All Things Considered	1	2	3	4	5
Boston Symphony	1	2	3	4	5
Chamber Music	1	2	3	4	5
Chicago Symphony	1	2	3	4	5
Cleveland Orchestra	1	2	3	4	5
Duke Ellington	1	2	3	4	5

Semantic-differential scales are most effective when used with a statistical procedure called *factor analysis,* which factors out and clusters the scales that correlate with each other. These groups of scales, which are called *dimensions,* can tell us a great deal about people's perceptions of everything from station personalities to musical programming. For example, if we are programming a hard-rock format on radio and find in a station-image survey that our listeners prefer programming that falls into those dimensions appropriate to classical music, then we might revise the format to soft rock. We may use a semantic scale to find that a competing newscaster who receives the highest ratings in town exhibits certain dimensions. In analyzing the personnel in our own news department, we find that one of our street reporters is perceived by the audience as having dimensions very similar to those of the popular newscaster. We move the street reporter to the anchor desk, and our ratings immediately improve.

Many more data-gathering instruments are available than the two mentioned here. All are designed to provide an in-depth look at how the audience perceives the station in every respect, from its standing in the community to its programming.

Sales and Marketing Surveys

The sales manager had worked for months on the account. But the drugstore owner was convinced the newspaper was the only place in which to advertise and could see no reason whatsoever for trying the broadcast media. Finally, after repeated calls, explanations, gentle persuasion, and a few lunches, the druggist decided to sponsor the local news. He demanded, however, that he be allowed to write the commercials and have an announcer at the station record them. The copy that reached the station told how long the drugstore had been in the community, how loyal its customers were, and the excellent service it provided. Now it was six months later and time to renew the contract. What the sales manager suspected happened. The drugstore canceled the account. The druggist claimed he just did not see how the commercials could increase sales. When he ran ads in the newspaper, the item he listed always sold out. The sales manager persuaded the druggist to try one more week of commercials, only this time to let the station write the commercials, which the druggist would then approve. It was June, and the sales manager suggested advertising a suntan oil. He also convinced the druggist not to advertise the oil in the newspaper. The commercial started on Monday, and by Wednesday afternoon the drugstore was out of suntan oil. The druggist extended the contract for another six months and took a new look at advertising over the broadcast media.

Our example shows the importance of another type of research—sales and marketing surveys.[12] The sales manager surveyed the marketing mix used by the drugstore and discovered that the tactic of advertising a single product generated noticeable sales. The manager used this information, and the result convinced the client to renew his contract. Monitoring sales is just as important to broadcasters as station-image surveys and community-needs and ascertainment surveys are. Some broadcasters would argue that it is even more important.

Focus Groups

Some stations find focus groups an efficient way to conduct research on listener and viewer preferences. Focus groups are small groups of people brought together to discuss, under the guidance of a trained group leader, topics selected by the station. The station staff records the discussions and analyzes them for trends in audience opinions about the station and its programming.

BEHIND THE SCENES OF A NETWORK ELECTION POLL

"They told me at the doughnut shop we had a reporter from NBC here, and by golly we do!" The pollster looked up from her interviewing sheets to see a weathered farmer in bib overalls smiling as if he had just reaped the biggest corn harvest in three counties. The woman's quick explanation that she was just freelancing for NBC as a precinct pollster for this election day did not seem to bother him in the least. It was obvious that his stories of meeting a real live "network person" would be heard in front of many a crackling fire.

Planning the Poll and Selecting the Pollsters

Public-opinion polls in radio and television are mainly the domain of the broadcast journalist and are usually concentrated around election time. We take for granted the election-night predictions of state and national winners that are made only a few hours after the polls close and before all the votes are counted. We no longer sit in amazement as computers, network commentators, and sample precincts determine the fate of democracy. We expect it.

What is behind these public-opinion polls? It all starts in the network planning rooms, where statisticians and polling experts pour over mounds of computer data, analyzing voting trends in every state. How many persons voted in which county for what candidate? How do these figures correlate with state and national voting trends? Do they correlate often enough to produce a sample precinct, that tiny subdivision of each community used to predict a winner long before the local election officials finish their work? A sample precinct may be found in the heart of Los Angeles or a tiny Maine fishing village. They are chosen by the same random-sampling techniques we learned about when we studied broadcast ratings. Together, they become part of the state-by-state predictions of House representatives, senators, governors, and presidents.

Equally critical to the election poll are the precinct pollsters selected by the networks to interview voters. Some of the pollsters are associated with local broadcasting stations and are invited by the network to represent them at a polling place in their area. At the network's office in New York, other people are in charge of coordinating this national group of volunteers, who will receive a modest fee for their day's work. Coordinating a national core of pollsters and training them by mail are big jobs and must be carefully planned and executed.

Imagine yourself as an interviewer participating in a network election-day poll. What will your job be like? It will actually start about a month before the election with a call from a network executive asking you to represent the network as a precinct pollster. About two weeks later you will receive a large packet of instructions. You will be asked to read the instructions carefully and to call a special telephone number if you need advice or if something unexpected happens. The number belongs to a state supervisor hired by the network. The instructions will tell you where you will conduct the polling, give you the exact precinct and voting location, and list the name and telephone number of the local precinct official, along with a suggestion that you contact that person before election day. Since you are just one part of a national systematic effort you will be asked to follow the directions very carefully. You have two responsibilities: to conduct the poll and to report the results to the network.

Each pollster is assigned certain periods in which to conduct the precinct poll. For example, you might be assigned to interview people coming out of the polling place between 6:00 A.M. and 9:00 A.M. and then call in those results to the network at 9:15 A.M. The second interview time might be between 12:30 P.M. and 1:30 P.M., in which case you would call in your second report to the network at 1:45 P.M.

You will also be told which sequence of voters to interview—for instance, every fifth or every third voter. The interval depends upon the precinct's size. Your instructions would also tell you your quota of completed interviews—perhaps thirty within those two time periods.

Conducting the Poll

Finally election day arrives. In the predawn darkness you start your drive to the polling place, leaving yourself plenty of time to get there. You have been assigned to a precinct in a small rural area. The morning sun is just coming up when you roll into the sleepy little town. You pass an old general store, a gas station, and a cafe where a few people are downing their first morning coffee. The precinct voting place is in the town library. You have seen them before, one of the old Carnegie structures with an American flag outside. Inside, the precinct workers all are ready for the first voter. You are greeted by the local precinct official you talked to earlier on the phone. She eyes your official NBC badge and asks,

"How about a cup of coffee and some of Mabel's cookies?" You accept and begin to wonder what the day will bring.

"Who are you going to interview?" she asks.

"Well I'm supposed to interview every third person, starting with the first one to vote after 6:00 A.M."

Before the precinct official can answer, Mabel says, "I'll tell you who that's gonna be." She has a big grin on a face revealing years of toil on a farm. "You can betcha Harvey Clodfelter will be the first through that door. Twenty years and he ain't missed being first yet."

You sense that election day is one of those special days ranking with the church suppers, the day of the school picnic, and the beginning of the county fair. It seems light years away from the network control center in New York, where computers and statisticians are adding the finishing touches for the marathon telecast to follow that night.

But here is where it all begins. You begin, sure enough, with Harvey Clodfelter. Your day will be filled with Harveys. They will ask you who you are, where you live, why you are there, and when you will be back. They will offer you their own brand of election philosophy, tell you why this candidate or that candidate will win, explain why the electoral college should be abolished, and complain how the big city folks are going to sway the election. To each of them you will give a ballot, similar in some ways to the one they have just completed. The ballot will be labeled SECRET BALLOT, and when they have finished filling it out they will put it in a big envelope. Later you will open that envelope and tally the results.

The ballot requires information that is much more detailed than merely whom the respondents voted for. It asks them whether the TV debates affected their choice, who they voted for in the last presidential election, their ethnic background, the occupation of the head of their household, and such basic demographic information as age and sex. The ballot also asks what issues influenced their decisions, what the candidates' positions on the economy and foreign policy are, and whether those positions affected their decision.

If Harvey Clodfelter, the first person to finish voting after 6:00 A.M., refuses to be interviewed, then you continue counting until you reach the next interval. Remember, your goal is to interview every third person. It is a hard day. Some local people do not trust outsiders, and you get completed interviews from only three of those chosen people. Nevertheless, you keep working toward your quota. You make certain you offer a questionnaire only to those persons who have actually voted. That is one advantage the election-day polls have over preelection polls. You are also careful not to interfere in any way with the actual election process—voting and the checking of voter registration.

So as not to influence the results of your poll, you try to remain polite while refraining from talking about candidates, issues, political beliefs, or anything else that might bias the results. The only information you will supply is on the mechanics of completing the secret ballot; you will not answer any requests for political information. If a person does not understand a question or the directions, a polite suggestion to reread the ballot, not a rephrasing of the question or directions, is necessary. In other words, you will not want to influence, either by word or action, the response of the person being polled.

At precisely 9:15 A.M. you walk up the stairs to the library's office and call New York with the results of your first poll. To help make sure every item is understood by the data collector, you use word identifications for each of the possible answers: *alpha* for A, *bravo* for B, *Charlie* for C, *delta* for D, and so on. A typical conversation might go like this:

NBC OPERATOR: NBC. Your location code, please.
INTERVIEWER: This is Ohio, location 400. (The NBC operator will then repeat your code and give you the name of your polling location in order to be sure NBC has the correct information.)
NBC OPERATOR: I'm ready for the answers.
INTERVIEWER: "Question one, Alpha."
NBC OPERATOR: "One, Alpha, Okay. Go ahead."
INTERVIEWER: "Two, Charlie."
NBC OPERATOR: "Two, Charlie, right."
INTERVIEWER: Three, Delta.[13]

You then walk back down the stairs, nibble another cookie, and wait until the specified time of 12:30 P.M., when you will repeat the procedure.

In New York, the data from your poll and those of other pollsters scattered throughout the United States are fed into a computer, which tabulates them and predicts the winners. So why does the network not start predicting at noon on election day? The answer to that is a matter of geography. Since the West, because of the time-zone difference, votes later than the East, such predictions could influence western voters. A news report stating that a certain candidate has won by a landslide in New York may convince people in California that they should also vote for the probable winner. On the other hand, that news might make the candidate's California supporters so complacent that they stay home and give the opponent the election. Let's examine this reporting process more closely.

REPORTING PUBLIC-OPINION POLLS

As either a consumer of broadcast communication or someone who will someday report polls, you should be aware that there is more to an opinion poll than just the results. A gullible public and press are often the objects of persuasion campaigns based on public-opinion polls. Broadcast journalists, partly because of the time restrictions placed on them, find it difficult to report all of the pertinent data from an opinion poll. Because of this, the following could very likely happen. A wire service reports that a senatorial candidate is leading his opponent by twenty percent. The radio station reports the story, only to find out later that the poll consisted of twenty-five persons who stopped by for coffee at the candidate's of-

fice. The sampling error alone would make the results questionable, to say nothing of the probable bias. We can assume that anyone who takes the time to have coffee at a candidate's office is not vehemently opposed to that person.

Reporting a public-opinion poll can be just as important, perhaps more so, than conducting the poll itself. The American Association of Public Opinion Research and the National Council on Public Opinion Polls have adopted guidelines for reporting public-opinion polls. An emphasis on "precision journalism" has also fostered more responsible and intelligent interpretation of polls.[14] Other guidelines have been offered by both journalists and educators (Figure 22–4). The aim of this attention is to educate the public and the media in the polling pro-

FIGURE 22–4 Despite the fact a poll may be scientifically produced, the reporting of the poll can lead to distortion and misunderstanding. Broadcast news programs, because of time limitations, many times find it impossible to provide all of the qualifiers that might be used in reporting a poll. (*The Quill*, published by the Society of Professional Journalists, Sigma Delta Chi)

**CHECKLIST—
WHAT TO LOOK FOR IN A POLL STORY:**

✔ *Was a probability sample used?*

✔ *Who sponsored, and who conducted, the polling?*

✔ *Is the population sampled adequately defined?*

✔ *How were those polled contacted—by mail, by telephone or in person?*

✔ *Is exact wording of questions specified?*

✔ *How many people were surveyed?*

✔ *Is it clear when analysis and interpretation concern only part of the full sample?*

✔ *Does the story specify an error margin for results, and does interpretation outrun that error margin?*

✔ *Does the story provide data to compare the sample with demographic characteristics of the population from which the sample was drawn?*

✔ *Is the headline or teaser accurate?*

---

cess. Even if the press is unable, because of space or time limitations, to report exactly how the poll was set up, it should be able to decide intelligently whether even to use the poll, and if so whether it warrants detailed interpretation.

What are the important considerations in reporting polls?[15] The first is the sample. If it is not a random-probability sample, then it may be questionable. In other words, for the poll to be credible, the probability of one person being selected should equal that of all other persons who might be selected. If the sample covers only your state, then it is not good sense to apply predictions based on it to the entire country.

A second important consideration is who sponsored and conducted the poll. A poll favoring a Democratic governor that is sponsored by the state's Democratic committee and conducted by Democratic precinct workers would be suspect.

Third, it is important to define the sample population. If a poll taken among Maine voters states that the senator from Maine has a 60-percent chance of winning his party's nomination for president, the chances are that the estimate is inflated. Knowing who was sampled permits a better judgment of the poll's results.

A fourth consideration in reporting polls is how the respondents were contacted. A telephone survey, for example, would automatically eliminate all those who could not afford to have a telephone.

Fifth, it is important to know what questions were asked. "Will you be voting for our fine Senator Claghorn?" will elicit answers favoring Senator Claghorn.

Sixth, it is important to know how many people were surveyed. In this way we can determine the margin of error.

Seventh, the poll should distinguish samples and subsamples in interpreting its findings. For instance, a poll may be reported to have a sampling error of ± 4 percent, based on a random sample of 600 persons. However, if 50 of those respondents were Indians, it would not be correct to predict how the Indian population would vote and still claim the sampling error was ± 4 percent. Because only 50 Indians were sampled, the margin of error would be closer to ± 14 percent.

Eighth, it is important to report the error margin. Merely knowing what it is but not telling the listening or viewing audience has little purpose. Error margins are one of the easiest and best-understood factors in an opinion poll. If you claim that a candidate has a 5-percent edge over his opponent but do not tell the public that the margin for error is 10 percent, then you have misled them. Moreover, if you predict a winner when the margin of error makes a contest too close to call, then you also have misled the public.

A ninth important consideration in reporting polls is how the sample compares with the total population. If the population is 50-percent Hispanic yet only 33 percent of your sample is Hispanic, then you would be asking for trouble by predicting the election without compensating for that variation.

The tenth consideration is the all-important headline. People can be persuaded by headlines. The radio or television reporter who announces, "Opinion poll predicts Senator Doolittle will sweep the state," and then comes back after the commercial to report a poll of the senator's precinct workers has been irresponsible.

Public-opinion polls are not foolproof and can be used incorrectly. The key is to understand them and know their pitfalls. The broadcast manager who editorializes in favor of a candidate may be in hot water if he bases that support on a sloppy opinion poll. A television news director who sends her staff out to conduct an opinion poll on election eve and violates all the rules of random sampling is asking for trouble if she reports the results of the poll as though they were representative of the total population. Take the opportunity to read more about opinion polling. Design a sample poll. Ask yourself if it meets all of the criteria discussed above. Would you be able to draw general conclusions from your results?

ALTERNATIVE FORMS OF DATA COLLECTION AND APPROACHES TO RESEARCH

New technology is accelerating the polling process even beyond the computer analyses so common in today's surveys. With this technology broadcasters will be able to conduct opinion polls faster and with fewer personnel than in the past. One of the newer polling systems uses a series of tape recorders and a single operator. The operator dials a telephone number. When the phone is answered, the tape recorder takes over and plays a recorded message to the party answering the phone. It then records the person's response. Meanwhile, the operator is busy dialing another number for one of the other tape recorders. This system permits a single operator to make as many as one thousand calls per day. Of course, the results of such a poll are only as accurate as the information being asked. If the questions are poorly phrased or if there are errors in the sampling procedure, then it is difficult for the poll to reflect the opinions of the population accurately.

Researchers have used an electronic device called an *oculometer* to examine how people watch television commercials. Utilizing a sensor that monitors the eye movements of viewers, the oculometer has shown, for example, that people are attracted immediately to people in television commercials, that their attention span is rather short, and

that certain visual elements in a television commercial can actually distract the viewer from the product being advertised.

In research centers, colleges and universities, advertising-research firms, and almost any other place where broadcast-related research goes on, paper-and-pencil questionnaires are often being replaced by still other electronic data-gathering instruments.

Electronic Response Systems

Electronic data gathering, a process in which a member of an audience punches a button or has his or her pulse read electronically, is not new to broadcasting.[16] In 1937 Frank Stanton of CBS and Paul Lazarsfeld, a well-known social scientist, developed Big Annie, perhaps the first electronic response indicator (ERI) used to measure how an audience reacts to radio shows. The listener could push one of three buttons labeled *like, dislike,* and *neutral*. Big Annie had a short life, but she did spark interest in electronic data gathering.

One instrument designed to gather data was invented by a professor of telecommunication at the University of Oregon, Elwood Kretsinger. He called it a *chi-square meter*. It simultaneously records an individual's responses to whatever he or she happens to be listening to or watching. Researchers compare responses among different individuals or groups by using a statistical test called the chi square. The chi-square meter was not Kretsinger's first venture into response systems. In the late 1940s he invented a device called the *wiggle meter* that measured how much people fidget. The device had three components. A wire strung on the back of a chair was fed into an amplifier, which in turn measured the amount of wiggling on a long roll of graph paper.[17]

The increased interest in ERIs has resulted in a number of commercial firms that manufacture the systems. They are usually installed in a large auditorium, one to every seat or desk. Each unit has five buttons that can electronically record anything from an answer to a five-part multiple-choice question to one of five attitudinal responses such as "strongly agree," "agree," "neutral," "disagree," and "strongly disagree." The entire auditorium of ERIs can be monitored by a computer and can register continuously the response of the entire room or sections of the room, or calculate statistical comparisons between various groups of people.

Assume you have produced an instructional television program and now want to test its effectiveness. You arrange for a physical-education class to use a room equipped with ERIs, and at periodic intervals in the program you ask the class to respond to a series of questions with which they will evaluate your program's effectiveness. When the program is over, a computer printout tells you how the class scored on every question. Those questions the students missed may indicate that you need to revise one or more sections of the program. If you had not been using ERIs, you could have waited until the program was over and given the students a paper-and-pencil test to evaluate what they had learned. However, you then would have had to score the tests and calculate the statistical computations yourself or wait until they could be done by computer.

Galvanic Skin Response

Not all of the methods that test audience reaction necessitate pushing a button or wiggling. There are also systems that measure changes in the conductivity of the skin, which are called galvanic skin responses (GSRs). One data-collection firm uses electrodes attached to the palm to test audience reaction to such things as commercials, records, and radio-station formats.[18] About one hundred persons are selected for each study, and the system's developers have claimed that it has as high as 91-percent accuracy in predicting whether records will appear among the top twenty of the national charts. Another system uses a computer to analyze the data from about eighty subjects wired for GSR readings. The developers claim that it enables radio stations to figure out how to "recycle" listeners—that is make them return to the station once they have sampled it.[19] Still other systems have used brain waves to measure audience response. For example, researchers at the Princeton Medical Center used an electroencephalograph to examine the brain waves of people watching television.[20]

Gathering data from either ERIs or GSRs has two advantages over older methods of data collection. First, it is fast, especially when monitored by a computer. What formerly took hours of work and computation can now be calculated almost instantaneously. Second, it can measure detailed aspects of audience reaction, thus providing much more sophisticated data bases. When decision makers can monitor audience reaction every few seconds, they have a more useful account of how an audience is reacting to a message.

The two systems can be installed even in mobile vans. These vans can stop outside a grocery store and ask shoppers to come in. There they watch a television commercial and have their reactions to it recorded. Then the operators watch the shoppers enter the grocery store and directly monitor sales of a certain product.

A disadvantage of the systems is the limited number of responses they can monitor at any one time. Although a major rating service can obtain feedback from an audience large enough to enable it to predict national trends, most electronic response systems are designed for a group no larger than can be accommodated in a small auditorium. This limitation is not, however, a technological weakness. Electronic response systems that connect the home to a computer, much as a two-way cable system does, already enable researchers to measure large audiences. The future may see national populations' reactions to television programs being monitored on a second-to-second basis. It is not beyond the reach of current technology.

Role Observation: Producing an Ethnography

Although such data-collection measures as the ERI and the GSR are useful in highly controlled laboratory conditions, the very artificiality of those conditions can sometimes limit the applicability of research results. Recently, researchers have been turning less to laboratory-oriented methods of data collection and more to real-life settings. Living with families and observing how they use radio and television is becoming a more frequent research approach. Such approaches can produce an *ethnography,* an account of how individuals have interacted with their environment and with each other, and, in the case of broadcasting, how radio and television have functioned in this interaction.

Research is telling us of the increasingly important role media play in structuring our daily activities and interpersonal exchanges.[21] Further ethnographic approaches to the study of how radio and television affect our lives will provide new perspectives on how we interact with our media-filled society.

SUMMARY

This chapter has examined the telecommunication research process. There are four kinds of research: historical, descriptive, experimental, and developmental. Of these, descriptive research is the kind most commonly used in the broadcasting industry. Experimental research manipulates an independent variable, then observes any phenomenon resulting from that manipulation. The phenomenon to be observed is the dependent variable. Research extends from that done at academic research centers to individual studies by students and faculty, to doctoral dissertations. Besides that done by the government and rating services, research is conducted by local stations and networks.

Survey research common in local stations includes community-needs and ascertainment surveys, station-image surveys, and sales and marketing surveys. Surveys should also take into consideration the ''voiceless'' members of a community. Station-image surveys often use more sophisticated methodology than community-needs and ascertainment surveys do. Ranking of programs, questions on station operating procedures, and semantic-differential scales are just some of the many methods researchers use to discover an audience's perceptions of a station and its programming. Sales and marketing surveys determine if systematic broadcast advertising campaigns have had satisfactory results.

Focus-group research brings together small groups of people who discuss topics under the guidance of a trained moderator.

Public-opinion polls are usually the domain of the broadcast journalist and are frequently used around election time. But merely conducting a good poll is not enough. Reporters should consider information about the sample, sponsor, population, contact method, questions, sampling error, and headlines in order to communicate responsibly the results of a poll to a broadcast audience.

New technology is significantly altering the way in which research data are collected. Such methods as electronic response indicators and galvanic skin responses are being used more often to hasten the collection and processing of raw data. Role observation that produces an ethnography is also gaining increased attention.

OPPORTUNITIES
FOR FURTHER LEARNING

ALKIN, M. C., and L. C. SOLMON, eds., *The Costs of Evaluation.* Beverly Hills, Calif.: Sage, 1983.

ALTSCHULER, B. E., *Keeping a Finger on the Public Pulse: Private Polling and Presidential Elections.* Westport, Conn.: Greenwood, 1982.

BLALOCK, H. M., JR., *Conceptualization and Measurement in the Social Sciences.* Beverly Hills, Calif.: Sage, 1982.

BOHRNSTEDT, G. W., and E. F. BORGATTA, eds., *Social Measurement: Current Issues.* Beverly Hills, Calif.: Sage, 1981.

A Broadcast Research Primer. Washington, D.C.: National Association of Broadcasters, 1974.

BUDD, J., comp., *Register of Current British Research on Mass Media and Mass Communication.* Leicester, England: Center for Mass Communication Research, 1980.

CAMPBELL, J. P., R. L. DAFT, and C. L. HULIN, *What to Study: Generating and Developing Research Questions.* Beverly Hills, Calif.: Sage, 1982.

CANTRIL, A. H., ed., *Polling on the Issues: Twenty-one Perspectives on the Role of Opinion Polls in the Making of Public Policy.* Cabin John, Md.: Seven Locks Press, 1980.

Demonstration Report and User's Manual: Nielsen Station Index. Northbrook, Ill.: A. C. Nielsen, 1975.

Description of Methodology: Arbitron Television Market Reports. Beltsville, Md.: American Research Bureau, 1975.

EDELSTEIN, A. S., *Comparative Communication Research.* Beverly Hills, Calif.: Sage, 1982.

GANTZ, W., *Public Television Pilot Testing Instrument: A User's Handbook.* Washington, D.C.: Corporation for Public Broadcasting, 1981.

Guidelines for the Public Use of Market and Opinion Research. New York: Advertising Research Foundation, 1981.

HAKEL, M. D., M. SORCHER, M. BEER, and J. L. MOSES, *Making It Happen: Designing Research With Implementation in Mind.* Beverly Hills, Calif.: Sage, 1982.

HEISE, D. R., ed., *Microcomputers and Social Research.* Sociological Methods and Research Series, Vol. 9, No. 4. Beverly Hills, Calif.: Sage, 1981.

HIRSCH, P. M., P. V. MILLER, and F. G. KLINE, *Strategies for Communication Research.* Beverly Hills, Calif.: Sage, 1977.

HOUSE, E. R., *Evaluating With Validity.* Beverly Hills, Calif.: Sage, 1980.

How Arbitron Measures Radio. Beltsville, Md.: American Research Bureau, 1974.

HUNTER, J. E., F. L. SCHMIDT, and G. B. JACKSON, *Meta-Analysis: Cumulating Research Findings Across Studies.* Beverly Hills, Calif.: Sage, 1982.

JAMES, L. R., S. A. MULAIK, and J. M. BRETT, *Causal Analysis: Assumptions, Models, and Data.* Beverly Hills, Calif.: Sage, 1982.

KNORR-CETINA, K., and M. MULKAY, eds., *Science Observed: New Perspectives on the Social Study of Science.* Beverly Hills, Calif.: Sage, 1983.

KRIPPENDORFF, K., *Content Analysis: An Introduction to Its Methodology.* Beverly Hills, Calif.: Sage, 1980.

MARSDEN, P. V., ed., *Linear Models in Social Research.* Beverly Hills, Calif.: Sage, 1981.

McGRATH, J. E., J. MARTIN, and R. A. KULKA, *Judgment Calls in Research.* Beverly Hills, Calif.: Sage, 1982.

MONGE, P. R., and J. N. CAPPELLA, eds., *Multivariate Techniques in Human Communication Research.* New York: Academic, 1980.

MORGAN, G., ed., *Beyond Method: Strategies for Social Research.* Beverly Hills, Calif.: Sage, 1983.

NIELSEN, A. C., *Greater Prosperity Through Marketing Research: The First 40 Years of A. C. Nielsen Company.* New York: Newcomen Society in North America, 1964.

PATTON, M. Q., *Practical Evaluation.* Beverly Hills, Calif.: Sage, 1982.

———, *Qualitative Evaluation Methods.* Beverly Hills, Calif.: Sage, 1980.

POPE, J. L., *Practical Marketing Research.* New York: AMACOM, 1981.

Reference Supplement: NSI Methodology, Techniques and Data Interpretation. Northbrook, Ill.: A. C. Nielsen, 1974.

ROGERS, E. M., and D. L. KINCAID, *Communication Networks: Toward a New Paradigm for Research.* New York: Free Press, 1981.

ROSENGREN, K. E., ed., *Advances in Content Analysis.* Beverly Hills, Calif.: Sage, 1981.

SAXE, L., and M. FINE, *Social Experiments: Methods for Design and Evaluation.* Beverly Hills, Calif.: Sage, 1981.

SHAW, DAVID, "Political Polls: Use and Abuse," in *Journalism Today,* Chapter 3. New York: Harper & Row, 1977.

Six Experiments in Ascertainment Methodology. Washington, D.C.: Corporation for Public Broadcasting, 1977. Authors include Robert K. Avery, Paige Birdsall, Antonio Rey, Alfred G. Smith, Patrick A. Nester, D. Lynn Pulford, James A. Anderson, Thomas A. McCain, C. Richard Hofstetter, Navita Cummings James, and James E. Hawkins.

STEMPEL, G. H., III, and B. H. WESTLEY, eds., *Research Methods in Mass Communication.* Englewood Cliffs, N.J.: Prentice-Hall, 1981.

WEAVER, D. H., D. A. GRABER, M. E. McCOMBS, and C. H. EYAL, *Media Agenda-Setting in a Presidential Election: Issues, Images, and Interest.* New York: Praeger, 1981.

WILHOIT, G. C., and M. McCOMBS, "Reporting Surveys and Polls," in *Handbook of Reporting Methods,* ed. Maxwell McCombs, Donald Lewis Shaw, and David Grey, pp. 81-95. Boston: Houghton Mifflin, 1976.

WINICK, C., and others, *Children's Television Commercials: A Content Analysis.* New York: Praeger, 1973.

WOELFEL, J., and E. L. FINK, *The Measurement of Communication Processes: Galileo Theory and Method.* Human Communication Research Series. New York: Academic, 1980.

ZIKMUND, W. G., W. J. LUNDSTROM, D. SCIGLIMPAGLIA, *Cases in Marketing Research.* Chicago: Dryden, 1982.

23

THE BROADCAST AUDIENCE: APPROACHES TO STUDYING USES AND EFFECTS

Imagine you are media director for an advertising agency. Selecting a magazine in which to advertise your client's products requires you to examine the magazine's audience. Naturally you need to know the circulation, but you also want to know something about how the readers think, what their interests are, how old they are, what their income is, and how much education they have had. If the magazine is well established, this information will be readily available to you in a readership survey.

Now assume you need to buy time on a major television network. Here, identifying the audience becomes much more difficult. Although you could choose certain types of programming that would reach certain audiences, such as Saturday-morning programs for children, you are dealing mainly with a large, unidentified audience.

To say only that a broadcast audience is too big and complex to study would be to admit defeat much too soon. Instead, this chapter will examine what we *do* know about the broadcast audience, realizing all the time that researchers are continually working to learn more about it. We have been able only to scratch the surface of this inquiry, partly because human behavior is a highly complex phenomenon. Our studies of television violence and the effects of broadcast programming overlap with research in many other disciplines. Moreover, cooperative research across international boundaries, if political conditions permit it, would be invaluable.

UNDERSTANDING THE AUDIENCE

Electronic media have been studied by scholars, organizations, and the industry itself. Some of the more classic studies remain landmarks in the history of research and have influenced the way we are affected by and interpret the media. Studies such as Harry Field and Paul L. Lazarsfeld's *The People Look at Radio* (Figure 23–1), completed under the auspices of the National Association of Broadcasters, The National Opinion Research Center at the University of Denver, and the Bureau of Applied Social Research at Columbia University, opened up a new era in systematic evaluation of electronic media. Published in 1946 by The University of North Carolina Press at Chapel Hill, *The People Look at Radio* examined such fundamental questons as: "Do you have a radio in working order?" and "If you had to give up either reading the newspaper or listening to the radio, which one would you give up?" Eighty-seven percent of the more than three thousand people interviewed had a radio in working order and sixty-two percent said they would rather give up the newspaper.

Since 1946 we have changed the way we measure people's perceptions about the mass media, partially because of more sophisticated means of analysis aided by the computation power of the computer. We have also altered our views and theories on the way media affect us and the way we use media.

FIGURE 23–1 One of the classic studies of early radio research was Field and Lazarsfeld's *The People Look at Radio*, published in 1946 by The University of North Carolina Press at Chapel Hill.

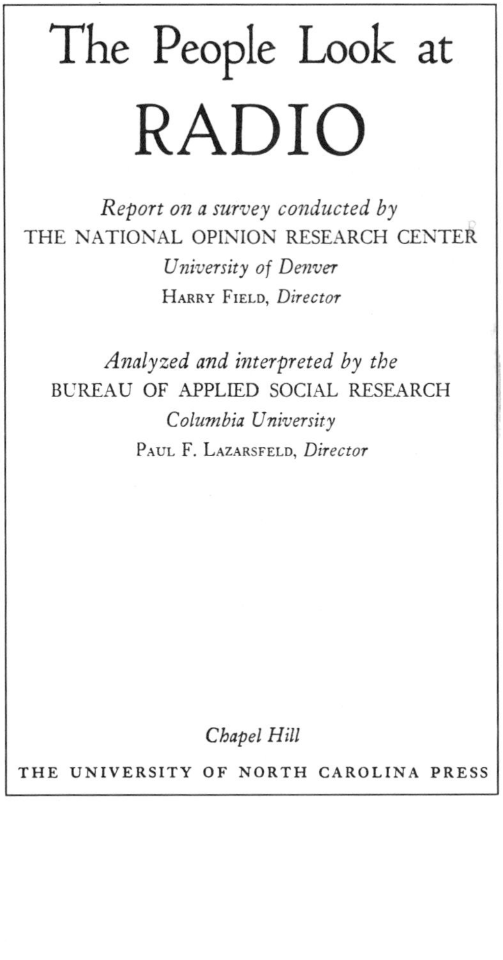

The People Look at
RADIO

Report on a survey conducted by
THE NATIONAL OPINION RESEARCH CENTER
University of Denver
HARRY FIELD, *Director*

Analyzed and interpreted by the
BUREAU OF APPLIED SOCIAL RESEARCH
Columbia University
PAUL F. LAZARSFELD, *Director*

Chapel Hill
THE UNIVERSITY OF NORTH CAROLINA PRESS

Early Perceptions of the Audience: The Bullet Theory

Theorists used to look at the audience as a disconnected mass of individuals who received communication in much the same way that sitting ducks receive birdshot. This approach to media effects was labeled the *bullet theory,* or sometimes the *hypodermic theory.* Part of this misconception developed during World War I as a result of scare tactics employed in propaganda campaigns. As researchers began to realize that the behavior of humans was more complex than that of sitting ducks, their perception of the mass audience began to change.

The first change was in the concept of the mass. Instead of being viewed as a huge body of isolated persons exhibiting similar reactions to media messages, the audience gradually came to be studied as a group of individuals held together by different social systems and reacting to messages partly on the basis of their interaction with others within these systems. A political commercial may affect different persons in different ways. Those same persons may interact with others about the commercial. These other persons may determine, just as much as and perhaps many times more than the media does, how a person reacts to the commercial.

The Individual-Differences, Categories, and Social-Relations Approaches

In revising the bullet theory, researchers have used three approaches to the study of audience reaction to media messages. The *individual-differences approach* "implies that media messages contain particular stimulus attributes that have differential interaction with personality characteristics of audience members. Since there are individual differences in personality characteristics among such members, it is natural to assume that there will be variations in effect which correspond to these individual differences."[1] In other words, we each have individual qualities that cause us to react differently to media messages. These differing effects of media messages are caused partially by the audience's exposure to and perception and *retention* of media content, all of which we shall examine later in this chapter.

The *categories approach* originated in the needs of advertisers to reach audiences with specific characteristics. Although the simplest way to group an audience into categories is by demographics—sex, age, and so on —researchers are looking more and more at psychographics—values, beliefs, attitudes,

and life-styles. The categories approach to the mass audience can be as simple or as involved as the purpose to which it is put. For the ad buyer wanting to reach eighteen- to twenty-one-year-old females, the application of the theory is mechanical. But for social scientists wanting to know how categories of people think and how they interact with other categories of people, the approach becomes much more complex. Moreover, if we want to use these interrelationships to understand how people react to broadcast messages, the process becomes even more sophisticated. Buying an ad to reach the homemaker is one thing; buying an ad to reach the homemaker who interacts with another homemaker viewing a competing commercial is something else.[2]

Concentrating on such interaction and the persons taking part in it would describe the *social-relations approach* to studying the audience and the effects of media on it. Interpersonal communication is thus important to this approach, as is the realization that although the media can help disseminate the initial message, how it is retransmitted, discussed, and rediscussed among audience members will in great part determine its effect.

We can readily see that these three approaches not only overlap but are in some ways all part of the communicative process. Different persons may view that process through different-colored glasses. A psychologist concerned with an individual's behavior might feel more comfortable with an individual-differences approach but would be foolish to ignore the other approaches. Similarly, an advertiser wanting to reach a specific audience might be concerned with categories but could not ignore the relationships among people that receive the attention of the social-relations approach.

FLOW AND PROCESSING
OF MESSAGES

Interaction among members of the broadcast audience is part of the natural process of information dissemination and processing.

Opinion Leaders
and the Two-Step Flow

Imagine for a moment that you are discussing a new television series with your friend. Your friend tells you how great the series is, says you would enjoy the fast action, and suggests you watch it. Since you value your friend's opinion, you decide you will take a break from studying to watch the show. Why did you make that decision? Undoubtedly because you valued your friend's opinion enough to be influenced to take action—to watch the program. In doing so you demonstrated how other persons, whom we shall call *opinion leaders,* influence opinions concerning media messages.[3]

Since you had not seen the program, your friend's description was all you knew about it. By first hearing about the program from your friend, you demonstrated how messages flow to and through the mass audience. We call this process the *two-step flow,* even though many more than two steps may be taken before the information reaches all the people who eventually learn about it. Remember that the two-step flow can apply to both acquiring information and being persuaded by it.

Selective Exposure, Perception,
and Retention

In discussing the individual-differences approach, we talked about exposure, perception, and retention. Each influences our interaction with the media and how it affects

us. First of all, research has taught us that we selectively expose ourselves to certain types of programming, a process called *selective exposure.* If a politician is delivering a televised address, you might tune in the program because you agree with the politician's views. On the other hand, you might tune in the program because you disagree with the politician. In either case, you selectively exposed yourself to the program.

Second, the perceptions you hold before watching the televised address will affect how you react to it. If you are extremely loyal to the politician, you might agree with everything she says regardless of *what* she says, so much so that even if her opponent said the very same thing, you might totally disagree with him. You would be guilty of *selective perception.* It is not a serious crime, but one that can distort how you react to messages.

Third, because of your selective perception you might retain only those portions of the address with which you agree. If you perceive the entire address as favorable, you may remember all of it. If you perceive it as unfavorable, you may wipe it entirely from your mind. If parts of the address affect you positively, you remember those parts while forgetting the negative ones. Or the negative ones may be the very ones you remember. Either way, how you originally perceived the address determines what you retain, a process called *selective retention.*

An interesting study conducted by Neil Vidmar and Milton Rokeach among viewers of the television program "All in the Family" showed that selective perception caused different opinions about two of the show's main characters—Archie Bunker, a very conservative factory worker, and his son-in-law Mike, a liberal college student. The two researchers found that highly prejudiced people identified more with Archie and perceived him as making better sense than Mike and winning arguments with him more often. Moreover, they disliked Mike's personality much more than they disliked Archie's. Vidmar and Rokeach found that "persons who like Archie reported he is down-to-earth, honest, hard-working, predictable, and kind enough to allow his son-in-law and daughter to live with him."[4] Conversely, less prejudiced persons disliked Archie's personality traits more than they disliked Mike's. People who liked Mike felt that he was tolerant and stood up for his beliefs. Those disliking him saw him as stupid, narrow-minded, prejudiced against the older generation, rebellious, lazy, and a "banner waver."

Source Credibility and Media Credibility

Two other factors that can affect how we perceive broadcast messages are source credibility and media credibility. Source credibility is the credibility of the original source of the communication. In the case of the politician's televised address, it would be the credibility of the politician. If you perceive the politician as highly credible, then the chances are that your reaction to her will be favorable. Research has assigned many subordinate factors to source credibility, among them dynamism, trustworthiness, and competence.

Source credibility lies partially in the source and partially in how the source is perceived by the audience. In other words, how broadcast messages affect us is related to how we perceive the source of those messages. Source credibility and both interpersonal communication and mass communication all are part of the communication process.

Media credibility is the overall credibility of a medium, such as a local radio station. Two types of media credibility are important. *Intermedia credibility* is the relative credibility of various media. For example, you might determine that television is a more credible medium than radio or newspapers. *Intramedia credibility* is the relative credibility within the same medium. Here you might decide that one radio station is more credible than another. Over a number of years, studies on media credibility have asked such questions as, "In the face of conflicting news reports, which medium would you be most likely to believe: television, newspapers, radio, magazines, or other people?" Much of the research has found television to be the most frequent response. Notice that we said "most frequent response," not "most credible medium." Such studies fail to allow for the many possible intervening variables that truly reflect media credibility.

On the basis of such research we might justifiably ask whether television is listed first because it is the most credible medium or because we spend more time with it than with other media? Is there a wide variance among different media in different communities? In some communities would radio or newspapers come out on top because of the credibility of the local press? How many times do we really hear or even recognize conflicting news reports? Is television really the most credible medium, or do we just think so because two of our senses, sight and hearing, can consume the information instead of one, and can do so in color and in motion?

Some of the research that listed television as the most credible medium listed radio as the least credible. If we were to interpret those results literally, we might have some difficulty explaining some of the effects of radio programming. Back in 1938 many people became hysterical because they believed a report by Orson Welles, acting in the radio play of H. G. Wells's *War of the Worlds,* of an invasion from outer space. Those who said it could not happen again were proved wrong in 1977, when Swiss radio aired a program containing mock news bulletins about neutron bombs being dropped in a war between East Germany and West Germany. Mock casualty reports listed 480,000 persons killed. Panicked listeners called the station and received an official apology over Swiss radio.

The broadcast media do not seem so credible when they are involved in advertising. Research has shown that newspapers are a more credible advertising source than other media. One survey asked, "Some advertising seems honest and believable, while other advertising seems hard to believe. In this area, considering radio, newspapers, television, and magazines—which one is likely to carry the most believable advertising?" Newspapers were listed first by the different categories of respondents.[5]

Further research on media and source credibility can be invaluable to both the business and consumer communities. Our access to the media, its availability, our interests in specific programming, our attitudes, and the video or audio techniques used to communicate broadcast programming are all part of our perceptions.

CATEGORIZING THE BROADCAST AUDIENCE

We have talked about some of the approaches we use to examine the audience—individual-differences, categories, and social-relations. All of these approaches will eventually concentrate on two broad categories of audience classification: demographics and psychographics.

Demographics

Demographics refers to such things as the *age, sex, education, income, and race of an audience.* Partly because the data are easily obtainable—everything from courthouse records to census figures—demographic characteristics are the most commonly used types of broadcast-audience classification. The rating services, for example, use age and sex as their two principal categories, producing such classifications as women eighteen to twenty-four years of age and men thirty-four to forty-nine.

Arbitron has developed questionnaires approved by its legal counsel that provide demographic breakdowns of ethnic audiences. The questionnaire asked "how do you describe your family." It was then validated through personal interviews with respondents who had indicated their race or nationality in the Arbitron diary.

For advertisers, the demographic audience becomes something to reach, something to identify, and something to persuade. Using data from rating services and broadcasting stations, advertisers make time buys based on such considerations as when the highest concentration of women is watching and what the cost-per-thousand is for those women who are reached. Others need data to reach children, males, minorities, or teenagers. The key is to match the product to the audience, and the more specialized the product becomes, the greater the need to reach a specialized audience.

Demographics will most likely continue to be the main identifier of broadcast audiences, for four reasons. First, the information is easily obtained from different sources. Second, the industry is geared to using demographic data. Although psychographics are becoming more important, the average radio-station manager is much more at ease with data on age, sex, and income than with psychological constructs, media-involvement scales, or value profiles. Third, advertisers are comfortable with demographic data. An account executive selling a local druggist a radio commercial is on much safer ground talking about the station's high-income audience than attempting to teach a course in psychology while explaining the station's rate card. Fourth, information other than demographics is still subject to conflicting methodologies, not so much in the minds of the researchers collecting the data as in the minds of the industry that uses them. Although a research firm that claims to analyze an audience's value structure may be compared with a firm that analyzes its personality, the broadcast manager may simply groan and say, "Just tell me if they're men or women and how much money they make."

Psychographics

Psychographics refers to such things as *attitudes, values, beliefs, and opinions*. Psychographics methodologies range from dividing an audience according to its attitudes about brand preferences to discovering that audience's subconscious reactions to broadcast programming. Asking consumers if they prefer brand *X* or brand *Y* is one way of obtaining psychographic information. Interviewing prison inmates to determine how they react to television crime shows entails a far more complex psychographic profile.

One example of widely used psychographic information—audience program preferences—has been applied to television programming in adjacent time blocks on the basis of the theory of *cluster programming.* Using the work of clinical psychologists, a group of researchers at Ohio State University classified viewers into different types of audiences,[6] such as people who like situation

comedies and people who like westerns. The idea of program preferences among these audience types was carried one step further by a member of the same research team, Joseph Plummer, a research executive with Leo Burnett, U.S.A. Plummer subjected data on viewing habits to statistical measures, which showed different programs tended to cluster together. That is, if you like "T.J. Hooker," you will probably like the other police-action shows, such as "Hill Street Blues." If you like situation comedies, then "Three's Company," "9 to 5," and "Archie Bunker's Place" could be your favorites. "Dallas," "Falcon Crest," and "Dynasty" are another group of similar programs. Basing decisions on both program preferences and how different programs cluster together, networks now find it profitable to schedule blocks of similar types of programs.

FUNCTIONAL USES OF MEDIA

We can use psychographics to study the functional uses of broadcasting. If someone were to ask "What function does broadcasting play in our lives?" We might answer "I use broadcasting to escape from reality," "I use broadcasting to be entertained," or "I use broadcasting to learn what's happening in the world." In doing so we have mentioned three functions of broadcasting—escape, entertainment, and information.

Stephenson's Play Theory

Using a data-gathering procedure called *Q-sort,* William Stephenson completed extensive research on how individuals representative of different audience types feel about the media. From this research has come Stephenson's play theory, which, applied to broadcasting, suggests that we use radio and television as a means of escaping into a world of play not accessible at other times.[7] Some researchers have severely criticized this theory. David Chaney, for example, contends that "Stephenson . . . fails to move beyond an individualistic level of description. While the importance of audience commitment is understood, his concern with finding a methodological demonstration of his argument leads his audience to be conceived as only a conglomeration of individuals."[8]

But those researchers familiar with Q methodology have supported Stephenson's theory as well as his methodologies. Deanna Campbell Robinson, for example, offers a more generous view of Stephenson's methodologies. In her study of the uses of television and film by upper-middle-class professionals, she suggests that Stephenson's research methods could be used to directly examine people's attitudes toward the media and could demonstrate "(1) that within any single, demographically defined audience group several attitude or 'taste' groups exist and (2) that similar taste groups exist within other classes."[9] Wilbur Schramm, another supporter, claims that Stephenson, the possessor of a style of writing like Marshall McLuhan's, could have been the guru of modern media.[10]

Uses and Gratifications

Stephenson's play theory is part of a wider body of research and theory focusing on what uses we make of media and what gratification we get from exposing ourselves to them. This research has been conducted among populations ranging from farmers in less-developed countries to American homemakers. The researchers have vigorously debated not only the different types of uses and gratifications but the very methodologies that attempt to identify them.

Part of the debate arises from a conflict between the individual-differences approach and the categories approach to the study of media effects. Consider a television program. We could argue that a soap opera provides certain role models for homemakers or college students. We also could contend that audience reaction to soap operas can be classified not in demographic terms but rather in psychographic terms. Soap operas have certain *uses* for people having certain motivations or psychological characteristics. We could argue, however, that even this approach is unsatisfactory, since each individual is different and many different individuals may have many different uses for the same soap opera. How we learn what uses these many different individuals or groups of individuals make of the media is another dilemma. Do we test them individually in tightly controlled laboratories, "wiring" them psychologically in order to get at the depths of their thought processes? Or do we sample a large population of respondents in a survey?

What has the research on uses and gratifications told us about these two concepts? By sampling a few of these studies, Robinson examined upper-middle-class professionals portrayed in some of these studies. She discovered that some of them were *information absorbers,* people who absorb information from television without actively interpreting it. Another group, which she labeled *analytical artists,* used television to increase their understanding of themselves, others, and the world.[11] Neil T. Weintraub has suggested that radio makes teenagers feel more aware, makes their day pass more quickly, and lets them know what is happening.[12] Lawrence Wenner found that one use of television among the elderly was companionship.[13]

One of the earliest studies on the uses of the broadcast media was conducted by Herta Herzog, who used in-depth interviews to examine the uses of radio soap operas by listeners. Herzog found three uses: compensation, wish fulfillment, and advice. In the first category were people who wanted to compensate their own behavior by identifying with a soap opera character. A second group listened vicariously, achieving in the soap opera what was missing in their own lives. The third group sought advice on how to conduct their lives.[14] More recently, Joseph Foley examined a viewing audience and found eight functions of television viewing: withdrawal, play, conversation, togetherness, para-social interaction, education, background (the set on but not being watched), and learning about social norms.[15]

The studies continue. No matter what methodology they use or what theory they give rise to, they all add fuel to the debate over what use we gain from broadcasting and how broadcasting should be studied.[16]

Agenda Setting

Of all the recent research on the functional uses of media, some of the best and most systematic deals with their *agenda-setting function.* Agenda setting means that the media not only inform us but inform us about what we should be informed. In other words, media set an agenda for our thought processes; they tell us what is important and what we should know and need to know.

Sophisticated analyses have made it possible to isolate those media that are dominant agenda setters—no small task since many communities have more than fifty different media. Newspapers, radio, television, books, and magazines are all important. By keeping track of which media are important to specific populations and then concentrating on those media, researchers can build a theoretical base for agenda setting.

The agenda-setting function becomes more pertinent when we realize that media have suddenly become some of the main determinants of how we perceive our world. The media, in effect, structure our world, and we in turn reinforce this structure. Bernard Cohen summarized the agenda-setting concept when he said that the mass media may not be very successful in telling people what to think, but are stunningly successful in telling them what to think about.[17]

This agenda-setting function can be divided into the *interpersonal agenda,* the things we not only think about but talk about, and the *intrapersonal agenda,* the things we merely think about.

An empirical test of the agenda-setting function took place in 1968, when Maxwell McCombs and Donald Shaw examined the presidential elections.[18] Since then, McCombs and others have continued to research agenda setting.

Research on agenda setting is also winding its way into media decision making—specifically, how and why gatekeepers select the news they do and feed it to the public. The gatekeeper agenda appears to originate in the wire services. Thus, although the local press sets the public's agenda, the wire services set the agenda for the gatekeeper.

SOCIALIZATION

Closely aligned with how we use broadcasting is its effect on our acquisition of culture and social norms. Although a significant amount of research concentrates on broadcasting's effects on the socialization of children, we all know that socialization continues throughout our lives, and broadcasting can affect this socialization at any time. Here as with other approaches to studying the effects of broadcast messages on the audience, the content of these messages can mean different things to different people. For example, the effect of a television program containing violence on a group of male adults can contrast sharply with its effect on a group of small children, whose world and ideas are just being formed and whose socialization is much less developed than that of the adults. The adult might go to bed thinking how great John Wayne was as the hero. The child may have nightmares about evil forces affecting his or her ability to survive in the world.

As with research on other functions of broadcasting, research on its socializing function has opened up a Pandora's box of results, theory, and debate. Different methodologies are used. In this research, and as a responsible consumer of broadcasting in society we should recognize them. Since a person is not socialized simply by watching a single program, we must gather data from research across many disciplines in order to begin to theorize exactly how media in general and broadcasting in particular affect our socialization. Moreover, that data must be gathered over time. Few studies examine socialization over time. Most ask a given group of individuals what meaning television or radio has for them and then group the results under the heading of research on the socialization of uses and gratification. Although examining a great deal of research about these different audiences is valuable, studying the same individuals over a longer period is much more desirable.

Stages in Studying the Effects of Broadcasting on Socialization

Research on the socializing function of broadcasting has three stages. First, it examines the content of broadcast messages. Such content as the image of women in television

commercials, hero figures in prime-time television, and acts of violence are representative of much of what we see or hear on television and radio. The second stage of this research attempts to find whether the people exposed to the broadcast messages actually recognize them. Were children who saw a given program able to recognize examples of good behavior? The third stage of investigation must determine what effect the messages have once they are received.

Results of the Research

From socialization research we have learned that children can identify certain prosocial themes. CBS has actively supported various research projects on this finding, which have benefited its public relations. This research has been conducted under responsible surveillance.[19] Research in three cities—Cleveland, Philadelphia, and Memphis—on the program "Fat Albert and the Cosby Kids" revealed that close to nine out of ten children who had seen an episode of the program received one or more messages of social value. Some of the prosocial messages reported to have been received were "Take care of younger children," "Father's job is important," "Support a friend in trouble," "Be honest," and "Be friendly; don't be rude, nasty, jealous, or mean."

Another CBS study showed older children were more likely than younger children to receive abstract messages. For example, in watching "Shazam," a program about a Superman figure, about half of the seven-to-eight-year-olds in the study received the message "Obey your parents," as opposed to about three-fourths of the ten-to-eleven-year-olds and the thirteen-to-fourteen-year-olds. Only 4 percent of the seven-to-eight-year-olds received the message "Be independent," in contrast with 11 percent of the ten-to-eleven-year-olds and 25 percent of the thirteen-to-fourteen-year-olds. In watching "Isis," a program about a superhuman female figure, girls were more likely than boys to comment on Isis's concern for others and her beauty; boys mentioned her superhuman qualities as often as girls did.

After analyzing the effects of broadcasting on socialization, we can conclude that parents have a major responsibility to not permit television to become a surrogate parent.[20] Watching television with very young children and then discussing their reactions and referring to possible prosocial lessons is one positive use of the medium. This same process was common in pretelevision times, when parents read storybooks to children, then discussed their content. Children apparently learn from television, and such broadcasting practices as stereotyping the roles of certain classes of people can shape a child's perception of reality.

The amount of television children watch and when and how it becomes part of their lives can also influence how children relate to their environment. In studying three towns in Australia that offered three different types of television programs, researchers found that the content that was viewed was directly related to the context in which it was viewed.[21] When television experience was restricted mostly to an informative-educational context, children perceived it to be far more than just entertainment. When high levels of television viewing tended initially to reduce participation in such outside activities as sports, participation returned to normal levels after the novelty wore off.

Content and context variables are also included in research on the political socialization of children. Political knowledge, news discussion, public-affairs interest, and seeking of information about news events were investigated by Charles K. Atkin and Walter Gantz.[22] They found the amount of news

viewing to be somewhat associated with a child's political awareness; the highest correlations were exhibited by older children. The amount of exposure to television news has some relation to the child's knowledge of politics, more so among middle-class youngsters than among working-class youngsters. Many children in the research reported being stimulated to seek further information after watching television news, and to some degree this desire for more information increased with the amount of news exposure.

Advertising can also influence socialization. For example, one study showed children three different eyeglass commercials in which a woman gave a testimonial.[23] One commercial showed her dressed as a court judge, another as a computer programmer, and the third as a television technician. The children who saw that woman as a particular role model were more apt to choose that occupation as appropriate for women.

There is still much to be learned about the effects of broadcast messages on socialization. In the case of children, part of our knowledge will be gained from examining what psychologists have long taught about learning theory and formative development.

THE VIOLENCE DEBATE

Of all the effects of broadcasting, none has attracted more attention than the effect of the portrayal of violence on television. It has been the subject of research and debate by academicians, government agencies, local schools, and international research organizations alike.

Violence Gains Attention

The issue of televised violence had been raised in 1952 by Senator Estes Kefauver's committee on juvenile delinquency. But in

1952, television was too new to draw pertinent conclusions, despite testimony by psychiatrists and other recognized authorities. The attention currently given to televised violence is the result not only of its very presence but also of research indicating a possible causal relationship between violence and behavior. Two articles appearing in the *Journal of Abnormal and Social Psychology* set the stage, examining exposure to filmed violence and subsequent aggressive behavior.[24] Other studies followed.

In 1969 Senator John O. Pastore wrote to the secretary of health, education, and welfare, saying, "I am exceedingly troubled by the lack of any definitive information which would help to resolve the question of whether there is a causal connection between televised crime and violence and antisocial behavior by individuals, especially children."[25] Pastore then called for a blue-ribbon committee of leading scholars to examine the relationship in detail. Members of the committee, which became known as the Surgeon General's Scientific Advisory Committee on Television and Social Behavior were chosen by a review of the names of experts on the subject. The final selection process was assigned to the three commercial networks and the National Association of Broadcasters. CBS, seeing its own research director as a possible appointee, withdrew from the selection committee to avoid a conflict of interest. Completed in 1972, the committee's report immediately drew praise, criticism, and varying interpretations. The most succinct summary statement of the report was this:

> There is a convergence of the fairly substantial experimental evidence for short-run causation of aggression among some children by viewing violence on the screen and the much less certain evidence from field studies that extensive violence viewing precedes some long-run manifestations of aggressive behavior. This convergence of the two types of evidence constitutes some preliminary evidence of a causal relationship.[26]

In other words, the report found that television violence may adversely affect some people. The report elicited widespread attention to the violence issue and encouraged researchers to get to the heart of the causal connection. Their research which has been funded by various foundations and government agencies, has not yet been finished.

The networks have also become involved in studies of televised violence. Undoubtedly because of the pressure from some citizens' groups to revamp American television, the networks, and for that matter their affiliate stations, are under fire. In some cases the affiliates are even worse offenders than the networks, preempting bland network fare to insert more violent programming.

Theories of the Effects of Televised Violence

The relationship between televised violence and aggressive behavior is best understood from the point of view of the various learning theories. There are four main theories. The *catharsis theory* suggests that in our daily lives we build up frustrations that are released vicariously when we watch violent behavior. Therefore, there are actual benefits from televised violence. This theory is the weakest of the four, although some studies have provided limited support for it.[27] The *aggressive-cues theory* suggests that exposure to violence on television will raise the level of excitement in the viewer, and that televised violent acts may be repeated in real life.[28] Closely aligned to this theory is the *reinforcement theory,* which suggests that televised violence will reinforce existing behavior in an individual.[29] Inherent in such a theory is the assumption that the violent person, because of violent tendencies, perceives televised violence as a real-life experience, whereas the nonviolent person perceives the violent program as entertainment and remains detached from it. The *observational theory* suggests that we can learn violent behavior from watching violent programs.[30]

Clearly, all of the theories have merits and none should be discounted. Researchers are examining new variations on these four principal approaches. The observational learning theory, for example, could be applied to children in their formative years of growth, when their environment has a significant effect on what they learn. In essence, if television becomes a surrogate parent, it could certainly teach behavior. Later in the child's life, when behavior is more firmly determined, violence learned in the formative years could be reinforced. For the hyperactive or easily excitable child, the aggressive-cues theory might be used to explain emotions easily aroused by exposure to televised violence. The catharsis theory could apply even to the business executive who uses television to unwind and vicariously vent his or her frustrations through the actions of others. We immediately begin to see all sides of the violence debate.

Current research is focusing primarily on children, partly because such research is being funded and partly because there is a general feeling that children may very well be those most affected by television violence. At the same time, the violence debate is becoming public as citizens' groups become more vocal and visible.

Along with suggesting the causal relationship of televised violence to aggression, the widely quoted research of George Gerbner, at the University of Pennsylvania, has fueled the arguments. For many years, Gerbner and his associates have compared violence on television among the major networks,

plotting their data over time and thereby providing a running record of the number of violent acts representing each new television season. Two often discussed measures are Gerbner's Violence Index, which measures the actual acts of violence, and the Risk Ratio, which describes the risk of encountering violence. The index is used mostly for counting violent acts on television. The ratio is a bit more complex. It measures the aggressors and the victims, dividing the larger number by the smaller. The final figure is preceded by a plus sign if the number of aggressors exceeds that of the victims and a minus sign if the number of victims exceeds that of the aggressors. CBS uses a different measure of violence, which has prompted debate over which measure is more accurate and more representative of actual violence.[31]

Effects of the Portrayal of Violence on Aggressive Behavior

The amount of research on televised violence is now tremendous, and more studies are in progress. According to one scholar, what this research is suggesting to us about the relationship between the portrayal of violence and aggressive behavior is that:

1. Cartoon as well as live portrayals of violence can lead to aggressive performance on the part of the viewer.

2. Repeated exposure to cartoon and live portrayals of violence does not eliminate the possibility that new exposure will increase the likelihood of aggressive performance.

3. Aggressive performance is not dependent on a typical frustration, although frustration facilitates aggressive performance.

4. Although the "effect" in some experiments may be aggressive but not antisocial play, implications in regard to the contribution of television violence to antisocial aggression remain.

5. In ordinary language, the factors in a por-

trayal which increase the likelihood of aggressive performance are: the suggestion that aggression is justified, socially acceptable, motivated by malice, or pays off; a realistic depiction; highly exciting material; the presentation of conditions similar to those experienced by the young viewer, including a perpetrator similar to the viewer and circumstances like those of his environment, such as a target, implements, or other cues resembling those of the real-life milieu.

6. Although there is no evidence that prior repeated exposure to violent portrayals totally immunizes the young viewer against any influence on aggressive performance, exposure to television portrayals may desensitize young persons to responding to violence in their environment.[32]

Policy Dilemmas

Where all this research and debate will lead is difficult to predict, but even if the evidence becomes conclusive, the result may be a constitutional crisis of sizable proportions. Although government has traditionally kept an ear open to complaints about violence, sympathy and rhetoric have been about as much as Congress or the FCC has been willing to offer. To offer more would be to collide head on with the First Amendment to the Constitution and the Communications Act of 1934. Even if the broad "public interest" standard were applied in an effort to curtail violence, court tests would be necessary so that it would not encroach on the Constitution. Although the debate and research will continue, the biggest battle of all may be fought in the political arena, in which no medium yet has been successfully curtailed, except superficially. Nor have the courts been responsive to the violence issue. When a Florida teenager claimed that television violence caused him to commit murder, the jury did not accept the idea.

Then there is the case of Japan, which is receiving more and more attention because of its high level of television violence and its low crime rate. Some possible explanations are that Japanese students are too busy with schoolwork to watch much television, Japan has strict gun laws, and Japanese citizens are becoming involved in crime protection.[33] Another possible explanation is Japanese society's emphasis on collective (family, school, company) responsibility, as opposed to American society's emphasis on individual responsibility. Although the attacks on television violence will continue, alternative causes of the ills of our society will remain of keen interest to policy makers.

Some changes may come as advertisers begin to place economic pressure on the networks to reduce televised violence. But support among local advertisers for such a movement is minimal, and stations wishing to preempt network programming with locally originated programs containing more violence are finding little to stop them. If televised violence is a serious threat, then at least in the immediate future the broadcast industry will best hold threat at bay by educating responsible consumers of broadcast communication, including parents, and exercising restraint and responsible decision making.

SUMMARY

This chapter has examined the broadcast audience and approaches to studying it in order to identify the effects of broadcast programming.

Early theories that the audience is a mass of unrelated individuals responding like sitting ducks to media messages have been greatly altered. Contemporary theorists believe that the audience interacts with the media, permitting them to be an important part of their lives.

Three approaches to studying the audience are the individual-differences, categories, and social-relations approaches. Information received from the media flows through the population in a multi-step process called the two-step flow.

At the heart of the two-step flow are opinion leaders, those individuals who influence other people's reactions to media content. How we react to media content can be determined by three factors: selective exposure, selective perception, and selective retention. The importance we place on a broadcast message can be based on source credibility, media credibility, or a combination of both.

Researchers use demographics and psychographics to classify the broadcast audience. *Demographics* refers to such characteristics as age, sex, income, occupation, and race. *Psychographics* refers to attitudes, beliefs, values, opinions, and other psychological characteristics of the audience. With these classifications in mind, three approaches to how we use media are Stephenson's play theory, the theory of uses and gratification, and the theory of agenda setting. Radio and television are important in the process of acquiring culture and social norms. One of the most visible issues concerning the effects of broadcast programming is that of televised violence.

OPPORTUNITIES
FOR FURTHER LEARNING

ADLER, R. P., and others, *The Effects of Television Advertising on Children: Review and Recommendations.* Lexington, Mass.: Lexington Books, 1980.

ADLER, R. P., ed., *Understanding Television: Essays on Television as a Social and Cultural Force.* New York: Praeger, 1981.

BERRY, G. L., and C. MITCHELL-KERNAN, *Television and the Socialization of the Minority Child.* New York: Academic, 1982.

BLUMLER, J. G., and E. KATZ, eds., *The Uses of Mass Communications: Current Perspectives on Gratifications Research.* Beverly Hills, Calif.: Sage, 1974.

CASSATA, M. B., and M. K. ASANTE, eds., *The Social Uses of Mass Communication.* Buffalo: Communication Research Center, Department of Communication, State University of New York, 1977.

CATER, D., and S. STRICKLAND, *TV Violence and the Child.* New York: Russell Sage Foundation, 1975.

CHAFFEE, S. H., ed., *Political Communication: Issues and Strategies for Research.* Beverly Hills, Calif.: Sage, 1975.

CISIN, I., and others, *Television and Growing Up: The Impact of Televised Violence.* Washington, D.C.: Superintendent of Documents, 1972.

COMSTOCK, G., and others, *Television and Human Behavior.* New York: Columbia University Press, 1978.

DAVIS, R. H., *Television and the Aging Audience.* Los Angeles: University of Southern California Press, 1980.

FESHBACH, S., and R. D. SINGER, *Television and Aggression.* San Francisco: Jossey-Bass, 1971.

GERBNER, G., L. GROSS, M. MORGAN, and N. SIGNORIELLI, *Trends in Network Television Drama and Viewer Conceptions of Social Reality, 1967-1979.* Philadelphia: Annenberg School of Communications, University of Pennsylvania, 1980.

GUERNICA, A., with IRENE KASPERUK, *Reaching the Hispanic Market Effectively: The Media, the Market, the Methods.* New York: McGraw-Hill, 1982.

HOTHI, H., *Light and Heavy Viewers: Television Patterns of Light and Heavy Viewers and other Demographic and Socioeconomic Groups.* Ottawa: Canadian Radio-Television and Telecommunications Commission, 1981.

JOHNSTON, J., and J. S. ETTEMA, *Positive Images: Breaking Stereotypes With Children's Television.* Beverly Hills, Calif.: Sage, 1982.

KATZ, E., and T. SZECSKO, eds., *Mass Media and Social Change.* Beverly Hills, Calif.: Sage, 1981.

KRAUS, S. and D. DAVIS, *The Effects of Mass Communication on Political Behavior.* University Park: Pennsylvania State University Press, 1976.

LARSON, R., and R. W. KUBEY, *Media Use in the Ecology of Adolescents' Lives*. Beverly Hills, Calif.: Sage, 1983.

LIEBERT, R. M., J. N. SPRAFKIN, and E. S. DAVIDSON, *The Early Window: Effects of Television on Children and Youth* (2nd ed.). Elmsford, N.Y.: Pergamon, 1982.

——, *Effects of Television on Children and Youth* (2nd ed.). Elmsford, N.Y.: Pergamon, 1982.

MCLAURIN, R. D., ed., *Military Propaganda: Psychological Warfare and Operations*. New York: Praeger, 1982.

MILGRAM, S., and R. I. SHOTLAND, *Television and Antisocial Behavior*. New York: Academic, 1973.

MONAHAN, J., *Predicting Violent Behavior: An Assessment of Clinical Techniques*. Beverly Hills, Calif.: Sage, 1981.

PETERSON, G. W., and D. F. PETERS, *Television, Peers and the Social Construction of Reality*. Beverly Hills, Calif.: Sage, 1983.

PIEPE, A., M. EMERSON, and J. LANNON, *Television and the Working Class*. Lexington, Mass.: Lexington Books, Heath, 1975.

ROWLAND, W. D., JR., *The Politics of TV Violence*. Beverly Hills, Calif.: Sage, 1983.

SCHWARZ, M., ed., *TV and Teens: Experts Look at the Issues,* Action for Children's Television. Reading, Mass.: Addison-Wesley, 1982.

SHAW, D., and M. E. MCCOMBS, eds., *The Emergence of American Political Issues*. St. Paul: West, 1977.

SINGER, J. L., and D. G. SINGER, *Television, Imagination, and Aggression: A Study of Preschoolers*. Hillsdale, N.J.: Lawrence Erlbaum, 1981.

STEIN, A. H., and L. K. FRIEDRICH, *Impact of Television on Children and Youth*. Chicago: University of Chicago Press, 1975.

TANNENBAUM, P. H., ed., *The Entertainment Functions of Television*. Hillsdale, N.J.: Lawrence Erlbaum, 1980.

Television and Behavior: Ten Years of Scientific Progress and Implications for the Eighties, Vol. 1, Summary Report. Rockville, Md.: United States National Institute of Mental Health, 1982.

URBAN, C., *Factors Influencing Media Consumption: A Survey of the Literature*. Cambridge, Mass.: Program on Information Resources Policy, Harvard University, 1981.

Uses and Gratifications Studies: Theory and Methods. Stockholm: Severiges Radio, 1974.

WEST, C., *The Social and Psychological Distortion of Information*. Chicago: Nelson-Hall, 1981.

WITHEY, S. B., and R. P. ABELES, eds., *Television and Social Behavior: Beyond Violence and Children*. Hillsdale, N.J.: Lawrence Erlbaum, 1980.

GLOSSARY

AAAA American Association of Advertising Agencies.

ABC (1) African Broadcasting Company; (2) American Broadcasting Company; (3) Australian Broadcasting Company.

Access to retrieve information from a disc through a computer.

Access channels cable-television channels for general public use.

Accountable programming term used in educational television to describe a program meeting a specified set of instructional objectives.

Acoustic coupler a device that connects a computer terminal to a telephone.

ACT Action for Children's Television.

ADI area of dominant influence; a term used in rating.

AEJ Association for Education in Journalism.

Affiliate a broadcasting station bound by contract with a particular broadcasting network or wire service.

Agenda-setting function the theory that media set an agenda for our thought processes; they tell us what is important and what we should know and need to know.

Aggressive-cues theory the theory that exposure to violence on television will raise the level of excitement in the viewer.

All-channel receiver receiver capable of receiving AM and FM radio signals.

Alternator developed by Ernst Alexanderson at the General Electric Laboratories. Used to modulate early voice broadcasting.

AM amplitude modulation.

AM stereo dual-channel broadcasting on AM frequencies. A common method is to use one channel as amplitude modulation and the other channel as frequency modulation.

Analog continuously operating, such as a telephone, radio, or television transmission. Analog computers accept and process continuous, or real-world, signals, such as voltage fluctuations.

Anik Canadian satellite system.

Annual billings broadcast station's bill to advertisers for commercials carried over a one-year period.

AP Associated Press, a print and broadcast wire service.

Application specific use to which a computer can be put.

Application software specific computer instructions for particular applications, such as payroll and purchasing.

AP Radio radio network of the Associated Press.

ARB Arbitron rating survey.

ARD Federal coordinator of West German radio broadcasting.

Armature revolving iron core of the alternator.

ARRL American Radio Relay League.

ASCAP American Society of Composers, Authors, and Publishers.

ATS Application Technology Satellite.

Audio actuality the recording of the actual sounds in the news for incorporation into radio newscasts.

Audion three-element vacuum tube invented by Lee De Forest.

Average quarter-hour persons an estimate of the number of persons listening to a station during any quarter-hour in a specified time period.

AWRT American Women in Radio and Television.

Banks groups of control switches on a master control console used to program various portions of an audio or video production.

Barter an advertising arrangement in which stations receive programming in return for providing advertising time; widespread in syndicated programming.

BBC British Broadcasting Corporation.

BEA Broadcast Education Association.

Binary two; refers to machine-readable information or software, which consists of the two digits *1* and *0*.

Bit a single binary digit; the memory capacity of a computer is described in *bits* of information.

BMI Broadcast Music Incorporated.

BRC Broadcast Rating Council.

Broadcast Signals sent via radio or television.

Buses see *Banks*.

Byte a series or pattern of bits—typically eight bits—that is a common unit of storage in a computer system; also called *character* or *text*.

Capital-intensive business a business in which maximum costs occur immediately from the start; exemplified by the cable industry.

Cash-flow statement a statement of the amount of money necessary to keep the station running smoothly and to avoid going into debt.

Catharsis theory the theory that in our daily lives we build up frustrations that are released vicariously when we watch violent behavior.

CATV community-antenna television, or cable TV.

CBC Canadian Broadcasting Corporation.

CCTV closed-circuit television.

Cellular radiotelephone systems a series of small transmitters with limited-coverage cells that make up the core of a mobile telephone system.

Chain broadcasting early term for *network broadcasting*.

Chart of accounts ledger used to record station finances.

Chip miniaturized electronic circuits; also called *integrated circuits* or *microelectronics.*

Clearance ratio the number of network affiliate stations that agree to air a network program.

Clear channel one on which dominant stations broadcast over wide areas virtually interference-free within their primary service areas and most of their secondary service areas.

Coaxial cable cable consisting of wire core surrounded by a layer of plastic, metal-webbed insulation, and a third layer of plastic.

Coherer small glass tube used in Marconi's experiments to create and break an electrical connection.

Columbia a label, developed in the early days of broadcasting, for such companies as the Columbia Broadcasting System (CBS) and the Columbia Phonograph Broadcasting System, Incorporated.

Common carrier a communications channel that handles interstate and international communications by electronic means, and whose services are open to the public for hire.

Communication the movement of messages between senders and receivers.

Communication model a stop-action picture of the communicative process.

Comparative balance sheet a comparison of assets and liabilities between two points in time.

Comparative income statement a comparison of income between two points in time.

Component television a television set whose monitor, tuner, speakers, video screen, and other attachments are sold separately.

COMSAT Communications Satellite Corporation. Formed by the Communication Satellite Act of 1962.

COMSTAR satellite system launched by COMSAT and leased by AT&T.

Conduction the use of ground or water, both electrical conductors, to replace a second wire in a telegraph hookup.

Construction permit permission granted by the FCC to begin construction of a broadcast facility.

Co-ops (1) broadcast news networks, also called *informal networks,* created by a group of radio or TV news personnel; (2) trade-out advertising agreements between advertisers and the individual advertising outlet.

Co-op advertising a split in the cost of advertising, usually between a retail outlet and the manufacturer.

CPB Corporation for Public Broadcasting.

CPM Cost per thousand; the cost of reaching one thousand persons with a message.

CPS cycles per second.

CPU Central processing unit; the core of a computer, containing the processor and main memory, which reads and interprets the instructions from a computer program.

CRTC Canadian Radio-Television Commission.

CTNC Catholic Television Network of Chicago.

CTS Communication Technology Satellite.

CTV abbreviation for Canada's CTV Television Network, Ltd.

Cume persons (cumulative audience) the number of different persons or households watching or listening to a given station or program at least once during a certain time period.

CWA Communication Workers of America.

DAD Digital audio disc; recorded music captured and stored as a binary code.

Daytimers radio stations required by the FCC to sign off at sunset.

Delayed feedback noninstantaneous response to information received; differentiates mass communication from intrapersonal and interpersonal communication.

Demographics a term referring to such things as the age, sex, education, income, and race of an audience.

Descriptive research research that describes a current condition.

Developmental research the process of continually perfecting something, such as an ITV program.

Diary method in a rating survey, a method of data collection utilizing a diary.

Digital a term that describes operations, signals, or transmissions that are broken up into binary code for the computer—a series of on-off pulses (bits of information)—and transmitted virtually noise-free, unlike analog or continuous transmissions.

Direct-broadcast satellites high-powered satellites that beam signals directly to small home antennas.

Directional antennas a group of strategically placed broadcast antennas transmitting a signal in a specific direction so as to form an irregular rather than a circular contour.

Directional stations radio stations, primarily in the AM band, that use directional antennas in order to keep their signals from interfering with those of other stations.

Director the person responsible for the entire production of a program.

Direct-wave propagation radio-wave pattern in which signals are transmitted in a direct line of sight.

Dish dish-shaped antenna that receives signals from a satellite.

Dissolve a smooth change from an image produced by one television camera to an image produced by a second television camera, film, slide, or videotape.

Distribution system a system that disperses cable programming through various cables.

DMA Designated market area.

Double billing fraudulent practice of charging advertisers twice.

Drop cable cable from the subtrunk of a cable system to the home terminal.

Earth station a station that transmits microwave signals to a satellite and also receives those signals.

Electromagnetic spectrum the range of levels of electromagnetic energy, or frequencies.

Electromagnetic waves energy traveling through space at the speed of light; used to transmit radio and television signals.

ENG Electronic news gathering.

ERI Electronic response indicator.

ESPN the Entertainment and Sports Programming Network, a cable network.

ETV educational television; all noncommercial television programming and commercial programming produced especially for educational purposes, whether or not the program is used for direct classroom instruction.

Experimental research sophisticated research that entails a controlled experiment.

FACTS Federation of Commercial Television Stations (Australia).

Fairness Doctrine FCC rule requiring equal air time for controversial issues.

FBC Federal Broadcasting Corporation (Rhodesia).

Feedback information received in response to information already imparted.

Fiber optics the use of thin strands of glass to carry as many as a thousand or more cable channels. Also used for data communication.

Field of experience the accumulation of knowledge, experiences, values, beliefs, and other qualities that make up a person's self.

Filament one of the elements in a three-element vacuum tube. The other two are the plate and the grid. Early tubes used just a plate and filament.

Fixed position an advertising term referring to a commercial placed at the same time every day.

Floor manager the person who communicates the commands of the director to the performers.

Floppy disc a single flexible plastic magnetic device that stores computer programs and information.

FM frequency modulation.

Focus groups small groups of people brought together to discuss topics selected by the researcher or station and guided by a trained group leader.

Forfeiture the most common sanction imposed on a station by the FCC; it is based on the violation and on the ability of the station to pay.

Franchise a contractual agreement between a local governmental unit and a cable company.

Frequency (1) broadcast-rating term indicating how often a viewer has tuned to a given station; (2) position on the electromagnetic spectrum.

FR3 French Regional Broadcasting Service.

Gatekeeper the person directly involved in relaying or transferring information from one individual to another through a mass medium.

Geostationary (synchronous) satellite an orbiting satellite traveling at a speed proportional to that of the earth's rotation, and thus appearing to remain stationary over one point on the earth.

GHz gigahertz (one billion hertz, or cycles per second). (See *kHz* and *MHz*.)

Grid one of the elements in a three-element vacuum tube. The other two are the filament and the plate.

Ground wave wave adhering to the earth's surface.

Ham informal term for amateur radio operators.

Hard interconnects physically connected cable systems linked together by wires or microwaves.

Hardware the machinery of a computer, as opposed to its instructions, or *software.*

HDTV high-definition television; produces large-screen television without a grainy effect.

Head end the combination of humans and hardware responsible for originating, controlling, and processing signals over the cable system.

Hertz (Hz) last name of Heinrich Rudolph Hertz; commonly used as an abbreviation for *cycles per second* in referring to electromagnetic frequencies.

Heterodyne circuit improved detector of radio waves invented by Reginald A. Fessenden.

Holography a combination of photographic film and laser light that makes images appear to float in space.

Home terminal (1) receiving set for cable-TV transmissions, either one-way or two-way; (2) device connecting the drop cable of a cable system to the receiving set.

Homophily the extent to which such things as beliefs, experiences, background, and culture are shared by two different communicators.

HUT households using television.

Hypoing using promotional efforts to increase the size of an audience during a rating period.

IBA Independent Broadcasting Authority (British Television Network).

IBEW International Brotherhood of Electrical Workers.

IBM International Business Machines Corporation.

ICA International Communication Association.

ILR Independent Local Radio (British Radio Network).

Image orthicon one of the first pickup tubes used in early television broadcasting.

INA Institute Nationale de l'Audiovisuel (France).

Induction process by which a current in one antenna produces a current in a nearby antenna.

Informal networks broadcast news networks created by a professional group of radio or TV news personnel; also called *co-ops.*

Input information entered into a computer.

Integrated circuit one or more electronic circuits combined on a chip.

INTELSAT International Telecommunications Satellite Organization.

Interactivity the ratio of user activity to system activity in teletext and videotex systems.

Interface the connection among computer hardware, software, and people.

Intermittent service area an area that receives service from the ground wave but is beyond the primary service area and thus experiences some interference and fading.

Interpersonal communication communication between two or more persons in a face-to-face situation.

Intrapersonal communication communication within ourselves.

Ionosphere the upper level of the atmosphere, which reflects radio waves back to earth.

ITU International Telecommunication Union.

ITV (1) instructional television (programming designed specifically for direct or supplemental teaching); (2) the Independent Television Network.

JCET Joint Committee on Educational Television.

Jingles a set of short musical recordings, all designed around a common musical theme and usually related to a station's call letters.

kHz kilohertz (one thousand hertz or cycles per second); measure of a position on the electromagnetic spectrum.

Local channels AM channels located at the upper end of the AM band and operating with a power no greater than 250 watts at night and 1,000 watts during the day.

Long lines term used by AT&T to describe long-distance-telephone communication links.

Lowest unit charge minimum charge on a station rate card.

LPTV Low-power television; stations that rebroadcast the signals of TV stations to outlying areas, much like translator stations. LPTV can also originate programming.

Mainframe computer a large computer.

Marisat a COMSAT satellite that makes data, telex, and voice communications available interference-free; especially valuable for marine operations.

Mass audience the audience reached by the mass media.

Mass communication the process by which messages are communicated to a large number of persons by a mass medium.

Master control console the heart of a television control room through which both the audio and the video images are fed, joined together, and improved, perhaps by special effects, for the on-air image.

MBS Mutual Broadcasting System.

MDS Multipoint distribution systems; systems that use microwaves to transmit television signals from a master omnidirectional microwave antenna to smaller microwave antennas.

Media plural of *medium*.

Media credibility the effect of various media on how mass-communication messages are perceived.

Medium channel of communication, such as radio or television; singular of *media*.

Memory the primary work space in a computer; its working storage, which consists of chips.

Menu a display of all the options in an interactive computer program, that are available to the user at the computer terminal.

Message intensity the value or importance of an event or its potential impact in relation to other events or potential news stories.

Meter method a method of broadcast ratings in which a monitoring device installed on TV sets is connected to a central computer, which then records channel selection at different times of the day.

MGM Metro Goldwyn Mayer.

MHz megahertz (one million hertz or cycles per second). (See kHz and GHz.)

Microcomputer a small-scale computer, such as a personal computer.

Microwave a very short wave of higher frequency than that of standard broadcast transmission; usually measured in gigahertz (billions of cycles per second).

Millimeter waves a generic term referring to electromagnetic waves that are between a centimeter and a millimeter long.

Minicomputer a small-to-medium-scale computer, midway in size and capability between the microcomputer and the mainframe computer.

Mix to join and separate the pictures from various television cameras for a composite on-air image.

Modem a device that adapts digital transmissions, as from a computer, to analog transmissions, such as a voice or broadcast transmission, and vice versa.

MPATI Midwest Program for Airborne Television Instruction.

MSA metro survey area (rating term).

NAB National Association of Broadcasters.

NAEB National Association of Educational Broadcasters.

NAPTS National Association of Public Television Stations.

NARBA North American Regional Broadcasting Agreement.

NASA National Aeronautics and Space Administration.

NBC National Broadcasting Company.

NCTA National Cable Television Association.

NET National Educational Television.

Network clipping the fraudulent billing practice whereby a station certifies to a network that a network commercial has been aired when in fact it has not.

NHK Nippon Hōsō Kyōkai (Japanese broadcasting system).

NOS Netherlands Broadcasting Foundation.

NPR National Public Radio.

NRBA National Radio Broadcasters Association.

OCLC Online Computer Library Center; stores computer holdings from thousands of libraries.

OCR Optical character recognition; the capability of an optical scanner to recognize character images for the computer.

Opinion leader person interpreting messages originally disseminated by the mass media.

Optical scanner a computer hardware device that recognizes and reads images on paper, film, and other media and converts them to digital form.

ORTF Office de Radiodiffusion-Television Française.

Oscillation valve an early tube that constituted the main component in a wireless receiver (term used by inventor J. Ambrose Fleming).

OT Office of Telecommunication.

Output information generated by a computer.

Page sequencing the way teletext systems designate pages: A-type pages are single textual pages sent over the system to users, whereas B-type pages are sequences of pages.

Pay cable a system in which cable subscribers pay a fee in addition to the standard monthly rental fee in order to receive special programming.

Pay-per-view cable a pay-cable arrangement that charges the subscriber on a per-program basis.

PBS Public Broadcasting Service.

Perigee the closest point to the earth of a satellite's orbit.

Photophone a device invented by Alexander Graham Bell whereby the voice could be transmitted over light waves; the forerunner of today's fiber-optic light-wave communication.

Physical noise breakdown in communication caused by some physical quality or object interfering with the communicative process.

Plate one of the elements in a three-element vacuum tube. The other two are the filament and the grid. Early tubes used just a plate and filament.

Plumbicon a device that superseded both the image orthicon and the vidicon; it can capture color images with the sensitivity of the human eye. It is a trademarked name of the Amperex Corporation.

Prime time the time of the largest audience, when a station charges the highest price for advertising: 7 to 11 P.M. for TV, 7 to 9 A.M. and 4 to 6 P.M. for radio. (Radio prime time varies with the market and lifestyle trends.)

Process any action, usually by a computer, that changes the content or form of information or merely transfers it from one source to another.

Production companies businesses that produce broadcasting programs for adoption either by networks or by individual stations through syndication; commonly called *production houses.*

Program managers persons responsible for selecting programs for airing, scheduling their air time, and overseeing the production and direction of locally produced programs.

Program 1,2,3 Swedish radio networks.

Projection an estimate of the characteristics of a total universe based on a sample of that universe.

Psychographics a term referring to such things as the attitudes, values, beliefs, and opinions of an audience.

PTA National Congress of Parents and Teachers.

Public broadcasting the operation of the various noncommercial radio and television stations in the United States.

Public service advertising (PSA) advertising designed to support a nonprofit cause or organization. Most of the time or space for this advertising is provided free as a service to the public by the print or broadcast media.

Quad abbreviation for *quadraphonic.*

Quadraphonic four-channel sound.

RAB Radio Advertising Bureau.

RAM Random-access memory; that portion of computer memory where information can be transferred in and out. It is not permanent, as is ROM.

Random sampling selection process in which each unit of the larger portion has an equal chance of being selected.

Rating percentage of a given population who are tuned to a radio or television station during a given time period.

RCA Radio Corporation of America.

Record rotation how often records are changed on the playlist plus how frequently they are played on the air.

Regional channels channels assigned where several stations operate, none having a power of more than five thousand watts.

Relay satellite A satellite capable of bouncing messages back to earth. Echo I was the first.

Repeater satellite A satellite that can both receive signals and retransmit them back to earth. Courier I-B of the United States was the first of the series.

ROM Read-only memory; contains predetermined functions stored permanently in the computer.

ROS run of schedule.

RTNDA Radio Television News Directors Association.

SABC South African Broadcasting Corporation.

Sales network a group of broadcasting stations linked together by a financial agreement that benefits all member stations by offering advertisers a joint rate.

Sampling the process of examining a small portion of something in order to estimate its characteristics.

Satcom domestic satellite system operated by RCA American Communications, Incorporated.

SATNET a COMSAT satellite system that employs multiple services on a single satellite communication channel by using Time-Division Multiple Access.

Saturation schedule the airing of a heavy load of commercials over a short period of time.

SBC Swedish Broadcasting Corporation.

SBS Satellite Business System; a cooperative, all-digital network employing Time-Division Multiple Access and devoted to business use.

SCA (1) Speech Communication Association; (2) Subsidiary Communication Authority.

Secondary service area an area served by sky waves and not subject to objectionable interference.

Selective exposure exposing oneself to communication believed to coincide with one's preconceived ideas.

Selective perception perceiving only those things that agree with one's preconceived ideas.

Selective retention remembering only those things that agree with one's preconceived ideas.

Semantic noise breakdown in communication caused by misunderstanding the meaning of words.

Share an estimate of the percentage of listeners to a particular station in comparison with listeners to all other stations or programs during a given time period.

Silicone detector crystal used in early radio receiving sets to detect radio waves.

SIN Spanish International Network.

Skip a section of the earth's surface that neither ground nor sky waves reach.

Sky-wave propagation a radio-wave transmission pattern in which the signals travel up, bounce off the ionosphere to the earth, and rebound from the earth in a continuing process.

SMATV Satellite Master-Antenna Television; a system that receives signals from satellites.

Soft interconnects cooperative associations of cable operators who work together to attract advertisers and air commercial programming, but whose systems are not physically connected.

Software the information the computer processes; the computer's instructions.

SPC Station program cooperative. Program-acquisition method used in public television.

Spectrum plan a medium level of commercials distributed equally throughout the broadcast day.

SPF Société Française de Production et de Creation Audiovisuelles.

SPJ, SDX Society of Professional Journalists, Sigma Delta Chi.

Spot schedule a series of commercials aired in one or two day-parts only.

STV Subscription television; a system whereby the signal from a TV station is scrambled and the subscriber pays a monthly fee for a decoder that unscrambles it.

Subtrunk cable a secondary cable that branches out from the main trunk in a cable TV system and carries the signal to outlying areas.

Superheterodyne circuit an improvement on Fessenden's heterodyne circuit; developed by Edwin H. Armstrong.

Supering positioning a picture from one television camera on top of another picture from a second camera; special effect controlled by the master control console.

Superstation a radio or television station that has expanded its listening and viewing audiences by beaming its signals to satellites, which in turn relay those signals to cable systems and their subscribers.

Sweep the period of a rating survey.

Switcher (technical director) the person responsible for operating the master control console.

Synchronous see *Geostationary*.

Syndicated programming programming distributed directly to the stations, not through a network, although it may have first appeared on a network.

Syndicator company supplying syndicated programming to local stations.

System community unit a cable-TV system, or a portion of it, that operates within a separate and distinct community or municipal entity, including unincorporated areas.

System software computer instructions that perform common functions for all users of the computer.

Talent raid CBS's acquisition of talent from other networks in 1948; sometimes refers to similar actions by ABC in 1976.

TDF Télédiffusion de Française.

TDMA Time-Division Multiple Access; a process that lumps together many different messages on one satellite channel by converting all information to digital format and then sending different bundles, or packets, of information, each of which is only part of a message. The parts of the messages are put back together at the receiving end and transposed into their original format.

TDRSS Tracking Data Relay Satellite System; a Western Union satellite system that supplements NASA's system for ground-tracking U.S. manned space missions.

Telecommunication electronic communication involving both wired and unwired, one-way and two-way communications systems.

Teleconference a video conference conducted over a long distance.

Teletext one-way transmission of textual information employing the unused scanning lines (the vertical blanking interval) of a television signal.

Television household a broadcast-rating term used for any home merely having a television set, as distinguished from a household actually using television.

Telstar early satellite used for the first transatlantic television broadcast.

TF1 Télévision Français 1.

Tiering a process whereby cable operators lump different channels or services into tiers and charge their subscribers an additional fee to receive the channels offered by a particular tier.

Toll broadcasting an early term for commercial broadcasting; first used by WEAF.

Trade-out an agreement in which a product or service is traded for advertising on a station.

Transaction the process whereby information is sent and received and feedback occurs.

Transfer to send and receive information.

Transistor wafer-thin three-layer crystal used extensively in electronic equipment; performs many of the functions of the three-element vacuum tube.

Translators television transmitting antennas, usually located on high natural terrain.

Transmit to send information.

Transponder a receiver/transmitter in a communications satellite.

Trunk cable the primary cable or main transmission line of a cable-TV system.

TSA total survey area (rating term).

Two-step flow the process by which information disseminated by mass media is (1) received by a direct audience and then (2) relayed to other persons.

Two-way cable cable system capable of both sending and receiving data.

UHF Ultrahigh frequency.

Universe the whole from which a sample is being chosen. In broadcast ratings, this can be the sample area, metro area, or rating area.

Untouchables a term used in the cable business for potential subscribers who for some reason choose not to hook up to cable.

UPI United Press International, a print and broadcast wire service.

UPI Audio audio network of United Press International.

Valve an early two-element vacuum tube.

VBI vertical blanking interval; the thick black bar that appears on a TV screen when the vertical-hold adjustment is manipulated.

VCR Video-cassette recorder.

VHF very high frequency.

Videodisc a device like a long-playing record that produces both a television picture and sound.

Videotex a two-way interactive wired system providing textual information; it can transmit over cable and telephone lines.

Vidicon a sensitive television tube that followed the image orthicon.

VOA Voice of America.

Voltaic pile the first practical energy cell, developed by Alessandro Volta.

VTR videotape recorder.

WARC World Administrative Radio Conference.

Wavelength the distance between two waves.

Westar Western Union Satellite System.

WICI Women In Communication, Inc.

Wireless term used for early radio.

Wireless telephone term used for an early invention by Nathan B. Stubblefield.

YLE (YLEISRADO) state-controlled Finnish broadcasting monopoly.

APPENDIX

LIBRARY AND DATA–BASED SEARCH GUIDE FOR BROADCASTING AND TELECOMMUNICATION

Whether writing a term paper, preparing a report, or just expanding our knowledge about broadcasting and telecommunication, knowing how to use the library is the first step in a successful search for information.

USING THE CARD CATALOGUE

In most library searches the card catalogue is the first source of information.

Using Subject, Title, and Author Heading Cards

Subject heading cards are most useful when seeking general works in a field or when the author or title of a particular book are unknown. A newcomer to a field will find the subject heading cards the best place to start. If you are unsure what subjects to look under, consult the *Library of Congress Subject Headings*. For example, if we were searching in the field of broadcasting and telecommunication, the following subject headings would be beneficial:

Broadcast journalism
Broadcasters
Broadcasting
Broadcasting policy
Communict antenna television
Radio

Radio—U.S.—Laws and Regulations
Radio advertising
Radio announcing
Radio as a profession
Radio audiences
Radio authorship
Radio broadcasting
Radio in education
Radio journalism
Radio plays
Telecommunication
Telecommunication cables
Telecommunication lines
Telecommunication policy
Telecommunication systems
Television
Television—Apparatus and Supplies
Television—Law and Legislation—U.S.
Television—production and direction
Television and children
Television announcing

Television audiences
Television authorship
Television in education
Television in politics
Television plays
Television programs

As an example, we'll assume our search through the subject headings of the card catalogue located a card for the book *Broadcast Law and Regulation,* written by the author of the text you are now reading. The subject heading card is illustrated in Figure LG-1. Notice at the top of the card is the word "Broadcasting" which conformed to one of the subject headings in the *Library of Congress Subject Headings.* As we looked through the card catalogue and got to the "Ls" we located the card under the subject heading "Broadcasting—Law and Legislation—United States."

FIGURE LG-1

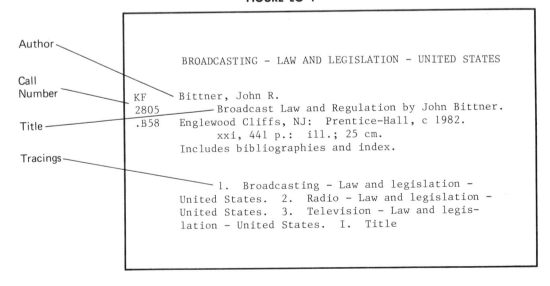

We could have located the same information on two other cards in the card catalogue, a title card or an author's card. The bibliographic information on each of these cards would be identical except the heading at the top of the card would be different. The heading at the top of the title card would read "Broadcast Law and Regulation," the same title as the book. The heading at the top of the author card would read "John R. Bittner." Tracings indicate other headings under which the book may appear or the reader can go to locate similar information about the field of study. The call number of the book is in the upper left hand corner of the catalogue card. It refers to the location of the book, and it is assigned so that books on similar subjects are shelved together.

Call numbers may be used to peruse the shelves and find relevant books on a topic. This is not as efficient as using the card catalogue but still may be useful. Usually a particular subject heading card is not assigned to a book unless a significant portion of the book is on that topic. We may want to use subject headings to find several areas of the library to examine. While doing so, check the index in the back of each book for terms relating to the topic of research.

Using References

References provide definitions of terms, biographical information, bibliographies, and introductory essays about a topic. Information from references can aid us in searching for information in more extensive library sources.

Bibliographical Sources Most libraries are equipped with numerous sources of bibliographical information. Three major sources are *Contemporary Authors, Current Biography* 1940-date, and *Who's Who in America.*

Dictionaries and Encyclopedias Because many disciplines include topics relating to broadcasting and telecommunication, specialized dictionaries and encyclopedias such as the *Encyclopedia of Psychology,* the *International Encyclopedia of the Social Sciences,* and the *Encyclopedia of Educational Research* can be helpful.

Other References Other references more directly related to the study of broadcasting and telecommunication are *Broadcasting Yearbook, BBC Handbook, Television Factbook,* and *The Standard Directory of Advertising Agencies.*

Using Indexes

Indexes are used to find relevant articles in magazines, journals, books, and newspapers. Some good ones to start with are:

Applied Science and Technology Index
Business Periodicals Index 1958–date
Current Index to Journals in Education
Education Index
Humanities Index
Index to Legal Periodicals
Index to Periodicals Relating to Law
International Index to Multimedia Information
New York Times Index
Public Affairs Information Services
Reader's Guide to Periodical Literature
Social Sciences Index
Social Sciences and Humanities Index
Topicator
Wall Street Journal Index

USING GOVERNMENT DOCUMENTS

Many libraries contain U.S. government publications. To get a head start in using government documents, check the following:

Indexes

Monthly Catalog of United States Government Publications

This is the standard guide to most U.S. government publications. Documents are arranged by issuing agency. See also the:

Cumulative Subject Index to the Monthly Catalog of the United States Government Publications

Selected Documents

The federal government publishes a variety of statistical reports, hearings, studies, and other documents relating to broadcasting. The following are major examples of various types of government documents.

United States Statutes at Large
As each law is enacted, it is published. Later, the laws passed during each session of Congress are included in the *Statutes at Large*. They are arranged chronologically by date of passage.

United States Code
This is the official compilation of U.S. laws in force. Laws from the *Statutes at Large* are consolidated and codified in this work. A completely revised edition is issued every six years with annual supplements between revisions.

Media Law Reporter
This contains the texts of major decisions affecting mass media.

Federal Register
Statutory laws prescribe general intent; Congress delegates to the executive and the various departments the detailed task of administration. Administrative rules and regulations have legal force. The *Federal Register* provides the medium through which new rules and regulations are disseminated.

Code of Federal Regulations
The regulations and rules in the *Federal Register* are codified annually and published in this source. It lists, among other things, all the permanent and general rules and regulations established by the Federal Communications Commission.

Federal Communications Commission Reports 1934—

This contains the administrative decisions of the Federal Communications Commission, including decisions regarding "the Fairness Doctrine," television station license renewal, cable television, and many more.

Federal Communications Commission Annual Report 1935—
This is a review of the major events for the year in the area of regulatory concern, including administrative matters, engineering, legal and legislative activities.

Congressional Hearings, Monthly Catalog
The *Monthly Catalog* is the index to use when researching congressional hearings.

JOURNALS AND TRADE PUBLICATIONS

Since broadcasting and telecommunication is a rapidly changing field of study, journals and trade publications are an excellent place to locate up-to-date information. Some of the more common publications in the field, and those found in many major libraries are:

AV Communications Review
Advertising Age
Billboard
Broadcast Management/Engineering
Broadcasting
Broadcasting and the Law (Perry's)
Communication Monographs
Communications News
Communication Research
Educational & Instructional Television
Feedback
Journalism Monographs
Journal of Advertising Research
Journal of Communication
Journal of College Radio
Journalism Quarterly
Mass Comm Review
The Quill
SMPTE Journal
Telecommunications Policy

Publications related to specific media and technologies such as satellite and cable communications are also relevant.

DATA—BASED SEARCHES

More and more libraries are placing their holdings in electronic data bases that can be accessed by a simple keyboard and visual-display terminal at the library (some schools prefer library staff members operate the system). Many data bases show holdings not only in individual libraries but also in libraries located in the same region, and nationally. Using these data-based services is easy and expedient, especially when we are searching for holdings that can be acquired only through interlibrary loan. Most data bases currently in use work better for books than for periodicals. This will gradually change as more and more periodicals are placed in data bases and individual journals and articles can be accessed. Achieving complete data-based collections, however, must wait on funding (much of it from government and foundation sources), which, because of recessionary economic conditions in the 1980s, has lagged behind technology.

To better understand how a data-based system works, we will examine one—the Online Computer Library Center (OCLC). Started in 1967 as the Ohio College Library Center, the OCLC is a nonprofit educational corporation that stores computer holdings from over two thousand libraries located in large research institutions on down to small towns.

If we were to use a traditional card-catalogue search method, we would select our topic, author, or title and then search the card catalogue until we located the appropriate card, which would tell us where in the library the book was located. In using the OCLC system, however, instead of going to the card catalogue we would go to the library's OCLC computer terminal and log on with a predetermined account number. We could then conduct any one of three primary searches: author-title search, author-name search, or title search.

Author–Name Search

We would key in the first four letters of the author's name (in the case of multiple authors, we would use the first author's name), then a comma, the first three letters of the author's first name, another comma, and the middle initial or first letter of the author's middle name. Thus, if we wanted to locate a book by the author of the book you are now reading, we would type the following:

bitt,joh,r

Our entry consists of the first four letters of the author's last name, the first three letters of the author's first name, and the middle initial or first letter of the author's middle name. Then by pressing the DISPLAY REC'D key and then the SEND key, we would call up on the screen before us books or other library holdings published by that author. For other authors we would use the same procedure. Each publication appearing on the screen before us would be numbered.

We would then select the publication by its number (1, 2, 3, 4, and so on). By pressing the appropriate numbered key we would call up on the screen a complete bibliographic entry of that book.

We will assume that in our search we chose Bittner, John R., *Broadcast Law and Regulation.* Englewood Cliffs, N.J.: Prentice-Hall, Inc., 1982. Figure LG–2 illustrates the OCLC entry for this book.

```
OCLC: 7573375      Rec stat: c Entrd: 810601      Used: 821206
Type: a Bib lvl: m Govt pub:   Lang:  eng Source:    Illus: a
Repr:    Enc lvl:   Conf pub: 0 Ctry:  nju Dat tp: s M/F/B: 10
Indx: 1 Mod rec:    Festschr: 0 Cont: b
Desc: a Int lvl:    Dates: 1982,
  1 010       81-8701
  2 040       DLC c DLC d OCL
  3 020       0130835927 : c $19.95
  4 039 0     2 b 3 c 3 d 3 e 3
  5 043       n-us---
  6 050 0     KF2805 b .B58
  7 082 0     343.73/0994 a 347.303994 2 19
  8 092       b
  9 049       NDDP
 10 100 10    Bittner, John R., d 1943-
 11 245 10    Broadcast law and regulation / c John R. Bittner.
 12 260 0     Englewood Cliffs, N.J. : b Prentice-Hall, c c1982.
 13 300       xxi, 441 p. : b ill. : c 25 cm.
 14 504       Includes bibliographies and index.
 15 650 0     Broadcasting x Law and legislation z United States.
 16 650 0     Radio x Law and legislation z United States.
 17 650 0     Television x Law and legislation z United States.
```

FIGURE LG-2

This information, especially lines 10 through 17, is the same as the card-catalogue card for the same book. Lines 15 through 17 are the *tracings*.

Let us assume the library where we are conducting our search does not have this book. We can therefore choose to search other libraries in the state, the region (bordering states), or the nation. We will assume we chose a national search. By keying in the appropriate information (in this case the three letters *dha*), we call up abbreviations for states followed by abbreviations for libraries in each state that include a copy of the book in their holdings and have placed this book in the OCLC system. Keep in mind that only libraries that are part of the OCLC system are included, not every library in the United States. As an example, and to save space, Figure LG-3 shows only the states Alabama thru Missouri.

FIGURE LG-3

```
ALL LOCATIONS -  FOR OTHER HOLDINGS DISPLAYS ENTER dhg, dhs, OR dhr, DISPLAY
RECD, SEND; FOR BIBLIOGRAPHIC RECORD ENTER bib, DISPLAY RECD, SEND

STATE      LOCATIONS
  AL       AAA ALM AMU
  AR       AKH AKU ALR AMK
  AZ       AZC AZL AZP AZS AZU MSA
  CA       CCH CDH CDL CDS CFI CLO CPF CSF CSO CTU CUI FUP
  CO       COD DVP
```

```
DC      DHU DLC DWP FCC GWL UCA USI WCL
FL      FGM FHS FNP FPS FSL FYM ORL
GA      GCD GLL GPM GUA
HI      HUH
IA      IOD IWA IWG NIU
IL      IAD IAF IAI IAQ IAS IAZ IBC IBQ ICI ICN ICS IFK ILK IUJ JNA SOI UIU
IN      IND ISU IUB IUL IUP IVV
KS      KFL KKC KKQ KKU KSW KWL
KY      KMS KSL
LA      LRL LSC LUL
MA      CUM FST MYG REG SLL SUF TFW WPG
MD      LOY LUM MSU TSC
MI      EEM EXH EYH EYP EYW EZC
MN      MHL MLL MNT MNV MNY MST SPP
MO      MCW MKN MOO MUU SLU UMK WUL
```

FIGURE LG-3 Continued

In an actual search more than one screen may be necessary. In that case we would need to select the screen that has the information most appropriate to our search. The directory accompanying each OCLC terminal tells which library corresponds to which abbreviation. Assume we are in a library in North Carolina. The library does not have the book we want, so we must order it through interlibrary loan. The abbreviations found after the North Carolina abbreviation (NC) are EWF, NCS, NDL, and NOC. By checking the OCLC directory we find these abbreviations correspond to the libraries at Wake Forest University, North Carolina State University, Duke University (Law Library), and the University of North Carolina at Chapel Hill, respectively. We would then choose one of the libraries and order the book through interlibrary loan.

There are several reasons why a library chooses to include a book in its holdings. For example, the librarian or someone else may decide to order it, or someone may donate it to the library. Unfortunately, in times of tight money library acquisitions suffer considerably. More general books may be given preference over books dealing with more narrow topics that interest only a few readers.

Author–Title Search

Another way to search the OCLC system is to use the author-title search. In this case we key in the first four letters of the author's last name and the first four letters of the title. Thus, to search for *Broadcast Law and Regulation* we would key in

bitt,broa

Appearing on the screen (Figure LG-4) will be two books by the author, each having a title whose first four letters are *broa*. Keep in mind all books written by an author do not appear, only those with the first four letters keyed into the search.

```
    1   Bittner, John R.,   Broadcast law and regulation /    Englewood Cliffs,
N.J. :    1982   DLC
    2   Bittner, John R.,   Broadcasting : an introduction /    Englewood Cliffs,
N.J. :    1980   DLC
```

FIGURE LG-4

Assume that we want the second book listed. We are able to have the bibliographic entry for *Broadcast Law and Regulation* appear on the screen simply by keying the number 1 on our keyboard.

If we wanted to do a national library search we would again key in the appropriate letters (*dha*) and the list of states with the corresponding library abbreviations would appear.

Title Search

Another alternative is the title search. Here we can locate a specific title or a selection of titles on a given topic. We locate a specific title by keying in the first three letters of the first word of the title, the first two letters of the second word of the title, the first two letters of the third word of the title, and the first letter of the fourth word of the title. Seem confusing? Not really.

For *Broadcast Law and Regulation,* we would key in the letters in bold type:

Broadcast Law and Regulation
bro,la,an,r

For this entry we find two listings, as shown in Figure LG-5:

We can now call up bibliographic entry 1 or entry 2. By keying in a national library search (again, by using the letters *dha*) we can determine which libraries in the OCLC system have the book.

Libraries are becoming as involved as many other institutions in our society with electronic processing of information. Telecommunication, in the form of interactive systems such as the OCLC, is becoming more and more common. Libraries are placing their complete holdings in in-house computers that may or may not interface with larger data bases. The card-catalogue search, while still useful, is cumbersome compared with an electronic search for library materials, which can be speedy and accurate. High-speed printers aid the search even more: information on any OCLC screen we have described can be obtained immediately as a printout.

When you consider the available technology, it does not take much imagination to see the library search of the future being made from the computer terminal in your own living room. If the actual pages of information, such as the contents of a book, are also available from a data base, this information can be placed at your side by the

FIGURE LG-5

```
    1   Broadcast law and regulation /    Bittner, John R.,    Englewood Cliffs,
N.J. :    1982   DLC
    2   Broadcasting law and regulation,    Ellmore, R. Terry.    Blue Ridge
Summit, Pa. :    1982   DLC
```

same system that searched for the publication. For example, a term-paper research strategy of the future could involve sitting at a computer terminal and calling up the books you want to use. You would then access the actual pages of the book, in much the same way you would look up pages in the index. With a simple keyboard command you can have the printer provide you with a hard copy of the pages. Without leaving your chair you have at your side the exact information, the exact quotes, the exact data and tables, from the very books and periodicals that will become part of your paper. This information will then be composed, typed, and edited on the same computer terminal you used to search your bibliography. The finished paper may even be transmitted electronically to your professor, who will read it at another terminal. As we have learned, that very scenario can occur right now in the case of newspapers and magazines, which are available in data banks that can be accessed by anyone having a modest home computer connected to a telephone.

As we approach the end of the twentieth century and experience the changing world of broadcasting and telecommunication we perhaps need to consider more and more what the human consequences of our electronic world and information society will be. How will the new technology affect our lifestyles, our ability to communicate with each other? Answers to these questions will be at the forefront of inquiry when the novelty of the technology wears off and we stop long enough to ponder its history and where it is taking us.

NOTES

CHAPTER 1

[1]We need to keep in mind that researchers disagree about what *transmit, transfer,* and *transact* mean and that definitions change across disciplines. Communication may mean one thing to a computer scientist and something entirely different to a philosopher. A manager of a large corporation might use all three terms interchangeably. He or she may communicate regularly with employees through letters or newsletters and not care if feedback is received or if communication has taken place. In the mind of the sender it *has* taken place and that is all that is important to his or her approach to running the business.

[2]S. L. Tubbs and S. Moss, *Human Communication: An Interpersonal Perspective* (New York: Random House, 1974), p. 6.

[3]K. E. Andersen, *Introduction to Communication Theory and Practice* (Menlo Park, Calif.: Cummings, 1972), p. 8.

[4]W. Schramm, "The Nature of Communication Between Humans," in *The Process and Effects of Mass Communication,* rev. ed., ed. W. Schramm and

D. F. Roberts (Urbana: University of Illinois Press, 1971), p. 8. Schramm first posited the *sharing* emphasis of communication in the first edition of *The Process and Effects of Mass Communication,* published in 1954.

[5]Some of the more well known models are found in C. E. Shannon and W. Weaver, *The Mathematical Theory of Communication* (Urbana: University of Illinois Press, 1964); G. Gerbner, "Toward a General Model of Communication," *Audio Visual Communication Review,* 4 (Summer 1956), 171–99; H. D. Lasswell, "The Structure and Function of Communications in Society," in *The Communication of Ideas,* ed. L. Bryson (New York: Harper & Row, 1948), p. 37; W. Schramm, "How Communication Works," in *The Process and Effects of Communication: An Introduction to Theory and Practice* (New York: Holt, Rinehart & Winston, 1960), p. 72; F. E. X Dance, "Toward a Theory of Human Communication," in *Human Communication Theory: Original Essays* (New York: Holt, Rinehart & Winston), 1967, p. 296. General works include Berlo, Dance, and others. See also the more recent collection of essays edited by R. W. Budd and B. D. Rubin, *Approaches to Human Com-*

munication (New York: Spartan Books, 1972). A classic work is C. Cherry, *On Human Communication* (New York: John Wiley, 1957).

[6]Components vary considerably, as we can see from the following terms, all of which are found in various communication models or discussions of them: communicator, message, receiver, channel, medium, noise, feedback, delayed feedback, information source, transmitter, signal, noise source, receiver signal, destination, perceptual dimension, percept, event, media, form, content, man, machine, encoder, decoder, interpreter, communication skills, attitudes, knowledge, social system, culture content, treatment code, seeing, hearing, touching, smelling, tasting, environment, point in time.

[7]The role of intrapersonal communication in overcoming stress is gaining attention in psychology. A general overview of this concept can be found in S. Worchel and W. Shebilske, *Psychology: Principles and Applications* (Englewood Cliffs, N.J.: Prentice-Hall, 1983), pp. 325–39.

[8]As conceptualized by Schramm in *The Process and Effects of Communication,* p. 8.

[9]K. K. Campbell, *Critiques of Contemporary Rhetoric* (Belmont, Calif.: Wadsworth, 1972), p. 33. This is Campbell's interpretation of Kenneth Burke, *A Grammar of Motives and a Rhetoric of Motives* (New York: Meridian Books, 1962).

[10]J. C. McCroskey and L. Wheeless, *Introduction to Human Communication* (Boston: Allyn & Bacon, 1976). The term's conceptual application is credited to P. F. Lazarsfeld and R. K. Merton, "Friendship as a Social Process: A Substantive and Methodological Analysis," in *Freedom and Control in Modern Society,* ed. Monroe Berger and others (New York: Octagon, 1964), p. 23. Recent perspectives on interpersonal communication and related dimensions can be found in B. D. Ruben, "Communication and Conflict: A System-Theoretic Perspective," *Quarterly Journal of Speech,* 64 (1978), 202–10; D. Barnlund, *Interpersonal Communication: Survey and Studies* (Boston: Houghton Mifflin, 1968); G. R. Miller, "The Current Status of Theory and Research in Interpersonal Communication," *Human Communication Research,* 4 (Winter 1978), 164–78; W. A. Donahue, D. P. Cushman, and R. F. Nofsinger, Jr., "Creating and Confronting Social Order: A Comparison of Rules Perspectives," *Western Journal of Speech Communication,* 44 (Winter 1980), 5–19; C. R. Berger and R. J. Calabrese, "Some Explorations in Initial Interaction and Beyond: Toward a Developmental Theory of Interpersonal Communication," *Human Communication Research,* 1 (Winter 1975), 99–112. W. Schultz's theories, specifically FIRO (fundamental interpersonal relations orientation) theory, can be found in his *FIRO: A Three-Dimensional Theory of Interpersonal Behavior* (New York: Holt, Rinehart & Winston, 1958); *The Three-Dimensional Underworld* (Palo Alto, Calif.:

Science and Behavior Books, 1966); *Here Comes Everybody* (New York: Harper & Row, 1973); *Elements of Encounter* (New York: Bantam, 1975); and *Leaders of Schools* (La Jolla, Calif.: University Associates, 1977). See also S. W. Littlejohn, *Theories of Human Communication* (Columbus, Ohio: Charles E. Merrill, 1978), pp. 212–17.

[11]K. Lewin, "Channels of Group Life: Social Planning and Action Research," *Human Communication Research,* (1947), 143–53.

[12]K. Starck and J. Soloski, "Effect of Reporter Predispositions in Covering a Controversial Story," *Journalism Quarterly,* 55 (Spring 1977), 120–25; B. S. Greenberg and P. H. Tannenbaum, "Communicator Performance Under Cognitive Stress," *Journalism Quarterly,* 39 (Spring 1962), 169–78; J. S. Kerrick, T. E. Anderson, and L. B. Swales, "Balance and Writers' Attitude in News Stories and Editorials," *Journalism Quarterly,* 41 (Spring 1964), 207–15; and I. De Sola Pool and I. Shulman, "Newsmen's Fantasies, Audiences, and Newswriting," and W. Gieber, "News Is What Newspapermen Make It," in *People, Society, and Mass Communications,* ed. L. Anthony and D. M. White (Glencoe, N.Y.: Free Press, 1964), pp. 141–59 and 173–82.

[13]Although many studies have examined the various relationships, the concept of opinion leader was first reported and applied to current mass communication in P. F. Lazarsfeld, B. Berelson, and H. Gaudet, *The People's Choice* (New York: Columbia University Press, 1948). Opinion leaders can also act in strictly interpersonal communication. However, it is in reference to mass media that we use the term here.

[14]R. A. Dutch, ed., *Roget's Thesaurus* (New York: St. Martin's, 1965), p. 711.

[15]Minow made the remarks in a speech to the 1961 meeting of the National Association of Broadcasters.

[16]W. Schramm and J. Alexander, "Broadcasting," in *Handbook of Communication,* ed. I. De Sola Pool and others (Chicago: Rand McNally, 1973), p. 586.

CHAPTER 2

[1]Much of the background information for this chapter is contained in G. G. Blake, *History of Radio Telegraphy and Telephony* (1928; reprint ed., New York: Arno Press, 1974); J. Brooks, *Telephone: The First Hundred Years* (New York: Harper & Row, 1975); C. Domb, ed., *Clerk Maxwell and Modern Science* (London: Athlone Press, 1963); J. J. Fahie, *A History of Wireless Telegraphy* (1901; reprint ed., New York: Arno Press, 1971); and E. A. Marland, *Early Electrical Communication* (London: Abelard-Schuman, 1964). In

addition, a number of telephone-company publications provided important background information. Especially valuable was William Chauncy Langdon's account of the early history of AT&T published in the July 1925 edition of *Bell Telephone Quarterly*. It has been reprinted by the Bell System, most recently in 1979. Other information of general interest can be found in *Events in Telecommunications History* (New York: AT&T, 1979); L. K. Lustig, ed., *IMPACT: A Compilation of Bell System Innovations* (New York: Bell System, 1981); *Communicating and the Telephone* (New York: Bell System, 1979); K. P. Todd, ed., *A Capsule History of the Bell System* (New York: Bell System, 1979); *The Computer and Telecommunications* (New York: Bell System, 1980); and *Connecting: The Social Impact of the Telephone in America* (New York: Bell System, 1979).

[2]Readers interested in early electrical communication should consult Hugh G. J. Aitken, *Syntony and Spark: The Origins of Radio* (New York: John Wiley, 1976); Blake, *History of Radio Telegraphy and Telephony;* Silvanus P. Thompson, *Michael Faraday: His Life and Work* (Macmillan 1898); Fahie, *The History of Wireless Telegraphy;* W. Rupert MacLaurin, *Invention and Innovation in the Radio Industry* (1949; reprint ed., New York: Arno Press, 1971); Gleason L. Archer, *History of Radio to 1926* (New York: American Historical Society, 1938); J. A. Fleming, *The Principles of Electric Wave Telegraphy* (London: Longmans, Green, 1908); Richard T. Glazebrook, *James Clerk Maxwell and Modern Physics* (New York: Macmillan, 1896); and Marland, *Early Electrical Communication.*

[3]Chauncy, *Bell Telephone Quarterly,* July, 1923, p. 5. (Page references are to the 1979 reprint.)

[4]Ibid.

[5]Ibid.

[6]Ibid., p. 6.

[7]Ibid.

[8]Of interest is the account that:

Bell had been carrying on studies with a laboratory device called the phonautograph, which made mechanical tracings of sound vibrations. He made an improved phonautograph, using the bones and drum of a human ear procured for him by a friend, Dr. Clarence Blake. Bell explained how his experiments with this improved instrument led him to his conception of the telephone as follows: "I was much struck by the disproportion in weight between the membrane and the bones that were moved by it; and it occurred to me that if such a thin and delicate membrane could move bones that were, relatively to it, very massive indeed, why should not a larger and stouter membrane be able to move a piece of steel in the manner I desired? At once the conception of the membrane speaking telephone became complete in my mind. . . . The arrangement thus

conceived in the summer of 1874 was substantially similar to that shown . . . in my patent of March 7, 1876." Bell described to his father, while on a visit to the family home at Brantford, Ontario, on this date (1874) his conception of his electric speaking telephone using his undulating current principle. (*Events in Telecommunications History,* pp. 2–3.), date (1874) added.

[9]Prior to the formation of the company, on August 10, 1876,

the world's first long distance telephone call (one-way) was received at Paris, Ontario, by Bell from his father and uncle at Brantford, Ontario, over telegraph lines 8 miles and 68 miles long. Referring to this call, Bell said: "This Brantford experiment is of historical interest . . . because it led to the discovery of the proper combination of parts in a telephone to enable it to become operative upon a long line; and because upon this occasion occurred the first transmission of the human voice over a telegraph line in which the transmitting and receiving telephone was miles apart."

Permission to use this telegraph line was granted by Lewis B. McFarlane, a telegraph manager, who entered the telephone business in 1879, was president of The Bell Telephone Company of Canada from 1915 to 1925 and chairman of the board from 1925 to 1930. (*Events in Telecommunications History,* p. 3.)

[10]Hubbard offered to sell the telephone invention to Western Union for $100,000, but the offer was refused (*Events in Telecommunications History,* p. 3.)

[11]Chauncy, *Bell Telephone Quarterly,* p. 8.

[12]Ibid., p. 10.

[13]Ibid.

[14]Ibid., p. 13.

[15]Ibid., p. 14.

[16]The District Telephone Company of New Haven, organized by licensee George W. Coy along with Walter Lewis and H. P. Frost, had twenty-one subscribers. (*Events in Telecommunications History,* p. 5.) "First" exchanges the following year (1879) included:

February	Louisville, Ky.
February 15	Minneapolis, Minn.
February 24	Denver, Colo.
March	Indianapolis, Ind.
March 15	New Orleans, La.
April 1	Richmond, Va.
April 2	Providence, R.I.
April 26	Toronto, Canada
May 1	Montreal, Canada
June	Omaha, Nebr.
June 1	Burlington, Vt.
June 4	Topeka, Kans.
June 15	Dubuque, Ia.

August 1 .... Augusta, Ga.
August 15 .... Camden, N.J.
August 21 .... Galveston, Tex.
August 26 .... Charleston, S.C.
September 1 .... Portland, Me.
September 1 .... Brantford, Canada
September 20 .... Raleigh, N.C.
September 22 .... London, Canada
November 1 .... Little Rock, Ark.
November 15 .... Mobile, Ala.
December .... Nashville, Tenn.

(Events in Telecommunications History, p. 7)

[17][Elisha Gray.] worked his way through Oberlin College as a carpenter. His work in physics at Oberlin quickly narrowed to electrical applications. He invented a self-adjusting telegraph relay, a telegraphic switch and a repeater. He continued in the firm of Gray and Barton only two years, after which he devoted himself entirely to electrical research. Gray was working on a harmonic telegraph at the same time as Bell, and perfected what he called a telephone to transmit musical sounds. The idea of transmitting vocal sounds occurred to him, and on Feb. 14, 1876, he filed a caveat (a confidential report of an invention which is not fully perfected) in the U.S. Patent Office. His caveat indicated that he was on the same track as Bell, but had not worked out his transmitter as fully. And on that same day, but a few hours earlier, Alexander Graham Bell had filed a patent application for his telephone, thus anticipating Gray. Gray's most important invention thereafter probably was the telautograph which transmits facsimile handwriting and drawings. At the time of his sudden death in 1901, he was experimenting on underwater signaling to vessels at sea. *(Events in Telecommunications History,* p. 2)

[18]Competition in the telephone business developed from the Western Union Telegraph Company through its newly established subsidiaries, the American Speaking Telephone Company and the Gold & Stock Telephone Company. These companies used Thomas A. Edison transmitters and Elisha Gray receivers.

The Handset Telephone—Robert G. Brown, who became chief operator at the Western Union (Gold & Stock) exchange in New York City, devised in 1878 (possibly in April but more probably in May) the first handset, mounting an Edison transmitter and a Gray receiver on a bar of metal. Brown was sent to France in 1879 to open an exchange at Paris. There, his handset was lightened to make it more easily handled by women operators. It became popular in France and Europe despite limitations that made it unacceptable in the United States, and for years was known as the French or Continental telephone. Brown died at St. Petersburg, Florida, October 2, 1947, at the age of 93. *(Events in Telecommunications History,* p. 5)

[19]Chauncy, *Bell Telephone Quarterly,* pp. 23–24.

[20]Ibid., p. 24.

[21]Ibid.

[22]Ibid., p. 25

[23]The consent decree and the information of the AT&T subsidiary American Bell were reported extensively in the press and in the Bell System's booklet "Let's Talk About Change" (1982).

CHAPTER 3

[1]Keep in mind that not all of the players in any epoch of scientific achievement can be recognized, for three reasons. First, many conducted research but never took the time to publish their results so that other scientists could share in their discoveries. Second, others conducted research and in some cases published it, but never patented their inventions. Thus, someone else was given their place in history. Third, still others were interested in pure science as opposed to the practical application of their discoveries to society. Any historical overview, then, shows us that those who made practical application of their research were recognized, sometimes more than their academic peers. They also tended to reap the greatest economic rewards, not only from patents but also from the development of full-scale corporate endeavors that sometimes extended worldwide.

[2]Accounts of Marconi's life may be found in Orrin E. Dunlap, *Marconi: The Man and His Wireless* (1937; reprint ed., New York: Arno Press, 1971); W. P. Jolly, *Marconi* (Briarcliff Manor, N.Y.: Stein & Day, 1972); Degna Marconi, *My Father Marconi* (New York: McGraw-Hill, 1962); Niels H. de V. Heathcote, *Nobel Prize Winners in Physics: 1901–1950* (New York: Henry Schuman, 1953); R. N. Vyvyan, *Marconi and Wireless* (East Ardsley, England: E P Publishing, 1974).

[3]Marconi, *My Father Marconi,* p. 27.

[4]Ibid., p. 28.

[5]Ibid., pp. 38–39.

[6]Ibid., p. 36.

[7]Ibid., pp. 100–104.

[8]"Wireless Signals Across the Ocean," *New York Times,* December 15, 1901, pp. 1–2; "Wireless Telegraphy Across the Atlantic," *Times* (London), December 16, 1901, p. 5.

[9]P. T. McGrath, "Marconi and His Transatlantic Signal," *Century Magazine,* 63 (March 1902), 769; George Iles, "Marconi's Triumph," *World's Work,* February 1902, p. 1784.

[10]McGrath, "Marconi and His Transatlantic Signal," p. 781.

[11]"Signor Marconi's Experiments," *Times* (London), December 19, 1901, p. 5.

[12]Much has been written on the early development of the Marconi companies. Particularly useful to this text were W. J. Baker, *A History of the Marconi Company* (New York: St. Martin's, 1971); Gleason L. Archer, *History of Radio to 1926* (New York: American Historical Society, 1938); L. S. Howeth, *History of Communications: Electronics in the United States Navy* (Washington, D.C.: Bureau of Ships and Office of Naval History, 1963); Hiram L. Jome, *Economics of the Radio Industry* (London: A. W. Shaw, 1925); Thorn Mayes, "History of the American Marconi Company," *The Old Timer's Bulletin,* 13 (June 1972), 11–18; as cited in Lawrence W. Lichty and Malachi C. Topping, ed., *A Source Book on the History of Radio and Television* (New York: Hastings House, 1975); and Jolly, *Marconi.*

[13]The first proposed title of the company was Marconi's Patent Telegraphs Ltd., to which Guglielmo Marconi himself objected (Baker, *A History of the Marconi Company,* p. 35).

[14]*Investors World,* October 7, 1898, p. 484.

[15]Howeth, *History of Communications,* p. 36.

[16]Archer, *History of Radio to 1926,* pp. 81–82.

[17]See Lee De Forest, *The Father of Radio* (Chicago: Wilcox & Follett, 1950). Fleming's work is discussed in J. A. Fleming, *An Elementary Manual of Radio Telegraphy and Radio Telephony* (London: Longmans, Green, 1908), pp. 204–11; and George G. Blake, *History of Radio Telegraphy and Telephony* (1928; reprint ed., New York: Arno Press, 1974), pp. 238–40.

[18]Harlow, *Old Wires and New Waves,* pp. 462–63, as cited in Archer, *History of Radio to 1926,* p. 92.

[19]"October Meeting of the American Institute of Electrical Engineers," *Electrical World,* 43 (November 3, 1906), 836–37; also published by De Forest as "The Audion: A New Receiver for Wireless Telegraphy," *Scientific American Supplement,* November 30, 1907, pp. 348–56.

[20]J. A. Fleming, "Wireless Telegraph Receiver," *Electrical World,* 43 (December 8, 1906), 1117.

[21]Lee De Forest, "Wireless Telegraph Receiver," 43 *Electrical World* (December 22, 1906), 1206. See also note 40.

[22]Jome, p. 208; *Marconi Wireless Telegraphy Company of America* v. *De Forest Radio Telephone and Telegraph Company,* 236 Fd. 942, affirmed by the Circuit Court of Appeals in 243 Fd. 560.

[23]De Forest, *Father of Radio,* pp. 325–26.

[24]Ibid., p. 457.

[25]Charles Susskind, "De Forest, Lee," in *Dictionary of Scientific Biography, Volume 3,* ed. Charles Coulston Gillispie (New York: Scribner's, 1975), pp. 6–7.

[26]See Elliot N. Sivowitch, "A Technological Survey of Broadcasting's Prehistory," *Journal of Broadcasting,* 5 (Winter 1970–71), 1–20. For the most part, research into the role of induction and conduction in the development of the radio has been overlooked by historians, partly because such approaches became scientifically obsolete in later years. Research focusing on the political, economic, and social implications is still needed. It would provide some important "micro"-insights into how new scientific knowledge is applied to the invention process. Sources for such research studies are still available and more easily accessible than those of inventors in the early nineteenth century.

[27]For accounts of Stubblefield, see Sivowitch, "Technological Survey," pp. 20–22; Thomas W. Hoffer, "Nathan B. Stubblefield and His Wireless Telephone," *Journal of Broadcasting,* 15 (Summer 1971), 317–29; and Harvey Geller, "The Man History Overheard," *Circular-Warner/Reprise,* 7 (December 8, 1975), 1–4.

[28]Geller, "The Man History Overheard," p. 2.

[29]*Washington Post,* August 10, 1940, cited in Hoffer, "Stubblefield," 322.

[30]Hoffer, "Stubblefield," p. 322.

[31]Quoted in H. M. Fessenden, *Builder of Tomorrow* (New York: Coward-McCann, 1940), p. 77. The remainder of the letter read:

The Government cannot legally pay for the patents issued to you, but by the proposition herein made, you are allowed a salary that will enable you to easily bear such expense and thus own the patents, the Bureau reserving the right to make use of such patents or of such devices as you may invent for its use in receiving meteorological reports and transmitting Weather Bureau information.

I am of the opinion that you would have a better opportunity here not only to test your present devices, but also while enjoying a remunerative salary and having your traveling expenses paid be able to devise new apparatus that would inure both to the profit of the Government and to your own individual benefit.

Congress recently gave us $25,000 which we expended in making additions to our buildings in Washington. We therefore have plenty of room and can easily fit up such laboratory as you may need. You will also find instrument makers, blacksmiths, metal workers and artisans of many classes, the services of whom will be freely placed at your disposal.

If this general proposition meets with your approval, I would thank you to sign the enclosed agreement and return same to this office (p. 77).

[32]Ibid., p. 81.

[33]Ibid., p. 80, Quoting *Popular Radio,* 1923.

[34]Fessenden, *Builder of Tomorrow,* p. 94.

³⁵Ibid., p. 95.

³⁶Ibid., p. 98. The specific terms were outlined in Fessenden's letter to Queen & Company dated June 12, 1902:

About the contract, I note that you have made a mistake. I made a memorandum of our conversation, so that I should not forget it, within a few moments of its occurrence as my memory is rather poor sometimes. 'Mem. of agreement with Mr. Grey. 50 mile transmission to sell for $5,000 or $100 per mile. Allowing $500 for the cost of apparatus, and allowing Queen and Co. an additional $1,000 for manufacturers profit and office expenses, leaves $3,500 for division. Mr. Grey asked what portion of this I thought should be my share. Told him $2,000, leaving him $1,500 in addition to other $1,000. Said he thought this satisfactory.'

I see that the contract was drawn up hurriedly, so possibly the amount allotted to me, i.e., $1,250, is a mistake, as I do not think that you will say that a profit of $2,500 on apparatus which can be bought in the open market for $500 is too small. According to the agreement sent, your profit would be $3,250 and mine $1,250.

I have assumed that there has been a slip, and have had another contract drawn up, in agreement with my memorandum of the agreement made in our conversation and forward it for your signature, if agreeable. I think that if you get, as you will according to this agreement, $3,000 for each 50 mile transmission on outside work and $3,600 on each pair for the navy, your company will make a good thing. 30 pairs at this rate would make over $100,000 and there is little doubt but that you will get at least this.

My object was to give you such liberal terms that it would be an object for you to push matters, and that you should be enabled to make a good round sum before any company was formed. Even in case the company was formed it was my intention to see that Queen and Co. retained a profitable connection, if my influence could manage it, and in case the company were formed sooner than anticipated, it is my intention to see that the contract is continued, if I can possibly arrange this, (and my influence would naturally be strong to this end) until you have made an amount of profit which should be entirely satisfactory to you.

³⁷Ibid., p. 105. See the chapter in Fessenden's book entitled "National Electric Signalling Company." See also the accounts of Sivowitch, "Technological Survey;" Howeth, *History of Communications;* Archer, *History of Radio to 1926;* and Blake, *History of Radio Telegraphy and Telephony.*

³⁸Details of many of Fessenden's experiments can also be found in Sivowitch, "Technological Survey;" Howeth, *History of Communications;* Archer,

History of Radio to 1926; and Blake, *History of Radio Telegraphy and Telephony,* as well as other works cited.

³⁹Archer, *History of Radio to 1926,* pp. 102–3.

⁴⁰De Forest, *Father of Radio,* p. 268.

⁴¹Ibid., p. 260.

⁴²The information on ham radio is from Clinton B. DeSota, *Two Hundred Meters and Down: The Story of Amateur Radio* (West Hartford, Conn.: American Radio Relay League, 1936).

CHAPTER 4

¹R. Franklin Smith, "Oldest Station in the Nation," in *American Broadcasting: A Source Book on the History of Radio and Television,* ed. Lawrence W. Lichty and Malachi C. Topping (New York: Hastings House, 1975), pp. 114–16. (originally published in *Journal of Broadcasting,* Winter 1959–60, pp. 40–55.)

²Gordon R. Greb, "The Golden Anniversary of Broadcasting," in *American Broadcasting,* ed. Lichty and Topping, pp. 95–96 (originally published in *Journal of Broadcasting,* Winter 1958–59, pp. 3–13.)

³Ibid., p. 98.

⁴Ibid., p. 102.

⁵Two accounts of WHA's early history are Werner J. Severin, "WHA–Madison 'Oldest Station in the Nation' and the Wisconsin State Broadcasting Service" (paper presented at the meeting of the Association for Education in Journalism, Madison, Wisconsin, 1977); and *The First 50 Years of University of Wisconsin Broadcasting: WHA 1919–1969, and a Look Ahead to the Next 50 Years* (Madison: University of Wisconsin, 1970.)

⁶Our account of WWJ's early history is drawn from R. J. McLauchlin, "What the Detroit *News* Has Done in Broadcasting," in *American Broadcasting,* ed. Lichty and Topping, pp. 110–13 (originally published in *Radio Broadcast,* June 1922, pp. 136–41); *WWJ* (Detroit: WWJ, 1936); and the brochures "WWJ Broadcasting Firsts" and "WWJ Radio One," published by WWJ in 1970 in commemoration of the station's sixtieth anniversary.

⁷The account of KDKA's history is from *The History of KDKA Radio and Broadcasting* (Pittsburgh: KDKA, n.d.). See also *American Broadcasting,* ed. Lichty and Topping, pp. 13–110.

⁸*The History of KDKA,* p. 10.

⁹Besides WHA, WWJ, and KDKA there were many different licensees—including municipalities—of early radio stations. The first city station was WPG in Atlantic City, New Jersey. It went on the air on January 3, 1925, with 500 watts of power, broadcasting from a station in the rear of the Atlantic City Senior

High School building. The *Atlantic City Press* of May 27, 1927, reported a *Radio Fan* magazine survey (whose reliability has been questioned) showing that WPG was the seventh most popular radio station in the United States. The ten most popular stations, according to the survey, were (1) WJZ, New York; (2) WEAF, New York; (3) KDKA, Pittsburgh; (4) WLS, Chicago; (5) WGY, Schenectady, New York; (6) WBBM, Chicago; (7) WPG; (8) KFL, Los Angeles; (9) WBZ, Springfield, Massachusetts; and (10) WOC, Davenport, Iowa. (M. M. Anapol, "WPG Atlantic City: A Forgotten Chapter In the History of Broadcasting.") Paper presented at the annual meeting of the Speech Communication Association, San Antonio, Texas, November 1979.

[10]Gleason L. Archer, *History of Radio to 1926* (New York: American Historical Society, 1938), p. 164.

[11]Ibid., p. 157.

[12]Ibid., pp. 162–63.

[13]Ibid., pp. 112–13.

[14]There are many accounts of the formation of RCA. These include Archer's *History of Radio to 1926;* his *Big Business and Radio* (1939; reprint ed., New York: Arno Press, 1971), pp. 3–22; and Eric Barnouw, *A Tower in Babel* (New York: Oxford University Press, 1966), pp. 52–61.

[15]Barnouw, *A Tower in Babel,* pp. 44–45.

[16]Ibid., p. 49.

[17]W. R. MacLaurin, *Invention and Innovation in the Radio Industry* (1949; reprint ed., New York: Arno Press, 1971), p. 123.

[18]Ibid., p. 106.

[19]*Report on Chain Broadcasting* (Washington, D.C.: Federal Communications Commission, 1941), p. 10.

[20]Barnouw, *A Tower in Babel,* p. 181.

[21]Archer, *History of Radio,* p. 276.

[22]*American Radio Journal,* 1 (June 15, 1922), 4; cited in William Peck Banning, *Commercial Broadcasting Pioneer: The WEAF Experiment* (Cambridge, Mass.: Harvard University Press, 1946), p. 94.

[23]Banning, *Commercial Broadcasting Pioneer,* p. 93.

[24]Ibid., pp. 231–36.

[25]See Archer, *Big Business and Radio,* pp. 133–65.

[26]Ibid., p. 169.

[27]Quoted in Ibid., p. 173.

[28]*Report on Chain Broadcasting,* p. 17.

[29]Ibid., p. 92.

[30]Manuel Rosenberg, *Advertiser,* 14 (August 1943), 1–2, 24.

[31]FCC release (71159), October 12, 1943.

[32]Ibid.

[33]"Blues Sales Record an Outstanding One," Press release, Blue Network, 1942.

[34]Press release, American Broadcasting Company, March 29, 1945.

[35]Press release, American Broadcasting Company, June 15, 1945.

[36]*FCC Report on Chain Broadcasting,* p. 23.

[37]"The Way We've Been . . . and Are," *Columbine,* 2 (April-May 1974), 1. *Columbine* is a corporate publication of CBS.

[38]*FCC Report on Chain Broadcasting,* pp. 26–28.

[39]Eric Barnouw, *The Golden Web: The History of Broadcasting in the United States* (New York: Oxford University Press, 1968), p. 40.

[40]MacLaurin, "Detroit *News,"* p. 186.

[41]Archer, *Big Business and Radio,* p. 424.

[42]Barnouw, *The Golden Web,* p. 242.

[43]*Cox Looks at FM Radio: Past, Present and Future* (Atlanta: Cox Broadcasting Corporation), pp. 81–82.

[44]Ibid., p. 82.

[45]Stephen F. Hoffer, "Philo Farnsworth: Television's Pioneer," *Journal of Broadcasting,* Spring 1979, p. 157. Scholars who explore some of the earlier historical accounts of the telegraph will find that books written around 1850 elevate Bain's work above that of Samuel F. B. Morse. For his information on Bain Hoffer cites V. K. Zworykin, E. G. Ramberg, and L. E. Flory, *Television in Science and Industry* (New York: John Wiley, 1958), pp. 3–4.

[46]*From Semaphore to Satellite* (Geneva: International Telecommunication Union, 1965), p. 61.

[47]Hoffer, "Philo Farnsworth," p. 157; Zworykin, Ramberg, and Flory, *Television in Science and Industry,* pp. 3–4.

[48]Important sources for the material on Philo Farnsworth are Romaine Galey Hon, ed., *Headlines Idaho Remembers* (Boise: Friends of the Bishops' House, 1977), p. 39; *Idaho Statesman,* July 13, 1953; Stephen F. Hoffer, "Philo Farnsworth Television's Pioneer," *Journal of Broadcasting,* (Spring 1979), 153–65. Another valuable source is George Everson, *The Story of Television* (New York: Norton, 1949), p. 266. I am grateful to the staff of the Duke University Library for helping me locate many of the documents I needed in order to check facts and obtain early perspectives on the development of radio and television.

[49]Hoffer, "Philo Farnsworth," p. 154. Everson places it as near Bever City, Utah (*Story of Television,* p. 15).

[50]Hoffer, "Philo Farnsworth," p. 156.

[51]Ibid.

[52]Hoffer, "Philo Farnsworth," p. 160.

[53]Ibid., pp. 160–61, citing the following patents:

United States Patent #1,773,980, Philo T. Farnsworth of Berkeley, California, Assignor, by Mesne Assignments to Television Laboratories, Inc., of San Francisco, California, A Corporation of California, Television System, August 26, 1930, p. 1.

United States Patent #1,773,981, Philo T. Farnsworth of Berkeley, California, Assignor, by Mesne Assignments to Television Laboratories, Inc., of San Francisco, California, A Corporation of California, Television Receiving System, August 26, 1930, p. 1.

[54]See K. B. Benson, "A Brief History of Television Camera Tubes," *Journal of SMPTE,* 90 (August 1981), 708–12.

[55]Hoffer, "Philo Farnsworth," p. 158.

[56]Ibid., p. 159, in reference to the Farnsworth-Zworykin dispute.

[57]Ibid.

[58]Ibid., pp. 161–62.

[59]*Columbine,* 2 (April/May 1974), 8.

[60]See Benson, "Television Camera Tubes," p. 708.

[61]Ibid.

[62]Ibid.

[63]Ibid.

[64]Sources on the history of television recording include Albert Abramson, "A Short History of Television Recording," *Journal of SMPTE,* 64 (February 1955), 72–76, and "A Short History of Television Recording: Part II," *Journal of SMPTE,* 82 (March 1973), 188–98; and Joseph Roizen, "Video-tape Recorders: A Never-Ending Revolution," *Broadcast Engineering,* April 1976, pp. 26–30, and "The Video-tape Recorder Revolution," *Broadcasting Engineering,* May 1976, pp. 50, 52–53.

[65]See Roizen, "Video-tape Recorder Revolution."

[66]Ron Whittaker, "Super 8 in Broadcasting, CATV and CCTV: Current Technology and Applications" (unpublished paper, University of Florida, 1975).

CHAPTER 5

[1]Important to the development of this chapter were the following sources, which the author gratefully acknowledges: D. Peterson, *Big Things From Little Computers: A Layperson's Guide to Personal Computing* (Englewood Cliffs, N.J.: Prentice-Hall, 1982); N. Stern and R. A. Stern, *Computers in Society* (Englewood Cliffs, N.J.: Prentice-Hall, 1983); J. M. Nilles, *Exploring the World of the Personal Computer* (Englewood Cliffs, N.J.: Prentice-Hall, 1982); J. Frates and W. Moldrup, *Computers and Life* (Englewood

Cliffs, N.J.: Prentice-Hall, 1983); and L. K. Lustig, ed., *IMPACT: A Compilation of Bell System Innovations* (New York: Bell System, 1981). Information was provided by the following companies and used with their permission: Texas Instruments; Panasonic; Osborne Computer Corporation; Tandy Corporation and Radio Shack; Timex; International Business Machines Corporation (IBM); Apple Computer, Inc., including their copyrighted publication *A Personal Guide to Personal Computers, Personal Computers in Business: An Introduction and Buyer's Guide, Welcome to the World of Apple, and Lisa;* NEC; Digital; Epson, Universal Data Systems and Motorola, Inc.; AT&T; Hewlett-Packard; and Xerox.

[2]The History of computers is explained in more detail in Peterson, *Big Things from Little Computers,* pp. 3–23; Stern and Stern, *Computers in Society,* pp. 26–53; and Frates and Moldrup, *Computers and Life,* pp. 3–22.

[3]Among the other companies of this era that worked on computers were NCR, Burroughs, and GE (Stern and Stern, *Computers in Society,* p. 48).

[4]The development of computers within Bell Labs is chronicled in *IMPACT,* ed. Lustig, pp. 11–22 and 25–29.

[5]See Frates and Moldrup *Computers and Life,* pp. 19–22; and Nilles, *Personal Computer,* pp. 9–15.

[6]Sources for this discussion of Apple are cited in note 1, this chapter.

[7]See the Apple publication *Lisa.*

[8]E. Larson and F. Allen, "Apple to Sell 3,000 Portable Computers, Still to be Introduced, to Drexel University," *Wall Street Journal,* April 20, 1983, p. 60.

[9]Along with information supplied by IBM, an article in the IBM corporate publication *Think* was extremely helpful: H. Kinney, "Again: Something New," *Think,* July/August 1981, pp. 4–12. This article may become a classic in the history of personal computing.

IBM press releases of August 12–14, 1981, carried the story of the new computer. IBM's press release listed the following highlights of the IBM Personal Computer:

Features: Available with the system are an 83-key adjustable keyboard, up to 262,144 characters of user memory (16,384 standard), a printer that can print in two directions at 80 characters per second, self-testing capabilities that automatically check the system components and a high-speed, 16-bit microprocessor.

Performance: Operating at speeds measured in millionths of a second, the IBM Personal Computer can generate and display charts, graphs, text and numerical information. Business applications—including accounts receivable and word processing—can be run on the same system with applications covering personal finance and home entertainment.

Service: The IBM Personal Computer will be serviced by IBM and by a nationwide network of authorized IBM Personal Computer dealers designed to provide the high standards of service associated with all IBM products.

Color/Graphics: The capabilities provide users with a text system capable of displaying 256 characters in any of 16 foreground and 8 background colors. It is also capable of displaying graphics in four colors.

Compact Size: The main processor or system unit—about the size of a portable typewriter—contains expandable memory and a built-in speaker for audio and music applications.

Expandability: A starter system consisting of a keyboard and system unit can be connected to a home television set with a frequency modulator. It can then be expanded to a system with its own display, printer and auxiliary storage cassettes or diskettes. The computer can be used with color or black-and-white television sets. Information from centralized data banks such as Dow Jones News/Retrieval Service and THE SOURCE* can be accessed and displayed.

(*THE SOURCE—Source Telecomputing Corp.)

[10]Ibid.

[11]The author gratefully acknowledges the public information and marketing divisions of Tandy and Radio Shack for their cooperation in providing material on the TRS-80 series, as well as on the history of Tandy Corporation. History may show that just as KDKA received credit for being the first radio station mostly because of a well-oiled public-information effort, companies such as Radio Shack may achieve a more substantial place in history simply because they were willing to supply a wealth of information on their products during this early era of personal computers, which historians will be able to draw upon in years to come. Also helpful was S. Miastkowski, "Three New TRS-80 Computers: A Product Report," *onComputing,* Winter 1980, provided by the public-information office of Radio Shack.

[12]Early industry releases on the Model 100 and Tandy's move to more powerful yet portable computers are discussed in R. A. Shaffer, "Tandy May Have a Hot Seller in Planned Portable Computer," *Wall Street Journal,* January 28, 1983, p. 23, and "Tandy Hopes to Create Market In Notebook-Sized Computers," *Wall Street Journal,* March 25, 1983, p. 25.

[13]The advertising and marketing efforts behind the introduction of the Timex Sinclair 1000 are reported in R. Raissman, "Times Raises Its Ad Sights," *Advertising Age,* 53 (August 30, 1983), 3, 52.

[14]See "Tomorrow Has Arrived," *Forbes,* February 15, 1982, pp. 111–19.

[15]See J. Pournelle, "The Osborne Executive and Executive II," *Byte,* May 1983, pp. 38–44; and "Riding the Success of Hot Product, Osborne Computer is Going Public," *Wall Street Journal,* January 19, 1983, p. 23.

CHAPTER 6

[1]*American Heritage Dictionary* (New York: American Heritage Publishing Co. and Houghton Mifflin, 1973), p. 45. There are many applications of the term other than to physics and electronics. Mathematicians define amplitude as "the maximum ordinate value of a periodic curve," and astronomers view it as "the angular distance along the horizon from true east or west to the intersection of the vertical circle of a celestial body with the horizon" Ibid.

[2]Ibid., p. 696.

[3]See "FM Broadcast Channel Frequency Spacing," FCC/OCE RS 75–80.

[4]Lou Dorren, "Editorial," *FM 4-Channel Forum,* June, July 1976, p. 1.

[5]"California Quad 'Network' Broadcast a Resounding Success," *FM 4-Channel Forum,* 1 (October/November 1976), 4.

[6]Ibid.

[7]"Radio Production: Four Times Better in Quad," *FM 4-Channel Forum, 1* (October/November, 1976), *1.*

[8]See "Do We Want Discrete Four-Channel Stereo for FM?" *Broadcast Management/Engineering,* 12 (February 1976), 40–46.

[9]Ibid., p. 3. Emphasis on AM stereo was voiced at the 1976 meeting of the National Association of Radio Broadcasters.

[10]"The Road Ahead Looks Smooth for AM Stereo," *Broadcast Management/Engineering,* 12 (February 1976), 48–50. If a station already has FM stereo equipment, simulcasting stereo AM is possible, although the FCC has strict nonduplication-of-programming rules.

[11]The video portion of the signal is sent over AM, the audio signal by FM. "The effective radiated power of the aural transmitter shall not be less than 10 percent nor more than 20 percent of the peak radiated power of the visual transmitter" (FCC Rules 73.682 (a) (15)). The FCC Rules 73.881 define the television broadcast band as "the frequencies . . . extending from 54-890 megahertz which are assignable to television stations. These frequencies are 54 to 72 megahertz (channels 2 and 4), 76 to 88 megahertz (channels 5 and 6), 174 to 216 megahertz (channels 7 through 13), and 470

to 890 megahertz (channels 14 through 83).'' Because channel 6 is part of the FM broadcast band, it can be heard on the lower end of most FM radios. Approximately 4 mHz of the frequency range allocated to television stations are used for video transmission (FCC Rules 73.699, figure 5).

[12]Not to be confused with the three primary pigment colors: red, yellow, and blue.

[13]FCC Rules 73.11(a). There can be interference from either ground-wave or sky-wave propagation. In presenting charts to measure the coverage of ground waves, Section 73.184 of the FCC Rules defines ground-wave field intensity as ''that part of the vertical component of the electric field received on the ground which has not been reflected from the ionosphere nor the troposphere.''

[14]FCC Rules 73.11(b): ''The signal is subject to intermittent variations in intensity.''

[15]FCC Rules 73.11(c).

[16]FCC Rules 73.21(a).

[17]The specific definition of a regional channel in FCC Rules 73.21(b) (1) is ''one on which several stations may operate with powers not in excess of 5 kilowatts. The primary service area of a station operating on any such channel may be limited to a given field intensity contour as a consequence of interference.''

[18]The frequency 89.1 in New York City is reserved for the United Nations station.

[19]An inefficient and not necessarily distortion-free system.

[20]Information on ITU activities may be found in annual ITU reports and the *Yearbook of the United Nations.*

[21]FCC Rules 73.183(b), 73.183(c).

CHAPTER 7

[1]''Video Entertainment Offers Chicago Its First Pay TV Channel via Microwave,'' *Communications News,* 13 (September 1975), 14.

[2]See D. Dean VanUitert, ''Microwave Expands Campus Borders,'' *Educational and Industrial Television,* 6 (November 1974), 58–59, 60–63.

[3]This link is known as the Indiana Higher Education Telecommunications System (IHETS).

[4]See Richard Witkin, ''Live Images Transmitted Across Ocean First Time,'' *New York Times,* July 11, 1962, p. 16, and ''Europeans Beam First Television to Screens in U.S.,'' *New York Times,* July 12, 1962, pp. 1, 12. The specific agreement, ''Cooperative Agreement between the National Aeronautics and Space Administration and the American Telephone and Telegraph Company for the Development and Exper-

imental Testing of Active Communications Satellites'' provided backup launching systems and stipulated that all data resulting from the experiments were to be made available to NASA.

[5]Anthony Lewis, ''Sarnoff Suggests Industry Merger,'' *New York Times,* August 8, 1962, pp. 1, 14.

[6]Western Union eventually established its own satellite system.

[7]Jack Gould, ''TV: Telstar and World Broadcasting,'' *New York Times,* July 11, 1962, p. 71.

[8]Leonard H. Marks summarized these events in an article in the *Journal of Broadcasting* entitled ''Communication Satellites: New Horizons for Broadcasters,'' 9 (Spring 1965), 97–101. The article also summarized issues and asked probing questions.

[9]This account of the launch of Syncom II and Hughes Aircraft Company's part in it draws upon ''Mr. Watson I Want You,'' *Vectors,* 15 (Summer, Fall 1973), 7–9.

[10]Our account of INTELSAT organization is drawn from the 1980 Annual report to Congress COMSAT's pp. 29–32.

[11]''Interactive Satellite ATS-6 Brings People Together,'' *Broadcast Management Engineering,* 10 (November 1974), 30–44.

[12]Information on the Westar series was obtained from ''*Westar* Satellite Backgrounder,'' a publication of Western Union, July 1981.

[13]Specifications for Advanced Westar are as follows:

Frequency bands	Advanced Westar C-band coverage at 4-GHz transmit, 6-GHz receive; new K-band coverage at 12-GHz transmit, 14-GHz receive.
Solar cells	Solar arrays will provide 1,700 watts of power.
Coverage ''footprint''	C-band: 48 contiguous states—33 dbw EIRP; Alaska and Hawaii—26/28 dbw EIRP, respectively. K-band—three regional, plus four spot beams (40 to 50 dbw).
Relay capacity (each transponder)	C-band: 1,500 one-way voice circuits, or one color TV signal with audio or data at up to 60 Mbps. K-band (full system) will provide up to 1,000 Mbps transmission capacity.

Satellite manufacturer	TRW Inc., Redondo Beach, California.
Launch vehicle	NASA's Space Shuttle.
Major earth station	White Sands, New Mexico; will perform tracking, telemetry, and command functions.
Orbital location	79 degrees WL.
Overall dimensions of satellite	57.2 feet by 42.6 feet.
Number of antennas	Six—a combination of five C-band K-band antennas, three steerable by ground command, plus an S-band antenna for NASA/TDRSS use.
Diameter of two "umbrella type" antennas	16.0 feet.
Approximate weight of satellite in orbit at beginning of life	4,700 pounds.
Transmission channels	Twelve transponders at C-band, each with 36-MHz usable bandwidth; four transponders at K-band, each with 225-MHz bandwidth (250 Mbps capacity).

(Ibid.)

[14]See the discussion of the properties of K-band frequencies in James Martin, *Future Developments in Telecommunications,* 2nd ed. (Englewood Cliffs, N.J.: Prentice-Hall, 1977), pp. 412–15.

[15]The seven major Western Union earth stations are as follows:

1. Glenwood, New Jersey (near New York)	Serves the metro areas of Boston, Buffalo, Philadelphia, Baltimore, Wilmington, New York, Pittsburgh, and Washington, D.C. Performs tracking, telemetry, and command functions and directs station-keeping adjustments for Westar satellites.
2. Estil Fork, Alabama (near Atlanta)	Serves the Atlanta metro area and beams antenna-adjustment signals to the Westar satellites.
3. Lake Geneva, Wisconsin (near Chicago)	Serves the metro areas of Milwaukee, Detroit, Cleveland, St. Louis, Chicago, Indianapolis, Dayton, Columbus, and Minneapolis/St. Paul.
4. Steele Valley, California	Serves the Los Angeles area.
5. Cedar Hill, Texas (near Dallas)	Serves the metro areas of Kansas City, Dallas, and Houston. Performs as onshore terminal for Westar satellite service to offshore drilling rigs in the Gulf of Mexico and beams antenna-adjustment signals to the Westar satellites.
6. Sky Valley, California (near San Francisco)	Serves the San Francisco area.
7. Issaquah, Washington (near Seattle)	Serves the Seattle area.

(Ibid.)

[16]See "Satnet," *COMSAT,* 3 (1981), 26–27.

[17]A key component of the TDMA system are the four Satellite Interface Message Processors (Satellite IMPs), which handle both the packeting of messages and the sequence in which the packets are distributed. Each Satellite IMP is a partially pre-programmed Honeywell 316 computer.

The job of getting electronic packets on and off the radio-frequency equipment at the earth stations is handled by the four Packet Satellite Project terminals in the system.

Another component in the system is the Linear Predictive Vocoder, which provides live speech from the digital packetized message stream.

To keep the system synchronized, users program each Satellite IMP in SATNET to issue a signal burst of 30 to 40 milliseconds to every other terminal in its own separate time slot every 1.3 seconds. Each Satellite IMP issues a total of 66,000 such bursts a day.

The packeting of messages occurs in the Satellite IMP. The sender of the message has already coded into the message an indication of priority. For example, speech, because it must be "live" or "real time," receives first priority and will be held in "storage" by the Satellite IMP the shortest amount of time possible. Both computer-data and facsimile-data messages can be held longer. Using an algorithm programmed into it, the Satellite IMP will then break the message into packets no longer than two thousand bits or, in the case of speech, two hundred milliseconds. The Satellite IMP then directs the transmission of the packets at preassigned time slots. (Ibid., p. 27)

[18]See "Comsat Subsidiary Launches Proposal for Satellite-To-Home Subscription TV Service," COMSAT, December 17, 1980.

[19]See "Good News, Bad News in DBS Space-rush," *Broadcasting,* July 20, 1981, pp. 23–26.

[20]Ibid. See also "Another Satellite Plan from Comsat," *Broadcasting,* November 23, 1981, pp. 29–30.

[21]See R. T. Wigand, "Direct Satellite Broadcasting: Selected Social Implications," *Communication Yearbook 6,* ed. M. Burgoon (Beverly Hills, Calif.: Sage, 1982), pp. 250–88.

[22]Marks, "Communication Satellites," p. 100.

[23]Dallas W. Smythe, "Space-Satellite Broadcasting: Threat or Promise?" *Journal of Broadcasting,* 4 (Summer 1960), 193–94.

[24]Arthur D. Little, Inc., "Federal Regulatory System Seen as Inadequate to Requirement for Orderly Telecommunications Change" (Cambridge, Mass., 1976).

[25]Ithiel De Sola Pool, "The Communications Revolution in an Interdependent World," *Toward an American Agenda for a New World Order of Communications* (Washington, D.C.: U.S. National Commission for UNESCO, Department of State), p. 35. An interesting view from industry comes from COMSAT:

> One point that needs to be stressed is that research and development advances alone will not remove international political and social constraints. For example, applications in the 20-to-30-GHz range and new satellite configurations will be more costly than existing technology and thus less attractive to developing countries. In the specific case of the work in the 20-to-30-GHz range, high rainfall in the moist tropical areas where many developing countries are located presents a technological problem to be overcome in applications there. Any technology transfer must be carefully fitted to the economic, political, and technological capabilities of the recipient countries. Where the needs of developing countries are concerned, the major barriers to the transfer of satellite technology today are institutional rather than technological. *COMSAT,* 2 (1981), 25.

[26]See, for example, Michael Kinsley, "Is AT&T Hamstringing Comsat?" *New York Times,* June 13, 1976, sec. F, p. 11.

[27]AT&T, *1975 Annual Report to Shareholders,* p. 5.

CHAPTER 8

[1]Susan Q. Kelly (Public Affairs Coordinator, National Cable Television Association), letter to the author, December 8, 1976. Other sources that I found helpful while writing this chapter were D. M. Dozier and J. A. Ledingham, "Perceived Attributes of Interactive Cable Services Among Potential Adopters" (paper presented at the annual meeting of the International Communication Association, Boston, 1982); T. Rimmer, "Making Less Out of More: Cable TV and Some New Twists to Scarcity Theory" (paper presented at the annual meeting of the Speech Communication Association, Louisville, 1982); and L. R. Ekdom, "The First Rural Cooperative Non-Profit Cable System: The Trempealeau County, Wisconsin, Model" (paper presented at the annual meeting of the Speech Communication Association, Louisville, 1982).

[2]Figures are compiled from data supplied by the National Cable Television Association as well as from *Cable Sourcebook* (Washington, D.C.: Broadcasting Publications, 1983).

[3]For example, in Middletown, Connecticut, which TelePrompTer selected for a one-way pay-per-view experiment in 1982 (S. Spillman, "Pay-per-view Cable TV Test Set for Conn.," *Advertising Age,* January 11, 1982, pp. 1, 87).

[4]For an analysis of interconnects see "Cable Interconnects: Making Big Ones Out of Little Ones," *Broadcasting,* March 1, 1982, p. 59.

[5]For a perspective on the atmosphere surrounding the franchising process in the early 1980s, J. Neher, "Cable TV and Politics Mix," *Advertising Age,* 51 (March 24, 1980), 3, 64; "Prospecting for Cable Franchises: The Gold Rush of 1980," *Broadcasting,* March 31, 1980, pp. 35–56; and "Franchising: A Booby Trap for the Cable Industry?" *Broadcasting,* May 26, 1980, pp. 35–36.

[6]See "Prospecting for Cable Franchises," p. 35.

[7]See L. Landro and S. J. Sansweet, "HBO's Dominant Role in Pay-TV Field Faces Increasing Challenges," *Wall Street Journal,* November 8, 1982, pp. 1, 24.

[8]Ibid.

[9]S. Spillman, "Nickelodeon Aiming at Bill-Paying Parents," *Advertising Age,* June 21, 1982, p. 10.

[10]Examples of cable use in secondary education are presented in *Cable Television and Education: A Report From the Field* (Washington, D.C.: National Cable Television Association, 1973).

[11]PlayCable is a trademark of General Instrument. Intellivision is a trademark of Mattel.

[12]See, for example, J. E. Conney, "With Video Shopping Services, Goods You See on the Screen Can Be Delivered to Your Door," *Wall Street Journal,* July 14, 1981, p. 48; and "Vision Cable Airs Home-Shopping Show," *Advertising Age,* August 30, 1982, p. 39.

[13]L. Landro and J. Mayer, "Cable-TV Viewing Study Dims Prospect of Large Increase in Number of Channels," *Wall Street Journal,* November 16, 1982, p. 10.

[14]*Broadcast Management/Engineering* (February 1983), 16. The newspaper in question is the Omaha *World-Herald.*

[15]*Editor and Publisher,* August 7, 1982, p. 40.

[16]A. Radolf, "Cable Newspaper Network Aims for January Debut," *Editor and Publisher,* July 24, 1982, p. 12.

[17]*Cable Television and Education,* p. 8.

[18]*Communication Properties, Inc.,* in 1973 *Annual Report,* p. 11.

[19]Rolland C. Johnson and Donald Agostino, *The Columbus Video Access Center: A Research Evaluation of Audience and Public Attitudes* (Bloomington: Institute for Communication Research, Indiana University, 1974).

[20]Cited by Rudy Bretz, "Public-Access Cable TV: Audiences," *Journal of Communication,* 25 (Summer 1975), 29.

[21]Ibid., p. 30.

[22]Pamela Doty, "Public-Access Cable TV: Who Cares?" *Journal of Communication,* 25 (Summer 1975), 33–41. See also Alan Wurtzel, "Public-Access Cable TV: Programming," *Journal of Communication,* 25 (Summer 1975), 20.

[23]Doty, "Who Cares?"

[24]Ibid.

[25]Clifford M. Kirtland, Jr., "Room for All" (speech delivered at the annual meeting of the Institute of Broadcast Financial Management, Boston, 1976).

[26]Anne W. Branscomb, "The Cable Fable: Will It Come True?" *Journal of Communication,* 25 (Winter 1975), 52.

[27]Rolland C. Johnson and Robert T. Blau, "Single Versus Multiple-System Cable Television," *Journal of Broadcasting,* 18 (Summer 1974), 326.

[28]Ibid., p. 324.

[29]R. E. Park, *Prospects for Cable in the 100 Largest Television Markets* (Santa Monica, Calif.: Rand Corporation, 1971).

[30]For a perspective on the problem of disconnects see S. Spillman, "CATV Operators Churning Over Disconnects," *Advertising Age,* November 15, 1982, 52. "One out of every four consumers who subscribe to more than one pay service disconnects everything each year, and almost all who buy three or four services disconnect one or more of the channels they've purchased," said Charles Townsend, vice-president of marketing for United Cable. "It's incredible. Can you imagine if that many loyal Heinz ketchup users stopped using that brand every year? It's very, very bad news." According to Doug Wenger, director of marketing, for Storer Cable, "Selling subscribers multiple pay services is no problem; retaining them is. When we finally got around to looking at it, we realized a lot of it was never sticking."

Said Jerry Maglio, vice-president of marketing for Daniels & Associates, "Disconnect rates have increased excessively. So much so that some operators are re-evaluating their plans to introduce new services." (Ibid.)

[31]See "Wiring the Untouchables," *Broadcasting,* September 13, 1982, p. 38.

[32]S. Spillman, "Program Listings Plaguing Cablecasters," *Advertising Age,* June 10, 1982, p. 12.

[33]Ibid.

[34]Ibid.

[35]See J. B. Hull, "Cable-TV Service Is Often Shoddy; Industry's Rapid Growth is Blamed," *Wall Street Journal,* August 13, 1982, p. 19.

[36]"Cable's Weak Spot: 'Pathetic' Customer Service," *Advertising Age Electronic Media Edition,* June 10, 1982, p. 19.

[37]Ibid.

[38]Ibid.

[39]Issues affecting cable, including the new technologies of videotex (to be discussed in the next chapter), are dealt with in the following articles in the Spring 1983 issue of *Journal of Broadcasting:* J. G. Webster, "The Impact of Cable and Pay Cable Television on Local Station Audiences," pp. 119–26; L. B. Becker, S. Dunwoody, and S. Rafaeli, "Cable's Impact on Use of Other News Media," pp. 127–40; R. V. Ducey, D. M. Krugman, and D. Eckrich, "Predicting Market Segments in the Cable Industry: The Basic and Pay Subscribers," pp. 155–61; V. Sparkes, "Public Perception of and Reaction to Multi-Channel Cable Television Service," pp. 163–75; and J. Collins, J. Reagan, and J. D. Abel, "Predicting Cable Subscribership: Local Factors," pp. 177–83.

CHAPTER 9

[1]B. Loveless, "The Broadcasting of Teletext," *Educational and Industrial Television,* 16 (June 1979), 34–35.

[2]My discussion of A-, B-, and C-type pages is based on pp. 34–35 of the Loveless article.

[3]Ibid., p. 35. See also "U.S. in Need of Videotex Primer," *Advertising Age Electronic Media Edition,* June 10, 1982, p. 23.

[4]W. Paisley, "Computerizing Information Lessons of a Videotex Trial," *Journal of Communication,* Winter 1983, p. 155.

[5]Information on the Prestel system was provided by Prestel. See also M. Edwards, "Videotex/Teletext Services Poised for Major Growth in United States," *Communications News,* 19 (August 1982), 88–92.

[6]Edwards, ''Videotex/Teletext.''

[7]Ibid.

[8]See, for example, ''Teletext: TV Gets Married to the Printed Word,'' *Broadcasting,* August 20, 1979, pp. 30–36.

[9]Edwards, ''Videotex/Teletext,'' p. 90. Specific differences between the early British and French systems and the Telidon system can be seen in Edwards' account: The British and French systems use an *alphamosaic* coding scheme, whereby the picture is built from a matrix of individual dots; binary codes control the shape, color, and shading of picture elements formed from the dots. In the Telidon system images are described and stored in the data base as geometric shapes, which are placed at specific positions in the overall image. This *alphageometric* coding enables Telidon to provide a resolution of 240 by 320 picture elements, compared with 72 by 80 picture elements for the other systems. However, Telidon's improved resolution and other enhanced capabilities come at the expense of extra memory in the receiving terminal. (Ibid., pp. 89–90)

[10]Ibid., p. 90.

[11]Ibid.

[12]Ibid.

[13]Ibid.

[14]See P. K. McCarthy, ''Interactive Television: A Direct Marketing Tool,'' *Direct Marketing,* 42 (February 1980) 30–46.

[15]Ibid., p. 31.

[16]Ibid.

[17]The others were the Consumers Union, the American Cancer Society, Macmillan, the *New York Times,* Dow Jones & Company, HP Books, *Congressional Quarterly,* Addison-Wesley, the *Economist,* the Intercontinental Press Syndicate, and CBS Publications. See A. Radolf, ''Knight-Ridder to Test Home Electronic Info System,'' *Editor and Publisher,* April 12, 1980, pp. 7–8.

[18]The other advertisers were Shell Oil, Spec's Music, Bass Tickets, Service Merchandise, Cousins Associates, Shell's City Liquors, Master Host Dinner Service, Merrill Lynch, B. Dalton Booksellers, Grand Union, Southeast Banking, Official Airline Guides, AAA World Wide Travel Agency, and Goldberg's Marine Distributors.

[19]CBS–AT&T press release, October 1, 1981.

[20]For an account of the Green Thumb project, see W. Paisley, ''Computerizing Information: Lessons of a Videotex Trial,'' *Journal of Communication,* Winter 1983, pp. 153–61.

[21]Ibid., p. 156.

[22]K. K. Goodfriend, N. J. Bamberger, D. M. Dozier, and J. P. Witherspoon, *KPBS Interactive Videotex Project* (San Diego: KPBS-TV, 1982), p. 3.

[23]''Who's Doing What With Teletext: A Round Up of Teletext/Videotex Experiments in the United States and Canada,'' *Educational and Instructional Broadcasting,* October 1981, pp. 48–49.

[24]''Lotteries for LPTV; Go-Ahead for Teletext,'' *Broadcasting,* April 4, 1983, pp. 31–32.

[25]''U.S. in Need of Videotex Primer,'' p. 23.

[26]Ibid.

[27]Ibid.

[28]Ibid.

[29]Ibid.

[30]Ibid.

[31]The author is grateful to Time Video Information Services for providing material on the Time teletext experiments.

[32]R. Gingras, ''Design and Packaging of the Electronic Publication,'' *Videotex Teletext News,* October 1981, p. 1.

[33]Ibid.

[34]Ibid.

[35]Ibid., p. 4. See also T. Boulton, ''Perceptual Factors That Influence the Adoption of Videotex Technology: Results of the Channel 2000 Field Test,'' *Journal of Broadcasting,* 27 (Spring 1983), 141–53.

[36]*Viewtron Newsletter,* 2 (June 28, 1982), 5.

[37]Ibid.

[38]Ibid.

[39]*Synthesis of Findings for AP/Newspaper/Compuserve Program of Marketing Research* (Fair Lawn, N.J.: RMH Research, 1982), pp. 20–21.

[40]Ibid.

[41]*Viewtron Newsletter,* p. 5.

[42]As described in literature on the Cox INTAX System, Cox Broadcasting, Atlanta.

[43]Many of these examples of electronic-banking services are drawn from the Cox system.

[44]K. Bissell, ''A Break Through in Factfinding: Online World Book,'' *Today,* January/February, 1983, p. 27.

[45]Official Airline Guide press release, 1983.

CHAPTER 10

[1]A. C. Deichmiller, ''Advances in Fiber Optics are Spurring Broadband Services to Home and Office,'' *Communications News,* 18 (January 1981), 52–53.

[2]''First Network TV Program Via a Lightwave Link,'' *Communications News,* 17 (January 1980), 54.

[3]GTE press release, April 25, 1977.

4Literature from the Cable Television Division of Times Fiber Communications, Wallingford, Connecticut.

5Background on multipoint distribution service can be found in *New Technologies Affecting Radio and Television Broadcasting* (Washington, D.C.: National Association of Broadcasters, 1981), pp. 6–7.

6See, for example, "Small Earth Stations Blossom Into Big Businesses," *Broadcasting,* December 22, 1980, pp. 32, 34, 35, 38. See also *SMATV: Strategic Opportunities in Private Cable* (Washington, D.C.: National Association of Broadcasters, 1982).

7*SMATV,* pp. 28–29.

8See the National Association of Broadcasters research report *Subscription Television* (Washington, D.C., 1980).

9See, for example, *New Technologies,* p. 20.

10Ibid. Early tests of HDTV systems were reported in "Factoring HDTV in Planning for RARC," *Broadcasting,* June 21, 1982, pp. 79–80; "HDTV, Digital Star at Opryland," *Broadcasting,* February 8, 1982, pp. 34–35; B. Benson, "High Definition Television: An Update," *Broadcast Engineering,* August 1982, pp. 38, 42, 44, 46; "HDTV: The Look of Tomorrow Today," *Broadcasting,* March 2, 1981, pp. 34–35; "Clear Advantages to High Resolution," *Broadcasting,* February 16, 1981, pp. 30–32; "SONY Does it Again in HDTV," *Broadcasting,* March 4, 1981, p. 29; and J. B. Birge, "High Definition TV," *SAT Guide,* September 1982, pp. 17, 57.

11See *New Technologies,* pp. 14–16.

12For two perspectives on cellular radiotelephone services, see "Cellular Radio," *Broadcasting,* June 7, 1982, pp. 38–42; and W. Ginsberg, "New Cellular Radio Systems Promise Bright Future for Entrants and Users," *Broadcasting,* March 1982, pp. 36–37. Control over cellular radio telephone systems was initially a controversial regulatory issue, which centered on the stake AT&T would have in developing cellular radio in competition with other companies. The Justice Department said AT&T's involvement would be "blatantly anti-competitive." (United Press International, January 3, 1982)

13N. Sweet, "Airplane Phoning Gets Off the Ground," *Crains Chicago Business,* January 17, 1983, p. T10. This article describes one of the first plane-to-ground telephone services.

14Ibid. Refer also to the two articles cited in note 12. The same concept of cell-to-cell switching that is embodied in cellular radiotelephone systems is also utilized in plane-to-ground systems.

15Two reports from the trade press are E. Gold, "Trends in Teleconferencing Today Indicate Increasing Corporate Use," *Communications News,* 19 (October 1982), 48–49; and "Teleconferencing Today," *Communications News,* 19 (February 1982), 43–66.

16See, for example, R. Anderson, "Satellite-Aided Land Mobile Radio System Could Prove Cost Effective," *Communications News,* 18 (March 1981), 56–59.

17This system is based on the Dow Jones Alert News Service. See "Dow Alert Service Spawns New Generation for Radio," *Electronic Media,* January 13, 1983, pp. 5, 20.

18R. A. Shaffer, "Promising Uses Are Emerging for Millimeter Radio Signals," *Wall Street Journal,* June 26, 1981, p. 29.

19Ibid.

20A National Association of Broadcasters research report on radio services quoted Emil L. Torick, Director of Audio Development for the CBS Technology Center, as predicting the change to digital radio. See M. L. DeSonne, *Radio, New Technology, and You* (Washington, D.C.: National Association of Broadcasters, 1982), p. 24. A perspective on digital audio can be found in this same report on page 18.

21"Thin Is In," *Broadcasting,* May 5, 1980, p. 80.

22Mark R. Levy, "Home Video Recorders and Time Shifting," *Journalism Quarterly,* Autumn 1981, pp. 404–5.

23Ibid.

CHAPTER 11

1The author is grateful for material furnished by the three commercial networks, numerous syndication companies, and the wire services.

2The author is especially grateful to the staff of the public information department at ABC, which provided many original documents dealing with the history of that network.

3D. Mermigas, "ABC Basking in 'Winds' Glow," *Advertising Age Electronic Media Edition,* February 17, 1983, p. 1.

4Ibid.

5S. Flax, "Staying Tuned to Tomorrow," *Forbes,* 130 (July 19, 1982), 66–72.

6Ibid., pp. 68–69.

7Ibid.

8Martin Mayer, writing in *American Film,* April 1981, pp. 26, 28, noted that "Every reporter who feels the slightest pride in his calling must have glowed while watching The Secret Negotiations. Those who saw it will know, and those who missed it cannot hope entirely to understand, the enormous excitement one felt as this package was unwrapped."

9"Westinghouse, ABC to Joint Venture Into 24-

hour Cable News Programming," *Broadcasting,* August 17, 1981, pp. 27-29.

[10]An account of the incident can be found in "CBS Concedes Error in TV Documentary on War in Vietnam," *Wall Street Journal,* July 16, 1982, p. 29.

[11]ABC Radio Network promotional literature (New York). For more on the ABC radio networks, see the National Association of Broadcasters publication *Radioactive,* February, 1981, pp. 12-15.

[12]ABC Radio Network promotional literature.

[13]Ibid.

[14]Ibid.

[15]See "CBS Radio Readies New Youth Network," *Advertising Age,* 52 (July 20, 1981), 14.

[16]From the UPI Advisory Board bylaws provided the author by UPI.

[17]H. Allen, "Black America's All-News Radio," *Advertising Age,* 52 (June 29, 1981), S-9.

[18]*Changing Media: An Ogilvy and Mather Commentary on the New Media Technologies,* 1 (December 1981), 7.

[19]Ibid., p. 2.

[20]Ibid.

[21]Ibid., p. 3.

[22]For example, see J. Mayer, "NBC, ABC May Cut Some Reruns To Counter Cable-TV Competition," *Wall Street Journal,* February 1, 1983, p. 35.

CHAPTER 12

[1]The account of this broadcast is drawn from C. C. Clark, "Television in Education," *School and Society,* 48 (October 1, 1938), 431-32.

[2]"Metropolitan Art Is to Be Televised," *New York Times,* May 26, 1941, p. 21.

[3]The account of this series is based on "NBC's Educational Television Series," *School and Society,* 63 (February 16, 1947), 110.

[4]William M. Dennis, "Transition to Visual Education," *National Education Association Journal,* 35 (October 1946), 424.

[5]Amo DeBernardis and James W. Brown, "A Study of Teacher Skills and Knowledge Necessary for the Use of Audio-Visual Aids," *Elementary School Journal,* 46 (June 1946), 550-56.

[6]"A Research Fellowship in Television Education," *School and Society,* 69 (April 16, 1949), 278.

[7]"The U.S. Commissioner of Education on Television," *School and Society,* 72 (December 23, 1950), 427.

[8]"Colleges and Universities Prepare Television Programs," *School and Society,* 72 (September 2, 1950), 155-56.

[9]Ibid., *School and Society,* 72 (October 3, 1951), 44.

[10]These issues were summarized by Vivian Powell, then president of the National Education Association's Department of Classroom Teachers, in "Here's How Teachers Look at ITV," *National Education Association Journal,* 57 (November 1957), 506.

[11]For a history of the MPATI, see Norman Felsenthal, "MPATI: A History 1959-1971," *Educational Broadcasting Review,* 5 (December 1971), 36-44.

[12]See Richard J. Stonesifer, "The Separation Needed Between ETV and ITV," *AV Communication Review,* 14 (Winter 1966), 489-97.

[13]Ibid., p. 490, quoting Doris Willens, "ETV: An Uncertain Trumpet," *Television Magazine,* 21 (February 1964).

[14]A recent assessment of the relationship of learning to the educational process is found in J. Bryant, A. Alexander, and D. Brown, "Learning From Educational Television Programmes" (paper presented at the annual meeting of the Speech Communication Association, Louisville, 1982); to appear in *Learning From Television,* ed. M.J.A. Howe (London: Academic Press, 1983).

[15]The accountability issue has appeared in all instructional media, not just ITV.

[16]The answer to this question frequently attracts the attention of teachers' unions.

[17]*Public Television: A Program for Action. Report of the Carnegie Commission on Educational Television* (New York: Bantam, 1967), Preface.

[18]Ibid.

[19]*Corporation for Public Broadcasting, 1981 Annual Report* (Washington, D.C.: Corporation for Public Broadcasting, 1981), p. 11.

[20]Ibid., p. 18.

[21]Ibid., supplement sheet.

[22]J. Alter, " 'Anointed Ten' Hash Out Rules for PBS Ad Test," *Advertising Age,* March 15, 1982, p. 48.

[23]"PBS Ends 'Sponsor' Taboos," *Advertising Age,* July 5, 1982, p. 4.

[24]For accounts of these ventures in cable and pay TV, see " 'Grand Alliance' Now 'PBS/Cable,' " *Broadcasting,* July 6, 1981, p. 34; "PBS Begets PSN," *Broadcasting,* February 9, 1981, p. 31; "PBS Opts for Pay," *Broadcasting,* November 24, 1980, p. 63; and D. Mermigas, "PBS Studies STV Shift," *Advertising Age Electronic Media Edition,* January 27, 1983, pp. 1, 22. See also D. Agostino, "Cable Television's Impact on the Audience of Public Television," *Journal of Broadcasting,* 24 (Summer 1980), 347-65.

[25]*Corporation for Public Broadcasting, 1981 Annual Report,* supplement sheet.

[26]Ibid.

[27]See "NPR Explains New Data Service," *Broadcasting,* June 28, 1981, p. 59.

[28]See M. Gelman, "NPR Adopts Pay Radio for Revenue," *Electronic Media,* September 23, 1982, p. 3.

[29]See "NPR Joins Paging Venture," *Advertising Age Electronic Media Edition,* July 22, 1982, p. 1.

[30]H. B. McCarty, "Educational Radio's Role," *NAEB Journal,* 18 (October 1958), 3-6, 26-29.

[31]"Carnegie Commission II," *Public Telecommunication Review,* 5 (May/June 1977), 13-14.

CHAPTER 13

[1]In 1976 there were 600 companies using television and somewhat more than 700 commercial television stations. But the number of companies had grown twofold in three years, and thus seemed likely to soon overtake the number of commercial stations. Source of corporate estimate: Judith M. Brush, "Private Television Communications," *Matrix,* 62 (Winter 1976-77), 14-15, 30. Today, the figures are much higher.

[2]Ibid., p. 15.

[3]Ibid.

[4]William L. Cathcart, "Television and Industry: How a New Trend Relates to Students," *Feedback,* 18 (May 1976), 11-14.

[5]"Image Building Begins at Home," *Chemical Week,* November 19, 1975, p. 5.

[6]Ibid.

[7]Eugene Marlow, "Programming for a Company Television News Show," *Educational and Industrial Television,* 6 (April 1974), 30, 33-37.

[8]See Greg Stark and Rod Rightmier, "Around the Clock Video for Employee Communication," *Educational and Industrial Television,* 7 (February 1975), 18, 20-21.

[9]The discussion of Deere draws upon "What's on JDTV?" *JD Journal,* 5 (Summer 1976), 7-9; and "Deere and Company: All Out for Quality," *IVC Field Report,* International Video Corporation, 1975.

[10]"Tube Power: Reaching New Frontiers With Reliance Television," *Intercom,* February 1976, pp. 4-5.

[11]"Television Turns on at Owens-Corning," *Dialogue,* October 1974, pp. 4-5.

[12]See the Honeywell brochure *Honeywell Education: Multimedia Instructional Systems* (Wellesley Hills, Mass.: Honeywell, 1976).

[13]See "Holiday Inn's Vidnet System Helps in Training Employees," *Communications News,* 14 (October 1976), 36.

[14]See Warren R. Wille, "The Dana Approach: A Management Information System," *Educational and Industrial Television,* 6 (January 1974), 10-12.

[15]"Extending Our Vision with the Video Communication System," *Viewpoints,* November/December 1976, pp. 16-18.

[16]J. Martin, *The Future of Telecommunications,* 2nd ed. (Englewood Cliffs, N.J.: Prentice-Hall, 1977), p. 387 (italics added).

CHAPTER 14

[1]Sources helpful in the completion of this chapter include E. Shane, "Increasing Your Profits Is the Name of the Game," *Broadcast Communications,* February 1981, pp. 70, 72, 74; "McGavren-Guild Ranks Radio's Most Popular Program Formats," *Broadcasting,* May 2, 1977, pp. 51-52, 54, 56-58; "The Many Worlds of Radio in 1976: A Special Report," *Broadcasting,* September 27, 1976, pp. 34-64 passim, 66-82; T. Ervin, "How Similar Strategy Helps Three Different Stations Maintain Popularity in the Same Market," *Broadcast Magazine,* September 1976, pp. 46, 48; A. Holt, "What Radio Programming Will Be Like in the 80's," *Broadcast Magazine,* March 1977, pp. 28-29, 31-32; "The More Things Change in TV Programming . . . ," *Broadcasting,* February 18, 1980, pp. 72, 74, 78, 82, 92; "Tug of War for the Hearts of Programmers," *Broadcasting,* February 18, 1980, pp. 68, 70; "KING-TV Wins Higher Ratings by Making Its Audience Care," *Broadcast Communications,* February 1981, pp. 64, 66, 68; R. Tomsho, "Wake Up!" *Pittsburgher Magazine,* December 26, 1980, pp. 25-29; "Radio News: Satellites and Narrower Demographics," *Broadcasting,* December 1, 1980, pp. 68, 72, 76, 78; "Radio Syndicators Flourish at NAB," *Broadcast Magazine,* July 1982, pp. 19-20; "Radio Syndication: Offering a World of Programming," *Broadcasting,* August 30, 1982, pp. 76, 78, 80-84; J. Forkan, "Local Stations Block First-Run Fare," *Advertising Age,* July 8, 1982, p. 22; D. Mermigas, " 'Dr. Who' a Surprise Syndication Success," *Electronic Media,* November 4, 1982, p. 16; "A Sour Note for Beautiful Music," *Broadcasting,* August 23, 1982, pp. 52-54; K. McManus, "Music Giant Goes Talk," *Advertising Age,* June 7, 1982, pp. M-10, M-12; B. Rock, "The Way We Were: Tracing the Evolution of Adult Contemporary," *RadioActive,* February 1982, pp. 10-11; C. Reiss, "Ad Outlook Bright for TV Syndication," *Electronic Media,* December 2, 1982, pp. 1, 22; S. Storms, "Hitting the Demographics With Dick

Clark," *RadioActive,* December 1982, p. 10; C. Reiss, "Advertisers in Syndication Shift," *Advertising Age,* November 29, 1982, pp. 1, 70; J. Forkan, "Off-network 'Mandrell' a New Area for Syndicast," *Electronic Media,* February 10, 1983, p. 12; M. Christopher, " 'M*A*S*H,' 'Family Feud' Tops in Syndication Report," *Electronic Media,* September 23, 1982, p. 5; J. Forkan, "Paramount High on Barter Syndication," *Advertising Age,* July 1, 1982, p. 8; B. Marich, "Adults Keep 'Lone Ranger' Riding High in TV Syndication," *Electronic Media,* September 2, 1982, p. 10; and "Programming: Winds of Change Blowing Harder," *Broadcasting,* January 3, 1983, pp. 72–73.

[2]*Radio Program Department Handbook* (Washington, D.C.: WAB, n.d.), p. 10.

[3]*Research Guide for Programming Decision Makers* (Beltsville, Md.: Arbitron, n.d.), p. 9.

[4]*Third Report and Order* in Docket No. 19622, FCC 75-542, May 13, 1975.

CHAPTER 15

[1]*BBC Handbook* (London: BBC, 1977), p. 207. This publication is updated annually.

[2]*Australian Broadcasting Commission Annual Report, 1975–1976.* Updated annually.

[3]Canadian Broadcasting Act of 1968.

[4]The CFCF case is chronicled in both the 1975–76 and 1976–77 CRTC annual reports.

[5]*NKH 1976–77* (Tokyo: NHK, 1977), p. 2.

[6]See Milton Hollstein, "French Broadcasting After the Split," *Public Telecommunication Review,* 6 (January/February 1978), 15–19.

[7]The author acknowledges the generous help he received from MTV and YLE while preparing the paragraphs on Finnish broadcasting. One of the most concise summaries of French broadcasting is found in M. Hollstein, "French Broadcasting After the Split," *Public Telecommunication Review,* 6 (January/February, 1978), 15–19.

[8]See David E. Powell, "Television in the U.S.S.R.," *Public Opinion Quarterly,* 39 (Fall 1975), 287–300.

[9]For additional perspectives on West German and East German broadcasting, see M. S. Snow, "Telecommunications and Media Policy in West Germany: Recent Developments," *Journal of Communication,* 32 (Summer 1982), 10–32; and D. Marks, "Broadcasting Across the Wall: The Free Flow of Information Between East and West Germany," *Journal of Communication,* 32 (Winter 1983), 46–55.

[10]The quotation is from CRTC Annual Report, 1976–1977. For some perspectives on Canadian regulation of the content of broadcasting, E. Allebes and B. H. Petty, "Resurgence of Canadian Nationalism and Its Effect on American-Canadian Communications Relations," *Journal of International Law and Economics,* 9 (1974), 149–73; C. D. Asher, "Purging Madison Avenue From Canadian Television," *Law and Policy in International Business,* 6 (1975), and "Purging Madison Avenue From Canadian Television II," *Law and Policy in International Business,* 9 (1977), 1009–27; W. T. Howell, Jr., "Broadcast Spillover and National Culture: Shared Concerns of the Republic of Ireland and Canada," *Journal of Broadcasting,* 24 (Spring 1980), 225–39; A. Ichikawa, "Canadian-U.S. News Flow: The Continuing Asymmetry," *Canadian Journal of Communication,* 5 (1977), 8–20; D. R. LeDuc, "Cable TV Control in Canada: A Comparative Policy Study," *Journal of Broadcasting,* 20 (Fall 1976), 436–48; R. E. Miller, "The CRTC: Guardian of the Canadian Identity," *Journal of Broadcasting,* 17 (Spring 1973), 189–99; R. P. Nielsen and A. B. Nielsen, "Canadian TV Content Regulations and US Cultural 'Overflow,' " *Journal of Broadcasting,* 20 (Fall 1976), 460–66; K. Swinton, "Advertising and Canadian Cable Television: A Problem in International Law," *Osgoode Hall Law Journal,* 15 (1977), 543–90; E. D. Tate, "Canada and US Differences in Similar TV Story Content," *Canadian Journal of Communication,* 5 (Fall 1977), 1–12; and A. Toogood, "The Canadian Broadcasting System: Search for a Definition," *Journalism Quarterly,* 48 (Fall 1971), 331–36.

[11]Emile G. McAnany, *Radio's Role in Development: Five Strategies of Use* (Washington, D.C.: Academy for Educational Development, 1973), pp. 5–21. McAnany's review of research from international sources is comprehensive, and the student doing serious research on instructional radio will find it valuable.

CHAPTER 16

[1]The Wireless Ship Act of 1910, Public Law 262, 61st Congress, June 24, 1910.

[2]The Radio Act of 1912, Public Law 264, 62nd Congress, August 13, 1912, Sec. 1.

[3]See Edward F. Sarno, Jr., "The National Radio Conferences," *Journal of Broadcasting,* 13 (Spring 1969), 189–202.

[4]Ibid., For a summary of commerce department action during this period, see Marvin R. Bensman, "Regulation of Broadcasting by the Department of Commerce, 1921-1927," in *American Broadcasting: A Source Book on the History of Radio and Televi-*

sion, ed. Lawrence W. Lichty and Malachi C. Topping (New York: Hastings House, 1975), pp. 544–55.

[5]*Hoover* v. *Intercity Radio Co., Inc.* 286 F. 1003 (D. C. Cir), February 25, 1923.

[6]*United States* v. *Zenith Radio Corporation et al.* 12F. 2d 614 (N. D. Ill.), April 16, 1926.

[7]See Eric Barnouw, *A Tower in Babel: A History of Broadcasting in the United States* (New York: Oxford University Press, 1966), p. 175.

[8]Attorney General's Opinion, 35 Ops. Att'y Gen. 126, July 8, 1926.

[9]See H. Doc. 483, 69th Congress, 2nd Session.

[10]The Radio Act of 1927, Public Law 632, 69th Congress, February 23, 1927, Sec. 3.

[11]S. Doc. 144, 73d Congress, 2d Session, February 26, 1934.

[12]Communications Act of 1934, Sec. 326.

CHAPTER 17

[1]*FCC Annual Report, 1974,* pp. 2–3.

[2]The discussion of what the FCC does not control is based on *The FCC and Broadcasting,* FCC Broadcast Bureau publication 8310-100.

[3]However, "staged" news events are not considered to be in the public interest.

[4]*The FCC and Broadcasting.*

[5]The commission's first open meeting is chronicled in "Like a Day With the Sunshine at the FCC," *Broadcasting,* 46 (March 28, 1977), 29. Procedural policy was announced in "FCC in the Sunshine," NAB *Highlights,* 3 (March 7, 1977), 2.

[6]See Nicholas Johnson and John Jay Dystel, "A Day in the Life: The Federal Communications Commission," *Yale Law Journal,* 82 (1973), 1575–1634.

[7]Ibid.

[8]Johnson and Dystel are critical of the rule permitting a maximum of seven AM, FM, or TV stations to be owned by the same company. What was intended as a "per se maximum" has been converted into a "presumptively permissible number." Ibid.

[9]On December 13, 1972. Ibid.

[10]See Lawrence W. Lichty, "Members of the Federal Radio Commission and the Federal Communications Commission 1927-1961," *Journal of Broadcasting,* 6 (Winter 1961-62), 23-24, and "The Impact of FRC and FCC Commissioners' Background on the Regulation of Broadcasting," *Journal of Broadcasting,* 6 (Spring 1962), 97-110.

[11]Wenmouth Williams, Jr., "Impact of Commissioner Background on FCC Decisions: 1962-1975," *Journal of Broadcasting,* 20 (Spring 1976), 239-60.

[12]The discussion of FCC offices is drawn from FCC publications; *FCC Annual Reports; Broadcasting Yearbook;* "How the FCC Is Organized Into Offices and Bureaus," *Communication News,* 14 (January 1977), 46-48; and "FCC Makes Over Broadcast Bureau," *Broadcasting,* 45 (April 5, 1976), 53.

[13]See "FCC Lab Tests Radios for Rule Compliance," *Communication News,* 14 (January 1977), 50.

[14]See *FCC Annual Report,* 1974.

[15]Ibid., p. 78.

[16]Donald M. Gillmor and Jerome A. Barron, *Mass Communication Law* (St. Paul: West, 1974), p. 889, citing Richard Sneed, 15 P. & F. Radio Reg. 158 (1967).

[17]Gillmor and Barron, *Mass Communication Law,* p. 78, citing Mile High Stations, Inc., 28 FCC 795, 20 P. & F. Radio Reg. 345 (1960).

[18]Reported in *Broadcasting,* 46 (June 20, 1977), 68.

[19]*FCC Annual Report,* 1974, pp. 37–38.

[20]Charles Clift III, Fredric A. Weiss, and John D. Abel, "Ten Years of Forfeitures by the Federal Communications Commission," *Journal of Broadcasting,* 15 (Fall 1971).

[21]Ibid., pp. 379-85. The categories are those defined in the Communications Act. The period covered by the study was 1961 through June 1971.

[22]The FCC's authority to issue short-term renewals was granted by the same statute permitting it to issue forfeitures.

[23]*FCC Annual Report,* 1974, p. 37.

[24]Maurice E. Shelby, Jr., "Short-Term License Renewals: 1960-1972," *Journal of Broadcasting,* 18 (Summer 1974), 277-88.

[25]Ibid., p. 282.

[26]Johnson and Dystel, *A Day in the Life.*

[27]Ibid.

[28]Marc C. Franklin, *The First Amendment and the Fourth Estate* (Mineola, N.Y.: Foundation Press, 1977), pp. 465-66.

[29]Ibid., p. 466. Franklin points out the peculiar nature of the electromagnetic spectrum as a resource. For example, although not adhering to regional assignments of frequencies on a domestic scale, international agreements on frequency management are regional. When the overall territory (the world) is big enough, regional allocations are practical. Moreover, the political realities of trying to localize spectrum management on a world scale make such a task almost impossible.

[30]*A Study of the Federal Communications Commission's Equal Employment Opportunity Regulation: An Agency in Search of a Standard* (Washington, D.C.: Citizens Communications Center, 1976).

[31]*Window Dressing on the Set: Women and Mi-*

norities in Television (Washington, D.C.: United States Commission on Civil Rights, 1977).

³²Joseph A. Grundfest, *Citizen Participation in FCC Decision Making* (Santa Monica, Calif.: Rand Corporation, 1976).

³³Erwin G. Krasnow and Lawrence D. Longley, *The Politics of Broadcast Regulation* (New York: St. Martin's, 1973), p. 24.

³⁴Robert R. Smith and Paul T. Prince, "WHDH: The Unconscionable Delay," *Journal of Broadcasting,* 18 (Winter 1973-74), 85-86.

³⁵Sterling Quinlan, *The Hundred Million Dollar Lunch* (Chicago: J. Philip O'Hara, 1974), p. 4.

³⁶"FCC Berated for Policy on Stockholdings of the Employees," *Broadcasting,* 46 (May 30, 1977), 28, 30.

³⁷Johnson and Dystel, *A Day in the Life.*

³⁸*Your FTC: What It Is and What It Does* (Washington, D.C.: Federal Trade Commission, 1977), p. 19.

³⁹Ibid., p. 17.

⁴⁰Ibid., p. 16.

⁴¹Ibid., pp. 13-15.

⁴²See "The FTC Advertising Review Process," *Advertising Age,* 48 (July 11, 1977), 142.

⁴³*Your FTC,* p. 26.

⁴⁴*OTA Priorities 1979* (Washington, D.C.: Office of Technology Assessment, 1979), p. i.

⁴⁵Ibid., p. 15.

⁴⁶Discussions of the history, organization, and function of the ITU and of issues it faces can be found in David M. Leive, *International Telecommunications and International Law: The Regulation of the Radio Spectrum* (Dobbs Ferry, N.Y.: Oceana, 1971); and *Global Communications in the Space Age: Toward a New ITU* (New York: John and Mary R. Markle Foundation and the Twentieth Century Fund, 1972).

⁴⁷Harold K. Jacobson, "The International Telecommunication Union: ITU's Structures and Functions," in *Global Communications in the Space Age,* p. 40.

⁴⁸Final Protocol, Documents of the Berlin Preliminary Conference (1903), cited in Leive, *International Telecommunications and International Law,* pp. 83-85. The thrust of the protocol agreement survives in contemporary broadcast regulations.

⁴⁹International Telecommunication Convention (Montreux, 1965). See also Jacobson, "The International Telecommunication Union," pp. 40-41.

⁵⁰*United Nations Yearbook,* 27 (1973), 955.

⁵¹The discussion of ITU organization draws upon Leive, *International Telecommunications and International Law,* pp. 32-40; and *Global Communications in the Space Age,* pp. 6-7.

CHAPTER 18

¹Lee Loevinger, "The Role of Law in Broadcasting," *Journal of Broadcasting,* 8 (Spring 1964), 115-17.

²Ibid.

³See, for example, V. Blasi, "The Newsman's Privilege: An Empirical Study," 70 *Michigan Law Review,* 233 (December 1971).

⁴Loevinger, "The Role of Law in Broadcasting," pp. 115-17.

⁵Section 73.120. Two publications have updated rules and regulations and have provided broadcasters with guidelines for interpreting Section 315: *Uses of Broadcast and Cablecast Facilities by Candidates for Public Office,* Fed. Reg. 5796; and *Licensee Responsibility Under Amendments to the Communications Act of 1971,* FCC Public Notice, June 5, 1974, 47 FCC 516 (1974).

⁶Gillmor and Barron, *Mass Communication Law,* p. 230. The case in question is *Farmers Educational and Cooperative Union of America, North Dakota Division* v. *WDAY,* 89 N. W. 2d 102, 109 (N. D. 1958).

⁷*Farmers Educational and Cooperative Union of America* v. *WDAY Inc.,* 360 U.S. 525, 79 S. Ct. 1302, 3 L. Ed. 2d 1407 (1959).

⁸"Reinterpretation of Equal Time Passes First Court Challenge," *Broadcasting,* 45 (April 19, 1976), 26-27.

⁹74 Sta. 554 (1960). See also Gillmor and Barron, p. 797.

¹⁰*Use of Broadcast and Cablecast Facilities by Candidates for Public Office,* FCC Public Notice, March 16, 1972; 37 Fed. Reg. 5804, March 21, 1972.

¹¹*In the Matter of Editorializing by Broadcast Licensees,* 13 FCC 1246, June 1, 1949.

¹²Great Lakes Broadcasting Co., 3 F. R. C. Ann. Rep. 32 (1929), modified on other grounds, 37, F. 2d 993 (D. C. Cir.) certiorari dismissed, 281 U. S. 706 (1930), cited in Franklin, p. 601.

¹³*In the Matter of the Mayflower Broadcasting Corporation and The Yankee Network, Inc. (WAAB),* 8 FCC 333, 338, January 16, 1941.

¹⁴Ibid.

¹⁵*In reference to United Broadcasting Co. (WHKC),* 10 FCC 515 June 26, 1945.

¹⁶*In reference to Petition of Robert Harold Scott for Revocation of Licenses of Radio Stations KQW, KPO and KFRC,* 11 FCC 372, July 19, 1946.

¹⁷Ibid.

¹⁸*In the Matter of Editorializing by Broadcast Licensees,* 13 FCC 1246, June 1, 1949.

¹⁹*Applicability of the Fairness Doctrine in the*

Handling of Controversial Issues of Public Importance, 29 Fed. Reg. 10416, July 25, 1964.

[20]*Red Lion Broadcasting Co.* v. *Federal Communications Commission,* 127 U. S. App. D. C. 129, 381 F. 2d 908 (1967). This case and the ones cited in notes 21 and 22 are well documented in numerous legal texts. The reader is referred to the latest edition of Gillmor and Barron, for a detailed discussion as well as for pertinent questions on the decision.

[21]*Radio-Television News Directors Association* v. *United States,* 400 F.2d 1002 (7th Cir. 1968).

[22]*Red Lion Broadcasting Co., Inc.* v. *Federal Communications Commission. United States* v. *Radio-Television News Directors Association.* 395 U.S. 367, 89 S. Ct. 1794, 23 L. Ed. 2d 371 (1969).

[23]The Fairness Doctrine, as amended.

[24]Ibid.

[25]See "Fairness Case Goes Against Eight California Radio Stations," *Broadcasting,* 45 (May 24, 1976), 40, 42. A discussion of the legal aspects of editorial advertising is found in Milan D. Meeske, "Editorial Advertising and the First Amendment," *Journal of Broadcasting,* 17 (Fall 1973), 417–26.

[26]*In the Matter of Handling of Public Issues Under the Fairness Doctrine and the Public Interest Standards of the Communications Act,* 48, FCC 2d 1 (1974).

[27]For the early development of legal precedent in the area of regulating obscene, indecent, and profane programming, see James Walter Wesolowski, "Obscene, Indecent, or Profane Broadcast Language as Construed by the Federal Courts," *Journal of Broadcasting,* 13 (Spring 1969), 203–19.

[28]Title 18, United States Code (Codified June 25, 1948, Ch. 645, 62 Stat. 769).

[29]Sonderling Broadcasting Corporation, WGLD-FM, 27 Radio Reg. 2d 285 (FCC, 1973). The appeals case affirming the FCC ruling is *Illinois Citizens Committee for Broadcasting* v. *Federal Communications Commission,* 515 F. 2d 397 (D. C. Cir. 1975). See also Charles Feldman and Stanley Tickton, "Obscene/Indecent Programming: Regulation of Ambiguity," *Journal of Broadcasting,* 20 (Spring 1976), 273–82.

[30]*Pacifica Foundation,* 56 FCC 2d 94 (1975).

[31]Ibid.

[32]See "Origins of the Format Change Controversy," *Broadcasting,* 45 (August 2, 1976), 21.

[33]*Citizens' Committee to Preserve the Voice of the Arts in Atlanta* v. *F.C.C.,* 436 F. 2d 263 (D.C. Cir. 1970).

[34]*Citizens' Committee to Save WEFM* v. *FCC,* 506 F. 2d 246 (D.C. Cir. 1974).

[35]"FCC Defends Licensee Right to Choose Radio Formats," *Broadcasting,* 45 (August 2, 1976), 21.

[36]"FCC Urged to Take Another Look at Its Format Ruling," *Broadcasting,* 45 (September 6, 1976), 42.

[37]The issue surfaced in a number of cases in addition to *Citizens Committee to Save WEFM* v. *FCC,* (cited in note 32) *Citizens Committee to Keep Progressive Rock* v. *FCC,* 156 U.S. App. D.C. 16, 478 F. 2d 926 (1973); *Lakewood Broadcasting Service, Inc.* v. *FCC,* 156 U.S. App. D.C. 9, 478 F. 2d 919 (1973); *Hartford Communications Committee* v. *FCC,* 151 U.S. App. D.C. 9, 467 F. 2d 408 (1972); and *Citizens Committee to Preserve the Voice of the Arts in Atlanta* v. *FCC,* (cited in note 33).

[38]*FCC* v. *WNCN Listeners Guild,* 450 U.S. 582 (1981).

[39]*Third Report and Order* in Docket No. 19622, FCC 75–542, May 13, 1975. The different times result from different network feed times to affiliates in the various time zones. For two perspectives on the sports-antiblackout issue, see Ira Horowitz, "Sports Telecasts: Rights and Regulations," *Journal of Communication,* 27 (Summer 1977), 160–68; and John J. Siegfried and C. Elton Hinshaw, "Professional Football and the Anti-Blackout Law," *Journal of Communication,* 27 (Summer 1977), 169–74.

[40]*National Association of Independent Television Producers and Distributors et al* v. *FCC,* CA No. 75–4021, April 21, 1975.

[41]*Head* v. *New Mexico Board of Examiners in Optometry,* 374 U.S. 424 (1963), cited in Robert P. Sadowski, "Broadcasting and State Statutory Laws," *Journal of Broadcasting,* 18 (Fall 1974), 435.

[42]Sadowski, "Broadcasting and State Statutory Laws."

[43]Ibid.

[44]*NAB Highlights,* 3 (May 9, 1977), 4. Station liability for deceptive advertising is discussed in Leon C. Smith, "Local Station Liability for Deceptive Advertising," *Journal of Broadcasting,* 25 (Winter 1970–71), 107–12.

[45]Earl W. Kinter, *Michigan Law Review,* 64 (May 1966), 1280–81. Reprinted by permission.

[46]*Federal Trade Commission* v. *Colgate-Palmolive Co.,* 380 U.S. 374, 85 S. Ct. 1035 (1965). See also Harold L. Nelson and Dwight L. Teeter, Jr., *Law of Mass Communications* (Mineola, N.Y.: Foundation Press, 1973), pp. 537–40.

[47]"Firestone Agrees To Pay for Remedial Ads," *Broadcasting,* 45 (February 23, 1976), 73.

[48]"Williams Settles With FTC Over Geritol Ads," *Broadcasting,* 45 (January 19, 1976), 45.

[49]See *Applicability of Fraudulent Billing Rule* (FCC 70–513), 35 FR 7906, May 18, 1970; and B. Fox, "Points of Law," *Radioactive,* 3 (April 1977), 6–7.

[50]FCC Docket No. 20550, FCC 76–426, adopted June 22, 1976.

[51]Ibid. For a concise explanation of this program, see Ford and Lovett, "New EEO Rules."

[52]*EEOC Sexual Harassment Guidelines.* Additional perspectives on sexual harassment in the workplace can be found in K. A. Thurston, "Sexual Harassment: An Organizational Perspective," *Personnel Administrator,* December 1980, pp. 59–64; and C. R. Klasoon, D. E. Thompson, and G. L. Luben, "How Defensible Is Your Performance Appraisal System?" *Personnel Administrator,* December 1980, pp. 77–83. A summary advisory and procedural statement—NAB Counsel L–026—has been authored by communications attorney Wade H. Hargrove of the firm of Tharrington, Smith & Hargrove, Raleigh, North Carolina.

CHAPTER 19

[1]Source of quote and information for the sections on common carriers was provided by the Federal Communications Commission and included the FCC publication *Common Carrier Services* (1977) and updated information on important court and FCC decisions.

[2]*Common Carrier Services,* p. 2.

[3]*Ibid.*

[4]*Hush-a-Phone* v. *United States,* 238 F. 2d 266 (D.C. Cir. 1956).

[5]*Carterfone Device,* 13 FCC 2d 420, 423 (1968).

[6]*International Tel. & Tel. Co.* v. *General Tel. & Electronics Corp.,* 351 F. Supp. 1153 (D. Hawaii 1972). Refer also to *United States* v. *Western Elec. Co.,* 1956 Trade Cas. 68,246 (D. N.J. 1956) (consent decree).

[7]Information for this section on cable regulation was derived from FCC rules and publications. Especially helpful was the FCC Information Bulletin *Cable Television* (March 1982).

[8]*United States* v. *Southwestern Cable Co.,* 392 U.S. 157 (1968).

[9]A discussion of the compromise made in the 1972 rules and an example of the issues that can confront a local change of service can be found, respectively, in Harvey Jassem, "The Selling of the Cable TV Compromise," *Journal of Broadcasting,* 17 (Fall 1973), 427–36; and Norman Felsenthal, "Cherry-Picking, Cable, and the FCC," *Journal of Broadcasting,* 19 (Winter 1975), 43–53. The 1972 rules were issued in *Cable Television Report and Order,* 36 FCC 2d 143 (1972). Discussion of specific cable rules can be found in the definitions cited on pp. 7–8 of *Regulatory Developments in Cable Television* (Washington, D.C.: Federal Communications Commission, 1977); see also FCC Information Bulletin 13632, *Cable Television* (March 1979) and the most recent editions of the *Cable Sourcebook.*

[10]*Cable Television* (March 1982), p. 2.

[11]Ibid., pp. 5–6.

[12]Ibid.

[13]Ibid., p. 7.

[14]Vernone Sparkes, "Local Regulatory Agencies for Cable Television," *Journal of Broadcasting,* 19 (Spring 1975), 228–29.

[15]*Regulatory Developments in Cable Television.* These standards are also discussed in *Cable Television* (March 1982).

[16]Keep in mind, franchises do vary from city to city.

[17]See Frederick W. Ford and Lee G. Lovett, "State Regulation of Cable Television, Part I: Current Statutes," *Broadcast Management/Engineering,* 10 (June 1974), 18, 21, 50; "Part II: States With No CATV Statutes: Short-Term and Long-Term Trends," *Broadcast Management/Engineering,* 30 (June 1974), 20, 21, 22.

[18]A commercial should be registered as a copyrighted work, however.

[19]The disc jockey's program would typically be copyrighted if it were placed in syndication, except in the case of cable-radio transmission.

[20]Most publishing contracts and other copyright agreements provide for monies received from the sale of a deceased artist's work or performance to go automatically to his or her beneficiaries.

[21]As reported in "Guidelines on 'Fair Use' of Videotapes for Educational Purposes," *Chronicle of Higher Education,* December 16, 1981, p. 12.

[22]The discussion of these four requirements is adapted from *Statement of Account for Secondary Transmission by Cable Systems,* Forms CS/SA-1-3 (Washington, D.C.: Licensing Division, United States Copyright Office), p. ii.

[23]Ibid., p. 1.

[24]Ibid.

[25]Ibid., p. ii.

[26]*Statement of Account,* Short Form (CS/SA-1), p. iii.

[27]Ibid.

[28]Ibid.

[29]T. G. Mahn, "FCC Regulation of Personal- and Home-Computing Devices," *BYTE,* 5 (September 1980). The author gratefully acknowledges this important source as the basis for the material on regulation of frequency interference.

[30]Ibid.

[31]Ibid.

[32]Ibid.

[33]J. J. Myrick and J. A. Sprowl, "Patent Law for Programmed Computers and Programmed Life Forms," *American Bar Association Journal,* 68 (August 1982), 921. The author gratefully acknowledges this article as the basis for the material on patent law. (The case in question is *LeRoy* v. *Tatham,* 1 How. 156 (1852).)

[34]Ibid. (*O'Reilly* v. *Morse,* 1 How. 62 (1853).)

[35]Ibid. (*Funk Brothers Seed Company* v. *Kalo Inoculant Company,* 333 U.S. 127 (1948).)

[36]Ibid., p. 922. (*Gottschalk* v. *Benson,* 409 U.S. 63 (1972).)

[37]Ibid.

[38]Ibid., p. 923. (*Diamond* v. *Diehr,* 450 U.S. 175 (1981))

[39]A discussion of this subject can be found in K. Hohmann, "Software: Creators and Crooks Play Hardball," *Today,* January/February 1983, pp. 8–12. For a perspective on the regulation of videotex and teletext, see T. Rimmer, "Videotex and Teletext: Regulation of the Electronic Publisher?" (paper presented at the annual meeting of the International Communication Association, Minneapolis, 1981).

CHAPTER 20

[1]From *Radioactive* (NAB).

[2]Dick Stein, "Co-Op Q & A, Part I," *Radioactive,* 3 (May 1977), 16.

[3]See Brenda Fox, "AM–FM Advertising Packages: Are They Legal?" *Radioactive,* 3 (April 1977), 6–7; and *NAB Counsel,* September 1977—L–711.

[4]See John Coughlan, *Accounting Manual for Radio Stations* (Washington, D.C.: National Association of Broadcasters, 1975), p. 21.

[5]Interview with the late Richard A. Shaheen.

[6]For example, see Barry J. Dickstein, "True Station Value Is Key Ingredient in Broadcast Financing," *Broadcast Management/Engineering,* September 1976, pp. 41–42; and Harold Poole, "What's Your Station's Worth," *Radioactive,* July 1977, pp. 16–17.

CHAPTER 21

[1]From RKO Radio's "Breakthrough Course in Radio Selling," cited in *Radioactive,* 2 (July 1976), 1.

[2]Level of confidence is at the 95-percent level. Detailed discussions of sampling can be found in various statistics books. One detailed source is William L. Hays, *Statistics for the Social Sciences,* 2nd ed. (New York: Holt, Rinehart & Winston, 1973). A good general description of the sampling process is Maxwell McCombs, "Sampling Opinions and Behaviors," in *Handbook of Reporting Methods,* ed. Maxwell McCombs, Donald Lewis Shaw, and David Grey (Boston: Houghton Mifflin, 1976), pp. 123–38.

[3]Peter D. Fox, "Television Ratings and Cultural Programs," *Industrial Management Review,* 5 (Fall 1963), 37–43.

[4]See, for example, John Colombotos, "Personal Versus Telephone Interviews: Effect of Responses," *Public Health Reports,* 84 (September 1969), 773–82; D. A. Dillman and others, "Reducing Refusal Rates for Telephone Interviews," *Public Opinion Quarterly,* 40 (Spring 1976), 66–67; and T. F. Rogers, "Interviews by Telephone and in Person: Quality of Responses and Field Performance," *Public Opinion Quarterly,* 40 (Spring 1976), 51–65. The actual questions asked in surveys can also affect the results: Bradley S. Greenberg, Brenda Dervin, and Joseph Dominick, "Do People Watch 'Television' as 'Programs'?" *Journal of Broadcasting,* 12 (Fall 1968), 367–76.

[5]*Television Ratings Revisited* (New York: Television Information Office, 1971).

[6]There are many useful sources on interpreting the ratings. Those that were helpful in the preparation of this section include *A Broadcast Research Primer* (Washington, D.C.: National Association of Broadcasters, 1971); *Standard Definitions of Broadcast Research Terms* (Washington, D.C.: National Association of Broadcasters, 1973); *Probability Sampling* (Princeton, N.J.: Opinion Research Corporation, 1973); *How Arbitron Measures Radio* (Beltsville, Md.: American Research Bureau, 1974); *Description of Methodology: The Arbitron Television Market Reports* (Beltsville, Md.: American Research Bureau, 1975); *Understanding and Using Radio Audience Estimates* (Beltsville, Md.: American Research Bureau, 1976); *Arbitron Radio: Dayton, Ohio* (Beltsville, Md.: American Research Bureau, 1976); William L. Hays, *Statistics for the Social Sciences,* 2nd ed. (New York: Holt Rinehart & Winston, 1973); *Nielsen Station Index: Methodology* (Northbrook, Ill.: A. C. Nielsen, 1973–74); *Nielsen Station Index: Demonstration Report and User's Manual* (Northbrook, Ill.; A. C. Nielsen, 1974–75); and *Improvements in Your Arbitron Television Report* (Beltsville, Md.: American Research Bureau, 1975).

Although the formulas listed in Arbitron publications are used as a basis for defining some of the terms, in no way should they be construed as directly applicable to every rating company. Like the terms, the formulas are used in common by different rating companies, but there is considerable diversity in how these companies use them. The reader will want to keep this in mind.

[7]*Understanding and Using Radio Audience Estimates,* p. 4.

[8]Adapted from Ibid., p. 6.

[9]"Spanish-Language Net Still Battling Ratings," *Advertising Age,* February 26, 1973.

[10]"Language Problem," *Broadcasting,* 45 (April 26, 1976), 5.

[11]Spanish International Network press release, 1974.

[12]A. Howard to A. C. Nielsen Company, February 10, 1977. A copy of this letter was given to the author by Mr. Howard.

[13]Neil Hickey, "The Case of the Missing Viewers," *TV Guide,* 24 (May 8, 1976), 5.

[14]Ad agencies also become concerned as reflected in "Television Viewing: An Update on Hypocrisy," *Media Message,* February 1, 1977.

[15]Associated Press press release to subscribers during the week of May 1, 1976.

[16]This discussion of ADI is based on listenership surveys for ABC Radio by Arbitron.

[17]Among these efforts are the Committee on Nationwide Television Audience Measurement (CONTAM), established by ABC, CBS, NBC, and the National Association of Broadcasters: Three well-publicized studies by Martin Mayer, *How Good Are Television Ratings?* (New York: New York Television Information Office, 1966), *How Good Are Television Ratings?* (New York: New York Television Information Office, 1969), and *Television Ratings Revisited* (New York: New York Television Information Office, 1969–70); and a 1974 study commissioned by Arbitron and reported in R. D. Altizer and R. R. Ridgeway, Jr., *Arbitron Replication: A Study of the Reliability of Broadcast Ratings* (Beltsville, Md.: American Research Bureau, 1974).

[18]Robert Edward Balon, "The Future of Broadcast Audience Measurement" (paper presented to the Southern States Communication Convention, 1977).

CHAPTER 22

[1]Thomas E. Coffin, "Progress to Date in Radio and Television Research" (paper presented at the 1960 conference of the American Association for Public Opinion Research).

[2]Thomas E. Coffin, "What's Been Happening to the Media Research Budget? A Case History," Proceedings of the 1974 conference of the Advertising Research Foundation.

[3]Lyn Garson of the PBS Research Office to the author, October 31, 1977.

[4]*A Broadcast Research Primer* (Washington, D.C.: National Association of Broadcasters, 1974).

[5]Orville C. Walker, Jr., and William Rudelius,

"Ascertaining Programming Needs of 'Voiceless' Community Groups," *Journal of Broadcasting,* 20 (Winter 1976), 89–99.

[6]Ibid.

[7]Ibid.

[8]Ibid.

[9]Ibid.

[10]One type of analysis would be factor analysis. See R. J. Rummel, *Applied Factor Analysis* (Evanston, Ill.: Northwestern University Press, 1970).

[11]See Charles E. Osgood, George J. Suci, and Percy H. Tannenbaum, *The Measurement of Meaning* (Urbana: University of Illinois Press, 1957). A related study of image in broadcast media is Joseph C. Philport and Robert E. Balon, "Candidate Image in a Broadcast Debate," *Journal of Broadcasting,* 19 (Spring 1975), 181–93. Two studies examining newscaster credibility are James C. McCroskey and Thomas A. Jenson, "Image of Mass Media News Sources," *Journal of Broadcasting,* 19 (Spring 1975), 169–80; and D. Markham, "The Dimensions of Source Credibility of Television Newscasters," *Journal of Communication,* 18 (March 1968), 57–64.

[12]See W. Wayne DeLozier, *The Marketing Communications Process* (New York: McGraw-Hill, 1976), pp. 31–32.

[13]Adapted from guidelines for NBC pollsters.

[14]See D. Charles Whitney, "The Poll Is Suspect," *Quill,* 65 (July–August 1976), 23; G. Cleveland Wilhoit and Maxwell McCombs, "Reporting Surveys and Polls," in *Handbook of Reporting Methods,* ed. Maxwell McCombs, Donald Lewis Shaw, and David Grey (Boston: Houghton Mifflin, 1976), pp. 81–95; and Philip Meyer, *Precision Journalism* (Bloomington: Indiana University Press, 1973).

[15]The ten considerations that follow are adapted from Whitney, "The Poll Is Suspect," p. 25.

[16]See Samuel L. Becker, "Reaction Profiles: Studies in Methodology," *Journal of Broadcasting,* 4 (Summer 1960), 253–68.

[17]See "Tell If Speaker Is Boring," *Science News Letter,* May 24, 1952, p. 325; and Elwood A. Kretsinger, "Gross Bodily Movement as an Index of Audience Interest," *Speech Monographs,* 19 (1952), 244–48.

[18]See "Sweaty Palms Over TV Commercials," *Broadcasting,* 44 (November 17, 1975), 48.

[19]See Claude Hall, "Doomsday Machine Will Evaluate," *Billboard,* December 24, 1974, pp. 1, 25–28.

[20]See Ralph Schoenstein, "Watching Howard Cosell for the Love of Science," *TV Guide,* 24 (February 21, 1976), 18–21.

[21]Typical of such studies are James T. Lull, "Ethnomethods of Television Viewers," and James A. Anderson, Timothy P. Meyer, and Thomas Donohue,

"Ethnography and the Sphere of Effects" (papers presented at the annual meeting of the International Communication Association, Chicago, 1978); and Paul J. Traudt, "Families and Television: Implications From an Ethnomethodological View" (paper presented at the annual meeting of the Southern Speech Communication Association, Biloxi, Mississippi, 1979). See also S. J. Sigman "Why Ethnographers of Communication Do Ethnography: Issues in Observational Methodology" (paper presented at the annual meeting of the Speech Communication Association, Louisville, 1982) and J. Lull, "The Social Uses of Television," *Human Communication Research,* 6 (1980), 197–209.

CHAPTER 23

[1]Melvin De Fleur and Sandra Ball-Rokeach, *Theories of Mass Communication,* 3rd ed. (New York: McKay, 1975), p. 205.

[2]A discussion of how the categories approach evolved from the bullet theory and how it fits into current communication theory is found in Wilbur Schramm and Donald Roberts, *The Process and Effects of Mass Communication* (Urbana: University of Illinois Press, 1971), pp. 4–53.

[3]See Paul Lazarsfeld, Bernard Berelson, and H. Gaudet, *The Peoples' Choice* (New York: Columbia University Press, 1948).

[4]Neil Vidmar and Milton Rokeach, "Archie Bunker's Bigotry: A Study in Selective Perception and Exposure," *Journal of Communication,* 24 (Winter 1974), 43–44.

[5]Lee B. Becker, Raymond A. Martino, and Wayne M. Towers, "Media Advertising Credibility," *Journalism Quarterly,* 53 (Summer 1976), 216–22.

[6]Robert Monaghan, Joseph T. Plummer, David L. Rarick, and Dwight Williams, "Predicting Viewer Preference for New TV Program Concepts," *Journal of Broadcasting,* 18 (Spring 1974), 131–42.

[7]William Stephenson, *The Play Theory of Mass Communication* (Chicago: University of Chicago Press, 1967).

[8]David Chaney, *Processes of Mass Communication.* (London: Macmillan, 1972), pp. 20–21.

[9]Deanna Campbell Robinson, "Television/Film Attitudes of Upper-Middle Class Professionals," *Journal of Broadcasting,* 19 (Spring 1975), 196.

[10]Wilbur Schramm, *Men, Messages, and Media: A Look at Human Communication* (New York: Harper & Row, 1973).

[11]Robinson, "Television/Film Attitudes," p. 199.

[12]Neil T. Weintraub, "Some Meanings Radio Has for Teenagers," *Journal of Broadcasting,* 2 (Spring 1971), 147–52.

[13]Lawrence Wenner, "Functional Analysis of TV Viewing for Older Adults," *Journal of Broadcasting,* 20 (Winter 1976), 77–88.

[14]Herta Herzog, "What Do We Really Know About Daytime Serial Listeners," in *Radio Research, 1942–1943,* ed. Paul F. Lazarsfeld and Frank Stanton (New York: Duell, Sloan & Pearce, 1944).

[15]Joseph Foley, "A Functional Analysis of Television Viewing" (Ph.D. dissertation, University of Iowa, 1968) cited in Wenner, "Functional Analysis," p. 79. See also: R. Compesi, "Gratifications of Daytime TV Serial Viewers," *Journalism Quarterly,* 57 (Spring 1980), 155–58; and M. R. Levy, "The Audience Experience With Television News," *Journalism Monographs,* 55 (April 1978).

[16]Characteristic of the debate is a series of articles appearing in the 1975 issues of the *Journal of Broadcasting:* James A. Anderson and Timothy P. Meyer, "Functionalism and the Mass Media," *Journal of Broadcasting,* 19 (Winter 1975), 11–22; Calvin Pryluck, "Functions of Functional Analysis: Comments on Anderson-Meyer," *Journal of Broadcasting,* 19 (Fall 1975), 413–20; James A. Anderson and Timothy P. Meyer, "A Response to Pryluck," *Journal of Broadcasting,* 19 (Fall 1975), 421–23; and Calvin Pryluck, "Rejoinder to Anderson-Meyer," *Journal of Broadcasting,* 19 (Fall 1975), 424–25.

[17]Bernard Cohen, *The Press, the Public, and Foreign Policy* (Princeton, N.J.: Princeton University Press, 1963), p. 13.

[18]Maxwell E. McCombs and Donald Shaw, "The Agenda Setting Function of Mass Media," *Public Opinion Quarterly,* 36 (1972), 176–87.

[19]CBS Office of Social Research, *Communicating With Children Through Television* (New York: CBS, 1977).

[20]See, for example, Charles R. Corder-Bolz, "Television Content and Children's Social Attitudes," in *Progress Report to the Office of Child Development* (Washington, D.C.: Department of Health, Education, and Welfare, 1976).

[21]John P. Murray and Susan Kippax, "Children's Social Behavior in Three Towns With Differing Television Experience," *Journal of Communication,* 28 (Winter 1978), 19–29.

[22]Charles K. Atkin and Walter Gantz, "The Role of Television News in the Political Socialization of Children" (paper presented at the 1975 meeting of the International Communication Association).

[23]Charles K. Atkin and Mark Miller, "The Effects of Television Advertising on Children: Experimental Evidence" (paper presented at the 1975 meeting of the International Communication Association). A

review of research on television and advertising can be found in the *Journal of Communication,* (Winter 1977).

[24]A. Bandura, D. Ross, and A. Ross, "Imitation of Film Mediated Aggressive Models," *Journal of Abnormal and Social Psychology,* 66 (1963), 3–11; and L. Berkowitz and E. Rawlings, "Effects of Film Violence on Inhibitions Against Subsequent Aggression," *Journal of Abnormal and Social Psychology,* 66 (1963), 405–12.

[25]*Surgeon General's Scientific Advisory Committee on Television and Social Behavior,* 1972.

[26]Ibid.

[27]See, for example, Seymour Feshbach, "The Stimulating vs. Cathartic Effects of a Vicarious Aggressive Experience," *Journal of Abnormal and Social Psychology,* 63 (1961), 381–85.

[28]See Leonard Berkowitz, *Aggression: A Social Psychological Analysis* (New York: McGraw-Hill, 1962).

[29]See Joseph Klapper, *The Effects of Mass Communication* (New York: Free Press, 1960).

[30]Albert Bandura and Richard Walters, *Social Learning and Personality Development* (New York: Holt Rinehart & Winston, 1963).

[31]The *Journal of Broadcasting,* Summer 1977, features a discussion of the Gerbner methodology, CBS criticism, and the Gerbner response.

[32]George Comstock, "Types of Portrayal and Aggressive Behavior," *Journal of Communication,* 27 (Summer 1977), 189–98.

[33]Charles N. Barnard, "An Oriental Mystery," *TV Guide,* 26 (January 28, 1978), 2–4, 6, 8.

INDEX

SUBJECT

1941
Mayflower decision discourages editorializing.

1954
Edward R. Murrow confronts Senator Joseph McCarthy's "Red Scare" tactics on *See It Now*.

1943
Edward G. Noble buys NBC Blue, becomes ABC in 1945.

1953
KUHT signs on as first educational television station under new FCC allocations for ETV.

1956
Ampex engineers demonstrate videotape recording.

1935
Dr. Frank Stanton leaves position at The Ohio State University to join CBS's research efforts.

1953
ABC merges with United Paramount Theatres, Inc.

1961–1968
Midwest Program for Airborne Television Instruction (MPATI).

1938
First over-the-air ETV programming.

1948–1953
FCC freezes television allocations.

1941
FCC issues *Report on Chain Broadcasting*.

1956
United Press International launches audio service, first for a wire service.

1939
G.R. Stibitz and S.B. Williams build Complex Number Calculator.

1950
First successful recording of color television.

1937
Howard Aiken develops electromechanical computer.

1946
J.P. Eckert and J. Mauchley develop ENIAC computer.

1955
Association for Professional Broadcasting Education is founded. Later becomes Broadcast Education Association (B.E.A.).

1948
CBS conducts the first of various "talent raids" the networks participate in during the late 1940s.

1958
J.S. Sibley of Texas Instruments develops integrated circuit.

1939
Television is introduced at the World's Fair.

1947
Transistor is invented at Bell Laboratories.

1957
RCA demonstrates color videotape recording.

1948
Cable systems begin in Oregon and Pennsylvania.

1960
First televised Presidential debates between John F. Kennedy and Richard M. Nixon.

1945
Blue network changes name to American Broadcasting Company.

1955
Radio programming begins to specialize. Rock and roll formats develop.

1938
Orson Welles makes famous "War of the Worlds" broadcast.

1949
Fairness Doctrine is issued.

1961
Spanish International Network (SIN) begins operation.